GLR FM

Essential

FILM GUIDE

SIMON ROSE

Research Assistance
BILL REISS

*Title & logo
licensed by BBC Enterprises Ltd*

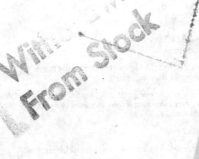

HarperCollinsPublishers

Dedicated to

Marisa, Jamie, Gabrielle, Barbara, Lara, Dana, Susan, Michelle, Tia, Halle, Laurie, Mädchen & Marcia

The Guide was produced on an Apple Macintosh IIsi. The information on which the book is based is stored in the Helix Express database. Those entries needed for the Guide were then downloaded to Quark Xpress and automatically formatted.

HarperCollins Publishers
P.O. Box, Glasgow G4 0NB

Reprint 10 9 8 7 6 5 4 3 2 1 0

Copyright © 1993 Simon Rose

BBC Radio One logo © BBC 1990
Licensed by BBC Enterprises Ltd

BBC, Radio 1 and the BBC Radio One logo are trade marks of the British Broadcasting Corporation and are used under licence.

The Author hereby asserts his moral right to be identified as the Author of the Work and the Publishers undertake to observe such assertion and to impose the same condition on its licencees.

ISBN 0 00 470434 7

A Catalogue record for this book is available from the British Library.

Printed in Great Britain by
HarperCollins Manufacturing, Glasgow

Contents

Introduction

To some extent it's all Jamie Lee Curtis's fault. After seeing *A Fish Called Wanda* on holiday I was wondering, like every other male, where I could see more of her. If only there was a film guide up-to-date enough to list all of her films and yet light enough to carry with me. Ideally, I'd be able to read something about those films too, without having to consult another book. It would be more useful still, if the ratings for the films were listed by her personal entry as well as against each movie.

There were some good lines of dialogue in the film, too. Wouldn't it be nice if the same book included one or two as a memory jogger? Some background details about the making of the film are always intriguing, while it surely couldn't have all that and yet omit one of the great pleasures of movie-viewing, spotting the many gaffes that slip through the film-makers' fingers and make it on to the screen?

Unfortunately for my sanity and peace of mind, when I couldn't find such a guide I foolishly began making a few notes. Five years later, they've grown into the book you have in your hand.

I was determined that the guide not be so thick that you could risk a hernia just by picking it up. Preferring to be reasonably comprehensive within a period, I settled on the last ten years. After all, it's usually the most recent movies people want to know about.

So the Guide includes the vast majority of those films shown in British cinemas from the beginning of 1983 (I cheated and put in a few like *E.T.* which fell just ouside the period) up to the middle of 1993. There are also some films that haven't yet been released in the cinema at the time of going to press and details on a dozen or so large-scale projects in the pipeline.

This isn't primarily a book for film buffs. I'm not particularly interested in whether a film has won prizes. Nor am I too bothered who the second assistant director is. What I want to know about a movie is simply, 'Is it worth seeing?'.

As far as I'm concerned, movies are all about entertainment, something too many film-makers seem to have forgotten. Whether I'm watching a film in a cinema or on TV, I want to be entertained. I want a story with a beginning, a middle and an end, and preferably in that order. So although there are plenty of arthouse films in here, some of the weirder ones that I couldn't imagine anyone of sane mind wanting to watch have simply been omitted. Films which went straight to video are also not usually in the Guide. It was the only way I could keep the book to a manageable size.

It's never easy to find good old-fashioned entertainment, the sort of movie that makes you feel you've had good value for your money. Films are more sluggish these days, with ad- and video-trained directors showing us in appallingly intricate detail exactly how a hero closes a car door or puts on his clothes in the morning. If you think there are some dull patches in many films, it's not just your imagination: the average movie script has shrunk in size by 25% in the past fifty years, yet the average length of a film has risen from just over one and a half hours to almost two hours. If only more film-makers took to heart Alfred Hitchcock's dictum that 'the length of a film should be directly related to the endurance of the human bladder'.

As with any other film guide, you'll have to make some allowances for my prejudices. My main concern is that films have a decent, well-structured story. So many movies are now high-concept, sold on an idea alone – Kathleen's a tough detective; Arnie's the Tooth Fairy; Eddie's a cop teamed with a three-legged horse – that the script almost seems an afterthought. If it's a comedy, then I expect it to make me laugh. If it's a thriller, then similarly, I expect thrills, and from something more exciting than the old standby of having a cat leap into shot at a moment of tension. I expect to be able to hear what the actors are saying and I have very little patience with a film where the whole plot has already been revealed in the trailer, a pernicious and all too common practice.

One other thing that drives me mad is the ease with which characters park in the movies. Of all the aspects of a film nothing is so designed to destroy credibility. Take Albert Brooks in *Lost in America*, for instance, who parks his mobile home right outside his old office in Manhattan in the middle of the day. Or John Cleese conveniently having his car parked in the street right outside the Law Courts in the Strand at the crucial moment in *A Fish Called Wanda!*

I've tried to highlight in the Guide those movies that are so indescribably bad that, in the right mood, they can be screamingly funny. Among them are *Shining Through*, *Midnight Crossing*, *Bitter Moon*, *Double X*, *Daydream Believer*, *Two Moon Junction*, *Lifeforce*, *Monsignor*, *The Lonely Lady*, *Scream for Help* and *Zandalee*.

As there is no shortage of female flesh in movies, it also seemed only fair to highlight wherever possible, those rare occasions when the male actors cast aside their modesty for the cameras.

If you like this book, do hang on to it, because many of the films won't be in future editions. The intention is that with each new version of the Guide, the earlier films will be dropped to make way for new movies. Because of space constrictions, the cast lists are sadly rather shorter than those contained in the database from which the book is produced. Still, who knows? Perhaps there'll be a Writer's Cut before too long?

N.B. The 'Revealed Within' posers on the back cover refer, respectively, to *Batman Returns*, Jamie Lee Curtis and *Licence to Kill*.

Appeal It's impossible for me to spot every boo-boo in every film, to jot down every good line or discover every piece of trivia. I'd be only too delighted if you wanted to share some examples of your own for future editions, particularly outrageous examples of characters finding it easy to park. They don't need only to be from the films of the past ten years either, as the scope of the Guide may be expanded in future. Write to me c/o The Essential Film Guide, PO Box, Glasgow G4 0NB.

Thanks I would like particularly to thank Mark Pearse and Paul Jackson of Pulsar Business Programs who developed the Helix Express database on which the information that makes up the Guide is stored. Mark's dedication to duty at one point involved a 24-hour non-stop programming session. I am indebted to Joe Sudwarts, too, for always being on hand to answer idiotic questions about my computer. For letting me catch those films that I had missed, my thanks to Ritz Video of Wimbledon, part of the Blockbuster UK Group. My undying gratitude goes to Bill Reiss, without whose assistance with research and reviews I would undoubtedly still be working on the Guide. His encyclopedic knowledge of the subject, amazing memory, hard work and unfailing good humour were invaluable. I must also thank my wife Jane for her extraordinary patience while the book was in preparation.

Rose's Rules of Movie Watching

*H*ere are ten, tell-tale signs that a movie is likely to be below par. If you don't have the Guide to hand, just memorise these rules and watch the quality of your viewing increase. Although not cast iron, they are accurate in nine out of ten cases. Some truly awesomely bad films qualify in more than one category.

Rose's Rule 1 The longer the title, the worse the film.
Scenes from the Class Struggle in Beverly Hills; The Adventures of Buckaroo Banzai Across the Fifth Dimension; Allan Quatermain and the Lost City of Gold; Delta Force 2: The Colombian Connection; The Favour, the Watch and the Very Big Fish; Friday the 13th: Jason Takes Manhattan; Harley Davidson and the Marlboro Man; Metalstorm: The Destruction of Jared-Syn. [Exception: Fried Green Tomatoes at the Whistle Stop Café.]

Rose's Rule 2 Steer clear of single-word titles designed to evoke exoticism or mysticism. If it sounds like a perfume, it stinks!

Sahara; Bolero; Harem; Havana; Zandalee; Sunset; Siesta; Eleni; Dune; Yentl; Ishtar.

Rose's Rule 3 No film with Shelley Long is funny.

See any film with Shelley Long. Or rather, don't.

Rose's Rule 4 Exclamation marks or dots in a title are a sign of desperation.

18 Again!; Howard...a New Breed of Hero; ¡Three Amigos!; Hot Dog...The Movie; Turk 182!; Ferngully...The Last Rainforest; Top Secret!; Baby...Secret of the Lost Legend; Stop! Or My Mom Will Shoot.

Rose's Rule 5 The Longer any lead character spends in make-up, the worse the film.

Krull; For the Boys; Shining Through; Mr. Saturday Night; Coming to America; True Identity; Nothing But Trouble; Another Country; Legend; The Hunger.

Rose's Rule 6 If there's a pun in the title, don't get your hopes up.

Splitting Heirs; Once Upon a Crime; Transylvania 6-5000; The Crackdown; Raising Cain; Foreign Body; Stepping Out; House 2: The Second Story; K-9.

Rose's Rule 7 If the title explains the plot, don't waste your money finding out what they've allready told you.

Don't Tell Mom the Babysitter's Dead; The Boy Who Could Fly; Stop! Or My Mom Will Shoot; Ernest Saves Christmas; Don't Tell Her It's Me; Not Without My Daughter.

Rose's Rule 8 No movie with a lead character called 'Hawk' or any variation thereof can possibly be any good. {There are no exceptions to this rule}

Hudson Hawk (qualifies twice, for title and character); Hawks; Ladyhawke; Over the Top (Lincoln Hawk); Navy SEALS (Dale Hawkins); The Distinguished Gentleman (Elijah Hawkins); Death Warrant (Hawkins); Two Moon Junction (Earl Hawkins); The January Man (Hawkes); Alone in the Dark (Allison Hawkins); Bullshot (Hawkeye McGillicuddy).

Rose's Rule 9 If there's a year in the title, sitting through it will seem like twelve months.

2010; Class of 1984; '68; Star 80; 1969; 1492: Conquest of Pardise; 1984.

Rose's Rule 10 If the title is changed when it crosses the Atlantic, you can bet your bottom dollar there's a good reason.

Too Hot to Handle/The Marrying Man; Wings of the Apache/Firebirds; Filofax/Taking Care of Business; The Honorary Consul/Beyond the Limit/ Howard the Duck/Howard...a New Breed of Hero; Knight Moves/Face to Face; Diamond Skulls/Dark Obsession; Mr. Mum/Mr. Mom; The Pope Must Die/The Pope Must Diet. [Exceptions include Truth or Dare/In Bed with Madonna & Diggstown/Midnight Sting]

The Best of the Best
All the 4 Star Movies at a glance

Accidental Hero
Aladdin
Aliens
Angel at My Table, An
Babette's Feast
Back to the Future
Back to the Future, Part III
Beauty and the Beast
Best Seller
Big
Big Easy, The
Blade Runner: The Director's Cut
Blood Simple
Book of Love, The
Born on the Fourth of July
Boyz N the Hood
Brazil
Breaking In
Christmas Story, A
Cinema Paradiso
City Slickers
Commitments, The
Coupe de Ville
'Crocodile' Dundee
Cyrano de Bergerac
Dances With Wolves
Dead Calm
Dead Poets Society
Deep Cover
Defence of the Realm
Delicatessen
Die Hard
Diner
Dirty Rotten Scoundrels
Do the Right Thing
Dream Team, The
E.T. The Extra-Terrestrial
Enchanted April
Eureka
Falling Down
Fanny and Alexander
Few Good Men, A
Field of Dreams
Flirting
Fly, The
Freshman, The
Fried Green Tomatoes

Ghost
Ghostbusters
Glory
Gods Must Be Crazy, The
GoodFellas
Grand Chemin, Le
Grey Fox, The
Handful of Dust, A
Hannah and Her Sisters
Hard Way, The
Hear My Song
Hearts of Darkness
Henry V
Henry: Portrait of a Serial Killer
Homicide
Honeymoon in Vegas
Hope and Glory
Howard's End
Indiana Jones and the Last Crusade
Jean de Florette
Jesus of Montreal
Karate Kid, The
King of Comedy, The
Kiss of the Spider Woman
Lethal Weapon 3
Local Hero
Man of Flowers
Manhunter
Manon des Sources
Matewan
Midnight Run
Midnight Sting
Miller's Crossing
Misery
Missionary, The
Monkey Shines
Moonstruck
Mountains of the Moon
My Cousin Vinny
My Favourite Year
My Left Foot
My Life as a Dog
Name of the Rose, The
Once Upon a Time in America
Paradise
Patriot Games
Pelle the Conqueror

Playboys, The
Player, The
Postcards from the Edge
Proof
Queen of Hearts
Rain Man
Raising Arizona
Rambling Rose
Re-Animator
Reservoir Dogs
Reversal of Fortune
Right Stuff, The
River's Edge
Roger & Me
Room With a View, A
Roxanne
Ruthless People
Salvador
Singles
Someone to Watch Over
Sommersby
Splash
Star Trek IV
Star Trek VI
Strictly Ballroom
Talk Radio
Terminator, The
Thelma & Louise
Thin Blue Line, The
This is Spinal Tap
Thunderheart
Tootsie
Toto the Hero
Trading Places
Turtle Diary
Two Jakes, The
Under Fire
Untouchables, The
Verdict, The
WarGames
Waterdance, The
Wayne's World
When Harry Met Sally
White Men Can't Jump
Witness
Working Girl
Year of the Dragon

The Best Soundtracks
of the Past Ten Years
by Steve Williams of New York's Newsday

The three most successful soundtrack albums of the past decade really have nothing to do with film music. *Flashdance* and *Footloose* danced to the top of the charts in 1983 and 1984 respectively while *Beverly Hills Cop* reached No.4 in 1985.

Film scores? Hardly; all were driven to popularity by hit singles, songs like *Neutron Dance* by the Pointer Sisters, Glenn Frey's *The Heat is On* and Kenny Loggins' *Footloose*.

Traditionally, film–score albums contain bits and pieces, or cues, of the dramatic background music. To most who purchase these recordings they are, essentially, souvenirs of the movie. These folks didn't buy the album because they heard some of it on the radio, but because they admired the film's star or its director or cinematographer or – sometimes – the composer.

The more zealous collectors and aficionados devoted themselves to a genre of films and film music – British spy thrillers, Biblical epics, Westerns, Sci-fi – or to a particular writer. Cults sprang up for this composer or that one: Jerry Goldsmith, Alex North, Elmer Bernstein, John Barry, Miklos Rosza. This in turn spawned fanzines, and even 'soundtrack' labels, like Varese Sarabande and Silva Screen.

Neither *Flashdance* nor *Beverly Hills Cop* were the first film soundtracks to break the mould with a hit song: Elvis Presley's scores on RCA Victor were chock full of singles while Henry Mancini had *Moon River* from *Breakfast at Tiffany's*. Perhaps the most spectacular example of a pop–driven soundtrack is 1977's *Saturday Night Fever*, 120 weeks on the Billboard charts.

The manner in which soundtracks were ordered, recorded and marketed changed mightily after that. 'Give us hits!', cried the studios and the music divisions complied.

Still, purists – me included – would argue that a true soundtrack shouldn't compromise. So I've limited my list to records within the past decade that reflect the 'pure' art of the film–score composer, hit songs notwithstanding.

Gorky Park (Varese Sarabande, 1983): Just enough Volga Boatman/Tchaikovsky notes to strike an authentic chord, but James Horner's music is strikingly modern – nearly progressive – and under-stated.

The Natural (Warner Bros., 1984): Blatantly heroic themes for a film that shamelessly pushed everybody's buttons. Randy Newman's folksy strains aren't nearly as hokey taken on their own merits. *The Natural* isn't the best baseball film (my vote goes to *Bang the Drum Slowly*) but Newman's music is sweet and evocative, the way America's national pastime used to be.

Witness (Varese Sarabande/That's Entertainment, 1985): Subdued and honest and never intrusive, Maurice Jarre's score colors this Harrison Ford effort perfectly. *Building the Barn* is a classic.

The Untouchables (A&M, 1987): Blustery in parts, warm and soothing in others. Ennio Morricone has great fun summing up, musically, the characters of Al Capone and Elliot Ness.

Empire of the Sun (Warner Bros., 1987): Composer John Williams employs most of the weighty symphonic artillery in his considerable musical arsenal in this Steven Spielberg tale of a boy caught up in a war. Not the best of many Spielberg–Williams collaborations – that's *Jaws* – but the best since '83.

Glory (Virgin, 1989): Memorable anthems from James Horner. Terrifically in sync with the movie, terrifically listenable without it.

The Mission (Virgin, 1986): Another score that shows Morricone's versatility, and his knack for integrating source music and melodies with thoroughly modern techniques. Gorgeous.

Robin Hood: Prince of Thieves (Morgan Creek/Polydor, 1991): No doubt every troubadour in Sherwood Forest in the 12th century sounded like Bryan Adams crooning *Everything I Do I Do It For You*. Michael Kamen's swashbuckling score sounds a little more appropriate to the time.

Basic Instinct (Varese Sarabande, 1992): Gritty and mesmerizing stuff from Jerry Goldsmith. Familiar snare drums, billowing Bernard Hermann–esque violins and a positively addictive theme. Goldsmith, who rarely misses completely, hits a home run here.

Honeymoon in Vegas (Epic Soundtrax, 1992): Alright, alright. So it's not a pure soundtrack. This is an album solely of Elvis Presley covers: *Heartbreak Hotel* by Billy Joel, *Suspicious Minds* from Dwight Yoakam, Amy Grant crooning *Love Me Tender* and John Mellencamp unloading *Jailhouse Rock*. Just buy it.

Bill Reiss adds: *Love and Menace* (Milan): Taken on by De Palma after Bernard Herrmann's death, Pino Donnagio lacks the Maestro's emotional depth, but still fills his scores full of stylish, seductive menace. This compilation album is the best introduction. *Blue Velvet* (That's Entertainment): Much of the eerie moodiness of David Lynch's films is due to the wistful, sinister scores of Badalamenti. The most varied is *Twin Peaks*, although strictly that's TV. But both that and *Blue Velvet* are enhanced by the ethereal voice of Julee Cruise.

Film Ratings

Ratings Many critics are rather snooty about the films they review. Anything which doesn't match up to the standards of *Citizen Kane* – which, let's face it, hadn't one decent car chase in it – tends to get slagged off. Yet, providing you're in a receptive mood, the vast majority of films serve to while away the time. Those films which qualify as okay, though nothing more, get 2 points; while I may quibble about some aspects of them, they're still passable. It's those with 1 point that I regard as a waste of time. I've given 3 points to films of above–average entertainment value and 4 stars to what I regard as must–sees. Opinions about films vary widely, of course, so it's very unlikely that you will agree with me in many cases. Over time, you'll probably be able to make allowances for my prejudices.

Year Generally this is the year of first theatrical release, unless it's a for–eign language film in which case the earlier of the American or British release date is used.

Length Timings are becoming ever more approximate with so many dif–ferent versions of some films floating around and some television stations butchering movies to fit into time slots. If you're watching a film on TV, bear in mind that they're shown slightly faster, at 25 frames per second rather than 24, so that a film lasting 100 minutes in the cinema only takes 96 mins.

Certificate These are original cinema certificates. They may be slightly dif–ferent for video releases. 'U' signifies films are suitable for everyone, 'PG' is an indication that Parental Guidance is called for, while '12', '15' and '18' films should be restricted to people of thoses ages and above.

Oscars Only the main categories, Best Actors, Best Supporting Actors, Best Director, Best Screenplay and Best Film are listed.

Blurb Good or memorable tag lines from advertising campaigns.

Showing A movie or movies shown within a movie, sometimes only for a few moments. Not knowing what they are can be immensely irritating.

Quotes Where it is important that a speaker is identified, a character name is given if the quote is used in the film. If a real name is used then it's some–thing somebody's said about the movie.

Oops! A variety of blunders and howlers that should never have got to the screen. If you're looking for these yourself, the most fruitful areas of study are usually wounds, bandages, food, dirt, clocks and unimportant charac–ters in the background who are hoping, vainly, to be discovered.

Key to the Actors' Entries

Almost 300 actors and directors are covered, some very famous and some who look headed for stardom. Also included is a selection of some of the many supporting actors whose faces are seen in umpteen movies.

Within the period covered by the book (from 1983 onwards) listings should include every mainstream cinema release in Britain. Before that period, usually only the more interesting or well-known films are listed.

Those films for which there's an entry in the main book are in ordinary type, those mentioned only in the back in italics. Some films that haven't yet come out and a few that have only just entered the production process have been included.

(a) Indicates an actor's role is just a small bit-part.

(c) Indicates an actor only played a cameo in the film.

(v) Indicates just the actor's voice is used in the film.

> Other abbreviations:
> a = actor;
> s = screenplay;
> d = director.

Star Satisfaction Score
Who gives the most pleasure in the dark?

Which stars are most frequently in good movies? We've taken those actors in the back of the book and worked out the average rating of those films of theirs covered by the main section of the book. Rosie Perez, sassy, wise-cracking star of films like *White Men Can't Jump* and *Do the Right Thing*, leads the list with an average satisfaction score of 3.25, followed closely by James Woods with 3.167, Harrison Ford with 3.091 and then Joe Pesci with 3.083. That's not to say that they're the best actors, or my favourite stars, simply that their films get the highest average rating. Close on their heels, all with an average of 3.00 are Lorraine Bracco, Cher, Billy Crystal, Danny Glover, Woody Harrelson, Bruno Kirby, Oliver Platt, Laura San Giacomo, Kyra Sedgwick and Emma Thompson.

Poor Mädchen Amick lags the list, achieving the lowest possible score of 1.00. Despite her splendid role in TV's *Twin Peaks*, each of her three films in the book got the minimum rating of 1. Chuck Norris is second to last with a score of 1.429 while Sharon Stone, despite currently being one of the hottest female stars, is dragged down by her pre-*Basic Instinct* roles in films like Police Academy 4 and *Allan Quatermain and the Lost City of Gold*. She and Andrew McCarthy both get 1.556. Kyle MacLachlan gets a paltry 1.571 while both Sherilyn Fenn and Robert Downey Jr. get just 1.60. Shelley Long, she of Rule #3, gets a surprisingly high 1.625.

The complete list of the most (and least) satisfying stars in the Hollywood firmament is on Page 464.

The Credits

Written by ....Simon Rose

Inspired by ....Jamie Lee Curtis

Research assistance ....Bill Reiss

Additional research ....Elizabeth Barrett

Reviewer.......................................Simon Rose

1st Asst Reviewer.............................Bill Reiss

2nd Asst Reviewer..James Cameron-Wilson

2nd second Asst Reviewer.......Charles Bacon

3rd second Asst Reviewer......Tom Cobbleigh

One measly review ....John Kane

One wonderful person ....John Kane

Only friend with in-house cinema ...John Kane

Soundtrack reviews ....Steve Williams

Designed by..........T. Carden & L. Roxburgh

Edited by ....Edwin Moore

Cutter & Splicer ....Caroline Smart

Unit Publicist...........................Jenny Seymour

Mr Cameron-Wilson's hyphen....In-breeding

Introduction to Mr. Reiss ....Sara Jubb

Agenting by...............................Patrick Walsh

Nice voice on the phone..............Janine Quick

Video facilities ....Ritz Video of Wimbledon

Satellite consultant ....Timothy Rose

Fuzzy undecoded foreign films.......Paul Micou

Database programmed by ....Mark Pearse

Additional programming ....Paul Jackson

Additional assistance.......Stig, Pavla & Alison

24-hour computer aid.................Joe Sudwarts

Fielding panicky phone calls.....Clare Sudwarts

Quark consultant ....Tony Tyler

Backup ....Kitty Alvarez & Paul Martin

Amazing computer widgets........John Langdon

New York Bed........Steve & Marta Williams

'Frisco Bed ..Marlene Arnese & Bill O'Neill

L A Bed.......................Peter & Diane Dennis

Introduction to Dudley Moore ...Peter Dennis

Mr Rose's hair.........Tony of Hair by Tonino

Mr Rose's tap dancing coach .....Julie Chapman

Mr Rose's personal trainer............Ron Niblo

Mr Rose's personal assistant ....Vacant

Mr Rose's current heroine ....Marisa Tomei

Patience supplied by ....Jane of Southfields

Moral support ....Maryon Tysoe

Immoral support ....Michael Bywater

Sympathetic barman.....Matthew Glendinning

Refreshments by ....Pippa, Martha, Paula,
                    Julia, Josephine, Lucy & Phillippa

Ernst Lubitsch's relation...............Gail Renard

Silly Christmas cards.............David Renwick

Smoked salmon wrangler.............Dorée Rose

Glasses ......On the table where you left them

Quofit supplied by ....Simon Richards

Financial advice by....................Oofy Prosser

Disreputable tittle-tattle by..........Guttersnipe

Toccata & Fugue by ..........................J.S. Bach

Nicest ever interviewee .....Penelope Spheeris

Best boy ....Joseph

Best girl ....Isabel

Best bagels..................................Bagel Express

Special appearance by.....................Sig Ruman

'Embonpoint' courtesy of......Mitchell Symons

'Stamp collection' joke ......© Amanda Roberts

Blatant plug for freebies ......Apple Macintosh

Unit manager...................................Gill Steene

Film Clipper Extraordinaire..............Sue Cole

Photocopying...Jan

Biology lessons ....Karen Krizanovich

Political education.......................Geoff Sawtell

Amazing jacket................David MacGillivray

Rhubarbing ambience artists .....Quentin Falk,
    Sue Heal, Hugo Davenport, Christopher
    Tookey, Alan Frank & John Marriott

Swing gang ....Terence Blacker, Stephen
    Hargrave, John Mole & Penny Harris

Mr Rose's body double ....Al Pacino

About Last Night... •• [1986]

Director: Edward Zwick
Screenplay: Tim Kazurinsky & Denise DeClue

David Mamet's play about long-time singles coming to terms with commitment, *Sexual Perversity in Chicago*, is flattened out for the screen. But it's still a passable romantic comedy. [113m/18]

Danny	Rob Lowe
Debbie	Demi Moore
Bernie	James Belushi
Joan	Elizabeth Perkins

Above the Law

SEE: Nico

Absolute Beginners •• [1986]

Director: Julien Temple
Screenplay: Christopher Wicking, Richard Burridge & Don MacPherson

Lively but vacuous attempt at a British film musical, set in the 50s, about the emergence of that strange creature the teenager. It's let down by weak performances from the central characters and a distracting subplot about racism. Brave. Some might say foolhardy. Still, where else would you see the Notting Hill riots set to music? [108m/15]

Colin	Eddie O'Connell
Suzette	Patsy Kensit
Vendice Partners	David Bowie
Henley of Mayfair	James Fox
Arthur	Ray Davies
Mum	Mandy Rice-Davies

Also: Eve Ferret, Steven Berkoff, Bruce Payne, Anita Morris, Paul Rhys, Julian Firth, Lionel Blair, Robbie Coltrane, Ronald Fraser, Irene Handl

The Abyss •• [1989]

Director: James Cameron
Screenplay: James Cameron

Abyss-mal. *Aliens* director Cameron dives under the sea. A group of oil rig workers, among them Harris and estranged wife Mastrantonio, are trying to rescue a sunken nuclear sub. But there's something else down there! Despite staggering special effects, it's about as nerve-wracking as an episode of *Stingray*. The Special Edition, 171 minutes long, makes more sense, has more thrills and gets a rating of 3. [140m/12]

Virgil 'Bud' Brigman	Ed Harris
Lindsey	Mary Elizabeth Mastrantonio
Lt. Coffey	Michael Biehn
Catfish De Vries	Leo Burmester
Alan 'Hippy' Carnes	Todd Graff
Jammer Willis	John Bedford Lloyd
'Sonny' Dawson	J.C. Quinn
Lisa 'One Night' Standing	Kimberly Scott

OOPS! When a body is discovered as the divers enter the sunken submarine, watch it blink in the bright light.

Psst! The cast and crew were issued with T-shirts saying 'Life's Abyss and then you dive.' • This was the first film to use 'morphing', computer-animated techniques that came of age with *Terminator 2*.

Accidental Hero •••• [1992]

Director: Stephen Frears
Screenplay: David Webb Peoples

In this superbly witty satire from the writer of *Unforgiven* and *Blade Runner*, Hoffman's a crooked sleazebag who is forced by circumstances into rescuing TV reporter Davis from a burning airplane. But when the station offers $1m for the 'Angel of Flight 104' to come forward, it's drifter Garcia who claims to be the hero. This is cinema entertainment at its finest. It's moving, absorbing and beautifully-acted, keeping us dying to know what's going to happen next. It starts brilliantly and just gets better as it goes along. With the exception of Davis's squirm-inducing onion-peeling scene, this is quite simply one of the greatest films of the past decade, whatever anyone else might tell you. [116m/15]

Bernie Laplante	Dustin Hoffman
Gale Gayley	Geena Davis

John Bubber..................................Andy Garcia
Evelyn ....Joan Cusack
Chucky (cameraman) ....Kevin J. O'Connor
Winston...................................Maury Chaykin
Wallace ....Stephen Tobolowsky
Conklin (reporter).........Christian Clemenson
Chick..Tom Arnold
Station head...............................Chevy Chase
Bradman (jumper) ....Edward Herrmann

Quote 'It's my story. I did the research.' ✦ 'Watch my shoes.'

OOPS! The all-important envelope handed to Davis by Garcia when he's on the ledge is never seen again — presumably forgotten by the film-makers.

Psst! Sharon Stone was beaten to the part by Davis ✦ So realistic was the crashed plane that pilots coming in to land at Los Angeles airport were reporting a disaster to the control tower.

The Accidental Tourist ●●● [1988]

Director: **Lawrence Kasdan**
Screenplay: **Frank Galati & Lawrence Kasdan**

Hurt's a diffident travel writer advising businessmen how to make their destination seem as much like home as possible. Davis is the ditzy dog-trainer who gets the choke-chain around his neck and begins training him to enjoy life. Although slow in places, this is a gentle, wryly amusing study of love triumphing over indifference. There's also a nicely under-stated performance from Bud as Edward the dog, so uncontrived compared to some of the awfully hammy over-acting we've seen from our canine chums in recent years.   **[121m/PG]**

Macon......................................William Hurt
Sarah...................................Kathleen Turner
Muriel......................................Geena Davis
Rose...Amy Wright
Porter ....David Ogden Stiers
Charles......................................Ed Begley Jr.
Julian..Bill Pullman
Alexander........................Robert Hy Gorman
Edward the dog...Bud

Oscars Geena Davis

Quote 'I make bottle-caps, but it isn't as exciting as it sounds' ✦ 'There are very few necessities in this world that don't come in travel-sized packets.'

The Accused ●● [1988]

Director: **Jonathan Kaplan**
Screenplay: **Tom Topor**

The great performance from Foster is the best thing about this truth-based tale of the waitress who goes to court after being gang-raped in a bar. Despite the interesting questions that the film raises, McGillis is unbelievably tedious as Foster's lawyer while the flashback rape sequence at the end is wholly gratuitous.
                                     [110m/18]

Kathryn Murphy ....Kelly McGillis
Sarah Tobias................................Jodie Foster
Ken Joyce ....Bernie Coulson
Cliff "Scorpion" Albrecht ....Leo Rossi
Sally Fraser......................................Ann Hearn
D.A. Paul Rudolph.........Carmen Argenziano

Oscars Jodie Foster

OOPS! At the opening of the film, Foster makes her escape in flat white shoes. But when we see the rape later, she's wearing black high heels.

Action Jackson ●● [1988]

Director: **Craig R. Baxley**
Screenplay: **Robert Reneau**

Loud and furious comedy-thriller with what little plot there is revolving around black, Harvard Law School-educated cop, Weathers, trying to nail the nasty Nelson. It's directed by the stunt director of the A-Team, something you could guess from the on-screen action.

                                     [95m/18]

"Action" Jackson......................Carl Weathers
Peter Dellaplane ....Craig T. Nelson
Sydney Ash...Vanity
Patrice Dellaplane........................Sharon Stone
Officer Kornblau..............Thomas F. Wilson
Capt. Armbruster ....Bill Duke
Tony Moretti................................Robert Davi

The Addams Family ••• [1991]

Director: **Barry Sonnenfeld**
Screenplay: **Caroline Thompson & Larry Wilson**

The cartoons of Charles Addams brought entertainingly to life. Although the weakness of the storyline means we're offered little more than a series of comedy skits strung together, the characters, their lifestyle and the gags, visual and verbal, are enough to keep us chortling. A standout comedy performance, shamelessly ignored at Oscar time, was that of Christopher Hart as Thing. **[99m/PG]**

Morticia Addams	Anjelica Huston
Gomez Addams	Raul Julia
Gordon	Christopher Lloyd
Tully Alford	Dan Hedaya
Abigail Craven	Elizabeth Wilson
Granny	Judith Malina
Lurch	Carel Struycken
Margaret Alford	Dana Ivey
Judge Womack	Paul Benedict
Wednesday Addams	Christina Ricci
Pugsley Addams	Jimmy Workman
Thing	Christopher Hart

Quote 'Don't torture yourself, Gomez. That's my job.' ✦ 'When we first met, it was an evening like this. A boy. A girl. An open grave.'

OOPS! As Fester and Gomez slide down the helter-skelter chute to the vaults, first one leads, then the other ✦ Although Margaret has to ask Morticia to get the finger trap off, we've already seen her once without it ✦ The fence is burned by Lurch breathing fire after drinking Wednesday's lemonade, but is miraculously repainted for the next shot.

Psst! The startled passenger glimpsed briefly on the doomed toy train is Barry Sonnenfeld, the director.

The Adjuster •• [1992]

Director: **Atom Egoyan**
Screenplay: **Atom Egoyan**

He's a loss adjuster. She's a film censor who videos porn for her sister. You're the audience. Guess who's the one who's lost? Although some intriguing ideas keep bubbling up in this weird Canadian film it ends up being rather depressing and aimless. **[102m/18]**

Noah Render	Elias Koteas
Hera Render	Arsinee Khanjian
Bubba	Maury Chaykin

Adventures in Babysitting •• [1987]

Director: **Chris Columbus**
Screenplay: **David Simkins**

Mildly amusing comedy about babysitter Shue having to drag her charges around Chicago late at night. Also known as *A Night on the Town*. **[102m/PG]**

Chris	Elisabeth Shue
Sara	Maia Brewton
Brad	Keith Coogan
Daryl	Anthony Rapp
Joe Gipp	Calvin Levels
Dawson	Vincent D'Onofrio

Psst! Lolita Davidovich appears in a small role, billed on the credits as 'Lolita David'.

The Adventures of Baron Munchausen ••• [1989]

Director: **Terry Gilliam**
Screenplay: **Terry Gilliam & Charles McKeown**

A teller of tall tales tells the biggest whopper of all: 'Of course I can bring this film in under budget.' This haphazard fantasy, based on stories told by the infamous liar Baron von Munchausen, is certainly flawed and has its dull spots. But it's also as imaginative as you'd expect from Gilliam, with some amazing effects. Underrated, but no doubt there'll be a director's cut before too long. **[126m/PG]**

Baron Munchausen	John Neville
Desmond/Berthold	Eric Idle
Sally Salt	Sarah Polley
Vulcan	Oliver Reed
Rupert/Adolphus	Charles McKeown

Bill/Albrecht ....Winston Dennis
Also: Jack Purvis, Valentina Cortese, Robin Williams, Jonathan Pryce, Bill Paterson, Peter Jeffrey, Uma Thurman, Alison Steadman, Don Henderson, Sting

Quote 'I got tides to regulate. I got no time for flatulence and orgasms!' ◆ 'The great thing was that we only shot seven days over schedule and we *still* went $20m over budget. Nobody's ever done that one!' [Terry Gilliam]

Psst! With the eventual cost around $50m after the budget ran out of control, not only was this the most expensive European film ever made, but it holds the record as the biggest flop in movie history, losing $48.1m ◆ Robin Williams cameo is uncredited, the actor being listed as Ray D. Tutto.

The Adventures of Buckaroo Banzai Across the 8th Dimension ●● [1987]

Director: W.D. Richter
Screenplay: Earl MacRauch

Sprawling sci-fi comedy has our poly-math hero (brain surgeon, singer, nuclear physicist, all-round troubleshooter) tangling with aliens who want his supercar. Half of the movie seems to have been left on the cutting-room floor; the wrong half judging by what's left. An unentertaining mess.   [102m/PG]

Buckaroo Banzai ....Peter Weller
Dr. Emilio Lizardo ....John Lithgow
Penny Priddy ....Ellen Barkin
New Jersey ....Jeff Goldblum
Also: Christopher Lloyd, Lewis Smith, Ronald Lacey, Vincent Schiavelli

The Adventures of Ford Fairlane ● [1990]

Director: Renny Harlin
Screenplay: Daniel Waters, James Cappe & David Arnott

Andrew Dice Clay is an American comic who gives sexism a bad name. He trans-fers his moronic stage persona perfectly to this dire flick about a rock 'n' roll detective investigating a groupie's disap-pearance.   [102m/18]

Ford Fairlane ....Andrew Dice Clay
Julian Grendel........................Wayne Newton
Colleen Sutton........................Priscilla Presley
Blurb Ford Fairlane, Rock 'N' Roll Detective. To Clients, He's The Great-est. To Everyone Else, He's Just A Dick.

Afraid of the Dark ●● [1992]

Director: Mark Peploe
Screenplay: Mark Peploe

A very peculiar psychological thriller, with a young boy obsessed by a local killer stalking blind women. Nothing is quite what it seems and it's immensely irritating to realise half way through that you've got to forget everything already seen and start again.   [91m/18]

Frank...James Fox
Miriam...Fanny Ardant
Tony Dalton ....Paul McGann
Rose...Clare Holman
Dan Burns ....Robert Stephens

After Dark, My Sweet ●● [1990]

Director: James Foley
Screenplay: Bob Redlin & James Foley

Ex-boxer Patric gets tangled up with gor-geous widow Ward, her nasty uncle Dern and their nefarious little kidnapping scheme. Despite looking wonderful, the story's flabby and never really grips as a Jim Thompson adaptation should.   [111m/18]

Kevin "Collie" Collins....................Jason Patric
Bert..Rocky Giordani
Fay Anderson..............................Rachel Ward
Uncle Bud.....................................Bruce Dern

After Hours ●● [1985]

Director: Martin Scorsese
Screenplay: Joseph Minion

In this rather draggy comedy, Dunne's the yuppie trapped without cash at night among the weirdos in New York's SoHo area. Overrated, but then can any movie with Cheech and Chong in possibly be any good?   [97m/15]

Paul Hackett .... Griffin Dunne
Marcy .... Rosanna Arquette
June .... Verna Bloom
Pepe .... Tommy Chong
Also: Linda Fiorentino, Teri Garr, John Heard, Cheech Marin, Catherine O'Hara, Dick Miller, Will Patton, Martin Scorsese

Psst! The writer was a film student who penned the script for his class ✦ Scorsese has a tiny cameo as the spotlight operator in the black leather bar ✦ He ordered star Dunne to refrain from sleep and sex during filming so that he would give a suitably nervy performance.

Against All Odds •• [1984]

Director: **Taylor Hackford**
Screenplay: **Eric Hughes**

Yet another dreary film noir update, with Ward so wooden as a femme fatale she should be treated for dry rot. As usual, only the presence of James Woods makes it worth watching.   [121m/15]

Jessie Wyler .... Rachel Ward
Terry Brogan .... Jeff Bridges
Jake Wise .... James Woods
Hank Sully .... Alex Karras
Mrs. Wyler .... Jane Greer
Ben Caxton .... Richard Widmark

Psst! Based on the 1947 film *Out of the Past* in which Greer played Ward's part.

Agnes of God ••• [1985]

Director: **Norman Jewison**
Screenplay: **John Pielmeier**

When nun Tilly murders her new-born baby, chain-smoking psychiatrist Fonda has to decide whether she's sane enough to stand trial, battling Mother Superior Bancroft along the way. The excellently-acted battle of wills between these two makes for compelling drama.   [98m/15]

Dr. Martha Livingston .... Jane Fonda
Mother Ruth Miriam .... Anne Bancroft
Sister Agnes .... Meg Tilly
Dr. Livingston's mother .... Anne Pitoniak

Air America •• [1989]

Director: **Roger Spottiswoode**
Screenplay: **John Eskow & Richard Rush**

Downey and Gibson are devil-may-care pilots, part of a Smugglers-R-Us operation during Vietnam. The drugs side of the real-life operation is ignored. Instead it's played for laughs. It doesn't get them.
                                                  [112m/15]

Gene Ryack .... Mel Gibson
Billy Covington .... Robert Downey Jr.
Corrine Landreaux .... Nancy Travis
Also: Ken Jenkins, David Marshall Grant, Lane Smith, Burt Kwouk

Psst! In *Lethal Weapon* two years earlier, the villains are all ex-Air America people, as is explained to Gibson just before his run-in with the helicopter.

Airplane II: The Sequel •• [1982]

Director: **Ken Finkleman**
Screenplay: **Ken Finkleman**

More a space shuttle than an airplane, this sequel's cobbled together by a different crew from the original. Not as good, but still a few chuckles to be had during the ride.   [84m/12]

Striker .... Robert Hays
Elaine .... Julie Hagerty
McCroskey .... Lloyd Bridges
Capt. Oveur .... Peter Graves
Murdock .... William Shatner

Blurb Just When You Thought It Was Safe To Go Back In The Departure Lounge.

Psst! There are cameos from the likes of Raymond Burr, Chuck Connors, Rip Torn and Sonny Bono ✦ Notice after 'Best Boy' in the credits, Adolph Hitler cropping up as 'Worst Boy'.

Aladdin •••• [1992]

Director: **John Musker & Ron Clements**
Screenplay: **John Musker, Ron Clements, Ted Elliott & Terry Rossio**

Vastly different to recent Disney cartoons, this is so frenetic and off-the-wall it's more watching a full-length version of

Bugs Bunny or Tex Avery than something like, say, *The Little Mermaid*. They have given Robin Williams his head as the genie, letting him improvise wildly and then devising the animation to go with it. Madcap, fast and immensely funny, Aladdin is a delight for the eye and the ear. **[90m/U]**

Aladdin	Scott Weinger
Genie	Robin Williams
Jasmine	Linda Larkin

Also: Jonathan Freeman, Frank Welker, Gilbert Gottfried, Douglas Seale

Psst! After three years in development and six months of actual production, the first rough screening was a disaster. Studio head Jeffrey Katzenberg told the animators that the story didn't work and made them start all over again ✦ Robin Williams received a $7m Picasso painting in lieu of cash ✦ Tim Rice won an Oscar for his songs.

Alamo Bay •• [1985]

Director: **Louis Malle**
Screenplay: **Alice Arlen**

Uninvolving tale of the mounting tension between hard-up Texas fishermen and the Vietnamese refugees who have settled in the area. **[98m/18]**

Glory	Amy Madigan
Shang	Ed Harris
Dinh	Ho Nguyen
Wally	Donald Moffat

Alice ••• [1990]

Director: **Woody Allen**
Screenplay: **Woody Allen**

A nervous, well-off housewife, discovering husband Hurt's adultery, decides to have an affair of her own with Mantegna. A constantly-surprising joy from beginning to end, although some didn't like the mystical elements or the air of playful whimsy. Most remarkable of all is that Farrow comes across as a female replica of Woody. **[105m/12]**

Alice	Mia Farrow
Joe	Joe Mantegna
Doug	William Hurt
Dr. Yang	Keye Luke
Vicki	Judy Davis
Nancy Brill	Cybill Shepherd
Ed	Alec Baldwin

Also: Blythe Danner, Gwen Verdon, Judith Ivey, Bernadette Peters

Quote 'So what number reed do you use, Joe?'

Alien Nation •• [1988]

Director: **Graham Baker**
Screenplay: **Rockne S. O'Bannon**

Aliens have begun emigrating to the earth and human cop Caan is forced to work with one of them. What ought to have been a clever way of looking at racism comes across as nothing more than a conventional buddy cop movie, which just happens to use rather more latex than usual. By setting it in 1992, it also looks a mite dated now. **[90m/18]**

Matthew Sykes	James Caan
Sam Francisco	Mandy Patinkin
William Harcourt	Terence Stamp

Aliens •••• [1986]

Director: **James Cameron**
Screenplay: **James Cameron**

Ripley wakes after 57 years, only to be told that the planet she found the alien on has been colonised. When contact is lost with the inhabitants, Weaver's sent in with the Marines. Nail-biting, pants-wetting suspense mixed with superb action sequences, on top of which Ripley has to mother young Henn as well. An outstanding sci-fi actioner. **[137m/18]**

Ripley	Sigourney Weaver
Newt	Carrie Henn
Corp. Hicks	Michael Biehn
Burke	Paul Reiser
Bishop	Lance Henriksen
Pte. Hudson	Bill Paxton
Lt. Gorman	William Hope
Pte. Vasquez	Jenette Goldstein
Sgt. Apone	Al Matthews
Pte. Drake	Mark Rolston

Quote 'Get away from her, you *bitch!*'

Psst! The almost complete absence of blood was at the insistence of Weaver, who hadn't liked the excess of gore in the original ◆ There's an even better Special Edition on video, which has almost 20 minutes not seen in the cinema release.

Alien³ ●   [1992]

Director: **David Fincher**
Screenplay: **David Giler, Walter Hill & Larry Ferguson**

Shaven-haired Weaver crash-lands on Prison Planet Fury 161 and guess who she's brought with her? The plot and dialogue are largely incomprehensible and the only action comes from interminable chases down dark tunnels as yet another prisoner has his sentence terminated prematurely. The best thing about it? There definitely won't be an *Alien⁴*.   **[115m/18]**

Ripley	Sigourney Weaver
Dillon	Charles S. Dutton
Clemens	Charles Dance
Golic	Paul McGann
Andrews	Brian Glover

Quote 'In space no one can hear you yawn.' [Critic Sue Heal]

Psst! The almost complete absence of guns was at the insistence of Weaver, who hadn't like the excess of weaponry in *Aliens* ◆ Weaver received $5m ◆ 8 scriptwriters and 3 directors were involved in bringing this to the screen. Fincher's main experience beforehand had been on Madonna videos ◆ The largely British cast referred to the film as 'Skinheads in Space'.

Alive ●●●   [1993]

Director: **Frank Marshall**
Screenplay: **John Patrick Shanley**

After the most terrifying plane crash yet put on film, the members of a college rugby team find themselves fighting for survival in horrendous conditions in the Andes. Based on a true story, the film glosses over the cannibalism, giving us a breath-takingly photographed and stirring – if occasionally slightly corny – rendering of one of the most extraordinary feats of human courage and fortitude. **[126m/15]**

Nando Parrado	Ethan Hawke
Antonio Balbi	Vincent Spano
Roberto Canessa	Josh Hamilton
Carlitos Paez	Bruce Ramsey

Also: John Haymes Newton, David Kriegel, Kevin Breznahan, Illeana Douglas

Quote 'To be fair to this dilemma, it is a beautiful spot.'

OOPS! When one of them falls off the mountain ledge, look for the sudden appearance of the boom mike top right as they struggle to pull him up on the left side of the screen.

Psst! To look convincing as people who went 70 days with little to eat, the actors were put on a rapid weight-loss diet of just 1,100 calories a day, almost a third of the average intake ◆ The credits include an 'avalanche dog' ◆ Illeana Douglas seems to be cornering the market in women who get eaten, her previous role being the lawyer who gets her cheek bitten off in Cape Fear ◆ Look out for John Malkovich's uncredited cameo as one of the survivors.

Allan Quatermain and the Lost City of Gold ●   [1987]

Director: **Gary Nelson**
Screenplay: **Gene Quintano, Alex Phillips & Frederick Elmes**

Almost worth introducing a lower movie rating just for this stinker, made back-to-back with *King Solomon's Mines*. Cardboard cutouts resembling Richard Chamberlain and Sharon Stone are propped up in the jungle and made to mouth inane dialogue. Anytime Stone boasts about her acting prowess, somebody should remind her of this trussed and basted turkey.   **[111m/PG]**

Allan Quatermain	Richard Chamberlain
Jesse Huston	Sharon Stone
Umslopogaas	James Earl Jones
Agon	Henry Silva

All Dogs Go to Heaven •• [1989]

Director: Don Bluth, Dan Kuenster &
Gary Goldman
Screenplay: David N. Weiss

As with other Bluth cartoons, the animation is fine but the story, involving a dead mutt returning to a canine world to do a good deed, is a right dog's breakfast.

[84m/U]

Itchy	Dom DeLuise
Charlie	Burt Reynolds

All I Want For Christmas • [1991]

Director: Robert Lieberman
Screenplay: Thom Eberhardt & Richard
Kramer

It isn't just two front teeth that are wanted. The whole set's gone from this toothless Xmas offering. Not even the presence of the wonderful Nielsen or Bacall can rescue this icky tale of children asking Santa to get their parents together again. It's enough to turn the kids from Santa to Satan.

[90m/U]

Santa	Leslie Nielsen
Lillian Brooks	Lauren Bacall
Catherine O'Fallon	Harley Jane Kozak
Michael O'Fallon	Jamey Sheridan
Ethan O'Fallon	Ethan Randall

All of Me ••• [1984]

Director: Carl Reiner
Screenplay: Phil Alden Robinson

This occasionally hysterical comedy has lawyer Martin's body part-occupied by crabby millionairess Tomlin. But unfortunately, they can't agree on anything. Although starting slowly, the laughs come ever thicker and faster. Martin is so good it's surprisingly easy to believe in the film's daft premise.

[91m/15]

Roger Cobb	Steve Martin
Edwina Cutwater	Lily Tomlin
Terry Hoskins	Victoria Tennant
Peggy Schuyler	Madolyn Smith
Prahka Lasa	Richard Libertini

Psst! Bitchy Tennant is now Mrs. Martin.

Almost an Angel • [1990]

Director: John Cornell
Screenplay: Paul Hogan

Hogan's a thief who reforms after a little chat with God, bearing an uncanny resemblance to Charlton Heston. This awful load of mush, written by Hogan, is so unbelievably sentimental they should be handing out sick bags to the audience.

[95m/PG]

Terry Dean	Paul Hogan
Steve	Elias Koteas
Rose Garner	Linda Kozlowski

Almost You •• [1984]

Director: Adam Brooks
Screenplay: Mark Horowitz

A moderately amusing romantic trifle about a New York couple going through the usual problems in their relationship. It wasn't released in the UK until 1987.

[96m/15]

Erica	Brooke Adams
Alex	Griffin Dunne
Lisa	Karen Young
Kevin	Marty Watt
David	Josh Mostel
Susan	Dana Delaney

Quote 'I'm an actor.' – 'Which restaurant?'

Alone in the Dark •• [1982]

Director: Jack Sholder
Screenplay: Jack Sholder

Anyone who saw it in the cinema probably *was* alone in the dark. Despite an interesting cast and some flair in the set-pieces, this tale of a trio of psycho mental patients menacing a shrink is really just another predictable slasher.

[93m/18]

Hawkes	Jack Palance
Dr. Bain	Donald Pleasence
Preacher	Martin Landau
Don	Dwight Schultz

Always •• [1985]

Director: Henry Jaglom
Screenplay: Henry Jaglom

A wife with divorce papers to sign turns up in the middle of a Fourth of July party. An unbelievably talky film with occasional flashes of wit and insight. **[105m/15]**

David..Henry Jaglom
Judy....................................Patrice Townsend
Lucy..Joanna Frank
Eddie..Alan Rachins

Quote 'The bravest film ever to come out of Hollywood.' [Orson Welles]

Psst! Jaglom and Townsend are, as in the movie, divorced ◆ Bob Rafelson, director of *Five Easy Pieces*, plays the neighbour.

Always •• [1989]

Director: **Steven Spielberg**
Screenplay: **Jerry Belson**

Spielberg's remake of the 1943 film *A Guy Named Joe* is a rather inconsequential and sentimental piece of fluff. Dreyfuss is the fire-fighting pilot who, as a ghost, helps young Johnson out with former girlfriend Hunter. With a heavier dose of the Spielberg sentiment than usual, no wonder this film has trouble getting airborne. **[123m/PG]**

Pete Sandich ....Richard Dreyfuss
Dorinda Durston ....Holly Hunter
Ted Baker....................................Brad Johnson
Al Yackey ....John Goodman
Hap......................................Audrey Hepburn

Psst! The burning forests are the real McCoy, filmed during the Yellowstone National Park fires of 1988 ◆ The film title was inspired by a 1925 Irving Berlin song, but he refused permission to use it.

Amadeus ••• [1984]

Director: **Milos Forman**
Screenplay: **Peter Shaffer**

Has-been composer Salieri confesses to his jealousy of the uncouth but brilliant Mozart and the efforts he went to to keep the upstart in obscurity. Hulce's Mozart is so extraordinarily annoying, we can easily sympathise with Salieri. Even those who don't care for the music should get swept up in the fascinating story. **[158m/PG]**

Antonio Salieri...............F. Murray Abraham
Wolfgang Amadeus Mozart...........Tom Hulce
Constanze Mozart..............Elizabeth Berridge
Emmanuel Schikaneder..............Simon Callow
Leopold Mozart............................Roy Dotrice
Katerina Cavalieri.............Christine Ebersole
Emperor Joseph II........................Jeffrey Jones

Oscars Best Picture, F. Murray Abraham, Best Director, Best Screenplay (adapted)

Quote 'Why would God choose an obscene child to be his instrument?'

Psst! The part of Constanze was Meg Tilly's, but she tore a leg ligament in a soccer game the day before filming began ◆ The two stars identified closely with their roles and formed separate cliques on set, barely speaking to each other ◆ The premiere of *Don Giovanni* was filmed in the Tyl Theatre in Vienna where it had been premiered two hundred years earlier, although it took some persuasion to allow the use of candle-lit chandeliers in the wooden building ◆ Prague, where most of the filming took place, was the only European city with buildings of the right period that had not been damaged in World War II.

Amazing Grace and Chuck
SEE: Silent Voice

The Ambassador ••• [1985]

Director: **J. Lee Thompson**
Screenplay: **Max Jack**

Implausible but pretty gripping thriller, with Mitchum the American ambassador trying to mediate in the Arab-Israeli conflict while having to contend with straying wife Burstyn at the same time. **[95m/18]**

Hacker..................................Robert Mitchum
Alex..Ellen Burstyn
Stevenson....................................Rock Hudson
Hashimi...Fabio Testi

American Anthem
SEE: Take It Easy

American Dreamer • [1984]

Director: Rick Rosenthal
Screenplay: Jim Kouf & David Greenwalt

A housewife who wins a trip to Paris starts thinking she's the heroine of her favourite airport novel. A comedy that is mild to the point of feeblemindedness.

[105m/PG]

Cathy	JoBeth Williams
Alan	Tom Conti
Victor	Giancarlo Giannini
Margaret	Coral Browne
Kevin Palmer	James Staley

American Friends ••• [1991]

Director: Tristram Powell
Screenplay: Michael Palin & Tristram Powell

A fusty Oxford tutor falls for a girl he meets on an Alpine walking holiday in the mid-1860s. From such a slight story, Palin creates a charming romance. He is superb as the confirmed bachelor being drawn, reluctantly, out of his lifelong shell. A gentle, bewitching gem. [95m/PG]

Francis Ashby	Michael Palin
Miss Elinor Hartley	Trini Alvarado
Miss Caroline Hartley	Connie Booth
Oliver Syme	Alfred Molina
Dr. Weeks	Alun Armstrong

Psst! Palin based the story on the diaries of his great-grandfather who resigned as an Oxford don to marry an American girl he had met in the Alps.

American Ninja • [1985]

Director: Sam Firstenberg
Screenplay: Paul De Mielche

Below-par, below the belt, chop-socky. Also known as *American Warrior*. [95m/18]

Joe	Michael Dudikoff
Hickock	Guich Koock
Patricia	Judie Aronson

An American Tail •• [1986]

Director: Don Bluth
Screenplay: Judy Freudberg & Tony Geiss

Little Fievel gets separated when the family of mice escapes from Russia and heads for America. Spielberg's attempt to rival Disney is superbly animated, but let down by insipid songs and a dull story. Kids should still enjoy it, though. [81m/U]

With: Erica Yohn, Nehemiah Persoff, Amy Green, Phillip Glasser, Christopher Plummer, Madeline Kahn, Dom DeLuise

An American Tail: Fievel Goes West •• [1991]

Director: Phil Nibbelink & Simon Wells
Screenplay: Flint Dille

The mice have to do what mice have to do and head West. Not even the presence of John Cleese and James Stewart (as Wylie Burp) can disguise the fact that this cheese is extremely thinly sliced. [74m/U]

Fievel Mousekewitz	Philip Glasser
Wylie Burp	James Stewart
Cat R. Waul	John Cleese
Miss Kitty	Amy Irving
Tiger	Dom DeLuise
Mama Mousekewitz	Erica Yohn
Tanya Mousekewitz	Cathy Cavandini
Papa Mousekewitz	Nehemiah Persoff
Also: Jon Lovitz	

American Warrior

SEE: American Ninja

The American Way •• [1986]

Director: Maurice Phillips
Screenplay: Scott Roberts

Very strange comedy about a group of oddball Vietnam veterans who set up a pirate radio station in a B-52 bomber to hound right-wing politicians. On this evidence, they are obviously hoping to bore them to death. Not released in the UK until 1989. Also known as *Riders of the Storm*. [140m/15]

Captain	Dennis Hopper
Tesla	Michael J. Pollard
Ace	Eugene Lipinsky
Also: James Aubrey, Al Matthews	

Amityville 3-D • [1983]

Director: **Richard Fleischer**
Screenplay: **William Wales**

The moment you see the dreaded '3-D', you know film-makers are desperately searching for something, *anything*, to make the film more interesting. They've failed. You'll need special glasses to appreciate the effects, but you'd be better off wearing earplugs and a blindfold. If you don't have them, a bag over the head will do. **[93m/15]**

John Baxter	Tony Roberts
Nancy Baxter	Tess Harper
Elliott	Robert Joy
Melanie	Candy Clark
Lisa	Meg Ryan

Amsterdamned ••• [1988]

Director: **Dick Maas**
Screenplay: **Dick Maas**

A psycho frogman paddles up and down the Amsterdam canals, attacking unsuspecting tourists and layabouts. An enjoyably stylish and nasty thriller, it won't have done much for the Dutch tourist trade, but does contain one of the best speed-boat chases ever. **[105m/18]**

Eric Visser	Huub Stapel
Laura	Monique Van De Ven
Vermeer	Serge-Henri Valcke

And God Created Woman • [1988]

Director: **Roger Vadim**
Screenplay: **R.J. Stewart**

...And Vadim Created this tedious remake of his 1956 Bardot classic. De Mornay marries the prison electrician to get out of prison, bonks everything in trousers on the outside and then joins a rock band. It does take great talent to make all this so utterly tiresome.

[94m/18]

Robin Shay	Rebecca De Mornay
Billy Moran	Vincent Spano
James Tiernan	Frank Langella
Peter Moran	Donovan Leitch

Android ••• [1982]

Director: **Aaron Lipstadt**

Kinski is the archetypal mad professor working on a space station with his male android Max 404, who is to be replaced when the newly-built female is ready. An inventive and enjoyable piece of low-budget sci-fi. **[80m/15]**

Dr. Daniel	Klaus Kinski
Maggie	Brie Howard
Keller	Norbert Weisser

Showing *Metropolis.*

Angel • [1984]

Director: **Robert Vincent O'Neil**
Screenplay: **Robert Vincent O'Neil**

High school student by day, Hollywood hooker by night, Wilkes is worried when a psycho starts murdering her nocturnal colleagues. Those who love exploitation movies will be disappointed. So will everybody else. **[92m/18]**

Angel/Molly	Donna Wilkes
Kit	Rory Calhoun
Billy Boy	John Diehl
Lt. Andrews	Cliff Gorman

An Angel at My Table •••• [1990]

Director: **Jane Campion**
Screenplay: **Laura Jones**

A hauntingly effective portrait of the life and times of New Zealand novelist Janet Frame, at one point banged up and treated, wrongly, for schizophrenia. Acutely observed, this is an original and intelligent approach to the literary biopic and the best indication of the arrival of the Kiwi film industry. **[158m/15]**

Janet Frame	Kerry Fox
Janet (as teenager)	Karen Fergusson
Janet (as girl)	Alexis Keogh
Myrtle Frame	Melina Bernecker
Isabel Frame	Glynis Angell

Psst! Originally made as a three-part mini-series for Australian television.

Angel Heart •• [1987]

Director: **Alan Parker**
Screenplay: **Alan Parker**

Private eye Rourke is hired to do a bit of investigating by De Niro. Once you know that Bob's character is called Louis Cyphre, then you can guess the rest. The set design is great, the story predictable. Wildly overrated. **[113m/18]**

Harry Angel	Mickey Rourke
Louis Cyphre	Robert De Niro
Epiphany Proudfoot	Lisa Bonet
Margaret Krusemark	Charlotte Rampling

Psst! A brief glimpse of a cockfight was cut by the censors. It is forbidden to show them in Britain.

Angelo My Love •• [1983]

Director: **Robert Duvall**
Screenplay: **Robert Duvall**

This dull, slow story of modern-day gypsies in New York was written, produced and directed by Duvall. **[116m/15]**

With: Angelo Evans, Michael Evans, Ruthie Evans, Tony Evans, Debbie Evans

Psst! It took Duvall 4 years to make the film, raising the money himself and casting the real-life Evans family in it, together with other gypsies. As many couldn't read English, much of the dialogue is improvised.

Anna ••• [1987]

Director: **Yurek Bogayevicz**
Screenplay: **Agnieszka Holland**

This variation on *All About Eve* has Kirkland as a Czech ex-movie star who befriends a young fan down on her luck, only to see her star soar. Porizkova is staggeringly good in this taut, occasionally melodramatic movie. It is scandalous that her only role after this was with Tom Selleck in *Her Alibi*. **[100m/15]**

Anna	Sally Kirkland
Daniel	Robert Fields
Krystyna	Paulina Porizkova
Baskin	Larry Pine

Annie's Coming Out ••• [1984]

Director: **Gil Brealey**
Screenplay: **John Patterson**

A moving true-life Australian drama of a therapist fighting to get a cerebral palsy victim out of an asylum. It may not sound much fun, but not only is it touching and thought-provoking, it is also very droll. Also known as *A Test of Love*. **[93m/PG]**

Jessica Hathaway	Angela Punch McGregor
David Lewis	Drew Forsythe
Sally Clements	Liddy Clark
Vera Peters	Monica Maughan
Annie O'Farrell	Tina Arhondis

Another Country •• [1984]

Director: **Marek Kanievska**
Screenplay: **Julian Mitchell**

The reason Burgess and Maclean betrayed their country, it transpires, was because people were so beastly to them at school. It's surprising half the country didn't end up in Moscow. This slightly flat adaptation of the play is most memorable for the hilarious make-up job on the aged Everett at the end of the film. [See Rose's Rule #5] **[90m/15]**

Guy Bennett	Rupert Everett
Tommy Judd	Colin Firth
Barclay	Michael Jenn
Delahay	Robert Addie
Imogen Bennett	Anna Massey
Julie Schofield	Betsy Brantley
Harcourt	Cary Elwes

Psst! The Princess of Wales' brother Viscount Althorp is in the background playing (what else?) a public schoolboy.

Another 48 HRS. •• [1990]

Director: **Walter Hill**
Screenplay: **John Fasano, Jeb Stuart & Larry Gross**

Eight years to think about it and all we get is a virtual remake of the fun *48 HRS*, but without the wit, panache or style. Such an obvious attempt to part us from our cash under false pretences is infuriating. **[95m/18]**

Reggie Hammond	Eddie Murphy
Jack Cates	Nick Nolte
Ben Kehoe	Brion James
Blake Wilson	Kevin Tighe
Frank Cruise	Ed O'Ross

OOPS! When Murphy and Nolte are in the back of a police car, they just open the doors and climb out. Someone more well versed in these matters than me has pointed out that the cops usually have child locks on the back doors.

Another Time, Another Place •• [1983]

Director: **Michael Radford**
Screenplay: **Michael Radford**

Farmer's wife Logan has an affair with an Italian prisoner-of-war sent to work on her Scottish farm in World War II. So languid is the pacing, it's a toss-up whether they'll hit the sack before the war finishes. **[101m/15]**

Janie	Phyllis Logan
Luigi	Giovanni Mauriello
Umberto	Gian Luca Favilla
Dougal	Paul Young
Beel	Gregor Fisher

Another Woman • [1988]

Director: **Woody Allen**
Screenplay: **Woody Allen**

...And Another Serious Woody Movie. If you actually *like* being plunged into the depths of despair, then you'll have a whale of a time with this. Others will be put off by the sub-Bergmanesque tale of unemotional Rowlands suddenly having to face the real world head on. A feel-good movie only in the sense that you feel much better when you stop watching it. **[81m/PG]**

Marion	Gena Rowlands
Hope	Mia Farrow
Ken	Ian Holm
Lydia	Blythe Danner

Also: Sandy Dennis, Gene Hackman, John Houseman, Martha Plimpton, David Ogden Stiers, Philip Bosco, Betty Buckley

Apartment Zero ••• [1989]

Director: **Martin Donovan**
Screenplay: **Martin Donovan & David Koepp**

A cinema manager in Buenos Aires takes in a lodger. Presumably his cinema hasn't shown *Pacific Heights*. A little-seen but quirkily enjoyable British suspenser, full of in-jokes for buffs. **[120m/15]**

Jack Carney	Hart Bochner
Adrian LeDuc	Colin Firth
Margaret McKinney	Dora Bryan
Mary Louise McKinney	Liz Smith

The Applegates
SEE: Meet the Applegates

Appointment with Death •• [1988]

Director: **Michael Winner**
Screenplay: **Anthony Shaffer, Peter Buckman & Michael Winner**

Someone has killed an Agatha Christie story. Poirot narrows it to three suspects, a cigar-smoking director called Winner, a cigar-smoking producer called Winner and a cigar-smoking co-writer called Winner. A who-dunnit is here turned into a who-cares. **[102m/PG]**

Hercule Poirot	Peter Ustinov
Lady Westholme	Lauren Bacall
Nadine Boynton	Carrie Fisher
Col. Carbury	John Gielgud
Emily Boynton	Piper Laurie
Miss Quinton	Hayley Mills
Dr. Sarah King	Jenny Seagrove
Jefferson Cope	David Soul

Arachnophobia •• [1990]

Director: **Frank Marshall**
Screenplay: **Don Jakoby & Wesley Strick**

Lethal spiders threaten a small American town. A 'thrillomedy', one of those horror movies that tiresomely pretends it isn't. The thrills are okay, but anyone who's ever panicked at a spider coming up the plughole should steer well clear.

[110m/PG]

Ross Jennings ....Jeff Daniels
Molly Jennings ....Harley Jane Kozak
Delbert McClintock.................John Goodman
Dr. James Atherton ....Julian Sands

Blurb Eight Legs, Two Fangs And An Attitude.

Psst! The film was originally called *Along Came the Spider* but the studio worried that people wouldn't go to see a movie about spiders. Presumably they figured nobody would know what the new title meant ◆ This is one film where the audience might be sorry how much care the film-makers took with the animals. Not one spider died. In the scene where Goodman stamps on one, a hole in his boot protected the spider. The noise you hear is that of crisps being scrunched ◆ Credits include a 'spider spotter'.

Aria • [1987]

Director: Nicolas Roeg, Ken Russell, Robert Altman, Bill Bryden, Charles Sturridge, Jean-Luc Godard, Julian Temple, Bruce Beresford, Franc Roddam, Derek Jarman

Opera MTV-style, with rapid cutting and lots of glitzy smut. A highly variable selection of opera highlights by ten highly variable directors. They say it's all over when the fat lady sings. Unfortunately, as the ladies here are so slim, the film seems to go on forever. **[89m/18]**

Pagliacci...John Hurt
King Zog................................Theresa Russell
Also: Buck Henry, Beverly D'Angelo, Bridget Fonda

Psst! This was Bridget Fonda's first film. She said not many actors get to make love and commit suicide within ten minutes in their film debut.

Army of Darkness: The Medieval Dead • [1993]

Director: Sam Raimi
Screenplay: Sam Raimi & Ivan Raimi

After surviving two *Evil Deads*, Campbell finds himself in the middle ages, still confronting screeching, high-speed zombies. The wisecracks are certainly medieval, but otherwise the film's simply silly when it tries to be funny, nasty when it tries to be scary, and crass everywhere else. Presumably the *Primeval Dead* is next?

[89m/15]

Ash...Bruce Campbell
Sheila......................................Embeth Davidtz
Arthur ....Marcus Gilbert

Psst! Bridget Fonda appears in a cameo.

Arthur 2: On the Rocks •• [1988]

Director: Bud Yorkin
Screenplay: Andy Breckman

This belated sequel to the wonderful *Arthur*, the inebriate millionaire, is nothing like as bad as some critics said, but nothing like as good as we'd like either. While there are fewer good gags, you could choke on all the extra sentiment they've piled on. **[112m/PG]**

Arthur Bach............................Dudley Moore
Linda Marolla Bach....................Liza Minnelli
Hobson.................................John Gielgud
Martha Bach ....Geraldine Fitzgerald
Burt Johnson..............................Stephen Elliott
Fairchild......................................Paul Benedict
Susan Johnson...........................Cynthia Sikes
Mrs. Canby ....Kathy Bates
Mr. Butterworth............................Jack Gilford

Quote 'Your regular, sir.' – 'Yes I am, thank you.'

Psst! Brogan Lane, the ex-Mrs. Moore, turns up as 'Cindy'.

The Assam Garden ••• [1985]

Director: Mary McMurray
Screenplay: Elisabeth Bond

An unassuming but captivating tale of Kerr, the widow of an ex-tea planter. She's trying to keep her late husband's garden going with the help of Jaffrey, who lives on a nearby council estate. Without ever resorting to polemic, it examines class, race and friendship in a moving and gently humorous way. A very British film, but none the worse for that. **[92m/U]**

Helen	Deborah Kerr
Ruxmani	Madhur Jaffrey
Mr. Philpott	Alec McCowen
Mr. Lal	Zia Mohyeddin

Psst! This was Deborah Kerr's first film in 15 years.

Assassin •• [1993]

Director: John Badham
Screenplay: Robert Getchell & Alexandra Seros

This remake of *Nikita* is virtually a photocopy of the original. A female cop killer is offered a reprieve if she'll become a government assassin. Although watchable, when the action stops, the film becomes rather embarrassing. The viewer is left with a choice of which black mini-skirted girl with a big gun they want to watch, Fonda or Parillaud – or both. Also known as *Point of No Return*. **[108m/18]**

Maggie	Bridget Fonda
Bob	Gabriel Byrne
J.P.	Dermot Mulroney

Also: Miguel Ferrer, Anne Bancroft, Olivia D'Abo, Richard Romanus, Harvey Keitel

Asterix and the Big Fight •[1989]

Director: Philippe Grimond
Screenplay: Yannik Voight & Adolf Kabatek

This Asterix adventure was the biggest animation project ever undertaken in Europe. It is extraordinarily tedious. Enough said. **[80m/U]**

With: Bill Oddie, Bernard Bresslaw, Ron Moody, Sheila Hancock, Peter Jones, Brian Blessed, Michael Elphick

Asterix in Britain •• [1988]

Director: Keith Ingham
Screenplay: Pierre Tchernia

The Romans take over Britain by attacking at the weekend – the cads! Help is forthcoming from the gallant Gauls who not only save Britain, but invent tea as well. Adults won't find it a patch on the original books but young kids will probably love it. **[75m/U]**

Asterix	Jack Beaber
Obelix	Bill Kearns
Anticlimax	Graham Bushnell
Totalapsus	Herbert Baskind

As You Like It • [1992]

Director: Christine Edzard
Screenplay: William Shakespeare

...Not as *I* like it. Updating Shakespeare's fine, but change the Forest of Arden to a Docklands wasteland and you know that yet another generation have been put off the Bard for life. **[117m/U]**

| Adam | Cyril Cusack |
| Jacques | James Fox |

Also: Don Henderson, Miriam Margolyes, Emma Croft, Griff Rhys Jones

At Close Range •• [1986]

Director: James Foley
Screenplay: Nicholas Kazan

Sean Penn's a little bored until his long-departed father turns up. As he is the particularly evil Walken, boredom's soon a thing of the past. This grim stuff is even more chilling for being based on a true story. **[115m/18]**

Brad Whitewood Jr.	Sean Penn
Brad Whitewood Sr.	Christopher Walken
Terry	Mary Stuart Masterson
Tommy	Christopher Penn
Julie	Millie Perkins
Grandmother	Eileen Ryan
Mary Sue	Candy Clark
Tim	Kiefer Sutherland

At Play in the Fields of the Lord •• [1991]

Director: Hector Babenco
Screenplay: Jean-Claude Carriere & Hector Babenco

A group of missionaries brings the word of God and the diseases of man to the

Amazonian Indian. As the missionaries' position becomes increasingly desperate, they throw off all their clothes (even Bates) in a vain attempt to make the front cover of National Geographic. Beautifully shot, the initially interesting plot gets lost somewhere in the jungle and spends over three hours trying to find its way out again. [186m/15]

Lewis Moon	Tom Berenger
Martin Quarrier	Aidan Quinn
Hazel Quarrier	Kathy Bates
Leslie Huben	John Lithgow
Andy Huben	Daryl Hannah
Wolf	Tom Waits

Quote 'Why did God create mosquitos?' [Dying Billy to Father Martin]

OOPS! Although Berenger has stripped naked, we clearly see his G-string from behind when he first enters the Indians' huts.

Psst! It was twenty-four years after first reading the book that producer Saul Zaentz finally acquired the rights to it
♦ The Berenger part was originally going to be played by Dennis Quaid.

Aunt Julia and the Scriptwriter ●● [1991]

Director: **Jon Amiel**
Screenplay: **William Boyd**

Weird little comedy with Reeves falling, understandably, for aunt Barbara Hershey, only to find that manic, Albanian-hating, scriptwriter Falk is using their romance in his soap-operas. Despite a bravura performance from Falk, the film doesn't live up to its promise of oddball fun. Also known as *Tune in Tomorrow*. [107m/12]

Aunt Julia	Barbara Hershey
Martin Loader	Keanu Reeves
Pedro Carmichael	Peter Falk
Aunt Olga	Patricia Clarkson
Uncle Luke	Richard Portnow
Sam & Sid	Jerome Dempsey
Leonard Pando	Richard B. Shull

Also: Henry Gibson, Peter Gallagher, Dan Hedaya, Buck Henry, Hope Lange, John Larroquette, Elizabeth McGovern

Quote 'When it's raining shit, the best umbrella you can buy is art.'

Psst! Nellie, the girl at the radio station stuck on Reeves, is Dedee Pfeiffer, Michelle's sister.

Avalon ●● [1990]

Director: **Barry Levinson**
Screenplay: **Barry Levinson**

Levinson's story of a Jewish immigrant family in Baltimore is perhaps a little less successful than his other films set in his old home town, *Diner* and *Tin Men*. Although there are some wonderful moments, not all the family are totally convincing and we are left with a good many unanswered questions. [128m/U]

Sam Krichinsky	Armin Mueller-Stahl
Michael Kaye	Elijah Wood
Dottie Kirk	Eve Gordon
Gabriel Krichinsky	Lou Jacobi
Ann Kaye	Elizabeth Perkins
Eva Krichinsky	Joan Plowright
Izzy Kirk	Kevin Pollak
Jules Kaye	Aidan Quinn

Also: Leo Fuchs, Israel Rubinek, Grant Gelt, Ronald Guttman, Tom Wood

Awakenings ●●● [1990]

Director: **Penny Marshall**
Screenplay: **Steven Zillian**

Heart-warming drama of shy doctor Williams discovering a way of waking patients from their sleeping sickness. Despite being unashamedly sentimental in places, the tugging on the heart-strings is offset by a very witty script. De Niro gives his usual dedicated performance, but Williams and Kavner are also splendid. [121m/12]

Leonard Lowe	Robert De Niro
Dr. Malcolm Sayer	Robin Williams
Eleanor Costello	Julie Kavner
Mrs. Lowe	Ruth Nelson
Dr. Kaufman	John Heard
Paula	Penelope Ann Miller

Lucy ....Alice Drummond
Dr. Peter Ingham ....Max Von Sydow

Quote 'If you were right, I would agree with you.'

OOPS! Watch Williams as he runs downstairs to Kavner near the end, with his coat open or shut depending on the shot ✦ As De Niro leaves the model he's working on to talk to Miller, a paper bag appears on the still-warm seat.

Psst! Williams accidentally broke De Niro's nose. He denied it was in a fit of anger, saying, 'If that was true, I don't think I'd be here today. I mean, not with my own teeth.'

A.W.O.L. — Absent Without Leave •• [1990]

Director: **Sheldon Lettich**
Screenplay: **Sheldon Lettich & Jean-Claude Van Damme**

Van Damme runs *away* from the Foreign Legion to beat the living daylights out of the guys who beat the living daylights out of his brother. An endless series of kick-boxing fights are occasionally interrupted by the usual imbecilic plot. Also known as *Lionheart*. **[110m/18]**

Lyon ....Jean-Claude Van Damme
Cynthia ....Deborah Rennard
Joshua ....Harrison Page
Helene ....Lisa Pelikan

B

Babar: The Movie ••• [1989]

Director: **Alan Bunce**
Screenplay: **Peter Sauder, Raymond Jafelice, Alan Bunce & Others**

For young kids who don't prefer turtles to elephants, this is a pleasant adaptation of the well-known books. The animation is uninspired, but that's unlikely to worry its target audience. **[70m/U]**

With: Gordon Pinsent, Gavin Magrath, Elizabeth Hanna, Sarah Polley

Babette's Feast •••• [1988]

Director: **Gabriel Axel**
Screenplay: **Gabriel Axel**

In this Danish film set in the late 19th century, Parisian exile Audran, working for two sisters in a primly religious Danish fishing village, wins a fortune in the Paris lottery and decides to use it to lay on an enormous banquet. Although this may sound rather tedious, in fact it is a masterful, magical film that has us enraptured as we watch the suspicious villagers succumb to the delights of the 'pagan' feast. Trust me. It's brilliant. **[102m/U]**

Babette Hersant ....Stephane Audran
Achille Papin ....Jean-Philippe Lafont
Lorens (young) ....Gudmar Wivesson
Lorens Lowenhielm (old) ....Jarl Kulle

Psst! The original story was by Karen Blixen, portrayed by Meryl Streep in *Out of Africa*. It was written as a bet with a friend who told her the best way to get Americans to buy her stuff was to write about food! ✦ In New York, one restaurant did a related promotion. After the film, cinemagoers could sit down to the same gargantuan banquet served up by Audran.

Baby Boom •• [1987]

Director: **Charles Shyer**
Screenplay: **Nancy Meyers & Charles Shyer**

Drably predictable yarn of workaholic yuppie Keaton 'inheriting' a baby and decamping to the country. Being from the big, bad city, naturally she can't cope with rural life until she finds true love and a recipe for baby food she can turn into a successful business. I wonder who wrote this drivel? The baby? **[111m/PG]**

J.C. Wiatt ....Diane Keaton
Steven Buchner ....Harold Ramis
Fritz Curtis ....Sam Wanamaker
Ken Arrenberg ....James Spader
Hughes Larrabee ....Pat Hingle
Verne Boone ....Britt Leach
Dr. Jeff Cooper ....Sam Shepard

Psst! In Latin America, its title was changed to *Who Called the Stork?* ◆ Meyers and Shyer, who wrote the screenplay, tackily dedicated the film to their daughter Annie.

Baby, It's You ••• [1983]

Director: **John Sayles**
Screenplay: **John Sayles**

A better than average coming-of-age drama with Arquette falling for bad boy Spano, the only lad in school to admire Sinatra, then outgrowing him when she goes to college. Mainly thoughtful and interesting, it loses its grip somewhat once school's out.   **[105m/15]**

Jill ....Rosanna Arquette
Sheik ....Vincent Spano
Mrs. Rosen ....Joanna Merlin
Dr. Rosen ....Jack Davidson
Capadilupo ....Nick Ferrari
Steve ....Matthew Modine
Stewart ....Robert Downey Jr.

Psst! Robert Downey Jr. is credited as Stewart. He is just about visible on the right-hand side as one of the college boys in the restaurant with Arquette.

Baby... Secret of the Lost Legend •• [1985]

Director: B.W.L. Norton
Screenplay: Clifford Green & Ellen Green

A couple find a brontosaurus family in the African jungle and have to contend with a villainous professor who can doubtless sense the immense merchandising opportunities. Rather typical, but pleasant, old-fashioned Disney fare.

[93m/PG]

George Loomis ....William Katt
Susan Matthews-Loomis ....Sean Young
Dr. Eric Kiviat ....Patrick McGoohan
Nigel Jenkins ....Julian Fellowes

Bachelor Party • [1984]

Director: **Neal Israel**
Screenplay: **Neal Israel & Pat Proft**

The usual teen nerd sex comedy, with Hanks the bridgegroom getting the predictable tasteful send-off from his mates. Only his presence makes it bearable.

[105m/18]

Rick Gassko ....Tom Hanks
Debbie Thompson ....Tawny Kitaen
Jay O'Neill ....Adrian Zmed
Mr. Thompson ....George Grizzard

Backdraft •• [1991]

Director: **Ron Howard**
Screenplay: **Gregory Widen**

They were all ready to make a gritty picture about squabbling firefighting brothers and a dangerous arsonist on the loose when the script must have got burnt up in one of the fires. They went ahead anyway, even though they had no real story you'd notice. While the fire is so real and frightening it's almost like an uncredited member of the cast, sitting in the garden watching your own home burn down would be just as entertaining.   **[136m/15]**

Stephen McCaffrey ....Kurt Russell
Brian McCaffrey ....William Baldwin
John Adcox ....Scott Glenn
Jennifer Vaitkus ....Jennifer Jason Leigh
Helen McCaffrey ....Rebecca De Mornay
Ronald Bartel ....Donald Sutherland
Donald Rimgale ....Robert De Niro
Tim Krizminski ....Jason Gedrick
Martin Swayzak ....J. T. Walsh

Psst! The script was written by a former fireman and there are several real firefighters among the cast ◆ In Connecticut, a cinema had to be evacuated when a real fire broke out, caused by nesting pigeons shorting a circuit.

Backfire •• [1987]

Director: **Gilbert Cates**
Screenplay: **Larry Brand & Rebecca Reynolds**

This film noir in which Allen wants hubby Fahey disposed of has bags of style. But its extraordinarily convoluted plot doesn't conceal its lack of originality, particularly with Carradine giving us yet another disturbed Vietnam vet. [91m/18]

Donny McAndrew	Jeff Fahey
Mara	Karen Allen
Reed	Keith Carradine
Sherrif Clint	Bernie Casey

Back to School • [1986]

Director: **Alan Metter**
Screenplay: **Steven Kampmann, Will Porter, Peter Torokvei & Harold Ramis**

Dangerfield's an American comic rather like Bernard Manning, only not so shy. Here he's a wealthy tycoon who enrols in his son's school. Rather than do any work, he pays Kurt Vonnegut to do his English essay and NASA to help out with astronomy. How clever that the certificate for the movie matches the IQ needed to enjoy it. [96m/15]

Thornton Melon	Rodney Dangerfield
Diane	Sally Kellerman
Lou	Burt Young
Jason Melon	Keith Gordon
Derek	Robert Downey Jr.
Coach Turnbull	M. Emmet Walsh
Dean Martin	Ned Beatty

Quote 'Bring a pitcher of beer every seven minutes until someone passes out. Then bring one every ten minutes.'

OOPS! If it doesn't spoil the magic of the cinema and destroy your faith in movies, you should know that it isn't really the portly Dangerfield doing the Triple Lindy highdive. Watch the double's hair come adrift slightly on the way down.

Back to the Future •••• [1985]

Director: **Robert Zemeckis**
Screenplay: **Bob Gale & Robert Zemeckis**

Cracking sci-fi adventure yarn, full of verve, originality, excitment and wacky humour. Inventor Lloyd sends teenager Fox (actually 24) back to the 50s where, to ensure his own existence, he has to bring his parents together, a feat complicated when his mother falls for him. A delight from start to finish. [116m/PG]

Marty McFly	Michael J. Fox
Dr. Emmett Brown	Christopher Lloyd
George McFly	Crispin Glover
Lorraine Baines	Lea Thompson
Jennifer Parker	Claudia Wells
Biff Tannen	Thomas F. Wilson
Dave McFly	Marc McClure
Linda McFly	Wendie Jo Sperber
Sam Baines	George DiCenzo
Stella Baines	Frances Lee McCain
Mr. Strickland	James Tolkan

OOPS! How come nobody notices that the money Marty hands over in the café for his coffee is 20 years ahead of its time? • Watch the mileometer lose a few miles as Marty tries to escape from the terrorists • Doc obviously invented Velcro and didn't tell anybody. It's on his trainers when he's hanging from the clock, several years too early.

Psst! Rejected by all the major studios, it was Spielberg who gave the writers their chance • Eric Stoltz was the original lead, but was replaced 5 weeks into production. Matthew Modine and Ralph Macchio turned the part down • Fox was working on his TV show *Family Ties* all day. For a month and a half he worked on *BTTF* from 6 till midnight each day as well • Glover lost his voice through nerves on the first day and had to dub his entire part later • Look out for Billy Zane as 'Match' and Huey Lewis, who sings 'The Power of Love', in a cameo as a schoolteacher.

Back to the Future, Part II •• [1989]

Director: **Robert Zemeckis**
Screenplay: **Bob Gale**

The weakest of the series has some stunning effects, with Fox at one point playing three characters at one and the very same time. But the story, involving parallel worlds in which villain Biff can be married to mum, is overcomplicated while the jokes (*Jaws 19* is playing in the future) aren't so plentiful. The cliff-hanger ending, forcing you to watch the next one, is a bit of a cheek. Shue, however, is delightful as the new Jennifer. [107m/PG]

Marty/Marlene McFly	Michael J. Fox
Dr. Emmett Brown	Christopher Lloyd
Lorraine	Lea Thompson
Biff Tannen/Griff	Thomas F. Wilson
Jennifer	Elisabeth Shue

Also: James Tolkan, Harry Waters Jr., Charles Fleischer, Jeffrey Weissman, Billy Zane, Joe Flaherty, Flea

Quote 'Something's got to be done about your kids, Marty!'

Psst! Crispin Glover thought he was indispensible as Marty's dad but Universal wouldn't pay the $1m he asked for. Instead they put in some out-takes from the first film and used a double ♦ Judy Ovitz, wife of Mike Ovitz, Hollywood's most powerful agent, appears as the 'antique store sales-woman', while Elijah Wood, perhaps the best (if not best-paid) child actor appears in an early role as a 'video game boy'.

Back to the Future, Part III •••• [1990]

Director: Robert Zemeckis
Screenplay: Bob Gale

In some ways the best of them all, with Fox nipping back to the 1880's to stop Lloyd being shot. The fun of the original is recreated along with the spirit of the Wild West in a rollicking romp that never lets up. Doc gets a love interest too, in the person of the lovely Steenburgen. Perfect entertainment. [118m/PG]

Marty/Seamus McFly	Michael J. Fox
Dr. Emmett Brown	Christopher Lloyd
Clara Clayton	Mary Steenburgen
"Mad Dog" Tannen/Biff	Thomas F. Wilson
Maggie McFly/Lorraine	Lea Thompson

Jennifer	Elisabeth Shue
Bartender	Matt Clark

Blurb They've Saved The Best Trip For Last...But This Time They May Have Gone Too Far.

Psst! Unusually, because of the work schedules of Fox and director Zemeckis, parts II & III were filmed back-to-back.

Backtrack
SEE: Catchfire

The Bad Boys ••• [1983]

Director: Rick Rosenthal
Screenplay: Richard Di Lello

Rough Chicago teenagers take their quarrels with them into the local juvenile nick. It seems hard now to credit the criticism the film attracted at the time for its violence. It's still pretty absorbing. [109m/18]

Mick O'Brien	Sean Penn
Ramon Herrera	Reni Santoni
Gene Daniels	Jim Moody
Horowitz	Eric Gurry
Paco Moreno	Esai Morales
J.C. Walenski	Ally Sheedy
Viking Lofgren	Clancy Brown

Bad Influence •• [1990]

Director: Curtis Hanson
Screenplay: David Koepp

Yuppie Spader befriends bad boy Lowe and then finds him taking over his life. The script never quite lives up to the promising idea and remains strictly by-the-numbers stuff. It has, of course, been done many times before, never better than in Hitchcock's *Strangers on a Train*. [100m/18]

Alex	Rob Lowe
Michael Boll	James Spader
Claire	Lisa Zane
Pismo Boll	Christian Clemenson
Leslie	Kathleen Wilhoite

Psst! The movie uncannily reflects Lowe's off-screen life, containing as it does yet another video of him cavorting naked with a girl ♦ The scene where Lowe tries to blow up a car by connecting a busted tail-light with a petrol tank is apparently a terrorist trick, from which one important step has been omitted.

Bad Lieutenant • [1992]

Director: **Abel Ferrara**
Screenplay: **Zoe Lund & Abel Ferrara**

Only Keitel could play this role of the corrupt, sleazy, drug-taking, gambling, self-destructive New York detective. Just as well, because Keitel is probably the only actor who'd want to, particularly considering his full-frontal. Keitel's sudden attack of conscience when a raped nun refuses to condemn her attackers, comes out of left field and never convinces. Dramatically turgid, it's about as much fun as being whopped about the skull with a nightstick. **[96m/18]**

Lt.	Harvey Keitel
Nun	Frankie Thorn
Zoe	Zoe Lund
Lite	Anthony Ruggiero

Bad Taste •• [1989]

Director: **Peter Jackson**
Screenplay: **Peter Jackson**

Aliens from space view earth as a source of nourishment for their junk food chain – and we're not talking vegeburgers. An aptly-titled introduction to the wholesome world of Peter Jackson with epic quantities of blood, macabre humour, wild make-up and uneven quality. **[93m/18]**

Derek	Peter Jackson
Frank	Mike Minett
Barry	Terry Potter

Quote 'I'm a Derek and Dereks never give up.'

Bagdad Cafe ••• [1988]

Director: **Percy Adlon**
Screenplay: **Percy Adlon & Eleonore Adlon**

Left by her husband in the middle of the Californian desert, calorifically-challenged Sägebrecht cools her heels at a roadside caff which she gradually livens up. Despite the lack of plot, the charm and wit should win you over. You certainly see Jack Palance as never before, a deliciously dandified painter desperate to run the brush over Sägebrecht. **[91m/PG]**

Jasmin	Marianne Sägebrecht
Brenda	C.C.H. Pounder
Rudi Cox	Jack Palance
Debby	Christine Kaufman
Phyllis	Monica Calhoun

The Ballad of Gregorio Cortez ••• [1983]

Director: **Robert M. Young**
Screenplay: **Robert M. Young**

This unusual Western is based on a true story of a Spanish-speaking Mexican cowhand mistakenly arrested in Texas. Trying to escape from a situation he can't understand, he kills a sheriff and manages to evade a massive posse for a fortnight. A trifle worthy in places, but fascinating nonetheless. **[105m/15]**

Gregorio Cortez	Edward James Olmos
Frank Fly	James Gammon
Boone Choate	Tom Bower
Reporter Blakly	Bruce McGill

Psst! The jail and courtroom are the originals where Cortez was held and tried.

The Ballad of the Sad Café • [1991]

Director: **Simon Callow**
Screenplay: **Michael Hirst**

Really peculiar film of a Depression-era Southern town run by despotic Redgrave. Callow's debut behind the camera scores a few points for atmosphere but none for keeping us interested in what happens to these weirdoes. **[100m/15]**

Miss Amelia Evans	Vanessa Redgrave
Marvin Macy	Keith Carradine
Cousin Lymon	Cork Hubbert
Rev. Willin	Rod Steiger
Lawyer Taylor	Austin Pendleton

Psst! The film was shot at Wille Nelson's ranch in Texas, converted at a cost of

$500,000 into a small town with church, mill and café ✦ The slap given to 12-year-old Zane Rockenbaugh by Redgrave is the real thing. It took six takes!

Bamba, La

SEE: La Bamba

Band of the Hand ✦ [1986]

Director: Paul Michael Glaser
Screenplay: Leon Garen & Jack Baran

A Vietnam vet gives some street toughs a bit of P.E. then sends them out to rid Miami of drugs. Deadeningly dull stuff from the creators of *Miami Vice*. [109m/18]

Joe	Stephen Lang
Ruben	Michael Carmine
Nikki	Lauren Holly
J.L.	John Cameron Mitchell
Cream	Larry Fishburne

Psst! This was the directorial debut of Glaser, best remembered as Starsky from *Starsky and Hutch*.

Barbarosa ••• [1982]

Director: Fred Schepisi
Screenplay: William D. Wittliff

Nelson is the legendary old outlaw involved in a family feud who adopts farmhand Busey as his protégé. This delightful film was shunned by audiences who felt at the time, wrongly, that old-style Westerns couldn't give them the entertainment they sought. [90m/PG]

Barbarosa	Willie Nelson
Karl	Gary Busey
Josephina	Isela Vega
Don Braulio	Gilbert Roland

Barfly ••• [1987]

Director: Barbet Schroeder
Screenplay: Charles Bukowski

Rourke's in the seedy milieu in which he is happiest, as the hard-drinking writer who takes up with alcoholic down-and-out Dunaway. Both are superb in this tough, but sometimes funny film that's

about as far from *Cheers* as you can get. [99m/18]

Henry	Mickey Rourke
Wanda Wilcox	Faye Dunaway
Tully	Alice Krige
Detective	Jack Nance
Jim	J.C. Quinn
Eddie	Frank Stallone

Psst! Director Barbet Schroeder turned up in producer Menahem Golan's office with an electric saw, threatening to cut off a finger if Golan didn't back the film. Knowing Schroeder, and not wanting blood on his hands (nor, indeed, his desk), Golan agreed ✦ Frank Stallone is Sylvester's brother.

Barton Fink ✦ [1992]

Director: Joel Coen
Screenplay: Ethan Coen & Joel Coen

Ludicrously over-praised by the artier critics, this yarn of a left-wing hack suffering writer's block on a boxing pic is all style and no substance. Despite some tricksy camera shots, this weird film becomes pretentious and mightily dull. Fine, perhaps, for those who actually like watching wallpaper peel. Lerner is brilliant as the bombastic studio head. [116m/15]

Barton Fink	John Turturro
Charlie Meadows	John Goodman
Audrey Taylor	Judy Davis
Jack Lipnick	Michael Lerner
W.P. Mayhew	John Mahoney
Ben Geisler	Tony Shalhoub
Lou Breeze	Jon Polito

Blurb Between Heaven And Hell, There's Always Hollywood.

Quote 'We all want it to have that Barton Fink feeling and I guess we all have that Barton Fink feeling. But since *you're* Barton Fink I'm assuming you have it in spades.'

OOPS! If there's any logic to this film, then surely Goodman's shoes shouldn't still be in the corridor waiting to be shone after he's left the hotel? ✦ Watch studio head Lerner's medals. They're are all over the shop.

Basic Instinct •• [1992]

Director: Paul Verhoeven
Screenplay: Joe Eszterhas

Strip out the steamy sex and you're left with a confusing and rather nasty little thriller that would've died a death were it not for the suspiciously useful public protests. Stone's certainly a knockout as the knickerless, bisexual novelist suspected by Douglas of ice-picking her lover to death (how different from the home life of our own dear Barbara Cartland). But the plot's wildly implausible, as well as being identical to the one Eszterhas uses in most of his pics. [128m/18]

Det. Nick Curran	Michael Douglas
Catherine Tramell	Sharon Stone
Gus	George Dzundza
Dr. Beth Garner	Jeanne Tripplehorn
Lt. Walker	Denis Arndt
Roxy	Leilani Sarelle
Andrews	Bruce A. Young
Capt. Talcott	Chelcie Ross

Blurb Flesh Seduces. Passion Kills.

Quote 'It's like ballet. In the rough sex scene between me and Jeanne Tripplehorn it was well rehearsed to the point of boom, up against the wall, kiss, kiss, kiss, boom, her leg comes up, kiss, rip open her blouse etc etc.' [Douglas]

OOPS! In the interrogation room, keep your eye on Stone's cigarette, rather than her legs, and you'll see it vanish and then pop back before disappearing again ✦ When she dresses to go with Douglas to be interrogated, not only her clothes change, but her hairstyle too ✦ The door of Tripplehorn's office spells her first name differently from the record on the computer.

Psst! Michael Douglas was paid $14m, while scriptwriter Eszterhas got a record $3m ✦ Sharon Stone got just $300,000, but for *Sliver*, her next film, she was paid $2.5m plus a percentage of profits ✦ She complained that her thighs were rubbed raw by Douglas's stubble after several hours of filming a love scene ✦ Britain got a stronger version than America,

with 43 seconds that were cut in the States ✦ Douglas lost 25 lb to get in shape for the part.

Basil, the Great Mouse Detective ••• [1986]

Director: John Musker, Ron Clements & Others
Screenplay: Ron Clements, John Musker & Others

Fun Disney tale about a Sherlock Holmes-type mouse who tangles with the dastardly Professor Ratigan (voiced by Vincent Price) when he plots to overthrow the mouse queen. A strong story and high-quality animation should keep everyone entertained. Also known as *The Great Mouse Detective*. [74m/U]

With: Vincent Price, Barrie Ingham, Val Bettin

Basket Case ••• [1982]

Director: Frank Henenlotter
Screenplay: Frank Henenlotter

A strange young man rents a room in a grungy New York hotel, bringing something strange with him in a basket. A zero-budget, tongue-in-cheek shocker which is perverse enough to hold the attention despite the drab sleaze. [90m/18]

Duane	Kevin Van Hentenryck
Sharon	Terri Susan Smith
Casey	Beverly Bonner
Hotel manager	Robert Vogel

Blurb The Tenant In Room Seven Is Very Small, Very Twisted And Very Mad.

Batman •• [1989]

Director: Tim Burton
Screenplay: Sam Hamm & Warren Skaaren

Nice pictures, shame about the story. In a film far removed from the camp TV series, the dark and moody design is everything. The uncharismatic Keaton's an odd choice for the lead and he's overacted off the screen by Nicholson's Joker.

Blurring the boundary between goodie and baddie is one thing, but making the baddie so much more fun unbalances everything. Let's have three cheers, though, for Gough as Alfred. **[126m/12]**

Batman/Bruce Wayne.............Michael Keaton
The Joker/Jack Napier..............Jack Nicholson
Vicki Vale.................................Kim Basinger
Alexander...................................Robert Wuhl
Commissioner Gordon ....Pat Hingle
Harvey Dent.....................Billy Dee Williams
Alfred.......................................Michael Gough
Grissom..Jack Palance
Alicia..Jerry Hall

Quote 'Have you ever danced with the devil in the pale moonlight?' ✦ 'What kind of world do we live in where a man dressed up as a *bat* gets all my press?'

OOPS! One give-away sign that the film was made in Britain is the anglicised spelling of 'moisturising' on the foam bath the Joker is peddling ✦ In the scene where the hoods are trashing pictures, watch the pink handprints vanish ✦ Although the Batmobile is supposedly driving on its own at one point, if you look carefully you can see a hand on the wheel ✦ When Vicki goes to see Bruce Wayne after hearing about his parents' death, she arrives in a different dress and with her hair redone.

Psst! Nicholson is said to have made over $50 million from the film and its attendant merchandising. That's more than the $40m the film is estimated to have cost ✦ The set was the biggest since *Cleopatra*. One man became wealthy just supplying the 60 miles of scaffolding used ✦ Sean Young was the original Vicki, but had a riding accident just before filming began. The last-minute replacement put an extra $500,000 on the budget ✦ Designer Anton Furst said he wanted Gotham City to look like 'New York without planning permission for 300 years.' ✦ Look out for Prince in the Joker's procession ✦ The '12' Certificate was introduced into the UK specifically so that *Batman* could reach its target audience.

Batman Returns ••• [1992]

Director: **Tim Burton**
Screenplay: **Daniel Waters**

Armed with even more impressive toys than in *Batman*, the Caped Crusader rides to the rescue of a Gotham City menaced by not one but three villains. Burton's wonderful-looking sequel is crammed with entertaining set-piece action scenes. However, like *Batman*, the plot has more loose ends than Spaghetti Junction. You'd think if they were spending $80 million, they could have afforded a script that made sense. It's worth seeing for Pfeiffer alone as the whip-wielding leather-clad Catwoman, the stuff dreams – naughty dreams – are made of. **[127m/12]**

Batman/Bruce Wayne.............Michael Keaton
Penguin/Oscar Cobblepot ....Danny DeVito
Catwoman/Selina Kyle ....Michelle Pfeiffer
Max Shreck....................Christopher Walken
Alfred.......................................Michael Gough
Mayor ....Michael Murphy
Also: Cristi Conaway, Andrew Bryniarski, Pat Hingle, Vincent Schiavelli

Quote 'Life's a bitch. Now so am I' ✦ 'You're only jealous because I'm a genuine freak and you have to wear a mask.'

OOPS! When Penguin visits his parents' grave, watch for the tombstone that wobbles as he brushes past.

Psst! Pfeiffer studied kick-boxing, yoga, martial arts and weight-lifting. All the tricks with the whip are done by her, though the derrière of her costume was apparently padded ✦ A scene with Catwoman chaining Batman to a bed was cut, as was the idea that she should swallow the bird ✦ DeVito ate raw fish to get into the part ✦ Pfeiffer and Keaton revived an old fling during the making of the film ✦ Annette Bening was to have been Catwoman, but became pregnant with Warren's baby. Madonna, Cher and Sean Young particularly coveted the part, with Young apparently turning up in a catsuit on the lot to argue her case ✦ The penguins had their own refrigerated trailer and swimming pool ✦ Pee-Wee

Herman, disgraced star of Burton's first movie, appears briefly, and almost unrecognizably, as the Penguin's father.

*batteries not included • [1987]

Director: **Matthew Robbins**
Screenplay: **Matthew Robbins, Brad Bird, Brent Maddock & S.S. Wilson**

A group of New Yorkers fight the planned demolition of their home, helped by a group of tiny little aliens. Spielberg, who executive-produced this, has thrown the scripts of *E.T.* and *Cocoon* into a pot, and forgotten to turn the heat on. So bad, you're willing the ball and chain to start swinging.   [106m/PG]

Frank	Hume Cronyn
Faye	Jessica Tandy
Harry	Frank McRae
Marisa	Elizabeth Pena

BAT 21 ••• [1988]

Director: **Peter Markle**
Screenplay: **William C. Anderson & George Gordon**

A different slant on Vietnam, with Hackman the backroom bigwig in uniform shot down behind enemy lines, and Glover the pilot trying to get him out. Straightforward, old-fashioned storytelling based on a true story.   [105m/15]

Lt. Col. Iceal Hambleton	Gene Hackman
Capt. Bartholomew Clark	Danny Glover
Col. George Walker	Jerry Reed
Ross Carver	David Marshall Grant
Sgt. Harley Rumbaugh	Clayton Rohner

The Bay Boy •• [1984]

Director: **Daniel Petrie**
Screenplay: **Daniel Petrie**

Yet another coming-of-age yarn, this time set in Canada in the 30s but otherwise similar to all the rest. For heaven's sake, when is this genre going to come of age?   [101m/15]

Donald Campbell	Kiefer Sutherland
Mrs. Campbell	Liv Ullmann
Mr. Campbell	Peter Donat

Beaches • [1988]

Director: **Garry Marshall**
Screenplay: **Mary Agnes Donoghue**

Beaches can be such a nuisance. All that irritating, scratchy sand getting everywhere. Mix it up with a hefty dose of syrup and you've got yourself a gooey, unpleasant mess. Add an overdose of Midler and you're ready to part with your dinner. This weepy, tacky tale of rich girl, poor girl friendship across the years seems interminable. For once, the ad for the film got it right. It does seem to last forever. However, that's a male view. Some women apparently like it.   [124m/15]

C.C. Bloom	Bette Midler
Hillary Whitney Essex	Barbara Hershey
John Pierce	John Heard
Dr. Richard Milstein	Spalding Gray

Also: Lainie Kazan, James Read, Grace Johnston, Hector Elizondo

Blurb Once In A Lifetime, You Make A Friendship That Lasts Forever.

OOPS! As Midler and Hershey go through revolving doors, the camera crew are reflected in the glass.

Psst! Although Kazan plays Midler's mother, she was only three years older at the time, 45 to Midler's 42.

The Bear ••• [1989]

Director: **Jean-Jacques Annaud**
Screenplay: **Gérard Brach**

A delightful family film about an orphaned bear taking up with a giant Kodiak grizzly being tracked by a couple of hunters. A remarkable cinematic feat which took several years to film, the animals do everything actors do except talk. A superb acting debut from La Douce as Youk.
                                          [94m/PG]

Youk	La Douce
Bill	Jack Wallace
Tom	Tcheky Karyo
Dog handler	Andre Lacombe

Psst! Probably the first movie to have a bear hallucinating on magic mushrooms ✦ The entire budget for the film, at $25m the most expensive ever French movie, came from producer Claude Berri. Remarkably, it made over $100 million before it even opened in America.

The Beastmaster •   [1982]

Director: **Don Coscarelli**
Screenplay: **Don Coscarelli & Paul Pepperman**

Beefcake hunk meets cheesecake bimbo and plans to avenge his father's death. Singer has the ability to communicate with animals, which perform beautifully at his bidding. What a shame this ability escapes the man himself.   **[117m/PG]**

Dar ....Marc Singer
Kiri ....Tanya Roberts
Maax ....Rip Torn

Beat Street ••   [1984]

Director: **Stan Lathan**
Screenplay: **Andrew Davis, David Gilbert & Paul Golding**

Young graffiti artists, nascent DJs and breakdancers in the Bronx. Lots of music, but all a bit five minutes ago.   **[105m/PG]**

Tracy ....Rae Dawn Chong
Kenny ....Guy Davis
Ramon ....John Chardiet
Chollie ....Leon W. Grant

Beauty and the Beast ••••   [1991]

Director: **Gary Trousdale & Kirk Wise**
Screenplay: **Linda Wolverton**

One of the greatest animated films ever. The feminist updating of the story works wonderfully and is mercifully free of the treacly sentiment of so many recent Disney pics. The supporting characters are splendidly drawn, in both senses of the word. If Belle had any sense, however, she'd have stuck with the Beast, rather than turned him into a Chippendale bimbo of a Prince.   **[84m/U]**

Belle ....Paige O'Hara
Beast ....Robby Benson

Lumiere ....Jerry Orbach
Mrs. Potts ....Angela Lansbury
Gaston ....Richard White
Cogsworth/Narrator ....David Ogden Stiers

Psst! The best-selling video ever in the US, surpassing *Fantasia's* record in only a few months.

The Bedroom Window ••   [1987]

Director: **Curtis Hanson**
Screenplay: **Curtis Hanson**

In the tried-and-tested Hitchcock way, Guttenberg has to prove his innocence when he's believed to be a multiple murderer. Despite flashes of excitement, there's one coincidence too many in a plot that takes some swallowing.   **[112m/15]**

Terry Lambert ....Steve Guttenberg
Denise...........................Elizabeth McGovern
Sylvia ....Isabelle Huppert
Collin ....Paul Shenar
Quirke ....Carl Lumbly
Henderson's attorney ....Wallace Shawn

Beethoven •••   [1992]

Director: **Brian Levant**
Screenplay: **Edmond Dantes & Amy Holden Jones**

A 13-stone St. Bernard on the lam from animal experimenters invades Grodin's home and behaves like any normal dog, saving lives, matchmaking, advising on business deals and slobbering a lot. This nifty, heart-warming family pic is strongly reminiscent of 60's Disney movies. The humour's more self-assured than many adult entertainments, too. Be warned, though, the baddies are so nasty they could spook really young kids. **[87m/U]**

George Newton ....Charles Grodin
Alice Newton ....Bonnie Hunt
Dr. Varnick....................................Dean Jones
Ryce ....Nicholle Tom
Ted.................................Christopher Castile
Also: Sarah Rose Karr, Oliver Platt, Stanley Tucci, David Duchovny, Patricia Heaton

Psst! A Dutch cinema offered free tickets

to St. Bernard dogs and their owners. 80 took up the offer ✦ Although the star of a film costing $15m, Chris playing Beethoven, got just $500 a day ✦ He did, however, have 8 stand-ins, doubles and understudies, with 16 further dogs needed to portray him as he was growing up.

Beetlejuice •• [1988]

Director: **Tim Burton**
Screenplay: **Michael McDowell &**
Warren Skaaren

Dearly departed couple Davis and Baldwin have difficulty adjusting to the hereafter and to the ghastly new inhabitants of their beloved home. So they call in mad ghoul Keaton to get rid of them. Despite the wonderful special effects, Keaton's energetic performance and the interesting look of the picture, it all gets rather tiresome and repetitive. [92m/15]

Adam	Alec Baldwin
Barbara	Geena Davis
Betelgeuse	Michael Keaton
Charles Deetz	Jeffrey Jones
Delia Deetz	Catherine O'Hara
Lydia Deetz	Winona Ryder
Juno	Sylvia Sidney

Also: Robert Goulet, Glenn Shadix, Dick Cavett, Annie McEnroe

Blurb The Name In Laughter From The Hereafter.

OOPS! If you can't see the ghosts in mirrors, how come you can see them reflected in a window?

The Believers • [1987]

Director: **John Schlesinger**
Screenplay: **Mark Frost**

A sinister religion advocates human sacrifices, not in some green jungle but in the urban jungle of New York, causing Sheen a few problems when he moves his family there. Schlesinger's attempt to dignify this trashy story is way off beam for this sort of schlock. [114m/18]

Cal Jamison	Martin Sheen
Jessica Halliday	Helen Shaver
Chris Jamison	Harley Cross
Lt. Sean McTaggert	Robert Loggia

Also: Elizabeth Wilson, Harris Yulin, Lee Richardson, Richard Masur, Jimmy Smits

Bellman and True •• [1988]

Director: **Richard Loncraine**
Screenplay: **Desmond Lowden, Richard**
Loncraine & Michael Wearing

An occasionally enjoyable offbeat British robbery movie, which suffers from having been cut down from a TV series. Hill's computer expert forced into participating in a bank heist by a group of ruthless crooks. [121m/15]

Hiller	Bernard Hill
The boy	Kieran O'Brien
Salto	Richard Hope
Anna	Frances Tomelty

The Belly of an Architect •• [1987]

Director: **Peter Greenaway**
Screenplay: **Peter Greenaway**

An American architect visiting Rome suspects his wife of adultery and fears he's been poisoned when he develops stomach pains. Dennehy's superb lead performance only exposes the weakness of the rest of the cast. The Rome Tourist Board must love Greenaway; the city's never looked so beautiful. [118m/15]

Stourley Kracklite	Brian Dennehy
Louisa Kracklite	Chloe Webb
Caspasian Speckler	Lambert Wilson

Psst! Note for pseuds: The nine-month timespan of the storyline reflects Brian Dennehy's baby, from conception to birth ✦ Another note for pseuds: The buildings are all shot straight on, so that they resemble architects' plans.

Benny & Joon ••• [1993]

Director: **Jeremiah Chechik**
Screenplay: **Barry Berman**

Since the death of their parents, Quinn has looked after his disturbed sister

Masterson. But their lives are turned upside-down when mad clown Depp, in another *Edward Scissorhands*-type role, comes onto the scene. Depp is glorious as the chap obsessed with Keaton and Chaplin, well-fitted to this sort of physical comedy . There's a refreshing, unusual magical quality about the film which constantly surprises the viewer. **[98m/PG]**

Sam	Johnny Depp
Joon	Mary Stuart Masterson
Benny	Aidan Quinn
Ruthie	Julianne Moore
Eric	Oliver Platt
Dr. Garvey	C.C.H. Pounder

Quote 'Did you have to go to school for that?' – 'No, I got thrown out of school for that.'

Psst! Woody Harrelson left the picture to make *Indecent Proposal* and was sued by the producers, settling later out of court.

Bert Rigby, You're a Fool • [1989]

Director: **Carl Reiner**
Screenplay: **Carl Reiner**

...But not as big a one as the studio head who gave this one the green light. An embarrassing musical misfire with Lindsay the song-and-dance miner who wants to dig his way into showbiz. **[94m/15]**

Bert Rigby	Robert Lindsay
Meredith Perlestein	Anne Bancroft
Jim Shirley	Corbin Bernsen
Sid Trample	Robbie Coltrane

Also: Cathryn Bradshaw, Jackie Gayle, Bruno Kirby, Liz Smith

Best Defense • [1984]

Director: **Willard Huyck**
Screenplay: **Gloria Katz & Willard Huyck**

Hideously unfunny star comedy remarkable in that the two stars never actually appear on screen together. Moore invents a new tank. Murphy has to try it out. You think they've both made some dogs before? This is practically rabid. **[94m/15]**

Wylie Cooper	Dudley Moore
Landry	Eddie Murphy
Laura	Kate Capshaw
Morgan	Michael Scalera
Loparino	George Dzundza

Best Friends •• [1982]

Director: **Norman Jewison**
Screenplay: **Valerie Curtin & Barry Levinson**

Screenwriter lovers Hawn and Reynolds spoil it all by getting married. A light, frothy soufflé which can't possibly rise when made with such a limp script and such terrible over-acting. **[116m/PG]**

Richard Babson	Burt Reynolds
Paula McCullen	Goldie Hawn
Eleanor McCullen	Jessica Tandy
Tim McCullen	Barnard Hughes

Also: Audra Lindley, Keenan Wynn, Ron Silver, Richard Libertini

Psst! The script is supposedly autobiographical. Curtin (who appears in a playpen) and Levinson were 'best friends' who then spoilt it all by getting married – and later divorced.

Best of the Best • [1989]

Director: **Robert Radler**
Screenplay: **Paul Levine**

Wholly inappropriately named martial arts movie. **[95m/18]**

Alex Grady	Eric Roberts
Coach Couzo	James Earl Jones
Wade	Sally Kirkland
Tommy	Phillip Rhee
Travis Brickley	Christopher Penn

Best of the Best 2 • [1993]

Director: **Robert Radler**
Screenplay: **Max Strom & John Allen Nelson**

Worst of the worst. **[99m/18]**

Alex Grady	Eric Roberts
Tommy Lee	Phillip Rhee
Travis Brickley	Christopher Penn

Also: Edan Gross, Ralph Moeller, Meg Foster, Sonny Landham, Wayne Newton

Best Seller •••• [1987]

Director: John Flynn
Screenplay: Larry Cohen

An excellent underrated thriller with Dennehy as the cop turned novelist who's approached by assassin Woods, who wants him to expose his former Mafia boss. An extremely ingenious plot, plenty of mayhem and strong acting from two of the best character actors in the business. A shame about Tennant, but you can't have everything. **[95m/18]**

Cleve	James Woods
Dennis Meechum	Brian Dennehy
Roberta Gillian	Victoria Tennant
Holly Meechum	Allison Balson
David Madlock	Paul Shenar
Graham	George Coe

Best Shot ••• [1987]

Director: David Anspaugh
Screenplay: Angelo Pizzo

Essentially the *Rocky* of basketball. Hackman's the coach fallen on hard times who whips into shape a tiny high school team. Despite fair doses of sentiment, it's entertaining and exciting stuff. Also known as *Hoosiers*. **[114m/PG]**

Coach Norman Dale	Gene Hackman
Myra Fleener	Barbara Hershey
Shooter	Dennis Hopper
Cletus	Sheb Wooley
Opal Fleener	Fern Persons
George	Chelcie Ross

Psst! The film is based on the true story of Milan High School which, despite having only 164 students, won the 1954 Indiana championships.

Betrayal •• [1983]

Director: David Jones
Screenplay: Harold Pinter

As if Pinter's plays weren't difficult enough to understand to begin with, this one starts at the end and works its way back to the beginning. Without this interesting idea, the tale of a long-standing affair between publisher Kingsley's wife Hodge and his mate Irons would have little to commend it. The usual Pinteresque silences are just as long backwards as forwards and come in handy if you want to make some tea. **[95m/15]**

Robert	Ben Kingsley
Jerry	Jeremy Irons
Emma	Patricia Hodge

Betrayed •• [1988]

Director: Costa-Gavras
Screenplay: Joe Eszterhas

The Ku Klux Klan is alive and sick and living in America's heartland. Undercover FBI agent Winger falls in love with their leader. This is an irritating film which has some chilling sequences, such as the killing of a black man as a field sport, but Costa-Gavras rarely manages to make it believeable. **[126m/18]**

Katie/Cathy	Debra Winger
Gary Simmons	Tom Berenger
Michael Carnes	John Heard
Gladys Simmons	Betsy Blair
Shorty	John Mahoney
Wes	Ted Levine

Psst! Timothy Hutton, Winger's husband, appears briefly in the fairground.

Betsy's Wedding • [1990]

Director: Alan Alda
Screenplay: Alan Alda

Alan Alda's daughter can't stand those wisecracks and that irritating grin any longer and decides the best escape is to get married. Unfortunately, there's the wedding to get through first. We've seen this all before, only funnier and without the daft Mafia subplot. Still, at least we get to see the glorious Madeline Kahn again. **[94m/15]**

Eddie Hopper	Alan Alda
Eddie's Father	Joey Bishop
Lola Hopper	Madeline Kahn
Gloria Henner	Catherine O'Hara
Oscar Henner	Joe Pesci
Connie Hopper	Ally Sheedy

Uncle Georgie...............................Burt Young
Betsy Hopper ....Molly Ringwald

Psst! Look out for Samuel L. Jackson as Mickey, the taxi dispatcher.

Betty Blue •• [1986]

Director: Jean-Jacques Beineix
Screenplay: Jean-Jacques Beineix

A frustrated novelist has a wild affair with a nubile teenager before realising that she's going bonkers in a big way. In the interim this pair go at it hammer and tongs. A typically Gallic tale of mad passion, complete with sombre voice-over and terrific style. But it becomes increasingly tiresome and, when the hero ends up in drag, you know the film has seriously lost its way. [121m/18]

Betty...Béatrice Dalle
Zorg ....Jean-Hugues Anglade
Lisa.............................Consuelo de Haviland

Quote 'I don't walk around naked like that, even at home. I don't like nudity. It's not my style.' [Dalle]

Psst! Dalle was discovered when Beineix saw her picture on a magazine cover. She wasn't a model. The photographer had just snapped her in the street ◆ This is one of those select films where, so we are led to believe, the actors got carried away and actually did make love in front of the camera ◆ There is also a director's cut of 182 minutes.

Beverly Hills Cop ••• [1984]

Director: Martin Brest
Screenplay: Daniel Petrie Jr.

Reasonably funny fish-out-of-water comedy, with Murphy a cop turning up in L.A. to get revenge for his mate's murder. Although Murphy is good, there's a nagging feeling that it should all be much funnier and sharper. Almost spoiled by the silly ending which has a couple of handguns that never run out of bullets triumphing over automatic weapons. [105m/15]

Axel Foley...................................Eddie Murphy
Det. Billy Rosewood.................Judge Reinhold

Sgt. Taggart...................................John Ashton
Jenny Summers ....Lisa Eilbacher
Lt. Bogomil......................................Ronny Cox
Victor Maitland.......................Steven Berkoff
Mickey Tandino ....James Russo
Zack ....Jonathan Banks
Chief Hubbard ....Stephen Elliott
Serge...................................Bronson Pinchot
Jeffrey ....Paul Reiser

Quote 'Tell Victor that Ramon...went to the clinic today and I found out that I had...er, herpy simplex ten, and I think Victor should go check himself out with his physician to make sure everything is fine before things start falling off the man.'

Psst! The movie was inspired by a cop stopping studio head Michael Eisner for speeding ◆ This was the film debut of comic Damon Wayans. His 15 seconds come as he gives Murphy some bananas ◆ Mickey Rourke and Sylvester Stallone had both been associated with the project when it was still a straight action pic. Stallone backed out when writer Petrie wouldn't let him monkey with the script. It didn't stop Nielsen, the then Mrs. Sly, being in the sequel.

Beverly Hills Cop II • [1987]

Director: Tony Scott
Screenplay: Larry Ferguson & Warren Skaaren

Noisy, plotless, tedious, money-making sequel. It seemed terrible at the time. It seems marginally better now, but only because the hyper-talented Murphy has made so many even worse turkeys since. When Murphy's good, he's brilliant. But when he's bad, boy do his films have an odour all their own. [102m/15]

Axel Foley...................................Eddie Murphy
Billy Rosewood ....Judge Reinhold
Maxwell Dent......................Jurgen Prochnow
Andrew Bogomil ....Ronny Cox
John Taggart...................................John Ashton
Karla Fry................................Brigitte Nielsen
Harold Lutz................................Allen Garfield
Chip Cain ....Dean Stockwell
Jeffrey Friedman.............................Paul Reiser
Nikos Thomopolis ....Paul Guilfoyle

OOPS! During the fight with the guard at the warehouse, his sunglasses fall off. Soon afterwards, they're back on again.

Psst! Look out for Hugh Hefner, appearing as himself.

Beyond the Limit
SEE: The Honorary Consul

Beyond Therapy • [1987]

Director: Robert Altman
Screenplay: Christopher Durang & Robert Altman

...Beyond the Pale. After watching this, it's far easier to understand why Hollywood ignored the talents of Robert Altman for so long. He displays none in this awful talky drivel about neurotic New Yorkers and their psychiatrists. [93m/15]

Prudence	Julie Hagerty
Bruce	Jeff Goldblum
Charlotte	Glenda Jackson
Stuart	Tom Conti

Big •••• [1988]

Director: Penny Marshall
Screenplay: Gary Ross & Anne Spielberg

One of the funniest, most delightful fantasies yet put on film. Hanks is perfect as the boy who wishes he were big – and wakes up twenty years older. Standing out in the adult world by virtue of his innocence (are 12-year-olds *really* that ignorant about sex?), he gets a job at a toy company. The scene with boss Loggia and him dancing out 'Chopsticks' on the giant piano is a classic, while the romance between Hanks and the excellent Perkins is perfectly handled. [105m/PG]

Josh Baskin	Tom Hanks
Susan	Elizabeth Perkins
Paul	John Heard
Billy	Jared Rushton
MacMillan	Robert Loggia
Young Josh	David Moscow
Scotty Brennen	Jon Lovitz
Mrs. Baskin	Mercedes Ruehl

Quote 'I'm a kid.' — 'Who isn't?'

Psst! At test screenings, audiences voted that they wanted Perkins and Hanks to live together happily ever after. It's one of the few films in recent years where the studio didn't insist on changing the ending as a result of such comments • The film was originally set to star Harrison Ford, with Spielberg directing.

The Big Blue •• [1988]

Director: Luc Besson
Screenplay: Luc Besson, Robert Garland, Marilyn Goldin, Jacques Mayol & Marc Perrier

Despite some wonderful underwater photography, this French tale of divers develops webbed feet when it's on dry land. Although absolutely magical in places, other parts remind you that magic sometimes means Paul Daniels. [119m/15]

Joanna	Rosanna Arquette
Jacques Mayol	Jean-Marc Barr
Enzo Molinari	Jean Reno
Dr. Laurence	Paul Shenar
Novelli	Sergio Castellitto
Duffy	Griffin Dunne

Big Business •• [1988]

Director: Jim Abrahams
Screenplay: Dori Pierson & Marc Rubel

Most people won't need to know any more than the fact that there is not one, but two Bette Midlers in this hit-and-miss comedy. Midler and Tomlin are sets of twins mixed up at birth. We are no doubt supposed to find the complications that result hilarious. We don't. [98m/PG]

Sadie Shelton/Ratcliff	Bette Midler
Rose Shelton/Ratcliff	Lily Tomlin
Roone Dimmick	Fred Ward
Graham Sherbourne	Edward Herrmann

OOPS! What is supposedly JFK airport in New York is clearly Los Angeles if you look carefully enough.

Psst! The credits include the line, far too late: 'Don't Go. It's Almost Over'.

The Big Chill ••• [1983]

Director: **Lawrence Kasdan**
Screenplay: **Barbara Benedek & Lawrence Kasdan**

When a friend kills himself, a group of 60's university students gets back together for a long weekend of talking, rediscovering, bonding, friendship remaking and the odd bit of nookie. Great music and acting, but perhaps a bit Thirtysomething and plotless for some tastes. [103m/15]

Sam	Tom Berenger
Sarah	Glenn Close
Michael	Jeff Goldblum
Nick	William Hurt
Harold	Kevin Kline
Meg	Mary Kay Place
Chloe	Meg Tilly
Karen	JoBeth Williams

OOPS! You can see that Kline is wearing a microphone when his sweatshirt sticks to him.

Psst! Kevin Costner was to play Alex, the dead friend, but his ten minutes of flashback were axed. All we see of him are his hands, torso and legs when the corpse is being dressed ♦ A leader in the Nepotism Handicap with Director's son, Jon Kasdan as Harold and Sarah's son, Jacob, as an autograph seeker and wife Meg as the airline hostess.

The Big Easy •••• [1987]

Director: **Jim McBride**
Screenplay: **Daniel Petrie Jr. & Jack Baran**

A series of Mafia murders are being investigated by a slightly corrupt New Orleans cop, himself under investigation by Internal Affairs. Although the whodunnit element is skimmed over pretty fast, the steamy Louisiana atmosphere and the steamy coupling of Quaid and Barkin make this one of the 80's smartest, most attractive thrillers. [108m/18]

Remy McSwain	Dennis Quaid
Anne Osborne	Ellen Barkin
Jack Kellom	Ned Beatty
Andrew De Soto	John Goodman
McCabe	Lisa Jane Persky
Ed Dodge	Ebbe Roe Smith

Psst! Jim Garrison, played by Costner in *JFK*, has a cameo as the judge.

Bigfoot and the Hendersons •• [1987]

Director: **William Dear**
Screenplay: **William Dear, William E. Martin & Ezra D. Rappaport**

Yet another variant on *E.T.*, this time with a family adopting the American equivalent of the abominable snowman, bearing an uncanny resemblance to Nick Nolte. Fine if you actually like long, sentimental yarns about big, furry creatures that teach us to be better human beings. Also known as *Harry and the Hendersons*. [111m/PG]

George Hendeson	John Lithgow
Nancy Henderson	Melinda Dillon
Sarah Henderson	Margaret Langrick
Ernie Henderson	Joshua Rudoy
Harry	Kevin Peter Hall
Jacques Lafleur	David Suchet
Irene Moffitt	Lainie Kazan
Dr. Wallace Wrightwood	Don Ameche
George Henderson Sr.	M. Emmet Walsh

OOPS! Even though Harry (Bigfoot in Britain) smashes the Hendersons' ceiling with his head, it miraculously mends.

Psst! Kevin Peter Hall, playing Bigfoot, is 7 feet 2 inches tall.

Big Girls Don't Cry... They Get Even

SEE: Stepkids

Biggles • [1986]

Director: **John Hough**
Screenplay: **John Grove & Kent Walwin**

I say, Biggles. Some blighter's gone and made a film about you. As well as lots of bandits-at-seven-o'clock derring-do against the Boche, they've added some drivel about a beastly Yank coming back in time to help you out...I say, Biggles. I don't think that sort of language is quite the ticket. [92m/PG]

Biggles	Neil Dickson
Jim Ferguson	Alex Hyde-White
Debbie	Fiona Hutchinson
Col. Raymond	Peter Cushing

The Big Man •• [1990]

Director: **David Leland**
Screenplay: **Don McPherson**

An unemployed miner agrees to a bare-knuckle fight for a cash purse but family and class tensions make him question his motives. The finale would give *Rocky* a run for its money, but elsewhere it's terribly muddled. Also known as *Crossing the Line.* [116m/18]

Danny Scoular	Liam Neeson
Beth Scoular	Joanne Whalley-Kilmer
Matt Mason	Ian Bannen
Frankie	Billy Connolly
Gordon	Hugh Grant

The Big Picture ••• [1989]

Director: **Christopher Guest**
Screenplay: **Michael Varhol, Christopher Guest & Michael McKean**

This unjustly neglected satire on the movie industry is partly written by two of the writers and performers of *Spinal Tap.* Bacon is the film student who has to decide just how far to compromise to get his film made. Full of malicious fun, the humour is gentle, rather than boffo, and provides a fascinating insight into the industry's power plays. Short, as usual, grabs the film and drops it over the touchline. [100m/15]

Nick Chapman	Kevin Bacon
Susan Rawlings	Emily Longstreth
Allen Habel	J.T. Walsh
Lydia Johnson	Jennifer Jason Leigh
Emmet Sumner	Michael McKean
Neil Sussman	Martin Short
Jenny Sumner	Kim Miyori
Gretchen	Teri Hatcher

Quote 'I don't know you. I don't know

your work. But I think you're a very, very talented young man.'

Showing *It's a Wonderful Life.* [Both black and white and colourised]

Psst! There are cameos from Elliott Gould, Roddy McDowall, Eddie Albert and John Cleese amongst others.

The Big Town •• [1987]

Director: **Ben Bolt**
Screenplay: **Robert Roy Pool**

This attempt to turn dice gambling into an exciting spectator sport doesn't come off. Despite the efforts of the good cast, the fact that it's all about craps seems all too appropriate. [110m/15]

J.C. Cullen	Matt Dillon
Lorry Dane	Diane Lane
George Cole	Tommy Lee Jones
Mr. Edwards	Bruce Dern
Ferguson Edwards	Lee Grant
Phil Carpenter	Tom Skerritt

Psst! Look out for Lolita Davidovich, here billed as Lolita David, in a small role as the 'black lace stripper'.

Big Trouble in Little China • [1986]

Director: **John Carpenter**
Screenplay: **Gary Goldman & David Z. Weinstein**

Once-great director Carpenter throws comedy, action, martial arts and magic together with a bizarre plot about The Yellow Peril lurking beneath San Francisco. As the odds are so overwhelmingly in favour of the thousands of Chinese, it's clear that they don't stand a chance against the might of Russell and Cattrall. They, like the viewer, look confused and lost throughout. A complete waste of everyone's time. [100m/PG]

Jack Burton	Kurt Russell
Gracie Law	Kim Cattrall
Wang Chi	Dennis Dun
Lo Pan	James Hong
Egg Shen	Victor Wong

Bill & Ted's Excellent Adventure ••• [1989]

Director: **Stephen Herek**
Screenplay: **Chris Matheson & Edward Solomon**

Winter and Reeves debut as those dim but bodacious dudes Bill & Ted, travelling through time rounding up famous characters to help them pass their history paper. The world is divided into those who love and those who hate B&T. For those who have seen the light, this is witty, inventive, uproarious, indeed, most excellent stuff. Nice to see such clean-living boys in a film like this too. **[89m/PG]**

Ted 'Theodore' Logan	Keanu Reeves
Bill S. Preston	Alex Winter
Rufus	George Carlin
Napoleon	Terry Camilleri
Billy the Kid	Dan Shor
Socrates	Tony Steedman
Freud	Rod Loomis
Ghenghis Khan	Al Leong
Joan of Arc	Jane Wiedlin
Abraham Lincoln	Robert V. Barron
Beethoven	Clifford David
Capt. Logan	Hal Landon Jr.
Mr. Ryan	Bernie Casey
Missy/Mom	Amy Stock-Poynton
Mr. Preston	Patrick McNamara

Blurb History Is About To Be Rewritten By Two Guys Who Can't Spell.

Showing *War and Peace* [1956].

Psst! The studio was so unsure about the movie that they didn't bother releasing it. Only when a writers' strike meant that cinemas were short of films did they let it out. It promptly cleaned up at the box office.

Bill & Ted's Bogus Journey ••• [1992]

Director: **Peter Hewitt**
Screenplay: **Edward Solomon & Chris Matheson**

Those most triumphant dudes Bill & Ted are back, being hunted by a couple of most heinous Bill & Ted lookalike robots from the future. Our heroes travel to Heaven and Hell and even do battle with Death himself. It's slightly less amusing than the original and the story is all over the place. However, Sadler is brilliant as the depressed Grim Reaper and the end credits are hilarious. **[93m/PG]**

Bill/Evil Ted	Alex Winter
Ted/Evil Ted	Keanu Reeves
Grim Reaper	William Sadler
Rufus	George Carlin
De Nomolos	Joss Ackland
Joanna	Sarah Trigger
Elizabeth	Annette Azcuy
Captain Logan	Hal Landon Jr.
Missy	Amy Stock-Poynton

Quote 'How's it hangin', Death?'

OOPS! The boom mike is pretty obvious in the first scene in the police station.

Billy Bathgate •• [1992]

Director: **Robert Benton**
Screenplay: **Tom Stoppard**

Young Dean joins Dutch Schultz's gang in the 1930s and finds himself falling for high-tone gangster groupie Kidman. Despite looking like a million dollars (it cost 40) and being more multi-layered than the average gangster movie, it's all a little flat. Although Kidman is a knock-out, Hoffman's mannered performance doesn't work. He was more frightening in *Hook*. **[107m/15]**

Dutch Schultz	Dustin Hoffman
Drew Preston	Nicole Kidman
Billy Bathgate	Loren Dean
Bo Weinberg	Bruce Willis
Otto Berman	Steven Hill

Psst! The 8th biggest failure in movie history, losing $33m ✦ Look out for Moira Kelly in a small role as 'Becky'.

Biloxi Blues ••• [1988]

Director: **Mike Nichols**
Screenplay: **Neil Simon**

The second of Simon's autobiographical trilogy follows him as he trains for the army and loses his virginity. Fortunately for the fate of the Allies in World War II, the shebang ends before this lot get into battle. We've seen it countless times before, but rarely with Simon's wit. Walken's superbly psychotic sergeant is spellbindingly terrifying. **[107m/15]**

Eugene Morris Jerome	Matthew Broderick
Sgt. Toomey	Christopher Walken
Joseph Wykowski	Matt Mulhern
Arnold Epstein	Corey Parker
Roy Selridge	Markus Flanagan
Don Carney	Casey Siemaszko
James Hennessy	Michael Dolan
Daisy Hannigan	Penelope Ann Miller
Rowena	Park Overall

Blurb The Army Made Eugene A Man. But Daisy Gave Him Basic Training.

Bird ••• [1988]

Director: **Clint Eastwood**
Screenplay: **Joel Oliansky**

A must for fans of sax man Charlie Parker, this Eastwood-directed biopic has a splendid lead performance from Whitaker and some fine, anguished, moments. But it's pretty long and a little turgid and arty in parts. **[161m/15]**

Charlie 'Bird' Parker	Forest Whitaker
Chan Parker	Diane Venora
Red Rodney	Michael Zelniker
Dizzy	Samuel E. Wright

Psst! Unreleased recordings of Parker were used for the film, although the original accompanying musicians were replaced by freshly-recorded ones.

Bird on a Wire •• [1990]

Director: **John Badham**
Screenplay: **David Seltzer, Louis Venosta & Eric Lerner**

It had to happen. The actor and the actress both renowned for their posteriors' love affair with the camera in one and the same movie. The excuse for an endless series of chases is that they're ex-lovers brought together after 15 years in order to go on the run from Carradine. **[111m/12]**

Rick Jarmin	Mel Gibson
Marianne Graves	Goldie Hawn
Eugene Sorenson	David Carradine
Albert Diggs	Bill Duke
Joe Weyburn	Stephen Tobolowsky

Blurb He's Every Woman's Dream And One Woman's Nightmare.

Birdy ••• [1984]

Director: **Alan Parker**
Screenplay: **Sandy Kroopf & Jack Behr**

All his life Modine's wanted to be a bird. After traumatic service in Vietnam, he thinks he's made it and so is confined in a mental hospital. Cage is the old friend who wants to clip his wings and bring him back to earth. A fascinating, weird and sometimes funny anti-war picture. The sort of film you think you aren't going to like and have trouble forgetting afterwards. **[120m/15]**

Birdy	Matthew Modine
Al Columbato	Nicolas Cage
Dr. Weiss	John Harkins
Mr. Columbato	Sandy Baron
Hannah Rourke	Karen Young
Mrs. Columbato	Crystal Field
Renaldi	Bruno Kirby

Psst! Feeling his face wasn't quite right for the part, Nicolas Cage had two of his teeth pulled out before filming.

Bitter Moon • [1992]

Director: **Roman Polanski**
Screenplay: **Roman Polanski, Gérard Brach & John Brownjohn**

Polanski's tale of obsessive love comes across like some badly-made 60's sex comedy. Wheelchair-bound Coyote tells the story of his steamy affair with Seigner to open-mouthed stiff Englishman Grant. A total load of old tosh, with some of the worst dialogue to be found outside an Australian soap, and sex scenes that look as though they belong to an early Woody Allen movie. Could be hysterically funny in the right mood. **[139m/18]**

Oscar	Peter Coyote

Mimi ....Emmanuelle Seigner
Nigel ....Hugh Grant
Fiona ....Kristin Scott Thomas
Blurb Some Lovers Never Know When
To Stop.

Quote 'I loved her too, but our credit was
running out. We were heading for sexual
bankruptcy.' ✦ 'Her belly was crying
famine, her organs in turmoil.'

Psst! Seigner is Mrs. Polanski.

The Black Cauldron •• [1985]

Director: **Ted Berman & Richard Rich**
Screenplay: **Various**

Technically splendid but heartless animated pic in desperate need of the Disney
magic. In the sort of sword and sorcery
caper that Arnie would revel in, a pig-
keeper has to stop the evil Horned King
getting his hands on the magic cauldron.
[80m/U]

With: John Huston, Grant Bardsley, Susan
Sheridan, John Hurt, Freddie Jones

Black Eagle • [1988]

Director: **Eric Karson**
Screenplay: **A.E. Peters & Michael
Gonzales**

Van Damme's the baddie, a Russkie what
is more, in this routine martial arts stuff
with Kosugi a James Bond type. [93m/15]

Ken Tani ....Sho Kosugi
Andrei ....Jean-Claude Van Damme
Patricia Parker ....Doran Clark
Father Joseph Bedelia ....Bruce French

Black Moon Rising •• [1986]

Director: **Harley Cokliss**
Screenplay: **John Carpenter**

A daft story about top secret papers being
stashed in a supercar which gets stolen, as
supercars always do. Forget the plot and
enjoy the nifty effects. [100m/18]

Quint ....Tommy Lee Jones
Nina ....Linda Hamilton
Ryland ....Robert Vaughn
Earl Windom ....Richard Jaeckel

Black Rain • [1989]

Director: **Ridley Scott**
Screenplay: **Craig Bolotin & Warren
Lewis**

Maverick American cop Douglas goes to
Japan to capture an escaped mobster.
Unpleasant, predictable thriller, with even
Ridley Scott's famous urban steamy vis-
uals looking second-hand. A nice head-
lopping sequence, though. [125m/18]

Nick Conklin ....Michael Douglas
Charlie Vincent ....Andy Garcia
Masahiro Matsumoto ....Ken Takakura
Joyce Kingsley ....Kate Capshaw

Black Rainbow ••• [1990]

Director: **Mike Hodges**
Screenplay: **Mike Hodges**

A fake carnival medium sees a murder
just before it happens, and puts her life and
her father's in danger. An intriguing little
thriller which gives a British perspective
to its North Carolina setting. [95m/15]

Martha Travis ....Rosanna Arquette
Walter Travis ....Jason Robards
Gary Wallace ....Tom Hulce
Lloyd Harley ....Mark Joy
Chief Det. Irving Weinberg ......Ron Rosenthal
Ted Silas ....John Bennes

Black Robe ••• [1992]

Director: **Bruce Beresford**
Screenplay: **Brian Moore**

A young Jesuit priest sets out to convert
the remote Canadian Huron Indians to
Catholicism in the mid-17th century.
Somewhat like *Dances With Wolves*
without the feel-good element, the culture
clash between 'civilised' and 'uncivilised'
is brilliantly explored, while the Indians
seem much more like real people than
Costner's perfect and environmentally-
conscious lot. The scenery, as bleak and
uncompromising as the story, is quite
staggering. [100m/15]

Father Laforgue ....Lothaire Bluteau
Daniel ....Aden Young

Annuka ....Sandrine Holt
Chomina ....August Schellenberg
Chomina's Wife ....Tantoo Cardinal
Psst! The credits include a 'raven trainer'.

The Black Stallion Returns •• [1983]

Director: Robert Dalva
Screenplay: Richard Kletter & Jerome Kass

This inferior sequel has a rather silly plot, involving Reno searching the Sahara when some Arabs steal the nag. Perhaps we should be thankful that it was a bust at the box office, as author Walter Farley wrote around a score of these horsey books! **[103m/U]**

Alec Ramsay...................................Kelly Reno
Raj ....Vincent Spano
Kurr ....Allen Goorwitz
Meslar.....................................Woody Strode

Black Widow ••• [1987]

Director: Bob Rafelson
Screenplay: Ronald Bass

To lose one rich husband may be regarded as a misfortune. To lose more looks like murder to workaholic cop Winger. Certainly being Russell's spouse doesn't look like a job with much in the way of prospects. A stylish, sexy film noir with a welcome absence of psychological claptrap, although perhaps not quite as good as the talent involved would lead you to expect. **[103m/15]**

Alexandra.................................Debra Winger
Catharine..............................Theresa Russell
Paul..Sami Frey
Ben...Dennis Hopper
William Macauley..............Nicol Williamson
Bruce......................................Terry O'Quinn
Psst! David Mamet, who wrote director Rafelson's *The Postman Always Rings Twice*, appears in a cameo as Herb, one of the poker players. He is a keen gambler himself.

Blade Runner: The Director's Cut •••• [1982]

Director: Ridley Scott
Screenplay: Hampton Fancher & David Webb Peoples

Ridley Scott's exciting and stylish futuristic thriller had a silly voiceover and implausible happy ending imposed when released in 1982. Although it was still seen as one of the best and most influential scifi pics ever, this 1992 release of the director's version makes an accomplished film even better. Ford's job is to 'retire' rogue androids but his dedication to the job in hand wavers when one of them turns out to be Sean Young. Disturbingly, the once amazingly futuristic look of the film looks less considerably less fantastical a decade later, as reality moves closer to Scott's bleak vision of future city life. **[116m/15]**

Deckard...................................Harrison Ford
Batty...Rutger Hauer
Rachael..Sean Young
Gaff..............................Edward James Olmos
Bryant.................................M. Emmet Walsh
Pris ....Daryl Hannah
Leon..Brion James
Zhora.....................................Joanna Cassidy
Quote 'More human than human, is our motto' • 'You think I'd be working in a place like this if I could afford a real snake?'

OOPS! Keep your eye on the snake girl's hair as she is shot. It changes colour, length and texture completely.

Psst! Ford's part was at one time a possibility for Dustin Hoffman, while Philip K. Dick, author of the original novel, was keen on Victoria Principal playing Sean Young's part! • Don't get involved in any arguments with friends about the number of escaped replicants. There is no right answer. You will go mad trying to work it out • When the film went over budget, the happy ending [in the original version] used an out-take from the opening of *The Shining* as its backdrop.

Blame it on Rio •• [1984]

Director: **Stanley Donan**
Screenplay: **Charlie Peters & Larry Gelbart**

On holiday in Rio, Caine falls in love with his best friend's teenage daughter. An unfunny, nudge–nudge farce. [110m/PG]

Matthew	Michael Caine
Victor	Joseph Bologna
Karen	Valerie Harper
Jennifer	Michelle Johnson
Nicole	Demi Moore

Blame it on the Bellboy •• [1992]

Director: **Mark Herman**
Screenplay: **Mark Herman**

A Dudley Moore farce in a Venice hotel. Instead of the bags getting mixed up, it's the names, with three chaps called Orton. Lawton and Horton. If this aimless farce really is the bellboy's fault, he should be strung up by his tagliatelli. [79m/12]

Melvyn Orton	Dudley Moore
Mike Lawton/Charlton Black	Bryan Brown
Maurice Horton	Richard Griffiths

Also: Andreas Katsulas, Patsy Kensit, Alison Steadman, Penelope Wilton, Bronson Pinchot, Jim Carter

Psst! British director Lindsay Anderson is the voice of Mr. Marshall, heard only on the phone.

Blaze •• [1989]

Director: **Ron Shelton**
Screenplay: **Ron Shelton**

The fictionalised story of the 50's affair between the Governor of Louisiana and the stripper Blaze Starr. Although Newman is good value, Davidovich is a little weaker. And, unlike Starr, when the script is stripped of its wrappings, there's nothing worthwhile underneath. [120m/18]

Earl Long	Paul Newman
Blaze Starr	Lolita Davidovich
Thibodeaux	Jerry Hardin
LaGrange	Gailard Sartain

Quote 'The real reason this movie got made is because Blaze Starr had been praying and putting the Bible on her chest every night for the last six years. Not even God can say no to that.' [Ron Shelton]

Psst! The real Blaze makes a cameo appearance as Lily in the Sho–Bar in New Orleans. She's the woman at the mirror who Newman kisses on the shoulder • Davidovich had already played a stripper in a bit part in *The Big Town*.

Blind Date •• [1984]

Director: **Nico Mastorakis**
Screenplay: **Nico Mastorakis & Fred C. Perry**

Although Bottoms is blind, he's got a gizmo that puts him on a par with bats, enabling him to track a psycho carving up women in Athens. Despite occasional moments of excitement, this thriller is just that bit too implausible. [100m/18]

Jonathon Ratcliff	Joseph Bottoms
Claire Simpson	Kirstie Alley
Dave	James Daughton
Rachel	Lana Clarkson

Psst! One of six 'girls in bikinis' is Valeria Golino, later the sultry psychiatrist in *Hot Shots*.

Blind Date • [1987]

Director: **Blake Edwards**
Screenplay: **Dale Launer**

Like some human Mogwai, Basinger is cute and fun until wet alcohol hits her throat, at which point she becomes mad, bad and dangerous to know. Willis foolishly ignores the 'don't get drunk' instructions and loses his job, possessions and sanity. Neither of the leads seem to have the slightest capacity for handling comedy and the only way to watch this without wincing is to tank up yourself beforehand. [93m/15]

Nadia Gates	Kim Basinger
Walter Davis	Bruce Willis
David Bedford	John Larroquette

Judge Harold Bedford............William Daniels
Quote 'Look on the bright side. What the hell else can happen?'

Blind Fury ••• [1990]

Director: **Phillip Noyce**
Screenplay: **Charles Robert Carner**

Hauer's pretty nifty at martial arts, but is always being underestimated by his opponents, possibly because he's totally blind. An above-average actioner which has little substance, but whizzes by with plenty of good fights and a fair bit of tongue-in-cheek humour. **[85m/15]**

Nick Parker...............................Rutger Hauer
Frank Devereaux....................Terry O'Quinn
Bill Devereaux............................Brandon Call
MacReady..........................Noble Willingham
Psst! Credits include an alligator wrangler.

Bliss •• [1986]

Director: **Ray Lawrence**
Screenplay: **Ray Lawrence & Peter Carey**

In this weird Australian satire, an advertising executive dies – for a few minutes – returning to life with a completely different perspective on life. Starting well, it runs out of steam and ideas too quickly. **[112m/18]**

Harry Joy ....Barry Otto
Bettina Joy ....Lynette Curran
Honey Barbara............................Helen Jones
Lucy Joy..Gia Carides

The Blob •• [1988]

Director: **Chuck Russell**
Screenplay: **Chuck Russell & Frank Darabont**

Remake of 50's horror classic, with those loveably giggly sex-mad teens that every American town has, meeting sticky ends from a rampant pink blancmange. Despite better effects than the original, it's just an okay horror comic. **[95m/18]**

Meg Penny ....Shawnee Smith
Brian Flagg..................................Kevin Dillon
Paul Taylor ....Donovan Leitch

Sheriff Herb Geller................Jeffrey DeMunn
Fran Hewitt ....Candy Clark
Blurb Terror Has No Shape.
Psst! Probably the first movie where a victim is sucked head–first down a sink drain ♦ Credits include 5 blob wranglers.

Blood Oath •• [1991]

Director: **Stephen Wallace**
Screenplay: **Denis Whitburn & Brian A. Williams**

The true-life story of a post-war trial in Australia of Japanese accused of murdering 300 Australian servicemen in Indonesia. A worthy but plodding recreation of the events. **[108m/15]**

Capt. Robert Cooper.................Bryan Brown
Vice-Adm. Baron Takahashi.....George Takei
Major Tom Beckett ....Terry O'Quinn
Major Frank Roberts........................John Bach
Psst! Despite just one line of dialogue near the end, a soldier played by someone called Jason Donovan seems to occupy a disproportionate amount of screen time.

The Blood of Heroes
SEE: Salute of the Jugger

Blood Red • [1989]

Director: **Peter Masterson**
Screenplay: **Ron Cutler**

Fortunately for the career of one Julia Roberts, her first film didn't come out for some time. This tedious turn of the century tale of squabbling over Californian wineries withers on the vine. **[91m/15]**

Marco Collogero ....Eric Roberts
Sebastian Collogero..........Giancarlo Giannini
William Bradford Berrigan.....Dennis Hopper
Andrews ....Burt Young
Also: Carlin Glynn, Lara Harris, Michael Madsen, Elias Koteas, Marc Lawrence, Aldo Ray, Julia Roberts
Psst! Julia Roberts got just $50,000 for her debut, made in 1986 ♦ The two Roberts are brother and sister in real life, as in the film.

Blood Simple •••• [1985]

Director: Joel Coen
Screenplay: Joel Coen & Ethan Coen

Bloody, complex thriller in which cuck-olded Hedaya hires Walsh to kill his wife and her lover. Occasionally implausible, but otherwise terrifically stylish, exciting and black. A dazzlingly original debut by the Coen brothers. [98m/18]

Ray..John Getz
Abby............................Frances McDormand
Julian Marty................................Dan Hedaya
Private detective...................M. Emmet Walsh
Debra..............................Deborah Neumann

Blurb Dead In The Heart of Texas.

Psst! Astonishingly, the budget was only $1.5 million.

Bloodsport •• [1988]

Director: Newt Arnold
Screenplay: Sheldon Lettich, Christopher Crosby & Mel Friedman

This early Van Dammer has him as an American soldier off to Hong Kong to compete in an illegal and very vicious martial arts competition. Supposedly based on a true story, it comes across as the usual chop-socky tale. [92m/18]

Frank Dux............Jean-Claude Van Damme
Jackson.......................................Donald Gibb
Janice...Leah Ayres
Helmer..................................Norman Burton

Blue Heat •• [1990]

Director: John Mackenzie
Screenplay: Jere Cunningham, Thomas Lee Wright & George Armitage

A mediocre tale of cops handing in their badges to pursue a drugs investigation themselves, only to uncover more than they expect. Not even Brian Dennehy can do much with the material. Also known as *Last of the Finest*. [106m/15]

Frank Daly..............................Brian Dennehy
Wayne Gross............................Joe Pantoliano
Ricky Rodriguez.................................Jeff Fahey
Howard 'Hojo' Jones.......................Bill Paxton

Blue Ice • [1992]

Director: Russell Mulcahy
Screenplay: Ron Hutchinson

Blue ice is frozen matter that falls from airplane lavatories to the ground. Not a lotta people know that. A bit drops on Michael Caine's head and makes him think he's back in one of his 60's spy thrillers. Old enough almost to be her grandfather, he takes up with Young, wife of the American ambassador (old enough to be her great-grandfather). This first film for Caine as producer is not going to revitalise the British film industry. It's crass, asinine and utterly boring. [105m/15]

Harry Anders..........................Michael Caine
Stacy Mansdorf.............................Sean Young
Sir Hector..Ian Holm
Osgood.................................Alun Armstrong

OOPS! Caine's been away so long, he's forgotten his London geography. Just watch as they leap from one bit of the capital to another in the twinkling of an eye at the beginning and the bizarre route to the docks taken towards the end.

Psst! Sharon Stone was first choice for Young's part, dropping out for personal reasons ◆ For the love scene, Young insisted that the camera crew strip to their underwear so that she wasn't the only one getting goosebumps ◆ Bob Hoskins' cameo was a return of Michael Caine's favour for appearing in *Mona Lisa*.

Blue Jean Cop •• [1988]

Director: James Glickenhaus
Screenplay: James Glickenhaus

An implausible action pic with Weller and Elliott investigating corruption in the Manhattan Police department, setting up some amazing stuntwork along the way. Also known as *Shakedown*. [96m/18]

Roland Dalton..............................Peter Weller
Richie Marks..................................Sam Elliott
Susan Cantrell..............Patricia Charbonneau
Gail Feinberger..........................Blanche Baker

Blue Steel •• [1990]

Director: Kathryn Bigelow
Screenplay: Kathryn Bigelow & Eric Red

Yuppie psycho Silver goes on a killing spree with rookie cop Curtis's gun. This disastrously unbelievable thriller gets sillier as it progresses. It's a pity, because Curtis does pretty well with her daft part.
[106m/18]

Megan Turner	Jamie Lee Curtis
Eugene Hunt	Ron Silver
Nick Mann	Clancy Brown
Tracy	Elizabeth Pena
Shirley Turner	Louise Fletcher
Frank Turner	Philip Bosco

OOPS! The opening credits make great play of the police revolver, showing us all six chambers being loaded. We also see later in target practice that it only holds six bullets. Yet in the final shoot-out on Wall Street, Curtis lets off seven shots.

Blue Thunder •• [1983]

Director: John Badham
Screenplay: Dan O'Bannon & Don Jakoby

Action pic with Scheider as a Vietnam vet cop. He's still flying despite that all too familiar Nam Flashback Syndrome, testing and then stealing a powerful new gadget-ridden, pistol-packing police helicopter. Some of the air fights are okay, but it does get rather silly and tiresome.
[110m/15]

Murphy	Roy Scheider
Braddock	Warren Oates
Kate	Candy Clark
Lymangood	Daniel Stern

Blue Velvet •• [1986]

Director: David Lynch
Screenplay: David Lynch

For some this weird view of small-town America is one of the greatest films of the 80s. But for everyone who swears by this movie, there's someone who swears at it, finding it a pretentious, violent, meaningless load of tosh. Even by the standards of Lynch's *Twin Peaks* it's bizarre, with MacLachlan doing some amateur detective work into the discovery of a severed ear, only to cross paths with beautiful but unstable Rossellini and demented psycho Hopper. •
[120m/18]

Jeffrey Beaumont	Kyle MacLachlan
Dorothy Vallens	Isabella Rossellini
Frank Booth	Dennis Hopper
Sandy Williams	Laura Dern
Mrs. Williams	Hope Lange
Ben	Dean Stockwell
Paul	Jack Nance
Raymond	Brad Dourif

Quote 'I don't know if you're a detective or a pervert.'

Bob Roberts ••• [1992]

Director: Tim Robbins
Screenplay: Tim Robbins

Actor turned writer-director-songwriter Robbins gives us a delicious political satire. He plays the wealthy right-wing country and western singer while Rickman is his marvellously smarmy *éminence grise*. The observation of political reality is keen and it's very funny in places. It would have been better still if he hadn't underestimated the audience's intelligence, spelling everything out two or three times to make sure we understand it. The songs, particularly *Wall Street Rap*, are wonderful.
[104m/15]

Bob Roberts	Tim Robbins
Bugs Raplin	Giancarlo Esposito
Chet MacGregor	Ray Wise
Terry Manchester	Brian Murray
Sen. Brickley Paiste	Gore Vidal

Also: Rebecca Jenkins, Harry J. Lennix, John Ottavino, Robert Stanton, Kelly Willis, John Cusack, Peter Gallagher, Pamela Reed, Alan Rickman, Susan Sarandon, James Spader, Fred Ward

Blurb Vote First. Ask Questions Later.

Quote 'Ask not what you can do for your country. Ask what you can do for yourself.'

Psst! Keep your eyes peeled for a raft of star cameos • Despite strong demand for it, Robbins refused to issue an album of the songs, worrying that extreme right-wingers would listen to them for all the wrong reasons.

Body Double • [1984]

Director: **Brian de Palma**
Screenplay: **Robert J. Avrech & Brian de Palma**

B-movie actor Wasson whiles away the hours spying on the disrobings of a beautiful woman, only to be drawn into a tortuous murder plot. Pillaging Hitchock as usual, De Palma displays none of the master's style or grace but majors instead in kinkiness and violence. Little of the plot makes sense and, although Griffith is excellent, Wasson is sadly only too believable as a bad actor. Saying he's wooden is an insult to trees. **[109m/18]**

Jake Skully ....Craig Wasson
Holly Body ....Melanie Griffith
Sam ....Gregg Henry
Gloria ....Deborah Shelton

OOPS! Towards the ending of the shooting of the porn film with Wasson, as they enter the loo you can see the camera and crew briefly reflected in a mirror. It's possible that this is intentional.

Psst! The video loses a couple of the raunchier sentences of Griffith's famous 'There are some thing that I like to get straight, right up front' speech ✦ Shelton's voice was dubbed afterwards by Helen Shaver ✦ Lovers of De Palma's camera technique might look out for the several-times-360-degree pan on the beach.

The Bodyguard •• [1992]

Director: **Mick Jackson**
Screenplay: **Lawrence Kasdan**

Bodyguard Costner reluctantly agrees to guard pop star Houston after she receives death threats. Soon the phrase 'personal protection' takes on a whole new meaning. Houston is fine in her debut role. Oddly enough it's Kev, with his Haircut From Hell, who seems uncomfortable,

displaying all the charisma of a dead pebble. The script doesn't give anyone anything to get their teeth into. Ostensibly a thriller, like a watched kettle, it takes forever to come to the boil. **[130m/15]**

Frank Farmer ....Kevin Costner
Rachel Marron ....Whitney Houston
Sy Spector ....Gary Kemp
Devaney...Bill Cobbs
Herb Farmer ....Ralph Waite

Quote 'Frank wasn't there the day Reagan was shot. He's never gotten over it.'

OOPS! Isn't it rather odd that a movie with at least one Oscar winner working on it should show actors turning up for the Oscar ceremony at night? Surely this is one time when the stars come out during the daytime? ✦ At one point, you can see the mike boom reflected quite clearly in Costner's hotel window.

Psst! The film he takes her to see is *Yojimbo*, the 1961 Japanese movie that inspired *A Fistful of Dollars*. Translated, it's *The Bodyguard*. ✦ Costner's terrible haircut was a tribute to Steve McQueen for whom the role was written almost twenty years earlier ✦ Much hilarity greeted the chasteness of the love scenes. The press reported her as insisting that the man rumoured to have the longest tongue in Hollywood keep his mouth closed ✦ As with *Robin Hood*, there were rumours that better scenes with Houston were cut at Costner's insistence ✦ The names of those receiving awards at the Oscar Ceremony are names of people working on the film ✦ If the last scene looks as though it's been tacked on, that's because it has, at great expense, after test audiences decided they didn't like the more downbeat ending originally planned.

Body of Evidence • [1993]

Director: **Uli Edel**
Screenplay: **Brad Mirman**

M'lud, the evidence is clear. The young woman Madonna is accused of wilfully attacking an audience with a rusty plot and a pair of pointy implements. No sooner had her learned counsel Dafoe picked up his brief than she dropped hers. Her acts of gross indecency, involving lifts, car bonnets, candlewax and broken glass raise nothing more than a titter, but she still persists. M'lud, how much more of this mental cruelty must ordinary citizens going about their business be expected to bear? **[99m/18]**

Rebecca Carlson .... Madonna
Frank Dulaney .... Willem Dafoe
Robert Tarrett .... Joe Mantegna
Joanne Braslow .... Anne Archer
Blurb An Act Of Love Or An Act Of Murder?

Psst! Archer's steamy scenes on the video are doubled by Shawn Lusader who, after being filmed naked for three days, came away with only $400 after taxes. Lusader was less than thrilled when Archer boasted on a chatshow how she managed to get into shape for the scenes.

Body Rock • [1984]

Director: **Marcelo Epstein**
Screenplay: **Desmond Nakano**

Does anything look more dated than a film rushed through to cash in on a dance craze? This one's even more still-born than all the other breakdancing movies. **[93m/15]**

Chilly D .... Lorenzo Lamas
Claire .... Vicki Frederick

Bolero • [1984]

Director: **John Derek**
Screenplay: **John Derek**

You should be able to sue for the wholly misleading subtitle: An Adventure In Ecstasy. This staggeringly boring and untitillating rubbish has the vacuous Bo unconvincingly trying to lose her virginity. It's about as riveting as watching somebody lose their glasses. Don't bother peeping at Bo this time. **[104m/18]**

Ayre McGillvary .... Bo Derek
Cotton Gray .... George Kennedy
Angel Contreras .... Andrea Occhipinti

The Bonfire of the Vanities • [1990]

Director: **Brian de Palma**
Screenplay: **Michael Cristofer**

Bonfire of the Inanities, more like. Arrogant Wall Street yuppie Hanks takes a wrong turning with his mistress (and his career) and lives to regret it. Overblown, miscast, misconceived bastardisation of a fine novel with only some directorial pyrotechnics from De Palma to keep you awake. **[126m/15]**

Sherman McCoy .... Tom Hanks
Peter Fallow .... Bruce Willis
Maria Ruskin .... Melanie Griffith
Judge White .... Morgan Freeman
Abe Weiss .... F. Murray Abraham
Also: Kim Cattrall, Saul Rubinek, John Hancock, Kevin Dunn, Donald Moffat, Mary Alice, Robert Stephens

Quote 'You're not important. You're dinner. This time next week they won't remember what they ate.'

Psst! The $5m paid for the rights to the novel was a record ◆ William Hurt was to have played McCoy, but his career was saved when his previous film ran over schedule ◆ F. Murray Abraham had his name taken off the credits ◆ Film buffs will want to check out that wonderful opening 4-minute Steadicam sequence ◆ Melanie Griffith had a boob job during filming, proudly showing them off to everyone on set and failing to understand that the change in *embonpoint* would not only necessitate her costumes being let out but might conceiveably be noticed by eagle-eyed viewers.

The Book of Love •••• [1991]

Director: **Robert Shaye**
Screenplay: **William Kotzwinkle**

Teenage angst and love in 50's high school America has been done to death. But this delightful little pic, beautifully acted by a cast of unknowns is fresh, funny, romantic and invigorating. A joy from start to finish, it was unjustly ignored on release.

Well worth seeking out. [87m/15]

Jack Twiller	Chris Young
Crutch Kane	Keith Coogan
Peanut	Aeryk Egan
Lily	Josie Bissett
Gina Gabooch	Tricia Leigh Fisher
Adult Jack Twiller	Michael McKean

Boomerang •• [1992]

Director: Reginald Hudlin
Screenplay: Barry W. Blaustein & David Sheffield

Murphy's a marketing man who has amazing success with the ladies, despite lines Mrs. Noah would recognise. But when new boss Givens treats him as he treats women, it drives him bananas. Although Murphy's endearing enough and there's a glowing performance from the stunning Berry, the movie as a whole is unremarkable. The best gags are from Murphy's friend who sees racism in everything, even the way the white ball dominates the game of pool. Odd, though, how there are almost no white actors.

[117m/15]

Marcus	Eddie Murphy
Angela	Halle Berry
Jacqueline	Robin Givens
Gerard Jackson	David Alan Grier

Also: Martin Lawrence, Grace Jones, Geoffrey Holder, Eartha Kitt

Quote 'That's Korean for "I'm sorry I shot you, but I thought you were robbing my store".'

Psst! Murphy's casual attitude to punctuality apparently cost the production $1m in wasted time. His reaction to the LA riots was not to turn up for reshoots, which cost another $300,000. His pay was $12m.

The Boost ••• [1988]

Director: Harold Becker
Screenplay: Darryl Ponicsan

A businessman gets hooked on drugs and goes downhill fast. A pretty good morality tale, given a boost of its own by Woods' manic performance. There is some voyeuristic fun to be had from these 'difficult' actors working together before their well publicised off-screen bust-up. [See Woods' biography.] [95m/18]

Lenny Brown	James Woods
Linda	Sean Young
Joel	John Kapelos
Max	Steven Hill
Rochelle	Kelle Kerr

Quote 'Does the word "nightmare" mean anything to you?' [Woods on his relationship with Young.]

Born on the Fourth of July •••• [1989]

Director: Oliver Stone
Screenplay: Oliver Stone & Ron Kovic

True story of Vietnam volunteer Ron Kovic, wounded in battle and confined to a wheelchair. The opening reels are a tad predictable, but otherwise a powerful, heartfelt scream of rage and despair, both shocking and human, in Stone's best style. Cruise gives a remarkably good performance in this masterpiece of modern cinema. [151m/18]

Ron Kovic	Tom Cruise
Donna	Kyra Sedgwick
Charlie	Willem Dafoe
Marine Recruiter	Tom Berenger
Mr. Kovic	Raymond J. Barry
Mrs. Kovic	Caroline Kava
Steve Boyer	Jerry Levine
Timmy	Frank Whaley
Jimmy Kovic	Jamie Talisman
Young Ron	Bryan Larkin

Oscars Best Director

Quote 'I'd give everything I believe in just to have my body again.'

OOPS! As Cruise visits the family of the guy he killed by mistake in Vietnam, the swing is hanging from just one chain. It's fixed by the time he leaves ◆ It's nice to hear *American Pie* again. Shame it wasn't released until three years after the film was set ◆ They shouldn't have Reeboks in 1972 at the Democratic Convention either. The vet wearing them is six years early.

Psst! The lead part was originally Al Pacino's, but he backed out ✦ Kovik himself appears in the opening parade sequence while Stone does his usual cameo, here as a reporter. Three of the Baldwin brothers pop their heads in, William as a member of the platoon, Daniel as one of a pair of vets and Stephen as Billy Vorosvich.

The Bostonians •• [1984]

Director: **James Ivory**
Screenplay: **Ruth Prawer Jhabvala**

This attempt by Merchant-Ivory to repeat the success of their other Henry James' adaptation, *The Europeans*, doesn't come off. The tale of a 19th-century early feminist is, despite the good acting and lovely photography, carried out at the pace of a rather leisurely funeral. **[122m/PG]**

Basil Ransom	Christopher Reeve
Oliver Chancellor	Vanessa Redgrave
Verena Tarrant	Madeleine Potter
Miss Birdseye	Jessica Tandy
Mrs. Burrage	Nancy Marchand
Dr. Prance	Linda Hunt
Mr. Pardon	Wallace Shawn

Psst! William Styron, author of *Sophie's Choice*, was on the verge of suicide when he saw this film on TV. A piece of music used was the same as his mother played to him as a boy, and he was so moved, he checked into hospital instead.

Bounty •• [1984]

Director: **Roger Donaldson**
Screenplay: **Robert Bolt**

Hopkins has the volume turned right up as Cap'n Bligh, cheesed off because first mate Christian, as played by Gibson, is more successful with the native Tahitian girls than him. Eventually the sailors mutiny and martinet Bligh is set adrift. Despite Hopkins' excellently believable Bligh, Gibson's vacuous performance nearly sinks the ship. The scenery is amazing, though. **[130m/15]**

Fletcher Christian	Mel Gibson
Lt. William Bligh	Anthony Hopkins
Admiral Hood	Laurence Olivier
Capt. Greetham	Edward Fox
Fryer	Daniel Day-Lewis
Cole	Bernard Hill
Young	Philip Davis
Churchill	Liam Neeson

Psst! For those who care about these things, historically this is the most accurate of all the screen versions of the story ✦ It cost $4m to build an exact replica of the Bounty ✦ Although the Tahitian girls used as extras looked beautiful, their teeth were rotten, and dentures had to be provided. These were collected at the end of each day's filming to ensure they returned the next day. They were given to them at the end of the film. ✦ Gibson's part was originally intended for Sting.

The Boys Next Door •• [1985]

Director: **Penelope Spheeris**
Screenplay: **Glen Morgan & James Wong**

A couple of teenagers figure that if they're heading for a dead end, they may as well hit it hard. So they embark on a murderous crime spree. Depressing, only occasionally distracting, stuff. **[91m/18]**

Roy Alson	Maxwell Caulfield
Bo Richards	Charlie Sheen
Angie	Patti D'Arbanville
Det. Mark Woods	Christopher McDonald

The Boy Who Could Fly •• [1986]

Director: **Nick Castle**
Screenplay: **Nick Castle**

Beware of films bearing titles that give away the plot [see Rose's Rule #7]. Bedelia's family move next door to an autistic boy, Underwood, and Deakins befriends him. A surprisingly downbeat fantasy that never really gets off the ground until its rather silly ending. **[114m/PG]**

Milly	Lucy Deakins
Eric	Jay Underwood
Charlene	Bonnie Bedelia
Louis	Fred Savage
Mrs. Sherman	Colleen Dewhurst

Boyz N the Hood ••• [1991]

Director: John Singleton
Screenplay: John Singleton

A father tries to keep his son on the straight and narrow in a black ghetto suburb of LA. One of the best depictions of life in such a violent, depressed community, it's staggering such a mature and balanced film was written and directed by Singleton at just 23. Gritty, realistic and well worthwhile. [111m/15]

Doughboy Baker	Ice Cube
Tre Styles	Cuba Gooding Jr.
Ricky Baker	Morris Chestnut
Furious Styles	Larry Fishburne
Brandi	Nia Long
Mrs Baker	Tyra Ferrell

Quote 'Increase the peace.'

Psst! This was the most profitable film of 1991, taking over $60m against a cost of just $6m • Although the film was intended to preach peace, when it opened three people were killed and thirty injured in shootings throughout the States.

Brain Damage •• [1988]

Director: Frank Henenlotter
Screenplay: Frank Henenlotter

A parasitic bug called Elmer gives its host highs with injections to his brain. The host comes to wish he'd Just Said No. Not as lively as Hennenlotter's *Basket Case*, it's worth seeing just for the creature's rendition of Elmer's Tune. [94m/18]

Brian	Rick Herbst
Mike	Gordon MacDonald
Barbara	Jennifer Lowry
Morris	Theo Barnes

Psst! Probably the first movie in which someone pulls their brains out through their ear.

Braindead ••• [1993]

Director: Peter Jackson
Screenplay: Peter Jackson, Stephen Sinclair & Frances Walsh

More gore than the sum total of all the horror films you've ever seen. In 1950's New Zealand, where the usual Sumatran virus is zombiefying the Kiwis, there are entrails everywhere. Repulsive but very funny. [101m/18]

Lionel	Timothy Balme
Paquita	Diana Penalver
Mum	Elizabeth Moody
Uncle Les	Ian Watkin

Psst! Probably the first movie in which a Flymo is used as a multiple murder weapon • How did they achieve all that gore? With pork fat, latex, sisal, polyfoam, human hair, ultra slime and hundreds of gallons of maple syrup!

Brainstorm •• [1983]

Director: Douglas Trumbull
Screenplay: Robert Stitzel & Philip Frank Messina

Scientists come up with a wonderful sensory device that, surprise, surprise, attracts the attention of the evil military. There's little to the film apart from some glorious special effects from FX wizard Trumbull, whose finest hour was *2001*. [106m/15]

Michael Brace	Christopher Walken
Karen Brace	Natalie Wood
Lillian Reynolds	Louise Fletcher
Alex Terson	Cliff Robertson

Psst! Natalie Wood died during the making of the film.

Bram Stoker's Dracula ••• [1992]

Director: Francis Ford Coppola
Screenplay: James V. Hart

When his wife tops herself, Vlad the Impaler renounces God, gets himself a Princess Leia hair-do and becomes a vampire, offering a free blood transfusion service without the tea and biscuits. 400 years later he turns up in Victorian London, wearing blue glasses and long hair and looking as if he's stopped off at Woodstock on the way. The Boy's Own-style story is a trifle weak, as are

some of the accents. The film isn't particularly frightening, either. But visually it's
a feast for the eye, one of the most sump-
tuous-looking and inventive movies in
ages, constantly surprising with both new
and old tricks. Far more erotic than is
given credit for, the main question is why
on earth Reeves would *want* to escape
from the attentions of Dracula's brides.

[123m/18]

Dracula	Gary Oldman
Mina/Elisabeta	Winona Ryder
Van Helsing	Anthony Hopkins
Jonathan Harker	Keanu Reeves
Dr. Jack Seward	Richard E. Grant
Lord Arthur Holmwood	Cary Elwes
Quincy P. Morris	Bill Campbell
Lucy Westenra	Sadie Frost
R.M. Renfield	Tom Waits

Quote 'I never drink...wine.' ✦ 'Vampires,
submission, domination, rape, bestiality,
guilt, biblical overtones, Satan, God,
Christian motifs, the dead, undead, blood,
murder, revenge, opera, classicism and
oral sex.' [Keanu Reeves]

OOPS! How is it that Dracula dreads the
daylight, yet spends part of the film
wandering round London by day quite
happily? ✦ Although one might have
expected the sight of Dracula to send
someone's hair grey, that's about the
only colour Reeves doesn't sport during
the film.

Psst! After a few people fainted at early
test screenings, the amount of blood was
toned down and the bones of the story
beefed up ✦ The film opened in America
on a Friday the 13th ✦ This was
Oldman's second outing as Dracula.
Aged 5, he entered a fancy dress competition at Butlin's in a cape of crepe paper
made by his mum. He lost ✦ Florina
Kendrick, one of Dracula's brides, was
born in Transylvania. She taught
Romanian to Oldman, Ryder, Hopkins
and the other two brides ✦ Reeves spent
some time at Eton, boning up on his
English accent ✦ The lid of the coffin
containing Sadie Frost was too heavy to
lift from the inside, apparently giving her

a panic attack on one occasion when
everybody knocked off for a break, forgetting she was inside ✦ Bram Stoker
was said to have been inspired to write
Dracula during a nightmare brought on
by a bad shellfish supper.

The Brave Little Toaster ●● [1989]

Director: **Jerry Rees**
Screenplay: **Jerry Rees & Joe Ranft**

A set of household appliances gets tired of
waiting for their young friend and sets off
in search of him. Despite being highly
praised at the time, it's dull uninspired
stuff from an adult's point of view,
although kids will probably like it for its
strange storyline and characters. [87m/U]

With: Jon Lovitz, Tim Stack, Timothy E.
Day, Thurl Ravencroft, Deanna Oliver

Brazil ●●●● [1985]

Director: **Terry Gilliam**
Screenplay: **Terry Gilliam, Tom Stoppard
& Charles McKeown**

There has never been and there never
will be another movie quite like this
bizarre, black and bleakly funny fantasy
about a Kafka-esque, bureaucratically
strangled future world. Pryce is the clerk
in Information Retrieval who won't stop
dreaming, particularly when he discovers
dream-girl Greist. Like a hard-nosed
version of Gilliam's Python animations
brought to life, Brazil may take more than
one viewing to appreciate fully and still
may not make complete sense. Certainly a
mite too long, but boy does it stick in the
memory. [142m/15]

Sam Lowry	Jonathan Pryce
Tuttle	Robert De Niro
Ida Lowry	Katherine Helmond
Kurtzmann	Ian Holm
Spoor	Bob Hoskins
Jack Lint	Michael Palin
Warren	Ian Richardson
Helpmann	Peter Vaughan
Jill Layton	Kim Greist

Also: Jim Broadbent, Charles McKeown, Derrick O'Connor, Bryan Pringle, Nigel Planer, Gordon Kaye

Quote 'I generally describe *Brazil* in a pretentious way as a post–Orwellian view of a pre–Orwellian world. That description bores everyone stiff, so they leave me alone.' [Gilliam]

Psst! The studio wasn't happy about the film and wanted it cut heavily and given a happy ending. Gilliam took an ad in Variety that said: 'Dear Sid Sheinberg. When are you going to release my film?' Only when it won three awards from the LA Film Critics Association was it released.

Breakdance •• · [1984]

Director: Joel Silberg
Screenplay: Charles Parker, Allen DeBevoise & Gerald Scaife

The first of the breakdancing movies is mildly engaging but something of a museum piece almost a decade later. Also known as *Breakin'*. [90m/PG]

Kelly	Lucinda Dickey
Ozone	Adolfo Quinones
Turbo	Michael Chambers

Breakdance 2: Electric Boogaloo • [1984]

Director: Sam Firstenberg
Screenplay: Jan Ventura & Julie Reichert

Property developers want to bulldoze the place where the local breakdancers strut their stuff. We sympathise with them. Also known as *Breakin' 2*. [94m/PG]

Kelly	Lucinda Dickey
Ozone	Adolfo Quinones
Turbo	Michael Chambers

The Breakfast Club •• [1985]

Director: John Hughes
Screenplay: John Hughes

A group of high school students are locked in the library for detention on a Saturday morning. Instead of picking their noses and staring at the wall, they talk...and talk, and talk, and talk. Despite hitting the button occasionally with some sensible truths about teenagerdom, it's still a relief when they unlock the fire doors and the lights come up. [97m/15]

Andrew	Emilio Estevez
John/"Bender"	Judd Nelson
Claire	Molly Ringwald
Brian	Anthony Michael Hall
Allison	Ally Sheedy

Quote 'It's unavoidable. When you grow up, your heart dies.'

Psst! Not yet up to the speed he achieved with *Weird Science*, Hughes took three days to write this script.

Breakin'
SEE: Breakdance

Breakin' 2: Electric Boogaloo
SEE: Breakdance 2: Electric Boogaloo

Breaking In •••• [1989]

Director: Bill Forsyth
Screenplay: John Sayles

Burglar Reynolds takes on a new partner and leads him astray. A little gem, with an intelligent script by Sayles, warmly quirky direction from Forsyth and Reynolds never better. Why Hollywood can't generate more of these low–budget charmers is one of the unsolved mysteries of the age. [94m/12]

Ernie Mullins	Burt Reynolds
Mike	Casey Siemaszko
Carrie	Sheila Kelley
Delphine	Lorraine Toussaint
Johnny Scat	Albert Salmi
Shoes	Harry Carey Jr.
Tucci	Maury Chaykin
District Attorney	Stephen Tobolowsky

Breathless • [1983]

Director: Jim McBride
Screenplay: L.M. Kit Carson

So devoid of breath that it's a complete

stiff. This pointless re-make of the classic French 1959 Godard film shifts the action to Los Angeles. Gere's a crook on the lam falling for foreign student Karpisky. Despite the pair of them showing off their lovely bodies, it is all too easy to understand why Gere's career went into reverse after this.   **[100m/18]**

Jesse	Richard Gere
Monica	Valerie Kaprisky
Birnbaum	Art Metrano
Lt. Parmental	John P. Ryan

Showing *Gun Crazy.*

Psst! To audition for the part of Monica, a three-day kissathon took place between Gere and 40 would-be starlets in a Paris hotel room. Kaprisky was apparently the hottest ♦ One of the few films with male nudity, with Richard Gere stripping off completely for the shower scene

Brewster's Millions • [1985]

Director: **Walter Hill**
Screenplay: **Herschel Weingrod**

They keep filming this play, but they never get it right. In this seventh version, Pryor has to spend $30m and end up without any money if he is to inherit an even bigger fortune. Shouldn't be too hard if it's this easy to spend $30m on a comedy and end up without any laughs.   **[97m/PG]**

Montgomery Brewster	Richard Pryor
Spike Nolan	John Candy
Angela Drake	Lonette McKee
Warren Cox	Stephen Collins
Charley Pegler	Jerry Orbach
Edward Roundfield	Pat Hingle

The Bride • [1985]

Director: **Franc Roddam**
Screenplay: **Lloyd Fonvielle**

Baron Frankenstein creates a mate for his monster, only to develop a pash on her himself. This feminist twist on the old tale has little going for it except the much missed Rappaport's performance. A shame someone couldn't get the lightning to ignite the script.   **[119m/15]**

Frankenstein	Sting
Eva	Jennifer Beals
Clerval	Anthony Higgins
Vicktor	Clancy Brown

Also: David Rappaport, Geraldine Page, Alexei Sayle, Quentin Crisp, Cary Elwes

Bright Lights, Big City • [1988]

Director: **James Bridges**
Screenplay: **Jay McInerney**

Michael J. Fox is once more miscast as he desperately tries to convince us that he's no longer still fifteen. Here he plays a cocaine-taking New Yorker whose life is falling to pieces. Despite giving his all, we don't really give a fig for the character. Sporadic flashes of insight do not a movie make.   **[110m/18]**

Jamie Conway	Michael J. Fox
Tad Allagash	Kiefer Sutherland
Amanda	Phoebe Cates
Megan	Swoosie Kurtz
Clara Tillinghast	Frances Sternhagen

Also: Tracy Pollan, John Houseman, Charlie Schlatter, Jason Robards, Dianne Wiest, Kelly Lynch

Psst! Fox spent three days working for Esquire magazine as a fact-checker on the food pages to prepare for the role ♦ He and Tracy Pollan married in July 1988, three months after the movie was released.

Brighton Beach Memoirs •• [1986]

Director: **Gene Saks**
Screenplay: **Neil Simon**

The first of the trio of films based on Neil Simon's semi-autobiographical plays (followed by *Biloxi Blues* and *Broadway Bound*). This one, about the slightly cooky family of teenager Silverman growing up in Brooklyn before the war, is pleasant enough but not as funny or interesting as the other two.   **[108m/15]**

Kate	Blythe Danner
Jack	Bob Dishy
Stanley	Brian Drillinger

Laurie..Stacey Glick
Blanche..Judith Ivey
Eugene.............................Jonathan Silverman

Quote 'You mean Dad used to do it!'

Broadcast News ••• [1987]

Director: James L. Brooks
Screenplay: James L. Brooks

Excellent satire on the world of televison news with Hunter the tough producer who has to choose between Brooks, the unphotogenic reporter who's a good friend and Hurt, the pretty but oh so dim new anchorman. Not only funny, but frighteningly realistic. Turn off before the daft, tacked-on ending.   [132m/15]

Tom Grunick ....William Hurt
Jane Craig....................................Holly Hunter
Aaron Altman............................Albert Brooks
Ernie Merriman........................Robert Prosky
Jennifer Mack................................Lois Chiles
Blair Litton ....Joan Cusack
Paul Moore..................................Peter Hackes
Bobby ....Christian Clemenson
Anchorman ....Jack Nicholson
Angry messenger..........................John Cusack

Quote 'If anything happens to me, tell every woman I've ever gone out with I was talking about her at the end. That way, they'll have to re-evaluate me.'

Psst! Jack Nicholson appears, unbilled, in a cameo as an anchorman while John Cusack, Joan's brother, pops up as the 'angry messenger.' ♦ The part was written with Debra Winger in mind, but she became pregnant. Kathleen Turner was also considered. Writer-director Brooks hadn't even heard of Hunter when she read for the part ♦ Hunter noticed when researching the part at CBS that everyone had dirty hands, so she rubbed hers with newspapers at the start of each day's filming.

Broadway Bound ••• [1992]

Director: Paul Bogart
Screenplay: Neil Simon

The third of Neil Simon's semi-autobio-

graphical plays transferred (the others are *Brighton Beach Memoirs* and *Biloxi Blues*). Here the fictionalised Simon brothers begin their comedy-writing careers. Although pretty stagey, it's witty and wise stuff, with Bancroft and Cronyn both turning in superb performances.   [87m/PG]

Eugene Morris Jerome ....Corey Parker
Stanley ....Jonathan Silverman
Kate ....Anne Bancroft
Ben..Hume Cronyn
Jack..Jerry Orbach

Quote 'Grandfather hasn't laughed since the stock market crashed.'

Psst! Although Silverman was in the early *Brighton Beach Memoirs*, confusingly he then played Eugene.

Broadway Danny Rose ••• [1984]

Director: Woody Allen
Screenplay: Woody Allen

Pleasant, though far from riotously funny, black-and-white Allen pic. He's the small-time agent who becomes the target for the mob when they wrongly think he's running round with gangster's moll Farrow. In fact, he's covering for lounge singer Forte, the only client of his making money.   [86m/PG]

Danny Rose ....Woody Allen
Tina Vitale ....Mia Farrow
Lou Canova.......................Nick Apollo Forte
Himself ....Milton Berle
Himself..Sandy Baron

The Brother from Another Planet ••• [1984]

Director: John Sayles
Screenplay: John Sayles

This bizarre but quietly amusing variation on the *E.T.* theme has a mute black alien landing in Harlem, pursued by a couple of bounty hunters. It shows just how much can be achieved on a small budget. [108m/15]

The Brother....................................Joe Morton
Fly ....Darryl Edwards

Odell	Steve James
Smokey	Leonard Jackson
Walter	Bill Cobbs

Psst! Writer–director Sayles appears as one of the alien bounty hunters.

Buddy's Song ••   [1991]

Director: **Claude Whatham**
Screenplay: **Nigel Hinton**

Rather dull British musical drama which revolves round a dysfunctional working-class family, with Hawkes the hopeful musician and Daltry his ex-con father.

[106m/12]

Terry Clark	Roger Daltrey
Buddy	Chesney Hawkes
Carol	Sharon Duce
Des	Michael Elphick
Bobby Rosen	Douglas Hodge

Buffy, the Vampire Slayer •   [1992]

Director: **Fran Rubel Kuzui**
Screenplay: **Joss Whedon**

Someone should have driven a stake through this Valley-girl vampire movie long before it reached the screen. Swanson's the shopping-mad teenager told by Sutherland she's got to stop the blood-suckers taking over Los Angeles (too late!). Only when it goes for laughs near the end does this stiff show any signs of opening its eyes.

[94m/12]

Buffy	Kristy Swanson
Merrick	Donald Sutherland
Amilyn	Paul Reubens
Lothos	Rutger Hauer
Pike	Luke Perry

Quote 'All I want to do is graduate, go to Europe, marry Christian Slater and die.' • 'I ain't no movie star and *Buffy, the Vampire Slayer* ain't no movie' [Luke Perry]

Psst! Reubens, the number two vampire, is Pee-Wee Herman. He replaced *Twin Peaks* Joan Chen when she dropped out.

Bugsy ••   [1992]

Director: **Barry Levinson**
Screenplay: **James Toback**

Beatty carries off his portrayal of the suave yet psychotic Bugsy Siegel with aplomb, while Bening is mesmerising as sultry starlet, Virginia Hill. More a love story than a gangster pic, this true story of the half-crazed Siegel's creation of the town that would become Las Vegas is as scintillating as watching someone play the slots for a couple of hours. **[135m/18]**

Bugsy Siegel	Warren Beatty
Virginia Hill	Annette Bening
Mickey Cohen	Harvey Keitel
Meyer Lansky	Ben Kingsley
Harry Greenberg	Elliott Gould
George Raft	Joe Mantegna
Countess di Frasso	Bebe Neuwirth

Quote 'Why don't you run outside and jerk yourself a soda?' • 'Twenty dwarves took turns doing handstands on the carpet.'

Showing *Scarface*.

OOPS! Although Bugsy sells his house to pay for the Flamingo, when he runs the screen test of himself near the end, it's in the house he sold.

Psst! Annette Bening became pregnant wth Warren Beatty's baby during filming. Some scenes, particularly when she leaves the Flamingo in the ballgown, reveal her condition.

Bull Durham •••   [1988]

Director: **Ron Shelton**
Screenplay: **Ron Shelton**

Sarandon is the baseball groupie who takes a member of the local minor-league team each year and coaches him in some of the finer things in life, believing that good sex produces higher batting averages. Robbins and Costner are the chaps competing for her affections in this lovely, sassy, often sexy, romantic comedy. Sarandon's performance is so good, it soars out of the ball park completely.

[108m/15]

Crash Davis	Kevin Costner
Annie Savoy	Susan Sarandon
'Nuke' LaLoosh	Tim Robbins
Skip	Trey Wilson
Larry	Robert Wuhl
Jimmy	William O'Leary

QUOTE 'This is the damnedest season I ever seen. The Durham Bulls can't lose and I can't get laid.' ♦ 'I believe in the soul, the small of a woman's back, the hanging curve ball, high fibre, good scotch, long foreplay, show tunes...I believe that Lee Harvey Oswald acted alone, I believe that there ought to be a constitutional amendment outlawing astroturf, I believe in the sweet spot, voting every election, soft core pornography, chocolate chip cookies...and I believe in long, slow, deep, soft, wet kisses that last for three days.'

Psst! There were no takers for this movie from first time writer-director Shelton until Costner picked up the ball and ran with it ♦ Shelton, who later made *White Men Can't Jump*, was in the minor-leagues for five years himself ♦ The scene in the pool hall where Robbins tells Costner he's joining the major league was originally set and filmed in a brothel, then changed a couple of months later.

Bullet Proof ●   [1987]

Director: **Steve Carver**
Screenplay: **T.L. Lankford & Steve Carver**

Plot Proof thriller about a half-mad cop sorting out baddies in Mexico. Pathetic. **[94m/15]**

Bulletproof McBain	Gary Busey
Lt. Devon Shepard	Darlanne Fluegel
Col. Kartiff	Henry Silva
Pantaro	Juan Fernandez

Bullseye! ●   [1990]

Director: **Michael Winner**
Screenplay: **Leslie Bricusse, Laurence Marks & Maurice Gran**

Forget about hitting the bull's-eye. The darts are so off-target, the entire pub should be evacuated. Lots of furious action, pathetic jokes, double doses of Caine and Moore and a script that stinks so badly you could use it on the rhubarb. Not even Moore's self-confessed 'left eyebrow raised, right eyebrow raised' acting technique can save it. **[102m/15]**

Dr. Hicklar/Sidney Lipton	Michael Caine
Bavistock/Bradley-Smith	Roger Moore
Willie Metcalfe	Sally Kirkland
Flo Fleming	Deborah Maria Moore
Club receptionist	Jenny Seagrove
Man on beach	John Cleese

Psst! Never one to waste money [see *Chorus of Disapproval*], Winner here set a record for the smallest crew on a major film. For the scene in Barbados, Winner operated the camera while the camera-man held the device that reflects the sun's rays. The microphone was hidden in the book that Cleese, acting in the scene, was carrying ♦ Deborah Maria Moore, best known from the Scottish Widows com-mercial, is Roger's daughter, here acting under the name 'Barrymore' ♦ The Duke and Duchess of Argyll appear as them-selves.

Bullshot ●   [1983]

Director: **Dick Clement**
Screenplay: **Ron House, Diz White & Alan Shearman**

There's one vowel wrong in the title of this dreadful, unamusing spoof of the old Bulldog Drummond detective movies. They are a lot funnier, both intentionally and unintentionally, than this load of bullshot. **[85m/PG]**

Capt. 'Bullshot' Crummond	Alan Shearman
Rosemary Fenton	Diz White
Count Otto von Bruno	Ron House
Also: Frances Tomelty, Michael Aldridge, Mel Smith, Billy Connolly	

The 'burbs ●●● ●   [1989]

Director: **Joe Dante**
Screenplay: **Dana Olsen**

A group of paranoid suburbanites suspect evil happenings at their new neighbour's house. This mildly amusing comedy keeps threatening to be brilliant, but never quite makes it. Nonetheless, the characters are so much fun that it's still all quite a laugh.

[102m/PG]

Ray Peterson	Tom Hanks
Mark Rumsfield	Bruce Dern
Carol Peterson	Carrie Fisher
Art Weingartner	Rick Ducommun
Ricky Butler	Corey Feldman
Bonnie Rumsfield	Wendy Schaal
Dr. Werner Klopek	Henry Gibson

Burning Secret •• [1988]

Director: **Andrew Birkin**
Screenplay: **Andrew Birkin**

Ponderous post–World War I tale of Baron Brandauer working his way into the confidences of a mother and son at an Austrian spa. Quite why something based on a short story takes so long to play out is more of a secret than the title's.

[104m/PG]

Edmund	David Eberts
Sonya	Faye Dunaway
Baron	Klaus Maria Brandauer
Father	Ian Richardson

Business as Usual •• [1987]

Director: **Lezli-An Barrett**
Screenplay: **Lezli-An Barrett**

A heavily political tale of shop manager-ess Jackson, in pre–MP days, being sacked after sticking up for a worker suffering sexual harrassment. Although well made, it's dry stuff and typical of a time when almost every British film also doubled as an attack on Thatcher. **[89m/15]**

Babs Flynn	Glenda Jackson
Kieran Flynn	John Thaw
Josie Patterson	Cathy Tyson
Stevie Flynn	Mark McGann

Buster •• [1988]

Director: **David Green**
Screenplay: **Colin Shindler**

Cheeky chappie Buster Edwards, flower-seller extraordinaire, is the only one of the Great Train Robbers to escape capture, but once in the sun he pines for the grey skies of England. Although moderately entertaining in the early stages, it soon goes off the rails and ploughs into the buffers. **[103m/15]**

Buster Edwards	Phil Collins
June Edwards	Julie Walters
Bruce	Larry Lamb
Franny Reynolds	Stephanie Lawrence
Insp. Jack Mitchell	Martin Jarvis
Mrs. Rothery	Sheila Hancock

Psst! This was Phil Collins' feature debut ✦ Although the Prince and Princess of Wales were to have attended a charity premiere of the film, such a fuss was made that they pleaded prior engagements.

The Butcher's Wife ••• [1992]

Director: **Terry Hughes**
Screenplay: **Ezra Litwak & Marjorie Schwartz**

Psychic Moore is brought to the Big Apple by her new butcher husband and there tangles with local shrink Daniels. The story's terribly predictable and it takes some getting used to Moore's blonde hair and deep-fried Southern accent. Nonetheless, for the tender-hearted this is a charming and amusing piece of old-fashioned romantic whimsy.

[105m/12]

Marina	Demi Moore
Dr. Alex Tremor	Jeff Daniels
Leo	George Dzundza
Stella	Mary Steenburgen

Also: Frances McDormand, Margaret Colin, Max Perlich, Miriam Margolyes

Psst! Credits include a psychic consultant.

Bye Bye Blues ••• [1990]

Director: **Anne Wheeler**
Screenplay: **Anne Wheeler**

A lovely, pleasantly sentimental Canadian tale of young mother Jenkins forced to cope on her own in wartime, uncertain even if her husband's still alive. Despite the familiarity of the storyline, it's handled so freshly, it's as if we're seeing it for the first time. Although it gives the tear-ducts a fair old workout, we never feel we're being manipulated. [116m/PG]

Daisy Cooper	Rebecca Jenkins
Max Gramley	Luke Reilly
Slim Godfrey	Stuart Margolin
Pete	Wayne Robson
Frances Cooper	Robyn Stevan
Teddy Cooper	Michael Ontkean
Mary Wright	Kate Reid

C

Cactus •• [1986]

Director: Paul Cox
Screenplay: Paul Cox, Norman Kaye & Bob Ellis

Isabelle Huppert fears she may lose her sight after a car accident but is comforted by a blind cactus grower. Another offbeat Australian film from Paul Cox, excellently made, but perhaps not as overwhelming as it should be. [96m/PG]

Colo	Isabelle Huppert
Robert	Robert Menzies
Tom	Norman Kaye
Bea	Monica Maughan

Cadillac Man •• [1990]

Director: Roger Donaldson
Screenplay: Ken Friedman

A womanising car salesman living near the edge comes close to being pushed off it when a gunman comes calling. Despite Williams' bravura performance and moments of brilliance, too many genres – comedy, melodrama, thriller – are thrown in for the film to cope. In the end, we simply don't give a monkey's for these people. [98m/15]

Joey O'Brien	Robin Williams
Larry	Tim Robbins
Tina O'Brien	Pamela Reed
Joy Munchack	Fran Drescher
Harry Munchack	Zack Norman
Donna	Annabella Sciorra
Lila	Lori Petty

Blurb If You Can't Trust A Car Salesman Who *Can* You Trust?

Quote 'You know what your problem is, Joey? You're a pig. And you're a chauvinist. And you have no respect for women.' – 'Oh. I guess dinner and a blow job is out of the question then, huh?'

Cal ••• [1984]

Director: Pat O'Connor
Screenplay: Bernard MacLaverty

A young Irishman involved with the IRA is racked with guilt when he has an affair with the widow of a policeman in whose murder he was involved. This finely-made film throws some compassionate light on The Troubles and is greatly helped by the sympathetic Lynch and the warmth of Mirren. There's a nice soundtrack by Mark Knopfler, too. [102m/15]

Marcella	Helen Mirren
Cal	John Lynch
Shamie	Donal McCann
Skeffington	John Kavanagh
Cyril Dunlop	Ray McAnally

California Man •• [1992]

Director: Les Mayfield
Screenplay: Shawn Schepps

Digging a pool in his back garden, Astin uncovers a frozen caveman. Thawed out, he's a great hit with the girls at school, lifting the curse of nerd status from Astin and weird-talking mate Shore. Far better than the critics allowed, this patchily amusing sub-Bill & Ted comedy could entertain those who are into weasel impressions in a big way. Also known as *Encino Man*. [88m/PG]

Dave Morgan	Sean Astin
Link	Brendan Fraser
Stoney Brown	Pauly Shore
Robyn	Megan Ward

Call Me •   [1988]

Director: **Sollace Mitchell**
Screenplay: **Karyn Kay**

An erotic thriller that's neither erotic nor thrilling. Charbonneau is the murder witness who starts receiving obscene phone calls which she enjoys. Don't call us.

[96m/18]

Anna	Patricia Charbonneau
Cori	Patti D'Arbanville
Alex	Sam Freed

Psst! Notable for including what many consider the most over-used line in the movies: 'There was blood everywhere.'

Came a Hot Friday •••   [1985]

Director: **Ian Mune**
Screenplay: **Dean Parker & Ian Mune**

A delightfully funny New Zealand comedy about a couple of itinerant con-men with amazing talent for picking up money and women. They may have met their match in the canny citizens of Tainula Junction, though. Great fun.   [101m/PG]

Wesley	Peter Bland
Cyril	Philip Gordon
Tainuia	Billy T. James
Don	Michael Lawrence
Sel	Marshall Napier

Cameron's Closet ••   [1988]

Director: **Armand Mastroianni**
Screenplay: **Gary Brandner**

Playing around with his son's mind, as parents are wont to do, Hunter unleashes something nasty in Cameron's cupboard. And it isn't a year-old Marmite soldier, either. Middle of the road horror. [87m/18]

Sam Talliaferro	Cotter Smith
Nora Haley	Mel Harris
Cameron	Scott Curtis

Campsite Massacre •   [1983]

Director: **Andrew Davis**
Screenplay: **Ronald Shusett**

Some teens go to a campsite in the woods. There is a massacre. They only have

themselves to blame. Early appearances by Ward and Hannah might generate some interest, but don't bank on it. Also known as *The Final Terror*.   [84m/18]

Zorich	John Friedrich
Margaret	Rachel Ward
Cerone	Adrian Zmed
Windy	Daryl Hannah

Psst! This was Rachel Ward's first film and Hannah's second.

Candyman •••   [1992]

Director: **Bernard Rose**
Screenplay: **Bernard Rose**

In the slums of Chicago residents are being butchered nastily. The locals believe a murdered ex-slave is responsible and that if you stand in front of your mirror saying 'Candyman' five times, he'll get you. Is academic Madsen foolish enough to do this? Of course she is. An attempt at an intelligent slasher movie has some interesting ideas and plenty of gore but an unconvincing storyline. Oddly, some people are unmoved by the movie, while others find it one of the most frightening they've ever seen.   [93m/18]

Helen Lyle	Virginia Madsen
Candyman	Tony Todd
Trevor Lyle	Xander Berkeley
Bernadette Walsh	Kasi Lemmons
Anne-Marie McCoy	Vanessa Williams
Jake	DeJuan Guy

Quote 'What's blood for if not for shedding?'

Psst! Originally set by Clive Barker in Birmingham, the location was switched to Chicago as the only way of raising the money • In the short story, her name was Helen Tate. Worried about echoes of Sharon Tate made them switch it. Instead of Tate, it's now Lyle!

Cannonball Run II •   [1984]

Director: **Hal Needham**
Screenplay: **Hal Needham, Albert S. Ruddy & Harvey Miller**

More silly cross-country car chases, with plenty of people whose names have long been forgotten popping in for cameo appearances. Dire. **[108m/PG]**

J.J..Burt Reynolds
Victor ....Dom DeLuise
Blake ....Dean Martin
Fenderbaum...........................Sammy Davis Jr.
Also: Jamie Farr, Marilu Henner, Telly Savalas, Frank Sinatra, Shirley MacLaine, Sid Caesar, Jackie Chan

Can She Bake a Cherry Pie? •• [1983]

Director: **Henry Jaglom**
Screenplay: **Henry Jaglom**

Two nervy New York neurotics meet up and talk an awful lot over endless cups of coffee. All performance and character, like Woody Allen without the laughs. **[90m/15]**

Zee ....Karen Black
Eli ....Michael Emil
Larry.....................................Michael Margotta

Psst! Black made the film for a nominal fee of $1,038. The Actors Guild fined her the same amount when it found out the film had been made without union approval.

Can't Buy Me Love •• [1987]

Director: **James Foley**
Screenplay: **Michael Swerdlick**

Fed up of his dweebish image at high school, Dempsey pays Peterson $1,000 to pose as his girlfriend for a month. His stock rises until she blows the gaff. Predictable and sentimental. Also rather pricey, when you consider that Gere gets a week's worth of hooker Julia Roberts doing whatever he wants in *Pretty Woman* for just $3,000. **[94m/PG]**

Ronald Miller.......................Patrick Dempsey
Cindy Mancini ....Amanda Peterson
Kenneth Wurman..................Courtney Gains
Barbara ....Tina Caspary

Cape Fear •• [1992]

Director: **Martin Scorsese**
Screenplay: **Wesley Strick**

Disappointing remake of the 1962 film.

De Niro – the only actor able to exude menace in a Hawaiian shirt – is released from prison after fourteen years, determined to revenge himself on Nolte, the lawyer whose incompetence put him there. Nolte's character is so flawed that it's difficult to root for him, while Scorsese's silly out-of-place camera tricks remind us we're watching a film and allow the tension to evaporate. At the climax plausibility, already stretched, snaps completely.

[127m/18]

Max Cady..............................Robert De Niro
Sam Bowden..................................Nick Nolte
Leigh Bowden...............................Jessica Lange
Danielle Bowden.......................Juliette Lewis
Claude Kersek..........................Joe Don Baker
Lieutenant Elgart ....Robert Mitchum
Lee Heller..................................Gregory Peck
Judge...Martin Balsam
Lori Davis...............................Illeana Douglas
Tom Broadbent..........Fred Dalton Thompson

Quote 'Jeez, I don't know whether to look at him or read him.'

Showing *All That Heaven Allows, Problem Child.*

OOPS! At the airport, De Niro asks at an airline desk if Nolte is on a particular flight. Everybody knows such information isn't given out nowadays, except for screenwriters needing a helping hand with the plot ◆ Keep an eye on Nolte's friend Lori in the bar scene where De Niro's chatting her up and see the top of her blouse pop open and shut several times.

Psst! Three of the stars of the original film, Robert Mitchum, Gregory Peck and Martin Balsam, appear in small cameo roles, acting some of their younger brethren off the screen ◆ De Niro worked out for 8 months to get his physique in shape for Cady ◆ When Scorsese directs, other Scorseses aren't far away. Mum Catherine [also in *Goodfellas*] and Charles Scorsese are customers at the fruit stand while Domenica Scorsese is Danny's girlfriend.

Captain America • [1989]

Director: **Albert Pyun**
Screenplay: **Stephen Tolkin**

Even Oliver Stone didn't blame The Red Skull for killing JFK but that's who does it here, with the evil one knocking off a few other US icons before Captain America, a former polio victim but now a regular superhero, comes back to save civilisation as we know it. A film so bad, it wasn't even shown in American cinemas. **[97m/PG]**

Captain	Matt Salinger
Tom Kimbell	Ronny Cox
Sam Kolowetz	Ned Beatty

Captive •• [1986]

Director: **Paul Mayersberg**
Screenplay: **Paul Mayersberg**

A sort of European version of the Patty Hearst story with a wealthy girl kidnapped and reeducated by a trio of terrorists. Despite a fair bit of nudity, this Anglo-French co-production is stylish but not always fathomable. Reed is surprisingly good. **[99m/18]**

Rowena	Irina Brook
Gregory	Oliver Reed
Hiro	Hiro Arai
D	Xavier Deluc

Psst! The original title was *Heroine*, but Mayersberg became fed up with irrelevant drugs-related questions about the title.

Caravaggio ••• [1986]

Director: **Derek Jarman**
Screenplay: **Derek Jarman**

The life and troubled times of the 16th-century Italian painter. One of Jarman's best films, it's sumptuous to look at despite its tiny budget and has more consistent acting than some of his earlier works. With its mixing of modern artefacts with the realities of 16th-century life, it's definitely an arthouse pic, but it still puts most Hollywood 'tortured artist' biopics to shame. **[93m/15]**

Caravaggio	Nigel Terry
Ranuccio Thomasoni	Sean Bean
Davide	Garry Cooper
Lena	Tilda Swinton
Cardinal Del Monte	Michael Gough
Marchese Giustiniani	Nigel Davenport
Cardinal Borghese	Robbie Coltrane

The Care Bears Movie •• [1985]

Director: **Arna Selznick**
Screenplay: **Peter Sauder**

This grotesquely unsubtle animated attempt to sell yet more of the bally toys might keep the kids quiet, but will drive adults up the wall. Come back, Pooh! All is forgiven. **[75m/U]**

With: Mickey Rooney, Georgia Engel, Harry Dean Stanton

The Care Bears Movie II: A New Generation • [1986]

Director: **Dale Schott**
Screenplay: **Peter Sauder**

When it became clear there were still a few kiddies left who hadn't bought a Care Bare, they brought out a sequel. Come back, Paddington! All is forgiven. **[77m/U]**

With: Hadley Kay, Bob Dermer, Eva Almos, Dan Hennessey

The Care Bears' Adventures in Wonderland! •• [1987]

Director: **Raymond Jafelice**
Screenplay: **Susi Snooks & John DeKlein**

Come on, now. There's still one child left who hasn't got one. This one's for him. Come back, *Sooty!* All is forgiven. **[75m/U]**

With: Bob Dermer, Eva Almos, Dan Hennessey

Careful, He Might Hear You ••• [1984]

Director: **Carl Schultz**
Screenplay: **Michael Jenkins**

A moving Australian tale, set in the time

of the Great Depression, with two very different sisters competing for custody of their late sister's boy. It's soap, but of a very high and utterly absorbing standard, topped off by three excellent performances. **[116m/PG]**

PS	Nicholas Gledhill
Vanessa	Wendy Hughes
Lila	Robyn Nevin
George	Peter Whitford
Logan	John Hargreaves
Agnes	Isabelle Anderson

Carry On Columbus • - [1992]

Director: **Gerald Thomas**
Screenplay: **Dave Freeman**

Rather sad attempt to revive the Carry On Series. Most of the jokes aren't worthy of a lolly stick, while some are so disgusting even Bernard Manning would wash his mouth out with soap. The only giggles come from the Indians who think Columbus is running a mobile laundry. As for Dale, he looks as if he'd have trouble crossing the road, let alone the Atlantic. It didn't tickle my fancy. **[91m/PG]**

Chris Columbus	Jim Dale
Mort	Bernard Cribbins
Countess Esmerelda	Maureen Lipman

Also: Peter Richardson, Alexei Sayle, Rik Mayall, Charles Fleischer, Larry Miller, Sara Crowe

Quote 'If you get lonely, you can come up my end.'

Psst! The ship was borrowed from Ridley Scott, who used it in *1492: Conquest of Paradise*. It cost more than the entire budget of *Carry On Columbus*.

Car Trouble •• [1986]

Director: **David Green**
Screenplay: **James Whaley & A.J. Tipping**

The urban myth of the woman and man making love in the car who get locked inextricably together was old when cars still had men with red flags walking in front of them. Here a whole film is spun around Walters' fateful bonk. A bootful of

nudge–nudge jokes raises a few half-hearted laughs. **[93m/18]**

Jacqueline Spong	Julie Walters
Gerald Spong	Ian Charleson
Kevin	Vincenzo Ricotta
Reg Sampson	Stratford Johns

Castaway •• [1987]

Director: **Nicolas Roeg**
Screenplay: **Allan Scott**

In this true–life story, Amanda Donohoe signs up to join a man for a year on a desert island, only to discover to her dismay that the man is Oliver Reed. Although Donohoe has her clothes off throughout much of her film debut, relatively little else happens. It all looks very pretty though. **[120m/15]**

Gerald Kingsland	Oliver Reed
Lucy Irvine	Amanda Donohoe

Also: Tony Rickards, Todd Rippon, Georgina Hale, Frances Barber, John Sessions

OOPS! Although it opens in London in 1980, you can distinctly see the 1985 *Witness* advertised in a video shop window.

Casualties of War ••• [1989]

Director: **Brian De Palma**
Screenplay: **David Rabe**

A soldier fights for justice after the appalling gang-rape of a Vietnamese woman by the rest of his platoon. The final scene is sentimental claptrap and Fox looks as if his mother shouldn't let him out to play on the street, never mind fight in Vietnam. Nonetheless, this was an underrated Vietnam movie giving a different slant to the conflict. Penn is brilliant as the gang leader and De Palma's full-blown portrayal of the horrors of war is terrifying and audacious. **[114m/18]**

Pfc. Eriksson	Michael J. Fox
Sgt. Meserve	Sean Penn
Clark	Don Harvey
Hatcher	John C. Reilly
Diaz	John Leguizamo
Oahn	Thuy Thu Le

Psst! Look out for a cameo from Woody Harrelson, it was as a favour to Michael J. Fox, with whom he became friendly when *Cheers* and *Family Ties* were being filmed on adjacent sound stages.

Cat Chaser ••• [1989]

Director: Abel Ferrara
Screenplay: Elmore Leonard, Jim Borrelli & Alan Sharp

Former soldier Weller meets up with old girlfriend McGillis whose hubbie, head of the San Domingo secret police, is up to no good. This accomplished thriller has a rather scrambled plot, but nevertheless has an agreeably stylish film noir tone and is tense and unpredictable. McGillis makes a good femme fatale and there are some fine examples of Ferrara's panache with mayhem. **[93m/18]**

Moran	Peter Weller
Mary	Kelly McGillis
Jiggs	Charles Durning
Nolan	Frederic Forrest

Catchfire ••• [1991]

Director: Dennis Hopper & Alan Smithee
Screenplay: Rachel Kronstadt-Mann & Ann Louise Bardach

A neon artist witnesses a killing and is in turn targetted by a hitman who then falls in love with her. This ludicrous thriller, much butchered by the studio, is nonetheless rather enjoyable. Full of lunatic quirks by director Dennis Hopper, it has an offbeat cast and a fiery finale which outburns *White Heat*. Try to see the long version if you can. Also known as *Backtrack*. **[119m/15]**

Milo	Dennis Hopper
Anne Benton	Jodie Foster
John Luponi	Dean Stockwell
Leo Carelli	Joe Pesci
Mr. Avoca	Vincent Price
Pinella	John Turturro
Pauling	Fred Ward
Greek	Tony Sirico
Bob	Charlie Sheen

Psst! When the studio mucked about with

the film, Hopper had his name changed to that of Alan Smithee, the all-purpose name designated by the Directors Guild when someone doesn't want to be associated with a project.

Catholic Boys ••• [1985]

Director: Michael Dinner
Screenplay: Charles Purpura

An excellent coming-of-age tale, set in a Catholic boys' school in Brooklyn in the 60s. Bright, witty and constantly sparky, this great little film shows how it should be done. Also known as *Heaven Help Us*. **[104m/12]**

Brother Thadeus	Donald Sutherland
Brother Timothy	John Heard
Michael Dunn	Andrew McCarthy
Dannie	Mary Stuart Masterson
Rooney	Kevin Dillon
Caesar	Malcolm Danare
Grandma	Kate Reid
Father Abruzzi	Wallace Shawn
Brother Paul	Philip Bosco

Cat's Eye •• [1985]

Director: Lewis Teague
Screenplay: Stephen King

A three-part anthology of Stephen King short stories, all revolving around moggies. Alright, if you like this sort of thing. **[93m/15]**

Our Girl	Drew Barrymore
Morrison	James Woods
Dr. Donatti	Alan King
Cressner	Kenneth McMillan

Cease Fire •• [1985]

Director: David Nutter
Screenplay: George Fernandez

Yet another 'Nam vet having nightmares years afterwards, suffering a bad attack of the flashbacks. Things get worse when his old wartime buddy kills himself. **[97m/18]**

Tim Murphy	Don Johnson
Paula Murphy	Lisa Blount
Luke	Robert F. Lyons
Badman	Richard Chaves

Celia ••• [1989]

Director: **Ann Turner**
Screenplay: **Ann Turner**

A small Australian girl finds that her nightmares spill out into the real world. Though not a perfect film, it's still a very convincing account of the cruelty and fears of childhood, full of monsters and gang rituals. A witty and shocking debut from writer–director Turner with an outstanding lead performance from Smart.

[103m/15]

Celia	Rebecca Smart
Ray	Nicholas Eadie
Pat	Maryanne Fahey
Alice	Victoria Longley

The Chain •• [1985]

Director: **Jack Gold**
Screenplay: **Jack Rosenthal**

This British variation on *La Ronde* is played out with removal vans and houses rather than lovers. Although there are odd moments that strike home, too few jokes have been packed into the van for the journey to seem worthwhile.

[96m/PG]

Des	Herbert Norville
Keith	Denis Lawson
Grandpa	Maurice Denham
Mr. Thorn	Nigel Hawthorne

Also: Billie Whitelaw, Judy Parfitt, Leo McKern, Bernard Hill, Warren Mitchell, Phyllis Logan, Anna Massey

Champions •• [1984]

Director: **John Irvin**
Screenplay: **Evan Jones**

The moving true story of Bob Champion, the jockey who not only beat cancer, but also all the other jockeys in the 1981 Grand National. Despite the magnitude of what he achieved, the film is a little less swift of foot than Champion's mount, Aldaniti.

[115m/PG]

Champion	John Hurt
Josh	Edward Woodward
Burly	Ben Johnson

Jo	Jan Francis
Nick	Peter Barkworth
Mary	Alison Steadman
Dr. Merrow	Judy Parfitt
Barbara	Kirstie Alley

Psst! The second film for Kirstie Alley who, after portraying a Klingon in *Star Trek II*, seemed to be specialising in movies to do with pointy ears ✦ Aldaniti plays himself.

Chaplin •• [1992]

Director: **Richard Attenborough**
Screenplay: **William Boyd, Bryan Forbes & William Goldman**

Despite its long running time, Attenborough tries to cram too much into this latest from the Madame Tussaud school of film-making. Characters come and go without us having the slightest idea who they are and the card saying 'X years later' is hardly off the screen. Dickie assumes too much knowledge on the audience's part and forgets to tell us a story. Good though Downey is at impersonating Chaplin, we can't imagine him making the entire world laugh as Charlie did.

[144m/12]

Charlie Chaplin	Robert Downey Jr.
Mack Sennett	Dan Aykroyd
Hannah Chaplin	Geraldine Chaplin
J. Edgar Hoover	Kevin Dunn
George Hayden	Anthony Hopkins
Mildred Harris	Milla Jovovich
Hetty Kelly/Oona O'Neill	Moira Kelly
Douglas Fairbanks	Kevin Kline
Paulette Goddard	Diane Lane
Edna Purviance	Penelope Ann Miller
Sydney Chaplin	Paul Rhys
Fred Karno	John Thaw
Mabel Normand	Marisa Tomei
Joan Berry	Nancy Travis
Lawyer Scott	James Woods

Quote 'Sorry luvs. It's only fish-heads again!'

Showing *Modern Times, The Great Dictator, City Lights, The Gold Rush, The Kid.*

Psst! The film was edited to its 144 minute length from a total of 65 hours ✦ When

Attenborough was visiting Chaplin's old haunts, he went to the great man's office. On the desk, wearing an LA Dodgers cap, was a bust of Gandhi. Spooky.

Chattahoochee ●● [1990]

Director: Mick Jackson
Screenplay: James Hicks

Harrowing truth-based tale of a sane individual in a Southern mental asylum straight out of a Hammer horror film. Gruelling stuff, the script never breaks free of its clichéd straitjacket. [97m/15]

Emmett Foley	Gary Oldman
Walker Benson	Dennis Hopper
Mae Foley	Frances McDormand
Earlene	Pamela Reed

Also: Ned Beatty, M. Emmet Walsh, Matt Craven, Richard Portnow

Checking Out ● [1989]

Director: David Leland
Screenplay: Joe Eszterhas

Don't bother checking out this woeful comedy about Daniels becoming a hypochondriac after a friend's death. After an hour and a half, you'll be praying for some fatal disease to put an end to your own suffering. [93m/15]

Ray Macklin	Jeff Daniels
Jenny Macklin	Melanie Mayron
Harry Lardender	Michael Tucker

Quote 'It's been re-cut and it's a mess. They'd have done much better to get a chimpanzee for post-production.' [Director David Leland]

Chicago Joe and the Showgirl ● [1990]

Director: Bernard Rose
Screenplay: David Yallop

An American soldier in World War II takes his English girlfriend on a crime spree. No film starring Kensit can be all good, but poor sets, a low budget and a dull script mean that this one never had a chance. Based on a true story. [103m/18]

Ricky Allen	Kiefer Sutherland
Georgina Grayson	Emily Lloyd
Joyce Cook	Patsy Kensit

Quote 'The best British film since *The Third Man*.' [Director Bernard Rose]
Showing *Double Indemnity*.

Children of a Lesser God ●●● [1986]

Director: Randa Haines
Screenplay: Hesper Anderson & Mark Medoff

Unusual love story, with Hurt the new teacher at a school for the deaf falling for the janitor, the intelligent but withdrawn Matlin. Romancing her is tough going as she won't use any form of communication other than sign language. As Hurt has to voice out loud what she's saying, following what's going on is at times more laborious than reading subtitles. But it's still an often charming and enlightening movie. [119m/15]

James	William Hurt
Sarah	Marlee Matlin
Mrs. Norman	Piper Laurie
Dr. Curtis Franklin	Philip Bosco
Lydia	Allison Gompf

Oscars Marlee Matlin

Psst! Matlin and Hurt became lovers off-screen and, according to those who can read sign language, their conversations often concern their private life and have nothing to do with the film at all.

Children of the Corn ● [1984]

Director: Fritz Kiersch
Screenplay: George Goldsmith

The kids in Iowa have done away with the adults and are now worshipping a corn god, presumably the Jolly Green Giant. The nice young couple that move into the area seem desperately slow to twig on. All done so much better a decade earlier with *The Wicker Man*. [93m/18]

Dr. Stanton	Peter Horton
Vicky	Linda Hamilton
Diehl	R.G. Armstrong

Child's Play •• [1988]

Director: Tom Holland
Screenplay: Don Mancini, John Lafia &
Tom Holland

Dying killer Dourif's soul passes into a
Chucky Doll, which then goes on a murderous rampage. One of those tiresome
mainstream horror movies which, by
desperately trying not to offend anyone,
ends up pleasing no-one. **[87m/15]**

Karen Barclay	Catherine Hicks
Mike Norris	Chris Sarandon
Andy Barclay	Alex Vincent
Charles Lee Ray	Brad Dourif

Child's Play 2 • [1990]

Director: John Lafia
Screenplay: Don Mancini

A dreadful sequel with its only merit
being its short running time. **[85m/15]**

Andy Barclay	Alex Vincent
Joanne Simpson	Jenny Agutter
Phil Simpson	Gerrit Graham
Kyle	Christine Elise
Chucky	Brad Dourif
Grace Poole	Grace Zabriskie

China Girl ••• [1987]

Director: Abel Ferrara
Screenplay: Nicholas St. John

When an Italian youth and a Chinese girl
fall in love, their respective gangs get
narked. Another New York story from
Ferrara, this time with a plot that was old
hat in Shakespeare's day. However, the
terrific style and energy make it a generally compelling retelling of R & J. **[90m/15]**

Alberto 'Alby' Monte	James Russo
Tony Monte	Richard Panebianco
Tyan-Hwa	Sari Chang
Johnny Mercury	David Caruso
Yung-Gan	Russell Wong
Tsu-Shin	Joey Chin

Choose Me ••• [1984]

Director: Alan Rudolph
Screenplay: Alan Rudolph

This superb, very funny, love story con-
cerns the interlinking stories of bar owner
Warren, radio agony aunt Bujold and the
drifter Carradine who comes into both
their lives. Although a low-budget production, it's highly inventive, oddball and
extremely enjoyable. **[106m/15]**

Nancy	Genevieve Bujold
Mickey	Keith Carradine
Eve	Lesley Ann Warren
Zack	Patrick Bauchau
Pearl	Rae Dawn Chong
Billy	John Larroquette
Mueller	Gailard Sartain

A Chorus Line • [1985]

Director: Richard Attenborough
Screenplay: Arnold Schulman

The *One Singular Sensation* here is that of
boredom. The superb stage musical in
which a group of young hopefuls have not
only to audition, but reveal something of
themselves and their backgrounds,
doesn't work on screen. What we get has
as much life as the boards on which they
tread. **[118m/PG]**

Zach	Michael Douglas
Cassie	Alyson Reed
Larry	Terrence Mann
Paul	Cameron English

A Chorus of Disapproval •• [1989]

Director: Michael Winner
Screenplay: Michael Winner & Alan
Ayckbourn

Neil Simon has *Too Hot To Handle* to live
down. Alan Ayckbourn has this. His play
about the romantic shenanigans within an
amateur dramatic group seems awfully
thin on screen. Winner, although beginning his career as a comedy director, has
had his touch blunted by all those *Death
Wish* films and allows some hideous
over-acting. **[100m/PG]**

Dafydd Ap Llewellyn	Anthony Hopkins
Guy Jones	Jeremy Irons
Hannah Ap Llewellyn	Prunella Scales

Fay Hubbard............................Jenny Seagrove
Also: Gareth Hunt, Richard Briers, Patsy Kensit, Lionel Jeffries, Sylvia Syms, Alexandra Pigg

Psst! According to Irons, producer–director Michael Winner, never one to waste money (see *Bullseye*), took him to Notting Hill for his shoes. There he found, in a shop having a sale, three pairs for a tenner each. Pointing out that Irons was a top British star, he asked for a special deal and only left when a duster and polish were thrown in!

Christine •• [1983]

Director: John Carpenter
Screenplay: Bill Phillips

A sleek red 1958 Plymouth Fury is possessed by the Devil and, when not treated with respect by the local kids, it runs amok. This slickly-produced Stephen King yarn gets depressingly bland and conventional direction from Carpenter. The scene where the wrecked car reconstructs itself is a dream for anyone wanting to keep their no-claims bonus intact. [110m/18]

Arnie Cunningham....................Keith Gordon
Dennis Guilder.........................John Stockwell
Leigh Cabot...............................Alexandra Paul
Will Darnell.............................Robert Prosky
Rudolph Junkins..............Harry Dean Stanton
Roseanne...................................Kelly Preston

A Christmas Story •••• [1983]

Director: Bob Clark
Screenplay: Jean Shepherd, Leigh Brown & Bob Clark

Why isn't this wonderful Yuletide film shown every Christmas along with *It's a Wonderful Life* instead of the yucky other modern Xmas rubbish we get endlessly repeated? Young Billingsley wants an airgun from Santa, but Mum's dead against it. This slight slice-of-life story of a mildly eccentric family is beautifully observed. A dose of fresh, charming and funny seasonal cheer that one would never tire of. [98m/PG]

Mother......................................Melinda Dillon
Old Man ....Darren McGavin
Ralphie ....Peter Billingsley
Randy...Ian Petrella
Flick...Scott Schwartz

Psst! Directed, though hard to believe, by the man who brought us not only *Porky's*, but also *Porky's II*.

Christopher Columbus: The Discovery • [1992]

Director: John Glen
Screenplay: John Briley, Cary Bates & Mario Puzo

This Columbus vessel springs its first leak when Tom Selleck appears improbably as King Ferdinand. It's shipping water badly when Brando does his Pythonesque turn as Torquemada and is practically water-logged by the time Corraface stops gazing out to sea and actually gets on a boat. So dull you feel you've travelled every inch of the way with them. They all laughed at Christopher Columbus when he said the world was round, says the song. They all laughed at the ridiculous dialogue, too. [120m/PG]

Torquemada ....Marlon Brando
King Ferdinand.............................Tom Selleck
Christopher Columbus .....Georges Corraface
Queen Isabella ....Rachel Ward
Martin Pinzon ....Robert Davi
Beatriz...........................Catherine Zeta Jones

Quote 'She's a fine vessel. Perhaps a little top heavy and narrow of beam. Not unlike someone else I know.'

Psst! Despite being paid over $5m, Brando wanted his name taken off the credits in protest at the portrayal of native Americans.

Cinema Paradiso •••• [1990]

Director: Giuseppe Tornatore
Screenplay: Giuseppe Tornatore

A cinema director returning home to Sicily recalls his childhood, his obsession with the local cinema and his friendship with gruff projectionist Noiret. An utterly delightful, moving and often very funny Italian tribute to the power of the movies. Understandably, this has become one of the favourite films of all those who love the cinema.   **[124m/PG]**

Alfredo	Philippe Noiret
Salvatore	Jacques Perrin
Salvatore as child	Salvatore Cascio
Salvatore as adolescent	Mario Leonardi
Elena	Agnese Nano
Father Adelfio	Leopoldo Trieste

Quote 'Life isn't like the movies. Life is harder.'

Showing *Modern Times, Stagecoach, Dr. Jekyll and Mr. Hyde, La Strada.*

City Heat •   [1984]

Director: **Richard Benjamin**
Screenplay: **Blake Edwards & Joseph C. Stinson**

Eastwood and Reynolds don 1930's costumes and trade jokes about the size of each other's gun. They may have enjoyed themselves, but it all seems lazy and self-indulgent to the paying audience.   **[97m/15]**

Lt. Speer	Clint Eastwood
Mike Murphy	Burt Reynolds
Addy	Jane Alexander
Caroline Howley	Madeline Kahn

Also: Rip Torn, Irene Cara, Richard Roundtree, Robert Davi

Psst! The credits show one writer as 'Sam O. Brown'. This was a pseudonym for Blake Edwards, who was to have directed the film, until he got fed up with the two stars' demands • In a fight scene, Reynolds was hit by a real chair instead of a fake one, breaking his jaw and landing him in hospital. He was in pain for years. The stories that Eastwood and he fought and that Clint socked him on the jaw are untrue.

City of Hope •••   [1991]

Director: **John Sayles**
Screenplay: **John Sayles**

Sayles' usual ensemble piece is a constantly interesting story of dying hopes and dreams set in a rundown small town. Spano, heavily mired in gambling debts, walks away from a cushy construction job arranged by his father and agrees to take part in a robbery.   **[129m/15]**

Nick Rinaldi	Vincent Spano
Wynn	Joe Horton
Joe Rinaldi	Tony Lo Bianco
Angela	Barbara Williams
Carl	John Sayles

Quote 'Marianne needed an instruction manual to chew gum.'

City of Joy ••   [1992]

Director: **Roland Joffé**
Screenplay: **Mark Medoff**

Stranded in Calcutta, a disillusioned American doctor is badgered into administering to the poor and ends up trying to improve their lot. Although the sassy Collins is great, it's hard to take Swayze seriously. Amazing coincidences and smothering sentimentality destroy the film's credibility, while the roving shots of the city make it seem more like a travelogue at times. Notable, however, for one of the most unpleasant birth scenes yet put on to celluloid.   **[135m/12]**

Max Lowe	Patrick Swayze
Joan Bethel	Pauline Collins
Hasari Pal	Om Puri
Kamla Pal	Shabana Azmi
Ashoka	Art Malik

Psst! Shooting was marred by an epidemic of protest at the way Calcutta would be portrayed in the film, with the cast and crew actually stoned on one occasion.

City Slickers ••••   [1991]

Director: **Ron Underwood**
Screenplay: **Lowell Ganz & Babaloo Mandel**

Three friends play at cowboys during a cattle drive, watched over by the bemused Palance who deservedly picked up an Oscar for his brilliant, deadpan performance. This comedy combines an engrossing story with some wonderfully

funny lines. A winner, despite a layer of
gooey sentiment at the finale.   [114m/12]

Mitch Robbins	Billy Crystal
Phil Berquist	Daniel Stern
Ed Furillo	Bruno Kirby
Barbara Robbins	Patricia Wettig
Bonnie Rayburn	Helen Slater
Curly	Jack Palance
Barry Shalowitz	Josh Mostel
Ira Shalowitz	David Paymer
Clay Stone	Noble Willingham

Oscars Jack Palance

Blurb Yesterday They Were Businessmen.
Today They're Cowboys. Tomorrow
They'll Be Walking Funny.

Quote 'The older you get, the younger your
girlfriends get. Pretty soon you'll be dating sperm.'

OOPS! The flowers on Curly's grave mysteriously vanish ◆ Earlier, as he's riding
with Billy Crystal, his cigarette keeps
changing length.

Psst! Bonnie is played by Helen Slater,
star of the disastrous 1984 film *Supergirl*
◆ Odd, isn't it, how despite all those
cows, we never once see a cowpat?

The Clan of the Cave Bear ●   [1986]

Director: Michael Chapman
Screenplay: John Sayles

The perfect movie for Hannah, you might
think. No words to trip over, only grunts
and groans in this tale of a prehistoric
feminist cavewoman who wields a mean
club. Sadly, not quite bad enough to be
funny.   [98m/15]

Ayla	Daryl Hannah
Iza	Pamela Reed
Creb	James Remar

Psst! More interesting than the film are the
credits for *Sign language, Clan vocalisa-
tions* and *Primitive skill trainer*.

Clara's Heart ●●   [1988]

Director: Robert Mulligan
Screenplay: Mark Medoff

Goldberg in rare acting mode as a know-
all housekeeper who befriends the difficult
young master. Sentimental in the extreme.
   [108m/PG]

Clara Mayfield	Whoopi Goldberg
Bill Hart	Michael Ontkean
Leona Hart	Kathleen Quinlan
David Hart	Neil Patrick Harris
Peter Epstein	Spalding Gray

Class ●   [1983]

Director: Lewis John Carlino
Screenplay: Jim Kouf & David Greenwalt

The ad says it all, but the film doesn't
deliver. Often more melodrama than
comedy, the script never gives the cardboard characters any life. Dull stuff.
   [98m/15]

Ellen	Jacqueline Bisset
Skip	Rob Lowe
Jonathan	Andrew McCarthy
Burroughs	Cliff Robertson

Also: Stuart Margolin, John Cusack, Alan
Ruck, Virginia Madsen

Blurb The Good News Is Jonathan's
Having His First Affair. The Bad News
Is She's His Roommate's Mother.

Psst! This was John Cusack's first film.

Class Action ●●●   [1991]

Director: Michael Apted
Screenplay: Carolyn Shelby, Christopher
Ames & Samantha Shad

Who should lawyer Hackman find strutting their stuff against him in a negligence
case but his own estranged daughter
Mastrantonio? Well-made and acted, it is
rather enjoyable despite a particularly
predictable plot.   [109m/15]

Jebediah Tucker Ward	Gene Hackman
Maggie Ward	Mary Elizabeth Mastrantonio
Michael Grazier	Colin Friels
Estelle Ward	Joanna Merlin
Nick Holbrook	Larry Fishburne

Also: Donald Moffat, Jan Rubes, Matt
Clark, Fred Dalton Thompson, Jonathan
Silverman

Class of 1984 •• [1982]

Director: **Mark L. Lester**
Screenplay: **Mark L. Lester, John Saxton & Tom Holland**

There haven't been that many revenge movies with teachers going after their pupils with murder in mind. The kids in this American high school are revolting and virtually run the school. Then new teacher King is pushed too far. Despite the premise, it's still mediocre. **[94m/18]**

Andy Norris	Perry King
Diane Norris	Merrie Lynn Ross
Terry Corrigan	Roddy McDowall
Peter Stegman	Timothy Van Patten

Psst! Look out for Michael J. Fox, when he really *was* young, as a nerd being bullied by the thugs in his class.

Clean and Sober ••• [1988]

Director: **Glenn Gordon Caron**
Screenplay: **Tod Carroll**

Clichéd and Sombre. Keaton's the estate-agent addict who checks into a rehab place after his druggie one-night stand doesn't manage to make it through one night. Despite the predictability of it all, the fine performances make it very watchable, if understandably a mite depressing. **[124m/18]**

Daryl Poynter	Michael Keaton
Charlie Standers	Kathy Baker
Craig	Morgan Freeman
Donald Towle	Tate Donovan
Xavier	Henry Judd Baker
Iris	Claudia Christian
Richard Dirks	M. Emmet Walsh
Ralston receptionist	Harley Jane Kozak

Cliffhanger [1993]

Director: **Renny Harlin**
Screenplay: **Michael France**

Stallone's the human St. Bernard, a mountain rescue team chap battling a gang of desperate criminals whose plane has brought down by a blizzard.

With: Sylvester Stallone, John Lithgow, Michael Rooker, Janine Turner, Leon,

Ralph Waite, Caroline Goodall

Psst! Both Stallone and Turner were afraid of heights. Whereas she was once too scared to enter a lift, Sly apparently played self-help tapes in his car to conquer his fear ✦ One of the most expensive movies ever made, with Stallone giving up a couple of his 15 million dollars' payment to cover the cost of the dangerous plane-to-plane leap ✦ Stallone insisted on having Guinness, his favourite drink, brought to Italy for cast and crew at the completion of filming.

Clockwise ••• [1986]

Director: **Christopher Morahan**
Screenplay: **Michael Frayn**

Punctuality-obsessed headmaster Cleese is set to be the first from a state school to speak to the Headmasters' Conference. Unfortunately, one minor mistake means that he's running just a teensy bit late. Cleese is superb in this hilarious, slow-building comedy in which he becomes ever more and more desperate to arrive on time. **[96m/PG]**

Timpson	John Cleese
Gwenda Stimpson	Alison Steadman
Pat Garden	Penelope Wilton
Mr. Jolly	Stephen Moore
Laura	Sharon Maiden
Mrs. Trellis	Joan Hickson

Psst! Apparently the moment where Cleese takes his frustration out on the phone boxes which don't work puzzled them in America. As public phones *do* usually work there, it only got a laugh in vandal-ridden New York.

Close My Eyes • [1991]

Director: **Stephen Poliakoff**
Screenplay: **Stephen Poliakoff**

Close them? It's only too easy. Brother and sister have an incestuous affair but her husband suspects something. Quite how such an accomplished team of actors and technicians could have generated something so drab and long-winded out of such potentially sizzling material remains a mystery. **[107m/18]**

Richard Gillespie...........................Clive Owen
Natalie Gillespie.........................Saskia Reeves
Sinclair Bryant............................Alan Rickman

Clue •. [1985]

Director: **Jonathan Lynn**
Screenplay: **Jonathan Lynn**

In this woefully unfunny comic version of the *Cluedo* board game, the only fun is speculating which weapon you'd use to do away with the actors, who overdo the ham dreadfully. **[87m/PG]**

Mrs. Peacock...........................Eileen Brennan
Wadsworth ....Tim Curry
Mrs. White.............................Madeline Kahn
Also: Christopher Lloyd, Michael McKean, Martin Mull, Lesley Ann Warren

Psst! Three different endings were filmed. However, few people were around to see any of them.

Cobra • [1986]

Director: **George Pan Cosmatos**
Screenplay: **Sylvester Stallone**

A maverick cop who makes Dirty Harry look talkative goes it alone against a vicious gang. The usual overblown, implausible nonsense, with Sly not perhaps the world's likeliest policeman. That there were no sequels tells you a lot. **[87m/18]**

Marion Cobretti ....Sylvester Stallone
Ingrid ....Brigitte Nielsen
Gonzales ....Reni Santoni
Det. Monte ....Andrew Robinson

Blurb Crime Is A Disease. Meet The Cure.

Psst! The script is similar to one Stallone had written for *Beverly Hills Cop* while it was in development ✦ Robinson, here playing the by-the-book cop, was the psycho in *Dirty Harry*.

The Coca-Cola Kid ••• [1985]

Director: **Dusan Makavejev**
Screenplay: **Frank Moorhouse**

Coca-Cola hotshot Roberts is sent to Australia to boldly sell Coke where nobody has sold it before. There he comes into conflict with wacky soft-drinks maker Kerr. Delightfully offbeat comedy is let down by Roberts, but as the sexy secretary Scacchi practically smoulders a hole in the screen. **[98m/15]**

Becker...Eric Roberts
Terri ....Greta Scacchi
T. George McDowell........................Bill Kerr
Kim.......................................Chris Haywood
Juliana ....Kris McQuade
Bushman.......................................Tony Barry

Quote 'It was worse than prostitution for me. You try spending three days naked with a man you despise.' [Scacchi on Roberts]

Psst! The credits contain the line: 'Catering...Kaos (Highly recommended by the whole cast and crew)' ✦ Among the crew were a 'camel wrangler' and a 'kangaroo wrangler'.

Cocktail •• [1988]

Director: **Roger Donaldson**
Screenplay: **Heywood Gould**

Popular but empty-headed drivel about Cruise learning about life and bartending from the droll, laid-back Brown. Initially keen to see how many chicks he can get to lie back, Cruise naturally matures into a warm, rounded human being. Yuk! **[104m/15]**

Brian Flanagan.............................Tom Cruise
Doug Coughlin...........................Bryan Brown
Jordan Mooney ....Elisabeth Shue
Bonnie..Lisa Banes
Mr. Mooney ....Laurence Luckinbill
Kerry Coughlin............................Kelly Lynch

Blurb When He Pours, He Reigns.

Quote 'A proctologist's dream. Assholes wall to wall.'

OOPS! When Cruise and Banes pass a cinema it's advertising the film *Barfly*. Shortly afterwards, the film's *Casablanca*.

Psst! The original script was a biting satire on yuppiedom but the studio decided that audiences weren't ready to see Cruise attempt dark comedy.

Cocoon •• [1985]

Director: **Ron Howard**
Screenplay: **Tom Benedek**

Alien things at the bottom of a swimming pool have a strange effect on people, making them soft in the head and amenable to a mushy, near plotless, load of poppycock. A bunch of wrinklies discover an alien fountain of youth. Despite the appearance of some of the finest mature actors around, this is sub-standard sci-fi with poor special effects and very few laughs.

[117m/PG]

Art Selwyn	Don Ameche
Ben Luckett	Wilford Brimley
Joe Finley	Hume Cronyn
Walter	Brian Dennehy
Bernie Lefkowitz	Jack Gilford
Jack Bonner	Steve Guttenberg
Mary Luckett	Maureen Stapleton
Alma Finley	Jessica Tandy
Bess McCarthy	Gwen Verdon
Rose	Herta Ware
Kitty	Tahnee Welch

Oscars Don Ameche

Quote 'If this is foreplay, I'm a dead man!'

OOPS! It's keep your eye on the bandage time, as Guttenberg's injured leg switches from the right to the left.

Psst! Director Robert Zemeckis, whose films have been the most financially successful ever made, was fired from the movie ◆ Ron Howard's dad Rance plays a detective ◆ Tahnee Welch is Raquel's daughter ◆ Frederick R. Newman is credited with 'additional dolphin voices'.

Cocoon: The Return • . [1988]

Director: **Daniel Petrie**
Screenplay: **Stephen McPherson**

The Twinklies pop down to earth on an Away-Day ticket, look up a few friends and decide whether to stay and decay or go back to their heavenly paradise. This shameless, violently sentimental, empty rip-off would be daylight robbery if you were watching in daylight. [115m/PG]

Art Selwyn	Don Ameche
Ben Luckett	Wilford Brimley
Sara	Courteney Cox
Joe Finley	Hume Cronyn

Also: Jack Gilford, Steve Guttenberg, Barret Oliver, Maureen Stapleton, Elaine Stritch, Jessica Tandy, Gwen Verdon, Tahnee Welch

Code of Silence •• [1985]

Director: **Andrew Davis**
Screenplay: **Michael Butler, Dennis Shryack & Mike Gray**

One of Norris's better films. He's a Chicago cop doing battle against the drug gangs as well as bad pennies in the force. Fast, furious stuff which may well be implausible and formulaic, but is so well-handled you don't mind. [101m/18]

Eddie Cusack	Chuck Norris
Luis Comacho	Henry Silva
Commander Kates	Bert Remsen
Tony Luna	Mike Genovese

Cold Dog Soup • [1991]

Director: **Alan Metter**
Screenplay: **Thomas Pope**

Ludicrous and mirth-free black comedy about the shenanigans that ensue when Harnos persuades Whaley to bury her dead dog. [85m/15]

Jack Cloud	Randy Quaid
Michael Latchmer	Frank Whaley
Sarah Hughes	Christine Harnos
Mrs. Hughes	Sheree North

Cold Feet • [1990]

Director: **Robert Dornhelm**
Screenplay: **Tom McGuane & Jim Harrison**

An attempt not only to modernise the Western, but to make it funny as well. It doesn't work. [94m/15]

Monte Latham	Keith Carradine
Maureen	Sally Kirkland
Kenny	Tom Waits
Buck Latham	Bill Pullman

Also: Rip Torn, Kathleen York, Vincent Schiavelli, Jeff Bridges

The Color of Money ••• [1986]

Director: **Martin Scorsese**
Screenplay: **Richard Price**

This exciting sequel to *The Hustler*, 25 years on, has Newman discovering hot-shot pool player Cruise and, although jealous of his talents, adopting him as his protégé. Even for those unfamiliar with pool, the stuff at the tables is great. A pity it tails off a little towards the end. **[119m/15]**

Eddie..Paul Newman
Vincent ....Tom Cruise
Carmen ....Mary Elizabeth Mastrantonio
Janelle ....Helen Shaver
Julian ....John Turturro
Orvis ....Bill Cobbs
Diane....................................Elizabeth Bracco
Lou ....Vito D'Ambrosio
Amos....................................Forest Whitaker

Oscars Paul Newman

Quote 'Money won is twice as sweet as money earned.' ◆ 'We had a few games for money. I won his house. I didn't collect.' [Newman on Cruise]

OOPS! They conveniently forget to mention the death threat that was responsible, at the end of the earlier film, for Eddie giving up the game.

Psst! Though the budget for the film was $13m, the actual filming only cost $6m. The rest was taken up with salaries and the costs of getting the project underway after years of the big studios passing it round.

The Color Purple ••• [1985]

Director: **Steven Spielberg**
Screenplay: **Menno Meyjes**

Superb story of Goldberg, down-trodden by cruel husband Glover and forcibly separated from her sister, who eventually finds freedom. Although it has a tendency towards melodrama and, like *Fried Green Tomatoes*, ignores the novel's lesbianism, this is a fine attempt by Spielberg to break away from his usual happy alien pics. If it had been directed by anyone else and had an all-white cast, it might not have been

so unfairly attacked at the time. **[152m/15]**

Celie ....Whoopi Goldberg
Albert Johnson ....Danny Glover
Shug Avery ....Margaret Avery
Sofia ....Oprah Winfrey
Harpo ....Willard Pugh
Nettie ....Akosua Busia
Young Celie ....Desreta Jackson
Old Mr. ....Adolph Caesar
Squeak................................Rae Dawn Chong
Miss Millie.....................................Dana Ivey
Pa...Leonard Judison
Swain....................................Larry Fishburne

OOPS! Oprah retains her modesty even when knocked out. Although she's unconscious, she pulls her skirt down when the wind threatens to lift it and reveal too much.

Psst! Currently the joint record-holder for the most number of Oscar nominations, eleven, without any wins. *The Turning Point* is the other ◆ Four of the main 7 actors had never acted on screen before. Goldberg had proposed Tina Turner for the part of Shug Avery, but Turner said it was 'too close to home' ◆ The National Association for the Advancement of Colored People objected to the 'perpetuation of stereotypes' in the movie.

Colors •• [1988]

Director: **Dennis Hopper**
Screenplay: **Michael Schiffer**

Brave but ultimately rather disappointing story of mismatched cops (what other sort is there?) Duvall and Penn assigned to gang duty in LA. Although it has its moments, it's not so different from every other movie of its kind, unless you count the extraordinary amount of swearing. Difficult to believe that it's Dennis Hopper, *the* Dennis Hopper, directing what is in effect a cop movie. **[121m/18]**

Danny McGavin.............................Sean Penn
Bob Hodges...............................Robert Duvall
Louisa Gomez...........Maria Conchita Alonso
Ron Delaney ....Randy Brooks

Psst! Some of the real gang members appear in small roles.

Come Back to the Five and Dime, Jimmy Dean, Jimmy Dean ••• [1982]

Director: **Robert Altman**
Screenplay: **Ed Graczyk**

Altman brings to the screen the play he staged on Broadway, about six former Woolies' workers reuniting twenty years after the 'Disciples of James Dean' fan club split up. Although it is pretty clear that it is based on a stage work, the actors really get their teeth into their parts as they face up to the difference between their dreams and the reality of their lives.

[109m/18]

Mona	Sandy Dennis
Sissy	Cher
Joanne	Karen Black
Juanita	Sudie Bond
Stella May	Kathy Bates

Psst! Filming took only nineteen days.

Come See the Paradise •• [1990]

Director: **Alan Parker**
Screenplay: **Alan Parker**

...Or not, as the case may be. An oddly unmoving tale of the internment of Japanese-Americans during World War II, with Quaid the union organiser separated from his Japanese wife and family when the camps are set up after Pearl Harbour. Working neither as a romance nor as a historical document, the film suffers from an attempt to cram too much into a fascinating period of American history. [131m/15]

Jack McGurn	Dennis Quaid
Lily Kawamura	Tamlyn Tomita
Mr. Kawamura	Sab Shimono
Mrs. Kawamura	Shizuko Hoshi

Showing *Oshidori Utagassen*

Comfort and Joy ••• [1984]

Director: **Bill Forsyth**
Screenplay: **Bill Forsyth**

A Glaswegian disc jockey gets involved in a local war between Mr. McCool and Mr. Bunny, two rival ice-cream empires, rubbing bosses and combatants up the wrong way. Although far from Forsyth's best work, there are plenty of incidental pleasures in this quirky comedy, among them a superb performance from the always-reliable Paterson.

[106m/PG]

Alan	Bill Paterson
Maddy	Eleanor David
Charlotte	C.P. Grogan
Trevor	Alex Norton
Colin	Patrick Malahide
Hilary	Rikki Fulton

The Comfort of Strangers • [1990]

Director: **Paul Schrader**
Screenplay: **Harold Pinter**

A repressed English couple in Venice encounter sinister Walken and his disabled wife and, before long, matters take a sinister turn. Despite the talent involved, it moves with the speed of a gondola through sludge. Imagine *Don't Look Now* with the video stuck in slow-motion and you won't be far wrong. [105m/18]

Robert	Christopher Walken
Colin	Rupert Everett
Mary	Natasha Richardson
Caroline	Helen Mirren

Quote 'Hansel and Gretel on a bad acid trip.' [Everett]

Coming to America •• . [1988]

Director: **John Landis**
Screenplay: **David Sheffield & Barry W. Blaustein**

Some impressive comic schtick from Murphy is undermined by an unconvincing and tiresome tale of an African prince journeying to New York to look for a wife who will love him for himself. Even when you're looking out for it, it's hard to believe that Murphy and Hall play all six people in the barber's shop. Hall appears as Morris, the ugly girl and Rev. Brown while Murphy gives us Clarence, Saul and Randy Watson.

[116m/15]

Prince Akeem	Eddie Murphy
Semmi	Arsenio Hall
Cleo McDowell	John Amos
King Jaffe Joffer	James Earl Jones
Lisa McDowell	Shari Headley

Psst! As usual with director Landis, the film is peppered with cameos, best of which is at the end when Murphy hands the money to the two tramps. They are Mortimer and Randolph Duke, played by Don Ameche and Ralph Bellamy, who gave Murphy such a hard time of it in the hit, *Trading Places* ◆ As in *Oscar*, there's a 'Face on the Cutting Room Floor', this time that of *Airplane* co-director Jim Abrahams ◆ While made-up as the old white Jew, Murphy was introduced to the high-ups at Paramount. None recognised him ◆ Columnist Art Buchwald sued Paramount, claiming they had stolen his idea. He was awarded $150,000, with the studio claiming that the film, which took $130m in the US, had made a loss ◆ During the case, it was revealed that Murphy had been paid $8m, plus a signing fee of $1.7m on top of which he got a $1m living allowance. Among his expenses was a bill for 200$ for breakfast for him and his entourage – at McDonalds!

Coming Up Roses ◆◆ [1987]

Director: **Stephen Bayly**
Screenplay: **Ruth Carter**

Undoubtedly the best Welsh-speaking comedy. Alright, so it's the only Welsh-speaking comedy, released outside the Principality with subtitles. Although it never reaches the heights of Ealing, it's still a gently amusing film about a closed cinema in a small town that is turned into a mushroom farm.

[93m/PG]

Trevor	Dafydd Hywel
Mona	Iola Gregory
Mr. Valentine	Bill Paterson

Commando ◆◆ [1985]

Director: **Mark L. Lester**
Screenplay: **Steven E. de Souza**

A vicious gang kidnap Arnie's daughter and naturally don't live to regret it. The usual mix of violence, macho bravado, muscle-rippling and dumb wisecracks. Neither brilliant nor terrible. **[90m/18]**

Matrix	Arnold Schwarzenegger
Cindy	Rae Dawn Chong
Arius	Dan Hedaya

Also: Vernon Wells, James Olson, David Patrick Kelly, Bill Duke

Quote 'Let off some steam.'

OOPS! The Porsche that Arnie rams amazingly loses all its dents and looks as good as new when he drives it later ◆ He doesn't pick up his wallet when he drops it in the car park. Yet he shows a picture from it later on ◆ If the truck he pushes down the hill won't go, why is the exhaust smoking?

The Commitments ◆◆◆◆ [1991]

Director: **Alan Parker**
Screenplay: **Dick Clement & Ian La Frenais**

Who needs expensive stars when a group of unknowns can light up the screen like this lot? A bunch of Dublin teenagers set up a cracking good soul band that's on the verge of cracking apart even at the first gig. Hysterical, albeit salty, dialogue, superlative music and sparkling performances make this a joy from start to finish. Unmissable, and a couple of great albums to boot. **[117m/15]**

Jimmy Rabbitte	Robert Arkins
Deco Cuffe	Andrew Strong
Steve Clifford	Michael Aherne
Imelda Quirke	Angeline Ball
Natalie Murphy	Maria Doyle
Mickah Wallace	Dave Finnegan
Bernie McGloughlin	Bronagh Gallagher
Dean Fay	Félim Gormley
Outspan Foster	Glen Hansard
Joey "The Lips" Fagan	Johnny Murphy
Mr. Rabbitte	Colm Meaney

Blurb They Had Absolutely Nothing. But They Were Willing To Risk It All.

Quote 'U2 must be shitting themselves.' ✦ 'You're working class, right?' – 'We would be if there was any work.' ✦ 'God sent him.' – 'On a Suzuki?'

OOPS! Imelda's caravan holiday in the Isle of Man wouldn't be much to write a postcard home about. Caravans are banned from the island.

Psst! Director Alan Parker appears in a cameo right at the end as 'Eejit Record Producer' ✦ Among the suggestions for the band's title is 'The Likely Lads' – the writers' famous TV sitcom.

The Company of Wolves ••• [1984]

Director: Neil Jordan
Screenplay: Angela Carter & Neil Jordan

'What a stylish and ambitious film you're making, Grandma.' 'Yes, my dear. What a shame we couldn't find a better 12-year-old than you for the part.' Grannie tells the little one mystical tales of wolves, all rampant with sexual symbolism. It has a wonderful fairytale feel to it, but it's a pity the violence ended up being stressed more heavily than the passion. **[95m/15]**

Granny................................Angela Lansbury
Father......................................David Warner
Old priest...........................Graham Crowden
Amorous boy's father..................Brian Glover
Young bride ....Kathryn Pogson
Young groom ....Stephen Rea
Rosaleen................................Sarah Patterson

Compromising Positions •• [1985]

Director: Frank Perry
Screenplay: Susan Isaacs

A bored housewife investigates the murder of a dentist who seems to have got more than just his drill into most of the women in the neighbourhood. The story lacks bite and Sarandon fails to get her teeth into her gauche character. Not only is the humour lacklustre but the promised sleaze never arrives. One of Sarandon's most disappointing films. **[98m/15]**

Judith Singer ....Susan Sarandon
Lt. David Suarez ....Raul Julia
Nancy Miller ....Judith Ivey
Bob Singer.........................Edward Herrmann
Peg Tuccio ....Mary Beth Hurt
Dr. Bruce Fleckstein...................Joe Mantegna

Showing *Jane Eyre.*

OOPS! When Sarandon and Ivey are in the car talking, a hand comes from the back seat to touch Sarandon's shoulder and give her the cue for her next line of dialogue. This is very hard to spot; you'll need the slo-mo on the video.

Comrades • [1987]

Director: Bill Douglas
Screenplay: Bill Douglas

The Tolpuddle martyrs upset the Establishment and are shipped out to Australia. A mind-numbingly tedious account of early trade unionists has many familiar faces, but they do nothing to alleviate over 3 hours of facile reconstruction. Deportation would be preferable. **[180m/PG]**

George Loveless ....Robin Soans
Betsy Loveless.........................Imelda Staunton
James Hammett.............................Keith Allen
Also: Robert Stephens, Michael Hordern, Freddie Jones, Barbara Windsor, Vanessa Redgrave

Conan the Destroyer •• · [1984]

Director: Richard Fleischer
Screenplay: Stanley Mann

Arnie returns as Conan and goes on a quest, because that is what people called Conan do. Although this time everyone's tongue is firmly in their cheek, that doesn't make matters any more interesting. It is fun, though, watching Arnie getting drunk. **[103m/15]**

Conan......................Arnold Schwarzenegger
Zula ....Grace Jones
Bombaara ....Wilt Chamberlain
Akjiro 'The Wizard'...............................Mako

Consenting Adults • [1992]

Director: **Alan J. Pakula**
Screenplay: **Matthew Chapman**

If you believe that Elvis is alive and well and working in your local supermarket then you *might* swallow this preposterous yarn. Kline and new neighbour Spacey cook up a bit of nocturnal wife-swapping. Not only does sexy Miller not wake up while Kline's doing the deed; she doesn't wake up at all. The ensuing thriller keeps throwing up questions: Why don't they call the police, why is he so trusting and why are we wasting our time watching drivel like this? [100m/15]

Richard Parker	Kevin Kline
Priscilla Parker	Mary Elizabeth Mastrantonio
Eddy Otis	Kevin Spacey
Kay Otis	Rebecca Miller
David Duttonville	Forest Whitaker

Psst! Dedicated actor that he is, Spacey shed 30 lb, learned to ride a motorbike, sail a yacht and box for the movie.

Consuming Passions • [1988]

Director: **Giles Foster**
Screenplay: **Paul D. Zimmerman & Andrew Davies**

Terrible British black comedy about a chocolate factory that discovers the odd dead body in the mix goes down a treat with its customers. Well past its sell-by date. [98m/15]

Mrs. Garza	Vanessa Redgrave
Farris	Jonathan Pryce
Ian Littleton	Tyler Butterworth
Graham Chumley	Freddie Jones

Cookie •• [1989]

Director: **Susan Seidelman**
Screenplay: **Susan Seidelman, Nora Ephron & Alice Arlen**

Having the wacky Falk in a comedy is one thing. Having Lloyd and Wiest trying to out-Falk Falk is another. Wildly over-baked cookie comedy about a daughter meeting her mobster father for the first time when he gets out of prison. These people soon become very tiresome. [93m/15]

Dino Capisco	Peter Falk
Lenore	Dianne Wiest
Cookie Voltecki	Emily Lloyd

Also: Michael V. Gazzo, Brenda Vaccaro, Jerry Lewis

Quote 'I was a single mother long before they talked about it on Oprah Winfrey.'

The Cook, the Thief, His Wife and Her Lover ••• [1989]

Director: **Peter Greenaway**
Screenplay: **Peter Greenaway**

Offal given the nouvelle cuisine treatment. Impressive to look at, but rather disgusting. This stylish but repellent allegory on 80's greed owes far more than its director might admit to fine performances from Gambon and Mirren. Although flawed by overwriting and by Greenaway's deep-frozen style, it's still a one-off. [120m/18]

Richard, the Cook	Richard Bohringer
Albert, the Thief	Michael Gambon
Georgina, his Wife	Helen Mirren
Michael, her Lover	Alan Howard
Mitchel	Tim Roth
Grace	Liz Smith

Quote 'Try the cock, Albert. It's a delicacy, and you know where it's been.'

Psst! Note for pseuds: The long tracking shots from the restaurant door to the toilet are supposed to represent the passing of food through the body.

Cool World • [1992]

Director: **Ralph Bakshi**
Screenplay: **Michael Grais & Mark Victor**

The film Basinger *should* have walked away from. She's a cartoon character who can only become human by having sex with a real person. Technically competent in its mix of live action and animation, it is incompetent in absolutely every other way. [102m/12]

Holli Would	Kim Basinger
Jack Deebs	Gabriel Byrne
Frank Harris	Brad Pitt

Cop ••• [1988]

Director: James B. Harris
Screenplay: James B. Harris

A maverick cop (could Woods be any other kind?) develops an unhealthy obsession with the serial killer he is tracking down. A not always plausible story nevertheless has an appropriately downbeat approach, wonderful atmosphere and gives us Woods on top manic form. Best scene is the one where he tells his daughter a chilling bedtime story.

[110m/18]

Lloyd Hopkins	James Woods
Kathleen McCarthy	Lesley Ann Warren
Dutch Peltz	Charles Durning
Whitey Haines	Charles Haid
Fred Gaffney	Raymond J. Barry
Joanie Pratt	Randi Brooks

Cop and a Half • [1993]

Director: Henry Winkler
Screenplay: Arne Olsen

A grotesquely ghastly comedy with Golden a kid obsessed with cops who witnesses a murder and Reynolds the kid-hating detective who...Arrrggghhh! Never mind it being an insult to children's intelligence. This one would outrage an amoeba.

[93m/PG]

Nick McKenna	Burt Reynolds
Devon Butler	Norman D. Golden II
Rachel	Ruby Dee

Corrupt
SEE: Order of Death

The Cotton Club •• [1984]

Director: Francis Ford Coppola
Screenplay: William Kennedy & Francis Ford Coppola

This potentially explosive meld of music and gangsters, based around the famous Harlem nightclub, lacks the most important ingredient that would make it go off bang – a coherent story. Although some of the musical numbers are great, they are the high spots, instead of the icing on the cake. Oddly enough, the less you concentrate, the more enjoyable it becomes.

[128m/15]

Dixie Dwyer	Richard Gere
Sandman Williams	Gregory Hines
Vera Cicero	Diane Lane
Lila Rose Oliver	Lonette McKee
Owney Madden	Bob Hoskins
Dutch Schultz	James Remar
Vincent Dwyer	Nicolas Cage

Also: Allen Garfield, Fred Gwynne, Gwen Verdon, Lisa Jane Persky, Julian Beck, Larry Fishburne, Tom Waits, Charles Honi Coles

Quote 'I saw *The Cotton Club* and I told Coppola, "After this disaster, there's only one thing for you to do. Commit suicide".' [Kenneth Anger]

Psst! The 5th biggest failure in Hollywood history, losing $38.1m ✦ This much-troubled production, went wildly over budget and is one of the few films on which the director went on strike. Coppola, brought in at the last minute, refused to work any longer without pay or a contract. Gere also walked off at one point ✦ The financial backers eventually hired a gangster-like watchdog from Las Vegas to hang around and report back on what was happening. Joey Cusumano not only stopped the squabbling, but became so interested in the process that he later went into acting for himself ✦ There were a total of 30 different versions of the script, which was still being written during filming ✦ Despite its length, 17 musical numbers that were filmed were left out of the final version ✦ Although Gere does actually play the cornet, the widespread belief that he performed his own solos here isn't true. They were dubbed by Warren Vaché.

The Couch Trip • [1988]

Director: Michael Ritchie
Screenplay: Steven Kampmann, Will Porter & Sean Stein

An escaped mental patient takes the place of an eminent radio shrink. This desperately disappointing comedy has barely a good gag in it and is dragged lower still by Matthau's disastrous cameo as a crusader for the rights of plants. **[98m/15]**

John Burns	Dan Aykroyd
Donald Becker	Walter Matthau
George Maitlin	Charles Grodin
Laura Rollins	Donna Dixon

Quote 'Nymphomaniacs in bus three with me.'

Psst! Had its title changed in France to *Talk to My Psyche, My Head is Sick* ◆ Donna Dixon is the real-life Mrs. Aykroyd ◆ Can anyone explain how Grodin gets from London to Los Angeles in what seems to be about ten minutes? ◆ Chevy Chase appears in a cameo as 'Condom Father'.

Count a Lonely Cadence
SEE: Stockade

Country ••• [1984]
Director: Richard Pearce
Screenplay: William D. Wittliff

One of a brace of mid-80's 'farmers having it tough coz the slickers in the banks done gone sold them out' movies. Lange (also the co-producer) is wonderful as the woman who takes over when her husband can't cope any more and who isn't going to let them take the family's farm, no matter what. **[109m/PG]**

Jewell Ivy	Jessica Lange
Gil Ivy	Sam Shepard
Otis	Wilford Brimley
Tom McMullen	Matt Clark
Marlene Ivy	Therese Graham
Carlisle Ivy	Levi L. Knebel

Coupe de Ville •••• [1992]
Director: Joe Roth
Screenplay: Mike Binder

Three quarrelling brothers are compelled by their tyrant of a father to drive a '54 Cadillac from Michigan to Florida. Set in the early 60s and complemented by a

great soundtrack, this is a witty, charming film that casts a delightful spell, captivating completely. **[98m/12]**

Bobby Libner	Patrick Dempsey
Buddy Libner	Arye Gross
Marvin Libner	Daniel Stern
Tammy	Annabeth Gish
Betty Libner	Rita Taggart
Uncle Phil	Joseph Bologna
Fred Libner	Alan Arkin

Psst! The only film to be directed by Roth, one of the top honchos in Hollywood.

Courage Mountain •• [1990]
Director: Christopher Leitch
Screenplay: Weaver Webb

A sort of sequel to *Heidi*, showing what happens when she goes off to boarding school in Italy just as the First World War is starting. One of those 'family' films you can never imagine a real family sitting down to, it's mild enough stuff although Sheen, who is a pipe-playing goatherd turned soldier, must cringe at the very mention of the film's name. **[98m/U]**

Heidi	Juliette Caton
Peter	Charlie Sheen
Jane Hillary	Leslie Caron
Grandfather	Jan Rubes

The Courier • [1988]
Director: Frank Deasy & Joe Lee
Screenplay: Frank Deasy

Although set amongst the criminals and drug-pushers of Dublin, this is a tedious, badly-made and wholly unoriginal thriller. **[86m/15]**

Mark	Padraig O'Loingsigh
Colette	Cait O'Riordan
Val	Gabriel Byrne
McGuigan	Ian Bannen
Christy	Patrick Bergin

Psst! Cait O'Riordan was once bass player for the Pogues, while the score is by husband Declan MacManus, better known as Elvis Costello.

Cousins ••• [1989]

Director: Joel Schumacher
Screenplay: Stephen Metcalfe

This American remake of the French film *Cousin Cousine* for once doesn't destroy all the charm of the original. It's an enjoyable comedy of two cousins, Danson and Rossellini, who discover at a big family wedding just how much they're attracted to each other. **[113m/15]**

Larry Kozinski	Ted Danson
Maria Hardy	Isabella Rossellini
Tish Kozinski	Sean Young
Tom Hardy	William Petersen
Uncle Vince	Lloyd Bridges

Crackers • [1984]

Director: Louis Malle
Screenplay: Jeffrey Fiskin

A group of bungling mates decide to rob their local pawnbroker while he's away. Criminally unfunny. **[92m/15]**

Weslake	Donald Sutherland
Garvey	Jack Warden
Dillard	Sean Penn
Turtle	Wallace Shawn

Crazy People •• [1990]

Director: Tony Bill
Screenplay: Mitch Markowitz

Adman Moore comes up with a series of true adverts ('Volvo – they're boxy but they're good' – 'Metamuesli: Helps you go to the toilet') and is forced into a mental asylum by his partner. Then, of course, the ads come good. But by then, Moore's discovered that the people in the asylum are saner than the ones outside. Mildly amusing. **[92m/15]**

Emory Leeson	Dudley Moore
Kathy Burgess	Daryl Hannah
Stephen Bachman	Paul Reiser
Charles F. Drucker	J.T. Walsh
Also: Bill Smitrovich, Ben Hammer, Mercedes Ruehl, Alan North	

Psst! John Malkovich was originally in this, but he left after an on-set disagreement.

Creator •• [1985]

Director: Ivan Passer
Screenplay: Jeremy Leven

O'Toole is an eccentric inventor trying to revive his wife 30 years after her death. What a shame he couldn't do it to the script. O'Toole is, however, a pleasure to watch as always. The film didn't come out in Britain until 1990. **[108m/15]**

Harry Wolper	Peter O'Toole
Meli	Mariel Hemingway
Boris	Vincent Spano
Barbara	Virginia Madsen
Sid	David Ogden Stiers

Creepers • [1985]

Director: Dario Argento
Screenplay: Dario Argento & Franco Ferrini

Decidedly offbeat and gruesome horror effort set in a girls' Swiss finishing school menaced by a psycho scyther. Connelly can communicate telepathically with insects – it's one of the first things they teach you in a Swiss finishing school – and uses her many-legged chums to win the day. The most horrific thing about the film is the appalling dubbed English. **[83m/18]**

Jennifer Corvino	Jennifer Connelly
Frau Bruckner	Daria Nicolodi
Insp. Rudolf Geiger	Patrick Bauchau
Prof. John McGregor	Donald Pleasence

Psst! The director likes to keep it in the family. Amongst those gruesomely killed off are his 14-year-old daughter Fiore and girlfriend Nicolodi • The credits include an 'entomology consultant'.

Creepshow 2 • [1987]

Director: Michael Gornick
Screenplay: George A. Romero

Creepshow was no classic but this trio of Stephen King stories, with Romero only writing, is passable at best. An interesting cast, which includes King in a cameo, are wasted. **[90m/18]**

Ray Spruce ....George Kennedy
Martha Spruce ....Dorothy Lamour
Annie Lansing ....Lois Chiles

Psst! Tom Savini, who appears as 'The Creep' is a special effects man, renowned for his way with gore, usually working with George Romero.

Crimes and Misdemeanors •• [1989]

Director: **Woody Allen**
Screenplay: **Woody Allen**

Although some people's favourite Allen pic, this rather unsatisfying movie is really two films running side by side that have little to do with each other. Dr. Landau goes to extreme lengths when mistress Huston threatens to spill the beans while documentary-maker Allen suffers the intolerable smug superiority of his successful sitcom-producing brother-in-law. In the end, despite its reputation, all you remember are the great lines. [104m/15]

Barbara.....................................Caroline Aaron
Lester...Alan Alda
Cliff Stern ....Woody Allen
Miriam Rosenthal ....Claire Bloom
Halley Reed ....Mia Farrow
Wendy Stern ....Joanna Gleason
Dolores Paley ....Anjelica Huston
Also: Martin Landau, Jerry Orbach, Sam Waterston, Jenny Nichols

Quote 'The last time I was inside a woman was when I visited the Statue of Liberty.' ◆ 'Show business is dog eat dog. It's worse than dog eat dog. It's dog doesn't return other dog's phone calls.' ◆ 'He wants to produce something of mine.' – 'Yes, your first child.'

Showing *Mr and Mrs Smith.*

Psst! One of the many films Sean Young was fired from ◆ As the killer is stalking his victim, the music is (clever, clever) Schubert's *Death and the Maiden.*

Crimes of Passion • [1984]

Director: **Ken Russell**
Screenplay: **Barry Sandler**

Turner is a successful dress designer by day and a cheap hooker by night. Although Turner is fine and Perkins is watchable as a psychotic preacher, it's let down by weird direction that makes it look like a horrendously long pop video and by acting from Laughlin so bad you think you're watching a badly dubbed foreign movie. [101m/18]

Joanna/China Blue.................Kathleen Turner
Shayne ....Anthony Perkins
Grady..John Laughlin

Quote ' I never forget a face, especially when I've sat on it.'

Psst! The 'European' version is much stronger than the one that went on release in America, where the scene with the policeman being sodomised with his nightstick was cut.

Crimes of the Heart •• [1986]

Director: **Bruce Beresford**
Screenplay: **Beth Henley**

Three slightly kooky sisters get together at their Carolina home and argue about which of them's going to go completely mad first. There's some wonderful acting but the script's wildly melodramatic. Very much an 'if you like that sort of thing' film. [105m/15]

Lenny Magrath ....Diane Keaton
Meg Magrath ....Jessica Lange
Babe Magrath.............................Sissy Spacek
Doc Porter ....Sam Shepard
Chick Boyle..................................Tess Harper

Quote 'Why, you're just as perfectly sane as anyone walking the streets of Hazlehurst, Mississippi.'

Crimewave •• [1986]

Director: **Sam Raimi**
Screenplay: **Sam Raimi, Joel Coen & Ethan Coen**

The credits are intriguing, with *Evil Dead* Raimi, joined by the amazing Coen brothers on the screenplay. Unfortunately, despite patchy moments of inspired weirdness, this story of a man about to be executed for a murder he didn't commit, is all over the shop.   **[86m/PG]**

Mrs. Trend	Louise Lasser
Ernest Trend	Edward R. Pressman
Crush	Paul L. Smith
Coddish	Brion James

Criminal Law •• [1989]

Director: **Martin Campbell**
Screenplay: **Mark Kasdan**

Lawyer Oldman has an attack of conscience when he discovers that Bacon, the serial-killer he got off, is guilty and starting up again. This ponderous thriller could well be the rainiest film of all time.

[117m/18]

Ben Chase	Gary Oldman
Martin Thiel	Kevin Bacon
Ellen Faulkner	Karen Young
Detective Mesel	Joe Don Baker
Detective Stillwell	Tess Harper

Critters • [1986]

Director: **Stephen Herek**
Screenplay: **Stephen Herek & Dominic Muir**

A group of toothy, furry, aliens escapes from their prison planet and land in Kansas. Presumably furious that they can't find Dorothy or Oz, they run amok. An interesting cast obviously hasn't seen *Gremlins*, of which this is a shameful rip-off, or it would be better prepared. **[86m/15]**

Helen Brown	Dee Wallace Stone
Harv	M. Emmet Walsh

Also: Billy Green Bush, Scott Grimes, Don Opper, Billy Zane

Critters 2: The Main Course • [1988]

Director: **Mick Garris**
Screenplay: **David Twohy & Mick Garris**

They open their toothy mouths to eat people. We open ours to yawn. The producers obviously forgot that if you're thinking of a sequel, you shouldn't kill off your cast in the first film. This lot are dreadful. Hard to believe that there are two more in this series on video.   **[87m/18]**

Brad Brown	Scott Grimes
Megan Morgan	Diane Curtis
Charlie McFadden	Don Opper

'Crocodile' Dundee •••• [1986]

Director: **Peter Faiman**
Screenplay: **Paul Hogan & Ken Shadie**

Delightful fish-out-of-water comedy has sceptical New York journalist shown around the Oz outback by Hogan, who is then just as baffled when he returns with her to the Big Apple. Often silly, but totally beguiling and frequently hilarious, the film is made by Hogan's disarming performance. At long last, a hero we chaps can identify with, who doesn't look as if he's worked out in a gym twenty-six hours a day.   **[98m/15]**

Mick Dundee	Paul Hogan
Sue Charlton	Linda Kozlowski
Wally Reilly	John Meillon
Richard Mason	Mark Blum
Sam Charlton	Michael Lombard
Nevile Bell	David Gulpilil
Con	Ritchie Singer

Quote 'That's not a knife. *THAT'S* a knife.'

Psst! An enormous success in Australia, Paramount bought the American rights. Even though they spent more than the original $5.5 million budget on ads, they had only moderate hopes for it. It became one of the biggest-ever sleeper hits ✦ Seven minutes were cut for the American version, with the Aussie slang that couldn't be cut being re-recorded ✦ After considering 200 possible names, they stuck with the original title, adding the quotation marks in case people thought it was a picture about reptiles! ✦ The insurance company wouldn't allow real crocodiles, so the one that gets close is a rubber model on an underwater rail ✦ So eager were Australian investors to put money into the film that, according to Hogan, some $3.5m had to be given back ✦ The video sadly lacks the funny scene where Dundee assumes that someone taking cocaine has a bad cold ◆ The Plaza Hotel in New York received many complaints from guests who couldn't find the bidet that so baffled Hogan.

'Crocodile' Dundee II •• [1988]

Director: **John Cornell**
Screenplay: **Paul Hogan & Brett Hogan**

This disappointing sequel forgoes most of the laughs and goes for action in a very tired and strung-out plot about Hogan chasing after some drug traffickers who've taken Koslowski. He's still a pleasure to watch, but the magic and believability have gone. **[111m/PG]**

Mick Dundee	Paul Hogan
Sue Charlton	Linda Kozlowski
LeRoy Brown	Charles S. Dutton
Rico	Hechter Ubarry
Miguel	Juan Fernandez

Quote 'I'll get out of any stunt I can. Except the love scenes.' [Hogan]

Psst! Hogan, once a rigger on the Sydney Harbour Bridge, left his wife of 30 years for Kozlowski.

Cross Creek •• [1983]

Director: **Martin Ritt**
Screenplay: **Dalene Young**

Despite its length, this is a pleasing true-ish tale of Marjorie Kinnan Rawlings who abandoned her husband and New York life to live in the backwoods of Florida. There, she used the colourful types around her in her fiction, best-known of which is *The Yearling*, made into a wonderful film.

[120m/U]

Rawlings	Mary Steenburgen
Marsh Turner	Rip Torn
Norton Baskin	Peter Coyote
Ellie Turner	Dana Hill
Geechee	Alfre Woodard
Mrs. Turner	Joanna Miles
Max Perkins	Malcolm McDowell

Psst! McDowell and Steenburgen were married at the time of the film.

Crossing Delancey ••• [1988]

Director: **Joan Micklin Silver**
Screenplay: **Susan Sandler**

A lovely, gentle comedy in the *Moonstruck* vein, only Jewish rather than Italian. Irving is the modern woman with the usual problems who kicks against the old ways of doing things, particularly when the marriage-broker tries to set her up with pickle man Riegert. Beautifully written, observed and acted, this is a little gem. **[96m/PG]**

Isabelle Grossman	Amy Irving
Sam Posner	Peter Riegert
Bubbie Kantor	Riezl Bozyk
Anton Maes	Jeroen Krabbé
Hannah Mandelbaum	Sylvia Miles
Lionel	George Martin
Nick	John Bedford Lloyd
Mark	David Pierce

Psst! At 74, Bozyk was making her film debut as the grandmother.

Crossing the Line
SEE: The Big Man

Crossover Dreams •• [1985]

Director: **Leon Ichaso**
Screenplay: **Leon Ichaso, Manuel Arce & Ruben Blades**

The singer is Spanish-American Blades and the music is Salsa, but otherwise it's the much-told story of a songster turning his back on his friends on the way up, only to find that he comes down again sooner than expected. **[86m/15]**

Rudy Veloz	Ruben Blades
Orlando	Shawn Elliot
Lou Rose	Tom Signorelli
Liz Garcia	Elizabeth Pena

Crush ••• [1993]

Director: **Alison Maclean**
Screenplay: **Alison Maclean & Anne Kennedy**

Promising debut pic with Harden seducing novelist Smith while his daughter takes up with the journalist hospitalised as a result of Harden crashing the car. Although parts of this tangled relationship drama are quite clumsy, others are highly imaginative. A moody atmospheric portrayal of modern New Zealand, with the opening bubbling mud pools setting the sombre tone. **[96m/15]**

Lane	Marcia Gay Harden
Christina	Donogh Rees
Angela	Caitlin Bossley
Horse	Pete Smith

Crusoe ••• [1989]

Director: **Caleb Deschanel**
Screenplay: **Walon Green**

Robinson Crusoe as he hasn't been seen on screen before, a bigoted slave trader. It's also far pacier than we're used to, with plenty of action as well as sumptuous photography and an underlying message about racism. **[95m/15]**

Crusoe	Aidan Quinn
Warrior	Ade Sapara
Runaway slave	Elvis Payne

Also: Richard Sharp, William Hootkins, Shane Rimmer, Jimmy Nail, Timothy Spall, Oliver Platt

Cry-Baby •• [1991]

Director: **John Waters**
Screenplay: **John Waters**

Supposedly a parody of 50's juvenile delinquent pics. Unfortunately, Waters has become so disappointingly mainstream that this musical–comedy, with Locane and Depp as the young lovers, doesn't seem all that different to the originals it's supposed to be spoofing. Lords is splendidly brassy, but the late Divine is sorely missed. **[93m/12]**

Wade 'Cry–Baby' Walker	Johnny Depp
Allison Vernon–Williams	Amy Locane
Ramona Rickettes	Susan Tyrrell
Mrs. Vernon–Williams	Polly Bergen

Psst! Traci Lords, playing Wanda, was once a leading porn actress, notorious in America because the majority of her

films were made before she was 18 ✦ Willem Dafoe, famous kidnap victim Patti Hearst (as Mrs. Woodward) and Iggy Pop also pop up in small parts.

Cry Freedom •• [1987]

Director: **Richard Attenborough**
Screenplay: **John Briley**

Richard Attenborough 'does' Steve Biko. Despite the worthiness of a film laying bare apartheid, it mostly follows not Steve Biko, but newspaperman Donald Woods, as he and his family escape to freedom. Despite the immense power of the roll–call of the dead at the end, even the trial of watching Sir Dickie collect another half dozen awards would be preferable to this liberal, preachy movie. **[158m/PG]**

Donald Woods	Kevin Kline
Wendy Woods	Penelope Wilton
Steve Biko	Denzel Washington
Bruce	John Hargreaves
High Commissioner	Alec McCowen

Also: Kevin McNally, Zakes Mokae, Ian Richardson, Josette Simon, John Thaw, Timothy West, Julian Glover

Psst! After veiled threats on his life, Attenborough had a bodyguard at all times while filming in Zimbabwe.

The Crying Game •• [1992]

Director: **Neil Jordan**
Screenplay: **Neil Jordan**

A bust in Britain but a phenomenal success in America, this confused film is part thriller, part romantic comedy. The middle section, with an IRA man seeking out the girlfriend of a dead squaddie, is touching and delightfully funny, sporting an incredible twist in the tale. The outer sections, involving the IRA, are tedious and in desperate need of a storyline to hold them together. While some of the actors look as if they'd have trouble acting their way out of a bag, Whitaker gives the best performance of the film *in* one. **[112m/18]**

Fergus	Stephen Rea
Jude	Miranda Richardson
Jody	Forest Whitaker

Col ....Jim Broadbent
Dave..Ralph Brown
Maguire ....Adrian Dunbar
Dil ....Jaye Davidson

Oscars Best Screenplay

Psst! Costing less than £3m, Jordan was turned down by every studio in Hollywood, yet the film was nominated for six Oscars ◆ British Palace Pictures financed it, but went bust in the middle of filming. The producer is said to have been using his ATM machine to get cash to pay the actors ◆ Rea drew on his personal experience for his role as an IRA gunman; his wife was once a member and served 8 years in prison for her part in car bombings.

A Cry in the Dark •• [1988]

Director: Fred Schepisi
Screenplay: Robert Caswell & Fred Schepisi

...And an occasional yawn too. Streep dons a black wig and an Aussie accent for this true story of the storm surrounding Lindy Chamberlain, sentenced to hard labour for life for killing her baby. She, however, maintained that a dingo had run off with it. Too long and sometimes a little bit clinical, but still an absolutely fascinating story. [121m/15]

Lindy..Meryl Streep
Michael..Sam Neill
Barker...Bruce Myles
Charlwood...Nick Tate
Phillips.....................................Neil Fitzpatrick
Barritt...Maurie Fields

Blurb ...It Could Be Yours.

Quote 'A dingow stowl mah bibey.'

Cujo •• [1983]

Director: Lewis Teague
Screenplay: Don Carlos Dunaway & Lauren Currier

A woman and her son are terrorised by a rabid dog. What is it? A rottweiler? A pitbull? No, a St. Bernard. That's the essential flaw in this well-made and tense thriller. You can't help feeling that instead of biting them, the dog intends slobbering them to death. [91m/18]

Donna ....Dee Wallace
Tad...Danny Pintauro
Vic...................................Daniel Hugh-Kelly
Steve....................................Christopher Stone

Curly Sue • [1991]

Director: **John Hughes**
Screenplay: **John Hughes**

Possibly the worst film John Hughes has ever thrown up. Indeed, throwing up is likely to be your reaction to this unbelievably sentimental, tear-jearking, uninventive concoction of conman Belushi and moppet Porter (a sort of Shirley Temple with attitude) thawing the heart of yuppie professional Lynch. [102m/PG]

Bill Dancer.................................James Belushi
Grey Ellison.................................Kelly Lynch
Curly Sue ....Alisan Porter
Also: John Getz, Fred Dalton Thompson, Cameron Thor

Quote 'I brushed my teeth in Detroit.' – 'So you brush them in Chicago.'

OOPS! The mike boom appears in this film more than some of the actors, bobbing into the very first shot.

The Curse of the Pink Panther • [1983]

Director: **Blake Edwards**
Screenplay: **Blake Edwards & Geoffrey Edwards**

...Is Blake Edwards, who wouldn't let go of Clouseau, even after Sellers died. He gets a similarly clumsy Waas to investigate Clouseau's disappearance, with various actors from the earlier films popping in and out in the hope you won't miss Sellers. Some hope. [110m/PG]

Sir Charles Litton ....David Niven
George Litton..........................Robert Wagner
Dreyfus.......................................Herbert Lom
Chandra ....Joanna Lumley
Lady Litton ....Capucine

Bruno...Robert Loggia
Clifton Sleigh ....Ted Wass

Psst! This was David Niven's last film. His voice was so frail that it was dubbed by Rich Little ✦ Although uncredited, Roger Moore appears as a facelifted Clouseau at the end.

The Cutting Edge ••• [1992]

Director: Paul Michael Glaser
Screenplay: Tony Gilroy

Formulaic but nonetheless delightful romantic comedy. Sweeney is the injured hockey player who is bullied into part-nering icy rich girl figure-skater Kelly. She, of course, hates him on sight. You know just what's going to happen, but that doesn't stop this being an immensely pleasurable, old-fashioned, mist-your-eyes-up delight. It's pure escapism.
[102m/PG]

Doug...D.B. Sweeney
Kate...Moira Kelly
Anton...Roy Dotrice
Jack..Terry O'Quinn
Hale ....Dwier Brown

Psst! Director Glaser is better known as Starsky ✦ As neither Sweeney nor Kelly are champion skaters, you can have a lot of fun watching the camera switch from their faces to other people's legs.

Cyrano de Bergerac •••• [1990]

Director: Jean-Paul Rappeneau
Screenplay: Jean-Claude Carriere & Jean-Paul Rappeneau

Brilliant French film version of the famous Rostand play about the guy with the Pinocchio nose, heavily and forlornly in love with his cousin Roxane. Depardieu is perfect for the part, Fairbanks-like in the duelling sequences and eminently believable in the more emotional moments. Although it was a clever idea to save money on latex by get-ting the already nasally-overendowed Depardieu to play the part, it was still, at $20m, France's second most expensive film.
[135m/U]

Cyrano de Bergerac ....Gérard Depardieu
Roxane ....Anne Brochet
Christian de Neuvillette ....Vincent Perez
Comte De Guiche....................Jacques Weber

Psst! The English subtitles were written in verse by Anthony Burgess.

Da ••• [1988]

Director: Matt Clark
Screenplay: Hugh Leonard

Irish playwright Sheen returns to the old sod for his dad's funeral, only to have the old sod himself pop up again a day later. Together, in this adaptation of a successful play, they revisit the past in a moving, often highly droll, examination of their father-son relationship.
[102m/PG]

Da ....Barnard Hughes
Charlie ....Martin Sheen
Drumm ....William Hickey
Young Charlie ....Karl Hayden
Mother ....Doreen Hepburn
Boy Charlie ....Hugh O'Conor

Dad •• [1989]

Director: Gary David Goldberg
Screenplay: Gary David Goldberg

Tear-jerker about businessman Danson returning to the family home to care for his dying father. Well-made, but some-what sloppy, Lemmon gives his usual splendid performance, even if it is through a mound of make-up.
[118m/PG]

Jake Tremont ....Jack Lemmon
John Tremont...............................Ted Danson
Bette Tremont.....................Olympia Dukakis
Annie..Kathy Baker
Also: Kevin Spacey, Ethan Hawke, Zakes Mokae, J.T. Walsh

Quote 'Dying's not a sin. Not living is.'

Daddy's Dying, Who's Got the Will? ••• [1990]

Director: Jack Fisk
Screenplay: Del Shores

A squabbling Texas family gather round their daddy's deathbed and try to conceal their eagerness for the old man to pop off. Despite the odd flat patch, it's mostly lively and amusing, with a good cast giving it all they've got. [96m/12]

Orville	Beau Bridges
Evalita	Beverly D'Angelo
Sara Lee	Tess Harper
Harmony	Judge Reinhold
Lurlene	Amy Wright

Damage •• [1992]

Director: Louis Malle
Screenplay: David Hare

Government minister Irons has a tempestuous affair with his son's girlfriend, with horrendous consequences. Despite the up-market cast, director and writer, it's really just raunchy Mills & Boon although the po-faced sex scenes result in tittering rather than titillation. Anyone who knows the novel will undoubtedly be disappointed. Others may find the plot fascinating. [112m/18]

Dr. Stephen Fleming	Jeremy Irons
Anna Barton	Juliette Binoche
Ingrid	Miranda Richardson
Martyn	Rupert Graves
Edward Lloyd	Ian Bannen
Elizabeth Prideaux	Leslie Caron

OOPS! They go into the wrong room in grandfather Bannen's house to make love, later emerging from the door of a completely different room. Perhaps the earth moved more than they expected?

Dancers • [1987]

Director: Herbert Ross
Screenplay: Sarah Kernochan

A ballet-dancing star becomes enamoured of a young dancer, who keeps him on his toes. This dreadful *pas de deux*, should give second thoughts to anyone contemplating taking up ballet. [99m/PG]

Tony	Mikhail Baryshnikov
Francesca	Alessandra Ferri
Nadine	Leslie Browne

Dances With Wolves •••• [1990]

Director: Kevin Costner
Screenplay: Michael Blake

A remarkable directing debut from Costner. Despite its irritating and inaccurate Politically Correct stance, this story of the Civil War hero befriending and then joining the Sioux is a marvel from beginning to end. Proving that epics *can* still work, there's hardly a dull moment in a film which is fascinating, touching, shaming and even pretty funny in places. Even though the Western is such an old genre, the photography dazzles the eye. Such a shame that Costner saw fit to bring out a 230 minute ego-puffing 'Special Edition'. [179m/12]

Lt. John J. Dunbar	Kevin Costner
Stands With A Fist	Mary McDonnell
Kicking Bird	Graham Greene
Wind In His Hair	Rodney A. Grant
Ten Bears	Floyd Red Crow Westerman
Black Shawl	Tantoo Cardinal
Timmons	Robert Pastorelli
Lt. Elgin	Charles Rocket

Oscars Best Picture, Best Screenplay (adapted), Best Director

OOPS! The Indians were ahead of us in many areas, one of them obviously being hair-styling. Or is that *not* mousse that Mary McDonnell's wearing? Her hair also changes length when Costner first encounters her ♦ Keep an eye on Timmons, the wagon driver. First he gets egg on his beard, which vanishes then reappears. Then, when he's killed, he still manages a last breath ♦ Isn't that a choke chain around the dead wolf's neck?

Psst! So sure was Hollywood that Costner would come unstuck with this troubled production, which ran 30 days over schedule, that they nicknamed it *Kevin's Gate*, a reference to the disastrous

Heaven's Gate ◆ Revisionist it may be, but the 90's-style Indians, pacifist and green, certainly aren't historically accurate. According to one scholar: 'The Sioux massacred. They pillaged. They raped. They burned. They carried women and children into captivity. They tortured for entertainment. All this was their long-established custom, carried out, indeed, far more frequently against other Indian tribes than against whites.'

Dance with a Stranger ••• [1985]

Director: Mike Newell
Screenplay: Shelagh Delaney

Richardson is superb as Ruth Ellis, the last woman hanged in Britain. Despite sticking closely to the facts, this is still a fascinating account of the Soho club 'hostess' who became obsessed with upper-class Hooray Henry Blakely. Despite losing its grip slightly in the latter stages, it's splendidly lurid as well as being a fascinating account of life in Britain in the 50s.   [102m/15]

Ruth Ellis	Miranda Richardson
David Blakely	Rupert Everett
Desmond Cussen	Ian Holm
Andy	Matthew Carroll
Anthony Findlater	Tom Chadbon
Carole Findlater	Jane Bertish
Morrie Conley	Stratford Johns

Dancing in the Dark • [1986]

Director: Leon Marr
Screenplay: Leon Marr

In this Canadian film, a long-married housewife reacts strongly when she learns of hubby's infidelity. It seems a bit much taking our money and then expecting us to act as her analyst for free as she talks and talks and talks at us. Depressing.   [98m/15]

Edna	Martha Henry
Henry	Neil Munro

Dancin' Thru the Dark •• [1990]

Director: Mike Ockrent
Screenplay: Willy Russell

On the eve of their wedding, both the bride's hen party and the groom's stag do end up at the same nightclub. The bride's ex-boyfriend is in the band, too. Another slice of Liverpool life from Willy Russell, but perhaps lacking a little of the bite and wit of some of his other work.   [95m/15]

Linda	Claire Hackett
Peter	Con O'Neill
Kav	Simon O'Brien
Maureen	Angela Clarke
Bransky's manager	Colin Welland
Drunk in pub	Willy Russell

Dangerous Liaisons ••• [1988]

Director: Stephen Frears
Screenplay: Christopher Hampton

Visually sumptuous adaptation of the play of the original book about two French aristos playing sexual games of conquest. Close promises Malkovich a return to her bed if he'll seduce Thurman. He's after the tougher challenge of the married Pfeiffer. Although modern accents intrude and it's a little hard to believe in Close as this all-powerful sexual being, Pfeiffer is painfully brilliant as the doomed Mme de Tourvel. Costume drama has rarely been so captivating.   [120m/15]

Marquise de Merteuil	Glenn Close
Vicomte de Valmont	John Malkovich
Madame de Tourvel	Michelle Pfeiffer
Madame de Volanges	Swoosie Kurtz
Chevalier Danceny	Keanu Reeves
Madame de Rosemonde	Mildred Natwick
Cecile de Volanges	Uma Thurman
Azolan	Peter Capaldi

Oscars Best Screen Play (adapted)

Psst! Malkovich and Pfeiffer became lovers during filming, though he later returned to his wife ◆ Any thoughts of keeping the original title, *Les Liaisons Dangereuses* were scuppered when a survey showed only 1 in 50 Americans were willing to see a film with a foreign title.

Daniel •• [1983]

Director: Sidney Lumet
Screenplay: E.L. Doctorow

In this adaptation, Doctorow doesn't quite manage to get across the fascination of his novel about the Rosenbergs, slightly disguised, the couple executed in America in the 50s for spying for the Russians. All a little dull. [129m/15]

Daniel Isaacson	Timothy Hutton
Jacob Ascher	Ed Asner
Paul Isaacson	Mandy Patinkin
Rochelle	Lindsay Crouse
Selig Mindish	Joseph Leon
Susan Isaacson	Amanda Plummer
Phyllis Isaacson	Ellen Barkin

Danny the Champion of the World •• [1989]

Director: Gavin Millar
Screenplay: John Goldsmith

Pleasant, pint-sized, Ealing-style comedy with Irons père et fils as the happy single-parent family in the 50s fighting off Coltrane who has designs on their property. Based on a Roald Dahl book. [98m/U]

William Smith	Jeremy Irons
Danny	Samuel Irons
Victor Hazell	Robbie Coltrane

Also: Cyril Cusack, Lionel Jeffries, Ronald Pickup, Jean Marsh

Dark Angel •• [1990]

Director: Craig R. Baxley
Screenplay: Jonathan Tydor & Leonard Maas Jr.

A detective is puzzled by an incredibly productive killer on the loose. Despite a relatively standard cop-whose-life's-shot-to-hell plot, Lundgren brings quite a bit of fun to the proceedings. [92m/18]

Jack Caine	Dolph Lundgren
Laurence Smith	Brian Benben
Diane Pollone	Betsy Brantley
Talec	Mathias Hues

Psst! Probably the first movie to use a compact disc as a murder weapon.

Dark Crystal •• [1982]

Director: Jim Henson & Frank Oz
Screenplay: David Odell

Good battles Evil and wins. What a shame that the story in this film from Muppet mastermind Jim Henson doesn't match up to the superb puppetry and imagery. The alien world they've created is imaginative enough to win over the children, but adults will probably weary of the limp plot. [93m/PG]

With: Stephen Garlick, Lisa Maxwell, Billie Whitelaw

Darkman •• [1990]

Director: Sam Raimi
Screenplay: Chuck Pfarrer, Sam Raimi, Ivan Raimi, Daniel Goldin & Joshua Goldin

Scientist Neeson is left for dead by a gang of thugs. He emerges from hiding as Darkman, wreaking dreadful revenge. Frequently rather unpleasant cartoon stuff, with no shortage of noise and swooping camerawork, but little presence of wit or originality to make it come alive. [91m/15]

Peyton Westlake/Darkman	Liam Neeson
Julie Hastings	Frances McDormand
Louis Strack Jr.	Colin Friels
Robert G. Durant	Larry Drake

Also: Nelson Mashita, Theodore Raimi, William Dear, Jenny Agutter, John Landis

Dark Obsession
SEE: Diamond Skulls

The Dark Wind ••• [1992]

Director: Errol Morris
Screenplay: Eric Bergren, Neal Jimenez & Mark Horowitz

This fascinating thriller is intriguingly set on an Indian reservation where the cops are native Americans. Although not to everyone's taste, it has a wonderful brooding atmosphere while the photography makes superb use of the locale.

Low-key it may be (soporific, said some critics), but it plays like a lost episode of the TV series *Twin Peaks* and I was gripped throughout.   **[112m/15]**

Officer Jim Chee ....Lou Diamond Phillips
Lt. Joe Leaphorn ....Fred Ward
Albert (Cowboy) Dashee ....Gary Farmer
Jake West......................................John Karlen
Mr. Archer ....Lance Baker

Psst! Hopi Indian religious leaders thought the way their ancient rites were depicted in the script were 'sacrilegious', so the film-makers changed it to mollify them.

D.A.R.Y.L. ••   [1985]

Director: **Simon Wincer**
Screenplay: **David Ambrose, Allan Scott & Jeffrey Ellis**

A couple's lives are transformed by a sweet little boy, who turns out to be some sort of Government-created robot. The fun is dampened by the heavy sentiment and a failure to gloss over moments of wild implausibility.   **[100m/PG]**

Joyce Richardson....................Mary Beth Hurt
Andy Richardson ....Michael McKean
Ellen ....Kathryn Walker
Elaine ....Colleen Camp
Dr. Stewart................................Josef Sommer
D.A.R.Y.L................................Barret Oliver

Dave •••   [1993]

Director: **Ivan Reitman**
Screenplay: **Gary Ross**

Hired as a double to impersonate the President, meek but decent Kline is suddenly thrown into the job for real when the President has a stroke. This charming and highly amusing tale only spins off into silliness in the final stretch.   **[110m]**

Dave Kovic/Bill Mitchell ....Kevin Kline
Ellen Mitchell..................Signourney Weaver
Bob Alexander ....Frank Langella
Alan Reed....................................Kevin Dunn
Vice President Nance..................Ben Kingsley
Murray Blum ....Charles Grodin

Quote 'You're very good, but *she* needs a lot of work.'

Psst! Although many of the cameos wheeled in to add verisimilitude will be unfamiliar to British audiences, most should be able to spot Arnie and Oliver Stone, spouting yet another conspiracy theory.

The Dawning •••   [1988]

Director: **Robert Knights**
Screenplay: **Moira Williams**

In Ireland during The Troubles in the 20s, a young girl helps a stranger, not realising that he is an IRA man on the run. Three fine actors, Howard, Simmons and particularly Hopkins, turn a low-budget TV-financed film into compelling viewing.   **[97m/PG]**

Maj. Angus Barry ....Anthony Hopkins
Nancy Gulliver......................Rebecca Pidgeon
Aunt Mary ....Jean Simmons
Grandfather ....Trevor Howard
Harry..Hugh Grant

Psst! This was Trevor Howard's last film.

Daydream Believer •   [1992]

Director: **Kathy Mueller**
Screenplay: **Saturday Rosenberg**

A film so dreadful it's almost worth watching. Otto's a girl who turns into a horse whenever stressed. Instead of training for the Grand National, she makes life miserable for wealthy stud-owner Kemp, eventually winning his love when her ability to speak horse fluently enables her to bring two equine lovers together. The horsey romance is less embarrassing than its human counterpart. Also known as *The Girl Who Came Late*.
                                [86m/15]

Nell ....Miranda Otto
Digby ....Martin Kemp
Margo..Anne Looby

Day of the Dead ••   [1985]

Director: **George A. Romero**
Screenplay: **George A. Romero**

Feeble follow-up to *Night of the Living*

Dead and *Dawn of the Dead*, with the world's last group of boffins and squaddies holed up in a bunker besieged by flesh-eating zombies. The butcher who supplied the film-makers with all that offal for the exciting finale has probably retired to Barbados on the proceeds. **[102m/18]**

Sarah	Lori Cardille
John	Terry Alexander
Capt. Rhodes	Joseph Pilato
McDermott	Jarlath Conroy

Days of Thunder • [1990]

Director: **Tony Scott**
Screenplay: **Robert Towne**

This attempt to reproduce *Top Gun* with racing cars gets a flat early on and has to limp back to the pits. It shows every sign of the enormous post-production rush that meant it was shown almost the moment they finished filming. **[107m/12]**

Cole Trickle	Tom Cruise
Harry Hogge	Robert Duvall
Dr. Claire Lewicki	Nicole Kidman
Tim Daland	Randy Quaid
Russ Wheeler	Cary Elwes
Rowdy Burns	Michael Rooker

OOPS! When Cruise is taken to hospital after crashing, it is his right eye that needs attention. Later on, the problem has switched to his left eye. Then it's the right again ◆ Cary Elwes' wife calls Cruise 'Tom' at one point.

Psst! Cruise is a keen racing driver himself. He took it up at Paul Newman's suggestion when they worked together on *The Color of Money* ◆ The film-makers were allowed to have two camera-cars within the real Daytona 500. Altogether there were 19 cameras filming the race as it happened ◆ Cruise received $9m plus a percentage of the profits ◆ One of Hollywood's top producers, Don Simpson (*Top Gun*, *Beverly Hills Cop*), appears as Aldo Bennedetti. Not even the mighty are safe from the knife, however. He ends up with only one line left ◆ Cruise and Kidman fell in love on the set.

D.C. Cab
SEE: **Street Fleet**

The Dead ••• [1987]

Director: **John Huston**
Screenplay: **Tony Huston**

Huston's last film is a faithful adaptation of the James Joyce short story. Slight on plot but heavy on atmosphere and with some excellent performances, it tells of a married woman recalling a doomed love affair years before. Much more effective in the cinema than on television, it is a very powerful film, though perhaps not for all tastes. **[83m/U]**

Gretta Conroy	Anjelica Huston
Gabriel Conroy	Donal McCann
Aunt Kate Morkan	Helena Carroll
Aunt Julia Morkan	Cathleen Delany
Mr. Brown	Dan O'Herlihy
Lily	Rachael Dowling

Psst! The house we see in the film is the actual one that Joyce wrote about, though the interiors were filmed in California.

Dead Again •• [1991]

Director: **Kenneth Branagh**
Screenplay: **Scott Frank**

West Coast private dick Branagh investigates the case of the amnesiac Thompson. Are they the reincarnations of a doomed couple from 40 years before? Or are the luvvies simply trying to hog two parts each? Camper than Butlin's in high season, the references to Hitchcock, Welles and others come so thick and fast that one loses interest in the rather predictable plot. **[101m/15]**

Roman Strauss/Mike	Kenneth Branagh
Gray Baker	Andy Garcia
Franklyn Madson	Derek Jacobi
Inga	Hanna Schygulla
Margaret Strauss/Grace	Emma Thompson
Dr. Cozy Carlisle	Robin Williams

Psst! Robin Williams' name didn't appear on the credits. He said he was worried about overshadowing the other names.

Dead-Bang •• [1989]

Director: John Frankenheimer
Screenplay: Robert Foster

Less *Miami Vice* than *Miami Lice*, as un-kempt Johnson goes after a bunch of neo-Nazi supremacists. Some good action sequences from veteran thriller director Frankenheimer, but the biggest mystery is what the title means. [102m/18]

Jerry Beck	Don Johnson
Linda	Penelope Ann Miller
Arthur Kressler	William Forsythe
Elliot Webly	Bob Balaban

Psst! Probably the first movie in which a cop throws up over a suspect.

Dead Calm •••• [1989]

Director: Phillip Noyce
Screenplay: Terry Hayes

Top-notch Australian thriller has mar-ried Neill and Kidman getting over the death of their child with a sailing trip, only for psycho Zane to hitch a lift. Made all the more frightening by there only being three characters who've got nowhere to go, it's all so slickly and terrifyingly done that the holes in the plot only become apparent later on. It works its spell much better on a large screen than the 12-inch portable in the bedroom. [95m/15]

John Ingram	Sam Neill
Rae Ingram	Nicole Kidman
Hughie Warriner	Billy Zane

The Dead Can't Lie ••• [1988]

Director: Lloyd Fonvielle
Screenplay: Lloyd Fonvielle

Maybe the dead *can't* lie, but they can still bonk apparently. So private eye Jones discovers when he encounters Madsen, a femme more than usually fatale. Enjoyably perverse, even though it loses its way in the last reel. [97m/15]

Eddie Martel Mallard	Tommy Lee Jones
Rachel Carlyle	Virginia Madsen
Father George	Frederic Forrest
Charlie Rand	Colin Bruce
Tim	Kevin Jarre

Deadline

SEE: War Zone

Deadly Friend •• [1986]

Director: Wes Craven
Screenplay: Bruce Joel Rubin

When a robot is destroyed a young man uses its brain to revive his murdered girlfriend. Unfortunately, she's not quite as grateful as he'd hoped. A middling Craven effort, half ingenious *Frankenstein* re-hash, half silly teen horror. [99m/18]

Paul	Matthew Laborteaux
Samantha	Kristy Swanson
Tom	Michael Sharrett
Jeannie	Anne Twomey
Elvira	Anne Ramsey

Deadly Pursuit ••• [1988]

Director: Roger Spottiswoode
Screenplay: Harv Zimmel, Michael Burton & Daniel Petrie Jr.

This tense thriller has Poitier, in his first role for a decade, as a city cop chasing a murderer up into the mountains with the help of guide Berenger. As implausible as so many modern films of this sort, that doesn't stop the tension racking up nicely. Also known as *Shoot to Kill*. [110m/15]

Warren Stantin	Sidney Poitier
Jonathan Knox	Tom Berenger
Sarah	Kirstie Alley
Steve	Clancy Brown
Norman	Richard Masur
Harvey	Andrew Robinson

Dead Men Don't Wear Plaid •• [1982]

Director: Carl Reiner
Screenplay: Carl Reiner, George Gipe & Steve Martin

Private eye Martin is hired by Ward to investigate her father's death and uncov-ers a fiendish Nazi plot to conquer the U.S. of A. The initially clever idea of mixing live actors in with old filmclips soon gets tiresome, particularly as the storyline is so trite. It was all done so much better later in the Griff Rhys Jones lager ads. However, Ward is deliciously sultry compensation. **[88m/PG]**

Rigby Reardon	Steve Martin
Juliet Forrest	Rachel Ward
Field Marshall VonKluck	Carl Reiner
Carlos	Reni Santoni
Dr. Forrest	George Gaynes

Blurb I'd Been Shot So Many Times You Could Use My Shirt As a Tea Strainer.

Quote 'Do you use a Dictaphone?' – 'No, I use a pencil.'

Showing *The Big Sleep, Suspicion, White Heat, The Killers, Double Indemnity, Dark Passage, In a Lonely Place*, etc.

Dead of Winter ••• [1987]

Director: **Arthur Penn**
Screenplay: **Marc Shmuger & Mark Malone**

A preposterous, yet highly entertaining, gothic tale about an actress being lured to a creepy house to play a role, only to discover that the part on offer is that of a prisoner. Forget the plot inconsistencies and enjoy the actors having fun going over the top. **[100m/15]**

Kate McGovern	Mary Steenburgen
Mr. Murray	Roddy McDowall
Dr. Joseph Lewis	Jan Rubes
Rob Sweeney	William Russ
Officer Huntley	Wayne Robson

Dead Poets Society •••• [1989]

Director: **Peter Weir**
Screenplay: **Tom Schulman**

Ignore the carpers and seize the chance to see this brilliant performance from Williams as the unconventional English teacher at a straight-laced 1959 boys' school. His love for poetry inspires them but doesn't always have the desired consequences. Yes, it's sentimental. Yes, the story's a little obvious. But it's one of those rare, life-enhancing films that make you feel so much better about things, even

if you can't later explain just why. **[129m/PG]**

John Keating	Robin Williams
Neil Perry	Robert Sean Leonard
Todd Anderson	Ethan Hawke
Knox Overstreet	Josh Charles
Charlie Dalton	Gale Hansen
Richard Cameron	Dylan Kussman
Steven Meeks	Allelon Ruggiero
Gerard Pitts	James Waterston
Mr. Perry	Kurtwood Smith
Mr. Nolan	Norman Lloyd
Ginny Danburry	Lara Flynn Boyle

Oscars Best Screenplay

Quote 'Carpe diem, lads. Seize the day. Make your lives extraordinary.' ✦ 'I was the intellectual equivalent of a 98-lb weakling. I would go to the beach and people would kick copies of Byron in my face.'

Psst! At different stages Alec Baldwin and Liam Neeson were considered for Williams' role. So was Dustin Hoffman, but he wanted to direct the film as well.

The Dead Pool •• [1988]

Director: **Buddy Van Horn**
Screenplay: **Steve Sharon**

A death list shows that a mysterious killer is not too wild about Harry. Nor were audiences for this fifth outing for Inspector Callaghan, the policeman who never actually arrests anybody. Neeson is enjoyably suspicious, though, as a director of video nasties. **[91m/18]**

Harry Callahan	Clint Eastwood
Samantha Walker	Patricia Clarkson
Peter Swan	Liam Neeson
Al Quan	Evan C. Kim

Psst! Probably the first movie in which a chase sequence involves a remote-controlled toy car.

Dead Ringers •• [1988]

Director: **David Cronenberg**
Screenplay: **David Cronenberg & Norman Snider**

Extraordinarily unpleasant, yet fascinating, tale of two gynaecologist brothers.

Identical twins, they share everything, even their women, until actress Bujold comes between them. The amazing cinematic trickery, giving us Irons playing opposite Irons, isn't enough to compensate for the film's lack of heart and its essential macabre nastiness. **[115m/18]**

Beverly/Elliot Mantle.................Jeremy Irons
Claire Niveau.....................Genevieve Bujold
Cary ....Heidi Von Palleske
Danuta ....Barbara Gordon
Laura ....Shirley Douglas

Quote 'The beauty of our business is you don't have to get out to meet beautiful women.'

Psst! Bizarrely, the film is based on a true story, although the brothers were gay rather than heterosexual.

The Dead Zone ••• [1983]

Director: **David Cronenberg**
Screenplay: **Jeffrey Boam**

Dave 'Depraved' Cronenberg in restrained mode. A clever Stephen King story about ESP is exquisitely shot and hauntingly scored. Walken is the English teacher who wakes from a five-year coma with second sight and a vision of disaster for presidential candidate Sheen. The first film in which Cronenberg showed a heart as well as an ability to revolt us. **[103m/15]**

Johnny Smith ....Christopher Walken
Sarah Bracknell........................Brooke Adams
Sheriff Bannerman ....Tom Skerritt
Dr. Sam Weizak.......................Herbert Lom
Roger Stuart ....Anthony Zerbe
Henrietta Dodd.................Colleen Dewhurst
Greg Stillson ....Martin Sheen

Dealers •• [1989]

Director: **Colin Bucksey**
Screenplay: **Andrew MacLear**

Like all young bloods in the City, McGann flies his own seaplane into work each day, landing it on the Thames. This preposterous thriller gets sillier by the minute. But it does have the wonderful De Mornay and a nice scene with McGann

wooing her by filling her flat with balloons. **[91m/15]**

Daniel Pasco.............................Paul McGann
Anna Schuman...............Rebecca De Mornay
Robby Barrell ....Derrick O'Connor
Frank Mallory...............................John Castle

Psst! The TV series *Capital City* was spun-off from this.

Death Becomes Her ••• [1992]

Director: **Robert Zemeckis**
Screenplay: **Martin Donovan & David Koepp**

The astounding special effects are the main attraction of this cast-against-type comedy. Hawn's the mousy writer who loses nerdy plastic surgeon husband Willis to glamorous actress Streep. Just when Streep fears she's losing her looks, she's offered a magic potion by vampish Rossellini. Although not quite as bellyachingly funny as it should be, this black comedy does have some lovely touches and, at long last, we finally find out what really has happened to Elvis. **[104m/PG]**

Madeline Ashton ....Meryl Streep
Ernest Menville............................Bruce Willis
Helen Sharp...............................Goldie Hawn
Lisle.....................................Isabella Rossellini
Chagall..Ian Ogilvy

Quote 'I'm glad you came. I didn't know if you would. I spoke to my PR woman and she said Madeline Ashton goes to the opening of an envelope.'

Psst! Body double Donna Baltron was used for the scene where Streep has her legs spray-painted. ◆ Catherine Bell doubled as the nude Rossellini from behind ◆ Hawn was scarred on the face when a shovel hit her during one of the fights with Streep ◆ The bewildered doctor is Sydney Pollack, director of films like *Tootsie* and *Out of Africa*.

Death in Brunswick • [1992]

Director: **John Ruane**
Screenplay: **John Ruane**

Supposed black Australian comedy about

the problems of low-life pizza cook Neill after an accidental murder. Despite the occasional flash of wit – usually pretty tasteless – Neill doesn't have what it takes to hold a comedy together. If you're in a really sick mood, you might enjoy the scene in the graveyard when they try to hide the body. **[109m/15]**

Carl Fitzgerald.................................Sam Neill
Sophie Papafagas ....Zoe Carides
Quote 'Dad thinks I'm a slut.' – 'Christ, Soph. This is Australia.'
Showing *Howling III: The Marsupials.*

Death of a Salesman ••• [1985]

Director: **Volker Schlondorff**
Screenplay: **Arthur Miller**

This straight transfer of Hoffman's Broadway revival of the Arthur Miller play shows us just what all the fuss was about. Necessarily stagey, it's still wonderful, powerful stuff with superb acting. **[135m/PG]**

Willy Loman..........................Dustin Hoffman
Charley.................................Charles Durning
Linda Loman.....................................Kate Reid
Happy Loman ....Stephen Lang
Also: Louis Zorich, David S. Chandler, Jon Polito, Linda Kozlowski

Death of a Soldier •• [1986]

Director: **Philippe Mora**
Screenplay: **William Nagle**

In wartime Australia, an American GI who murdered three women is found guilty by a military court. Although clearly insane, he is hanged to appease relations between locals and the Yanks. Based on a true story, it's vaguely unsatisfying even though the glimpse of Australia in the war is fascinating. **[93m/18]**

Maj. Patrick Dannenberg..........James Coburn
Edward J. Leonski ....Reb Brown
Dt. Sgt. Adams ....Bill Hunter
Det. Sgt. Martin.........................Maurie Fields

Death Warrant •• [1990]

Director: **Deran Sarafian**
Screenplay: **David S. Goyer**

The Muscles From Brussels is here a Mountie, of all things, going undercover in clink to find out who's been culling the prison population. Rather brutal, but well-made of its kind. **[88m/18]**

Louis Burke...........Jean-Claude Van Damme
Hawkins ....Robert Guillaume
Amanda Beckett ....Cynthia Gibb
Tom Vogler......................George Dickerson

Death Wish 3 • [1985]

Director: **Michael Winner**
Screenplay: **Michael Edmonds**

Even aged 63, Bronson's still running around blowing gangs away. As he even gets to use a missile launcher in this one, it's a wonder there are any left. **[90m/18]**

Paul Kersey ....Charles Bronson
Kathryn Davis.......................Deborah Raffin
Richard Striker.................................Ed Lauter
Bennett......................................Martin Balsam
Psst! Shot almost entirely in South London.

Death Wish 4: The Crackdown • [1987]

Director: **J. Lee Thompson**
Screenplay: **Gail Morgan Hickman**

New director. Same old story. Even older vigilante. Their imagination ran out after thinking up the punning title. **[99m/18]**

Paul Kersey ....Charles Bronson
Karen Sheldon....................................Kay Lenz
Nathan White..............................John P. Ryan

Deceived ••• [1992]

Director: **Damian Harris**
Screenplay: **Mary Agnes Donoghue**

This underrated Goldie Hawn thriller is hot stuff. She's the woman with the perfect marriage who uncovers disturbing details about her husband after he dies. All expectations to the contrary, Hawn actually acts here, emitting barely any of her girlish giggles. Though it's never clear why she doesn't just go to the police when things turn nasty, the tension builds nicely throughout, with a superbly tense finale that avoids most of the cliché traps other recent thrillers fall into. **[108m/15]**

Adrienne Saunders	Goldie Hawn
Jack Saunders	John Heard
Charlotte	Robin Bartlett
Mary Saunders	Ashley Peldon
Harvey Schwartz	Tom Irwin
Carol Gingold	Maia Filar
Tomasz Kestler	Jan Rubes

Psst! For those who are amazed at Hawn's perfect body, keep your eyes on her feet. – ample evidence that at least part of her is less than perfect ✦ The movie contains a line film writer David MacGillivray claims is one of the most over-worked in movies: 'Try and get some rest.'

The Deceivers ••   [1988]

Director: **Nicholas Meyer**
Screenplay: **Michael Hirst**

Slightly soggy adventure yarn has the less than charismatic Brosnan getting blacked-up to infiltrate the Thuggee cult in 19th-century India. Although supposedly based on fact, you don't believe it for a minute. **[100m/15]**

William Savage	Pierce Brosnan
Hussein	Saeed Jaffrey
Chandra Singh	Shashi Kapoor
Sarah Wilson	Helena Mitchell
Col. Wilson	Keith Michell

The Decline of the American Empire •   [1986]

Director: **Denys Arcand**
Screenplay: **Denys Arcand**

Decline this one. At a dinner party, a group of Canadian intellectuals rabbit on for over an hour and a half, mostly about sex. You'll fall asleep in the soup. **[101m/18]**

Dominique	Dominique Michel
Louise	Dorothee Berryman
Diane	Louise Portal
Pierre	Pierre Curzi

Deep Cover ••••   [1992]

Director: **Bill Duke**
Screenplay: **Michael Tolkin & Henry Bean**

A cracking good thriller, despite the conventional-sounding 'narcotics cop goes undercover' plot. Fishburne's the narc who discovers he's got a taste for the life of the drug dealer, while Goldblum is stunning as the wise-cracking, crooked lawyer with a penchant for gratuitous violence. Violent, gritty, exciting, funny and with great dialogue, this makes *Rush* look like a Government educational film. **[112m/18]**

John Q. Hull	Larry Fishburne
David Jason	Jeff Goldblum
Betty McCutcheon	Victoria Dillard
Jerry Carver	Charles Martin Smith
Felix Barbosa	Gregory Sierra
Ken Taft	Clarence Williams III
Hector Guzman	Rene Assa
Molto	Alex Colon

Quote 'A man has two things in this world. His word and his balls. Or is that three things?' ✦ 'What's the weirdest thing you did sexually?'

OOPS! Even though Fishburne's earring has been ripped out, it's back when he finds the young mother dead. In the next scene, it's gone again.

Psst! Director Duke, who also directed *A Rage in Harlem* appears as 'Cooke' in Arnie's *Commando*.

Deep in the Heart

SEE: Handgun

DeepStar Six •   [1989]

Director: **Sean S. Cunningham**
Screenplay: **Lewis Abernathy & Geoff Miller**

One of several underwater *Alien* variants at the end of the 80s, all of which displayed little of the excitement of their inspiration. Here it's difficult to tell which is the daftest – the script or the monster. **[99m/15]**

Capt. Phillip Laidlaw	Taurean Blacque
Dr. Joyce Collins	Nancy Everhard
Kevin McBride	Greg Evigan
Tony Snyder	Miguel Ferrer

Defence of the Realm •••• [1986]

Director: **David Drury**
Screenplay: **Martin Stellman**

They should slap a preservation order on this rare object, a cracking good British-made thriller. Byrne is the journalist digging into the background of a disgraced MP, uncovering something somebody had gone to great efforts to cover up in the first place. Despite making a few political points, it nonetheless fairly fizzes along, offering truly exciting entertainment. Why, oh why, was this just a one-off?   **[96m/PG]**

Nick Mullen	Gabriel Byrne
Nina Beckman	Greta Scacchi
Vernon Bayliss	Denholm Elliott
Dennis Markham	Ian Bannen
Victor Kingsbrook	Fulton Mackay
Jack MacLeod	Bill Paterson
Harry Champion	David Calder
Arnold Reece	Frederick Treves
Leo McAskey	Robbie Coltrane

Defending Your Life •• [1991]

Director: **Albert Brooks**
Screenplay: **Albert Brooks**

Another of those somewhat whimsical films about the afterlife in heaven, with writer-director Brooks finding he's expected to justify his life in Judgment City. Some splendid ideas raise a few smiles but the whole thing never really clicks.   **[112m/PG]**

Daniel Miller	Albert Brooks
Julia	Meryl Streep
Bob Diamond	Rip Torn
Lena Foster	Lee Grant
Dick Stanley	Buck Henry
Elderly woman on tram	Maxine Elliott
Herself	Shirley MacLaine

Delicatessen •••• [1992]

Director: **Jean-Pierre Jeunet & Marc Caro**
Screenplay: **Jean-Pierre Jeunet, Marc Caro & Gilles Adrien**

Bizarre and very funny black French comedy about a future world in which meat is hard to come by. Pity the new lodgers in Dreyfus's apartments, for the chap's a butcher as well. Far more enjoyable, and considerably less tasteless, than it sounds, this is one of the most innovative, gag-packed comedies of recent years, packing cannibalism, farce, love, satire, sex and guerilla warfare into a visually-splendid package.   **[97m/15]**

Louison	Dominique Pinon
Julie	Marie-Laure Dougnac
Butcher	Jean-Claude Dreyfus

The Delinquents •• [1989]

Director: **Chris Thomson**
Screenplay: **Clayton Frohman & Mac Gudgeon**

Kylie's big-screen debut is a tear-jerking tale of misunderstood young lovers in late 50's Australia. Nothing like as bad as many were hoping for, but it's hardly *Gone With The Wind* either.   **[103m/12]**

Lola	Kylie Minogue
Brownie	Charlie Schlatter
Mrs. Lovell	Angela Punch McGregor
Bosun	Bruno Lawrence

OOPS! Schlatter must have an amazing metabolism. Although getting soundly whipped by his stepfather, when he gets his togs off to make love to Kylie that evening, his body's in pristine condition.
Psst! The film is based on a novel by Criena Rohan, Pat Cash's auntie.

The Delta Force •• [1986]

Director: **Menahem Golan**
Screenplay: **James Bruner & Menahem Golan**

When an American plane is hijacked in the Middle East, Chuck Norris swings into action. Reasonably enjoyable, though occasionally silly, action pic. **[129m/15]**

Maj. Scott McCoy ....Chuck Norris
Col. Nick Alexander ....Lee Marvin
Ben Kaplan ....Martin Balsam
Harry Goldman ....Joey Bishop
Also: Lainie Kazan, George Kennedy, Hanna Schygulla, Susan Strasberg, Bo Svenson, Robert Vaughn, Shelley Winters

Delta Force 2: The Colombian Connection • [1990]

Director: Aaron Norris
Screenplay: Lee Reynolds

The Delta Force goes into action again, this time against a drugs baron in Latin America. Chuck Norris fans won't miss it, but the rest of us can. It's directed by Chuck's brother. **[105m/18]**

Col. Scott McCoy ....Chuck Norris
Ramon Cota ....Billy Drago
Gen. Taylor ....John P. Ryan
John Page ....Richard Jaeckel

Psst! The film is dedicated to those four members of the crew who died in a helicopter crash while making the movie.

Demolition Man [1993]

Director: Marco Brambilla
Screenplay: Daniel Waters & Jonathan Lemkin

A futuristic action thriller with Stallone as a former cop released from suspended animation to catch a psychopathic murderer. Before long, he discovers that being a cop in the future is more complicated than he thought.

John Spartan ....Sylvester Stallone
Simon Phoenix ....Wesley Snipes
Also: Lori Petty, Nigel Hawthorne, Melinda Dillon

Desert Bloom ••• [1986]

Director: Eugene Corr
Screenplay: Eugene Corr

This interesting family drama, set in Las Vegas in the early 50s and seen largely through the eyes of a young girl, would be good taken on its own account. But add the fascinating background of the first atmospheric atom bomb test and it becomes riveting. **[106m/PG]**

Rose ....Annabeth Gish
Jack ....Jon Voight
Lily ....JoBeth Williams
Starr ....Ellen Barkin
Robin ....Jay Underwood
Dee Ann ....Desiree Joseph
Mr. Mosol ....Allen Garfield

Desert Hearts ••• [1986]

Director: Donna Deitch
Screenplay: Natalie Cooper

Female academic Shaver is brought out of her shell by a lesbian encounter with Charbonneau. A sympathetic, wry and at times very passionate love story, with Shaver particularly moving as the repressed flower opening up. **[93m/18]**

Vivian Bell ....Helen Shaver
Cay Rivvers ....Patricia Charbonneau
Frances Parker ....Audra Lindley
Silver ....Andra Akers

Desperate Hours •• [1990]

Director: Michael Cimino
Screenplay: Lawrence Konner, Mark Rosenthal & Joseph Hayes

Actually it's only a desperate hour and three-quarters spent trapped watching a family being held hostage by escaped convicts. It has its moments, as it should with such a director and actors like Hopkins and Rourke. But if it's excitement you're after, watch the 1955 original. Kelly Lynch, as a micro-skirted bimbo whose blouse keeps flapping open, is the cinema's least convincing lawyer since Cher in *Suspect*. **[105m/15]**

Michael Bosworth ....Mickey Rourke
Tim Cornell ....Anthony Hopkins
Nora Cornell ....Mimi Rogers
Brenda Chandler ....Lindsay Crouse
Nancy Breyers ....Kelly Lynch
Wally Bosworth ....Elias Koteas

Desperately Seeking Susan ••• [1985]

Director: **Susan Seidelman**
Screenplay: **Leora Barish**

Once upon a time, there was a pop singer on the verge of fame who starred in a quirky, fast-paced farce that was funny and fresh. Ever since then, she's been desperately seeking Susan Seidelman – or a director as good as her – to make another successful film, failing miserably every time. Well this is the one film where Madonna really *does* get it right. She's excellent as the mysterious Susan who so fascinates bored housewife Arquette. A good, fun little movie. **[104m/15]**

Roberta	Rosanna Arquette
Susan	Madonna
Dez	Aidan Quinn
Gary	Mark Blum
Jim	Robert Joy
Leslie	Laurie Metcalf
Nolan	Will Patton
Larry	Steven Wright
Ray	John Turturro

Showing *Rebecca.*

Psst! Madonna won her part over two hundred other auditioning hopefuls ✦ Arquette was originally the star but, as the film was being made, Madonna's career suddenly took off and her part was rapidly rewritten to give her a more prominent role. Arquette's nose was put considerably out of joint by Madonna and objected to the way her song 'Into the Groove' was inserted into the movie ✦ Getting the film off the ground took some doing. Producer Midge Sanford said: 'Our standard joke was that if the film ever got made, no-one would be left to see it because everyone had read the screenplay.'

Diamond Skulls • [1990]

Director: **Nick Broomfield**
Screenplay: **Tim Rose Price**

Obscurely titled, predictable and totally irrelevant exposé on heartless aristocratic behaviour. Sets the cause of Marxism back yet another ten years. Also known as *Dark Obsession*. **[87m/18]**

Lord Hugo Buckton	Gabriel Byrne
Lady 'Ginny' Buckton	Amanda Donohoe
Lord Crewne	Michael Hordern
Lady Crewne	Judy Parfitt

Psst! Amanda Donohoe sets a personal best by baring her breasts within ten seconds of the opening titles. Until *Zandalee,* this was a movie record.

Dick Tracy •• [1990]

Director: **Warren Beatty**
Screenplay: **Jim Cash & Jack Epps Jr.**

The only one of the recent comic-book adaptations that actually *looks* like a comic, with all their garish colours and bold designs. It's a shame they didn't spend as much effort getting the script right. Still, much fun can be had from trying to spot the stars cameoing under all that make-up. Pacino's great as Big Boy, while others include Dustin Hoffman, Dick Van Dyke and James Caan. **[103m/PG]**

Dick Tracy	Warren Beatty
Kid	Charlie Korsmo
Big Boy Caprice	Al Pacino
Tess Trueheart	Glenne Headly
Breathless Mahoney	Madonna
Flattop	William Forsythe
Mumbles	Dustin Hoffman
Chief Brandon	Charles Durning
88 Keys	Mandy Patinkin
Lips Manlis	Paul Sorvino
DA Fletcher	Dick Van Dyke
Mrs. Green	Kathy Bates
Spaldoni	James Caan
Bug Bailey	Michael J. Pollard

OOPS! Watch the glass of milk as The Kid tries to leave the diner. As Tracy fetches him back, the glass he'd just polished off refills itself.

Psst! Although PG-rated, its 14 killings give it a higher body count than the original *Death Wish* film ✦ The film had the biggest-ever publicity budget [until beaten by Jurassic Park]. The $48m spent pushing the movie worldwide was marginally more than it cost ✦ Sean Young was fired as Tess Trueheart after a week, claiming it was because 'I wouldn't make out with Warren Beatty'. ✦ Madonna's breasts were glued into her tight-fitting gowns, causing the makeup man to lament: 'Each of those honeys is worth six, maybe seven million. What if she has an allergic reaction to the glue?...Not only will we be sued, we'll become known as the schmucks who destroyed a national treasure'.

Die Hard ••••   [1988]

Director: **John McTiernan**
Screenplay: **Jeb Stuart & Steven E. de Souza**

Terrorists take control of a skyscraper, not realising that supercop Willis is on hand to thwart their plans. Perhaps the best action thriller ever, with an excellent script backing up the rough stuff. The part fits Willis like a glove, while Rickman is superb as the intellectual, Jermyn Street–suited terrorist. One of those rare films that gets better on every viewing. **[131m/18]**

John McClane	Bruce Willis
Hans Gruber	Alan Rickman
Holly Gennaro McClane	Bonnie Bedelia
Karl	Alexander Godunov
Sgt. Al Powell	Reginald Veljohnson
Dwayne T. Robinson	Paul Gleason
Argyle	De'voreaux White
Thornburg	William Atherton
Ellis	Hart Bochner
Takagi	James Shigeta
Big Johnson	Robert Davi
Little Johnson	Grand L. Bush

Quote 'Welcome to the party, pal.' ✦ 'Only John can drive someone that crazy.'

OOPS! When the terrorists fire a missile at the police car, they obviously smash the window. Yet when they fire again, the glass is shattered once more ✦ Surely the terrorists would find McClane's shoes and socks after he leaves them in plain view in the bathroom?

Psst! Bruce Willis was not particularly popular when the film was launched,

which is why on the posters his face was half obscured by the skyscraper ✦ The building is the 20th Century Fox Tower, HQ of the company that made the pic.

Die Hard 2 •••   [1990]

Director: **Renny Harlin**
Screenplay: **Steven E. de Souza & Doug Richardson**

Yet another Christmas spoiled for tough cop McClane as he tackles a bunch of right-wing terrorists menacing Washington airport while his wife circles overhead. Fast and exciting and with plenty of wry humour, this sequel would be as good as the original were it not for some wild implausibilities. Not least of them is the idea that a man with a handgun not only never runs out of bullets but is invincible against baddies who play dirty by using automatic weapons. **[120m/15]**

John McClane	Bruce Willis
Holly McClane	Bonnie Bedelia
Dick Thornberg	William Atherton
Sgt. Al Powell	Reginald Veljohnson
Esperanza	Franco Nero
Col Stuart	William Sadler
Capt. Grant	John Amos
Carmine Lorenzo	Dennis Franz
Trudeau	Fred Dalton Thompson
Marvin	Tom Bower
Samantha Copeland	Sheila McCarthy
Garber	Don Harvey
O'Reilly	Robert Patrick
Burke	John Leguizamo
Pilot	Colm Meaney
Vito Lorenzo	Robert Costanzo

Blurb Die Harder

Quote 'Just the fax, ma'am. Just the fax.' ✦ 'How can the same shit happen to the same guy twice?'

OOPS! If the passengers can use the phones on the planes to contact the ground, why don't the pilots use them instead of flying blind? ✦ Although Willis rings his wife while she's in the air, it would be impossible. Calls only work the other way. ✦ Not long after we're told that Nashville airport is snowed up, flights are told to divert there ✦ Why does a plane with no fuel left burst into flames on crash-landing?

Psst! The bodycount is said to be 264, possibly the highest in mainstream Hollywood history ✦ The studio laughed when the director suggested filming this winter-set story in his native Scandinavia. An unusually mild American winter meant a frantic search for rapidly-vanishing snow and dry ice bills of $50,000 a day ✦ The video is an '18' certificate, with scenes not seen in the cinema version which was cut to get a '15' certificate.

Diggstown
SEE: Midnight Sting

Dim Sum: A Little Bit of Heart ••• [1985]

Director: **Wayne Wang**
Screenplay: **Terrel Seltzer**

A slow-paced but warm-hearted and amusing slice of Chinese life in San Francisco. An old Chinese woman is looked after by her more assimilated 30-year-old daughter and thinks the time is right for her to get married. The daughter has her own plans. It *is* a bit arty but, as they say, if you like that sort of thing...

[88m/U]

Geraldine Tam	Laureen Chew
Mrs. Tam	Kim Chew
Uncle Tam	Victor Wong
Auntie Mary	Ida F.O. Chung

Diner •••• [1982]

Director: **Barry Levinson**
Screenplay: **Barry Levinson**

Five young men on the verge of manhood spend much of their time in the Fells Point Diner trying to get to grips with what being an adult means, continually pressing each other for advice on women. An assured debut from Levinson, it's splendidly evocative and has extraordinarily

naturalistic dialogue. Full of memorable moments, particularly the scenes with the popcorn in the cinema and in the strip joint when they decide the music isn't fast enough. Wise, witty and wonderful.

[110m/15]

Eddie	Steve Guttenberg
Shrevie	Daniel Stern
Boogie	Mickey Rourke
Fenwick	Kevin Bacon
Billy	Timothy Daly
Beth	Ellen Barkin
Modell	Paul Reiser
Barbara	Kathryn Dowling
Bagel	Michael Tucker
Mrs. Simmons	Jessica James
Diane	Kelle Kipp

Blurb What They Wanted Most Wasn't On The Menu

Quote 'Fenwick. Put the damn sheep down.'

Showing *A Summer Place.*

Psst! The movie is based on Levinson's own experiences growing up in Baltimore. The original diners, upon whom he had based the characters, watched much of the film being shot.

Dirty Dancing •• [1987]

Director: **Emile Ardolino**
Screenplay: **Eleanor Bergstein**

Grey, on holiday in the Catskills with her family, falls for the attractions of dancing instructor Swayze. For some reason, her dad isn't happy. A pleasing but insubstantial soufflé that appeals to young girls but may leave others a little cold. The dancing's good fun, though it's a wonder they don't fall over all those clichés that are lying around the place.

[97m/15]

Baby Houseman	Jennifer Grey
Johnny Castle	Patrick Swayze
Jake Houseman	Jerry Orbach
Penny Johnson	Cynthia Rhodes
Max Kellerman	Jack Weston

OOPS! When Swayze returns for the final dance number, he takes off his jacket twice ✦ Soon afterwards, he leaps from the stage and gets dirt on his knees. But it vanishes in the next shot.

Dirty Rotten Scoundrels •••• [1988]

Director: Frank Oz
Screenplay: Dale Launer, Stanley Shapiro & Paul Henning

1964's *Bedtime Story* isn't a patch on this remake, a delicious battle between rival conmen Caine and Martin to see which of them must move away from the lucrative French Riviera. Despite a mite too much silliness from Martin, the jokes fly thick and fast and are supported by a wonderfully clever, twisting, plot that keeps you guessing. A comic delight.

[110m/PG]

Freddy Benson	Steve Martin
Lawrence Jamieson	Michael Caine
Janet Colgate	Glenne Headly
Inspector Andre	Anton Rogers
Fanny Eubanks	Barbara Harris
Arthur	Ian McDiarmid
Mrs. Reed	Dana Ivey

Psst! Originally developed as a musical vehicle for Mick Jagger and David Bowie! ◆ The scene in the trailer with Martin pushing the old woman into the water wasn't in the movie, being shot specially for the ad.

Distant Voices, Still Lives •• [1988]

Director: Terence Davies
Screenplay: Terence Davies

...Still Born, more like. Life in the slums of Liverpool in the 50s, chock-full of drunken, abusive fathers, nobly suffering wives and tearful pub singalongs. Shot in an attractively stylised manner, this film is an inspiration to some and an over-praised, bum-numbing puzzle to rather more. [85m/15]

Mother	Freda Dowie
Father	Pete Postlethwaite
Eileen	Angela Walsh
Tony	Dean Williams
Maisie	Lorraine Ashbourne

The Distinguished Gentlemen •• [1992]

Director: Jonathan Lynn
Screenplay: Marty Kaplan

A conman realises the big scams are carried out in Congress and so, with amazingly little effort, Mr. Murphy Goes To Washington. Although Eddie is back on form, this is little more than a vehicle for a series of his stand-up routines. Funny though they are, the script is flabby and lacks bite, turning yuckily sentimental once a young cancer victim is wheeled into his office. [114m/15]

Thomas Jefferson Johnson	Eddie Murphy
Dick Dodge	Lane Smith
Miss Loretta	Sheryl Lee Ralph
Olaf Andersen	Joe Don Baker
Celia Kirby	Victoria Rowell

Also: Grant Shaud, Kevin McCarthy, Charles S. Dutton, Victor Rivers, Noble Willingham

Quote 'We feel that the semi-automatic weapon's gotten a bad rap.'

Psst! Test audiences didn't like the original ending which had Murphy giving a Capraesque, don't-forget-the-little-man speech. He was paid half a million dollars to film a new ending ◆ Look out for a brief, un-Rockford-like cameo from James Garner.

D.O.A. (Dead on Arrival) •• [1988]

Director: Rocky Morton & Annabel Jankel
Screenplay: Charles Edward Pogue

This remake of a 1949 film noir has Quaid, given a slow-acting poison, setting out to find his own murderer before it's too late. Alternates between being gripping and silly throughout. [98m/15]

Dexter Cornell	Dennis Quaid
Sydney Fuller	Meg Ryan
Mrs. Fitzwaring	Charlotte Rampling
Hal Petersham	Daniel Stern

Psst! Directors Jankel and Morton were the creators of Max Headroom.

Doc Hollywood •• [1991]

Director: Michael Caton-Jones
Screenplay: Jeffrey Price, Peter S. Seaman & Daniel Pyne

En route to life as a rich plastic surgeon in Hollywood, doctor Fox crashes in Hicksville, South Carolina. Sentenced to community service in the local hospital, he falls for the charms of Warner but remains immune to the spell of rural life. A pleasing film with some nice touches, it keeps relapsing into the mundane and is marred by one extraordinary tasteless scene with Warner urinating to put hunters off their prey's scent. [104m/12]

Dr Benjamin Stone	Michael J. Fox
Lou	Julie Warner
Dr Hogue	Barnard Hughes
Henry "Hank" Gordon	Woody Harrelson
Mayor Nick Nicholson	David Ogden Stiers
Lillian	Frances Sternhagen
Dr Halberstrom	George Hamilton
Nancy Lee	Bridget Fonda

Showing *The General.*

Psst! Watch for the great in-joke at the end where Fonda asks if that's a star over there. 'No,' says Woody, 'That's Ted Danson.'

The Doctor and the Devils • [1986]

Director: Freddie Francis
Screenplay: Ronald Harwood

Thirty-two years after it was buried, a script is exhumed and brought fitfully to life. This uplifting tale of grave-robbers Burke and Hare keeping doctor Dalton supplied with fresh corpses is nearly so bad it's funny, with Twiggy as a hooker particularly worthy of derision. [93m/18]

Dr. Thomas Rock	Timothy Dalton
Robert Fallon	Jonathan Pryce
Jenny Bailey	Twiggy
Dr. Murray	Julian Sands

Also: Stephen Rea, Phyllis Logan, Beryl Reid, T.P. McKenna, Patrick Stewart

Psst! Until recently this held the record for the longest gap between script and film,

with 32 years elapsing after Dylan Thomas wrote it before it hit cinemas. The new record-holder, *Rebecca's Daughters*, is also, bizarrely, based on a Dylan Thomas script.

The Doctor •• [1992]

Director: Randa Haines
Screenplay: Robert Caswell

A doctor whose wise-cracking bedside manner stems from watching too much M*A*S*H, gets a dose of his own medicine when he develops cancer. In a gleaming hospital any National Health patient would die for, Hurt's inhumane treatment includes being kept waiting the odd half hour for an appointment and being compelled to fill out a few forms. Through his friendship with fellow patient Perkins, he becomes a better person and thus a better doctor. Quick, nurse! Pass the sick bag. [123m/12]

Jack MacKee	William Hurt
Anne MacKee	Christine Lahti
June Ellis	Elizabeth Perkins
Murray Caplan	Mandy Patinkin
Eli Blumfeld	Adam Arkin
Nicky	Charlie Korsmo

Quote 'Tell your husband you look like a Playboy centrefold and you've got the staples to prove it.'

Psst! Winner of the award for the Most Blatant Attempt To Plug A Soundtrack, when cancer patients Hurt and Perkins stop off for a three-minute dance in the desert ✦ Hurt replaced Warren Beatty.

Dogs in Space • [1987]

Director: Richard Lowenstein
Screenplay: Richard Lowenstein

This awful Australian film about the punk era in Melbourne is notable only for the film debut of Michael Hutchence of INXS. Pointless and extremely unpleasant. Never have end credits been more welcomed. [108m/18]

Sam	Michael Hutchence
Anna	Saskia Post
Tim	Nique Needles

Dominick and Eugene
SEE: Nicky and Gino

Don't Tell Her It's Me • [1992]

Director: Malcolm Mowbray
Screenplay: Sarah Bird

When Guttenberg gets nowhere with Gertz, he tries to turn himself into the macho man of her dreams. This nightmare of a film is a perfect example of Rose's Rule #3. [102m/12]

Gus Kubiak	Steve Guttenberg
Emily Pear	Jami Gertz
Lizzie Potts	Shelley Long
Trout	Kyle MacLachlan
Mitchell	Kevin Scannell
Mandy	Mädchen Amick

Don't Tell Mom the Babysitter's Dead •• [1992]

Director: Stephen Herek
Screenplay: Neil Landau & Tara Ison

No sooner has Mom popped off to Oz, than (in a plot twist that had audiences reeling with surprise) the baby-sitter pops her clogs, leaving the kids to fend for themselves. A great idea is largely wasted, although it gets funnier towards the end. If you've started, you may as well finish. [105m/12]

Sue Ellen Crandell	Christina Applegate
Rose Lindsey	Joanna Cassidy
Gus Brandon	John Getz
Bryan	Josh Charles
Kenny Crandell	Keith Coogan
Mom	Concetta Tomei

Quote 'Sue Ellen. Every girl over 25 should have a cucumber in the house.'

The Doors •• [1991]

Director: Oliver Stone
Screenplay: Oliver Stone & J. Randal Johnson

The Doors are unhinged by drugs, the adulations of crowds and groupies, and the egocentric behaviour of their lead singer. Kilmer is uncannily convincing as Jim Morrison but, as usual with the women in Stone's films, Ryan is totally wasted. So are we. After two-and-a-half hours of overkill and hallucinations, we're begging to go cold turkey. [141m/18]

Jim Morrison	Val Kilmer
Robby Krieger	Frank Whaley
John Densmore	Kevin Dillon
Pamela Courson	Meg Ryan
Ray Manzarek	Kyle MacLachlan
Dog	Dennis Burkley
Cat	Billy Idol
Bill Siddons	Josh Evans
Tom Baker	Michael Madsen

Quote 'Listen, anybody who throws his girlfirend into the closet and sets it on fire can't be all bad, huh?' [Oliver Stone on Jim Morrison]

OOPS! Ryan throws food at Kilmer during an argument, getting it over his face and clothes. But his face is clean in the next shot ✦ When Kilmer's in the shower, we hear him called 'Val' ✦ Near the end, as Kilmer is sitting on a ledge, you can catch a glimpse of a poster for *Another 48HRS*, twenty years too early.

Psst! Morrison's butt is not Kilmer's but a body double ✦ John Travolta had earlier been announced as having signed up for the lead ✦ Look out for cameos from the likes of Eric Burden, Mimi Rogers as a photographer and Crispin Glover as Andy Warhol. Stone, who crops up in most of his films, here has a walk-on as a film professor.

Do the Right Thing •••• [1989]

Director: Spike Lee
Screenplay: Spike Lee

Though not a perfect film, this is still a provocative, convincing portrait of American inner-city tensions as frustration boils over into violence. Witty and scorchingly shot, Lee erred only in predicting the uprising taking place in New York rather than Los Angeles. [120m/18]

Sal	Danny Aiello
Da Mayor	Ossie Davis

Mother Sister .... Ruby Dee
Vito .... Richard Edson
Buggin' Out .... Giancarlo Esposito
Mookie .... Spike Lee
Radio Raheem .... Bill Nunn
Pino .... John Turturro
Tina .... Rosie Perez

Psst! Robert De Niro was originally signed to play Sal but dropped out ✦ Joie, Lee's real-life sister, plays his sister in the film ✦ The credits have an appeal to audiences to vote. Lee hoped that people would kick out New York's Mayor Koch, perhaps best-known as a guest-star of *The Muppets Take Manhattan*.

Double Impact • [1992]

Director: **Sheldon Lettich**
Screenplay: **Sheldon Lettich & Jean-Claude Van Damme**

Two Van Dammes for your money is even worse value than one. Here he plays twins, separated when babies, who get together to avenge their parents' murder. The only interest in this violent actioner is watching Van Damme having trouble trying to remember which brother he's supposed to be playing. **[100m/18]**

Chad/Alex .... Jean-Claude Van Damme
Frank Avery .... Geoffrey Lewis
Nigel Griffith .... Alan Scarfe

Double X • [1992]

Director: **Shani S. Grewal**
Screenplay: **Shani S. Grewal**

Candidate for the funniest bad film ever. Gormless Norman Wisdom goes on the run from a criminal organisation led by Hill, hamming it up with the stagiest limp yet seen on screen. A thriller so atrociously made, it looks like one of those awful generic cinema ads that end with someone saying: 'For really great Chinese food, try Joe's in the High Street.' It's as funny as most of Wisdom's proper comedies. Lovers of all-time turkeys should seek it out. **[97m/15]**

Edward Ross .... Simon Ward
Michael Cooper .... William Katt

Arthur Clutton .... Norman Wisdom
Iggy Smith .... Bernard Hill
Jenny Eskridge .... Gemma Craven

OOPS! Keep an eye on the stuntmen. One of them dies at least twice.

Down and Out in Beverly Hills ••• [1986]

Director: **Paul Mazursky**
Screenplay: **Paul Mazursky & Leon Capetanos**

Tramp Nolte tries to drown himself in hanger-king Dreyfuss's pool then, when taken in by the family, takes over their lives and remoulds them, as well as schtupping a few. Although nothing like as sharp as it could be, there's still plenty to enjoy in this amusing satire on the lifestyles of the rich and famous in LA.
 [103m/15]

Jerry Baskin .... Nick Nolte
Davie Whiteman .... Richard Dreyfuss
Barbara Whiteman .... Bette Midler
Orvis Goodnight .... Little Richard
Jenny Whiteman .... Tracy Nelson
Carmen .... Elizabeth Pena

Psst! The film is based on the hysterical 1932 French film *Boudu Sauvé Des Eaux* ✦ When Nolte shows the dog the delights of canned pet food, that really is dog food he's eating ✦ Director Mazursky plays Sidney Waxman, Dreyfuss's accountant.

Down by Law •• [1986]

Director: **Jim Jarmusch**
Screenplay: **Jim Jarmusch**

Black and white comedy about a couple of losers joined in a Southern jail by Italian Benigni, whose command of English is somewhat tenuous. So slight you could blow it away, but it's fitfully amusing.
 [106m/15]

Zack .... Tom Waits
Jack .... John Lurie
Roberto .... Roberto Benigni
Nicoletta .... Nicoletta Braschi
Laurette .... Ellen Barkin

Dracula
SEE: Bram Stoker's Dracula

Dragnet •• [1987]
Director: Tom Mankiewicz
Screenplay: Dan Aykroyd, Alan Zweibel
& Tom Mankiewicz

This spoof of the 60's TV series unfortunately drags on for far too long. Aykroyd
and Hanks are good fun as the straight-
by-the-book cop and his rather looser
partner. But it loses pace and many jokes
will be lost on those who aren't word-
perfect on the original. [106m/PG]

Friday ....Dan Aykroyd
Streebek..Tom Hanks
Whirley........................Christopher Plummer
Bill Gannon.............................Harry Morgan
Also: Alexandra Paul, Elizabeth Ashley,
Dabney Coleman

Psst! Famous in Hollywood for having the
shortest pitch ever. Producer David
Permut (who invented those maps to the
stars' homes) reputedly did no more than
point at Dan Aykroyd and sing 'Dum-
da-dum-dum', the first four notes of the
Dragnet theme. It was enough for the
studio to sign on the dotted line ✦ It is
said that this has the first post-AIDS
scene in a mainstream American film
where Hanks loses out through having
no condoms.

Dragon: The Bruce
Lee Story •• [1993]
Director: Rob Cohen
Screenplay: Edward Khmara, John Raffo &
Rob Cohen

A well-made but overlong tale of the brief
life of martial arts star Bruce Lee.
Although entertaining in places with some
good fights, the story still suffers from
many of the usual biopic probems. [121m]

Bruce Lee................................Jason Scott Lee
Linda Lee....................................Lauren Holly
Bill Krieger.............................Robert Wagner
Vivian Emery........................Michael Learned

Dreamchild ••• [1985]
Director: Gavin Millar
Screenplay: Dennis Potter

An original, imaginative account of Lewis
Carroll and young Alice Hargreaves, and
how *Alice in Wonderland* haunted her and
subsequent generations, although for different reasons. For once Dennis Potter
keeps his libidinous obsessions under
control, but the film is slightly marred by
some appallingly unconvincing New
York settings. [94m/PG]

Mrs. Hargreaves ....Coral Browne
Rev. Dodgson ....Ian Holm
Jack Dolan ....Peter Gallagher
Sally..Caris Corfman
Lucy......................................Nicola Cowper
Mrs. Liddell...................................Jane Asher
Little Alice ....Amelia Shankley

Dream Demon • [1988]
Director: Harley Cokliss
Screenplay: Christopher Wicking

Below-par, pointless, British psychological horror movie. [89m/18]

Diana Markham ....Jemma Redgrave
Oliver................................Mark Greenstreet
Jenny...................................Kathleen Wilhoite
Also: Jimmy Nail, Timothy Spall

Dreamscape ••• [1984]
Director: Joseph Ruben
Screenplay: David Loughery, Chuck
Russell & Joseph Ruben

An intriguing sci-fi thriller has Quaid as
the psychic who becomes Von Sydow's
guinea pig in experiments to put someone
into somebody else's dreams. When the
President is having holocaustal nightmares, Quaid's the man to get him back to
counting sheep. Enjoyable stuff. [98m/15]

Alex...Dennis Quaid
Paul..:Max Von Sydow
Bob ....Christopher Plummer
President ....Eddie Albert
Jane...Kate Capshaw
Tommy Ray ....David Patrick Kelly
Charlie.......................................George Wendt

The Dream Team •••• [1989]

Director: Howard Zieff
Screenplay: Jon Connolly & David Loucka

Delightfully funny comedy thriller about four mental patients who have to fend for themselves in the middle of Manhattan when they become separated from their doctor escort. Some great performances and a nice old-fashioned plot with plenty of twists and turns make this a treat to watch. It's also screamingly funny, with laugh building on laugh. If only there were more comedies like this. **[113m/15]**

Billy Caulfield ....Michael Keaton
Henry Sikorsky ....Christopher Lloyd
Jack McDermott ....Peter Boyle
Albert Ianuzzi ....Stephen Furst
Riley ....Lorraine Bracco
Dr. Weitzman ....Dennis Boutsikaris
Dr. Newald ....Milo O'Shea
O'Malley ....Philip Bosco
Also: James Remar, Jack Gilpin, Brad Sullivan, Tico Wells

Quote 'It's great to be young and insane.'

The Dresser ••• [1983]

Director: Peter Yates
Screenplay: Ronald Harwood

Old-style actor manager Finney, trying to keep his touring troupe going during the war, is mollycoddled by his camp dresser Courtenay. Despite looking as if it's been adapted from a play, which it has, this is still wonderfully entertaining drama from two of the best troupers in the business. **[118m/PG]**

Sir ....Albert Finney
Norman ....Tom Courtenay
Oxenby ....Edward Fox
Her Ladyship ....Zena Walker
Madge ....Eileen Atkins
Frank Carrington ....Michael Gough

The Dressmaker • [1989]

Director: Jim O'Brien
Screenplay: John McGrath

Liverpudlian sisters Whitelaw and Plowright meddle in the wartime romance of their niece and a GI. A thin story is stitched together at a funereal pace. **[92m/15]**

Nellie ....Joan Plowright
Margo ....Billie Whitelaw
Rita ....Jane Horrocks
Jack ....Pete Postlethwaite

Driving Me Crazy ••• [1992]

Director: Peter Faiman
Screenplay: John Hughes

Underrated John Hughes comedy about a spoilt snob of a kid being dragged home for Thanksgiving by his mum's blue-collar boyfriend. Although a trifle sentimental in parts, in the usual Hughes manner, there's plenty of good sparky dialogue and the pace of the story-telling never lets up. Also known as *Dutch*. **[107m/12]**

Dutch Dooley ....Ed O'Neill
Doyle Standish ....Ethan Randall
Natalie Standish ....JoBeth Williams
Also: Christopher McDonald, Ari Meyers, E.G. Daily

Quote 'If you insult Natalie again I'll hit you so fucking hard your dog will bleed.'

Driving Miss Daisy ••• [1989]

Director: Bruce Beresford
Screenplay: Alfred Uhry

Oscar-winning, cosy, soft-centred adaptation of the cosy, soft-centred stage play about the cantankerous and bigoted old Jewish lady who is mellowed by her black chauffeur. The performances are great, but it's all a bit schmaltzy.. **[99m/U]**

Hoke Colburn ....Morgan Freeman
Daisy Werthan ....Jessica Tandy
Boolie Werthan ....Dan Aykroyd
Florine Werthan ....Patti LuPone
Idella ....Esther Rolle

Oscars Best Picture, Jessica Tandy, Best Screenplay (adapted)

OOPS! Hoke seems to be taking Miss Daisy for a ride in more senses than one. On the way back from the synagogue, they pass the same house with the same van in front of it twice • When they drive from Georgia into Alabama, the policemen they encounter are wearing Georgia patches.

Psst! At 80, Tandy became the oldest actor to win an Oscar.

Drop Dead Fred •   [1991]

Director: Ate de Jong
Screenplay: Carlos Davis & Anthony Fingleton

Cates is suddenly revisited by her noisy, prank-playing, imaginary childhood friend. Nothing she does will make him go away. Unfortunately, Mayall's manic performance must have put the cause of British comics in Hollywood back a fair few years.   [99m/12]

Elizabeth Cronin	Phoebe Cates
Drop Dead Fred	Rik Mayall
Polly	Marsha Mason

Also: Tim Matheson, Carrie Fisher, Keith Charles, Bridget Fonda

Drowning by Numbers •••   [1988]

Director: Peter Greenaway
Screenplay: Peter Greenaway

Three East Anglian woman, all called Cissie Colpitts, murder their husbands, seducing the local coroner to help them escape scot-free. Strong acting and evocative photography of the English landscape are the best parts of this typical Greenaway treatise on games-playing. Once you see where it's heading, you wish it would hurry up.   [118m/18]

Cissie Colpitts	Joan Plowright
2nd Cissie Colpitts	Juliet Stevenson
3rd Cissie Colpitts	Joely Richardson
Nery Madgettt	Bernard Hill
Smut	Jason Edwards
Jake	Bryan Pringle

Psst! Note for pseuds: The numbers 1 to 100 appear consecutively. Trying to spot them does help pass the time. ◆ There are credits at the end for a 'pyrotechnics expert' and an 'entomologist'.

Drugstore Cowboy ••   [1989]

Director: Gus Van Sant
Screenplay: Gus Van Sant & Daniel Yost

The sordid life of a bunch of addicts in the early 70s who don't bother with prescriptions when getting stuff from their local chemists. Downbeat, well-acted and convincing portrayal of junkies. Suffers from the usual problem of watching other people getting high.   [100m/18]

Bob Hughes	Matt Dillon
Dianne Hughes	Kelly Lynch
Rick	James Le Gros
Nadine	Heather Graham

Quote 'Don't get the idea that it was easy. Being a dope fiend was hard work.'

Psst! Based on an unpublished novel by addict and thief James Fogle, written while in prison ◆ William S. Burroughs, author of *Naked Lunch* appears as 'Tom the priest'.

A Dry White Season ••   [1989]

Director: Euzhan Palcy
Screenplay: Euzhan Palcy & Colin Welland

Worthy but often dull story of Afrikaner Sutherland waking up to the horrors of apartheid when his gardener is tortured and killed. Although he doesn't really fit into the film, Marlon Brando steals the show in a brief appearance as a world-weary lawyer.   [101m/15]

Ben du Toit	Donald Sutherland
Susan du Toit	Janet Suzman
Stanley	Zakes Mokae
Captain Stolz	Jurgen Prochnow
Melanie Bruwer	Susan Sarandon
Ian McKenzie	Marlon Brando

Psst! The first film for a major Hollywood studio (MGM) to be directed by a black woman.

Dudes •   [1987]

Director: Penelope Spheeris
Screenplay: J. Randal Johnson

Three punks heading from New York to California run foul of intolerant, violent redneck types in Arizona. Tiresome, peculiarly-handled, revenge tale. **[90m/15]**

Grant	Jon Cryer
Biscuit	Daniel Roebuck
Milo	Flea

Duet for One •• [1987]

Director: **Andrei Konchalovsky**
Screenplay: **Tom Kempinski, Jeremy Lipp & Andrei Konchalovsky**

A play that seemed so powerful on stage, when performed by just two characters is weakened by being opened out on screen, ending up nothing more than a bland eye-moistener. Andrews is better than you expect as the famous violinist who develops multiple sclerosis, but there's always that nagging worry that she might burst into song at any moment. **[107m/15]**

Stephanie Anderson	Julie Andrews
David Cornwallis	Alan Bates
Dr. Louis Feldman	Max Von Sydow
Constantine Kassani	Rupert Everett
Sonia Randvich	Margaret Courtenay
Totter	Liam Neeson

Psst! Rumour has it that Julie Andrews' husband Blake Edwards tried to buy up every print of the film to stop it being seen again. If only he'd done it to some of his other movies.

Dune • [1984]

Director: **David Lynch**
Screenplay: **David Lynch**

Special effects have rarely looked as good as in this David Lynch-directed version of the vast Frank Herbert sci-fi novel. But to what end? Lynch himself may understand what it all means, but nobody else on this planet appears to. **[140m/PG]**

Paul Atreides	Kyle MacLachlan
Lady Jessica	Francesca Annis
Piter DeVries	Brad Dourif
Feyd Rautha	Sting
Baron Harkonnen	Kenneth McMillan

Also: Dean Stockwell, Linda Hunt, Max Von Sydow, Jose Ferrer, Freddie Jones, Richard Jordan, Sian Phillips, Jurgen Prochnow, Patrick Stewart, Sean Young

Dust ••• [1986]

Director: **Marion Hansel**
Screenplay: **Marion Hansel**

Birkin has devoted herself to looking after grumpy father Howard on their South African farm. When he makes goggle-eyes at his black worker's young bride, she jumps off the deep end and starts sinking. The superb, controlled, performance from Birkin is mesmerising. **[87m/18]**

Magda	Jane Birkin
Father	Trevor Howard
Hendrik	John Matshikiza
Klein Anna	Nadine Uwampa

Dust Devil •• [1993]

Director: **Richard Stanley**
Screenplay: **Richard Stanley**

A lone, black-hatted hitcher with a penchant for murdering young ladies in the Namibian desert encounters Field after she's walked out on her husband. An intriguing, stylish, occasionally horrific, murder mystery flawed by some weak performances and dialogue. **[105m/18]**

Hitch	Robert Burke
Wendy Robinson	Chelsea Field
Ben Mukurob	Zakes Mokae
Joe Niemand	John Matshikiza
Dr. Leidzinger	Marianne Sägebrecht
Capt. Beyman	William Hootkins

Dutch

SEE: Driving Me Crazy

Dying Young • [1991]

Director: **Joel Schumacher**
Screenplay: **Richard Friedenberg**

...But still not young enough. This misjudged, mismanaged weepie has Roberts nursing the terminally-ill Scott. Surprise, surprise, they fall for each other. Even worse than it sounds. **[112m/12]**

Hilary O'Neal	Julia Roberts
Victor Geddes	Campbell Scott
Gordon	Vincent D'Onofrio

Estelle Whittier ....Colleen Dewhurst
Richard Geddes ....David Selby
Mrs. O'Neal ....Ellen Burstyn

Quote 'I have only one thing to give you – my heart.'

Psst! Colleen Dewhurst, playing Scott's mother in the film, is his real-life mom. George C. Scott is his father ✦ The original ending was tougher, with Roberts driving off with the boy next door.

E

Earth Girls Are Easy • [1989]

Director: Julien Temple
Screenplay: Julie Brown, Charlie Coffey & Terrence McNally

It's the old, old story. A bunch of hairy aliens crash-land in the pool of a dizzy Valley girl who just happens to be a hairdresser. Depilating them, she discovers that underneath they're cool, sexy guys. The idea of this comedy-cum-musical is great, the execution abysmal. The special effects make *Doctor Who* look like *Star Wars* while the jokes are pathetic. The highlight comes about three-quarters of the way through when Brown, who also co-wrote, does the great number *Coz I'm a Blonde*. [100m/PG]

Valerie Dale ....Geena Davis
Mac...Jeff Goldblum
Wiploc ....Jim Carrey
Zeebo.....................................Damon Wayans
Candy Pink....................................Julie Brown

Blurb He's From Outer Space. She's From Los Angeles. At Least They Have Something In Common.

Quote 'It just wouldn't work. You're from out of town. The phone bills would be hellish.'

Showing *Earth vs. the Flying Saucers* [among others].

Eating Raoul ••• [1982]

Director: Paul Bartel
Screenplay: Richard Blackburn & Paul Bartel

Black comedies don't come much blacker than this. Woronov and Bartel are the dry couple who want to start their own restaurant and stumble across the idea of luring sex-seekers through an ad in a singles magazine. They're such amiable people, these two, it's hard not to sympathise with them. A tasty little film. [87m/18]

Mary Bland ....Mary Woronov
Paul Bland ....Paul Bartel
Raoul...Robert Beltran
Mr. Leech ....Buck Henry
Mr. Kray ....Richard Paul
Hippy...Ed Begley Jr.

Quote 'It's amazing what you can do with a cheap piece of meat if you know how to treat it.'

Psst! Bartel raised the money from his family and friends and filmed whenever he had enough cash.

Eat the Peach ••• [1986]

Director: Peter Ormrod
Screenplay: Peter Ormrod & John Kelleher

A couple of Irish lads decide to build a motorcyle wall of death after seeing Presley in *Roustabout*. It's not as easy as they hoped. This uneven but charming film deserves credit for being an original take on an apparently true story. [95m/PG]

Vinnie ....Stephen Brennan
Arthur................................Eamon Morrissey
Nora.....................................Catherine Byrne

Eat the Rich • [1987]

Director: Peter Richardson
Screenplay: Peter Richardson & Pete Richens

Dated and extremely unfunny political satire from the Comic Strip, involving a cannabalist restaurant and a Home

Secretary who uses the Krays' methods for solving crises. Rightly belongs on the small screen, but anything bigger than 12 inches is too grand. **[90m/18]**

Commander Fortune....................Ronald Allen
Jeremy......................................Robbie Coltrane
Also: Sandra Dorne, Jimmy Fagg, Lemmy, Nosher Powell

Psst! Fast forward, and you'll catch glimpses of decaying 'personalities' like Paul and Linda McCartney, Bill Wyman, Fiona Richmond, Koo Stark and Sandy Shaw.

Echo Park •• [1986]

Director: **Robert Dornhelm**
Screenplay: **Michael Ventura**

This little film of three young wannabees in a mean part of Los Angeles is pleasing in parts, but unexceptional. The actress and the songwriter we can accept as artists who might one day make it. But the Austrian bodybuilder who wants to make it onto the screen? Come on. Some things are just too ridiculous, even for the movies! **[92m/15]**

May....................................Susan Dey
Jonathan...........................Tom Hulce
August..............................Michael Bowen
Henry...............................Christopher Walker

Eddie and the Cruisers •• [1983]

Director: **Martin Davidson**
Screenplay: **Martin Davidson & Arlene Davidson**

A reporter is trying to do a piece on a famous 60's rock band, which broke up in odd circumstances. We're into flashback territory but, without a decent script to guide us or the actors, it's fairly mundane stuff. **[92m/PG]**

Frank..................................Tom Berenger
Eddie.................................Michael Pare
Doc....................................Joe Pantoliano
Sal.....................................Matthew Laurance
Ann....................................Helen Schneider
Maggie..............................Ellen Barkin

Edge of Sanity • [1989]

Director: **Gerard Kikoine**
Screenplay: **J.P. Felix & Ron Raley**

The title seems an apt description of the mental state of the people who made this drivel. Over-twitchy, over-acting Perkins is not only Dr. Jekell but also Mr. Hyde and, just for good measure, Jack the Ripper as well. Poor Glynis Barber realises too late she's in a laughable porno slasher. **[90m/18]**

Dr. Jekyll/Mr. Hyde.............Anthony Perkins
Elisabeth Jekyll.........................Glynis Barber
Susannah.........................Sarah Maur-Thorp
Underwood.................................David Lodge

OOPS! This East European-filmed stab at Victorian London is rendered slightly less convincing by the presence of pound coins.

Educating Rita ••• [1983]

Director: **Lewis Gilbert**
Screenplay: **Willy Russell**

Caine and Walters make a great screen comedy team in this adaption of the successful play. He's the boozy English professor bullied by a Liverpudlian hairdresser into teaching her, despite the strains it places on her home life. This is Russell's best work. Peppered with home truths and superb dialogue, it makes for an often downright hilarious movie. Walters is brilliant in her film debut. **[110m/15]**

Dr. Frank Bryant......................Michael Caine
Rita...Julie Walters
Brian...................................Michael Williams
Trish....................................Maureen Lipman
Julia....................................Jeananne Crowley
Denny................................Malcolm Douglas

Quote 'Putting on 35 pounds for *Educating Rita* was simple. Taking it off took longer. I live in Beverly Hills so I took the Beverly Hills diet. I ate a lot of pineapple and it made me spotty. So I ate a lot of Nivea cream.' [Caine]

Psst! Director Gilbert and Caine had worked together almost twenty years earlier on *Alfie*.

Edward Scissorhands •• [1990]

Director: **Tim Burton**
Screenplay: **Caroline Thompson**

An inventor dies before completing his creation of a boy, leaving him with scissors for hands. Adopted by Avon lady Wiest, he is initially welcomed with open arms by the local community, before hostility to anything alien resurfaces. This imaginative modern fairy tale has some truly weird designs, but it's hard to get involved with the characters. Like Burton's *Batman* films, your view probably depends on whether you love his amazing visual style or whether you prefer a strong story. **[105m/PG]**

Edward Scissorhands ....Johnny Depp
Kim Boggs ....Winona Ryder
Peg Boggs ....Dianne Wiest
Jim ....Anthony Michael Hall
Joyce Monroe ....Kathy Baker
Bill Boggs ....Alan Arkin
Inventor ....Vincent Price

Psst! Tom Cruise was offered, but turned down, the lead role.

Edward II •• [1991]

Director: **Derek Jarman**
Screenplay: **Derek Jarman, Stephen McBride & Ken Butler**

Jarman's usual happy family movie. An adaptation of Marlowe's grim, gay play of court favouritism and lethal games of poker is stylish and boasts a terrific Queen Isabella in Tilda Swinton. Unfortunately, the two male leads are so tiresomely portrayed, you end up sympathising with their oppressors. **[90m/18]**

King Edward II ....Steven Waddington
Gaveston...............................Andrew Tiernan
Queen Isabella..........................Tilda Swinton
Mortimer ....Nigel Terry

Eight Men Out •• [1988]

Director: **John Sayles**
Screenplay: **John Sayles**

No doubt this immaculately detailed retelling of the infamous 1919 'Black Sox'

baseball scandal is fascinating to Americans. But the story of why eight Chicago White Sox should throw a match in the World Series is about as exciting to us as a film of the Bodyline affair would be to them. Baseball? I mean, it's just rounders really, isn't it? **[120m/PG]**

Buck Weaver................................John Cusack
Charles Comiskey.....................Clifton James
Arnold Rothstein.....................Michael Lerner
Bill Burns..........................Christopher Lloyd
Hap Felsch................................Charlie Sheen
Eddie Cicotte.........................David Strathairn
'Shoeless' Joe Jackson................D.B. Sweeney
Also: Jace Alexander, Perry Lang, John Mahoney, James Read, John Sayles, Maggie Renzi, Nancy Travis, Don Harvey

Psst! Studs Turkel appears as Hugh Fullerton the sportswriter while writer-director Sayles is Ring Lardner.

18 Again! • [1988]

Director: **Paul Flaherty**
Screenplay: **Josh Goldstein & Jonathan Prince**

Pretty unfunny addition to the crop of body-switch movies with Burns getting a knock on his head and turning into his 18-year-old grandson. Schlatter does a passable impression of Burns as a young man, but we see far too little of the wisecracker himself. If they'd just turned the camera on him alone for an hour and a half, we'd have something worth watching. **[100m/PG]**

Jack Watson...............................George Burns
David Watson.....................Charlie Schlatter
Arnold ....Tony Roberts

Psst! George Burns was 92 when he made the film. 'I'm at that age now,' he said, 'where just putting my cigar in its holder is a thrill.'

84 Charing Cross Road ••• [1987]

Director: **David Jones**
Screenplay: **Hugh Whitemore**

An adaptation of Helen Hanff's book of

correspondence between her, an avid New York book collector, and the somewhat stuffy Hopkins at the London bookshop. From such amazingly insubstantial material has been wrought a leisurely and wholly delightful film which highlights the essential differences between the two countries. **[97m/U]**

Helene Hanff	Anne Bancroft
Frank Doel	Anthony Hopkins
Nora Doel	Judi Dench
Maxine Bellamy	Jean De Baer
George Martin	Maurice Denham
Cecily Farr	Eleanor David
Kay	Mercedes Ruehl

Psst! The film was produced by Mel Brooks' company, the outfit that was also responsible for *The Elephant Man*, *The Fly* and *My Favourite Year* ◆ If Wendy Morgan looks familiar, it might be because she was Mollie in *Yanks* ◆ Anne Bancroft is, of course, Mrs. Brooks.

Electric Dreams •• [1984]

Director: Steve Barron
Screenplay: Rusty Lemorande

An architect programs his new computer to compose music for a cellist he wants to woo. Before long, the computer's hot for her, too. A daft idea, it has its moments and ends up being a little better than you might expect. **[111m/PG]**

Miles	Lenny Von Dohlen
Madeline	Virginia Madsen
Bill	Maxwell Caulfield
Edgar	Bud Cort

Eleni • [1985]

Director: Peter Yates
Screenplay: Steve Tesich

An author investigates the wartime story of his mother, killed by the Communists in Greece in World War II. A riveting true story is rendered aloof and dreary in this disappointing film, although Nelligan is excellent as usual. **[117m/PG]**

Eleni	Kate Nelligan
Nick	John Malkovich
Katina	Linda Hunt

Eliminators •• [1986]

Director: Peter Manoogian
Screenplay: Paul De Meo & Danny Bilson

Dotty sci-fi pic which tries to emulate Indiana Jones and comes out like a tatty episode of *Doctor Who*. Under the influence of the right stimulant this intentionally silly tale of a boffin who wants to zip back in time to become the Emperor of Rome *might* seem funny. Don't bank on it, though. **[96m/15]**

Harry Fontana	Andrew Prine
Nora Hunter	Denise Crosby
Madroid	Patrick Reynolds
Kuji	Conan Lee
Abbott Reeves	Roy Dotrice

Quote 'What is this, anyway? Some kind of comic book? We've got robots. We've got cavemen. We've got kung fu.'

El Norte ••• [1984]

Director: Gregory Nava
Screenplay: Gregory Nava & Anna Thomas

A brother and sister escape from Guatemala and make the perilous journey to the United States. But their efforts to enter the country as illegal immigrants is nothing like as tough as trying to survive and prosper in LA. Although occasionally mushy, this is a stark, moving look at the reality of the American dream and the strength of the human spirit. Also known as *The North*. **[139m/15]**

Rosa Xuncax	Zaide Silvia Gutierrez
Enrique Xuncax	David Villalpando
Arturo Xuncax	Ernesto Gomez Cruz
Lupe Xuncax	Alicia del Lago

Elvira, Mistress of the Dark • [1988]

Director: James Signorelli
Screenplay: Cassandra Peterson, Sam Egan & John Paragon

Elvira is a big-busted hostess of a late-night American horror movie show. Her feature film career starts (and probably ends) with this monstrously unfunny story of her going to collect her inheritance. Centring on her main assets, this is a horror spoof as Benny Hill might have done it, only without the jokes. **[96m/15]**

Elvira	Cassandra Peterson
Vincent Talbot	W. Morgan Sheppard
Bob Redding	Daniel Greene

Quote 'If I'd wanted your opinion, I'd have beaten it out of you.'

Showing *Attack of the Killer Tomatoes.*

The Emerald Forest ••• [1985]

Director: John Boorman
Screenplay: Rospo Pallenberg

The fascinating story of engineer Boothe, who spends ten years searching for his son, kidnapped by a rare Amazonian Indian tribe. Although it's almost impossible to believe that this extraordinary tale is based on a true story, it makes for compelling cinema. For once the message about the rainforests is incidental to the plot and all the more effective for that. **[113m/15]**

Bill Markham	Powers Boothe
Jean Markham	Meg Foster
Young Tommy	William Rodriquez
Young Heather	Yara Vaneau
Heather	Estee Chandler
Tommy	Charley Boorman

Quote 'When the toucan cries, danger is not far.'

Psst! Charley Boorman is director John Boorman's son.

Emily Brontë's Wuthering Heights

SEE: Wuthering Heights

Emma's War ••• [1985]

Director: Clytie Jessop
Screenplay: Peter Smalley & Clytie Jessop

Charming, languid Australian wartime story of mother Remick struggling to cope while her husband is away doing his bit. Enlivened by a splendid performance

from Otto as one of the daughters sent away to boarding school, this is one of those gentle films that leaves you with a smile on your face. **[90m/PG]**

Anne Grange	Lee Remick
Emma Grange	Miranda Otto
Laurel Grange	Bridey Lee
Frank Grange	Terence Donovan

Empire of the Sun ••• [1987]

Director: Steven Spielberg
Screenplay: Tom Stoppard

This semi-autobiographical J. G. Ballard story of a young boy's attempts to survive in a Japanese prison camp in World War II is Spielberg's second attempt at a thinking man's film. Although overlong, it's a generally intelligent and thought-provoking movie about the loss of childhood innocence through the horrors of war. Bale, as the boy, gives an extraordinarily believeable performance. **[153m/PG]**

Jim	Christian Bale
Basie	John Malkovich
Mrs. Victor	Miranda Richardson
Dr. Rawlins	Nigel Havers
Frank Demerest	Joe Pantoliano
Maxton	Leslie Phillips
Sgt. Nagata	Masato Ibu
Jim's mother	Emily Richard
Jim's father	Rupert Frazer

Psst! The movie was originally going to be made by David Lean ✦ They filmed for three weeks in China, Shanghai having changed very little in the interim. ✦ The mock-Tudor homes favoured by the British were still there, but filming in them was impossible as they were occupied by a dozen or more Chinese families. Homes in the stockbroker belt in Berkshire were used instead.

Enchanted April •••• [1991]

Director: Mike Newell
Screenplay: Peter Barnes

Slight but delightful little film about a quartet of Edwardian ladies breaking loose and taking an idyllic holiday in an Italian villa. Once you get used to the slowness of pace, the charm and magic wash over you and induce a splendid feeling of well-being. Atmosphere, acting and attention to detail are all top-hole. Financed by the BBC, the film got a shamefully limited cinema release here but was a big (by British standards) hit in the States. **[95m/U]**

Rose Arbuthnot .... Miranda Richardson
Mrs. Fisher .... Joan Plowright
Mellersh Wilkins .... Alfred Molina
Lottie Wilkins .... Josie Lawrence
Lady Caroline .... Polly Walker
George Briggs .... Michael Kitchen
Frederick Arbuthnot .... Jim Broadbent

Encino Man

SEE: California Man

Encounter at Raven's Gate •• [1988]

Director: **Rolf De Heer**
Screenplay: **Marc Rosenberg & Rolf De Heer**

In this off-the-wall Australian sci-fi thriller, aliens come to a sparsely-populated area of the outback. Lots of odd things happen in a mysterious, David Lynch-like way. Little of it makes much sense, but it's still way-out enough to hold the attention. Released in the UK in 1990. **[93m/15]**

Eddie Cleary .... Steven Vidler
Rachel Cleary .... Celine Griffin
Richard Cleary .... Ritchie Singer
Skinner .... Vince Gil

Enemies, A Love Story ••• [1989]

Director: **Paul Mazursky**
Screenplay: **Paul Mazursky & Roger L. Simon**

In this adaptation of the Isaac Bashevis Singer novel, Silver is a Jew who escaped the Nazis. Living in New York in the late 40s, he seems rather carelessly to have, effectively, collected himself three wives.

A moving, often wryly funny film with some wonderful acting. **[120m/15]**

Herman Broder .... Ron Silver
Tamara .... Anjelica Huston
Masha .... Lena Olin
Yadwiga .... Margaret Sophie Stein
Rabbi Lembeck .... Alan King
Masha's mother .... Judith Malina
Leon Tortshiner .... Paul Mazursky

Enemy Mine • [1985]

Director: **Wolfgang Petersen**
Screenplay: **Edward Khmara**

In this obvious sci-fi allegory, two battling astronauts crash land on an inhospitable planet after a dogfight. Although enemies, the only way they'll survive is if they help each other. All rather corny, but worth catching a glimpse of Gossett as a lizard giving birth. **[108m/PG]**

Davidge .... Dennis Quaid
The Drac .... Louis Gossett Jr.
Stubbs .... Brion James

Quote 'I believe I am the first male actor to give birth to a child on screen. I'd like to think this is going to get me a lot more pregnant woman parts.' [Louis Gossett Jr.]

Psst! British director Richard Loncraine was fired by the studio, which then had to junk four weeks of film shot in Iceland.

Enid is Sleeping

SEE: Over Her Dead Body

Enigma •• [1983]

Director: **Jeannot Szwarc**
Screenplay: **John Briley**

One of the last of the Cold War spy thrillers, only not so thrilling. Sheen's the East German defector who agrees, not for principle but for money, to go back East, only to discover that his mission's not so secret after all. You struggle through a complicated plot for little reward. **[101m/15]**

Alex Holbeck .... Martin Sheen

Dimitri Vasilkov...............................Sam Neill
Karen.......................................Brigitte Fossey
Also: Derek Jacobi, Michel Lonsdale, Frank Finlay, Kevin McNally, Michael Williams

Erik the Viking • [1989]

Director: **Terry Jones**
Screenplay: **Terry Jones**

Erik has doubts about the traditional Viking values of rape, pillage, violence and drink and sets off on a voyage of discovery. Unfortunately, we go with him. This Politically Correct Monty Python offshoot is screamingly unfunny, bar one or two moments. Best thing of all are the credits, including such worthies as Thorkatta the Indiscreet, Ulf the Unmemorable, Horribly Slain Warrior and Even More Horribly Slain Warrior. **[102m/12]**

Erik...Tim Robbins
Erik's Grandfather ....Mickey Rooney
Freya..Eartha Kitt
King Arnulf...................................Terry Jones
Also: John Cleese, Gary Cady, Imogen Stubbs, Antony Sher, John Gordon Sinclair, Freddie Jones, Jim Broadbent, Jim Carter

Blurb An Adventure To The End Of The Earth And Over It.

Ernest Saves Christmas • [1988]

Director: **John Cherry**
Screenplay: **B. Kline & Ed Turner**

Cross Norman Wisdom with Pee-Wee Herman. Add a little of the irritation of Jerry Lewis at his worst and you've got Ernest, here helping Santa out at Christmas. The other Ernest titles went straight to video. **[92m/U]**

Ernest P. Worrell ....Jim Varney
Santa ....Douglas Seale
Joe Carruthers ....Oliver Clark

Escape 2000
SEE: Turkey Shoot

E.T. The Extra-Terrestrial •••• [1982]

Director: **Steven Spielberg**
Screenplay: **Melissa Mathison**

Delightful, timeless family pic guaranteed to bring a lump to the throat and a tear to the eye, even if the effects look a little shaky a decade on. A bunch of kids adopt a wacky little alien and then fight off the adults when he wants to return home. Funny, fascinating and occasionally frightening, this spendidly-directed film (almost all shot from child's-eye view) deservedly became the most successful of all time, grossing over $700m worldwide. Full marks to Spielberg, too, for never spoiling it by giving us a sequel. **[115m/U]**

Mary...Dee Wallace
Elliott ....Henry Thomas
Keys...Peter Coyote
Michael ....Robert MacNaughton
Gertie...................................Drew Barrymore
Greg...K.C. Martel
Steve...Sean Frye

Blurb He Is Afraid. He Is Totally Alone. He Is 3 Million Light Years From Home.

Quote 'E.T. Phone home.' ✦ 'I've never driven forward before.'

OOPS! Watch Drew Barrymore's hamburger when she's eating dinner with Mom at the start of the film as it first becomes as good as new and then vanishes.

Psst! Both Disney and Universal passed on the film after tests showed the public wouldn't be interested. The film took more in its opening weekend alone than the $10.5m it cost to make ✦ The drunk scene was done by legless schoolboy Matthew de Merrit, walking on his hands inside the costume ✦ Stardom was too much for Drew Barrymore. She turned to drugs and drink and attempted suicide at 13. At 14 she became the youngest person ever to write an autobiography, recently bouncing back as a video star ✦ The little girl in school who kisses Elliott grew up to be a big girl indeed, *Baywatch's* Erika Eleniak, recently seen in *Under Seige* ◆ Sweden wouldn't allow children under eleven to see the film because it showed parents reprimanding their children ◆ M&M refused permission to use their sweets in the film so E.T. followed a trail of Reese's Pieces instead. Sales promptly doubled ◆ Spielberg designed the face of E.T. by taking a picture of a baby and putting Albert Einstein's eyes and forehead on top ◆ The voice was a combination of a heavy-smoking ex-schoolteacher, discovered talking in a supermarket, and Debra Winger ◆ Among the exotic plants in the spaceship were some made from polyester blown over inflated condoms.

Eureka •••• [1983]

Director: **Nicolas Roeg**
Screenplay: **Paul Mayersberg**

Dazzlingly powerful story, based on fact, of a gold prospector who strikes it fantastically lucky, only to have those around him close in for the kill 20 years later. Violent, sexy and superbly shot, Hackman and Russell as father and daughter have seldom been better. Disowned by the studio, its reputation is finally beginning to struggle out of the mire. [129m/18]

Jack	Gene Hackman
Tracy	Theresa Russell
Maillot van Horn	Rutger Hauer
Helen	Jane Lapotaire
Perkins	Ed Lauter
Aurelio	Mickey Rourke
Mayakofsky	Joe Pesci

The Everlasting Secret Family • [1988]

Director: **Michael Thornhill**
Screenplay: **Frank Moorhouse**

Young boys are whisked away from their schools to serve as catemites to top Government officials. This Australian film treats the idea with an extraordinary lack of interest or expertise. [94m/18]

The Senator	Arthur Dignam
The Youth	Mark Lee
Senator's Wife	Heather Mitchell

Everybody Wins • [1990]

Director: **Karel Reisz**
Screenplay: **Arthur Miller**

...Except the audience. Despite being written by Arthur Miller, this is an unfathomable and rather silly mystery with Nolte as a private eye stirring up a hornet's nest in a small town. [96m/15]

Angela Crispini	Debra Winger
Tom O'Toole	Nick Nolte
Jerry	Will Patton

Also: Judith Ivey, Kathleen Wilhoite, Jack Warden

Everybody's All-American
SEE: When I Fall In Love

Every Time We Say Goodbye • [1986]

Director: **Moshe Mizrahi**
Screenplay: **Moshe Mizrahi, Rachel Fabien & Leah Appet**

Quite dreadful B-grade slush about World War II flyer Hanks in Jerusalem falling for a strict Jewish girl. [97m/15]

David	Tom Hanks
Sarah	Cristina Marsillach
Peter	Benedict Taylor

The Evil Dead •• [1983]

Director: **Sam Raimi**
Screenplay: **Sam Raimi**

Ultra-low-budget shocker, in which a group of gormless teens are turned into homicidal demons after one of the girls is raped by a tree. After that, sadly, it loses its grip on reality and branches out in all directions. It's energetic stuff and admirable considering the budget, but it's still badly-acted rot. [85m/18]

Ash................................Bruce Campbell
Cheryl..............................Ellen Sandweiss
Linda......................................Betsy Baker
Scott....................................Hal Delrich

Psst! At 19, Sam Raimi was then Hollywood's youngest-ever director. He made the film for less than £200,000 ◆ Almost a minute was cut for the cinema release, with a further minute axed for the video.

The Evil Dead 2 • [1987]

Director: **Sam Raimi**
Screenplay: **Sam Raimi & Scott Spiegel**

Although a bigger budget meant better effects, this is just a tame reworking of the first film's plot, played entirely for laughs. It isn't long before the audience, too, turn into zombies. Cheekily ends with a blatant trailer for the next one, *Army of Darkness*.

[85m/18]

Ash................................Bruce Campbell
Annie....................................Sarah Berry
Jake..Dan Hicks

The Evil that Men Do • [1984]

Director: **J. Lee Thompson**
Screenplay: **David Lee Henry & John Crowther**

The quote may be by Shakespeare, but the script certainly isn't. A dire *Death Wish* rip-off. If you want to know what it's about, just read the synopsis for any one of them.

[89m/18]

Holland..............................Charles Bronson
Rhiana..................................Theresa Saldana
Moloch..................................Joseph Maher
Lomelin..Jose Ferrer

The Exorcist III •• [1990]

Director: **William Peter Blatty**
Screenplay: **William Peter Blatty**

Writer-director Blatty disowned John Boorman's *Exorcist II* and integrates this tale of a serial killer with the diabolical goings-on in the first film. It's intriguing, but rather passé twenty years down the line.

[109m/18]

Lt. Kinderman......................George C. Scott
Father Dyer..................................Ed Flanders
The Gemini Killer........................Brad Dourif
Patient X..Jason Miller
Father Morning..................Nicol Williamson

Explorers •• [1985]

Director: **Joe Dante**
Screenplay: **Eric Luke**

A group of kids catch the episode of *Blue Peter* where they teach you how to make your own spaceship out of bottle tops and sticky-back plastic and are soon soaring off into space, mixing it up with aliens who've learnt all about earth from watching TV. All rather silly. There's not enough spectacle or action for the kids and not enough meat for adults.

[110m/U]

Ben Crandall..............................Ethan Hawke
Wolfgang Muller......................River Phoenix
Darren Woods..........................Jason Presson
Lori Swenson......................Amanda Peterson
Charlie Drake..............................Dick Miller

Exposed • [1983]

Director: **James Toback**
Screenplay: **James Toback**

Model Kinski gets involved with concert violinist Nureyev who's really an agent out to kill Keitel who's a terrorist responsible for killing his mother. Every bit as silly as it sounds, although looking quite stylish in places. Worth catching a few moments just for Nureyev's wildly over-the-top performance.

[99m/15]

Elizabeth..............................Nastassja Kinski
Daniel....................................Rudolf Nureyev
Rivas..Harvey Keitel
Greg...Ian McShane

Extreme Prejudice • [1987]

Director: **Walter Hill**
Screenplay: **Deric Washburn & Harry Kleiner**

This disappointing modern Western from thriller specialist Hill is phenomenally violent and yet still manages to be tedious. Set on the Mexican border, Nolte is the

Texas ranger up against former chum Boothe who's now a wrong 'un. If the locals could only strike oil that flowed as freely as the blood here, they'd be stinking rich. **[104m/18]**

Jack Benteen	Nick Nolte
Cash Bailey	Powers Boothe
Maj. Paul Hackett	Michael Ironside
Sarita Cisneros	Maria Conchita Alonso
Sheriff Hank Pearson	Rip Torn

OOPS! Keep an eye on Boothe's chin during the final shootout as he sprouts the fastest five o'clock shadow ever seen.

Extremities •• [1986]

Director: **Robert M. Young**
Screenplay: **William Mastrosimone**

When a rapist bursts into Fawcett's home, she manages to overcome and capture him, as any ex-*Charlie's Angel* would be expected to. The problems really start when she has to decide what to do with him. The play doesn't translate well to film, particularly with Fawcett in the lead. **[89m/18]**

Marjorie	Farrah Fawcett
Joe	James Russo
Terry	Diana Scarwid
Patricia	Alfre Woodard

The Fabulous Baker Boys ••• [1989]

Director: **Steve Kloves**
Screenplay: **Steve Kloves**

A pair of lounge-playing brotherly pianists ginger up their act by taking on a singer. Although the slight story peters out towards the close, it's well worth seeing for Pfeiffer's electrifying performance. This is her first singing role since

Grease 2 and her jaw-dropping rendition of *Makin' Whoopie* on the piano top is one of the highlights of 80's cinema.

[113m/15]

Jack Baker	Jeff Bridges
Susie Diamond	Michelle Pfeiffer
Frank Baker	Beau Bridges
Nina	Ellie Raab
Lloyd	Xander Berkeley
Monica Moran	Jennifer Tilly

Quote 'We didn't want it looking like choreographed dance [Makin' Whoopie]. The dress had to be open enough so I could move in it. My only concern was not flashing my knickers.' [Michelle Pfeiffer]

Showing *It's a Wonderful Life*.

OOPS! When the brothers are fighting in the alley and the view is through the fence, look out for the chap leaping out of the way of the fisticuffs. You'll need slo-mo to see that he's holding a camera.

Face to Face
SEE: Knight Moves

Fade to Black • [1980]

Director: **Vernon Zimmerman**
Screenplay: **Vernon Zimmerman**

A potty film buff goes on a killing spree, while dressed up as characters from his favourite violent movies. He's undone when he comes across Marilyn Monroe. Not released in Britain until 1983. **[101m/18]**

Eric	Dennis Christopher
Marilyn	Linda Kerridge
Dr. Moriarty	Tim Thomerson

Psst! Look out for Mickey Rourke in a bit part as Richie.

The Falcon and the Snowman •• [1985]

Director: **John Schlesinger**
Screenplay: **Steve Zaillian**

This true story of two well-off young Californians who become spies for

Russia isn't completely convincing either as a thriller or as a study of loyalty and betrayal. It's all a bit so—whatish.   **[131m/15]**

Christopher Boyce	Timothy Hutton
Daulton Lee	Sean Penn
Mr. Boyce	Pat Hingle
Mrs. Boyce	Joyce Van Patten
Dr. Lee	Richard Dysart
Mrs. Lee	Priscilla Pointer

Falling Down ••••   [1993]

Director: Joel Schumacher
Screenplay: Ebbe Roe Smith

Like many of us, Douglas is fuming in a never—ending traffic jam. But something snaps and he abandons his car, setting off to walk to his estranged wife and daughter's house. As he encounters the horrors of everyday life, he reacts to them in stronger and stronger ways. Soon he's become a consumer vigilante, insisting on being served breakfast even though it's three minutes after the proper time. Despite his appalling behaviour, it's extraordinary how far we are prepared to sympathise with him. Nothing like the bleak film many expect, it's exciting, scary and blackly humorous.   **[115m/18]**

D–Fens	Michael Douglas
Prendergast	Robert Duvall
Beth	Barbara Hershey
Sandra	Rachel Ticotin
Mrs. Prendergast	Tuesday Weld
Surplus store owner	Frederic Forrest
D–Fens' mother	Lois Smith

Quote 'I'm the bad guy?...How did that happen? I did everything they told me.'

Falling in Love ••   [1984]

Director: Ulu Grosbard
Screenplay: Michael Cristofer

De Niro and Streep, indifferently married, fall for each other on a commuter train but agonise over beginning an affair. Despite the stars, it never gets over the major problem of implausibility, the idea that two commuters travelling to work on a train would actually talk to each other.   **[106m/PG]**

Frank Raftis	Robert De Niro
Molly Gilmore	Meryl Streep
Ed Lasky	Harvey Keitel
Ann Raftis	Jane Kaczmarek
John Trainer	George Martin
Brian Gilmore	David Clennon
Isabelle	Dianne Wiest

OOPS! Look out for the camera clearly visible in a mirror.

Family Business ••   [1989]

Director: Sidney Lumet
Screenplay: Vincent Patrick

The family that robs together, stays together. Father, son and grandson Connery, Hoffman and Broderick, plan one of those heists that can't possibly go wrong. Despite the quality of the lead actors, you never for one moment believe they are related to each other. The drama is emphasised more heavily than the comedy, but the script simply isn't up to supporting all the implausibilities.   **[110m/15]**

Jessie McMullen	Sean Connery
Vito McMullen	Dustin Hoffman
Adam McMullen	Matthew Broderick
Elaine McMullen	Rosana DeSoto

Psst! Although Connery plays Hoffman's father, he is actually only 7 years older.

Fanny and Alexander ••••   [1983]

Director: Ingmar Bergman
Screenplay: Ingmar Bergman

Young Alexander's father dies and he and his sister find they have a hard time of it when mom marries a severe pastor. How can the plot do justice to a Bergman film, particularly one as brilliant as this? Autobiographical in nature, it's a collage of echoes from his previous films, with an attractive balance between humour and gloom. Don't be put off by the length or the fact that it's in Swedish.   **[189m/15]**

Helena Ekdahl	Gunn Wallgren
Prof. Carl Ekdahl	Boerje Ahlstedt
Lydia Ekdahl	Christina Schollin
Oscar Ekdahl	Allan Edwall

The Fantasist • [1987]

Director: Robin Hardy
Screenplay: Robin Hardy

The ability to produce silly stalk–and–slash thrillers isn't just restricted to Hollywood. This Irish effort has Harris terrorised by a psycho topping the maidens so pretty in Dublin's fair city. Promises much more than it delivers.

[98m/18]

Patricia Teeling	Moira Harris
Insp. McMyler	Christopher Cazenove
Danny Sullivan	Timothy Bottoms

Far and Away •• [1992]

Director: Ron Howard
Screenplay: Bob Dolman

A period epic about a poor farm lad and haughty lady (named, for some reason, after an airport), forced to flee Ireland for America, where they endure life on the potato–line before racing for free land in Oklahoma. It's lusciously filmed but woodenly acted. The electricity generated by this real–life couple couldn't power a 40–watt bulb. The film does, however, have far and away the silliest ending to any movie in the past decade and had audiences hooting with laughter.

[140m/12]

Joseph Donelly	Tom Cruise
Shannon Christie	Nicole Kidman
Stephen	Thomas Gibson
Daniel Christie	Robert Prosky
Nora Christie	Barbara Babcock
Kelly	Colm Meaney

Quote '*Sister?* Our blood's not even the same temperature.' • 'You're a corker, Shannon.'

OOPS! Although the Oklahoma Land Rush did take place, if Cruise and Kidman arrived in 1892, as in the film, they'd be three years too late.

Psst! Apparently sensitive about his squeaky voice, Cruise insisted on using a sound system developed by the Scientologists to deepen his diction • The look of surprise on Kidman's face when she lifts the pot covering Cruise's privates is genuine. After several takes, the flannel covering his modesty was removed without her knowledge • Although much was made of this being the first live–action film to be shot in 70mm since *Ryan's Daughter*, the cameras weren't used for the final epic scene for fear they'd be damaged.

Farewell to the King • [1989]

Director: John Milius
Screenplay: John Milius

A rambling mess of a movie, with Nolte a deserter in World War II who ends up chief of a Borneo tribe, trying to protect his people from all outside influences, be they Japanese or British. The man from del Monte, he say: NO! [117m/PG]

Learoyd	Nick Nolte
Capt. Fairbourne	Nigel Havers
Col. Ferguson	James Fox

Far North • [1988]

Director: Sam Shepard
Screenplay: Sam Shepard

Stilted and pretentious yarn about a rural American family of the sort that only stays together in the movies and the torment they go through when daddy orders the death of a much–loved horse that almost killed him. [89m/12]

Kate	Jessica Lange
Bertrum	Charles Durning
Rita	Tess Harper
Uncle Dane	Donald Moffat

Fatal Attraction •• [1987]

Director: Adrian Lyne
Screenplay: James Dearden

With his family away, lawyer Douglas has a brief fling with Close. But once he zips his trousers up and says goodbye she becomes somewhat unhinged, threatening him and his family. Despite the quality of the acting, as a thriller it's appallingly unsubtle. Although it probably cut the incidence of infidelity for a while, the over-the-top ending has now been copied by so many other films that it looks plain silly. [119m/18]

Dan Gallagher	Michael Douglas
Alex Forrest	Glenn Close
Beth Gallagher	Anne Archer
Ellen Gallagher	Ellen Hamilton Latzen
Jimmy	Stuart Pankin
Hildy	Ellen Foley
Arthur	Fred Gwynne

Quote 'I will *not* be ignored.'

OOPS! No wonder Michael Douglas was treated for sex addiction. When he and Close begin making love at the sink, the clock says 4.45. They're still bonking at 6.15 ♦ Time's a big problem for the family. According to Douglas's watch, when he tucks his daughter in for the night, it's 3.15 ♦ Watch the sheet jump about between shots when Close is in bed chatting to Douglas.

Psst! The original ending had Close committing suicide, making sure that Douglas would be blamed for her murder. Test audiences didn't like it, so they reshot the new ending seven months after they'd finished filming. The original version can be seen on the special video edition ♦ The original downbeat ending was retained for Japan ♦ The rumours that writer Dearden based the character of Alex on actress Sean Young appear not to be true.

Fatal Beauty • [1987]

Director: Tom Holland
Screenplay: Hilary Henkin & Dean Riesner

Fatal is right. This deathly comedy thriller has Goldberg as a wacky LA narcotics cop, lashings of gratuitous violence and a script that was most probably written under the influence of the drug she's trying to eradicate. [104m/18]

Rita Rizzoli	Whoopi Goldberg
Mike Marshak	Sam Elliott
Carl Jimenez	Ruben Blades

Father of the Bride •• [1991]

Director: Charles Shyer
Screenplay: Frances Goodrich, Albert Hackett, Nancy Meyers & Charles Shyer

This remake of the old Spencer Tracy movie has Martin as the harrassed father facing the loss of his daughter to another man, as well as the bill that goes with it. It's amiable enough, but ultimately rather tiresome, particularly when the inevitable mawkish sentimentality gatecrashes the party. Short steals the film from Martin as the hilarious wedding organizer. [105m/PG]

George Banks	Steve Martin
Nina Banks	Diane Keaton
Annie Banks	Kimberly Williams
Matty Banks	Kieran Culkin
Bryan MacKenzie	George Newbern
Franck Eggelhoffer	Martin Short

Quote 'Drive carefully. And don't forget to fasten your condom.'

Fat Man and Little Boy
SEE: Shadow Makers

The Favour, the Watch and the Very Big Fish • [1992]

Director: Ben Lewin
Screenplay: Ben Lewin

In this surreal farce, Goldblum poses as Christ for photographer Hoskins, only for it to go to his head. Surreal here means unfunny. A perfect example of Rose's Rule #1: The longer the title, the worse the film. [87m/15]

Louis Aubinard	Bob Hoskins
Pianist	Jeff Goldblum
Sybil	Natasha Richardson
Norbert	Michel Blanc

Fear •• [1991]

Director: Rockne S. O'Bannon
Screenplay: Rockne S. O'Bannon

In this canny re-think of *The Eyes of Laura Mars*, not only does Sheedy have psychic

powers but so does the killer she's helping the Police to trap. Sadly, the story is
unsatisfactorily resolved.   **[95m/18]**

Cayce Bridges...............................Ally Sheedy
Shadow Man....................Pruitt Taylor Vince
Jessica Moreau.........................Lauren Hutton
Jack Hays.............................Michael O'Keefe

Fellow Traveller •••   [1990]

Director: Philip Saville
Screenplay: Michael Eaton

One of the better, less heavy-handed,
films about the McCarthy era is British-
made. Scriptwriter Silver escapes the
blacklist by coming to work in England.
As interesting as the political background
is the insight into the early days of British
TV, with Silver working on the wonderful *Adventures of Robin Hood* series that
Python was to spoof so memorably years
later.   **[97m/15]**

Asa Kaufman.................................Ron Silver
Clifford Byrne.............................Hart Bochner
Sarah Aitchison........................Imogen Stubbs
Jerry Leavy.........................Daniel J. Travanti
Joan Kaufman..................Katherine Borowitz
Sir Hugo Armstrong.............Richard Wilson

FernGully...The Last Rainforest •   [1992]

Director: Bill Kroyer
Screenplay: Jim Cox

This ghastly sugary animated tale of forest
fairy folk fighting evil loggers is so irritat-
ingly right-on that you want to rush out
and buy armfuls of aerosols, fill the house
with hardwood furniture and convert the
car back to leaded petrol. While the kiddies might not be too bored, the only
saving grace for anyone else is the marvellously batty Robin Williams.   **[76m/U]**

Hexxus...Tim Curry
Crysta.................................Samantha Mathis
Pips.......................................Christian Slater
Zak...Jonathan Ward
Batty Koda.............................Robin Williams
Also: Grace Zabriskie, Geoffrey Blake,
Robert Pastorelli, Cheech Marin

Ferris Bueller's Day Off ••   [1986]

Director: John Hughes
Screenplay: John Hughes

This slightly disappointing Hughes' pic
has Broderick skipping school to have a
riotious day round and about Chicago.
The invention and humour sadly run out
before the film does but Jones is as good
as always as the rightly suspicious headmaster.   **[103m/15]**

Ferris Bueller...................Matthew Broderick
Cameron Frye.................................Alan Ruck
Sloane Peterson..............................Mia Sara
Ed Rooney ....Jeffrey Jones
Jeanie Bueller...........................Jennifer Grey

Quote 'Cameron's so tight, if you stuck a
piece of coal up his ass, in two weeks
you'd have a diamond.'

Psst! Keep watching the credits to the end
and you'll see a little more of Broderick ✦
Apparently Dan Quayle's favourite
movie ✦ Jack Nicholson said after watching it that it 'made me feel totally irrelevant to anything that any audience could
want and made me feel 119 years old...I
literally walked out of there thinking my
days are numbered in the Hollywood
film industry' ✦ Watch out for a cameo
from Charlie Sheen in the police station
and Kristy Swanson in a tiny part as one
of four 'economics students'.

A Few Good Men ••••   [1992]

Director: Rob Reiner
Screenplay: Aaron Sorkin

One of the best, all-round Hollywood
entertainments for years. Cruise is the
inexperienced, devil-may-care navy
lawyer assigned to defend two Marines
accused of murdering a colleague. Along
the way, he tangles with base commander
Nicholson. Despite only having three
scenes, Jack dominates the film. Cruise
still proves himself a fine actor, though,
while Moore does the best with her sadly
underwritten part. The film fizzes and
crackles throughout, the actors firing off

their lines like bullets. Bar a moment of sentimental Stars-and-Stripes waving at the end, this is as near a perfect film as you could hope to get. **[138m/15]**

Lt. J.G. Kaffee	Tom Cruise
Col. Jessep	Jack Nicholson
Lt. Cdr. Galloway	Demi Moore
Capt. Ross	Kevin Bacon
Lt. Kendrick	Kiefer Sutherland
Lt. Weinberg	Kevin Pollak
Pfc. Downey	James Marshall
Lt. Col. Markinson	J.T. Walsh
Dr. Stone	Christopher Guest
Judge Randoplph	J.A. Preston
Lt. Spradling	Matt Craven
Lance Cpl. Dawson	Wolfgang Bodison

Quote 'Walk softly and carry an armoured tank division, I always say.'

Psst! In Cruise's apartment is *Misery's Child* by Paul Sheldon, the novel that caused so much grief in Rob Reiner's previous film *Misery* ◆ William Goldman, writer of *Butch Cassidy* and *Marathon Man* is said to have been paid $300,000 just to hold the hand of Sorkin who had written the play, but never a film before ◆ Bodison was another first-timer. He had run errands for Reiner on *Misery* and bumped into him a couple of years later just when the director was despairing of ever finding the right person for the part. Within a couple of days, Bodison was rehearsing with the others.

The Field •••   [1990]

Director: **Jim Sheridan**
Screenplay: **Jim Sheridan**

Learning that American Berenger is to buy the field he's rented for years, Irish farmer Harris goes to extreme lengths to stand in his way. All the Oirish movie clichés are here, but worth seeing for the conviction of Harris' superb performance and the all-stops-out production. **[110m/12]**

'Bull' McCabe	Richard Harris
Tadgh McCabe	Sean Bean
Widow	Frances Tomelty
Maggie McCabe	Brenda Fricker
'Bird' O'Donnell	John Hurt
The American	Tom Berenger

Field of Dreams ••••   [1989]

Director: Phil Alden Robinson
Screenplay: Phil Alden Robinson

A failing farmer hears voices in the corn-field telling him that if he builds a baseball diamond then Shoeless Joe Jackson, one of the greatest players of all time, will pop in for a quick match. Don't be put off by the weird-sounding plot. True, it's as corny as Costner's fields, but unless you're wholly immune to whimsy, it is also a magical, heart-warming tale which not only grips totally but is even surprisingly believable. In its own way, a modern *It's a Wonderful Life.*

[106m/PG]

Ray Kinsella	Kevin Costner
Annie Kinsella	Amy Madigan
Karin Kinsella	Gaby Hoffman
Shoeless Joe Jackson	Ray Liotta
Mark	Timothy Busfield
Terence Mann	James Earl Jones
Dr. "Moonlight" Graham	Burt Lancaster

Quote 'If you build it, he will come.' ◆ 'Hey, is this heaven?' — 'No, it's Iowa.'

Showing *Harvey.*

Psst! Filming took place in 1988, during a drought. It cost $200,000 to irrigate the fields ◆ When filming was over, the farmer kept the diamond in place and it became a massively popular tourist attraction for a while.

52 Pick-Up •••   [1986]

Director: John Frankenheimer
Screenplay: Elmore Leonard & John Steppling

When tough businessman Scheider is blackmailed by a gang, he fights back. This enjoyably sleazy thriller has a good star performance and Frankenheimer's direction approaching something like its best, tense form after too many years in the doldrums.

[114m/15]

Harry Mitchell	Roy Scheider
Barbara Mitchell	Ann-Margret
Doreen	Vanity

Flatliners •   [1990]

Director: **Joel Schumacher**
Screenplay: **Peter Filardi**

A group of film-makers conduct an experiment. Can they bring a moribund script back to life? They can't. This tale of a bunch of irritating medical students playing around on the brink of death is annoyingly trivial poppycock.   **[114m/15]**

Nelson Wright	Kiefer Sutherland
Rachel Mannus	Julia Roberts
David Labraccio	Kevin Bacon
Joe Hurley	William Baldwin

Blurb They Are About To Experience The Adventure Of A Lifetime...Death

OOPS! When Sutherland gets out the sewing basket for some do-it-yourself surgery on the cut on his right cheek, watch the gash disappear, then switch to his left cheek.

Psst! Kiefer Sutherland's father, Donald, once 'died' briefly while suffering from acute meningitis.

Flesh + Blood •••   [1985]

Director: **Paul Verhoeven**
Screenplay: **Gerard Soeteman & Paul Verhoeven**

Ludicrously implausible medieval romp, not helped by the usual mishmash of American and European accents. However, the story of noble daughter Leigh being brutally kidnapped by a bunch of Hauer's vagabonds has plenty of energy and imagination and is really rather enjoyable. Director Verhoeven, here making his first English-language movie, gives us an early sign of the OTT panache he brought to *Robocop*. For once, you can trust the film's title: there's an abundance of both.   **[127m/18]**

Martin	Rutger Hauer
Agnes	Jennifer Jason Leigh
Steven	Tom Burlinson
Hawkwood	Jack Thompson
Arnolfini	Fernando Hillbeck
Celine	Susan Tyrrell
Cardinal	Ronald Lacey
Karsthans	Brion James

Fletch •   [1985]

Director: **Michael Ritchie**
Screenplay: **Andrew Bergman**

Thanks to his penchant for disguises, you get not just one Chevy Chase here but seemingly hundreds. If you like Chevy Chase, then fine. There is probably medication you can take for it. But despite the odd amusing wisecrack, the rest of us will weary of this tale of the investigative reporter who gets offered a job as a hitman. Could anything else ever be this unfunny? Try the sequel.   **[96m/PG]**

Fletch	Chevy Chase
Chief Karlin	Joe Don Baker
Gail Stanwyk	Dana Wheeler-Nicholson

Also: Richard Libertini, Tim Matheson, M. Emmet Walsh, George Wendt, Kenneth Mars, Geena Davis

Quote 'You know, if you shoot me you'll lose a lot of those humanitarian awards.'

OOPS! Look at Chase's stethoscope when he's pretending to be a doctor. From one side, it's in his ears. From the other, it's round his neck.

Fletch Lives •   [1989]

Director: **Michael Ritchie**
Screenplay: **Leon Capetanos**

...More's the pity. If you're contemplating watching this, it can only be because you enjoyed *Fletch*. Extraordinary. Still, after viewing this lamentably unfunny sequel in which reporter Chase inherits a Southern mansion, the first one might conceivably seem funny in comparison.   **[95m/PG]**

I.M. Fletcher	Chevy Chase
Ham Johnson	Hal Halbrook
Becky Culpepper	Julianne Phillips
Jimmy Lee Fransworth	R. Lee Ermey

The Flight of the Navigator •••   [1986]

Director: **Randal Kleiser**
Screenplay: **Michael Burton & Matt MacManus**

Kid's sci-fi adventure has a lad whisked

away by aliens, only to find that while he hasn't aged a day when he gets back, everyone else has moved on eight years. Hardly original, but it's good fun.

[90m/U]

David Freeman	Joey Cramer
Helen Freeman	Veronica Cartwright
Bill Freeman	Cliff De Young
Carolyn McAdams	Sarah Jessica Parker
Jeff (16 years)	Matt Adler
Dr. Faraday	Howard Hesseman

Showing *Grease* [on the car radio].

Psst! The voice of Max, although credited to Paul Mall, is actually Pee-Wee Herman (Paul Reubens).

Flirting •••• [1990]

Director: John Duigan
Screenplay: John Duigan

Bullied but bright boarder Taylor falls for Newton, the only African at the nearby girls' school. This Australian sequel to *The Year My Voice Broke* is an utterly absorbing and charming tale of boarding-school life and love. Sometimes biting, sometimes tender, it is also extremely funny. The performances are excellent, with Kidman particularly good as a snooty head-girl. [100m/PG]

Danny Embling	Noah Taylor
Thandiwe Adjewa	Thandie Newton
Nicola Radcliffe	Nicole Kidman
'Gilby' Fryer	Bartholomew Rose
Jock Blair	Felix Nobis

Quote 'They can be pretty desperate, these black women. Look at National Geographic.'

Flowers in the Attic • [1986]

Director: Jeffrey Bloom
Screenplay: Jeffrey Bloom

Mummy and granny lock the kids in the attic after daddy dies. As granny is Louise Fletcher, things don't look too promising. Neither does this film. [92m/15]

Grandmother	Louise Fletcher
Mother	Victoria Tennant
Cathy	Kristy Swanson

The Fly •••• [1986]

Director: David Cronenberg
Screenplay: Charles Edward Pogue & David Cronenberg

Director Cronenberg conducts an experiment and mixes two film genres together, horror with romantic tragedy, coming up with great results. Loopy scientist (is there any other sort?) Goldblum develops an unhealthy taste for sugar while Davis, worried perhaps about the ozone layer, is just too slow with the fly-spray. The transformations are gross, but terrifically done. A contender for best horror pic of the 80s. [96m/18]

Seth Brundle	Jeff Goldblum
Veronica Quaife	Geena Davis
Stathis Borans	John Getz
Tawny	Joy Boushel
Dr. Cheevers	Les Carlson

Blurb Be Afraid...Be Very Afraid.

OOPS! At one point, when Goldblum is in the pod, the camera and crew can be seen reflected in the glass.

Psst! Director Cronenberg appears as the gynaecologist. He claims this was at Geena Davis's insistence as she didn't want a stranger between her legs.

The Fly II • [1989]

Director: Chris Walas
Screenplay: Mick Garris, Ken Wheat, Jim Wheat & Frank Darabont

An experiment to transform the special effects man from *The Fly* into a fully-fledged director goes horribly wrong, leaving a photogenic but laughable mess all over everyone's faces. Goldblum's son starts growing *really* fast and this time it's Zuniga who's too slow with the fly-killer. [105m/18]

Martin Brundle	Eric Stoltz
Beth Logan	Daphne Zuniga
Bartok	Lee Richardson
Stathis	John Getz

Blurb Like Father, Like Son.

Folks! •   [1992]

Director: Ted Kotcheff
Screenplay: Robert Klane

Tom Selleck shaves off his moustache for this tasteless, laugh-free comedy. It does no good. He's *still* recognisable as the stockbroker whose father develops Alzheimer's Disease, creating untold havoc. As no-one should have to sit through this disaster movie for themselves, suffice to say that Selleck loses not only his sanity, but also one ear, one eye, a couple of toes and a testicle. Although no-one had a good word to say about this at the time, there is one; it just happens to be unprintable!   [106m/PG]

Jon Aldrich ....Tom Selleck
Harry Aldrich ....Don Ameche
Mildred Aldrich ....Anne Jackson
Arlene Aldrich ....Christine Ebersole

Quote 'The furniture isn't all that's missing.' [Selleck to wife]

Psst! In the film, Don Ameche wreaks havoc by driving a car backwards. The week before the film came out a woman in New York, also with Alzheimer's, lost control of her car and killed five people.

The Fool ••   [1991]

Director: Christine Edzard
Screenplay: Christine Edzard & Olivier Stockman

From the same team that put together *Little Dorrit* comes another Victorian adaptation. This time it's from the diaries of Henry Mayhew, with Jacobi a man flitting between the highest and lowest strata of London society. As before, atmosphere and character are superb. But the storytelling is just a mite confusing and unsatisfying.   [137m/U]

Sir John/Mr. Frederick.................Derek Jacobi
The Ballad Seller..........................Cyril Cusack
The Girl ....Ruth Mitchell
Lady Amelia ....Maria Aitken
Also: Irina Brook, Paul Brooke, Jim Carter, Jonathan Cecil, Patricia Hayes, Don Henderson, Michael Hordern, Stratford Johns, Miriam Margolyes, Michael Medwin, Corin Redgrave, Miranda Richardson, Joan Sims, Frederick Treves

Fool for Love ••   [1985]

Director: Robert Altman
Screenplay: Sam Shepard

Two ex-lovers find it isn't as easy to shake off the past as they thought. Despite Altman helming, Shepard's play still works better on stage. It probably works better without Basinger, too.   [107m/15]

Eddie..Sam Shepard
May...Kim Basinger
Old Man ....Harry Dean Stanton
Martin ....Randy Quaid

Fools of Fortune •   [1990]

Director: Pat O'Connor
Screenplay: Michael Hirst

The Irish Troubles after World War I are the background to upheavals within one particular family. Coming across more like soap opera than anything else, the plot is about as easy to make sense of as the Irish question today.   [104m/15]

Marianne ....Mary Elizabeth Mastrantonio
Willie...Iain Glen
Mrs. Quinton ....Julie Christie
Mr. Quinton ....Michael Kitchen

Footloose ••   [1984]

Director: Herbert Ross
Screenplay: Dean Pitchford

Slightly daft *Flashdance*-type film has Bacon mean as a hog when he's moved from Chicago to a dull backwater where local preacher Lithgow has banned degenerate music and dancing. You just know that he'll have a daughter and that she'll fall for the lad. There's lots of music of the sort that should be beneath contempt, but which still gets hummed inadvertently afterwards.   [107m/15]

Ren..Kevin Bacon
Ariel..Lori Singer
Rev. Shaw Moore ....John Lithgow

Vi Moore.................................Dianne Wiest
Willard.............................Christopher Penn
Rusty...............................Sarah Jessica Parker

Psst! It was originally to have been helmed by *Deer Hunter* director Michael Cimino, but he left after disagreements with the producer.

Foreign Body •• [1986]

Director: **Ronald Neame**
Screenplay: **Celine La Freniere**

The 60s are alive, in particular the rather twee British sex comedies of the period, in this tale of an unemployed Indian posing as a doctor. Before long, he has a brass plate in Harley Street and a bevy of pretty women queueing up to be bedded by him, among them Amanda Donohoe. [108m/15]

Ram Das ....Victor Banerjee
I.Q. ....Warren Mitchell
Lady Ammanford.............Geraldine McEwan
Also: Denis Quilley, Amanda Donohoe, Eve Ferret, Anna Massey, Stratford Johns, Trevor Howard

Forever Young ••• [1992]

Director: **Steve Miner**
Screenplay: **Jeffrey Abrams**

Distraught when his childhood sweetheart goes into a coma, 30's test-pilot Gibson volunteers to be frozen for a year. Rip Van Gibson wakes up fifty years later and, defrosted, gives us the usual Mel butt-shot before taking refuge with single mother Curtis and son Wood. The sci-fi's just the framework for a delightful, unashamed, cuddling-in-the-back-row romance about the longevity of love, complete with laughter and tears. If only Mel's flight from the curious military didn't stretch the elastic band of credibility beyond breaking-point. [102m/PG]

Daniel..Mel Gibson
Claire....................................Jamie Lee Curtis
Nat..Elijah Wood
Helen......................................Isabel Glasser
Harry......................................George Wendt
Cameron......................................Joe Morton

Quote 'This is a matter of national security. I'm sorry, but I'm going to have to tickle you.'

Psst! Mel received $5om from the film ◆ Director Miner and George Wendt had worked together before, on the horror pic *House* ◆ The designer confessed that the inspiration for the cryogenic chamber came from an Electrolux vacuum cleaner. Included in its design were a toilet plunger and an old mining pan.

For Keeps

SEE: **Maybe Baby**

For Queen and Country •• [1989]

Director: **Martin Stellman**
Screenplay: **Martin Stellman & Trix Worrell**

This tale of black Falklands' hero Washington suffering the ingratitude, indifference and racism of his countrymen is weakened by having the central part played by an American. Grim stuff, and rather violent too. [105m/15]

Reuben............................Denzel Washington
Fish..Dorian Healy
Stacey....................................Amanda Redman
Bob..Sean Chapman

For the Boys •• [1992]

Director: **Mark Rydell**
Screenplay: **Marshall Brickman, Neal Jimenez & Lindy Laub**

What starts out as an entertaining down-the-years review of the career of a pair of popular singing stars, turns rapidly into a mawkish, syrupy, never-ending mess that gets as bogged down as the trucks in Korean mud. As the years pass, every liberal cause – be it McCarthyism, Vietnam, or the rainforests – seems to be crammed in, even while the Stars and Stripes is waved aggressively in our faces. Worth watching for the first half-hour and for Midler's grannie routine, hampered by one of the worst make-up jobs in movies. [140m/15]

Dixie Leonard	Bette Midler
Eddie Sparks	James Caan
Art Silver	George Segal
Shepard	Patrick O'Neal

Also: Christopher Rydell, Brandon Call, Arye Gross

Quote 'What would I have to give you for a little kiss?' – 'Chloroform.'

Psst! To date, this holds the record as the most expensive musical ever made.

48 HRS. ••• [1982]

Director: **Walter Hill**
Screenplay: **Roger Spottiswoode, Walter Hill, Larry Gross & Steven E. de Souza**

Cop Nolte gets fast-talking con Murphy out of prison for a couple of days to help him track down a killer. Needless to say, they hate each other on sight and natural-ly...well, you know the plot. But it's funny, full of great action and highly entertaining. Murphy, in his film debut, shows what he's capable of when his tal-ents are kept in check. Who can forget the scene in the redneck bar? Followed by *Another 48 HRS.* [97m/18]

Jack Cates	Nick Nolte
Reggie Hammond	Eddie Murphy
Elaine	Annette O'Toole
Haden	Frank McRae
Ganz	James Remar
Luther	David Patrick Kelly
Billy Bear	Sonny Landham
Kehoe	Brion James
Algren	Jonathan Banks

1492: Conquest of Paradise • [1992]

Director: **Ridley Scott**
Screenplay: **Roselyne Bosch**

A man with a big nose sails west and dis-covers he's 500 years too early for plastic surgery. If only it *were* that interesting. It's all very pretty and full of directorial tricks, but indescribably boring. It's like being asked to look at Ridley Scott's stamp collection for two-and-a-half hours. The jungle scenes are like an advert, but for

what? It can't be shampoo, because Depardieu obviously hasn't washed his hair since 1492. This jarringly Politically Correct Columbus, extremely violent in places, deserves to sink without trace. [155m/15]

Columbus	Gérard Depardieu
Sanchez	Armand Assante
Queen Isabel	Sigourney Weaver
Older Fernando	Loren Dean
Beatrix	Angela Molina
Marchena	Fernando Rey

Quote 'Ridley Scott is mad, a force of nature. If I were a woman, I'd have made love with him.' [Depardieu]

OOPS! There's a vapour trail from a jet visible at one point at sea ✦ The boom mike pops into the top of the frame when they're in the cabin on the first trip.

Psst! Could somebody explain how, if they have such trouble raising that bell, they got it off the boat or even why the boat didn't sink carrying it?

The Fourth Protocol •• [1987]

Director: **John Mackenzie**
Screenplay: **Frederick Forsyth**

The real reason the Cold War ended was that Russia wanted to put an end to the stream of spy thrillers. In this wildly implausible, but moderately entertaining, adaptation by Forsyth of his own novel, Caine is – singlehandedly – to stop the Russkies exploding one of the atomic bombs America keeps in Britain. [119m/15]

John Preston	Michael Caine
Petrofsky	Pierce Brosnan
Vassileva	Joanna Cassidy

Also: Ned Beatty, Julian Glover, Michael Gough, Ray McAnally, Ian Richardson

The Fourth War •• [1990]

Director: **John Frankenheimer**
Screenplay: **Stephen Peters & Kenneth Ross**

It's back to the Cold War with Scheider the Vietnam vet general assigned to duty along the East–West border and getting an itchy trigger finger. An interesting idea – what can happen when soldiers trained to fight don't have a convenient war handy – is botched here. Despite the director's track record, this wasn't one of his finest moments.   **[91m/15]**

Col. Jack Knowles	Roy Scheider
Col. N. A. Valachev	Jurgen Prochnow
Lt. Col. Timothy Clark	Tim Reid
Elena	Lara Harris
Gen. Hackworth	Harry Dean Stanton

Frances ••   [1982]

Director: **Graeme Clifford**
Screenplay: **Eric Bergren, Christopher De Vore & Nicholas Kazan**

The strife and times of 1930's Hollywood star Frances Farmer, who ended up in an asylum being lobotomised. This okay biopic tells a little known, yet horrific, story but is over-Hollywoodised. Lange, however, shines as she is too rarely allowed to do.   **[139m/15]**

Frances Farmer	Jessica Lange
Harry York	Sam Shepard
Lillian Farmer	Kim Stanley
Ernest Farmer	Bart Burns
Bebe	Allan Rich

Psst! Yet another film in which the budding actor Kevin Costner had his part cut to ribbons.

Frankenstein Unbound

SEE: Roger Corman's Frankenstein Unbound

Frankie & Johnny •••   [1991]

Director: **Garry Marshall**
Screenplay: **Terrence McNally**

Shy cook Pacino and dowdy waitress Pfeiffer (well, this is the movies!) are both lonely. It takes them forever to realise what the audience does from the opening credits, namely that they are destined for each other. Although the will-they, won't-they, stuff goes on far too long and the caff in which they work is so wonderful people would fight to work there, this is a pleasing, old-fashioned starry

romance from the director of *Pretty Woman*. The kiss in front of the truck is corny but inspired.   **[117m/15]**

Johnny	Al Pacino
Frankie	Michelle Pfeiffer
Nick	Hector Elizondo
Tim	Nathan Lane
Cora	Kate Nelligan
Nedda	Jane Morris
Tino	Greg Lewis

Psst! Although the play was written for Kathy Bates, who played it on Broadway, apparently she was not considered to play it on screen ◆ Hector Elizondo, best-known for his part as the hotel manager in *Pretty Woman*, has been in every one of director Marshall's films.

Frantic ••   [1988]

Director: **Roman Polanski**
Screenplay: **Roman Polanski & Gérard Brach**

Surgeon Ford and wife Buckley discover on arrival in Paris that they've got the wrong suitcase. When she disappears and the police prove less than helpful, Ford sets out to find her himself. The problem with this Hitchock homage is that, despite the potential, it's really rather boring. Somebody ought to tell Polanski that the point of thrillers is that they're supposed to thrill.   **[120m/15]**

Richard Walker	Harrison Ford
Sondra Walker	Betty Buckley
Michelle	Emmanuelle Seigner
Williams	John Mahoney

Psst! Credits include a 'nightlife adviser'.

Freddie as F.R.O.7 •   [1992]

Director: **Jon Acevski**
Screenplay: **Jon Acevski & David Ashton**

A prince turned frog turned secret agent saves Britain when Buckingham Palace, Nelson's Column and assorted other monuments are stolen. This disastrous UK animated pic is a splendid argument in favour of tadpoling, a croak-and-dagger tale that fails to engage at any level. If, as the producers claim, Freddie is the hip hero for the 90s, then we need a hip replacement. **[91m/U]**

Freddie ....Ben Kingsley
Daffers...Jenny Agutter
El Supremo ....Brian Blessed
Also: Nigel Hawthorne, Michael Hordern, Phyllis Logan, Victor Maddern, Jonathan Pryce, John Sessions, Billie Whitelaw

Freddy's Dead: The Final Nightmare •
[1992]

Director: Rachel Talalay
Screenplay: Michael DeLuca

If only we could be sure that it was. By now the *Nightmare* series is so worn out, we don't really care one way or the other. Not even a ten-minute, 3-D sequence can stave off that seen-it-all-before feeling. Goodness knows what it looks like on video without the special glasses.

[90m/18]

Freddy Kruger.........................Robert Englund
Maggie Burroughs ....Lisa Zane
John...Shon Greenblatt

OOPS! In Britain, many cinemas got faulty glasses so that all the audience saw during the 3-D sequence was a blur.

Psst! As well as cameos from Alice Cooper, Roseanne Arnold and hubbie Tom, Johnny Depp also drops in, having made his debut with the first *Nightmare* film ◆ The evil ticket seller is Robert Shaye, head of New Line, the company that has grown rich on the talents and talons of Freddy and Jason.

Freejack •
[1992]

Director: Geoff Murphy
Screenplay: Steven Pressfield, Ronald Shusett & Dan Gilroy

A rock star's film career is frozen in 1970 after *Performance*, only to be revived twenty years later for a disastrous sci-fi actioner. Racer Estevez is saved from death, only to be revived twenty years later so that some rich guy can transplant his mind into his body. **[110m/15]**

Alex Furlong............................Emilio Estevez
Vacendak ....Mick Jagger
Julie Redlund................................Rene Russo
McCandless........................Anthony Hopkins

French Lesson
SEE: The Frog Prince

Fresh Horses ••
[1988]

Director: David Anspaugh
Screenplay: Larry Ketron

College – Plot #5. Well-off student McCarthy falls for Ringwald from the wrong side of the tracks. Could it possibly be that we have seen all this before?

[103m/15]

Jewel..Molly Ringwald
Larkin ....Andrew McCarthy
Jean ....Patti D'Arbanville
Tipton ....Ben Stiller

The Freshman ••••
[1990]

Director: Andrew Bergman
Screenplay: Andrew Bergman

Funny, charming, yet little-known comedy about a penniless student in New York who goes to work for Godfather-like figure Brando. But when Brando's daughter falls for him, his problems really begin. A superb cast and a witty, offbeat script make this a delight. Surprisingly, Brando proves himself adept at comedy, spoofing his most famous role. **[103m/PG]**

Carmine Sabatini ....Marlon Brando
Clark Kellogg..................Matthew Broderick
Victor Ray ....Bruno Kirby
Tina Sabatini ....Penelope Ann Miller
Steve Bushak ....Frank Whaley
Chuck Greenwald ....Jon Polito
Arthur Fleeber ....Paul Benedict
Edward ....B.D. Wong
Larry London.....................Maximilian Schell

Quote 'You know, when people laugh their bodies produce endorphins and I would like to be responsible for producing an endorphin or two.' [Brando]

Showing *42nd Street, The Godfather Part II.*

Psst! This is the only film in which you'll see Marlon Brando roller-skating ✦ Paramount, makers of the *Godfather* films were annoyed about the film. So was Brando, claiming that: 'It's going to be a flop. After this, I'm retiring.' The following month, after the studio lawyers had made him an offer he couldn't refuse, he said: 'Clearly, I was wrong. It contains moments of high comedy that will be remembered for decades to come.'

Friday the 13th, Part 3 • [1982]

Director: **Steve Miner**
Screenplay: **Martin Kitrosser & Carol Watson**

Jason's obviously killed the scriptwriter by mistake, because there's nothing new here as Jason continues to carve his gory way through a gang of dim-witted teens. It was made in 3-D, a clever ploy, ensuring that those punters still awake would nudge those who weren't to tell them to put on their glasses. The pokes in the eyes with sharp sticks don't work quite as well on video. **[95m/18]**

Chris Higgins	Dana Kimmell
Rick	Paul Kratka
Debbie	Tracie Savage

Psst! Director Steve Miner, who went on to direct *Forever Young* appears as a newscaster.

Friday the 13th — The Final Chapter • [1984]

Director: **Joseph Zito**
Screenplay: **Barney Cohen**

As long as there are sex-mad teenagers swimming in the nude at night, there'll be a *Friday the 13th* movie. Even though Jason buys it in this, the fourth in the series, don't get too excited. He'll be back. **[91m/18]**

Jimmy	Crispin Glover
Trish	Kimberly Beck
Sara	Barbara Howard

Blurb Jason Is Back. And This Is The One You've Been Screaming For.

Friday the 13th, Part 5: A New Beginning • [1985]

Director: **Danny Steinmann**
Screenplay: **Martin Kitrosser, David Cohen & Danny Steinmann**

Jason's dead, but someone seems to be doing a pretty good impersonation of him in this fifth in the series. Surely there have now been more *Friday the 13th* films than there have been actual Fridays falling on the 13th of the month? **[92m/18]**

Tommy Jarvis	John Shepherd
Reggie	Shavar Ross
Pam	Melanie Kinnaman

Psst! In Latin America, the series is called *Tuesday the 13th*.

Friday the 13th, Part VI: Jason Lives • [1986]

Director: **Tom McLoughlin**
Screenplay: **Tom McLoughlin**

Some idiot digs up Jason's grave, a bolt of lightning strikes and...oops, that's the plot given away. **[87m/18]**

Tommy	Thom Mathews
Megan	Jennifer Cooke
Sheriff Garris	David Kagen

OOPS! There seem to be as many boom mike sightings as there are murders in this one.

Friday the 13th Part VII — The New Blood • [1988]

Director: **John Buechler**
Screenplay: **Daryl Haney & Manuel Fidello**

First Jason's dead, then he's alive, then he's dead again. Why can't he make his mind up? A foolish teen with powers of telekinesis wakes him up and Camp Crystal once again has a lot of sudden vacancies. **[90m/18]**

Tina	Lar Park Lincoln
Nick	Kevin Blair
Mrs. Shepard	Susan Blu

Friday the 13th Part VIII – Jason Takes Manhattan •• [1989]

Director: Rob Hedden
Screenplay: Rob Hedden

The best of the bunch, this is the one that bypassed British cinemas. Odd, because it shows a few – just a few – traces of wit and intelligence, though very few traces of Manhattan, as it's set mainly on a boat. [100m/18]

Rennie Wickham	Jensen Daggett
Sean Robertson	Scott Reeves
Charles McCulloch	Peter Mark Richman
Colleen Van Deusen	Barbara Bingham

OOPS! Jason gets on a cruise ship in British Columbia bound for New York. It must take an interesting route.

Fried Green Tomatoes at the Whistle Stop Cafe •••• [1992]

Director: Jon Avnet
Screenplay: Fanny Flag & Carol Sobieski

Bates strikes up a liberating friendship with the elderly Tandy, who regales her with stories of her Southern childhood. Tender, bitter-sweet and often amusing, this is old-fashioned film-making at its very best. The photography, story and acting is all topnotch. One of those surprising films people don't expect to enjoy and end up raving about. [130m/12]

Evelyn Couch	Kathy Bates
Ninny Threadgoode	Jessica Tandy
Idgie Threadgoode	Mary Stuart Masterson
Ruth	Mary-Louise Parker
Frank	Nick Searcy
Ed Couch	Gailard Sartain
Big George	Stan Shaw
Sipsey	Cicely Tyson
Grady Kilgore	Gary Basaraba
Buddy	Chris O'Donnell
Rev. Scroggins	Richard Riehle
Eva Bates	Grace Zabriskie

Blurb The Secret Is In The Sauce!

Quote 'Face it, lady. We're younger and faster.' – 'Face it, girls. I'm older and I have more insurance.'

OOPS! At the end, Tandy sits on a suitcase. When Bates arrrives, it disappears.

Psst! In the scene where Masterson charms the bees, she didn't use a stand-in but insisted on doing it herself.

Fright Night ••• [1985]

Director: Tom Holland
Screenplay: Tom Holland

What do you do when a vampire moves in next door? You get on-the-rocks TV horror film host McDowall to help you convince the bloodsucker that he's chosen the wrong neighbourhood to unfurl his cape. Spectacular, wonderfully tongue-in-cheek, vampire movie. [106m/18]

Jerry Dandridge	Chris Sarandon
Charley Brewster	William Ragsdale
Amy Peterson	Amanda Bearse
Peter Vincent	Roddy McDowall
Evil Ed	Stephen Geoffreys
Billy Cole	Jonathan Stark

Fright Night Part 2 •• [1989]

Director: Tommy Lee Wallace
Screenplay: Tommy Lee Wallace, Tim Metcalfe & Miguel Tejada-Flores

What Ragsdale and McDowall didn't realise when they despatched the vampire in Part 1 was that he had a sister. She thinks his death sucks and plans a little sucking herself by way of revenge. Suffers from sequelitis, in that it was all much better done the first time. [104m/18]

Peter Vincent	Roddy McDowall
Charley Brewster	William Ragsdale
Alexandra Goode	Traci Lin
Regine Dandridge	Julie Carmen

The Fringe Dwellers •• [1986]

Director: Bruce Beresford
Screenplay: Bruce Beresford & Rhoishin Beresford

An Aborigine family tries to integrate into a white suburb, but don't find it easy.

This is one of those well-made, well-intentioned movies you feel guilty about not liking more. Even though director Beresford is back on Oz territory, it doesn't help. **[98m/PG]**

Trilby	Kristina Nehm
Mollie	Justine Saunders
Joe	Bob Maza
Noonah	Kylie Belling

The Frog Prince •• [1985]

Director: **Brian Gilbert**
Screenplay: **Posy Simmonds**

A young English girl studying at the Sorbonne falls in love with a French student, rather more experienced in matters of the heart than she. Set wholly in France, but British made, this is quite a charming romantic tale, though it's so lightweight you'll need something heavy to stop it blowing away. Also known as *French Lesson*. **[90m/15]**

Jenny	Jane Snowden
Jean Phillippe	Alexandre Sterling
Ros	Diana Blackburn
Niels	Oystein Wilk

From Beyond • [1986]

Director: **Stuart Gordon**
Screenplay: **Dennis Paoli**

A scientist believes he has discovered a sixth sense in the human brain, but the breakthrough is not without its damaging side-effects. This group's second H.P. Lovecraft adaptation isn't as much fun as their outing with *Reanimator*. **[85m/18]**

Crawford Tillinghast	Jeffrey Combs
Catherine McMichaels	Barbara Crampton
Dr. Edward Pretorious	Ted Sorel

The Fruit Machine •• [1988]

Director: **Philip Saville**
Screenplay: **Frank Clarke**

This story of a couple of young Liverpool lads who witness a gangland killing and flee to Brighton tries to recapture some of the sparkle and life of the same writer's *Letter to Brezhnev*, but only partially suc-

ceeds. It has some splendid moments, though. Also known as *Wonderland*. **[103m/15]**

Eddie	Emile Charles
Michael	Tony Forsyth
Vincent Barbari	Robert Stephens

Also: Clare Higgins, Bruce Payne, Robbie Coltrane

The Fugitive [1993]

Director: **Andrew Davis**
Screenplay: **David Twohy**

The feature-film version of the cult 60's TV series has Ford as the man on the run, trying to prove his innocence by finding his wife's murderer before cop Jones catches up with him.

Dr. Richard Kimble	Harrison Ford
Lt. Gerard	Tommy Lee Jones

Psst! This was another film that was originally slated for Alec Baldwin. He had also been replaced by Harrison Ford on *Patriot Games*.

Full Metal Jacket ••• [1987]

Director: **Stanley Kubrick**
Screenplay: **Stanley Kubrick, Michael Herr & Gustav Hasford**

Private Joker goes through a hellish training programme and is then sent to Vietnam. A sometimes brilliant, occasionally tiresome, indictment of the war which starts and ends well but badly sags in the middle. Although not the masterpiece anticipated or proclaimed when released, it half succeeds in giving a new perspective on a well-worn theme. Ermey is superb, but then he *is* playing himself. **[116m/18]**

Pvt. Joker	Matthew Modine
Animal Mother	Adam Baldwin
Pvt. Pyle	Vincent D'Onofrio
Gny. Sgt. Hartman	R. Lee Ermey
Eightball	Dorian Harewood
Cowboy	Arliss Howard
Rafterman	Kevyn Major Howard
Lt. Touchdown	Ed O'Ross

Psst! Ermey was an ex-Parris Island

instructor hired to give technical advice. Because he made sure he kept appearing in all the test shots, he was given the part even though he hadn't acted before. Much of his extraordinary dialogue is his own ✦ Ermey broke six ribs in a car accident during filming, but refused to let it affect his schedule ✦ Apart from the time when he made *Barry Lyndon* in 1975, director Stanley Kubrick has not worked outside England since 1962. He is afraid of flying ✦ *Full Metal Jacket* was filmed entirely in England. Shooting took place in a barracks and an East End gasworks, with palm trees imported at a 1000$ a throw to simulate Vietnam ✦ D'Onofrio gained an extraordinary 70 lb (5 stone) for the part.

Full Moon in Blue Water •• [1988]

Director: Peter Masterson
Screenplay: Bill Bozzone

Bar-owner Hackman is depressed, not only because he's picked the wrong film to do yet again, but because he can't get over the death of his wife, despite attracting the attentions of Garr. A lot of people with Texan accents talk at each other for an hour and a half to no particular purpose.

[95m/15]

Floyd	Gene Hackman
Louise	Teri Garr
The General	Burgess Meredith
Jimmy	Elias Koteas

F/X Murder by Illusion •• [1986]

Director: Robert Mandel
Screenplay: Robert T. Megginson & Gregory Fleeman

Film special effects man Brown is asked to help fake a killing, but discovers he's been set up. Although Brown and cop Dennehy are a good team, the twists of the plot are obviously designed only to set up yet another series of spectacular effects. While these are fascinating, as a thriller it's pretty implausible. [107m/15]

Rollie Tyler	Bryan Brown
Leo McCarthy	Brian Dennehy
Ellen	Diane Venora
Lipton	Cliff De Young
Col. Mason	Mason Adams
Nicholas DeFranco	Jerry Orbach

F/X2 — The Deadly Art of Illusion •• [1991]

Director: Richard Franklin
Screenplay: Bill Condon

This sequel has special effects man Brown seeking the help of ex-cop Dennehy when he gets into trouble. Another excuse for the F/X boys to show off their skills, this one doesn't even attempt to give us a rational plot. [108m/15]

Rollie Tyler	Bryan Brown
Leo McCarthy	Brian Dennehy
Kim Brandon	Rachel Ticotin
Liz Kennedy	Joanna Gleason
Ray Silak	Philip Bosco

G

Gaby — A True Story ••• [1987]

Director: Luis Mandoki
Screenplay: Martin Salinas & Michael James Love

This true story of a girl born with cerebral palsy who refuses to make concessions to the disease is like a Mexican-set version of *My Left Foot*. Similarly heart-warming, inspiring and life-enhancing, it is brought to life by an amazing performance from Levin. [110m/15]

Sari	Liv Ullmann
Florencia	Norma Aleandro
Michel	Robert Loggia
Gaby	Rachel Levin

Also: Lawrence Monoson, Robert Beltran, Beatriz Sheridan, Tony Goldwyn

Gandhi ••• ....[1982]

Director: **Richard Attenborough**
Screenplay: **John Briley**

One of the best of all movie epics. Kingsley is brilliant as the Indian lawyer who devotes his life to ending the British occupation of India. Although it tapers off a little in the latter stages, the acting, photography and story are all strong enough to make us believe that we are witnessing history in the making.   **[188m/PG]**

Mahatma Gandhi	Ben Kingsley
Margaret Bourke-White	Candice Bergen
General Dyer	Edward Fox
Lord Irwin	John Gielgud
Judge Broomfield	Trevor Howard
Viceroy	John Mills
Walker	Martin Sheen
Kasturba Gandhi	Rohini Hattangady
Charlie Andrews	Ian Charleson
General Smuts	Athol Fugard
Patel	Saeed Jaffrey
Mirabehn	Geraldine James
Kahn	Amrish Puri
Collins	Richard Griffiths
Kinnoch	Nigel Hawthorne
G.O.C.	Bernard Hepton
Sir George Hodge	Michael Hordern
Nahari	Om Puri
Sir Edward Gait	Richard Vernon
Colin	Daniel Day-Lewis

Oscars Best Picture, Best Director, Best Screenplay, Ben Kingsley

Quote 'You have been guests in our home long enough. Now we would like you to leave.'

Psst! The funeral uses 300,000 extras, the most ever used in one scene on film ◆ Although there are only 138 actors on the credits, there are 430 speaking parts ◆ It took Attenborough around 20 years to get the film made. One studio executive turned him down saying nobody would want to see a film about 'a little brown man in a loincloth'. ◆ The film won a total of 8 Oscars, the most for any British film ◆ In preparation for the role, Kingsley turned vegetarian, did Yoga daily, lost 17 pounds and learned how to spin thread ◆ Tom Courtenay, Anthony Hopkins, Peter Finch, Dirk Bogarde and Alec Guinness had all turned the part down ◆ Sheen gave his pay to charity ◆ Long before he was a Mohican, Daniel Day Lewis can be seen in a bit part roundly abusing Gandhi in the street.

Gardens of Stone ••• [1987]

Director: **Francis Ford Coppola**
Screenplay: **Ronald Bass**

Almost as far from *Apocalypse Now* as you can get, Coppola here views the Vietnam War from the viewpoint of the soldiers guarding Arlington National Cemetery, where many of the bodies ended up. Caan is the veteran eager to stop the son of an old buddy, Sweeney, going into active service. A slow but extraordinarily powerful film.   **[111m/15]**

Clell Hazard	James Caan
Samantha Davis	Anjelica Huston
'Goody' Nelson	James Earl Jones
Jackie Willow	D.B. Sweeney
Homer Thomas	Dean Stockwell
Rachel Feld	Mary Stuart Masterson
Slasher Williams	Dick Anthony Williams

OOPS! The boom mike is clearly visible on the parade ground early on ◆, At the funeral, Caan rips a badge from his uniform to put on the coffin. But it's back on again in the next shot.

Psst! Coppola's son Giancarlo died during the making of the film in a boating accident ◆ Mary Stuart Masterson's parents in the movie are played by her real-life parents.

Gas Food Lodging ••• [1992]

Director: **Allison Anders**
Screenplay: **Allison Anders**

Totally delightful, small-scale tale of a mother trying to bring up two daughters in New Mexico, eager to stop them taking the same wrong turns as she did. Wonderful performances and a rich vein of humour make this a thoughtful little treat.   **[100m/15]**

Nora	Brooke Adams
Trudi	Ione Skye
Shade	Fairuza Balk
John	James Brolin
Dank	Robert Knepper
Hamlet	David Lansbury
Darius	Donovan Leitch

Psst! Notice the director's name is on the notepaper of Trudi's school as the head ◆ Skye's father was the 60's pop singer Donovan ◆ Donovan Leitch is Skye's real-life brother.

The Gate •• [1987]

Director: Tibor Takacs
Screenplay: Michael Nankin

Teenagers discover the gateway to hell in their own back garden. So-so Canadian horror yarn which, like so many, relies on special effects to carry the viewers through a predictable story. **[86m/15]**

Glen	Stephen Dorff
Al	Christa Denton
Terry	Louis Tripp
Lori Lee	Kelly Rowan

Getting It Right ••• [1989]

Director: Randal Kleiser
Screenplay: Elizabeth Jane Howard

31-year-old virgin Birdsall has trouble with women until one memorable evening. An often very funny modern version of those much-admired 60's British sex comedies, full of wonderful characters and great charm. **[102m/15]**

Gavin Lamb	Jesse Birdsall
Minerva Munday	Helena Bonham Carter
Mr. Adrian	Peter Cook
Sir Gordon Munday	John Gielgud
Jenny	Jane Horrocks
Joan	Lynn Redgrave
Anne	Shirley Anne Field

Ghost •••• [1990]

Director: Jerry Zucker
Screenplay: Bruce Joel Rubin

This amazingly popular film deserves every bit of its success. Swayze is the murdered man who refuses to lie down until he's saved the life of girlfriend Moore, communicating with the real world through wacky medium Goldberg. The ads made the film sound a sentimental weepie, but its splendid sense of humour keeps it balanced, making it one of the best ever all-round feel-good films. **[126m/12]**

Sam Wheat	Patrick Swayze
Molly Jensen	Demi Moore
Oda Mae Brown	Whoopi Goldberg
Carl Bruner	Tony Goldwyn
Willie Lopez	Rick Aviles
Subway Ghost	Vincent Schiavelli

Oscars Whoopi Goldberg, Best Screenplay
Blurb Believe.
Quote 'Ditto.' ◆ 'All I know is that ever since *Ghost* came out, there's been a high enrolment in pottery classes.' [Demi Moore]
OOPS! For two people who've got themselves all mucky with clay at the potter's wheel, Moore and Swayze are remarkably clean when they get down to the serious nookie straight after ◆ When Willie Lopez is run over, the body jumps from its position in the street to the car bonnet.
Psst! The director, Jerry Zucker, was one of the trio that brought us *Airplane* and *Naked Gun*. His brother David Zucker got his own back by spoofing the potter's wheel sequence in the second *Naked Gun* movie ◆ The studio spent $75,000 on illuminating poster billboards in an eerie blue light to make them look more romantic ◆ Amy Rochelle body-doubled for Moore in the sex scene, most of which was cut.

Ghostbusters •••• [1984]

Director: Ivan Reitman
Screenplay: Dan Aykroyd & Harold Ramis

Faced with academic scepticism, a trio of parapsychologists set up their own ghost-busting business just as the spirit world is about to make a concerted attack on the world. Packed with great gags and amazing effects, this is a wonderfully infectious movie with Murray, Weaver and Moranis giving particularly enjoyable performances. **[107m/PG]**

Dr. Peter Venkman	Bill Murray
Dr. Raymond Stantz	Dan Aykroyd
Dr. Egon Spengler	Harold Ramis
Dana Barrett	Sigourney Weaver
Louis Tully	Rick Moranis
Janine Melnitz	Annie Potts
Walter Peck	William Atherton
Winston Zeddmore	Ernie Hudson

Quote 'We came. We saw. We kicked its ass!' ✦ 'He *slimed* me.'

Psst! The film was originally intended to star Belushi and Aykroyd, although this became a little tricky after Belushi's untimely death. The 'eating and drinking ghost' is their tribute to 'Bluto', Belushi's character in *Animal House* ✦ The story grew out of Aykroyd's own interest in parapsychology ✦ A cinema on a New York street is showing *Cannibal Girls*, one of Ivan Reitman's first films ✦ The voice of the 'possessed' Weaver as she levitates is that of Reitman, who did many of the other alien voices too ✦ Roberto Goizueta, the head of Coca-Cola, Columbia's parent company, said on coming out of an early screening: 'Gee, we're going to lose our shirts'.

Ghostbusters II •• [1989]

Director: **Ivan Reitman**
Screenplay: **Harold Ramis & Dan Aykroyd**

This slightly disappointing sequel is haunted by the same plot as the first. As a result, although there are some reasonable gags, the fun is all a touch déjà vu. The effects seem a little off-key too, while the baby's something of a tactical error.

[108m/PG]

Dr. Peter Venkman	Bill Murray
Dr. Raymond Stantz	Dan Aykroyd
Dana Barrett	Sigourney Weaver
Dr. Egon Spengler	Harold Ramis
Louis Tully	Rick Moranis
Winston Zeddemore	Ernie Hudson
Janine Melnitz	Annie Potts

Quote 'I'm not doing *Ghostbusters II* for the dramatic challenge, that's for sure.' [Sigourney Weaver]

Psst! The film's opening weekend gross of $29.5m was a record. It lasted only a week. The following weekend *Batman* opened ✦ Cheech Marin, of Cheech and Chong, appears in a cameo as 'dock supervisor' while Judy Ovitz, wife of Mike Ovitz, Hollywood's most powerful agent, appears briefly as 'slimed restaurant patron'.

Ghost Chase • [1989]

Director: **Roland Emmerich**
Screenplay: **Roland Emmerich & Thomas Kubisch**

Two young horror film-makers, short of cash for their latest film, call up their dead uncle's butler's ghost to help. They probably dug the script up in a graveyard too.

[90m/PG]

Warren McCloud	Jason Lively
Fred	Tim McDaniel
Stan Gordon	Paul Gleason

Ghosts... of the Civil Dead ••• [1989]

Director: **John Hillcoat**
Screenplay: **John Hillcoat**

A creepily antiseptic prison providing 'humane containment' offers inhumane entertainment. An excellent, if grim, true-life drama which avoids all the clichés and makes you extraordinarily grateful you're on the outside. **[90m/18]**

Wenzil	Dave Field
David Yale	Mike Bishop
Lilly	Dave Mason

The Girl in the Picture ••• [1986]

Director: **Cary Parker**
Screenplay: **Cary Parker**

Although not a patch on *Gregory's Girl*, some of the same actors reunite for another quirkily delightful and gentle comedy. Sinclair still has girl trouble, this time while working at the 'Smile Please' photographic studio in Glasgow. **[91m/15]**

Alan	John Gordon-Sinclair
Mary	Irina Brook
Ken	David McKay
Bill	Gregor Fisher
Annie	Caroline Guthrie
Smiley	Paul Young

Psst! Gregor Fisher is perhaps better known as Rab C. Nesbitt.

Girls Just Want to Have Fun •• [1985]

Director: Alan Metter
Screenplay: Amy Spies

A teenager goes against her father's wishes and enters a dance competition. Something tells me we've seen something like this before. It's all pretty clichéd, but the endearing performers make it pass without too much pain. **[87m/PG]**

Janey Glenn	Sarah Jessica Parker
Jeff Malene	Lee Montgomery
J.P. Sands	Morgan Woodward
Drew	Jonathan Silverman
Lynne Stone	Helen Hunt
Col. Glenn	Ed Lauter
Maggie Malene	Shannen Doherty

Psst! Despite forking out a record $750,000 for the rights to a song, Cyndi Lauper's *Girls Just Want To Have Fun*, the film-makers didn't even use her version of it in the movie.

The Girl Who Came Late

SEE: Daydream Believer

Give My Regards to Broad Street •• [1984]

Director: Peter Webb
Screenplay: Paul McCartney

This big budget Valentine's card from Paul McCartney to himself is totally forgettable as a film, with its daft plot of lost

tapes from a recording session. There are twelve musical numbers, though, three of them new. **[108m/PG]**

Paul	Paul McCartney
Steve	Bryan Brown
Ringo	Ringo Starr

Also: Barbara Bach, Linda McCartney, Tracey Ullman, Ralph Richardson

Psst! This was the last film Ralph Richardson ever made.

Gladiator ••• [1992]

Director: Rowdy Herrington
Screenplay: Lyle Kessler & Robert Mark Kamen

Marshall, reprising his mumbling James Dean routine from *Twin Peaks*, gets involved in illegal boxing to pay off his father's debts. The romantic element detracts from a story we've seen umpteen times before. But if you aren't too squeamish about the vicious boxing bouts (the qualification for the referees appears to be an inability to count as far as ten), then it's reasonably slick and diverting. **[101m/15]**

Lincoln	Cuba Gooding Jr.
Tommy Riley	James Marshall
Pappy Jack	Robert Loggia
Noah	Ossie Davis
Horn,	Brian Dennehy
Dawn	Cara Buono
John Rile	John Heard

The Glass Menagerie ••• [1987]

Director: Paul Newman
Screenplay: Tennessee Williams

There are some wonderful performances in this adaptation of Tennessee Williams' masterpiece about the battles within a Southern family and the effect of an outside visitor. But, competent though it is, it's a shame Paul Newman's direction never lets us forget we're watching a stage play. **[143m/PG]**

Amanda	Joanne Woodward
Tom	John Malkovich
Laura	Karen Allen
Gentleman caller	James Naughton

Gleaming the Cube • [1989]

Director: Graeme Clifford
Screenplay: Michael Tolkin

This skateboarding teen action pic has Slater riding out to find his half-brother's killers. There are plenty of places you can go to watch skateboarders in action free without having to suffer Slater's irritating mannerisms. [105m/PG]

Brian Kelly	Christian Slater
Al Lucero	Steven Bauer
Ed Lawndale	Richard Herd

Glengarry Glen Ross ••• [1992]

Director: James Foley
Screenplay: David Mamet

Although doing little to cover up its stage origins, this is a superlative piece of old-fashioned ensemble acting that could give anyone who works in an office the screaming heebee-jeebees. A group of real-estate hustlers who make British estate agents look like angels are given one week to hit their target or join the dole queue. Blackly funny, it's like watching a modern-day gladiatorial contest. [100m/15]

Ricky Roma	Al Pacino
Shelley Levene	Jack Lemmon
Blake	Alec Baldwin
Dave Moss	Ed Harris
George Aaronow	Alan Arkin
John Williamson	Kevin Spacey
James Lingk	Jonathan Pryce

Blurb A Story For Everyone Who Works For A Living.

Quote 'Put that coffee down. Coffee's for closers only.'

Glory •••• [1989]

Director: Edward Zwick
Screenplay: Kevin Jarre

Superbly stirring telling of the story of the North's first regiment of black soldiers in the Civil War, led by rookie officer Broderick. Although one wonders about the superb quality of the soldiers' teeth, everything else is spot on. Exciting and moving, this is film-making of the very highest order, never putting a foot wrong. It's not surprising that the film won a chestful of medals, including an Oscar for British cinematographer Freddie Francis. [122m/15]

Col. Robert G. Shaw	Matthew Broderick
Pvt. Trip	Denzel Washington
Maj. Cabot Forbes	Cary Elwes
Sgt. Maj. John Rawlins	Morgan Freeman
Pvt. Jupiter Sharts	Jihmi Kennedy
Pvt. Thomas Searles	Andre Braugher
Gov. John A. Andrew	Alan North
Maj. Gen. George Strong	Jay O. Saunders
Quartermaster	Richard Riehle
Francis Shaw	Peter Michael Goetz

Oscars Denzel Washington

OOPS! You'll probably need the slo-mo on the video to spot it, but as the regiment is sent into the South, Freeman gives a pep talk to some kids. When they wave him off, one has a digital watch on his wrist ✦ In their first battle, keep an eye on the ends of the rifles. Sometimes bayonets are fixed. Sometimes they're not.

Psst! The film gives a credit for *Environmental Consultants and Dune Restoration* ✦ At one point, the film-makers were confronted by the noise of a piledriver working on a new bridge nearby. They came up with an ingenious solution: a blacksmith beat an anvil in exactly the same time ✦ The silver candlesticks in Broderick's family home belonged to the real Shaw.

Gobots: Battle of the Rock Lords • [1986]

Director: Ray Patterson
Screenplay: Jeff Segal

Partly financed by Tonka Toys, this is another of those animated films that may have a storyline – here the Gobots helping the suffering Rock People – but it's really just a feature-length commercial. [74m/U]

With: Margot Kidder, Roddy McDowall, Michael Nouri, Telly Savalas

The Godfather, Part III ••• [1990]

Director: Francis Ford Coppola
Screenplay: Mario Puzo & Francis Ford Coppola

Michael Corleone tries to buy salvation for his life of crime but finds that the Vatican is full of gangsters even bigger than him. Despite lacking the crispness of the brilliant originals and having a plot with a few loose ends, this is a severely underrated sequel. As a portrayal of repentance, salvation and spiritual decay, it remains very powerful. Had Winona Ryder played Mary instead of the dreadful Sofia Coppola, then it would have been a masterpiece. [160m/15]

Michael Corleone	Al Pacino
Kay Adams	Diane Keaton
Connie Corleone Rizzi	Talia Shire
Vincent Mancini	Andy Garcia
Don Altobello	Eli Wallach
Joey Zasa	Joe Mantegna
B.J. Harrison	George Hamilton
Grace Hamilton	Bridget Fonda
Mary Corleone	Sofia Coppola
Cardinal Lamberto	Raf Vallone
Anthony Corleone	Franc D'Ambrosio
Andrew Hagen	John Savage

Quote 'Never hate your enemies. It affects your judgement.'

OOPS! Popes Paul VI and John Paul I are much discussed in the film which is odd as they'd both died by 1979, when the movie is set.

Psst! Al Pacino had his teeth filed down and a yellow stain applied to make him look more realistic as an old man. When filming was over, he had them capped ✦ He received $8m for the film ✦ His part in the series was originally to be played by Robert Redford, but he pulled out ✦ The script was written by Coppola and Puzo between gambling sessions ✦ Sofia Coppola, the director's daughter, took over from Winona Ryder at the last minute when Ryder's doctor warned she was on the verge of a nervous break-down ✦ One of the two 'women in cafe'

is Catherine Scorsese who often appears in son Martin's movies ✦ The video is a director's cut, with an extra ten minutes.

The Gods Must Be Crazy •••• [1982]

Director: Jamie Uys
Screenplay: Jamie Uys

One of the most extraordinary comedies ever, this Botswanan film has the produc-tion values of an episode of *Daktari* and features actors who can't act. Yet it is wonderfully, screamingly, tearfully funny. A bizarre piece of slapstick about the reaction of a tribe to a Coke bottle falling from an aeroplane, it begins slowly but will soon have you clutching your sides to stop the pain. The scene with the lan-drover and the tree is a classic. [108m/PG]

Andrew Steyn	Marius Weyers
Kate Thompson	Sandra Prinsloo
Xi	N!xau
Sam Boga	Louw Verwey
Mpudi	Michael Thys
Reverend	Jamie Uys

OOPS! The guns were set to single shot, but they're automatic again when the gunfight starts.

Psst! Though the film came out slightly before the 10-year limit of this book, it's been included because its impact was only felt some time after its release.

The Gods Must Be Crazy II ••• [1990]

Director: Jamie Uys
Screenplay: Jamie Uys

Although almost as amusing as the first, like so many sequels the originality is missing. There are still plenty of laughs, though. Here Nixau has to go after his children when they are accidentally taken to civilisation. [98m/PG]

Xixo	N!xau
Dr. Ann Taylor	Lena Farugia
Dr. Stephen Marshall	Hans Strydom
Mateo	Erick Bowen

The Golden Child • [1987]

Director: **Michael Ritchie**
Screenplay: **Dennis Feldman**

This is Murphy at rock bottom and striking fools' gold. Raising barely a smile, he drags himself through this tiresome bone-shaker of a plot about him having to save a Messiah-like child from the forces of evil.

[94m/PG]

Chandler Jarrell	Eddie Murphy
Sardo Numspa	Charles Dance
Kee Nang	Charlotte Lewis

The Golden Seal ••• [1983]

Director: **Frank Zuniga**
Screenplay: **John Groves**

A boy who befriends a valuable golden seal has to protect him from greedy grown-ups. Despite the occasional bit of over-sentimentality, it's one of those few Disneyesque 'family' films that could be watched by all the family without too much squabbling over the remote.

[94m/PG]

Jim	Steve Railsback
Crawford	Michael Beck
Tania	Penelope Milford
Eric	Torquil Campbell

Goodbye, New York • [1985]

Director: **Amos Kollek**
Screenplay: **Amos Kollek**

...And Hello Jerusalem. Hagerty over-sleeps on the plane and misses her stop, Paris, ending up without any means of support in Israel. A cabbie, torn between staring at her and the meter, takes her on a sightseeing trip. Get a travel brochure and gaze at that instead.

[90m/15]

Nancy Callaghan	Julie Hagerty
David	Amos Kollek
Albert	David Topaz

Psst! Kollek, who wrote, produced, directed and starred in the film, is son of the then-Mayor of Jerusalem.

The Good Father ••• [1986]

Director: **Mike Newell**
Screenplay: **Christopher Hampton**

Embittered by the breakdown of his marriage, lawyer Hopkins gives vent to his feelings by persuading Broadbent to fight for custody in *his* marriage break-up. Excellent performances complement a bleak but thought-provoking script.

[90m/15]

Bill Hooper	Anthony Hopkins
Roger Miles	Jim Broadbent
Emmy Hooper	Harriet Walter
Cheryl Miles	Fanny Viner
Mark Varda	Simon Callow
Mary Hall	Joanne Whalley-Kilmer
Jane Powell	Miriam Margolyes

GoodFellas •••• [1990]

Director: **Martin Scorsese**
Screenplay: **Nicholas Pileggi & Martin Scorsese**

A dazzlingly brilliant depiction of the allure and often sad reality of life within the Mafia, centring around the criminal career of Liotta. Although a violent film, direction, script, photography and performances are all out of the top drawer. One expects great things of Pesci and De Niro, but Liotta and Bracco, as the mistreated wife turned-on by the violence, are also both superb.

[146m/18]

James Conway	Robert De Niro
Henry Hill	Ray Liotta
Tommy DeVito	Joe Pesci
Karen Hill	Lorraine Bracco
Paul Cicero	Paul Sorvino
Frenchy	Mike Starr
Billy Batts	Frank Vincent
Morris Kessler	Chuck Low
Tommy's mother	Catherine Scorsese
Frankie Carbone	Frank Sivero
Sonny Bunz	Tony Darrow
Tuddy Cicero	Frank DiLeo
Janice Rossi	Gina Mastrogiacomo
Vinnie	Charles Scorsese
Stacks Edwards	Samuel L. Jackson

Oscars Joe Pesci

Quote 'As far back as I can remember, I've always wanted to be a gangster. To me, being a gangster was better than being President of the United States. You were treated like a film star.'

Showing *The Jazz Singer.*

OOPS! As the caption 'Idlewild Airport, 1963' comes up near the beginning of the film, two jumbos fly overhead. They didn't exist for another five years ◆ When Bracco drives off after believing De Niro is about to top her, watch the fake number plate of the brown estate car in front fall off just as she passes it. Apparently, New York license plates have changed colour since the 60s.

Psst! Based on the real-life story of gangster Henry Hill, now in the Witness Protection Plan. Hill's response to the film was: 'That's really the way it was. It's all true'. ◆ According to the Entertainment Research Group, the 'F'-word appears 246 times, beating the previous record-holder *Scarface*. Together with assorted 'S'-words, 'A'-words and others, there's an obscenity on average every thirty seconds, probably the current record ◆ Although often seen in his films, Scorsese's mother has a proper part this time as Pesci's screen mom.

Good Morning Babylon ••• [1987]

Director: Paolo Taviani & Vittorio Taviani
Screenplay: Paolo Taviani, Vittorio Taviani & Tonino Guerra

Two Italian brothers, from generations of cathedral-builders, end up in the States working on D.W. Griffith's 1915 epic *Intolerance*. This likeable, visually striking film is fascinating in its look at the early days of cinema. **[117m/15]**

Nicola	Vincent Spano
Andrea	Joaquim De Almeida
Edna	Greta Scacchi
Mabel	Desiree Becker
Bonanno	Omero Antonutti
D.W. Griffith	Charles Dance

Good Morning, Vietnam ••• [1987]

Director: Barry Levinson
Screenplay: Mitch Markowitz

Williams is superb as the outrageous forces DJ in Saigon who upsets his superiors by doing his own thing and giving the troops something to enjoy. Although it gets bogged down in silly mawkishness when Williams tries to get to help the natives, his routines at the microphone are so inspired that you are willing to forgive. **[121m/15]**

Adrian Cronauer	Robin Williams
Edward Garlick	Forest Whitaker
Tuan	Tung Thanh Tran
Lt. Steven Hauk	Bruno Kirby
Trinh	Chintara Sukapatana
Marty Lee Dreiwitz	Robert Wuhl
Sgt. Major Dickerson	J.T. Walsh
Gen. Taylor	Noble Willingham
Pvt. Abersold	Richard Edson
Phil McPherson	Juney Smith
Dan 'The Man' Levitan	Richard Portnow

Quote ' What do you think it's going to be like tonight? It's going to be *hot* and *wet*. That's nice if you're with a lady, but it ain't no good if you're in the jungle.'

Psst! After the film came out, the real Cronauer confessed that he was never as wacky or clever as Williams portrays him. The real man can be heard in the background of *Platoon*.

The Good Mother • [1988]

Director: Leonard Nimoy
Screenplay: Michael Bortman

The Bad Movie. No sooner has divorcée Keaton found herself a new lover than her ex pops up claiming custody of their daughter. Despite the best efforts of Keaton and Neeson, it's a stew we've seen all too often before. **[105m/15]**

Anna	Diane Keaton
Leo	Liam Neeson
Muth	Jason Robards
Grandfather	Ralph Bellamy
Grandmother	Teresa Wright

Good to Go •• [1986]

Director: Blaine Novak
Screenplay: Blaine Novak

The old journalist–framed–for–murder scenario, with Garfunkul the arm–bending Washington reporter. There's plenty of go–go music in the background. [87m/15]

S.D.	Art Garfunkel
Max	Robert DoQui
Harrigan	Harris Yulin
Little Beats	Reginald Daughtry

The Good Wife •• [1987]

Director: Ken Cameron
Screenplay: Peter Kenna

A bored wife in the Australian wilds finds some consolation in the slimy hands of Neill, the new barman in town. This competent romantic drama is a touch dry and pedantic. Also known as *The Umbrella Woman*. [92m/15]

Marge Hills	Rachel Ward
Sonny Hills	Bryan Brown
Sugar Hills	Steven Vidler
Neville Gifford	Sam Neill

Psst! Brown and Ward are married. She is the niece of the Earl of Dudley.
Apparently, on meeting her father for the first time, Brown said: 'I'm glad to be part of the family. I've always thought the English aristocracy needed a good injection of convict blood'.

The Goonies •• [1985]

Director: Richard Donner
Screenplay: Chris Columbus

This junior version of *Indiana Jones*, based on a story by Speilberg, has a bunch of kids finding a pirate map and going off on a hunt for booty. One the youngsters will probably enjoy, but there's no buried treasure here for adults. [114m/PG]

Mickey	Sean Astin
Brand	Josh Brolin
Chunk	Jeff Cohen
Mouth	Corey Feldman

Also: Kerri Green, Martha Plimpton, Ke Huy Quan, Robert Davi, Joe Pantoliano

Gorillas in the Mist ••• [1988]

Director: Michael Apted
Screenplay: Anna Hamilton Phelan

Anthropologist Weaver, playing the true–life Dian Fossey, goes slightly bananas trying to protect her beloved mountain gorillas. Remarkably, it's almost impossible to tell the real monkeys from the guys wearing the suits and, partly because they have no dialogue, they are often more interesting to watch than the humans. Although the love affair seems a little spurious, it's still a highly entertaining movie. [129m/15]

Dian Fossey	Sigourney Weaver
Bob Campbell	Bryan Brown
Roz Carr	Julie Harris
Sembagare	John Omirah Miluwi
Dr. Louis Leakey	Iain Cuthbertson

Psst! Weaver didn't wash for 6 weeks and smoked 100 cigarettes a day so she could copy Dian Fossey's croaky voice ◆ First choice for the role was Jessica Lange, who became pregnant.

Gorky Park •• [1983]

Director: Michael Apted
Screenplay: Dennis Potter

Amongst those things apparently in short supply in Russia are credible characters and plots. This thriller has to use cardboard imitations instead. Despite the shift of locale, this tale of Moscow investigator Hurt unearthing a cover–up during a murder enquiry only occasionally comes alive and is remarkably lacking in atmosphere. [128m/15]

Arkady Renko	William Hurt
Jack Osborne	Lee Marvin
William Kirwill	Brian Dennehy
Iamskoy	Ian Bannen
Irina	Joanna Pacula

Also: Michael Elphick, Richard Griffiths, Rikki Fulton, Alexander Knox, Alexei Sayle

Psst! Filmed largely in Helsinki.

The Gospel According to Vic
SEE: Heavenly Pursuits

Gothic •• [1987]

Director: Ken Russell
Screenplay: Stephen Volk

What could have been a hysterical horror movie on the origins of Frankenstein is hampered by too few shocks, too much running around aimlessly and an indescribably wooden performance from Sands. However, by having Myriam Cyr's nipples turn into eyes, Uncle Ken establishes yet another movie first.

[87m/18]

Byron..Gabriel Byrne
Shelley...Julian Sands
Mary...............................Natasha Richardson
Claire...Myriam Cyr
Dr. Polidori...............................Timothy Spall

Psst! Disgusting though it looks, the slime covering Richardson on the floor of the crypt is actually boiled spinach.

Grand Canyon •• [1991]

Director: Lawrence Kasdan
Screenplay: Lawrence Kasdan & Meg Kasdan

A feel-good movie only in the sense that it makes you feel good that you don't live in Los Angeles. Not only is the place incredibly violent (we are treated to one of the most horrible mugging scenes in the movies), but it's full of liberal Fortysomething do-gooders who never stop talking about how awful it is. The film's unstructured, haphazard and pretentious, with lots of slo-mo shots and time-lapse photography. A sort of *LA Story* without the jokes. Martin, as the producer of action movies, is by far the best thing in it.

[134m/15]

Simon.......................................Danny Glover
Mack...Kevin Kline
Davis...Steve Martin
Claire.................................Mary McDonnell
Dee...............................Mary-Louise Parker
Jane.......................................Alfre Woodard

Quote 'That's part of your problem, you know. You haven't seen enough movies. All of life's riddles are answered in the movies.'

OOPS! Kline's bandage on his finger grows during the earthquake. Compare it outside to the size it was when he put it on moments before.

Psst! Martin's character, complete with car number plate GRSS PTS, is obviously based on the action-pic producer Joel Silver [see rear of book] • Magic Johnson is in the opening basketball match as a member of the LA Lakers.

Grand Chemin, Le •••• [1988]

Director: Jean Loup Hubert
Screenplay: Jean Loup Hubert

An utterly delightful French coming of age story. A young lad gets sent to friends of his mum's while she's having a baby and there strikes up a friendship with a wonderfully naive yet knowing tomboy. Deliciously atmospheric and beautifully acted, it was remade, superbly, as *Paradise*. Also known as *The Grand Highway*.

[107m/15]

Marcelle...Anemone
Pelo....................................Richard Bohringer
Louis, the boy.........................Antoine Hubert
Martine, the girl......................Vanessa Guedj
Claire....................................Christine Pascal

The Grand Highway
SEE: Le Grand Chemin

Graveyard Shift • [1990]

Director: Ralph S. Singleton
Screenplay: John Esposito

In this redundant film, a redundant textile mill is re-opened and the rats have a field day. If they had any sense, they'd be deserting the sinking movie. Tacky horror pic continuing the decline of Stephen King's screen reputation. Also known as *Stephen King's Graveyard Shift*. [86m/18]

John Hall...............................David Andrews
Jane Wisconsky.............................Kelly Wolf
Warwick..................................Stephen Macht
The Exterminator..........................Brad Dourif

Great Balls of Fire •• [1989]

Director: **Jim McBride**
Screenplay: **Jack Baran & Jim McBride**

It hardly ranks as one of the great screen biographies, but there's still some fun in this rousing, stylised look at some of the life of rocker Jerry Lee Lewis. Ryder is particularly good as Lewis's third wife, who happened not only to be his cousin, but also only 13 years old. [107m/15]

Jerry Lee Lewis	Dennis Quaid
Myra Gale Lewis	Winona Ryder
J.W. Brown	John Doe
John Phillips	Stephen Tobolowsky
Sam Phillips	Trey Wilson
Jimmy Swaggart	Alec Baldwin

Quote 'Elvis didn't have no movie made on him while he was still living, did he?' [Jerry Lee Lewis]

Psst! Although Quaid is actually playing the piano in the movie, the voice is that of Lewis ◆ Appearing as 'Dewey "Daddy-O" Phillips' is hilarious Texan film critic Joe Bob Briggs, the drive-in specialist who rates films according to the 3 Bs – Blood, Breasts and Beasts.

The Great Mouse Detective

SEE: Basil, the Great Mouse Detective

Green Card ••• [1990]

Director: **Peter Weir**
Screenplay: **Peter Weir**

MacDowell needs to be married to get the apartment she covets. Depardieu needs to be married to stay in America. Cue the usual Boy Meets Girl, Boy Hates Girl but not as much as Girl Hates Boy story. Despite its pleasing light tone, many of the gags shoot wide of the mark while the wafer-thin plot threatens to break under the weight of Depardieu's heavy-handed comic turn. Only in the movies could MacDowell find a rent-controlled miniature Kew Gardens with two bedrooms, central heating and kitchen attached. [107m/12]

George Faure	Gérard Depardieu
Brontë Parrish	Andie MacDowell
Lauren	Bebe Neuwirth
Phil	Gregg Edelman
Brontë's laywer	Robert Prosky
Mrs. Sheehan	Mary Louise Wilson
Mrs. Parrish	Lois Smith
Mr. Parrish	Conrad McLaren

Blurb The Story Of Two People Who Got Married, Met And Then Fell In Love.

Psst! If it bugs you where you've seen Bebe Neuwirth before, it could be as Lilith in *Cheers*.

Gremlins ••• [1984]

Director: **Joe Dante**
Screenplay: **Chris Columbus**

Billy's Christmas present is an eminently merchandisable cuddly creature bought from Creatures-R-Us in Chinatown. For a townful of instant little monsters, just add water. Some great gags and some occasionally OTT violence. Film buffs could spend a year trying to find all the in-jokes. [111m/15]

Billy	Zach Gilligan
Rand Peltzer	Hoyt Axton
Kate	Phoebe Cates
Lynn	Frances Lee McCain
Mrs. Deagle	Polly Holliday
Sheriff	Scott Brady
Hanson	Glynn Turman
Pete	Corey Feldman
Futterman	Dick Miller
Grandfather	Keye Luke
Gerald	Judge Reinhold

Blurb Cute. Clever. Mischievous. Intelligent. Dangerous.

Quote 'Keep him out of the light...don't get him wet. And never, never feed him after midnight.' ◆ 'Gremlins are not good. You can't trust them. You don't want one for a pet. You don't want your daughter to marry one.' [Director Joe Dante]

Showing *It's a Wonderful Life*.

OOPS! After Billy drops Gizmo into the bin, you can catch a glimpse of another Gizmo by his feet. [Not spottable on the video.]

Psst! Columbus thought up the pic after dreaming that mice were nibbling his fingers ◆ The cinema is advertising *A Boy's Life* and *Watch the Skies*, the working titles for producer Spielberg's films *E.T.* and *Close Encounters* respectively ◆ There are cameos from the likes of Bugs Bunny animator Chuck Jones and Steven Spielberg.

Gremlins 2: The New Batch ••• [1990]

Director: Joe Dante
Screenplay: Charlie Haas

One of those rare sequels that's more out-and-out enjoyable than the original. Whereas the first was a horror film that was funny, this one goes all out for the laughs. The story is similar – 'This is a Mogwai. Whatever you do, don't get it wet...Whoops!' Set in a New York sky-scraper owned by smarmy Trump-like entrepreneur Donald Clamp, the jokes come thick and fast. You'll need to watch it several times before you get them all, and then there are the film buff in-jokes to unravel. [107m/12]

Billy Peltzer	Zach Galligan
Kate Beringer	Phoebe Cates
Daniel Clamp	John Glover
Grandpa Fred	Robert Prosky
Forster	Robert Picardo
Dr. Catheter	Christopher Lee
Marla Bloodstone	Haviland Morris
Murray Futterman	Dick Miller

Also: Keye Luke, John Capodice, Paul Bartel, Ken Tobey, Kathleen Freeman, John Astin, Henry Gibson

Quote 'Casablanca in living colour with a happier ending.'

OOPS! If Gremlins don't like bright lights, how come they have such a great time in the TV studio?

Psst! This is yet another film where you should stick with it through the closing credits ◆ Leading film composer Jerry Goldsmith has a cameo as 'yogurt customer', Hulk Hogan appears as himself while bearded film critic Leonard Maltin,

who had hated the first film, is also in there ◆ Note the cinema advertising *Gremlins 2* ◆ If it's bothering you where you've seen John Astin before, he was Gomez in the TV *Addams Family* ◆ This was Christopher Lee's 203rd movie.

The Grey Fox •••• [1983]

Director: Phillip Borsos
Screenplay: John Hunter

Stagecoach hold-up man Farnsworth is released from prison after 33 years to find the world much changed. Unwilling to give up his line of business, he turns his attention towards locomotives. Superb, quirky, true-life Western is a little-known delight, with the laid-back performance of the mature Farnsworth a particular joy. [92m/PG]

Bill Miner	Richard Farnsworth
Kate Flynn	Jackie Burroughs
Shorty	Wayne Robson
Jack Budd	Ken Pogue
Fernie	Timothy Webber
Det. Seavey	Gary Reineke

Showing *The Great Train Robbery.*

Greystoke: The Legend of Tarzan, Lord of the Apes ••• [1984]

Director: Hugh Hudson
Screenplay: Robert Towne & Michael Austin

An attempt to make the Tarzan story a little more realistic for the 80's audience. Lambert's the baby of aristocratic birth raised by apes and found and returned to grandfather Richardson back in England. There, the attempts to integrate him into Victorian society aren't always successful. Outside the jungle, which is magnificently filmed, it's the scenes with the delightfully cherubic Richardson that work best. Although Lambert seemed like a great acting discovery at the time, it is now clear that the role of someone half-ape, half-man was perfect for him. [129m/PG]

John Clayton/Tarzan .....Christopher Lambert
Lord Greystoke....................Ralph Richardson
Capt. Phillippe D'Arnot....................Ian Holm
Jane Porter.........................Andie MacDowell
Lord Esker ....James Fox
Lady Alice Clayton ....Cheryl Campbell

Also: Paul Geoffrey, Nigel Davenport, Ian Charleson, Richard Griffiths, Nicholas Farrell, David Suchet

Psst! It may look like Andie MacDowell, but the voice is that of Glenn Close, who was called in to dub the part after filming ended! ◆ P.H. Vazak appears on the credits as one of the writers. Robert Towne wanted his name taken off, and used that of his sheepdog instead.

The Grifters ••• [1990]

Director: **Stephen Frears**
Screenplay: **Donald E. Westlake**

Superbly moody, bleak tale of three small-time, big-aspiration con artists – Cusack, mother Huston and girlfriend Bening – who bring about each other's downfall. The performances are stunning, particularly the gorgeous Bening as the girl who never uses cash when her body will do, and Hingle as one of the nastiest hoods yet seen on the screen.

[119m/18]

Lilly Dillon ....Anjelica Huston
Roy Dillon...................................John Cusack
Myra Langtry..........................Annette Bening
Bobo Justus ....Pat Hingle
Simms ....Henry Jones
Jeweller ....Stephen Tobolowsky
Cole ....J.T. Walsh
Hebbing..................................Charles Napier

Quote 'If you can't trust your mother, who can you trust?'

OOPS! Look out for the boom mike popping into view in the scene with Anjelica Huston and John Cusack in his flat ◆ Huston gets out of Pat Hingle's car weaing a belt. But she didn't have it on when she got into the car.

Groundhog Day ••• [1993]

Director: **Harold Ramis**
Screenplay: **Danny Rubin & Harold Ramis**

Obnoxious weatherman Murray, reluctantly covering a small town festival, wakes up to discover that he is cursed to live through the same day again...and again and again. From this slender idea is spun of comedy of great delight and charm, as Murray's character explores first the impish fun that's to be had from knowing what everyone will do and then the misery of being unable to break out of a recurring nightmare. **[103m/PG]**

Phil...Bill Murray
Rita....................................Andie MacDowell
Larry ....Chris Elliott
Ned...............................Stephen Tobolowsky
Buster..........................Brian Doyle-Murray
Nancy....................................Marita Geraghty

OOPS! The groundhog at the steering wheel? Honestly!

Psst! All that snow in the final scene is real. Just as they were about to spend a fortune on the artificial stuff, the area was struck by the biggest blizzard of the year, just as happens in the film ◆ Buster, the guy saved from choking by Bill Murray, is Murray's elder brother ◆ Writer-director Harold Ramis appears in a cameo as the neurologist ◆ There really is a Punxsutawney and they really do have a Groundhog Day.

The Guardian • [1990]

Director: **William Friedkin**
Screenplay: **Stephen Volk, Dan Greenburg & William Friedkin**

English nanny Seagrove moves into the home of a squeaky-clean American couple. As she's into sacrificing kids to a tree, perhaps they're right to worry about her qualifications. It's hard to decide who gives the most wooden performance in this ludicrous load of poppycock, Seagrove or the tree? **[93m/18]**

Camilla...................................Jenny Seagrove
Phil..Dwier Brown
Kate ....Carey Lowell

Guilty by Suspicion •• [1991]

Director: Irwin Winkler
Screenplay: Irwin Winkler

Dull-as-ditchwater drama about the anti-Communist witchhunt in the film industry in the 50s. It plays up the human element, showing how long-standing friendships were torn apart. But although we can marvel that such appalling behaviour happened so recently, the film comes across like a bland and depressing lecture.

[105m/15]

David Merrill	Robert De Niro
Ruth Merrill	Annette Bening
Bunny Baxter	George Wendt
Dorothy Nolan	Patricia Wettig
Felix Graff	Sam Wanamaker
Paulie Merrill	Luke Edwards
Larry Nolan	Chris Cooper

Showing *Gentleman Prefer Blondes, The Boy With Green Hair.*

Psst! Wanamaker was himself a victim of the MacCarthyite witchhunt ✦ Martin Scorsese appears in a cameo as Joe Lesser, based on real-life director Joseph Losey.

Gung Ho •• [1986]

Director: Ron Howard
Screenplay: Lowell Ganz & Babaloo Mandel

Despite persuading a Japanese firm to reopen the defunct car plant in his home town, Keaton hasn't reckoned just how few laughs will stem from the idea that the Japanese are hard-working automatons while Yanks take a more relaxed view of the work ethic. Now that the Japanese have invested so heavily in Hollywood, there's unlikely to be a sequel to this over-long film that shows every sign of having been made on a Monday. [112m/PG]

Hunt Stevenson	Michael Keaton
Kazihiro	George Watanabe
Buster	George Wendt
Audrey	Mimi Rogers
Willie	John Turturro

Quote 'Well, who lost the big one then?'

Hairspray ••• [1988]

Director: John Waters
Screenplay: John Waters

In this spoof of the innocent teen musicals of the late 50s, Lake's the large teenager who upsets the apple cart on a TV dance show by calling for white and black to be able to dance together. Infectious fun, even if it does lack the usual Waters' bad taste.

[88m/PG]

Franklin Von Tussle	Sonny Bono
Motormouth Maybell	Ruth Brown
Edna Turnblad/Arvin Hodgepile	Divine
Amber Von Tussle	Colleen Fitzpatrick
Link Larkin	Michael St. Gerard
Velma Von Tussle	Deborah Harry
Tracy Turnblad	Ricki Lake
Beatnik Chick	Pia Zadora

Psst! The amazing Divine, the large transvestite who starred in most of Waters films and who ate dog excrement in *Pink Flamingos*, died of a heart attack 2 weeks after *Hairspray* opened ✦ Pia Zadora has a cameo as a pot-smoking beatnik, while Waters appears as Dr. Fredrickson.

Half Moon Street • [1986]

Director: Bob Swaim
Screenplay: Bob Swaim & Edward Behr

The potential for telling a fascinating story of academic-cum-hooker Weaver becoming embroiled with diplomat Caine isn't realised here. London is poorly evoked, the plot is scrambled and the two usually reliable stars are left at sea. Like the novel, it's all trousers and no mouth.

[89m/18]

Lauren Slaughter	Sigourney Weaver
Lord Bulbeck	Michael Caine
Gen. Newhouse	Patrick Kavanagh

Halloween III: Season of the Witch •• [1983]

Director: Tommy Lee Wallace
Screenplay: Tommy Lee Wallace

The joker in the *Halloween* pack: no Michael Myers. A sinister toy maker plans to use new-fangled Halloween masks to wipe out American children, but it's not clear if this is intended as a trick or treat. Although better than *Halloween II*, the potentially good script is wasted by poor production.

[96m/15]

Dr. Challis	Tom Atkins
Ellie	Stacey Nelkia
Conal	Dan O'Herlihy
Buddy	Ralph Strait

Halloween 4: The Return of Michael Myers • [1988]

Director: Dwight H. Little
Screenplay: Alan McElroy

After the unrelated *Halloween III*, Michael Myers is back, and he's not selling double-glazing. Shrink Pleasence returns as well, although unfortunately, Jamie Lee Curtis begged a prior engagement. Never mind, the same old story's back in her place. As deathly as Myers' intentions.

[88m/18]

Dr. Loomis	Donald Pleasence
Rachel Carruthers	Ellie Cornell
Jamie Lloyd	Danielle Harris
Michael M. Myers	George P. Wilbur

Psst! The earlier *Halloween* sequels used Roman numerals. It was decided not to call this one *Halloween IV* because it was thought that American youngsters would not know what it meant

• Michael Myers is the man who handled the UK distribution of Carpenter's early film, *Assault on Precinct 13*, and who succeeded in making it a hit here after it failed across the Pond. As thanks, Carpenter named the *Halloween* character after him.

Hambone and Hillie •• [1984]

Director: Roy Watts
Screenplay: Sandra K. Bailey, Michael Murphy & Joel Soisson

A sort of early *Kennel Alone*, with Gish's mongrel getting separated from her at the airport and going through umpteen adventures and 3,000 miles to get back to her. Although the dog's every bit as inventive as Macaulay Culkin, it's still thin stuff for adults. [89m/U]

Hillie	Lillian Gish
Michael	Timothy Bottoms
Nancy	Candy Clark
Tucker	O.J. Simpson

Hamburger Hill •• [1987]

Director: John Irvin
Screenplay: James Carabatsos

Forget all the philosophising and psychological claptrap of so many Vietnam movies. This is a straightforward account of a platoon's attempt to wrest just one hill from the enemy. Realistic to the point where we know no more about what's happening than the soldiers, it's let down by a lack of characterisation and story. Fascinating as documentary, it's less gripping as entertainment. [110m/15]

Languilli	Anthony Barrile
Motown	Michael Patrick Boatman
Washburn	Don Cheadle
Murphy	Michael Dolan
Frantz	Dylan McDermott

Psst! Both director and writer served in Vietnam, the former as a cameraman and the latter as a squaddie.

Hamlet ••• [1990]

Director: Franco Zeffirelli
Screenplay: Christopher De Vore & Franco Zeffirelli

The Danish prince isn't too keen on his new father-in-law and suspects him of foul play. This is a pretty good version of Shakespeare's tragedy, with Mad Mel acquitting himself better in the impulsive action scenes than the soliloquising, contemplative bits. Surprisingly, it's Zeffirelli's direction that slows things up towards the end.   [133m/U]

Hamlet	Mel Gibson
Gertrude	Glenn Close
Claudius	Alan Bates
The Ghost	Paul Scofield
Plonius	Ian Holm
Ophelia	Helena Bonham Carter
Horatio	Stephen Dillane
Laertes	Nathaniel Parker

Quote 'I'm playing Shakespeare – and I may not win.' [Mel Gibson]

OOPS! During the opening scene, look out for trucks going down to Dover docks.

A Handful of Dust •••• [1988]

Director: **Charles Sturridge**
Screenplay: **Charles Sturridge, Tim Sullivan & Derek Granger**

An excellent adaptation of Evelyn Waugh's novel about an upper-class marriage falling apart in the 1930s, with some startling consequences. British film-making at its finest. It looks good, the characters are well-acted and the script keeps you gripped. The haunting ending leads to involuntary shudders for some considerable time afterwards.   [118m/PG]

Tony Last	James Wilby
Brenda Last	Kristin Scott Thomas
John Beaver	Rupert Graves
Mrs. Rattery	Anjelica Huston
Mrs. Beaver	Judi Dench
Mr. Todd	Alec Guinness
Marjorie	Beatie Edney
Mr. Graceful	Graham Crowden
Reggie	Stephen Fry

Handgun •• [1983]

Director: **Tony Garnett**
Screenplay: **Tony Garnett**

A raped schoolteacher takes the law into her own hands. This exposé of gun-toting machismo is creditably unexploitative but it's still not a patch on *Thelma & Louise*. Also known as *Deep in the Heart*.   [99m/18]

Kathleen Sullivan	Karen Young
Nancy	Suzie Humphreys
Miss Davis	Helena Humann
Larry	Clayton Day

The Handmaid's Tale •• [1990]

Director: **Volker Schlondorff**
Screenplay: **Harold Pinter**

In the future, those women who can still conceive are being used by the ruling class for breeding purposes. Margaret Atwood's feminist novel becomes wholly daft and unconvincing in this adaptation.
                                    [108m/18]

Kate	Natasha Richardson
Serena Joy	Faye Dunaway
Nick	Aidan Quinn
Moira	Elizabeth McGovern
Aunt Lydia	Victoria Tennant
Commander	Robert Duvall

The Hand That Rocks the Cradle •• [1992]

Director: **Curtis Hanson**
Screenplay: **Amanda Silver**

The Nanny From Hell! Sciorra puts her kids in the care of an unhinged woman who blames her for her own baby's death. Big mistake. De Mornay is superb as the virginal-looking incarnation of evil, rightfully getting her big break after years of second-string roles. But Sciorra's family is so perfect they're sickening, while the tension is thrown out of the window by some daft *Fatal Attraction*-type silliness in the final confrontation scenes. Will somebody please tell me why people in these situations always insist on going into the cellar when that creepy music starts up?   [110m/15]

Claire Bartel	Annabella Sciorra
Peyton Flanders	Rebecca De Mornay
Michael Bartel	Matt McCoy
Solomon	Ernie Hudson
Marlene	Julianne Moore
Emma Bartel	Madeline Zima
Dr. Mott	John de Lancie

Quote 'I can't move. My leg's broken.'

Hangin' with the Homeboys ••• [1991]

Director: **Joseph B. Vasquez**
Screenplay: **Joseph B. Vasquez**

An entertaining weekend spent in the company of four boisterous young blacks and Puerto Ricans living in the Bronx. This is a slice of life we don't often see in the movies. They're guys who aren't criminals, who don't deal in drugs. They're just out for a good time. And we have one with them. [90m/15]

Willie	Doug E. Doug
Tom	Mario Joyner
Johnny	John Leguizamo
Vinny	Nestor Serrano
Vanessa	Kimberly Russell
Luna	Mary B. Ward

Hannah and Her Sisters •••• [1986]

Director: **Woody Allen**
Screenplay: **Woody Allen**

Astoundingly brilliant Allen film about three sisters and the intertwining stories of the characters involved with them. Shot through with wit, intelligence and little of Woody's tiresome, guilt-ridden angst, this is a perfect ensemble movie with excellent performances from everyone, but particularly Caine, never better than as Farrow's husband who falls for sister Hershey. Endlessly rewatchable. [107m/15]

Micky	Woody Allen
Elliot	Michael Caine
Hannah	Mia Farrow
April	Carrie Fisher
Lee	Barbara Hershey
Hannah's Father	Lloyd Nolan
Hannah's Mother	Maureen O'Sullivan
Dusty	Daniel Stern
Frederick	Max Von Sydow
Holly	Dianne Wiest
The Architect	Sam Waterston
Mickey's Friend	Tony Roberts
Himself	Bobby Short
Gail	Julie Kavner
Ed Smythe	J.T. Walsh

Writer	John Turturro

Oscars Michael Caine, Dianne Wiest, Best Screenplay

Quote 'How the hell would I know why there were Nazis? I don't know how the can opener works.'

Showing *Duck Soup.*

Psst! A large part of the movie was filmed in Farrow's apartment, which presumably made it pretty easy to get to work in the morning ◆ According to Caine, Farrow would disappear off to the kitchen to make food for the children, several of whom appeared in the film, taking off her apron and going into the other room when needed for filming. Caine had to do love scenes with Farrow with Woody and, on one occasion, former husband André Previn, watching ◆ An old man who turned up on the set trying to sell watches was, says Caine, Woody's father ◆ O'Sullivan plays Farrow's mother, as she is in real life ◆ This was veteran actor Lloyd Nolan's last role. He died before the film came out ◆ The doctor giving Allen the bad news on his sperm count is Benno C. Schmidt, Jr., president of Yale.

Hanna's War • [1988]

Director: **Menahem Golan**
Screenplay: **Menahem Golan**

The true story of Hanna Senesh, a Jewish resistance leader fighting the Nazis in Hungary in World War II, is here turned into a remarkably uninteresting, cliché-ridden film, which lasts for an eternity. [148m/15]

Katalin	Ellen Burstyn
Hanna	Maruschka Detmers
McCormack	Anthony Andrews
Rosza	Donald Pleasence
Capt. Simon	David Warner

Hard to Kill • [1990]

Director: **Bruce Malmuth**
Screenplay: **Steven McKay**

This tale of shot cop Seagal falling into a

coma, only to emerge after 7 years aching for revenge is so superbly made, brilliantly acted and stunningly photographed that it makes *Citizen Kane* look like a student film. Just kidding. It's the same old formulaic action–muscle stuff, but sadly not even up to the usual standard. **[95m/18]**

Mason Storm	Steven Seagal
Andy Stewart	Kelly LeBrock
Vernon Trent	William Sadler

Psst! Kelly LeBrock is Mrs. Seagal.

Hardware •• [1990]

Director: **Richard Stanley**
Screenplay: **Richard Stanley**

Stylish, atmospheric horror tale of a US military android reviving itself after the Big One and going on the rampage. Takes way too long to get going, but does build to a tense finale. Made for £1m and shot almost entirely in London's Roundhouse Theatre, a one-time railway shed. **[95m/18]**

Mo	Dylan McDermott
Jill	Stacey Travis
Shades	John Lynch
Lincoln	William Hootkins
Angry Bob	Iggy Pop

The Hard Way •••• [1991]

Director: **John Badham**
Screenplay: **Daniel Pyne & Lem Dobbs**

Exciting comedy thriller with plenty of laughs. Fox is the smug LA actor foisted on New York cop Woods to research a role. Sparks really fly when these two lock antlers, with both splendidly spoofing their screen images. **[111m/15]**

Nick Lang	Michael J. Fox
John Moss	James Woods
Party Crasher	Stephen Lang
Susan	Annabella Sciorra
Capt. Brix	Delroy Lindo

Quote 'I used to have a speech impediment. I couldn't say "no".' • 'It's like a movie, it's so real.'

OOPS! Although Fox loses a shoe when he's dangling above Times Square from the cigarette ad, it magically reappears.

Psst! Woods' personal hairdresser cost the production $6,000 a week. • One person was employed simply to insert Fox's contact lenses • Fox's agent Angie is Penny Marshall, director of films like *A League of Their Own* and *Big*.

Harem • [1986]

Director: **Arthur Joffe**
Screenplay: **Arthur Joffe & Tom Rayfiel**

Overdosing on Mills and Boon romances, Sheikh Kingsley has New York stockbroker Kinski kidnapped and installed in his harem. But he is a New Sheikh and wants her to fall for him of her own accord. The sort of film that gives tosh a bad name. **[97m/15]**

Diane	Nastassja Kinski
Selim	Ben Kingsley
Massoud	Dennis Goldson

Harlem Nights • [1989]

Director: **Eddie Murphy**
Screenplay: **Eddie Murphy**

This Murphy-written, Murphy-directed, Murphy-executive produced, Murphy-starring gangster pic is the low-point of his career. Set in prohibition-era New York, it's nastily violent, sleazy and lamentably unfunny. **[116m/15]**

Quick	Eddie Murphy
Sugar Ray	Richard Pryor
Bennie Wilson	Redd Foxx
Phil Cantone	Danny Aiello
Bugsy Calhoune	Michael Lerner

Quote 'The script was shitty. I wrote it in two weeks. And it shows.' [Eddie Murphy]

OOPS! If you get bored, listen out for the anachronistic 80's lines like "I'll let you have your space" and "Can we get back to you?".

Psst! Someone has counted 262 swear words in the film, making an average of one every 33 seconds • Chat-show host Arsenio Hall, co-star of *Coming to America* has a cameo as 'crying man'.

Harley Davidson and the Marlboro Man • [1991]

Director: **Simon Wincer**
Screenplay: **Don Michael Paul**

Imagine how your bum feels after sitting on a motorbike for twenty-four hours. Now imagine that feeling all over your body and you get a fair idea of the appeal of this Mickey Rourke biker pic. Two product names in one title is pretty good going, though.   **[98m/12]**

Harley Davidson......................Mickey Rourke
Robert Lee Anderson..................Don Johnson
Virginia Slim...............................Chelsea Field
Alexander..................................Daniel Baldwin

Psst! Vanessa Williams was 1984 Miss America, but lost her title for posing nude in Penthouse.

Harry and Son •• [1984]

Director: **Paul Newman**
Screenplay: **Ronald L. Buck & Paul Newman**

A somewhat aimless drama with Newman an unsympathetic construction worker who gets grumpy when he loses his job and starts quarrelling with his son. Although nicely acted, it never seems to go anywhere.   **[117m/15]**

Harry ....Paul Newman
Howard.....................................Robby Benson
Katie ....Ellen Barkin
Tom.......................................Wilford Brimley
Also: Judith Ivey, Ossie Davis, Morgan Freeman, Katherine Borowitz, Maury Chaykin, Joanne Woodward

Harry and the Hendersons
SEE: Bigfoot and the Hendersons

Haunted Honeymoon • [1986]

Director: **Gene Wilder**
Screenplay: **Gene Wilder & Terence Marsh**

Wilder is a radio star of the 30s, set to marry Radner in his ancestral home. This appallingly unfunny variation on the old Bob Hope film *The Cat and the Canary* reveals one interesting fact: Dom DeLuise is even unfunnier in drag than wearing trousers.   **[83m/PG]**

Larry Abbot ....Gene Wilder
Vickie Pearle ....Gilda Radner
Aunt Kate ....Dom DeLuise
Charles....................................Jonathan Pryce
Dr. Paul Abbot ....Paul L. Smith
Francis Sr.................................Peter Vaughan

Psst! Wilder and Radner were married. She died of cancer in 1989.

Haunted Summer • [1988]

Director: **Ivan Passer**
Screenplay: **Lewis John Carlino**

It's those wild cats Lord Byron, Percy Shelley and Mary Shelley as we discover yet again how she thought up Frankenstein. Like an arty version of Ken Russell's similarly-themed *Gothic* without the speed or the maggots. Indescribably dull.   **[106m/18]**

Percy Shelley ....Eric Stoltz
Lord Byron................................Philip Anglim
Mary Godwin...............................Alice Krige
Claire Clairmont..........................Laura Dern

Psst! Stoltz reveals all under a waterfall.

Havana • [1990]

Director: **Sydney Pollack**
Screenplay: **Judith Rascoe & David Rayfiel**

The last days of capitalism in Cuba in the 50s, with the plot of *Casablanca* drafted on top. An embarrassing, extremely long mistake by everyone concerned.   **[145m/15]**

Jack Weil...............................Robert Redford
Bobby Duran ....Lena Olin
Joe Volpi ....Alan Arkin
Also: Tomas Milian, Daniel Davis, Tony Plana, Raul Julia, Mark Rydell

Psst! Although American film-makers would never be given permission to film in Cuba, a second-unit crew did sneak in and take some footage surreptitiously.

Hawks • [1988]

Director: Robert Ellis Miller
Screenplay: Roy Clarke

Two terminal cancer patients throw caution and bedsheets to the wind and head to Holland for a brief spot of high-living and low-life. The mild dose of humour isn't enough to counteract the massive injection of sentiment. [A prime example of Rose's Rule #8] [110m/18]

Bancroft	Timothy Dalton
Deicker	Anthony Edwards
Hazel	Janet McTeer
Maureen	Camille Coduri

Hear My Song •••• [1992]

Director: Peter Chelsom
Screenplay: Peter Chelsom & Adrian Dunbar

One of the most unashamedly joyful films of the past decade. Unscrupulous nightclub owner Dunbar risks losing his love unless he can persuade a reclusive Irish singer to warble for him. As his girlfriend's the delectable Fitzgerald, his extraordinary efforts are understandable. With a similar feel to films like *Gregory's Girl*, this tale is heart-warming, hysterically funny and romantic. A delight from start to finish, there are two scenes that would surely go in anybody's *Desert Island Filmclips* list. [103m/15]

Josef Locke	Ned Beatty
Micky O'Neill	Adrian Dunbar
Cathleen Doyle	Shirley Anne Field
Nancy Doyle	Tara Fitgerald
Mr X	William Hootkins
Benny Rose	Harold Berens
Jim Abbott	David McCallum
Fintan O'Donnell	James Nesbitt

Quote 'I was born in peacetime. I haven't seen what you've seen. I haven't been where you've been.'

Psst! The story is based in part on the life of popular post-war singer Josef Locke, who fled England to avoid charges of tax evasion • The video contains some scenes not seen in the cinema.

Heartbreakers •• [1985]

Director: Bobby Roth
Screenplay: Bobby Roth

Sex and Friendship in Los Angeles. Coyote's the avant-garde artist and Mancuso the businessman living and loving amongst the trendies of the City of Angels. Not to everyone's tastes, perhaps, but perceptive stuff for those willing to stick with it. [98m/18]

Blue	Peter Coyote
Eli	Nick Mancuso
Liliane	Carole Laure
King	Max Gail

Heartbreak Ridge ••• [1986]

Director: Clint Eastwood
Screenplay: James Carabatsos

Gunnery sergeant Clint knocks a bunch of rookies into shape in time for them to invade Grenada. Eastwood is great, even if the film itself is a recyling of umpteen others. No-one ever understood just *why* the Grenada war happened. Surely it couldn't just have been to help the makers of this film out? [130m/15]

Highway	Clint Eastwood
Aggie	Marsha Mason
Maj. Powers	Everett McGill
Sgt. Webster	Moses Gunn

Also: Eileen Heckart, Bo Svenson, Boyd Gaines, Mario Van Peebles

Psst! The US Defence Department wouldn't cooperate with the film-makers.

Heartburn • [1986]

Director: Mike Nichols
Screenplay: Nora Ephron

What do you do when your husband leaves you for another woman? Nora Ephron stitched him up on screen in this barely-fictionalised tale of pregnant mum Streep discovering that journalist hubby Nicholson has been filing his copy elsewhere. Despite the leads, it's very dull talky stuff. For most of the movie, you wonder what accent Streep is using this

time, until eventually it occurs to you that
it's American.   [109m/15]

Rachel	Meryl Streep
Mark	Jack Nicholson
Richard	Jeff Daniels
Vera	Maureen Stapleton
Julie	Stockard Channing
Arthur	Richard Masur
Betty	Catherine O'Hara

Psst! Look out for Kevin Spacey as the
thief who follows Streep from the
Underground and Mercedes Ruehl in an
even smaller part as a member of the
encounter group ◆ Milos Forman, director of films like *One Flew Over the
Cuckoo's Nest*, makes his acting debut as
the Yugoslavian capitalist in the restaurant when they're playing that game ◆
When Streep leaves her father's building
after leaving the baby with the cleaning
lady, the sax player on the pavement is
playing the movie's theme music.

Heart Condition ••   [1990]

Director: **James D. Parriott**
Screenplay: **James D. Parriott**

A moderately entertaining piece of nothing, with Hoskins a bigoted cop who has a
black heart transplanted into him and then
has to solve a crime with the donor's
ghost. The premise is silly, but the acting
just about carries it along.   [100m/15]

Jack Mooney	Bob Hoskins
Napoleon Stone	Denzel Washington
Crystal Gerrity	Chloe Webb
Capt. Wendt	Roger E. Mosley

Heart Like a Wheel •••   [1983]

Director: **Jonathan Kaplan**
Screenplay: **Ken Friedman**

Bedelia is great in this amazing true story
of Shirley 'Cha-Cha' Muldowney who
overcame sexism at the hot rod track to
win the World Championship three
times. Unlike so many films of this type,
the off-track stuff doesn't develop a flat
but complements the racing perfectly.
                                   [113m/PG]

Shirley Muldowney	Bonnie Bedelia
Connie Kalitta	Beau Bridges
Jack Muldowney	Leo Rossi
Tex Roque	Hoyt Axton
Don 'Big Daddy' Garlits	Bill McKinney
John Muldowney (15-23)	Anthony Edwards

Heart of Midnight •   [1989]

Director: **Matthew Chapman**
Screenplay: **Matthew Chapman**

Claustrophobic psychological thriller, set
almost entirely in a night club. The story
is too sleazy for the average viewer, yet
not sleazy enough for the plastic mac
brigade. Unsurprisingly, Jennifer Jason
Leigh is the neurotic who inherits the
place.   [105m/18]

Carol Rivers	Jennifer Jason Leigh
Sharpe/Larry	Peter Coyote
Sonny	Gale Mayron
Ledray	Frank Stallone

Showing *The 39 Steps.*

Hearts of Darkness ••••   [1991]

Director: **Eleanor Coppola**

Fascinating account of the much-troubled
making of Coppola's *Apocalypse Now*.
This was film-making in the raw, no star
trailers, no catering trucks at lunchtime,
not even any T-shirts with the words
'Apocalypse When?' for the crew. Not
only is it the best behind-the-scenes look
at a film, but it also gives us a completely
spaced-out Dennis Hopper and exposes
the pretentiousness of Marlon Brando
who appears not to be from the same
planet. Unmissable.   [96m/15]

Psst! When told that the film cost $31m,
Clint Eastwood said that with that, 'I
could have invaded some country'.

Hearts of Fire •   [1987]

Director: **Richard Marquand**
Screenplay: **Scott Richardson & Joe
Eszterhas**

A desperately bad fictional yarn about a
female rock star. Quite why Dylan both-

ered to make this his film comeback is not clear, but he's not helped by the turkey of a performance given by Everett. Amazing to think writer Joe Eszterhas is involved and that he and Marquand had earlier made *Jagged Edge*.   [95m/15]

Molly	Fiona Flanagan
Billy Parker	Bob Dylan
James Colt	Rupert Everett

Heat and Dust ••   [1983]

Director: James Ivory
Screenplay: Ruth Prawer Jhabvala

Not even Merchant-Ivory get it right all the time. Christie goes to India to dig into the scandal involving great-aunt Greta sixty years before. Wouldn't you know it? The same thing happens all over again. Rather tiresome and overrated.   [130m/15]

Anne	Julie Christie
Olivia	Greta Scacchi
Douglas Rivers	Christopher Cazenove
Crawford	Julian Glover
Also: Susan Fleetwood, Shashi Kapoor, Madhur Jaffrey, Nickolas Grace

Heathers ••   [1989]

Director: Michael Lehmann
Screenplay: Daniel Waters

Despite the outrageous premise of Ryder's boyfriend Slater doing away with the most unpopular kids at high school and faking their suicide notes, the black humour quickly palls when it is clear that the script has taken us into a cul-de-sac. Though not living up to its cult reputation, you can relish some nicely macabre touches and the interesting lingo.   [103m/18]

Veronica Sawyer	Winona Ryder
J.D.	Christian Slater
Heather Duke	Shannen Doherty
Heather McNamara	Lisanne Falk
Heather Chandler	Kim Walker
Quote 'Fuck me gently with a chainsaw.'
Psst! In America, a 14-year-old girl organized a copycat game of croquet with accompanying picnic, at which she poisoned two of her best friends.

Heaven Help Us
SEE: Catholic Boys

Heavenly Pursuits ••   [1987]

Director: Charles Gormley
Screenplay: Charles Gormley

A pleasant, mildly funny, tale of Catholic schoolteacher Conti miraculously finding that a fall from a roof clears up his brain cancer nicely. Also known as *The Gospel According to Vic*.   [91m/15]

Vic Mathews	Tom Conti
Ruth Chancellor	Helen Mirren
Jeff Jeffries	David Hayman
Father Cobb	Brian Pettifer

Hellbound: Hellraiser II •   [1988]

Director: Tony Randel
Screenplay: Peter Atkins

Disappointing follow-up to *Hellraiser*, with the protagonists spending much of their time lost in a maze. So unfrightening and dull, you might as well be at Hampton Court, although Cranham has a bit of fun as a psychiatrist.   [93m/18]

Julia	Clare Higgins
Kristy	Ashley Lawrence
Channard	Kenneth Cranham
Tiffany	Imogen Boorman
Pinhead	Doug Bradley

Hello Again ••   [1987]

Director: Frank Perry
Screenplay: Susan Isaacs

...And Goodbye! A housewife chokes to death on a chicken ball. A year later she comes back to life again. It's got Shelley Long in. What do you expect? Laughs? [See Rose's Rule #3]   [96m/PG]

Lucy Chadman	Shelley Long
Zelda	Judith Ivey
Kevin Scanlon	Gabriel Byrne
Jason Chadman	Corbin Bernsen
Also: Sela Ward, Austin Pendleton

Hellraiser ••• [1987]

Director: **Clive Barker**
Screenplay: **Clive Barker**

This debut Clive Barker shocker shows much imagination and offers warped enjoyment for the sick at heart. Higgins is terrific as the vamp, luring men to provide blood for her undead former lover. It's rather a pity about some of the other actors, though. The sequel is *Hellbound: Hellraiser II*.   [93m/18]

Larry Cotton	Andrew Robinson
Julia Cotton	Clare Higgins
Kirsty	Ashley Laurence
Frank Cotton	Sean Chapman
Frank the Monster	Oliver Smith
Steve	Robert Hines

Psst! Bradley, who plays 'Pinhead' was at grammar school with Clive Barker ✦ His make-up takes four hours to put on and another hour to take off.

Hellraiser III: Hell on Earth ••• [1992]

Director: **Anthony Hickox**
Screenplay: **Peter Atkins**

In horror movies, the bad actors always die first. You just know from the woeful standard of acting here that there are going to be an awful lot of gory deaths. Farrell's the telly journalist led by dreams of her dead dad to Pinhead, the guy who looks as if he's been used for darts practice. The fate of the earth is in the spirited and personable Farrell's hands. Hokum, but it's pretty enjoyably done and the grisly special effects aren't bad at all.   [92m/18]

Joey Summerskill	Terry Farrell
Pinhead/Elliott Spencer	Doug Bradley
Terri	Paula Marshall
J.P. Monroe	Kevin Bernhardt

Psst! In Japan, Pinhead is the second most popular poster pin-up after Madonna ✦ In the street battle, note the 'Elm Street Café' in the background ✦ Can anyone explain why the music from the old style radio is the song from *Toto the Hero*?

Henry and June • [1990]

Director: **Philip Kaufman**
Screenplay: **Philip Kaufman & Rose Kaufman**

This steamy adaptation of Anaïs Nin's diaries of her 30's Paris love affair with writer Arthur Miller and his wife is, despite the sex, as bald in places as Ward. Despite the controversy over its alleged steaminess, it emerges as tiresome stuff, good to look at, but with talent wasted on both sides of the camera.   [136m/18]

Henry Miller	Fred Ward
June Miller	Uma Thurman
Anaïs Nin	Maria De Medeiros
Hugo	Richard E. Grant
Osborn	Kevin Spacey

Showing *Un Chien Andalou, Mädchen in Uniform*.

Psst! Such a stink was raised by the film in the States that, rather than give it the 'X' rating – the kiss of death in many of the more staid areas of the country – the censors created a new 'NC–17' rating to cover rude but artistically worthwhile movies ✦ One thing the censors didn't like was a shot of a postcard showing a woman and an octopus in a compromising position ✦ Ward replaced Alec Baldwin, who decided he didn't want to have his head shaved. 'I wanted to play June,' he said, 'But they wouldn't let me'.

Henry V •••• [1989]

Director: **Kenneth Branagh**
Screenplay: **Kenneth Branagh & William Shakespeare**

Following an insult from the French Dauphin, young King Henry, the fifth of that ilk, leads a reluctant British nation to an away win at Agincourt. Despite budgetary limitations which occasionally make the army look like an amateur soccer side struck by illness, this is a courageous and largely successful adaptation, excellently acted, bringing out Shakespeare's ambiguous feelings about patriotism and war.   [135m/PG]

Henry V	Kenneth Branagh
Chorus	Derek Jacobi
Exeter	Brian Blessed
Ely	Alec McCowen
Fluellen	Ian Holm
MacMorris	John Sessions
Pistol	Robert Stephens
Bardolph	Richard Briers
Falstaff	Robbie Coltrane
Mistress Quickly	Judi Dench
French King	Paul Scofield
Dauphin	Michael Maloney
Katherine	Emma Thompson
Alice	Geraldine McEwan

OOPS! During the long tracking shot of the field of Agincourt, keep an eye out for the corpse leaning on a couple of staves who begins to grin as the camera passes him.

Henry: Portrait of a Serial Killer •••• [1990]

Director: John McNaughton
Screenplay: John McNaughton & Richard Fire

Quietly spoken Henry introduces a new friend to his hobby, that of bumping people off. An immensely chilling, under-stated and creepily-acted portrayal of a modern nightmare. Black humour and blacker psychology are skilfully employed, even in the mutilated corpse of the slashed-up video version. Be warned, this is a *really* disturbing movie. **[83m/18]**

Henry	Michael Rooker
Otis	Tom Towles
Becky	Tracy Arnold

Showing *Becket.*

Psst! The video had almost 50 seconds cut, mostly from the scene where Henry and Otis are playing their home video of the family being killed.

Her Alibi •• [1989]

Director: Bruce Beresford
Screenplay: Charlie Peters

Thriller writer Selleck provides an alibi for beautiful murder suspect Porizkova, only to wonder if he's next for the chop.

This less than thrilling mystery should go and stand in the corner for including that old shaggy dog story about the family with the dead pet getting their stomachs pumped! **[95m/PG]**

Philip Blackwood	Tom Selleck
Nina	Paulina Porizkova
Sam	William Daniels
Frank Polito	James Farentino
Troppa	Hurd Hatfield

Psst! Selleck and Porizkova didn't get on and she 'wasn't available' when it came to posing for the poster together. So although it's her head on the poster, it isn't her body.

Hero

SEE: Accidental Hero

The Hidden •• [1987]

Director: Jack Sholder
Screenplay: Bob Hunt

An alien moves around from human stomach to human stomach, driving its hosts bananas. Luckily, extra-terrestrial cop MacLachlan is on its tail, or whatever it uses for one. Quite enjoyably silly *Alien/The Thing* hybrid which although marred by sluggish directing, still has entertaining highlights. **[97m/18]**

Tom Beck	Michael Nouri
Lloyd Gallagher	Kyle MacLachlan
Cliff Willis	Ed O'Ross
Ed Flynn	Clu Gulager
Brenda Lee	Claudia Christian

Hidden Agenda •• [1990]

Director: Ken Loach
Screenplay: Jim Allen

The investigation into a murdered American civil rights activist in Northern Ireland uncovers a huge conspiracy with-in the RUC. The film's agenda is anything but hidden, unfortunately. Although important issues are raised, without Oliver Stone's energy at the helm, it is all fatally preachy. **[108m/15]**

Peter Kerrigan................................Brian Cox
Ingrid............................Frances McDormand
Paul..Brad Dourif
Moa..Mai Zetterling

Blurb Every Government Has One.

Hider in the House •• [1989]

Director: **Matthew Patrick**
Screenplay: **Lem Dobbs**

Gary Busey hides in the loft of a squeaky clean family, but they aren't quite as keen on him as he is on them. An ever so unlikely plot premise (despite a similar real-life episode), made palatable only by the dependable Busey and Rogers. [105m/18]

Tom Sykes ....Gary Busey
Julie Dryer..................................Mimi Rogers
Phil Dryer............................Michael McKean
Neil Dryer..............Kurt Christopher Kinder
Holly Dryer...............................Candy Hutson

High Heels •• [1991]

Director: **Pedro Almodovar**
Screenplay: **Pedro Almodovar**

After fifteen years abroad, a larger-than-life actress returns to Spain to find that her daughter has married her ex-lover. After a sparky start, this disappointingly straight tale of revenge and murder turns into melodrama. Only a couple of oddball scenes live up to Almodovar's reputation as the king of camp kinkiness. [115m/18]

Rebecca ....Victoria Abril
Becky Del Paramo ....Marisa Paredes
Judge Dominguez ....Miguel Bosé

High Hopes ••• [1989]

Director: **Mike Leigh**
Screenplay: **Mike Leigh**

A working-class couple have strained relations with the in-laws and neighbours. Matters come to a head at a birthday party for the elderly mother. A warm, humane, yet incisive comedy of bad manners, offering more optimism than the average 80's British film and also better structured than most Mike Leigh offerings. [110m/15]

Cyril..Philip Davis
Shirley ....Ruth Sheen
Mrs. Bender....................................Edna Dore
Martin ....Philip Jackson
Valerie ....Heather Tobias
Laetitia Boothe-Braine...........Lesley Manville

Highlander •• [1986]

Director: **Russell Mulcahy**
Screenplay: **Gregory Widen, Peter Bellwood & Larry Ferguson**

A 16th-century nobleman battles a villain across Continents and centuries. Having a bad French actor playing a Scot and a Scottish actor doing a Spaniard shows just how seriously one is supposed to take the historical aspects of the movie. As a souped-up romp, it's enjoyable enough providing the lagers are extra-strength.
[116m/15]

Connor MacLeod..........Christopher Lambert
Brenda Wyatt ....Roxanne Hart
Kurgen......................................Clancy Brown
Ramirez ....Sean Connery

Highlander II – the Quickening • [1990]

Director: **Russell Mulcahy**
Screenplay: **Peter Bellwood**

It certainly doesn't quicken the pulse. An incomprehensible sequel to a fairly silly original. Connery should be ashamed of himself, while Madsen is criminally wasted. [100m/12]

Connor MacLeod..........Christopher Lambert
Louise Marcus ....Virginia Madsen
Juan Villa-Lobos Ramirez........Sean Connery
General Katana ....Michael Ironside

High Road to China •• [1983]

Director: **Brian G. Hutton**
Screenplay: **Sandra Weintraub Roland & S. Lee Pogostin**

Poor Tom Selleck. Not only did he not become *Indiana Jones*, but he then agreed to this tepid Indy wannabe in which he's a flyer hired by an heiress to help her find her father. I'll take the Low Road, if it's all the same to you. [104m/PG]

O'Malley	Tom Selleck
Eve	Bess Armstrong
Struts	Jack Weston
Bradley Tozer	Wilford Brimley
Bentik	Robert Morley
Suleiman Khan	Brian Blessed

High Season •• [1987]

Director: Clare Peploe
Screenplay: Clare Peploe & Mark Peploe

This supposed British satire on English tourists in Greece does have the delectable Bisset, but also some rubbish about Branagh as a spy. More an excuse for the cast and crew to get a nice tan. [101m/15]

Katherine	Jacqueline Bisset
Patrick	James Fox
Penelope	Irene Papas
Basil Sharp	Sebastian Shaw
Rick	Kenneth Branagh

High Spirits • [1988]

Director: Neil Jordan
Screenplay: Neil Jordan

This tale of O'Toole turning his ramshackle Irish castle into a haunted tourist attraction is brash, boring and monstrously unfunny. Guttenberg's the hen-pecked tourist who breaks the spell that has bound Hannah for centuries. The jokes are more transparent than the ghosts. [96m/15]

Mary Plunkett	Daryl Hannah
Peter Plunkett	Peter O'Toole
Jack	Steve Guttenberg
Sharon	Beverly D'Angelo

Also: Jennifer Tilly, Peter Gallagher, Liam Neeson, Martin Ferrero, Ray McAnally, Connie Booth, Liz Smith

Quote 'Look! You're a ghost. I'm an American. It would never work out.'

Psst! Director Jordan found making a film in Hollywood vastly different from Britain: 'What happens is you slowly go insane and at the end of it all you get this vast, noisy and unfunny movie'.

High Tide ••• [1987]

Director: Gillian Armstrong
Screenplay: Laura Jones

The superb Davis scores again in this Australian drama about a down-at-heel backing singer who has to face the teenage daughter she abandoned years before. Mercifully lacking in sentiment, this is a powerful and intelligent movie with some excellent acting. [104m/15]

Lilli	Judy Davis
Bet	Jan Adele
Ally	Claudia Karvan
Mick	Colin Friels
Col	John Clayton

Highway to Hell •• [1984]

Director: Mark Griffiths
Screenplay: Mark Griffiths

Stoltz is on the run after being wrongly accused of killing his dad. Hooker Carrico's on the run after her chap died rather abruptly. Plenty more will die yet, but we're not particularly interested in where this couple, or the film, is heading. Also known as *Running Hot*. [95m/18]

Charlene	Monica Carrico
Danny	Eric Stoltz
Trent	Stuart Margolin
Tom	Richard Bradford

The Hit ••• [1984]

Director: Stephen Frears
Screenplay: Peter Prince

Quirky British comedy-thriller about hitman Hurt unearthing supergrass Stamp in Spain and dragging him off to Paris to be topped. Occasionally brilliant, even if the implausibilities are sometimes a bit much to swallow.

[98m/18]

Willie Parker	Terence Stamp
Braddock	John Hurt
Myron	Tim Roth
Maggie	Laura Del Sol
Harry	Bill Hunter
Chief Inspector	Fernando Rey

The Hitcher ••• [1986]

Director: **Robert Harmon**
Screenplay: **Eric Red**

Howell unwisely picks up Hauer when he gives him the thumb, while Leigh splits from her man in spectacular fashion. A wildly implausible, but highly energetic and enjoyable horror-thriller.

[97m/18]

John Ryder	Rutger Hauer
Jim Halsey	C. Thomas Howell
Nash	Jennifer Jason Leigh
Capt. Esteridge	Jeffrey DeMunn
Sgt. Starr	John Hackson

Psst! Probably the first movie to include a finger in a bowl of fries and ketchup.

Hoffa •• [1992]

Director: **Danny DeVito**
Screenplay: **David Mamet**

One of the biggest crooks in America is here turned into something of a hero. Even Nicholson, handicapped by a gum shield, cotton wool in his cheeks and a plastic nose, can't bring the moribund script to life. We have no idea what motivated Hoffa or why he is important enough to make a pic about him. Little happens in two hours and, what is more, it doesn't happen extremely slowly.

[140m/15]

James R. Hoffa	Jack Nicholson
Bobby Ciaro	Danny DeVito
Carol D'Allesandro	Armand Assante
Fitzimmons	J.T. Walsh

Also: John C. Reilly, Frank Whaley, Kevin Anderson, John P. Ryan

OOPS! After they leave the wake, it is raining but in the shot looking back at the church, the puddles are clear ◆ During the rumpus at DeVito's place of work, watch the extras at the back give us one of the least convincing fights for years.

Psst! Nicholson and DeVito insisted that a special satellite dish be installed in their hotel during filming so they wouldn't miss any Laker games.

The Holcroft Covenant • [1985]

Director: **John Frankenheimer**
Screenplay: **George Axelrod, Edward Anhalt & John Hopkins**

Adolf Hitler's Right Hand Man Was My Father. So discovers Caine, who hares off after his father's fortune in this rather silly and convoluted thriller based on the Robert Ludlum novel. Even Caine can't make us swallow this tripe. **[112m/15]**

Noel Holcroft	Michael Caine
Johann von Tiebolt	Anthony Andrews
Helden von Tiebolt	Victoria Tennant
Althene Holcroft	Lilli Palmer

Hollywood Shuffle •• [1987]

Director: **Robert Townsend**
Screenplay: **Robert Townsend**

Townsend turned his experiences as a black actor trying to get work in Hollywood into an occasionally entertaining satire on racism in the film business. It's rough and the jokes don't always work but you have to admire the fact that he wrote, produced, directed and acted in the film as well as raising the finance himself. **[82m/15]**

Bobby Taylor	Robert Townsend
Lydia	Anne-Marie Johnson
Mother	Starletta Dupois
Grandmother	Helen Martin

Psst! Townsend got $40,000 of the $100,000 budget from his credit cards, though he didn't have a bank account. Plastic now seems to be one of the main sources of finance for young, independent film-makers in the US.

Home Alone •• [1990]

Director: **Chris Columbus**
Screenplay: **John Hughes**

A family leave smug, smart-alec 8-year-old Culkin behind when they go on holiday to Paris and try to pretend it's all a mistake rather than something they've been planning all year. Then burglars Pesci and Stern try to break in. Despite being the most popular comedy ever and the third-most popular film of all time, relatively little happens until the fun-filled final quarter of an hour. Although kids love to see one of their own making fools of a couple of adults, it's violent and nothing like as inventive as might be expected. There are those who find that a little Mac goes a long way. **[103m/PG]**

Kevin McCallister	Macaulay Culkin
Harry	Joe Pesci
Marv	Daniel Stern
Peter McCallister	John Heard
Kate McCallister	Catherine O'Hara
Marley	Roberts Blossom
Uncle Frank	Gerry Bamman
Gus Polinski	John Candy
Fuller	Kieran Culkin

Showing *It's a Wonderful Life* [in French].

OOPS! When Mom flies home, she arrives on a different type of plane than the one she left Paris on ◆ Watch Pesci forget which hand he's burnt on the hot doorknob. Its image on his palm is also upside down.

Psst! Hughes was inspired to write the script after he lost one of his own children briefly in a department store ◆ Culkins' goldfish died on the night of the end of filming party.

Home Alone 2: Lost in New York •• [1992]

Director: **Chris Columbus**
Screenplay: **John Hughes**

Rather than tinker with a successful formula, they've made the same movie again. He's not actually at home this time but in New York, where he runs into The Wet Bandits again. Rather more nastily violent than the original, it's also sickeningly slushy. Mac himself seems less charming and mugs mercilessly throughout. **[120m/PG]**

Kevin	Macaulay Culkin
Harry	Joe Pesci
Marv	Daniel Stern
Kate	Catherine O'Hara
Peter	John Heard
Buzz	Devin Ratray

Concierge	Tim Curry
Pigeon Lady	Brenda Fricker
Mr. Duncan	Eddie Bracken
Uncle Frank	Gerry Bamman

Blurb He's Up Past His Bedtime In The City That Never Sleeps.

Quote 'Funnily enough, we never lose our luggage.'

Showing *It's a Wonderful Life* [In Spanish].

Psst! American movie magazine *Premiere* worked out that by the end of their vacation, the McCallister's would have spent something like $39,000.

Homeboy •• [1989]

Director: **Michael Seresin**
Screenplay: **Eddie Cook**

As a keen boxer, Rourke was no doubt keen to play this role of a down-at-heel alcoholic pugilist. But despite his convincing performance, the script takes a serious punch early on and wanders round in circles, dazed and going nowhere. So realistic that it's extremely depressing. **[115m/15]**

Johnny Walker	Mickey Rourke
Wesley	Christopher Walken
Ruby	Debra Feuer
Grazziano	Kevin Conway

Homeward Bound: The Incredible Journey ••• [1993]

Director: **Duwayne Dunham**
Screenplay: **Caroline Thompson & Linda Wolverton**

This updating of Disney's 1963 *The Incredible Journey* should be titled *Look Who's Barking*. A couple of dogs and a cat, bearing the voices of Ameche, Fox and Field, left with a family friend, decide to head off on the long trek home. This delightfully sweet little film should keep the children well amused. **[84m]**

Voice of Shadow	Don Ameche
Voice of Chance	Michael J. Fox
Voice of Sassy	Sally Field
Bob	Robert Hays
Laura	Kim Greist

Homicide •••• [1991]

Director: **David Mamet**
Screenplay: **David Mamet**

New York cop Mantegna investigates the murder of an elderly Jewish shopkeeper. When evidence of neo-Nazism emerges, he is reluctantly forced to take sides. Director Mamet's best film cleverly uses the cop thriller format to explore ideas of loyalty and anti-Semitism in depth, without losing any of the accompanying suspense. [102m/15]

Bob Gold	Joe Mantegna
Tim Sullivan	William H. Macy
Chava	Natalija Nogulich
Randolph	Ving Rhames
Lieutenant Senna	Vincent Guastaferro
Ms Klein	Rebecca Pidgeon

Honey, I Shrunk the Kids ••• [1989]

Director: **Joe Johnston**
Screenplay: **Ed Naha & Tom Schulman**

A bunch of kids forget one of the first rules in life: If you have a crackpot inventor father, leave home. Accidentally shrunk, they have to fight their way across the back garden, menaced by giant insects, lawnmowers and a scorpion. This lively comedy manages the difficult feat of being both funny and thrilling. Great entertainment for all the family, a rarity these days. If only the ant hadn't been quite so pathetically nice... [93m/U]

Wayne Szalinski	Rick Moranis
Big Russ Thompson	Matt Frewer
Diane Szalinski	Marcia Strassman
Mae Thompson	Kristine Sutherland
Little Russ Thompson	Thomas Brown
Ron Thompson	Jared Rushton
Amy Szalinski	Amy O'Neill
Nick Szalinski	Robert Oliveri

Quote 'They broke up for religious differences. She thought she was God and he disagreed.'

Psst! If it bugs you where you've heard the voice of Frewer, the fishing-obsessed next door neighbour, it was probably in his incarnation as Max Headroom • Kimmy Robertson who plays Gloria, the woman who turns up for fishing in the camper, was Lucy in *Twin Peaks* • The cinema release was accompanied by the Roger Rabbit cartoon *Tummy Trouble*, Disney's first short for over 25 years.

Honey, I Blew Up the Kid •• [1992]

Director: **Randal Kleiser**
Screenplay: **Thom Eberhardt, Peter Elbling & Garry Goodrow**

A pale mirror-image imitation of its predecessor. This time the baby gets zapped and grows to 100 feet tall. When it heads off towards Las Vegas, it has to be stopped, presumably because it's too young to play the slots. This being Disney, we never learn what happens when its nappy needs changing. Amiable drivel for the really young, it's dull stuff for anyone whose age is less than their I.Q. [89m/U]

Wayne Szalinski	Rick Moranis
Diane Szalinski	Marcia Strassman
Nick Szalinski	Robert Oliveri
Clifford Sterling	Lloyd Bridges

Honeymoon in Vegas •••• [1992]

Director: **Andrew Bergman**
Screenplay: **Andrew Bergman**

This deliciously funny comedy has private eye Cage plucking up the courage to get married to Parker. Just before the wedding in Vegas, he loses her in a poker game to gangster Caan. There's a clever plot, some wonderfully quirky performances and a bizarre background of an Elvis convention. There are Elvises of every size, shape and even colour – even some Flying Elvises. A treat from start to finish. [95m/12]

Tommy Korman	James Caan
Jack Singer	Nicolas Cage
Betsy/Donna	Sarah Jessica Parker
Mahi Mahi	Pat Morita

Johnny Sandwich ....Johnny Williams
Sally Molars ....John Capodice
Sidney Tomashefsky ....Robert Costanzo
Bea Singer ....Anne Bancroft
Chief Orman ....Peter Boyle

Psst! There's a running joke about an ugly client of his believing that his wife is having an affair with Mike Tyson. Negotiations were under way for Tyson to appear with her at the end of the picture before another engagement took precedence ✦ Caan is said to have established a world record by sleeping with 17 consecutive Playboy Playmates of the Month.

Honkytonk Man •• [1982]

Director: **Clint Eastwood**
Screenplay: **Clancy Carlile**

Just to make sure we really understand that things are tough, Clint here plays an alcoholic country and western singer with TB in the midst of the Great Depression. All he wants out of what life's left to him is to get to Nashville to play the Grand Ole Opry. It's all pretty grim, but never grimmer than when Clint sings. [123m/15]

Red Stovall ....Clint Eastwood
Whit ....Kyle Eastwood
Grandpa ....John McIntire
Marlene...Alexa Kenin
Emmy..Verna Bloom

Psst! Kyle Eastwood is Clint's son.

The Honorary Consul • [1983]

Director: **John Mackenzie**
Screenplay: **Christopher Hampton**

If you can believe in Richard Gere as a guilt-ridden English doctor involved in political shenanigans in South America, then you'll believe anything. Despite Caine's bravura performance as the drunken British Consul of the title, the American title, *Beyond the Limit*, seems far more apt. [103m/18]

Charley Fortnum ....Michael Caine
Dr. Plarr ....Richard Gere
Col. Perez....................................Bob Hoskins
Clara..Elpidia Carrillo

Hook ••• [1991]

Director: **Steven Spielberg**
Screenplay: **James V. Hart & Malia Scotch Marmo**

A grown-up Peter Pan, now an investment banker, has to return to Never Never Land to rescue his children. The critics who savaged it missed the point. This is panto on film, and jolly good fun it is, too. Yes, it's too long. Yes, the plot's confusing. Yes, Roberts looks decidedly out of place as Tinkerbell. And yes, it's icky that The Lost Boys have been turned into the Politically Correct Benetton Boys (at least there aren't any girls!). But there's enough of the Spielberg magic and humour to keep the eye and the brain engaged and happy, with Hoffman and Hopkins a wonderful music-hall double-act. [144m/U]

Captain Hook.........................Dustin Hoffman
Peter Banning/Peter Pan ....Robin Williams
Tinkerbell......................................Julia Roberts
Smee ....Bob Hoskins
Granny Wendy..........................Maggie Smith
Moira...................................Caroline Goodall
Jack..Charlie Korsmo
Maggie...Amber Scott
Liza ....Laurel Cronin
Inspector Good..............................Phil Collins
Tootles..Arthur Malet

Quote 'Excuse me. Is there a payphone around here?'

OOPS! The flight across the Atlantic caused great hilarity in American cinemas. It shows the Bannings flying Pan Am, but the airline went bust just before the film opened ✦ Keep your eye on the pirates in the fight. Some of them aren't playing dead properly ✦ Surely, that's the skyline of Oxford that can be seen through Wendy's London window?

Psst! Keep an eye out for the bearded pirate, picked on by Hook and thrown into the chest of scorpions. It's a heavily disguised Glenn Close ✦ Among the uncredited writers working on the script was Carrie Fisher ✦ Hoffman made $20m from the film.

Hoosiers
SEE: Best Shot

Hope and Glory •••• [1987]
Director: John Boorman
Screenplay: John Boorman

A spellbinding evocation of family life in wartime suburban Britain, as seen through the eyes of a 9-year-old. Despite the privations and upheavals caused by the Blitz, for the youngsters it's a wildly exciting time. Often funny, occasionally sad, but always with the ring of truth, there has never been a better portrayal of life on the home front. [113m/15]

Bill Rohan	Sebastian Rice-Edwards
Sue Rohan	Geraldine Muir
Grace Rohan	Sarah Miles
Clive Rohan	David Hayman
Dawn Rohan	Sammi Davis
Mac	Derrick O'Connor
Molly	Susan Wooldridge
Cpl. Bruce Carey	Jean-Marc Barr
Grandfather George	Ian Bannen

Quote 'Thank you, Adolf.' [When school is bombed]

Psst! The voice narrating at the beginning is that of writer-director Boorman ✦ His son Charley Boorman, star of *The Emerald Forest* plays the downed Luftwaffe pilot.

Hot Dog... The Movie • [1984]
Director: Peter Markle
Screenplay: Mike Marvin

The film's resemblance to a hot dog is uncanny; it's limp, unpalatable and full of things you wouldn't want to step in. This teenage sex romp is ostensibly about ski-ing, although it's about as entertaining as doing a slalom into a fir tree. [98m/18]

Dan	David Naughton
Harkin	Patrick Houser

Also: Tracy N. Smith, John Patrick Reger, Shannon Tweed

Psst! Tweed was 1982 Playboy Playmate of the Year.

Hotel New Hampshire • [1984]
Director: Tony Richardson
Screenplay: Tony Richardson

John Irving's novel about a bevy of eccentrics setting up a hotel deserved to fail, if only for the crime of putting Nastassja Kinski into a bear suit. When they check in, you should check out. [110m/18]

Franny	Jodie Foster
Father	Beau Bridges
John	Rob Lowe
Susie	Nastassja Kinski
Iowa Bob	Wilford Brimley
Ernst	Matthew Modine

Hot Shots! •• [1991]
Director: Jim Abrahams
Screenplay: Jim Abrahams & Pat Proft

Although primarily a spoof of *Top Gun* this comedy from part of the *Airplane* and *Naked Gun* team also lays into a dozen other movies. While some of the jokes are hilarious, many of them take place in a vacuum. It would have been far better if the plot, involving pilot Sheen's attempt to wipe out the memory of his father's disastrous career, had been tighter. [85m/12]

Sean "Topper" Harley	Charlie Sheen
Kent Gregory	Cary Elwes
Ramada Thompson	Valeria Golino
Admiral Benson	Lloyd Bridges
Commander Block	Kevin Dunn

Showing *Flight of the Intruder.*

Psst! The credits are better than the movie, containing recipes for brownies and offering suggestions for things to do afterwards, such as 'Help someone learn to read', 'Visit a dairy and see how milk is handled and prepared for delivery' and 'If you had left this theater when the credits began, you'd be home by now'.

Hot Shots! Part Deux ••• [1993]
Director: Jim Abrahams
Screenplay: Jim Abrahams & Pat Proft

Far from being just a laugh a minute, this superb Rambo spoof (with a little roasting of *Casablanca, Terminator 2, Apocalypse Now* and *Robin Hood*, too) manages several excellent guffaws every 60 seconds. With a reasonable plot holding it all together, it's up to *Naked Gun's* standard.

[89m]

Topper Harley	Charlie Sheen
Tug Benson	Lloyd Bridges
Ramada Rodham Hayman	Valeria Golino
Col. Denton Walters	Richard Crenna
Michelle Rodham Huddleston	Brenda Bakke
Harbinger	Miguel Ferrer
Dexter Hayman	Rowan Atkinson

Blurb Just Deux It.

Psst! Look out for a hilarious cameo from Charlie's dad Martin ✦ As usual, the credits are as good as the movie, including 'Answer to tonight's scrambled movie title: "T–2"' and 'Secret of "The Crying Game"... She's a Guy'.

The Hot Spot ••• [1990]

Director: **Dennis Hopper**
Screenplay: **Nona Tyson & Charles Williams**

Drifter Johnson arrives in a small town in the Deep South, with Passion and Murder following close behind. A slow but underrated thriller, with a very steamy atmosphere and some cunning plot twists. Nance is hilarious as the bank manager while Madsen vamps it up splendidly.

[130m/18]

Harry Madox	Don Johnson
Dolly Harshaw	Virginia Madsen
Gloria Harper	Jennifer Connelly
Lon Gulik	Charles Martin Smith
Frank Sutton	William Sadler
George Harshaw	Jerry Hardin
Sheriff	Barry Corbin
Deputy Tate	Leon Rippy
Julian Ward	Jack Nance

Quote 'There are only two things to do around here. You got a TV?...No? Well, you're now down to one.'

Psst! Virginia Madsen used a body double for the sex scene with Johnson.

House •• [1986]

Director: **Steve Miner**
Screenplay: **Ethan Wiley**

Not the bingo movie you've all been waiting for, but another horror pic. A writer wanting to exorcise his Vietnam ghosts by writing about them moves into a Victorian house which doesn't exactly exude Ye Olde Worlde peace and charm. A passable, if highly familiar, romp with the usual elements.

[93m/15]

Roger Cobb	William Katt
Harold Gorton	George Wendt
Big Ben	Richard Moll
Sandy	Kay Lenz
Tanya	Mary Stavin

Psst! If you're wondering where you've seen Wendt, he's Norm from *Cheers*.

House II: The Second Story • [1987]

Director: **Ethan Wiley**
Screenplay: **Ethan Wiley**

In real life all these giant old houses have long since been turned into flats. Yet here's another of them, menacing a different hero with the same plot. This rickety structure's ripe for demolition.

[94m/15]

Jesse	Arye Gross
Charlie	Jonathan Stark
Gramps	Royal Dano
John	Bill Maher
Bill	John Ratzenberger

Psst! If you're wondering where you've seen Ratzenberger, he's Cliff from *Cheers*.

Housekeeper

SEE: Judgement in Stone

Housekeeping •• [1987]

Director: **Bill Forsyth**
Screenplay: **Bill Forsyth**

For his first film made outside Scotland, Forsyth chose this tale of two sisters in a remote part of Canada whose lives are turned upside down by an eccentric aunt.

Despite some of the usual splendid Forsyth eccentricity, this rather darker and bleaker picture than usual doesn't always hit the spot. **[116m/PG]**

Sylvie	Christine Lahti
Ruth	Sara Walker
Lucille	Andrea Burchill
Aunt Lily	Anne Pitoniak
Aunt Nona	Barbara Reese

House of Games ••• [1987]

Director: **David Mamet**
Screenplay: **David Mamet**

Crouse is the psychologist who gets involved with con man Mantegna and his chums and is drawn irresistibly into the world of confidence tricks. Cold and stagey at the start, we become just as fascinated as her by this unknown world where nothing is as it seems. Mesmerising on first viewing, it fails to grip a second time when you know the surprises in store. **[102m/15]**

Margaret Ford	Lindsay Crouse
Mike	Joe Mantegna
Joey	Mike Nussbaum
Dr. Littauer	Lilia Skala
The businessman	J.T. Walsh
Girl with book	Willo Hausman
Prison ward patient	Karen Kohlhaas

Psst! Crouse was then Mrs. Mamet ◆ The room number in the hotel is 1138. Is this a reference to the 1138 that has recurred in George Lucas's films since his *THX-1138*?

The House on Carroll Street •• [1988]

Director: **Peter Yates**
Screenplay: **Walter Bernstein**

This over-earnest and wildly unbelievable thriller, set against a background of McCarthyism, culminates in a tense finale high above Grand Central Station. For the rest, it's about as tense as a British Rail Away Day. **[101m/PG]**

Emily Crane	Kelly McGillis
Cochran	Jeff Daniels
Ray Salwen	Mandy Patinkin
Miss Venable	Jessica Tandy

House Party ••• [1990]

Director: **Reginald Hudlin**
Screenplay: **Reginald Hudlin**

Infectious, upbeat and boisterous look at a party held by a group of black teenagers. Its subject might be a little insubstantial compared to some black films, but it's funny, alive and extremely likeable. **[95m/15]**

Kid	Christopher Reid
Pop	Robin Harris
Play	Christopher Martin
Bilal	Martin Lawrence
Sidney	Tisha Campbell
Sharane	A. J. Johnson

Psst! Writer-director Reginald Hudlin and producer Warrington Hudlin play the 'crooks'.

House Party 2 • [1991]

Director: **Doug McHenry & George Jackson**
Screenplay: **Rusty Cundieff & Daryl G. Nickens**

Despite the presence of Iman and Whoopi Goldberg in cameos, this disappointing sequel only goes to show how difficult it was to bring off the first film successfully. The absence of the Hudlins can't have helped. **[94m/15]**

Kid	Christopher Reid
Play	Christopher Martin
Sidney	Tisha Campbell

Housesitter •• [1992]

Director: **Frank Oz**
Screenplay: **Mark Stein**

Spurned suitor Martin has a one-night stand with Hawn, only to find her moving into his house and taking over his life. Although the plot's mildly diverting, this comedy of complications, with the irritating Hawn digging Martin ever deeper into her hole, isn't terribly funny. What's more, Martin ends up with the wrong woman. **[102m/PG]**

Davis	Steve Martin
Gwen	Goldie Hawn
Becky	Dana Delaney
Edna Davis	Julie Harris
George Davis	Donald Moffat
Marty	Peter MacNicol
Ralph	Richard B. Shull

Psst! Hawn is apparently so proud of her bottom that she insists that the camera dwell on it. If you get bored, you could try counting the number of [clothed] butt shots.

Howard...A New Breed of Hero •   [1986]

Director: **Willard Huyck**
Screenplay: **Willard Huyck & Gloria Katz**

Known rather appropriately in the United States as *Howard the Duck,* it is hard to understand how a film as bad as this ever reached the screen. If there was ever a case for studio executives committing hari kari, this was surely it. An alien duck lands in Ohio, saves the world from baddies and ends up managing a girl rock group. One of the biggest bellyflops of the 80s.

[110m/PG]

Beverly Switzler	Lea Thompson
Dr. Jenning	Jeffrey Jones
Phil Blumburtt	Tim Robbins
Lt. Welker	Paul Guilfoyle

Psst! This was probably the first movie in mainstream Hollywood history to depict interspecies sex, with Lea Thompson putting out for the giant duck • Howard was apparently Marvel's most popular comic character in the 70s, immensely popular among American students • Hard to believe that the censor had his evil way with this one, but indeed a safe-sex joke about Howard having a duck condom in his wallet got chopped • Eight different people took their turn in the duck suit • The film cost over $30m.

Howard's End ••••   [1992]

Director: **James Ivory**
Screenplay: **Ruth Prawer Jhabvala**

At last an E.M. Forster adaptation that not only has the pretty frocks, meadows and steam trains, but a cracking good story, too. Independently-minded Thompson is bilked of the eponymous house by widower Hopkins, only to end up marrying him. A superb ensemble cast carry off this tale of class and family conflict brilliantly, showing up the horrors and hypocrisy of Edwardian society. A superlative entertainment.

[140m/PG]

Henry Wilcox	Anthony Hopkins
Ruth Wilcox	Vanessa Redgrave
Helen Schlegel	Helena Bonham Carter
Margaret Schlegel	Emma Thompson
Charles Wilcox	James Wilby
Leonard Blast	Samuel West
Evie Wilcox	Jemma Redgrave
Jacky Bast	Nicola Duffett
Aunt Juley	Prunella Scales
Lecturer	Simon Callow

Oscars Best Screenplay (adapted), Emma Thompson

OOPS! Jacky Bast has a vaccination scar on her upper arm.

Howard the Duck

SEE: Howard...A New Breed of Hero

How to Get Ahead in Advertising ••   [1989]

Director: **Bruce Robinson**
Screenplay: **Bruce Robinson**

An adman has a good head on his shoulders. Actually, he has two when, as a result of overwork, a second one develops from a boil. How could it miss? Unfortunately, an initially promising satire on the advertising business degenerates into a long rant, despite hard work from Grant.

[104m/15]

Dennis Bagley	Richard E. Grant
Julia Bagley	Rachel Ward
Bristol	Richard Wilson
Penny Wheelstock	Jacqueline Tong

Hudson Hawk • [1991]

Director: Michael Lehmann
Screenplay: Steven E. de Souza & Daniel Waters

...Or *Hudson the Duck*, as it was known at the time. This disastrous big-budget attempt to marry comedy with Willis's usual action stuff has him as a wise-cracking cat burglar involved in a Vatican art robbery and a chase after a gold-making machine invented by Da Vinci. If there was a lower grading, this film would have it. [The classic example of Rose's Rule #8] [100m/15]

Hudson Hawk	Bruce Willis
Tommy 'Five-Tone' Messina	Danny Aiello
Anna Baragli	Andie MacDowell
Darwin Mayflower	Richard E. Grant
Minerva Mayflower	Sandra Bernhard
Alfred, the butler	Donald Burton
George Kaplan	James Coburn

Psst! The third biggest flop in movie history, losing $47m • This was Willis's pet project for almost ten years. He co-wrote the story [and the title song] himself • Dutch actress Maruschka Detmers was to be have been Willis's love interest. Rumour has it that Demi Moore had her fired, to be replaced by happily-married MacDowell, but Mr. and Mrs. Willis have denied it • Before filming in Rome, producer Joel Silver had a priest bless the enterprise • The George Kaplan character is named after the fictional agent in *North by Northwest* • The life of Manhattan was disrupted for a week by this movie, when the out-bound lane of Brooklyn Bridge was closed to traffic for seven nights from 10 till 5.

The Hunger • [1983]

Director: Tony Scott
Screenplay: Ivan Davis & Michael Thomas

Catherine Deneuve needs regular supplies of blood to survive. Bowie misses a feed and ages at high speed. For those wishing to collect ad-director clichés such as billowing curtains, doves etc., Scott's debut is a must. But otherwise, even the famous Sarandon-Deneuve lesbian scene can't prevent matters disintegrating faster than Bowie. [97m/18]

Miriam	Catherine Deneuve
John	David Bowie
Sarah Roberts	Susan Sarandon
Tom Haver	Cliff De Young
Lt. Allegrezza	Dan Hedaya

Psst! The youth interrupting Sarandon in the phone booth is Willem Dafoe, later to star with her in *Light Sleeper*.

Hunter's Blood •• [1986]

Director: Robert C. Hughes
Screenplay: Emmett Alston

A group of city-boy hunters who obviously haven't seen *Deliverance* head into the woods and find that the locals aren't quite as friendly as the tourist brochures make out. [102m/18]

David Rand	Samuel Bottoms
Melanie	Kim Delaney
Mason Rand	Clu Gulager
Al Coleman	Ken Swofford
Snake	Billy Drago

The Hunt for Red October ••• [1990]

Director: John McTiernan
Screenplay: Larry Ferguson & Donald Stewart

Russian submarine commander Connery heads West with his top-secret vessel, confusing the Americans as to what he's up to, particularly intelligence expert Baldwin, playing the part of Jack Ryan that would soon pass to Harrison Ford. Although the Cold War evaporated before the film came out, it's still a tremendously exciting if complicated thriller, at its best in the underwater chase sequences. If you think the plot's a little unbelievable, wait till you hear Connery's Russian accent. Try to see it on the largest screen possible. [135m/PG]

Capt. Marko Ramius	Sean Connery
Jack Ryan	Alec Baldwin
Bart Mancuso	Scott Glenn

Capt. Borodin ....Sam Neill
Admiral James Greer............James Earl Jones
Ambassador Lysenko ....Joss Ackland
Jeffrey Pelt..................................Richard Jordan
Ivan Putin ....Peter Firth
Dr. Petrov ....Tim Curry
Seaman Jones.....................Courtney B. Vance
Capt. Tupolev.......................Stellan Skarsgard
Skip Tyler......................................Jeffrey Jones

Psst! Connery's part was to have been played by Klaus Maria Brandauer, but he pulled out at the last minute ♦ Connery was paid $10m

Husbands and Wives ••• [1992]

Director: **Woody Allen**
Screenplay: **Woody Allen**

Woody must have let one of his kids operate the camera. What other explanation can there be for the extraordinary, nausea-inducing, swaying picture? Without the fascination about whether or not the film mirrors Woody and Mia's real life, this is yet another Allen pic spent in the company of navel-gazing, angst-ridden, middle-class New Yorkers. Only the astounding performance of Davis marks it out from the others.   **[108m/15]**

Gabe Roth ....Woody Allen
Rain's mother............................Blythe Danner
Sally...Judy Davis
Judy Roth ....Mia Farrow
Rain ....Juliette Lewis
Michael..Liam Neeson
Jack ....Sydney Pollack
Sam ....Lysette Anthony

Quote 'Life doesn't imitate art. It imitates bad television.' ♦ 'It's over and we both know it. [Judy/Farrow to Gabe/Allen]

Psst! Britain's Emily Lloyd was fired from the picture.

I Bought a Vampire Motorcycle • [1990]

Director: **Dirk Campbell**
Screenplay: **Mycal Miller & John Wolskel**

How appropriate that two of the sorriest industries in Britain, motorbikes and films, should be combined in one movie. The title says it all. Grosser than you'd imagine, it has a sense of humour which is not so much infantile as foetal. A Chinese takeaway called Fu King? Laugh? I thought I'd never start.

[105m/18]

Nick Oddie.............................Neil Morrissey
Kim ....Amanda Noar
Insp. Cleaver..........................Michael Elphick
Priest.....................................Anthony Daniels

Psst! Probably the first movie to have a talking piece of excrement.

The Icicle Thief ••• [1990]

Director: **Maurizio Nichetti**
Screenplay: **Maurizio Nichetti & Mauro Monti**

Superb Italian comedy with clown Nichetti as a film director being interviewed about his latest film when a power cut causes the ads and the movie to get mixed up. Gorgeous model Komarek turns up in colour in the black-and-white film while the director tries to restore order by leaping into the frame as well. So unlike anything else it's well-nigh impossible to describe, this is a delightful hour and a half of madcap, surrealistic humour.

[90m/PG]

Nichetti/Antonio ....Maurizio Nichetti
Maria............................Caterini Sylos Labini
Bruno..Federico Rizzo
Don Italo ....Renato Scarpa
Model.....................................Heidi Komarex

If Looks Could Kill

SEE: Teen Agent

I Love You to Death • [1990]

Director: Lawrence Kasdan
Screenplay: John Kostmayer

...It isn't reciprocated. Despite being based on a true story, it is hard to believe a minute of this tale about Ullman and her mother trying to kill philandering pizzaman hubbie Kline. Black it certainly is. Funny it is not, even though it's unusual seeing Hurt as a spaced-out incompetent hitman. If only he'd been better at it, then we could have all gone home earlier. [98m/15]

Joey Boca	Kevin Kline
Rosalie Boca	Tracey Ullman
Nadja	Joan Plowright
Devo Nod	River Phoenix
Harlan James	William Hurt
Marlon James	Keanu Reeves

Quote 'If we keep shooting Joey, don't you think he'll start to get suspicious?'

Showing *Bridge on the River Kwai.*

Psst! Director Kasdan appears as the lawyer in the police station, although you don't get much of a view of him ✦ Phoebe Cates, the real-life Mrs. Kline, has a cameo in a disco as one of his flings ✦ The credits include a 'pizza consultant'.

I'm Gonna Git You Sucka •• [1988]

Director: Keenen Ivory Wayans
Screenplay: Keenen Ivory Wayans

Wayans wrote, directed and starred in this comedy spoofing the 70's black exploitation pictures. He plays an army veteran returning to avenge the death of his brother, a victim of too many gold chains! Although very funny to start with, the good ideas run out about half an hour before the movie does. [89m/15]

Jack Spade	Keenen Ivory Wayans
John Spade	Bernie Casey
Flyguy	Antonio Fargas

Also: Steve James, Isaac Hayes, Jim Brown, Ja'net DuBois

The Immaculate Conception •• [1993]

Director: Jamil Dehlavi
Screenplay: Jamil Dehlavi

A Western couple living in India visit a fertility shrine and become involved in social and political conflict. This brave and unconventional story of culture clash takes on too many issues to be able to resolve them all. [120m/15]

Alistair	James Wilby
Hannah	Melissa Leo
Samira	Shabana Azmi

Impromptu ••• [1991]

Director: James Lapine
Screenplay: Sarah Kernochan

Quirky biopic of the cross-dressing George Sand getting it together with Chopin, the megastar of his day. Uneven, but with welcome wit, pace and originality, this is a painless way to absorb High Culture. The ever-splendid Davis brings much fun to the proceedings. [107m/12]

George Sand	Judy Davis
Frederic Chopin	Hugh Grant
Alfred De Musset	Mandy Patinkin
Marie D'Agoult	Bernadette Peters
Franz Liszt	Julian Sands
Eugene Delacroix	Ralph Brown
Felicien Mallefille	Georges Corraface
Duke d'Antan	Anton Rodgers
Duchess d'Antan	Emma Thompson
George Sand's mother	Anna Massey

Quote 'A 19th-century *Big Chill.*' [Patinkin]

Impulse • [1984]

Director: Graham Baker
Screenplay: Bart Davis & Don Carlos Dunaway

An insignificant and rather unexciting thriller about a small town where, after something nasty gets in the milk supply, everyone goes bonkers and behaves in a reprehensible fashion. Not released in Britain until 1986. [91m/18]

Stuart	Tim Matheson
Jennifer	Meg Tilly
Dr. Carr	Hume Cronyn
Bob	John Karlen
Eddie	Bill Paxton

In Bed with Madonna ••• [1991]

Director: **Alek Keshishian**

This fascinating behind-the-scenes documentary following Madonna on her 1989 'Blonde Ambition' tour reveals more of the pop icon than anything else she's done, even 'Sex'. True, she doesn't take her togs off, but thanks to Keshishian, we learn much more about her than she must have guessed when she commissioned it. Absorbing stuff, whether you like her or not. Also known as *Truth or Dare*. [119m/18]

Quote 'We thought it was neat, really neat.'

Psst! Madonna insisted on the deletion of a couple of scenes, one where her father broke wind and another in the truth-or-dare game where she french-kissed one of her female backup singers.

In Country •• [1989]

Director: **Norman Jewison**
Screenplay: **Frank Pierson & Cynthia Cidre**

This very different role for Willis, as a shell-shocked Vietnam vet, was a brave effort but doesn't really come off. His niece, Lloyd, lost her father in war, but nobody wants to talk to her about it. It's the lacklustre script, rather than the acting, that lets it down. [115m/15]

Emmett Smith	Bruce Willis
Samantha Hughes	Emily Lloyd
Irene	Joan Allen
Lonnie	Kevin Anderson

Also: John Terry, Peggy Rea, Judith Ivey, Stephen Tobolowsky

Indecent Proposal ••• [1993]

Director: **Adrian Lyne**
Screenplay: **Amy Holden Jones**

Happy couple Woody and Demi find their marriage under pressure when, just as they are in desperate need of cash,

wealthy Redford offers one million dollars for just one night with her. An intriguing love story, this is one of those rare films where you genuinely want to know what's going to happen. Perhaps a little too slow, it's marred by a silly ending while the moral underpinning of the film is weakened by the fact that the millionaire in question is Redford and not, say, Danny DeVito. [117m/15]

John Gage	Robert Redford
Diana Murphy	Demi Moore
David Murphy	Woody Harrelson
Jeremy	Oliver Platt
Mr. Shackleford	Seymour Cassel
Auction Emcee	Billy Connolly
Day Tripper	Billy Bob Thornton
Mr. Langford	Rip Taylor

OOPS! The boom mike operator was keen to make his mark here, dipping his mike into the scene where Moore's opening the curtains in the bedroom suite and later as the two guys are leaving lawyer Platt's office ✦ When Moore is in Redford's car for the final time, it's pouring with rain and at night. When she gets out, the sun has risen on a glorious day.

Psst! Tom Cruise and Nicole Kidman were associated with the film in the early stages, but Cruise's involvement with Scientology led to him pulling out of such a risqué project ✦ The Redford part was originally to have been played by Warren Beatty ✦ Initially the couple were a construction worker and a waitress who were completely destitute ✦ Look out for Sheena Easton and Herbie Hancock, both of whom appear as themselves performing at private gatherings ✦ Amy Rochelle claims to have worked for 30 days on the film, body-doubling for Demi Moore in the sex scenes, apparently because husband Bruce Willis wouldn't let Moore be seen on screen naked ✦ Moore lived up to her nickname of 'Gimmee Moore' when the film company sent a jet to whisk her, hubby and entourage to the film's premiere. Apparently Moore decided the plane wasn't big enough and ordered another.

Indiana Jones and the Last Crusade •••• [1989]

Director: **Steven Spielberg**
Screenplay: **Jeffrey Boam**

An excellent outing for Indiana Jones, this time teamed up with dad Connery in a search for the Holy Grail. Although full of implausibilities (didn't anyone use passports in the 30s?), it's rollicking good fun, packed with great action sequences, villainous Nazis, great locations and wonderful bantering dialogue between Dad and Junior. [127m/PG]

Indiana Jones	Harrison Ford
Prof. Henry Jones	Sean Connery
Marcus Brody	Denholm Elliott
Dr. Elsa Schneider	Alison Doody
Sallah	John Rhys-Davies
Walter Donovan	Julian Glover
Young Indy	River Phoenix
Vogel	Michael Byrne
Kazim	Kevork Malikyan
Grail Knight	Robert Eddison
Fedora	Richard Young
Sultan	Alexei Sayle
Young Henry	Alex Hyde-White

Blurb He's Back, And This Time He's Brought His Dad ◆ You'll Have The Time Of Your Life Keeping Up With The Jones's

Quote 'Nazis! I hate these guys.' ◆ 'Does anyone here speak English, or even ancient Greek?'

OOPS! Where to start? After Dad and Junior escape from the castle, the signpost they stop at has directions to different places on each side ◆ When Hitler signs his autograph for Indy, the world's most notorious left-hander does so with his right hand ◆ The Jones boys would have had difficulty riding in the *Hindenberg* in 1938. It blew up the year before. Then again, Indy would have trouble with his transatlantic flight east. He made the journey a year before the service began ◆ In the airport lounge, a couple of passengers are reading a newspaper dated 1918 ◆ After the speedboat has been sliced up, watch the wheel of Indy's boat switch suddenly from right to left ◆ In the library in the old church, the all-important letter 'X' is clearly white when seen from the staircase but it's faint green when they're back downstairs again ◆ Despite the lettering on screen reading 'The Republic of Hatay', the ruler is immediately afterwards referred to as 'Your Royal Highness'.

Psst! Although Connery is playing Ford's father, he is actually only 12 years older ◆ The script originally had the relationship between Dad and Junior all lovey-dovey, with Dad a fount of much Yoda-like wisdom. It was changed at Connery's insistence ◆ Phoenix, here playing the young Indy, had starred with Ford 3 years earlier in *The Mosquito Coast* ◆ Lt. Col. Hugh Dickens, the C.O. of the 9th/12th Royal Lancers appears as a Nazi officer ◆ 3,000 rats were bred specially for the catacombs scene ◆ The original choice to play Indiana Jones in the first film was not Ford, but an unknown Tom Selleck. To his horror, he found his option taken up on a pilot he'd done for *Magnum*. He couldn't get out, even though Spielberg held up the project for five weeks. A TV actors' strike meant that *Raiders* actually finished before *Magnum* got off the ground.

Indiana Jones and the Temple of Doom •• [1984]

Director: **Steven Spielberg**
Screenplay: **Willard Huyck & Gloria Katz**

This prequel to *Raiders* is gruesome and unsubtle, undermined by a weak story involving Eastern religious fanatics. The endless succession of action set-pieces are suprisingly unconvincing, even the expensively-staged underground railway escape. [117m/PG]

Indiana Jones	Harrison Ford
Willie Scott	Kate Capshaw
Short Round	Ke Huy Quan
Mola Ram	Amrish Puri
Chattar Lal	Roshan Seth

Psst! The Club Obi-Wan, home to the opening sequence, is a *Star Wars* in-joke ✦ Keep an eye out early on for Dan Aykroyd in a cameo as 'Weber', leading Indy and the others to the plane. The cameo was a quid pro quo for Spielberg's appearance in *The Blues Brothers* ✦ Although the PG-13 rating was introduced for this film, The American National Coalition of Television Violence thought it should have been an X, logging 14 killings and 39 attempted murders by Indy and over a hundred other incidents of killing, maiming and torture ✦ A sacrifice involving a heart being ripped out was cut by the UK censor.

The Indian Runner ••   [1991]

Director: **Sean Penn**
Screenplay: **Sean Penn**

Sean Penn's first outing as a writer and director is a melodramatic tale of two very different brothers trying to come to terms with themselves, each other and their family. It is surprisingly moving and thoughtful and, what's more, bar the odd bit of self-indulgence, well scripted and directed.   [126m/15]

Joe Roberts	David Morse
Frank Roberts	Viggo Mortensen
Maria Roberts	Valeria Golino
Dorothy	Patricia Arquette
Father	Charles Bronson
Mother	Sandy Dennis
Caesar	Dennis Hopper

Showing *Rio Grande*.

Psst! The film was inspired by the Bruce Springsteen song 'Highway Patrolman'.

The Inner Circle •   [1991]

Director: **Andrei Konchalovsky**
Screenplay: **Andrei Konchalovsky &**
Anatoli Usov

I Was Stalin's Projectionist would be a better title. Hulce, sporting an accent so thick it's got snow on it, is so enamoured of the walrus-moustachioed tyrant that he is willing to sacrifice everything for him.

Based on a true story, it would have made a great documentary. As a film, it's messy and never gets a grip.   [137m/15]

Ivan Sanshin	Tom Hulce
Anastasia	Lolita Davidovich
Beria	Bob Hoskins
Stalin	Alexandre Zbruev

Showing *The Great Waltz*.

Psst! This was the first film allowed to shoot inside the Kremlin, which we can now see looks just like a seedy gentlemen's club.

Innerspace ••   [1987]

Director: **Joe Dante**
Screenplay: **Jeffrey Boam & Chip Proser**

Test pilot Quaid is shrunk in a scientific experiment, only to be mistakenly injected into Martin Short's backside. It's the sort of thing that is probably happening in Government labs worldwide every day. An intriguing idea disappointingly turns into the familiar bad-guys-after-the-secret chase although, as usual, Short is hilarious.   [120m/PG]

Lt. Tuck Pendleton	Dennis Quaid
Jack Putter	Martin Short
Lydia Maxwell	Meg Ryan
Victor Scrimshaw	Kevin McCarthy
Dr. Margaret Canker	Fiona Lewis

Also: Vernon Wells, Robert Picardo, Wendy Schaal

Psst! Quaid and Ryan became a couple during filming. Soon after, she arranged for a plane trailing a 'Happy Birthday Dennis' banner to fly over a rock concert where he was performing and got the 12,000-strong crowd to sing it to him ✦ Dick Miller, here the cab driver, appears in every Joe Dante film.

The Innocent ••   [1985]

Director: **John Mackenzie**
Screenplay: **Ray Jenkins**

Despite being well made, with lots of beautifully-filmed landscapes, this tale of a boy growing up during the Great Depression in Yorkshire is hardly gripping entertainment. Just because very little happened to boys growing up during the Great Depression in Yorkshire is no good reason to expect us to experience the same. [96m/15]

Tim Dobson	Andrew Hawley
Mrs. Dobson	Kika Markham
Win	Kate Foster
John Carns	Liam Neeson
Frank Dobson	Tom Bell

Innocent Blood ••• [1992]

Director: **John Landis**
Screenplay: **Michael Wolk**

In this splendidly funny vampire spoof, Parillaud is the gloriously sexy bloodsucker who brings a whole new meaning to the word 'necking'. When she goes after some mobsters, she hasn't reckoned on the Italian liking for garlic with their food. Cop LaPaglia falls for her, as would any red-blooded man, leading to one of the funniest sex scenes ever put on film. Full of over-the-top performances, particularly from Loggia as the Mafia guy envisaging zombie-Mob rule throughout America, this is a great tongue-in-cheek romp with lashing of gory effects. [113m/15]

Marie	Anne Parillaud
Sal (The Shark) Macelli	Robert Loggia
Joe Gennaro	Anthony LaPaglia
Lenny	David Proval
Emmanuel Bergman	Don Rickles
Tony	Chazz Palminteri
Pathologist	Frank Oz
Roma Meats Man	Sam Raimi
Photographer in car	Tom Savini
Refuse dump watchman	Michael Ritchie
Man with cello case	Alfred Hitchcock

Quote 'My first rule: Never play with the food.' ◆ 'I take lives.' – 'Yeh, well if you were perfect you wouldn't still be single.'

Showing Dracula, The Beast from 20,000 Fathoms, Murders in the Rue Morgue, Strangers on a Train, etc.

Psst! There are cameos from directors like Frank Oz, Sam Raimi, Dario Argento, Tom Savini and Michale Ritchie (the nightwatchman who says 'son of a bitch'), with even Hitchcock himself popping in ◆ The nurse shocked by the way Rickles dies is Linnea Quigley, 'Queen of the Bs', making a rare appearance with her clothes on.

An Innocent Man •• [1989]

Director: **Peter Yates**
Screenplay: **Larry Brothers**

This is the old 'framed guy surviving in prison' story. A plot that's been around since the 30s, Selleck has trouble carrying the weight of it on his shoulders. [114m/18]

Jimmie Rainwood	Tom Selleck
Virgil Cane	F. Murray Abraham
Kate Rainwood	Laila Robins
Mike Parnell	David Rasche
Danny Scalise	Richard Young

OOPS! Watch for Selleck locking the car but leaving its window wide open.

Insignificance •• [1985]

Director: **Nicolas Roeg**
Screenplay: **Terry Johnson**

Four people, bearing an uncanny resemblance to Monroe, Einstein, McCarthy and Di Maggio meet in a New York hotel. Watching a Blonde Actress explain the Theory of Relativity to a Famous Physicist is amusing, but despite the good acting the film's title remains the final verdict. Roeg has fun with a Big Bang finale, but by then it's too late. [105m/15]

The Ballplayer	Gary Busey
The Senator	Tony Curtis
The Professor	Michael Emil
The Actress	Theresa Russell
The Elevator Attendant	Will Sampson

Internal Affairs •• [1990]

Director: **Mike Figgis**
Screenplay: **Henry Bean**

Gere is a corrupt, libidinous, weasely cop. Garcia's the new guy in Internal Affairs out to nail him. Despite looking great, the far from original plot has about as much discipline as Gere's character, meandering all over the place. There's some interest in seeing Gere as a baddy (who rarely seems to do any proper cop work), but it's pretty average otherwise, with a vein of nastiness.　[115m/18]

Dennis Peck	Richard Gere
Raymond Avilla	Andy Garcia
Kathleen Avilla	Nancy Travis
Amy Wallace	Laurie Metcalf
Grieb	Richard Bradford
Van Stretch	William Baldwin

Psst! Look out for Annabella Sciorra as Heather.

In the Line of Fire　[1993]

Director: Wolfgang Petersen
Screenplay: Jeff Maguire

Clint is the secret service agent who's getting close to retirement, on the tail of a former CIA hitman with a grudge against the president. Willis in *The Last Boy Scout* failed to stop America's top politico getting shot. So did Costner in *The Bodyguard*. Can Clint succeed where they failed?

With: Clint Eastwood, John Malkovich, Rene Russo

In the Mood

SEE: The Woo Woo Kid

Into the Night ••　[1985]

Director: John Landis
Screenplay: Ron Koslow

A tongue-in-cheek thriller, following the ever-zanier things befalling insomniac Goldblum when he gets involved with Pfeiffer. Unfortunately, it never really gets going, in the main because the hero appears to be interested only in getting back to sleep. Pfeiffer's a knockout, though, the best Hitchcock blonde that the Master never had.　[115m/15]

Ed Okin	Jeff Goldblum
Diana	Michelle Pfeiffer
Jack Caper	Richard Farnsworth
Shaheen Parvizi	Irene Papas
Christie	Kathryn Harrold
Bud Herman	Paul Mazursky

Showing *Abbott and Costello Meet Frankenstein.*

Psst! Director Landis is the son of Jessie Royce Landis, who plays Cary Grant's mother in *North by Northwest* ♦ As usual with Landis, umpteen other directors crop up in cameos, among them Landis himself as an Iranian Villain, Jim Henson, David Cronenberg, Jonathan Lynn, Daniel Petrie, Paul Bartel, Don Siegel, Lawrence Kasdan, Jonathan Demme and Amy Heckerling. Dan Aykroyd and David Bowie are in there as well for good measure ♦ Dedee Pfeiffer appears momentarily in the one-line part that got her her equity card. She's the hooker approaching the car with her sister and Goldblum inside.

Into the West •••　[1992]

Director: Mike Newell
Screenplay: Jim Sheridan

This delightful adventure yarn has two young Irish gypsy lads grabbing back their confiscated horse and heading West, where the cowboys are. Byrne and Barkin are the father and friend trying to find the boys before the police. The mixture of comedy, chase, drama, myth and magic makes a deliciously heady brew. Several scenes stick in the memory, particularly the horse in the cinema. One of those rare family films enjoyed as much by adults as children.　[102m/PG]

Papa Reilly	Gabriel Byrne
Kathleen	Ellen Barkin
Ossie	Ciaran Fitzgerald
Tito	Ruaidhri Conroy
Grandpa Ward	David Kelly
Tracker	Johnny Murphy
Barreller	Colm Meaney

Showing *Back To The Future Part III.*

Invaders from Mars •　[1986]

Director: Tobe Hooper
Screenplay: Dan O'Bannon & Don Jakoby

This remake of the 1950's sci-fi classic, about the boy who sees the Martians landing, is so true to the original that it is extraordinarily anachronistic and old-fashioned. It was pointless remaking it. It is pointless watching it. **[100m/PG]**

Linda..Karen Black
David......................................Hunter Carson
Also: Timothy Bottoms, Laraine Newman, James Karen, Bud Cort, Louise Fletcher

Invasion U.S.A. •   [1985]

Director: Joseph Zito
Screenplay: James Bruner & Chuck Norris

Norris, here displaying the stature and acting ability of a Giant Redwood, discovers a plot by those fiendish Russkies to invade Florida out of season. Much action. Little plot. **[107m/18]**

Matt Hunter..............................Chuck Norris
Rostov..Richard Lynch
McGuire..............................Melissa Prophet

Iron Eagle •   [1986]

Director: Sidney J. Furie
Screenplay: Kevin Elders & Sidney J. Furie

Imbecilic tale of a lad who gets fed up of his dad being held hostage in the Middle East, learns to fly a fighter, borrows one and overcomes all resistance to his mission in what's undoubtedly supposed to be Libya. Although some of the action's competent, you'd need an I.Q. in single figures to swallow a minute of it. **[116m/PG]**

Chappy................................Louis Gossett Jr.
Doug..Jason Gedrick
Minister of Defense...................David Suchet

Iron Eagle II •   [1988]

Director: Sidney J. Furie
Screenplay: Kevin Elders & Sidney J. Furie

Not all sequels can match up to the original, but this succeeds in being almost as breathtakingly bad. A group of American and Russian pilots join together to destroy a nuclear facility in the Middle East. Crackpot drivel. **[98m/PG]**

Chappy................................Louis Gossett Jr.
Cooper.................................Mark Humphrey
Stillmore.................................Stuart Margolin

Iron Maze •   [1991]

Director: Hiroaki Yoshida
Screenplay: Tim Metcalfe

When a Japanese businessman who wants to build a theme park is attacked in a Pennsylvania steel town, different people have different versions of what happened. A wholly unnecessary reworking of the Japanese movie *Rashomon.* **[102m/15]**

Barry..Jeff Fahey
Chris..Bridget Fonda
Sugita................................Hiroaki Murakami
Jack Ruhle..J.T. Walsh
Showing *Bad Day at Black Rock.*

The Iron Triangle ••   [1989]

Director: Eric Weston
Screenplay: Eric Weston, John Bushelman & Larry Hilbrand

Captured in Vietnam, Bridges learns that in war, there are two sides to the argument as well as to the conflict. By trying to be totally apolitical, the film ends up a little flat, despite plenty of action. **[90m/18]**

Capt. Keene...............................Beau Bridges
Capt. Tuong............................Haing S. Ngor
Jacques.................................Johnny Hallyday
Ho...Liem Whatley

Ironweed ••   [1987]

Director: Hector Babenco
Screenplay: William Kennedy

Streep and Nicholson pretend to be down and outs in the 30s. They might be good actors but they're not *that* good. No wonder they called it The Depression. **[144m/15]**

Francis Phelan..........................Jack Nicholson
Helen...Meryl Streep
Annie Phelan............................Carroll Baker
Billy.......................................Michael O'Keefe
Also: Diane Venora, Fred Gwynne, Margaret Whitton, Tom Waits

Irreconcilable Differences • [1984]

Director: **Charles Shyer**
Screenplay: **Charles Shyer & Nancy Meyers**

A 9-year-old files for divorce from her squabbling parents. Although the central idea was years ahead of its time, the script simply isn't funny enough to hold our interest. The only reason for catching it is to see Stone as the gold-digger who gets her claws into O'Neal. [113m/15]

Albert Brodsky	Ryan O'Neal
Lucy	Shelley Long
Casey	Drew Barrymore
David Kessler	Sam Wanamaker
Phil	Allen Garfield
Blake	Sharon Stone

Ishtar • [1987]

Director: **Elaine May**
Screenplay: **Elaine May**

This isn't as bad as everyone says. But it is still appalling. Imagine Warren Beatty and Dustin Hoffman as Bob Hope and Bing Crosby, with Adjani as Dorothy Lamour. Imagine them a song-writing duo becoming involved in a civil war while, like their predecessors, they're Morocco-bound. Then imagine what it would be like with all the jokes taken out. *The Road to Oblivion.* [107m/PG]

Lyle Rogers	Warren Beatty
Chuck Clarke	Dustin Hoffman
Shirra Assel	Isabelle Adjani
Jim Harrison	Charles Grodin
Marty Freed	Jack Weston
Willa	Tess Harper

Psst! This was the second biggest flop of all time, which is reputed to have cost $50m and lost £47.3m of that. ♦ Hoffman and Beatty got $5.5m apiece ♦ This was the first film for Beatty in six years and the first for Hoffman in five ♦ Full marks to the marketing people in America who tried to sell the video as 'the most talked about comedy of the year'.

I've Heard the Mermaids Singing • [1987]

Director: **Patricia Rozema**
Screenplay: **Patricia Rozema**

If they *are* singing, it's impossible to hear them over the noise of the audience snoring. Ingratiating, pretentious Canadian nonsense about a woman discovering herself in an art gallery. [81m/15]

Polly Vandersma	Sheila McCarthy
Gabrielle St-Peres	Paule Baillargeon
Mary Joseph	Ann-Marie MacDonald

J

Jackie Chan's Police Story
SEE: **Police Story**

Jacknife •• [1989]

Director: **David Jones**
Screenplay: **Stephen Metcalfe**

Yet another hour and a half in the company of people trying to rid themselves of the ghosts of Vietnam. The best thing about this slow and obviously theatre-originated, film is the three superb performances of the leads. [98m/15]

Joseph 'Megs' Megessey	Robert De Niro
Martha	Kathy Baker
Dave	Ed Harris
Shirley	Sloane Shelton
Jake	Charles S. Dutton

Jack the Bear •• [1993]

Director: **Marshall Herskovitz**
Screenplay: **Steve Zaillian**

DeVito is a single parent who fronts a late-night TV movie horror show, bringing up his two boys in 1972 in a suburb populated by wackos. Most sinister of all is crippled neighbour Sinise, who eventually retaliates against his teasing by the local boys. Despite some lovely performances all round, the film is a strange mixture of humour and poignancy. *Thirtysomething* creator Herskovitz doesn't quite bring it off in his directorial debut. **[98m/12]**

John Leary	Danny DeVito
Jack Leary	Robert J. Steinmiller Jr.
Dylan Leary	Miko Hughes
Norman Strick	Gary Sinise
Peggy Etinger	Julia Louis-Dreyfus
Karen Morris	Reese Witherspoon

Jacob's Ladder •• [1990]

Director: **Adrian Lyne**
Screenplay: **Bruce Joel Rubin**

A Vietnam vet suffers from hallucinations and wanders round New York trying to get to the bottom of them. Creepy dream sequences and a script from *Ghost* writer Rubin still can't prevent the feeling that we're somehow having our legs pulled. **[113m/18]**

Jacob Singer	Tim Robbins
Jezzie	Elizabeth Pena
Louis	Danny Aiello
Michael	Matt Craven

Psst! Macaulay Culkin appears briefly. As the film was made before *Home Alone* was a success, he isn't credited. He was so hot when it came out, however, that they used his picture in the posters.

Jagged Edge ••• [1985]

Director: **Richard Marquand**
Screenplay: **Joe Eszterhas**

The age-old story of the lawyer falling for the accused murderer. Here it's Close getting steamed up over Bridges, suspected of having topped his wife for her money in a pretty grisly manner. Slickly produced and with some great performances from the leads, it just about moves fast enough to stop you thinking about the silliness of the plot, which has more holes than a string vest. Of course, to understand it now, you'll need some old-timer

to explain to you what a typewriter is. The countless attempts to imitate it since, including those by writer Eszterhas himself, only make you realise how well-crafted it is. **[108m/18]**

Jack Forrester	Jeff Bridges
Teddy Barnes	Glenn Close
Thomas Krasny	Peter Coyote
Sam Ransom	Robert Loggia
Judge Carrigan	John Dehner
Julie Jensen	Karen Austin
Matthew Barnes	Guy Boyd
Bobby Slade	Marshall Colt

OOPS! Keep an eye on Close's suit in court as it changes from grey on the way in, to dark blue and then to brown. Her blouse changes from white to brown as well.

Psst! There are those who maintain that this set the pattern for all Joe Eszterhas scripts. An entertaining parlour game is to spot the similarities in the plotlines of this, *Music Box* and *Basic Instinct* • Much of the opening of the film has been lost when shown on TV in the past.

Jake Speed • [1986]

Director: **Andrew Lane**
Screenplay: **Wayne Crawford & Andrew Lane**

Dreadful *Romancing the Stone* rip-off with the less-than-lively hero leaping from the pages of a book to rescue Kopins' kidnapped sister. Putting a real actor like Hurt in the midst of this lot is like putting a tiger in with the lambs. **[105m/15]**

Jake Speed	Wayne Crawford
Desmond Floyd	Dennis Christopher
Margaret Winston	Karen Kopins
Sid	John Hurt

Jane and the Lost City • [1987]

Director: **Terry Marcel**
Screenplay: **Mervyn Haisman**

Less-than-jolly japes in the jungle as our hunky hero tries to keep only his upper lip stiff despite the heroine's distracting habit of losing her clothes. The wartime *Mirror* comic strip on which it's based was ripping stuff and infinitely superior. **[91m/PG]**

Jungle Jack Buck	Sam Jones
Lola Pagola	Maud Adams
Jane	Kirsten Hughes
Heinrich	Jasper Carrott

The January Man • [1989]

Director: **Pat O'Connor**
Screenplay: **John Patrick Shanley**

It *may* be possible to make a comedy about a mass–murderer but this certainly isn't it. Kline is the ex–detective called in to help. He trips over an all–star cast who've fallen asleep, so little have they to do. A major let down. [97m/15]

Nick Starkey	Kevin Kline
Christine Starkey	Susan Sarandon
Bernadette	Mary Elizabeth Mastrantonio
Frank Starkey	Harvey Keitel
Vincent Alcoa	Danny Aiello
Eamon Flynn	Rod Steiger
Ed	Alan Rickman

Psst! Mastrantonio is married to director O'Connor.

Jaws 3-D • [1983]

Director: **Joe Alves**
Screenplay: **Richard Matheson & Carl Gottlieb**

Although the 3–D was pretty good in the cinema, without that gimmick it's just a moth–eaten sequel about a shark terrorising Florida's Sea World. No bite at all. [99m/PG]

Mike	Dennis Quaid
Kathryn	Bess Armstrong
Philip	Simon MacCorkindale
Calvin	Louis Gossett Jr.

Jaws the Revenge • [1987]

Director: **Joseph Sargent**
Screenplay: **Michael de Guzman**

Now that Scheider's dead, the shark's stalking his family, presumably with the help of a private eye. This utterly preposterous, thrill–free fourth outing ends extraordinarily abruptly, but not abruptly enough. The low spot of Caine's career. [100m/PG]

Ellen Brody	Lorraine Gary
Michael	Lance Guest
Jake	Mario Van Peebles
Carla	Karen Young
Hoagie	Michael Caine

Blurb This Time It's Personal.

OOPS! Watch Caine as he climbs out of the water after swimming to the boat to help Gary. His shirt is completely dry.

Psst! In a rare instance of a new ending for a movie being filmed after being released, another version was made in which Van Peebles didn't die. Unfortunately, this was the version exported to Europe ◆ Unbelievably, filming this rubbish meant that Caine couldn't get to the Oscar ceremony to collect his award for *Hannah and Her Sisters* ◆ The film was cut by ten minutes to get a PG rating. The cuts were restored for the video.

Jean de Florette •••• [1987]

Director: **Claude Berri**
Screenplay: **Claude Berri & Gérard Brach**

Magical, wholly captivating French story of hunchback Depardieu and his family trying to scratch a living on their new land, unaware that neighbour Montand and his half–witted nephew have blocked up their spring. A winner in every department, but particularly strong on photography and acting, it's one of those rare films that sticks in the memory long after you've seen it. It was made back-to-back with the sequel, *Manon des Sources*. [122m/PG]

Cesar Soubeyran	Yves Montand
Jean de Florette	Gérard Depardieu
Ugolin	Daniel Auteuil
Aimee	Elisabeth Depardieu
Manon	Ernestine Mazurowna

Jennifer 8 ••• [1992]

Director: **Bruce Robinson**
Screenplay: **Bruce Robinson**

An intelligent, well–made thriller with oodles of atmosphere. Garcia's the cop who disobeys orders and persists in pursuing a serial killer preying on blind women. Although a little slow for some tastes, the splendid characterisations make this a thinking-person's thriller, with a superbly tense climax.   [124m]

John Berlin.....................................Andy Garcia
Helena Robertson.....................Uma Thurman
Freddy Ross...........................Lance Henriksen
Margie Ross.................................Kathy Baker
Also: Graham Beckel, Kevin Conway, John Malkovich

Jersey Girl • [1992]

Director: **David Burton Morris**
Screenplay: **Gina Wendkos**

Feeble attempt to do for Joisey Goils what *Pretty Woman* did for hookers. Gertz is the personable lass who goes to great lengths to make wealthy McDermott fall for her. The actors do their best with this lame duck that's so schmaltzy it's obviously been force-fed with corn.
[95m/15]

Toby...Jami Gertz
Sal.....................................Dylan McDermott
Cookie...Molly Price
Also: Aida Turturro, Star Jasper, Sheryl Lee, Joseph Bologna

Jesus of Montreal •••• [1990]

Director: **Denys Arcand**
Screenplay: **Denys Arcand**

A Canadian acting troupe find that the events in their modern version of the Passion Play start to resemble the world around them. An often funny, imaginative, off-beat and iconolastic look at the role of religion in the modern world, with Bluteau outstanding in the title role.
[120m/18]

Daniel Coulombe...................Lothaire Bluteau
Mireille...........................Catherine Wilkening
Constance..............Johanne-Marie Tremblay
Martin..Rémy Girard
Psst! Writer-director Arcand appears as a judge.

The Jetsons: The Movie • [1991]

Director: **William Hanna & Joseph Barbera**
Screenplay: **Dennis Marks**

Even as a TV series, the futuristic cartoon wasn't much cop. This full-length outing stretches the idea beyond breaking point.
[82m/U]

With: George O'Hanlon, Mel Blanc, Penny Singleton

Jewel of the Nile •• [1985]

Director: **Lewis Teague**
Screenplay: **Mark Rosenthal & Lawrence Konner**

A pale imitation of *Romancing the Stone*. The contortions the plot has to go through to arrange for yet another 'thrilling' sequence are obviously extremely painful. Despite the odd good gag, this tale of Turner kidnapped by an Arab Sheikh is second-hand stuff.   [106m/PG]

Jack.......................................Michael Douglas
Joan ....Kathleen Turner
Ralph ....Danny DeVito
Omar...Spiros Focas
OOPS! As Turner leaps onto the train, her yachting shoes change briefly to leather sandals and then back again.

Psst! Douglas produced the picture. With just seven days filming left, the Moroccan government quarantined the film. Douglas had to charter a giant Hercules transport plane and ship the entire production to France ✦ The film is dedicated to Diane Thomas, writer of *Romancing the Stone*, who crashed in the Porsche given to her by Douglas.

JFK ••• [1991]

Director: **Oliver Stone**
Screenplay: **Oliver Stone & Zachary Sklar**

Can you remember where you were when JFK came out? Oliver Stone points the blame for Kennedy's assassination squarely at the industrial-military complex...the FBI, the CIA, Cuban dissidents, the Cuban Government, Lee Harvey Oswald, Ruby, Uncle Tom Cobbleigh and indeed anyone else who'd ever heard of the man. An undoubted filmic tour-de-force with some splendid acting, its overlong blend of fact and fiction muddies the waters for anyone hoping to understand events. Vietnam isn't forgotten, of course, Stone's slant here being that it wouldn't have happened if JFK hadn't been blown away. **[190m/15]**

Jim Garrison	Kevin Costner
Liz Garrison	Sissy Spacek
David Ferrie	Joe Pesci
Clay Shaw	Tommy Lee Jones
Lee Harvey Oswald	Gary Oldman
Lou Ivon	Jay O. Saunders
Bill Broussard	Michael Rooker
Susie Cox	Laurie Metcalf
Al Oser	Gary Grubbs
Dean Andrews	John Candy
Jack Martin	Jack Lemmon
Sen. Russell Long	Walter Matthau
Guy Bannister	Ed Asner
Colonel 'X'	Donald Sutherland
Willie O'Keefe	Kevin Bacon
Jack Ruby	Brian Doyle-Murray

OOPS! When Garrison and his colleagues meet in his house there's a Christmas tree. Yet a meeting with Clay Shaw the following Sunday turns out to be during Easter!

Psst! Earl Warren of the Commission of the same name is played by the real-life Jim Garrison.

Jimmy Reardon •• [1988]

Director: **William Richert**
Screenplay: **William Richert**

Yet another end-of-high-school, end-of-an-era, end-of-innocence film with very little to distinguish it from scores of others. Also known as *A Night in the Life of Jimmy Reardon*. **[92m/15]**

Jimmy Reardon	River Phoenix
Joyce Fickett	Ann Magnuson
Lisa Bentwright	Meredith Salenger
Denise Hunter	Ione Skye

Joe Versus the Volcano • [1990]

Director: **John Patrick Shanley**
Screenplay: **John Patrick Shanley**

Daft story of down-trodden office-fodder Hanks being told he's dying. Instead of taking it lying down, he accepts an offer to jump into a live volcano. In this highly peculiar movie, Ryan plays three different women while Hanks plays Hanks. Like several different movies thrown together in no particular order, without knowing what the aim of the film was, it's hard to know by how far they missed it. **[102m/PG]**

Joe Banks	Tom Hanks
DeDe/Angelica/Patricia	Meg Ryan
Graynamore	Lloyd Bridges
Dr. Ellison	Robert Stack

Johnny Dangerously •• [1984]

Director: **Amy Heckerling**
Screenplay: **Norman Steinberg, Bernie Kukoff, Harry Colomby & Jeff Harris**

The cast is the most interesting thing about this unfunny spoof of the gangster pic, with Keaton resorting to crime to pay his mum's medical bills. Firing jokes everywhere like bullets from a tommy-gun is fine just so long as *some* of them are funny. **[90m/15]**

Johnny Dangerously	Michael Keaton
Vermin	Jo Piscopo
Lil	Marilu Henner
Mom	Maureen Stapleton

Also: Peter Boyle, Griffin Dunne, Dom DeLuise, Danny DeVito, Ray Walston

Johnny Handsome •• [1989]

Director: **Walter Hill**
Screenplay: **Ken Friedman**

Disfigured criminal Rourke gets a second chance after plastic surgery, but is more interested in exacting revenge on his former buddies. An odd, quite enjoyable crime thriller which doesn't stick in the mind for long afterwards. Barkin fans will enjoy her foul-mouthed performance as a villain. **[94m/15]**

John Sedley	Mickey Rourke
Sunny Boyd	Ellen Barkin
Donna McCarty	Elizabeth McGovern
Lt. A.Z. Drones	Morgan Freeman
Dr. Steven Resher	Forest Whitaker
Rafe Garrett	Lance Henriksen

Johnny Suede ••• [1992]

Director: Tom DiCillo
Screenplay: Tom DiCillo

Inspired by a pair of suede shoes falling on his head, Pitt decides to be a musician. He isn't one to be stopped by lack of talent nor the fact that he wears underpants so distressed anyone else would turn them into dusters. Weird and slight it may be, but it's frequently very funny and surprisingly touching. How can you not like a film with the lyric: 'I've been a momma's boy since Daddy got the electric chair'? **[95m/15]**

Johnny Suede	Brad Pitt
Yvonne	Catherine Keener
Deke	Calvin Levels
Darlette Fontaine	Alison Moir

The Journey of Natty Gann ••• [1985]

Director: Jeremy Kagan
Screenplay: Jeanne Rosenberg

A lovely, old-style Disney movie about a young girl running away in the Great Depression to try to find her logging father. Her only companion is a wolf. Surprisingly unsentimental and enjoyable stuff. **[101m/PG]**

Natty Gann	Meredith Salenger
Harry	John Cusack
Sol Gann	Ray Wise
Connie	Lainie Kazan
Sherman	Scatman Crothers

Joyriders •• [1989]

Director: Aisling Walsh
Screenplay: Andy Smith

An Irish road movie with Kerrigan the mother who flees her husband and, with her children, hitches up with car thief Connolly. Although the central characters are fine, the parade of eccentrics flitting in and out of the diffuse story betrays too clearly that this is a debut film. **[96m/15]**

Mary Flynn	Patricia Kerrigan
Perky Rice	Andrew Connolly
Tammy O'Moore	Billie Whitelaw
Daniel Tracey	David Kelly

Judgement in Stone •• [1987]

Director: Ousama Rawi
Screenplay: Elaine Waisglass

This odd Canadian film has Tushingham as an obsessively-tidy housekeeper with a habit of tidying away anybody who mentions her reading disability. As she works for a doctor, this causes a few problems. Also known as *The Housekeeper*. **[100m/15]**

Eunice Parchman	Rita Tushingham
George Coverdale	Ross Petty
Jackie Coverdale	Shelley Peterson

Psst! Peterson, making her debut here, was at the time the wife of Ontario's leader.

Judgment in Berlin •• [1988]

Director: Leo Penn
Screenplay: Joshua Sinclair & Leo Penn

Dull, earnest, true-life courtroom drama with Sheen the judge having to decide the fate of a couple of East Germans who escaped to the West by hijacking an airliner. **[95m/PG]**

Herbert J. Stern	Martin Sheen
Bernard Hellring	Sam Wanamaker
Judah Best	Max Gail

Psst! Director Leo Penn is Sean's father.

Juice •• [1992]

Director: Ernest Dickerson
Screenplay: Ernest Dickerson & Gerard Brown

A black teenager, odds-on to win the Mixxmaster Massacre DJ competition is dragged down by his friends who believe that they'll only get anywhere through crime. A well-observed, often funny, character study from Spike Lee's cinematographer turns half-way into a violent and aimless thriller. **[91m/15]**

Q	Omar Epps
Bishop	Tupac Shakur
Steel	Jermaine Hopkins
Raheem	Khalil Kain

Jumpin' Jack Flash •• [1986]

Director: Penny Marshall
Screenplay: David Franzoni, J.W. Melville, Patricia Irving & Christopher Thompson

Terrible comic spy caper, with Goldberg the programmer getting messages from an agent on her terminal. Even Whoopi can't do much with this thin material. **[105m/15]**

Terry Doolittle	Whoopi Goldberg
Marty Phillips	Stephen Collins
Jeremy Talbot	John Wood
Cynthia	Carol Kane
Liz Carlson	Annie Potts

Also: Peter Michael Goetz, Jeroen Krabbé, Jonathan Pryce, Jon Lovitz, Phil Hartman, James Belushi, Tracey Ullman

Psst! Penny Marshall took over as director in the middle of filming from Howard Zieff • It was her first time as director. Brother Garry, director of films like *Pretty Woman*, has a cameo as the detective • Michael McKean of *Spinal Tap* appears at the party.

Jungle Fever ••• [1991]

Director: Spike Lee
Screenplay: Spike Lee

Black married yuppie Snipes has a fling with his white secretary Sciorra, with devastating consequences. A thoughtful, provocative and deeply-felt movie, its effect is sadly muffled by the over-emphasis on the drug subplot. **[132m/18]**

Flipper Purify	Wesley Snipes
Angela Tucci	Annabella Sciorra
Cyrus	Spike Lee
Lou Carbone	Anthony Quinn
The Good Rev. Dr. Purify	Ossie Davis
Lucinda Purify	Ruby Dee

Gator Purify	Samuel L. Jackson
Paulie Carbone	John Turturro
Mike Tucci	Frank Vincent
Orin Goode	Tyra Ferrell
Vivian	Halle Berry
Jerry	Tim Robbins

Jurassic Park [1993]

Director: Steven Spielberg
Screenplay: David Koepp & Malia Scotch Marmo

Why don't scientists realise that whenever they create living creatures, those creatures always turn on them? Sure enough, when mad boffin Attenborough sets up a theme park with dinosaurs instead of dodgems, the creatures demonstrate all too clearly the answer to that age-old question, are they vegetarians or carnivores?

With: Sam Neill, Laura Dern, Jeff Goldblum, Richard Attenborough, Samuel L. Jackson, Bob Peck, Martin Ferrero

Quote 'When Pirates of the Caribbean breaks down, the pirates don't eat the tourists.'

Psst! Filming on the Hawaiian island of Kauai was badly hit by Hurricane Iniki • Spielberg wasn't happy that the models of the Velociraptors were only 6 foot high and ordered the size to be doubled, realising that dinosaur enthusiasts would be furious. Then scientists discovered a cousin of the Velociraptor that was double the size.

Just Ask for Diamond • [1988]

Director: Stephen Bayly
Screenplay: Anthony Horowitz

This Children's Film Foundation spoof of the Sam Spade private eye genre, despite its commendable origins, raises barely a laugh. **[94m/U]**

Lauren Bacardi	Susannah York
Nick Diamond	Colin Dale
Himmell	Nickolas Grace

Also: Patricia Hodge, Saeed Jaffrey, Roy Kinnear, Jimmy Nail, Bill Paterson

Just Between Friends •• [1986]

Director: **Allan Burns**
Screenplay: **Allan Burns**

Moore, seemingly preserved in aspic, discovers not only that new friend Lahti was her dead husband's mistress but that she's pregnant. Does she try to murder her? No, that would deprive everyone of a good weep. Instead, they go in for multiple mothering. Nothing like as vomit-inducing as you expect, though that's not to say it's good. **[120m/15]**

Holly Davis	Mary Tyler Moore
Karen	Julie Payne
Judy	Beverly Sanders
Helga	Salome Jens
Chip Davis	Ted Danson
Sandy Dunlap	Christine Lahti
Harry Crandall	Sam Waterston

Just Like a Woman •• [1992]

Director: **Christopher Monger**
Screenplay: **Nick Evans**

Walters is the divorced landlady who takes a shine to her American banker lodger, only to discover that he's not only after her body, but her clothes as well. Patchily amusing, the dialogue is as full of life as a pair of falsies although Walters is good value as always. **[106m/15]**

Monica	Julie Walters
Gerald	Adrian Pasdar
Miles Millichamp	Paul Freeman
C.J.	Gordon Kennedy

K-9 • [1989]

Director: **Rod Daniel**
Screenplay: **Steven Siegel & Scott Myers**

K-9 is a dog. So is this film. Cop Belushi gets a canine partner but, try as they might, they can't come up with anything to match the Tom Hanks' cop-dog movie, and that isn't saying much. **[102m/15]**

Thomas Dooley	James Belushi
Tracy	Mel Harris
Lyman	Kevin Tighe
Lt. Brannigan	Ed O'Neill

K2 •• [1991]

Director: **Franc Roddam**
Screenplay: **Patrick Meyers & Scott Roberts**

K2 is a mountain. Boy, is it a long, long way to the top. Although the climbing sequences are superb, at the end of the rope there's the dead weight of a buddy-caring-sharing plot dragging the whole lot down. **[110m/15]**

Taylor Brooks	Michael Biehn
Harold Jamieson	Matt Craven
Philip Claiborne	Raymond J. Barry
Takane Shimuzu	Hiroshi Fujioka

Kangaroo •• [1986]

Director: **Tim Burstall**
Screenplay: **Evan Jones**

Davis is such a great actress, she could read the backs of cereal packets for two hours and still keep audiences spellbound. But when she's not on screen, this Australian tale of D.H. Lawrence (slightly disguised) going Down Under after World War I, and getting involved in politics is slightly soporific. **[110m/PG]**

Richard Somers	Colin Friels
Harriet Somers	Judy Davis
Jack Calcott	John Walton
Vicki Calcott	Julie Nihill

Psst! Friels and Davis are also married in real life.

Kansas • [1988]

Director: **David Stevens**
Screenplay: **Spencer Eastman**

Down on his luck, McCarthy makes the mistake of getting involved with ex-con Dillon. Don't make the same mistake. Steer well clear of this brainless, misconceived mess. **[106m/15]**

Doyle Kennedy	Matt Dillon
Wade Corey	Andrew McCarthy
Lori Bayles	Leslie Hope

Psst! Kyra Sedwick appears as a 'prostitute drifter'.

The Karate Kid •••• [1984]

Director: **John G. Avildsen**
Screenplay: **Robert Mark Kamen**

Forget the sneers. This is a brilliant movie about an underdog winning out, in the *Rocky* vein (they have the same director) but about karate. When Macchio moves with his mum to California, he's picked on by some bullies who are martial arts experts. Luckily, the janitor of his block knows a bit about chop-socky himself. Undoubtedly manipulative, if you just go with the flow, you'll have a hugely entertaining time. **[126m/PG]**

Daniel	Ralph Macchio
Miyagi	Pat Morita
Ali	Elisabeth Shue
Kreese	Martin Kove
Lucille	Randee Heller
Johnny	William Zabka

Quote 'Wax on. Wax off.'

Psst! In reality, Pat Morita knows nothing about karate. 'It mystifies me. All that stuff about breaking bricks. Why don't they just pick up the brick and hit 'em over the head with it?'.

The Karate Kid, Part II •• [1986]

Director: **John G. Avildsen**
Screenplay: **Robert Mark Kamen**

Morita has to go back to native Okinawa and protégé Macchio goes with him. Daft sequel has its moments, but little of the magic of the first film. **[113m/PG]**

Daniel	Ralph Macchio
Miyagi	Pat Morita
Yukie	Nobu McCarthy
Sato	Danny Kamekona

The Karate Kid III • [1989]

Director: **John G. Avildsen**
Screenplay: **Robert Mark Kamen**

Macchio's in trouble. He's in a series of karate movies that are getting worse with each outing. Will mentor Morita be able to save him from terrible embarrassment? Not this time. He's too busy opening a bonsai shop. Utterly hopeless and predictable sequel has no merits at all. **[111m/PG]**

Daniel LaRusso	Ralph Macchio
Mr. Miyagi	Pat Morita
Jessica Andrews	Robyn Lively

Psst! Credits list 2 'bonsai plant advisers'.

Hickboxer •• [1989]

Director: **Mark DiSalle & David Worth**
Screenplay: **Glenn Bruce**

To avenge his brother's death, the Muscles From Brussels trains as a kickboxer. Violent stuff, but those who like this sort of thing probably won't mind the quality of the acting or the plot. **[100m/18]**

Kurt Sloane	Jean-Claude Van Damme
Eric Sloane	Dennis Alexio
Xian Chow	Dennis Chan

Hickboxer 2: The Road Back • [1991]

Director: **Albert Pyun**
Screenplay: **David S. Goyer**

Don't expect Van Damme. He's gone on to better, or at least more profitable, things. Without him, there's no reason to catch this one at all. **[90m/18]**

Sloan	Sasha Mitchell
Justin	Peter Boyle
Xian Chow	Dennis Chan

Kid • [1990]

Director: **John Mark Robinson**
Screenplay: **Leslie Bohem**

Yet another attempt at a modern Western plunges to earth. Howell's the mysterious stranger with a score to settle. **[92m/18]**

The Kid	C. Thomas Howell
Kate	Sarah Trigger
Metal Louie	Brian Austin Green
Luke Clayton	R. Lee Ermey

Killing Dad • [1989]

Director: **Michael Austin**
Screenplay: **Michael Austin**

Lamentable British comedy dreadfully misuses the talents of Grant and Elliott in a tale of a son finding his long-lost father, only to wish he'd never bothered. We know how he feels. **[93m/PG]**

Alistair Berg	Richard E. Grant
Nathy Berg	Denholm Elliott
Judith	Julie Walters
Edith Berg	Anna Massey

The Killing Fields ••• [1984]

Director: **Roland Joffé**
Screenplay: **Bruce Robinson**

The harrowing, true-ish story of American journalist Sydney Schanberg and his Cambodian translator, who stay to cover the conflict after the Americans withdraw from Phnom Penh. While Schanberg receives the Pulitzer Price, Pran is imprisoned by the Khmer Rouge and 're-educated'. Schanberg vows to find him and bring him out. Although moving and well-made, the relationship between the two leads still lacks the essential spark. **[142m/15]**

Sydney Schanberg	Sam Waterston
Dith Pran	Haing S. Ngor
Al Rockoff	John Malkovich
Jon Swain	Julian Sands
Military Attaché	Craig T. Nelson
U.S. Consul	Spalding Gray
Dr. Macentire	Bill Paterson

Oscars Haing S. Ngor

Psst! Ngor, a doctor making his acting debut, won an Oscar for best supporting actor, one of only two non-professionals to win the statuette. He was a refugee who'd escaped from the Khmer Rouge ✦ The investors tried to foist Dustin Hoffman onto producer Puttnam, but he resisted ✦ Although based on a true story, in reality after the Khmer were driven out Pran became mayor of his home town and visited The Killing Fields as a tourist, rather than coming across

them when escaping ✦ The music is Barber's Adagio for Strings. If it sounds familiar, it could be because it's among the most over used in the movies, next only to Enya. You'll find it in *Platoon* and *The Elephant Man* among others.

Kill Me Again ••• [1989]

Director: **John Dahl**
Screenplay: **John Dahl & David W. Warfield**

A fiendishly complicated film noir, with Whalley-Kilmer faking her death in an attempt to steal mob money and drawing in infatuated private eye Kilmer. An enjoyable pastiche which keeps one step ahead of its audience, although Whalley-Kilmer doesn't really cut the mustard as a femme fatale. **[96m/18]**

Jack Andrews	Val Kilmer
Fay Forrester	Joanne Whalley-Kilmer
Vince Miller	Michael Madsen
Alan Swayzie	Jonathan Gries

The Kill-Off •• [1990]

Director: **Maggie Greenwald**
Screenplay: **Maggie Greenwald**

A black and bleak little thriller based on a Jim Thompson novel. The residents of a small town decide that it's time to silence the local gossip. Nice idea, but a bit drab. **[92m/18]**

Luane	Loretta Gross
Pete	Jackson Sims
Ralph	Steve Monroe
Danny Lee	Cathy Haase

Kindergarten Cop •• [1990]

Director: **Ivan Reitman**
Screenplay: **Murray Salem, Herschel Weingrod & Timothy Harris**

Trying to find a hoodlum's child, Arnie goes undercover as a kindergarten teacher, keeping order by turning the little darlings into infant members of the Hitler Youth. An intriguing idea is thrown away on a script that's flabby and badly in need of toning up. Despite occasional flashes of

fun, the laughter muscles get little exercise while the sentiment, although expected in this sort of thing, is still pretty schmaltzy.
[111m/12]

John Kimble	Arnold Schwarzenegger
Joyce Paulmarie	Penelope Ann Miller
Phoebe O'Hara	Pamela Reed
Miss Schlowski	Linda Hunt

Also: Richard Tyson, Carroll Baker, Cathy Moriarty, Jayne Brook, Richard Portnow

Blurb Go Ahead, *You* Tell Him You Didn't Do Your Homework.

Quote 'Kimble, if you were any stiffer we could take you surfing.'

OOPS! If the kid's already been told in the restaurant that Reed is Arnie's Austrian sister, why doesn't he say anything when she's introduced to the class as O'Hara?

Kindred •• [1987]

Director: Jeffrey Obrow & Stephen Carpenter
Screenplay: Jeffrey Obrow, Stephen Carpenter, John Penney, Earl Ghaffari & Joseph Stefano

...And, to my son, I leave my genetic experiments. Junior has to try to put mom's monster back in the test tube. Despite some unpleasant special effects this awful film appears to be acted out by a cast made of plaster of Paris cast, so stiff are they.
[91m/18]

John Hollins	David Allen Brooks
Dr. Phillip Lloyd	Rod Steiger
Melissa Leftridge	Amanda Pays
Sharon Raymond	Talia Balsam
Amanda Hollins	Kim Hunter

Psst! Stefano wrote the *Psycho* screenplay.

King David •• [1985]

Director: Bruce Beresford
Screenplay: Andrew Birkin & James Costigan

And the Studio said, 'Let there be a biblical epic and let it star Richard Gere'. And the Public said, 'Richard Gere as King David? Don't make us laugh'. But laugh they did, especially at his daft Dervish

dance. Not exactly a bad film, but not exactly good either. The book tie-in has done pretty well, though: it's sold more than any other book in history.
[114m/PG]

David	Richard Gere
Saul	Edward Woodward
Bathsheba	Alice Krige
Samuel	Denis Quilley

Also: Niall Buggy, Cherie Lunghi, Hurd Hatfield

Quote 'Must you record my every word?' [The dying King David] – 'It's for the book of Samuel. You ordered it yourself.'

Psst! Richard Gere prepared for the role by living with Bedouins ✦ Known in Hollywood as *An Israelite and a Gentleman* ✦ Costing almost $30m, it took less than $5m in the US.

The King of Comedy •••• [1983]

Director: Martin Scorsese
Screenplay: Paul D. Zimmerman

This superb black comedy from Scorsese was a failure on release, but its reputation is, deservedly, growing steadily. De Niro is the stage-door johnny Rupert Pupkin who believes he can be a great comic like his hero Jerry Langford. When Langford brushes him off, Pupkin and his friend take more drastic action. A frighteningly realistic satire on the world of entertainment, it is extremely funny, providing you like your comedy black, with no milk or sugar. What an actor Lewis turns out to be.
[108m/PG]

Rupert Pupkin	Robert De Niro
Jerry Langford	Jerry Lewis
Rita	Diahnne Abbott
Masha	Sandra Bernhard

Quote 'Look, I figure it this way: better to be king for a night than schmuck for a lifetime.'

OOPS! When Pupkin is in the restaurant with Abbot, watch how his glass keeps emptying and then refilling ✦ There's a wonderful moment when De Niro and Abbott are arguing on the street with a member of the public blatantly staring at the camera.

Psst! The credits thank the late Dan Johnson, Scorsese's former cook ✦ As usual Scorsese's mother Catherine plays her part, here as the off-screen voice of Pupkin's mother ✦ There are cameos from Scorsese as the director of the TV show, as well as Liza Minnelli, Victor Borge and Tony Randall ✦ If you look carefully at the start of the film, you'll see Mary Elizabeth Mastrantonio in the crowd. This was her first film part, but it was almost completely cut out of the final version.

King of New York •• [1990]

Director: **Abel Ferrara**
Screenplay: **Nicholas St. John**

From the luxurious Plaza Hotel, Walken wipes out his enemies and proceeds to take over the New York drug business. Although there's some great style and well-staged action on offer, there's little enough that's new to make it any sort of classic. Walken is his usual creepily-accomplished self. **[104m/18]**

Frank White	Christopher Walken
Dennis Gilley	David Caruso
Jimmy Jump	Larry Fishburne
Roy Bishop	Victor Argo
Thomas Flanigan	Wesley Snipes

King of the Wind • [1990]

Director: **Peter Duffell**
Screenplay: **Phillip Frey**

Dull, TV-financed tale of a dumb Arab boy and his horse. Definitely one for the knacker's yard. **[102m/U]**

Edward Coke	Frank Finlay
Hannah Coke	Jenny Agutter
Achmet	Nigel Hawthorne

Also: Ralph Bates, Barry Foster, Jill Gascoigne, Anthony Quayle

King Ralph ••• [1991]

Director: **David S. Ward**
Screenplay: **David S. Ward**

With the entire Royal Family wiped out in a freak accident, a hick American lounge-pianist, a *very* distant relation, ascends the throne. Although there's really only one joke, it's enjoyably played out and Goodman is goofily endearing in the title role. Come to think of it, a hick American lounge-pianist might be a better idea than some of the real heirs. **[95m/PG]**

Ralph Jones	John Goodman
Sir Cedric Willingham	Peter O'Toole
Lord Graves	John Hurt
Miranda	Camille Coduri
Duncan Phipps	Richard Griffiths
Princess Anna	Joely Richardson
Gordon	Leslie Phillips
P.M. Hale	James Villiers
King Gustav	Julian Glover
Queen Katherine	Judy Parfitt

OOPS! When Hurt goes to Coduri's flat, the inside pages of his newspaper are blank ✦ At one point Goodman is in residence as King, yet the flag isn't flying. Tut, tut! **Psst!** Ward also wrote *The Sting*.

King Solomon's Mines • [1985]

Director: **J. Lee Thompson**
Screenplay: **Gene Quintano & James R. Silke**

One suspects that if Sharon Stone could, she'd buy up and destroy all the movies she made before *Total Recall*. This is one of the most embarrassing, a pathetic attempt to marry Rider Haggard with Indiana Jones and getting Old Ma Haggard instead. Stone is cringe-making in her awfulness. The follow-up to this drivel is *Allan Quatermain and the City of Gold*. **[100m/PG]**

Quatermain	Richard Chamberlain
Jessie	Sharon Stone
Col. Bockner	Herbert Lom

The Kiss • [1988]

Director: **Pen Densham**
Screenplay: **Stephen Volk & Tom Ropelewski**

Pacula has a sinister snake in her body which has to be passed on to another woman via a kiss, and niece Salenger is the one she's chosen to give forked tongue to. Silly and tedious 'snake in the ass' story, cheaply made and supremely unfrightening. **[98m/18]**

Aunt Felice	Joanna Pacula
Amy	Meredith Salenger
Brenda	Mimi Kuzyk

Psst! The same producers, Pen Densham and John Watson, had better luck with *Robin Hood: Prince of Thieves*.

A Kiss Before Dying •   [1990]

Director: James Dearden
Screenplay: James Dearden

Ambitious Dillon kills one heiress sister and marries the other, plotting to take over from tycoon father Von Sydow. This truly risible thriller, a remake of a 1956 film, is rendered even worse by Young who, by playing twins, is doubly dreadful. **[92m/18]**

Jonathan Corliss	Matt Dillon
Ellen/Dorothy Carlsson	Sean Young
Thor Carlsson	Max Von Sydow
Mrs. Corliss	Diane Ladd

Showing *Vertigo*.

Psst! The original ending had Dillon dying by falling into a vat of molten copper.

Kiss of the Spider Woman ••••   [1985]

Director: Hector Babenco
Screenplay: Leonard Schrader

A flamboyant gay shares a South American prison cell with a radical activist and reminisces about old Hollywood movies. But the relationship between the two is not what it appears. This is one of those rare films which tackles a host of tricky issues and emerges with flying colours. Funny, scary, original and thought-provoking, it has a brilliant performance from Hurt. One of the great movies of the 80s. **[119m/15]**

Molina	William Hurt
Valentin	Raul Julia
Leni Lamaison/Marta	Sonia Braga

Oscars William Hurt

Quote 'It's just a romance. But it's *so* beautiful.'

Psst! Hurt's part was originally to have been played by Burt Lancaster, but he withdrew for a heart operation ✦ Julia lost 30 lb, reckoning that 'there are no fat revolutionaries' ✦ The actors worked for expenses only, deferring their salaries against box office receipts ✦ At one point, Hurt's beach house was broken into by thieves high on drugs. They held him hostage with a gun at his head, tormenting him for half an hour before escaping.

The Kitchen Toto ••   [1987]

Director: Harry Hook
Screenplay: Harry Hook

A young kitchen boy is caught up in the Mau Mau rising against the British in Kenya in 1950. An interesting story from a first-time director, told with clarity and succinctness. **[95m/15]**

Mwangi	Edwin Mahinda
John Graham	Bob Peck
Janet Graham	Phyllis Logan
D.C. McKinnon	Robert Urquhart

Knight Moves •   [1992]

Director: Carl Schenkel
Screenplay: Brad Mirman

Laughably bad thriller with more holes than a Swiss cheese. Lambert is the chess grandmaster who police suspect is nipping out from matches to murder young women before popping back to say 'checkmate'. Computers can now play chess brilliantly. The one that wrote this drivel can't. It's just taken lots of bits from other, more successful, films and plonked them in willy-nilly. [See Rose's Rule # 6]. Also known as *Face to Face*. **[116m/18]**

Sanderson	Christopher Lambert
Kathy Sheppard	Diane Lane
Frank Sedman	Tom Skerritt
Andy Wagner	Daniel Baldwin

Quote 'It doesn't make any sense.' – 'That's because we don't understand it yet.'

The Krays ••• [1990]

Director: **Peter Medak**
Screenplay: **Philip Ridley**

The Kemps are amazingly good as Ronnie and Reggie, the violent gangster twins who brought terror to London's East End. As much as an episodic study of their home life and relationship with their mother Whitelaw, as an account of their rise to infamy, this British *Goodfellas* would have been still better with a stronger story. Nonetheless, the Kemps portray the gruesome twosome with total believability. **[119m/18]**

Violet Kray	Billie Whitelaw
Ronald Kray	Gary Kemp
Reginald Kray	Martin Kemp
Rose	Susan Fleetwood
May	Charlotte Cornwell
Cannonball Lee	Jimmy Jewel
Jack "The Hat" McVitie	Tom Bell

Also: Avis Bunnage, Kate Hardie, Alfred Lynch, Steven Berkoff, Victor Spinetti

OOPS! A mike boom's clearly visible as Reg is brought sandwiches at his wife's wake.

Krull • [1983]

Director: **Peter Yates**
Screenplay: **Stanford Sherman**

Krudd's more like it. A pathetic plundering of the best of sci-fi, fantasy and sword and sorcery films which results in the worst of all worlds. Marshall's the young hero who has to save Anthony from the planet Krull. Save yourself from having to watch such rubbish. **[120m/PG]**

Colwyn	Ken Marshall
Lyssa	Lysette Anthony
Ynyr	Freddie Jones

Also: Francesca Annis, Alun Armstrong, Bernard Bresslaw, Liam Neeson

Psst! Francesca Annis's transformation into the Widow of the Web took over 8 hours each day and used 11 layers of latex. She wasn't able to eat when it was in place [See Rose's Rule #5] ◆ Lysette Anthony's voice was re-dubbed to make it more acceptable to US audiences.

Kuffs • [1992]

Director: **Bruce A. Evans**
Screenplay: **Bruce A. Evans & Raynold Gideon**

A Kuff around the ear's what Slater needs, so irritating are his smug asides to the camera. This dreadful comedy has him as a wastrel taking over a private police force in San Francisco when his brother is killed. The script is banal in the extreme, even resorting to silly sound effects. Worth seeing a minute or two, though, just to find out how Slater's imitation of Jack Nicholson's voice is coming along. **[101m/15]**

George Kuffs	Christian Slater
Ted Sukovsky	Tony Goldwyn
Maya Carlton	Milla Jovovich

Also: Bruce Boxleitner, Troy Evans

Psst! Contains the phrase: 'I don't know why I'm doing this.' This line, all too common in movies, is used by scriptwriters in the hope it stopd audiences asking themselves why a character is doing something incredibly stupid.

L

La Bamba ••• [1987]

Director: **Luis Valdez**
Screenplay: **Luis Valdez**

Well-mounted biography of Ritchie Valens, the rock 'n' roller who shot to fame at only 17 and died in a plane crash with Buddy Holly just eight months later. An unpretentious but lively and spirited film with Phillips excellent as the clean-cut Mexican. **[108m/15]**

Ritchi Valens	Lou Diamond Phillips
Bob Morales	Esai Morales
Connie Valenzuela	Rosana De Soto
Rosie Morales	Elizabeth Pena
Donna Ludwig	Danielle von Zerneck
Bob Keene	Joe Pantoliano

Labyrinth •• [1986]

Director: **Jim Henson**
Screenplay: **Terry Jones**

Another fantasy from the creators of the Muppets has Connelly having to navigate a maze full of puzzles set by the evil Demon King Bowie to rescue her little brother. As with *The Dark Crystal*, it's wonderful to look at but sadly lacking in substance, at least from an adult's viewpoint. **[101m/U]**

Jareth	David Bowie
Sarah	Jennifer Connelly
Toby	Toby Froud
Stepmother	Shelley Thompson

Quote 'I've never worked with an eight-year-old director before. It's wonderful fun.' [David Bowie]

Ladder of Swords • [1990]

Director: **Norman Hull**
Screenplay: **Neil Clark**

A strange British tale of travelling circus performer Shaw who has a caravan, a dancing bear, a disenchanted wife and an eye for the local talent but no plot to tie them all together. **[98m/15]**

Don Demarco	Martin Shaw
Denise Demarco	Eleanor David
Alice Howard	Juliet Stevenson
Det. Insp. Atherton	Bob Peck

Ladybugs • [1992]

Director: **Sidney J. Furie**
Screenplay: **Curtis Burch**

Rodney Dangerfield does his worst, and that's saying something, with this lamentable twaddle about him coaching a girls' soccer team (including his financée's son in drag). Words fail us. If only they'd fail *him* once in a while. **[90m/PG]**

Chester Lee	Rodney Dangerfield
Matthew/Martha	Jonathan Brandis

Ladyhawke • [1985]

Director: **Richard Donner**
Screenplay: **Edward Khmara, Michael Thomas & Tom Mankiewicz**

Hauer and Pfeiffer are star-crossed medieval lovers, turned into animals by a curse. Young thief Broderick comes to their rescue. Despite looking as if it can't miss on paper, actually the movie is overlong and amazingly dull. [See Rose's Rule #8] **[124m/PG]**

Phillipe	Matthew Broderick
Navarre	Rutger Hauer
Isabeau	Michelle Pfeiffer
Imperius	Leo McKern

Lady in White ••• [1988]

Director: **Frank LaLoggia**
Screenplay: **Frank LaLoggia**

Locked in his school overnight in the 60s, Haas encounters the ghost of a girl murdered there years before and sets out to find her killer. A gentle, chilling ghost story aimed at children, it achieves its spine-tingling aims without resorting to gore. **[112m/15]**

Frankie Scarlatti	Lukas Haas
Phil	Len Cariou
Angelo	Alex Rocco
Amanda	Katherine Helmond

Lady Jane ••• [1986]

Director: **Trevor Nunn**
Screenplay: **David Edgar**

Although history teachers will have trouble suppressing their mirth, others will be fascinated and moved by this story of the 15-year-old girl who became Queen of England for just nine days, before being toppled and then topped by Mary. This tragic tale makes the problems of the modern House of Windsor pale into insignificance. **[142m/PG]**

Lady Jane Grey	Helena Bonham Carter
Guilford Dudley	Cary Elwes
Duke of Northumberland	John Wood
Dr. Feckenham	Michael Hordern

Mrs. Ellen	Jill Bennett
Princess Mary	Jane Lapotaire
Duchess of Suffolk	Sara Kestelman
Duke of Suffolk	Patrick Stewart
Sir John Bridges	Joss Ackland

Psst! Bonham Carter is herself of aristo-cratic descent.

La Femme Nikita

SEE: Nikita

The Lair of the White Worm ••• [1988]

Director: Ken Russell
Screenplay: Ken Russell

The discovery of a mysterious skull attracts the attention of Donohoe. She's the head of a sinister vampire worm cult – which doesn't believe in overdoing the clothing – and has unspeakable designs on virginal Oxenberg. Underrated horror spoof, with our Uncle Ken making the most of the unusual story and English locations. Budget and acting limitations don't help, but Grant and more particu-larly Donohoe – luring boy scouts to their doom – embrace the proceedings with gusto. **[94m/18]**

Lady Sylvia Marsh	Amanda Donohoe
Lord James D'Ampton	Hugh Grant
Eve Trent	Catherine Oxenberg
Angus Flint	Peter Capaldi
Marcy Trent	Sammi Davis

Lamb •• [1986]

Director: Colin Gregg
Screenplay: Bernard MacLaverty

A young priest, disillusioned with the barbaric regime at the Irish remand home where he works, runs away with a mis-treated young epileptic. Well-made, but rather downbeat and depressing. **[110m/15]**

Michael Lamb	Liam Neeson
Priest	Harry Towb
Owen Kane	Hugh O'Conor
Mrs. Kane	Frances Tomelty
Brother Benedict	Ian Bannen

Lambada • [1990]

Director: Joel Silberg
Screenplay: Sheldon Renan & Joel Silberg

Possibly the worst dance-craze, cash-in movie ever made. **[98m/12]**

Kevin Laird/Blade	J. Eddie Peck
Sandy	Melora Hardin
Ramone	Shabba-Doo

The Land Before Time •• [1988]

Director: Don Bluth
Screenplay: Stu Krieger

This tepid attempt to cash in on kids' fas-cination for dinosaurs follows the cuddly little creatures' adventures as they search for a hidden green valley. This is only for the young at heart or the soft in head.
[69m/U]

With: Pat Hingle, Helen Shaver

Lassiter • [1984]

Director: Roger Young
Screenplay: David Taylor

An American cat burglar in wartime Britain is persuaded to rob the German embassy. A stylish caper wannabe, but Selleck isn't Cary Grant, Hutton isn't Grace Kelly and director Young most certainly isn't Hitchcock. **[100m/18]**

Lassiter	Tom Selleck
Sara	Jane Seymour
Kari	Lauren Hutton
Becker	Bob Hoskins

The Last Action Hero [1993]

Director: John McTiernan
Screenplay: Shane Black & Others

A lad obsessed with a Hollywood macho action man finds himself trapped on the other side of the screen, only to discover that partnering a violent, gung ho cop with an arsenal the size of a Middle Eastern country isn't such a happy experience. Using the cunning of an action movie buff, he's able to help Arnie out of his little local difficulties.

With: Arnold Schwarzenegger, Mercedes Ruehl, F. Murray Abraham, Art Carney, Anthony Quinn

Psst! The first ever film to be advertised on the side of a rocket, a stunt which cost $1m ✦ The trailer alone cost $300,000 ✦ Arnie's pay is $15m ✦ In New York a 75-foot high inflated Arnie aroused controversy because he was holding a stick of dynamite when the World Trade Centre was bombed. It was subsequently changed to a police shield.

The Last Boy Scout ••• [1992]

Director: **Tony Scott**
Screenplay: **Shane Black**

Willis is the ex-Presidential bodyguard, now a seedy private eye, who discovers that behind the murders he's trying to solve lies a dastardly plot to legalise sports gambling. The action bowls along at a rollicking pace and is backed up by a lively and witty script. The high body count and the violence with which that count is reached might not be to all tastes. [105m/18]

Joe Hallenbeck	Bruce Willis
Jimmy Dix	Damon Wayans
Sarah Hallenbeck	Chelsea Field
Sheldon Marcone	Noble Willingham
Milo	Taylor Negron
Darian Hallenbeck	Danielle Harris
Cory	Halle Berry
Mike Matthews	Bruce McGill
Senator Baynard	Chelcie Ross

Quote 'Just once I'd like to hear you scream with pain.' [Villain to Willis] – 'Play some rap music.'

Psst! The original ending was supposed to be a chase at sea. It was changed in order to save money ✦ Willis was paid over $10m ✦ The script was bought for $1.75m, $12,500 a page, then a record sum.

The Last Days of Chez Nous ••• [1993]

Director: **Gillian Armstrong**
Screenplay: **Helen Garner**

Australian director Armstrong brings us yet another little gem with this tale of novelist Harrow's life being turned upside down when her husband becomes enamoured of her sister. An acutely observed, bitter-sweet and low-key tale of love. How refreshing, too, to see such a convincingly warm, messy and awkward household on screen. [97m/15]

Beth	Lisa Harrow
J.P.	Bruno Ganz
Vicki	Kerry Fox
Annie	Miranda Otto
Tim	Kiri Paramore
Beth's father	Bill Hunter

The Last Dragon • [1985]

Director: **Michael Schultz**
Screenplay: **Louis Venosta**

Daft attempt to combine martial arts with rock music as our hero tries to save a pretty DJ from the unwanted attentions of some gangsters. It would be formulaic stuff except that somebody seems to have mislaid the formula. [109m/15]

Leroy	Taimak
Laura	Vanity
Eddie	Christopher Murney

The Last Emperor ••• [1987]

Director: **Bernardo Bertolucci**
Screenplay: **Mark Peploe & Bernardo Bertolucci**

The extraordinary life of Pu Yi, the boy Emperor living in the Forbidden City who ends up a gardener in Mao's Peking. Terrific camerawork and art direction, pretty good performances, but oh so hell-ishly overlong. [162m/15]

Pu Yi	John Lone
Wan Jung	Joan Chen
R.J.	Peter O'Toole
The Governor	Ying Ruocheng

Chen Pao Shen ....Victor Wong
Big Li..Dennis Dun
Oscars Best Picture, Best Director, Best
Screenplay (adapted)
Psst! Pu Yi's round glasses were mod-
elled on those of silent movie star
Harold Lloyd, the Emperor's favourite ◆
Chen had been one of the top Chinese
film stars. Her salary was increased
from $8 a month to $24 a month in 1980
when she won the Hundred Blossoms
award as the most popular actress in
the country ◆ This was the first Western
film allowed to shoot in the Forbidden
City ◆ The prison governor was played
by China's Vice Minister of culture ◆
2,000 soldiers of the People's Liberation
Army were among the 19,000 extras.

Last Exit to Brooklyn •• [1990]

Director: Uli Edel
Screenplay: Desmond Nakano

Hubert Selby Jr.'s novel of life and hard
times in 50's Brooklyn is a web of inter-
connecting stories involving work
lock-outs, domestic violence and Leigh
as local hooker Tralala. Despite some
powerful scenes, there's too much self-
importance in the narrative, no real
perspective and a woeful lack of humour.
[102m/18]

Harry Black................................Stephen Lang
Tralala.............................Jennifer Jason Leigh
Big Joe..Burt Young
Vinnie...Peter Dobson
Boyce..Jerry Orbach
Also: Stephen Baldwin, Alexis Arquette,
Ricki Lake

The Last of the Finest

SEE: Blue Heat

The Last of the Mohicans •• [1992]

Director: Michael Mann
Screenplay: Michael Mann & Christopher
Crowe

This may be the only war film more popular with women than men. The romance
between English lady Stowe and the wild,
frequently topless, fur trader Day-Lewis
struck some as wonderful, others as
ridiculous and stilted. Although the battle
scenes are among the best put on film, it's
dashed difficult to know what's going on
for much of the time. Although Day-
Lewis's use of 'ain't' may be historically
accurate, it jars and makes you think
you're watching a guy from Brooklyn on
an executive wilderness course. The
music is wholly inappropriate and the
scalpings horrendously realistic. [122m/12]

Hawkeye..........................Daniel Day-Lewis
Cora......................................Madeleine Stowe
Chingachgook..........................Russell Means
Uncas..Eric Schweig
Alice..Jodhi May
Heyward..........................Steven Waddington
Magua..Wes Studi
Col. Munro...........................Maurice Roeves
Quote 'Stay alive! No matter what occurs, I
will find you.'
Psst! To prepare for his role, Day-Lewis
was taught survival techniques by
America's equivalent of the SAS.
Wearing moccasins and a loincloth, he
learned to fight with a tomahawk and to
set traps although, being a concerned
animal rights activist, he would spring
them himself ◆ During the building of the
fort, 53 deadly copperhead snakes were
discovered. Despite several bites, no-
one actually died.

The Last Starfighter ••• [1984]

Director: Nick Castle
Screenplay: Jonathan Betuel

Chipper little film has Guest the teen who
breaks the record on a Starfighter video
game one night only to have Preston
appear from outer space and whisk him
off to play the game for real. A clever
idea, amusingly played out. [100m/PG]

Alex Rogan...................................Lance Guest
Grig...Dan O'Herlihy
Maggie Gordon.......Catherine Mary Stewart
Jane Rogan.............................Barbara Bosson
Xur...Norman Snow

The Last Temptation of Christ • [1988]

Director: **Martin Scorsese**
Screenplay: **Paul Schrader**

The story of Christ who, on the cross, dreams what life might have been like with a wife and kids. A rather dull retelling of the Gospel story, which only really becomes interesting when it deviates from scripture. It certainly doesn't justify all the ballyhoo whipped up at the time, with Scorsese clearly pulling his directorial punches. [164m/18]

Jesus	Willem Dafoe
Judas	Harvey Keitel
Mary Magdalene	Barbara Hershey
Saul/Paul	Harry Dean Stanton
Pontius Pilate	David Bowie

Quote 'Are you feeling alright?' [Asked of Lazarus as he rises from the dead]

OOPS! Although Hershey and other women are covered in tattoos, biblical law actually forbad tattoos of any sort ◆ Jesus's robe seems to have been machine–sewn and even bears signs of a label!

Psst! More than 25,000 people protested outside Universal Studios as the film was released, the biggest demonstration ever against a movie. The public demonstrated their disinterest by staying away: despite all the free publicity, it took only $7m in America, leaving the studio a hefty loss ◆ It was Hershey who originated the project, giving Scorsese a copy of the novel on which it's based back in 1972 ◆ The cast made the film for minimum union wages ◆ Hershey had collagen lip implants for the movie.

L.A. Story ••• [1991]

Director: **Mick Jackson**
Screenplay: **Steve Martin**

Okay, so LA's a weird and wacky place, but getting advice on life from a freeway sign? That's what happens to Martin the weatherman in this series of gags but little story peopled by lots of weird and wacky folk. There are some great laughs, but the lack of substance is rather galling, as is the spine–tinglingly embarrassing performance by Tennant, the real Mrs. Martin. [95m/15]

Harris K. Telemacher	Steve Martin
Sara McDowel	Victoria Tennant
Roland	Richard E. Grant
Trudi	Marilu Henner
SanDeE*	Sarah Jessica Parker
Ariel	Susan Forristal
Frank Swan	Kevin Pollak
Morris Frost	Sam McMurray
Maitre d' at L'Idiot	Patrick Stewart
June	Frances Fisher
Cynthia	Iman

Quote 'I could never be a woman because I'd spend all day at home playing with my breasts.' ◆ 'SanDeE*, your breasts feel weird.'–'Oh, that's coz they're real.'

OOPS! When Martin goes with Tennant to the talkative highway sign, he gets out of the driver's seat. Yet when they jumped into the car, it was she who got in on the driver's side ◆ Mozart's middle name is spelt 'Amedeus' in the museum.

Psst! SanDeE*'s name, which Parker is so concerned to get right in the film, is spelt 'Sandy' on the end credits ◆ Rick Moranis appears in a cameo as a grave digger. Who knows where he dug up his Cockney accent? Woody Harrelson and Chevy Chase also crop up.

Late for Dinner •• [1992]

Director: **W.D. Richter**
Screenplay: **Mark Andrus**

Two friends hop into the freezer in the 60s and emerge, well past their sell–by date, in the present. Although initially intriguing and amusing, the sci–fi is pushed out in the second half by suffocating sentiment as Wimmer seeks out his wife and daughter. *Forever Young* does it all so much better. Berg's a joy to watch, though, as the dimmer of the pair. [93m/PG]

Willie Husband	Brian Wimmer
Frank Lovegren	Peter Berg
Joy Husband	Marcia Gay Harden
Jessica Husband	Colleen Flynn

Laughterhouse ••• [1984]

Director: **Richard Eyre**
Screenplay: **Brian Glover**

A very funny, yet sadly overlooked, British comedy about goose farmer Holm, whose pluckers walk out just before Christmas. He resorts to taking his geese by road, walking them all the way from Norfolk to London, dogged by a TV crew. Why this charmer was forgotten so quickly is a mystery. **[93m/PG]**

Ben Singleton ....Ian Holm
Alice Singleton ....Penelope Wilton
Amos ....Bill Owen
Hubert..Richard Hope

The Lawnmower Man •• [1992]

Director: **Brett Leonard**
Screenplay: **Brett Leonard & Gimel Everett**

Although this sci-fi thriller claims to be the first-ever Virtual Reality movie, instead of the promised four dimensions, we barely get two. Scientist Brosnan gets retarded Fahey to be his guinea pig for experiments in which his computer generates another world. Pity it couldn't generate a better story or more credible characters. The much-vaunted F.X. are pretty naff while the famous VR sex scene may have moved the earth for them, but didn't register on my Richter Scale.
[105m/15]

Jobe Smith ....Jeff Fahey
Dr. Lawrence Angelo ....Pierce Brosnan
Marnie Burke............................Jenny Wright
Sebastian Timms ....Mark Bringleson
Quote 'He was the best chimp I ever had.'
Psst! Initially called *Stephen King's Lawnmower Man*, King successfully sued to have his name taken off it ♦ Credits include a 'sacred geometry consultant'.

A League of their Own •• [1992]

Director: **Penny Marshall**
Screenplay: **Lowell Ganz & Babaloo Mandel**

Disappointing story of the wartime women's baseball league. The off-field antics of the girls are incredibly clichéd and saccharine, particularly the emetic reunion fifty years later, which practically drags the tears out with pliers. Yet although way too long, the baseball scenes are surprisingly exciting. **[128m/PG]**

Jimmy Dugan.................................Tom Hanks
Dottie Hinson ....Geena Davis
Mae Mordabito.................................Madonna
Kit Keller...Lori Petty
Ernie Capadino................................Jon Lovitz
Ira Lowenstein ....David Strathairn
Walter Harvey......................Garry Marshall
Marla Hooch......................Megan Cavanagh
Quote 'Are you crying?...There's no crying in baseball.' ♦ 'It's been a thin slice of heaven.'
Psst! The cast went through baseball training beforehand. Just before filming started, however, Debra Winger left the movie, to be replaced at very short notice by Geena Davis ♦ A kiss between coach Hanks and the married Davis was cut out of the movie after test audiences objected.

Leap of Faith ••• [1992]

Director: **Richard Pearce**
Screenplay: **Janus Cercone**

Martin's an evangelist preacher touring the Southern States, fleecing each temporary flock before moving on again. As in every film involving crooked preachers, we know there'll be a miracle before too long. But the background details of the scams are so fascinating and the acting, particularly from Martin and the gutsy Winger, so good that we're caught up in the tale and swept along with the crowd. A mite sentimental in places, it's also funny, romantic and charming. **[107m/PG]**

Jonas Nightengale.......................Steve Martin
Jane ....Debra Winger
Marva...............................Lolita Davidovich
Will...Liam Neeson
Boyd..Lukas Haas
Hoover..Meat Loaf
Blurb Most People Believe That Miracles

Are Priceless. Here's Someone Who's
Willing To Negotiate.

Quote 'If God didn't mean us to take
advantage of suckers, why did He make
so many of them?'

Psst! Martin researched his role by
watching several examples of the real
thing in disguise ✦ The credits include a
'cons and frauds consultant' as well as
two 'butterfly handlers'.

Legal Eagles ••• [1986]

Director: **Ivan Reitman**
Screenplay: **Jim Cash & Jack Epps Jr.**

Although the plot's a trifle asinine, this
jokey tale of a DA and lawyer teaming up
to get performance artist Hannah off a
murder rap is lifted by the personable
performances of Redford and Winger.
The whole thing goes at a fair clip with
some clever dialogue and great special
effects, although any jury worth its salt
should convict Hannah just for her 'art'
alone. [116m/PG]

Tom Logan	Robert Redford
Laura Kelly	Debra Winger
Chelsea Deardon	Daryl Hannah
Cavanaugh	Brian Dennehy
Victor Taft	Terence Stamp
Bower	Steven Hill

Psst! The film was originally planned by
Reitman, director of *Ghostbusters*, as a
buddy movie with Bill Murray and
Dustin Hoffman ✦ The paintings and
sculptures used in the film were worth a
massive $10m, the most valuable collec-
tions of props ever used on a movie.

Legend • [1985]

Director: **Ridley Scott**
Screenplay: **William Hjortsberg**

Evil Tim Curry has plans for an innocent
princess and the unicorns. Luckily, Tom
Cruise is on hand in the magic forest to
set everything right. Even Ridley Scott
couldn't save this one, since the glossy
ad-like beauty goes for naught with such
a thin plot and insipid leads. [94m/PG]

Jack	Tom Cruise
Lili	Mia Sara
Darkness	Tim Curry
Gump	David Bennent

Psst! Shots of these unicorns crop up in
the director's cut of *Blade Runner*.

The Legend of Billie Jean • [1985]

Director: **Matthew Robbins**
Screenplay: **Mark Rosenthal & Lawrence
Konner**

Unjustly accused, Slater, her brother and
cronies decide that if they're going to be
accused of it, they may as well be outlaws.
Unfortunately, Billie and Lloyd are no
Bonnie and Clyde. [95m/15]

Billie Jean	Helen Slater
Lloyd	Keith Gordon
Binx	Christian Slater

Leon the Pig Farmer •• [1993]

Director: **Vadim Jean & Gary Sinyor**
Screenplay: **Gary Sinyor & Michael
Normand**

Honest estate agent Frankl discovers that
he's not North London Jewish but the off-
spring of a Yorkshire pig farmer. For a
low-budget debut, what's been achieved
is remarkable. Yet despite several funny
scenes, best of which is Brian Glover
doing Yorkshire Yiddish, the film's
somewhat uneven. [104m/15]

Leon Geller	Mark Frankel
Judith Geller	Janet Suzman
Brian Chadwick	Brian Glover
Yvonne Chadwick	Connie Booth
Also: David De Keyser, Maryam d'Abo,	
Gina Bellman	

Psst! The film was made for the almost
unbelievably paltry budget of £160,000,
with cast and crew accepting no money
against a percentage of possible profits ✦
The cod Kosher catering van – 'To You,
We Deliver' – went on location to
Yorkshire. It was stopped several times
in the middle of the Dales by people
hoping for salt beef, lox and bagels.

Les Patterson Saves the World • [1988]

Director: **George Miller**
Screenplay: **Barry Humphries & Diane Millstead**

As funny as Dame Edna is on stage, Barry Humphries on film is not. Here, as the infamous Australian cultural attaché to the Court of St. James he manages to insult every single ethnic, religious, national and sexual group on earth without raising more than a yawn. **[90m/15]**

Sir Les/ Dame Edna	Barry Humphries
Veronique Crudite	Pamela Stephenson

Lethal Weapon ••• [1987]

Director: **Richard Donner**
Screenplay: **Shane Black**

A cracking thriller with Gibson the Vietnam vet cop so unhinged by his wife's death that he doesn't care what happens, just so long as he brings down a few baddies. Glover, the more mature family man, has reservations about being teamed with someone so suicidal. The first in the series very much puts the top-notch action before the wisecracks.

[110m/18]

Martin Riggs	Mel Gibson
Roger Murtaugh	Danny Glover
Joshua	Gary Busey
The General	Mitchell Ryan
Michael Hunsaker	Tom Atkins
Trish Murtaugh	Darlene Love
Rianne Murtaugh	Traci Wolfe
Amanda Hunsaker	Jackie Swanson
Nick Murtaugh	Damon Hines
Carrie Murtaugh	Ebonie Smith
Psychologist	Mary Ellen Trainor

Quote 'You ever meet anybody you didn't kill?' [Murtaugh to Riggs]

Showing *A Christmas Carol.*

OOPS! Watch carefully as Riggs and the jumper leap from the ledge. The fake handcuffs come apart as the slow-motion begins, so they have to hold hands to make it look right.

Psst! A cinema claims to be showing 'The Lost Boys–This Year's Hit'. It was one of the studio's forthcoming films ✦ Isn't Mel just a touch boyish to have been a Vietnam vet?

Lethal Weapon 2 ••• [1989]

Director: **Richard Donner**
Screenplay: **Jeffrey Boam**

The weakest of the bunch, let down by a tiresomely illogical script about South African drug runners. Although the gags aren't bad and Pesci's great fun, you keep asking yourself questions. How can Riggs run after a BMW and nearly catch it? How come when he sets off on foot after those with transport have departed, he still arrives before them? How come automatic weapons are so popular with villains if they aren't a patch on Riggs' and Murtaugh's revolvers? **[111m/15]**

Martin Riggs	Mel Gibson
Roger Murtaugh	Danny Glover
Leo Getz	Joe Pesci
Arjen Rudd	Joss Ackland
Pieter Vorstedt	Derrick O'Connor
Rika Van Den Haas	Patsy Kensit

Quote 'We're back. We're bad. He's black. I'm mad.'

Psst! Probably the first movie in which a villain's head is removed with a surfboard ✦ A '15' in the cinema, the video is a slightly-longer '18'.

Lethal Weapon 3 •••• [1992]

Director: **Richard Donner**
Screenplay: **Jeffrey Boam & Robert Mark Kamen**

Murtaugh's just a few days away from retirement when he and Riggs discover weapons confiscated by the police turning up on the streets. The addition of tough woman cop Russo to the team is a bonus. When she and Riggs compare scars incurred in the line of duty, it turns into one of the cleverest foreplay scenes in the movies. With a clearer plot than usual, this is simply one of the greatest, funniest action pics of all time. **[118m/15]**

Martin Riggs	Mel Gibson
Roger Murtaugh	Danny Glover
Leo Getz	Joe Pesci
Lorna Cole	Rene Russo
Jack Travis	Stuart Wilson
Captain Murphy	Steve Kahan

Quote 'Nobody's dead.'–'Hey, the night's young.'

OOPS! Note the speed with which the bloodstains disappear after the killing in the police interrogation room ◆ Mel's boots change to shoes during the chase in the underground tunnel, then back again.

Psst! Keep watching the credits to the end ◆ After taking $100m in America, the stars were each presented with a new Range Rover ◆ Instead of Rene Russo, John Goodman was originally intended as the new addition to the team.

Let Him Have It ••• [1991]

Director: **Peter Medak**
Screenplay: **Neal Purvis & Robert Wade**

The tragic story of Derek Bentley, hanged for a murder he didn't commit, even though he had the mental age of an eleven-year-old. With attractive period detail, this is a well-acted reconstruction of the cause célèbre is directed with more panache than the usual true-life drama. It beggars belief that even this film hasn't led to Bentley's posthumous pardon. [115m/15]

Derek Bentley	Chris Eccleston
Chris Craig	Paul Reynolds
William Bentley	Tom Courtenay
Fairfax	Tom Bell

Also: Eileen Atkins, Clare Holman, Mark McGann, Michael Gough

Let's Get Harry • [1986]

Director: **Alan Smithee & Stuart Rosenberg**
Screenplay: **Charles Robert Carner**

Let's not. Standard 'mercenary taking greenhorns on a rescue mission in Central America' stuff put together in a sub-standard way. Also known as *The Rescue*. [107m/18]

Corey	Michael Schoeffling
Pachowski	Tom Wilson

Also: Glenn Frey, Gary Busey, Robert Duvall, Rick Rossovich

Psst! Real director Rosenberg had his name taken off the credits and replaced with that of Alan Smithee [see *Catchfire*].

Letter to Brezhnev ••• [1985]

Director: **Chris Bernard**
Screenplay: **Frank Clarke**

A Liverpool lass falls in love with a Russian sailor then struggles to follow him when he returns home. A generally charming and witty romantic fairy tale, with a good feel for Mersey feistiness and, given subsequent international events, rather prescient. [95m/15]

Sergei	Alfred Molina
Peter	Peter Firth
Teresa	Margi Clarke
Tracy	Tracy Lea
Elaine	Alexandra Pigg

Quote 'Drinking vodka, getting fucked and stuffing chickens, that's all I'm interested in.'

Leviathan • [1989]

Director: **George Pan Cosmatos**
Screenplay: **David Webb Peoples & Jeb Stuart**

Proliferating clones of *Alien* are running amok. Here, Weller and the rest of his underwater mining crew happen across a wrecked Soviet ship, but the vodka they nab has a few unexpected ingredients. This marine remake of *Alien* is far less enjoyable despite one bizarre scene where Pays takes a shower with her clothes on. [96m/18]

Beck	Peter Weller
Doc	Richard Crenna
Willie	Amanda Pays
Sixpack	Daniel Stern

Also: Ernie Hudson, Michael Carmine, Lisa Eilbacher, Hector Elizondo, Meg Foster

Quote 'Talk about having a bad day.'

Lianna ••• [1983]

Director: **John Sayles**
Screenplay: **John Sayles**

An unhappily married woman is drawn into a lesbian affair with a professor. This intelligent and entertaining film has Sayle's usual insight and wit and none of the heavy-handed earnestness that so often bedevils emotional dramas. [112m/18]

Lianna	Linda Griffiths
Ruth	Jane Hallaren
Dick	Jon DeVries
Sandy	Jo Henderson

Psst! Writer-director Sayles appears as the libidinous film professor.

Licence to Kill ••• [1989]

Director: **John Glen**
Screenplay: **Michael G. Wilson & Richard Maibaum**

Dalton shook and stirred a few Bond fans with this first film written specially for him. Adding a touch — just a touch — of realism to the character, he disobeys orders and goes after drug baron Davi. Lowell makes a wonderfully sassy heroine, and although the plot's as ropey as ever, the stunts are great. [133m/15]

James Bond	Timothy Dalton
Pam Bouvier	Carey Lowell
Franz Sanchez	Robert Davi
Lupe Lamora	Talisa Soto
Milton Krest	Anthony Zerbe
Sharkey	Frank McRae
Killifer	Everett McGill
Prof. Joe Butcher	Wayne Newton
Q	Desmond Llewelyn
Felix Leiter	David Hedison
M	Robert Brown
Miss Moneypenny	Caroline Bliss

Quote 'He disagreed with something that ate him.'

Psst! Although there's an unusual warning against the health dangers of tobacco at the end of the film, the film-makers accepted $350,000 from Philip Morris for the scene in which 007 lights up a *Lark* cigarette ✦ Originally the film had the book's title, *Licence Revoked*, until a survey found only 1 in 5 Americans knew what 'revoked' meant. Presumably, that didn't include the film-makers for, as Bond's licence *is* revoked in the film, the new title is nonsensical.

Liebestraum ••• [1992]

Director: **Mike Figgis**
Screenplay: **Mike Figgis**

An architectural critic returns to his home town where his mother's fatal illness exposes sexual secrets past and present. Thin on plot and long on atmosphere, the film is mesmerising if you're in the right mood and you like Figgis' lush style. [112m/18]

Nick Kaminsky	Kevin Anderson
Jane Kessler	Pamela Gidley
Paul Kessler	Bill Pullman
Mrs Anderssen	Kim Novak
Sheriff Ricker	Graham Beckel

Psst! The brothel scene was cut from the US release on the grounds that it was too intense for refined American sensibilities ✦ Kim Novak provides the obligatory nod to Hitchcock's *Vertigo*, in which she starred.

Lies •• [1983]

Director: **Ken Wheat & Jim Wheat**
Screenplay: **Ken Wheat & Jim Wheat**

An actress hired to stand in for a supposedly mad heiress finds that it's she who is trapped in a mental asylum. Considering the small budget, it's an entertaining, if occasionally preposterous, thriller. [102m/18]

Robyn Wallace	Ann Dusenberry
Jessica Brenner	Gail Strickland
Stuart Russell	Bruce Davison
Dr. Bartlett	Clu Gulager
Murray Haliday	Bert Remsen

Lifeforce •• [1985]

Director: **Tobe Hooper**
Screenplay: **Dan O'Bannon & Don Jakoby**

A beautiful woman descends from space and runs around with no clothes on.

Unfortunately, she's a vampire, turning those coming too close into zombies who run wild through a cardboard London that would disgrace a 50's British B-movie. One of those films so atrocious they're irresistable.   [101m/18]

Carlsens	Steve Railsback
Caine	Peter Firth
Fallada	Frank Finlay
Space Girl	Mathilda May
Dr. Armstrong	Patrick Stewart

Quote 'There's a naked female vampire in the building. Don't let her escape!'

OOPS! The BBC is employing American newsreaders now, is it? What is the world coming to?

Life is Sweet ••   [1991]

Director: Mike Leigh
Screenplay: Mike Leigh

One sister works as a plumber. The other is an unemployed neurotic with unconventional uses for chocolate spread. Mum Steadman does what she can to hold the family together. Starting hilariously and movingly, the film gets bogged down and never recovers. Leigh's skill with actors counts for naught when the structure of the film is so lopsided.   [102m/15]

Wendy	Alison Steadman
Andy	Jim Broadbent
Natalie	Claire Skinner
Nicola	Jane Horrocks
Patsy	Stephen Rea
Aubrey	Timothy Spall

Life Stinks ••   [1991]

Director: Mel Brooks
Screenplay: Mel Brooks, Rudy De Luca, Steve Haberman & Ron Clark

As you'd expect from Brooks, this satire on wealth and poverty, which has him living on the breadline for a month as a bet, is tasteless. Unfortunately, as it isn't terribly funny, it comes across as rather coarse and tawdry. Heaven help us from funnymen trying to teach us to be better people.   [95m/12]

Goddard Bolt	Mel Brooks
Molly	Lesley Ann Warren
Vance Crasswell	Jeffrey Tambor
Pritchard	Stuart Pankin

Quote 'I assumed that America understood irony, since it's an ironic title. I was wrong.' [Mel Brooks]

The Lighthorsemen ••   [1988]

Director: Simon Wincer
Screenplay: Ian Jones

The Australian cavalry charge on Beersheba in Palestine in World War I is the Oz equivalent of The Charge of the Light Brigade. The drama's a little leaden, but the well-captured battle scenes are extraordinarily exciting.   [110m/PG]

Dave	Peter Phelps
Scotty	Jon Blake
Bourchier	Tony Bonner

Also: Bill Kerr, John Walton, Sigrid Thornton, Anthony Andrews

Light of Day •   [1987]

Director: Paul Schrader
Screenplay: Paul Schrader

Unwise attempt to combine Schrader's dour tone — here examining a family falling apart — with a teen-orientated story about Fox and sister Jett making it in a rock 'n' roll band. Awful.   [107m/PG]

Joe Rasnick	Michael J. Fox
Jeanette Rasnick	Gena Rowlands
Patti Rasnick	Joan Jett
Bu Montgomery	Michael McKean

The Lightship ••   [1985]

Director: Jerzy Skolimowski
Screenplay: William Mai & David Taylor

A trio of crooks led by Duvall take refuge on a lightship captained by Brandauer. This odd little thriller is worthwhile only for the splendidly over-the-top performance by Duvall, a real collector's item for students of The School of Coarse Acting.   [89m/15]

Caspary	Robert Duvall
Capt. Miller	Klaus Maria Brandauer
Eddie	Arliss Howard
Gene	William Forsythe

Psst! The narration by Lyndon, the son of director Skolimowski, was added in post-production in a vain attempt to make things clearer.

Light Sleeper • [1992]

Director: **Paul Schrader**
Screenplay: **Paul Schrader**

Not a sleeper of any kind, but a desperately tedious study of the world of society drug dealing. Dafoe's a courier for Sarandon, an oddball who has trouble sleeping. He should watch this film. Devoid of almost all dramatic interest, it's the sort of movie that makes you resent how much less of your life is left as a result of watching it. **[103m/15]**

John LeTour	Willem Dafoe
Ann	Susan Sarandon
Marianne	Dana Delaney
Robert	David Clennon
Teresa	Mary Beth Hurt

Showing *Scorpio Rising.*

Psst! The story takes place during a dustmen's strike, with rubbish piling up on the streets. In fact, the real dustmen kept taking the it away, leaving the film-makers scrambling in the trucks to get it back
• Credits include a 'stunt cabbie'.

Like Father, Like Son •• [1987]

Director: **Rod Daniel**
Screenplay: **Lorne Cameron & Steven L. Bloom**

For a time, it seemed as if every comedy was about people switching identities. This was the first, with Moore swapping body with son Cameron. Highly amusing in places, it's screamingly unfunny in others. Moore over-acts dreadfully. **[100m/PG]**

Dr. Jack Hammond	Dudley Moore
Chris Hammond	Kirk Cameron
Ginnie Armbruster	Margaret Colin
Dr. Amy Larkin	Catherine Hicks

Limit Up • [1990]

Director: **Richard Martini**
Screenplay: **Richard Martini & Lu Anders**

Audiences can accept a degree of implausibility in supernatural comedies. But this yarn of a Chicago commodity trader doing a deal with the devil in return for riches, only to discover that world starvation could be the result, is pushing it a bit far. The daft ending makes you very sorry you've endured what's gone before. **[88m/12]**

Casey Falls	Nancy Allen
Peter Oak	Dean Stockwell
Marty Callahan	Brad Hall

Link • [1986]

Director: **Richard Franklin**
Screenplay: **Everett de Roche**

Stamp, experimenting on chimps with the assistance of Shue, finds that the primates have had enough and escape. Boring little British thriller that was probably put together by the monkeys while everyone else was on a tea break. **[116m/15]**

Dr. Steven Phillip	Terence Stamp
Jane Chase	Elisabeth Shue
David	Steven Pinner

Lionheart

SEE: A.W.O.L. — Absent Without Leave

Listen to Me • [1989]

Director: **Douglas Day Stewart**
Screenplay: **Douglas Day Stewart**

There have been teen movies about kids involved in every area of sporting activity but this must be the first time — and probably last — that the sport has been debating. You have one minute, without repetition, deviation or hesitation, to say why debating does *not* make for a gripping subject for a movie. **[107m/15]**

Tucker Muldowney	Kirk Cameron
Monica Tomanski	Jami Gertz
Charlie Nichols	Roy Scheider

Little Dorrit ••• [1987]

Director: **Christine Edzard**
Screenplay: **Christine Edzard**

Remarkable, though undeniably over-long, this adaptation of Dickens' novel exposing the horrors of Victorian debtors' prisons and the inhumanity of polite society, is full of life and character. Split into two parts of three hours each the first, *Nobody's Fault*, tells the story of debtor Guinness and daughter Pickering from the viewpoint of Jacobi, the man who tries to help them recover their fortune. The second, *Little Dorrit's Story*, is told from Pickering's point of view. The film is like those Sunday afternoon series the BBC used to do so brilliantly. As it's six hours in total, perhaps you should watch it in episode-sized bites. **[360m/U]**

Arthur Clennam	Derek Jacobi
William Dorrit	Alec Guinness
Pancks	Roshan Seth
Little Dorrit	Sarah Pickering
Flora	Miriam Margolyes
Frederick Dorrit	Cyril Cusack
Flintwinch	Max Wall
Mrs. Merdle	Eleanor Bron
Merdle	Michael Elphick
Mrs. Clennam	Joan Greenwood
Affery	Patricia Hayes
Decimus Barnacle	Robert Morley
Mr. Casby	Bill Fraser
Minnie	Sophie Ward
Tite Barnacle	John Savident

Psst! There are 211 people listed on the cast list, a record for a British film.

The Little Drummer Girl •• [1984]

Director: **George Roy Hill**
Screenplay: **Loring Mandel**

Le Carré's long and complicated novel about a pro-Palestinian English actress who is recruited by Israeli intelligence is undermined by the casting of Keaton. The ever-manic Klaus Kinski provides some compensation. **[130m/15]**

Charlie	Diane Keaton
Joseph	Yorgo Voyagis
Kurtz	Klaus Kinski
Khalil	Sami Frey

Psst! The character in the novel owed much to Le Carré's actress sister Charlotte Cornwell.

Little Man Tate ••• [1992]

Director: **Jodie Foster**
Screenplay: **Scott Frank**

Jodie Foster's first film as director is a delightful, bitter-sweet tale of an ill-educated single mother with a child prodigy for a son. Fascinating for its insight into such children, the film's also frequently funny. Hann-Byrd is wonderful in the title role while Foster is outstanding as the mother both proud and afraid of her child. Untypically, the weakest element is Wiest as a stereotypical head of a special institute, a former prodigy herself who can't cook. Highly enjoyable. **[99m/PG]**

Dede Tate	Jodie Foster
Dr Jane Grierson	Dianne Wiest
Fred Tate	Adam Hann-Byrd
Eddie	Harry Connick Jr.
Garth	David Pierce
Damon Wells	P.J. Ochlan

OOPS! Films are shot out of sequence, which probably explains why Adam Hann-Byrd has a plaster on his forehead some time before he is hit by the globe thrown by Connick.

Psst! Foster's own childhood was pretty remarkable. She spoke at 9 months, moving onto sentences three months later and teaching herself to read by the age of 3 ✦ Foster's nickname on set was 'BLT', Bossy Little Thing.

The Little Mermaid ••• [1989]

Director: **John Musker & Ron Clements**
Screenplay: **John Musker & Ron Clements**

Disney is almost back on top form with this Hans Christian Andersen story about the mermaid who wants to be human. The animation's great, the characters are fun and the songs are pretty good. Perhaps it's all a little unmemorable compared to the great features of Disney's past, but let us give thanks for the absence of icky sentimentality. **[82m/U]**

With: Rene Auberjonois, Christopher Daniel Barnes, Jodi Benson, Pat Carroll, Paddi Edwards, Buddy Hackett, Jason Marin, Kenneth Mars

Quote 'Look what the catfish dragged in.'

Psst! As if Disney hadn't had enough problems with *Three Men and a Baby* over the alleged ghost, they were inundated this time with calls from people who thought that an erect penis had been artfully drawn into the design of the towers on the video box.

Little Shop of Horrors •• [1986]

Director: **Frank Oz**
Screenplay: **Howard Ashman**

Timid florist Moranis finds a plant that thrives only on blood. As it grows, so it gets greedier, to the detriment of the local population. This transfer of the popular stage musical falls rather flat, although Martin's great as the sadistic dentist mistreating the wonderfully breathy-voiced Greene. **[94m/PG]**

Seymour Krelborn......................Rick Moranis
Audrey ....Ellen Greene
Mushnik..............................Vincent Gardenia
Orin Scrivello, D.D.S. ....Steve Martin
Also: James Belushi, John Candy, Christopher Guest, Bill Murray, Miriam Margolyes

Quote 'Feed me, Seymour. Feed me all night long.'

Psst! Almost twelve miles of cable were used in the creation of the final version of Audrey II, which weighed nigh on a ton • The voice of the plant was provided by Levi Stubbs of The Four Tops • The original, brilliant 1961 Roger Corman movie on which the stage musical was based was shot in just two days and three nights, while this version took seven months.

The Living Daylights ••• [1987]

Director: **John Glen**
Screenplay: **Richard Maibaum & Michael G. Wilson**

At 40, Dalton takes a bow as James Bond. Although he isn't as quick with the wisecracks as earlier incarnations of 007, there's plenty of great action, a delicious damsel in distress and some wonderful scenery. What more do you want from a Bond film? **[130m/PG]**

James Bond............................Timothy Dalton
Kara Milovy ....Maryam d'Abo
Gen. Georgi Koskov.................Jeroen Krabbé
Brad Whitaker.........................Joe Don Baker
Gen. Leonid Pushkin ....John Rhys-Davies
Kamran Shah ....Art Malik
Q ....Desmond Llewelyn
M......................................Robert Brown
Minister of Defence.................Geoffrey Keen
Miss Moneypenny....................Caroline Bliss
Felix Leiter.....................................John Terry
Rubavitch ....Virginia Hey

Quote 'I'm amazed at how fit Timothy Dalton is. His big sport is...fishing!' [Maryam d'Abo]

Psst! Ex-Royal girlfriend Katie Rabett appears in a small part as 'Liz' • This was the debut of Caroline Bliss as Miss Moneypenny, replacing the glorious Lois Maxwell.

Local Hero •••• [1983]

Director: **Bill Forsyth**
Screenplay: **Bill Forsyth**

Utterly delightful, magical comedy from the director of *Gregory's Girl*. Riegert is the oil executive sent to Scotland to buy an entire fishing village where his company wants to build a refinery. But dealing with slippery customers in suits hasn't adequately prepared him for the canniness of the villagers' negotiating tactics. Just as Riegert succumbs to the charms of the landscape, so you'll succumb to the charms of this warm-hearted film, peopled with wonderfully eccentric characters. **[111m/PG]**

Happer	Burt Lancaster
Mac	Peter Riegert
Ben	Fulton Mackay
Urquhart	Denis Lawson
Moritz	Norman Chancer
Oldsen	Peter Capaldi
Geddes	Rikki Fulton
Watt	Alex Norton
Marina	Jenny Seagrove
Stella	Jennifer Black
Ricky	John Gordon Sinclair

Psst! Apparently this film was the main influence behind the TV series *Northern Exposure*.

Lock Up •• [1989]

Director: **John Flynn**
Screenplay: **Richard Smith, Jeb Stuart & Henry Rosenbaum**

Convict Stallone comes up against his old adversary, the Warder From Hell Sutherland. It's Prison Film Plot #3, with no variations, but aside from the odd touch of worthiness it's still pretty slick and fast-paced. **[106m/18]**

Frank Leone	Sylvester Stallone
Warden Drumgoole	Donald Sutherland
Meissner	John Amos
Chink Weber	Sonny Landham

Quote 'This is hell, and I'm going to give you the guided tour.'

Psst! The movie was made at Rahway, the East Jersey State Prison. Many of the convicts seen are real ones. In return for their services, the film-makers bought them an outdoor athletics track.

London Kills Me • [1991]

Director: **Hanif Kureishi**
Screenplay: **Hanif Kureishi**

It won't kill you, but it may make you want to kill yourself. This daft tale of druggie Chadwick searching for some footwear so he can get a job is pointless, unpleasant and depressing, a perfect example of why people won't invest in British films. **[105m/18]**

Clint	Justin Chadwick

Muffdiver	Steven Mackintosh
Sylvie	Emer McCourt
Dr. Bubba	Roshan Seth
Headley	Fiona Shaw
Hemingway	Brad Dourif

Psst! This was the directorial debut of the writer of *My Beautiful Laundrette* ◆ There's apparently a glimpse of Jason Donovan somewhere. Watching filming in Portobello, he was asked to do a 'walk-on'.

Lonely Hearts ••• [1982]

Director: **Paul Cox**
Screenplay: **Paul Cox & John Clarke**

A delightful comedy about a love affair between two very timid people finding romance relatively late in life. Full of charm and wit, this is a gentle and lovely Australian film. **[95m/15]**

Patricia Curnov	Wendy Hughes
Peter Thompson	Norman Kaye
George, theatre director	Jon Finlayson
Pamela, Peter's sister	Julia Blake
Detective	Chris Haywood

The Lonely Lady • [1983]

Director: **Peter Sasdy**
Screenplay: **John Kershaw & Shawn Randall**

...Nothing like as lonely as the few lost souls watching this Zadora turkey. She soon discovered it takes more than just a wealthy husband to make it in the movies. The words 'talent' and 'little finger' spring to mind. Here she's a wannabe Hollywood scriptwriter who finds that people are more interested in producing her babies than her scripts. **[92m/18]**

Jerilee	Pia Zadora
Walter	Lloyd Bochner
Veronica	Bibi Besch
Joe	Ray Liotta
Bernie	Lou Hirsch

Quote 'But you're my daughter.' — 'I'm a woman too.' [Actually comes from the previous Zadora film, *Butterfly*, but far too good to waste.]

The Lonely Passion of Judith Hearne ••• [1987]

Director: Jack Clayton
Screenplay: Peter Nelson

Maggie Smith has rarely been better than as the middle-aged, tippling spinster who strikes up a relationship with Hoskins in repressed 50's Dublin. Although uncompromisingly realistic, this is a moving and sometimes wryly funny tale, superbly acted by its two principals and with one of the slimiest performances of the 80s from McNeice. **[110m/15]**

Judith Hearne	Maggie Smith
James Madden	Bob Hoskins
Aunt D'Arcy	Wendy Hiller
Mrs. Rice	Marie Kean
Bernard	Ian McNeice

Lone Wolf McQuade •• [1983]

Director: Steve Carver
Screenplay: B.J. Nelson

A reasonable Chuck Norris actioner. Here the man's a Texas Ranger battling the evil Carradine. All – presumably – done with tongue firmly in cheek. **[107m/18]**

J.J. McQuade	Chuck Norris
Rawley Wilkes	David Carradine
Lola	Barbara Carrera
Jackson	Leon Isaac Kennedy

The Long Day Closes • [1992]

Director: Terence Davies
Screenplay: Terence Davies

A perfect example of what is wrong with the British film industry. Ostensibly about a working-class childhood in 50's Liverpool, there's nothing so vulgar as a story, just a series of pretty pictures. These include a two-minute shot of sunlight playing on a carpet! Indescribably boring to everyone but insomniacs, who should rush out and rent the tape immediately. **[83m/12]**

Mother	Marjorie Yates
Bud	Leigh McCormack
Kevin	Anthony Watson

Longtime Companion ••• [1990]

Director: Norman Rene
Screenplay: Craig Lucas

A portrait of a group of gay New York men throughout the 80s, beginning with the outbreak of AIDS and ending with the decimation of their numbers. Intelligent, well-acted and moving. **[99m/15]**

Willy	Campbell Scott
Fuzzy	Stephen Caffrey
Sean	Mark Lamos
David	Bruce Davison
Paul	John Dossett
Lisa	Mary-Louise Parker

Look Who's Talking ••• [1989]

Director: Amy Heckerling
Screenplay: Amy Heckerling

Putting a talking baby in a comedy sounds ghastly, an idea that should have been suffocated at birth. Yet it works better than expected in this diverting tale of pregnant Alley, unable to force married Segal to do the right thing, setting out to find a suitable father. As soon as she gets in Travolta's cab, you just know what's in store. But this light and frothy concoction is still good fun. Willis is pretty good, but what sort of actor is it who can only succeed as either a macho hero or an infant? **[96m/12]**

James	John Travolta
Mollie	Kirstie Alley
Rosie	Olympia Dukakis
Albert	George Segal
Grandpa	Abe Vigoda
Voice of Mikey	Bruce Willis

Quote 'I look like a Russ Meyer movie.'
Showing *It's a Wonderful Life.*
OOPS! When Alley and Travolta are in the cab trying to find Mikey, see Travolta's shades keep appearing and disappearing.
Psst! Although Willis got no outright fee for voicing Mikey, his percentage netted him over $10 million, more than the film cost ✦ Some at the studio had wanted to stop the release of the film because they felt it was so bad. In fact, it was one of the highest grossing movies of the year.

Look Who's Talking Too • [1990]

Director: Amy Heckerling
Screenplay: Amy Heckerling & Neal Israel

A dismal sequel which, one assumes, was written by the babies themselves. Give thanks that despite the odd musical number and two additional screamers (one female, one black) filling their nappies, the film-makers still couldn't fill an hour and a half.   [81m/12]

James	John Travolta
Mollie	Kirstie Alley
Rosie	Olympia Dukakis
Stuart	Elias Koteas
Rona	Twink Caplan
Voice of Mikey	Bruce Willis
Voice of Julie	Roseanne Arnold
Voice of Eddie	Damon Wayans
Voice of Mr. Toilet Man	Mel Brooks

Quote 'Don't you just hate it when you get your head caught in your placenta.'

Psst! A wrangler on a film is someone who handles various animals. This is probably the first movie to have a 'Sperm Wrangler' on the credits!

Loose Connections •• [1984]

Director: Richard Eyre
Screenplay: Maggie Brooks

A minor British road movie, the road being that to Munich, with a feminist forced to endure the company of a Liverpool football supporter with an away ticket. The usual hate-each-other, come-together-at-end stuff doesn't really work, but there's some fun to be had along the way.   [95m/PG]

Harry	Stephen Rea
Sally	Lindsay Duncan

Lord of the Flies •• [1990]

Director: Harry Hook
Screenplay: Sara Schiff

A dull updating of Golding's powerful novel of civilised, shipwrecked children turning into savages. In this version, they're know-all American military cadets who are so Together that by the end of Day One they'd have built a nuclear bomb out of bottle tops.   [95m/15]

Ralph	Balthazar Getty
Jack	Chris Furrh
Piggy	Danuel Pipoly
Simon	Badgett Dale
Marine Officer	Bob Peck

OOPS! In one of the great movie boo-boos, they use short-sighted Piggy's glasses to start a fire with the sun's rays. This only works with lens for long sight. However, author Golding got it wrong in the book as well.

Psst! Getty is the great-grandson of the famous oil tycoon.

The Lords of Discipline ••• [1983]

Director: Franc Roddam
Screenplay: Thomas Pope & Lloyd Fonvielle

The other side of *Officer and a Gentleman*, with a black recruit at the Carolina Military Institute being given an unpleasantly rough time by his more reactionary colleagues. Keith is fantastic as the cadet who takes a stand against such reprehensible behaviour. Tough, but a solid, entertaining movie.   [103m/15]

Will	David Keith
Bear	Robert Prosky
Gen. Durrell	G.D. Spradlin
Abigail	Barbara Babcock
Alexander	Michael Biehn
Pig	Rick Rossovich
Macabbee	Judge Reinhold
MacKinnon	Jason Connery

Lorenzo's Oil •• [1992]

Director: George Miller
Screenplay: George Miller & Nick Enright

Extraordinary true-life story of two devoted parents who, discovering that their young son has the fatal disease ALD, set out to find a cure despite having no medical knowledge. Although it's not surprising that it is something of a weepie, the film suffers from undramatic, by-the-numbers storytelling. You might just as well read a Sunday colour sup-plement article on the Odones. Nolte's Chico Marx-like Italian accent might well be spot on, as claimed at the time, but it is nonetheless incredibly distracting.

[135m/12]

Augusto Odone	Nick Nolte
Michaela Odone	Susan Sarandon
Prof. Nikolais	Peter Ustinov
Deirdre Murphy	Kathleen Wilhoite
Dr. Judalon	Gerry Bamman
Wendy Gimble	Margo Martindale
Ellard Muscatine	James Rebhorn
Loretta Muscatine	Ann Hearn

OOPS! The boom mike appears as the first ALD conference opens, and jigs around a fair bit .

Psst! Although no great shakes as an actor, the endearing Don Suddaby appears as himself. He's the Yorkshire chemist who refracted the original Lorenzo's oil ✦ Nolte added 40 pounds for the part ✦ Director George Miller, responsible for the *Mad Max* films, was a practising doctor before moving into movies.

Losin' It •• [1983]

Director: Curtis Hanson
Screenplay: B.W.L. Norton

Apart from the curiosity value of seeing Cruise in one of his earliest roles, there's nothing exceptional about this tale of American teenagers popping down to Tijuana to pop their nuts. [See Rose's Rule #3] **[104m/18]**

Woody	Tom Cruise
Dave	Jackie Earle Haley
Spider	John Stockwell
Kathy	Shelley Long

Blurb The Last Word About The First Time.

Lost Angels
SEE: The Road Home

The Lost Boys •• [1987]

Director: Joel Schumacher
Screenplay: Janice Fischer, James Jeremias & Jeffrey Boam

A bratpack take on the vampire story, about a group of teens with a taste for blood. A humorous, moderately entertaining, timewaster. **[97m/18]**

Michael	Jason Patric
Sam	Corey Haim
Lucy	Dianne Wiest

Also: Barnard Hughes, Edward Herrmann, Kiefer Sutherland, Jami Gertz, Corey Feldman

Lost in America ••• [1985]

Director: Albert Brooks
Screenplay: Albert Brooks & Monica Johnson

Advertising executive Brooks, passed over for promotion, persuades wife Hagerty they should sell up, buy a motor home and tootle round America. Things don't quite go according to plan in this splendidly blackly funny satire on yuppiedom. **[91m/15]**

David Howard	Albert Brooks
Linda Howard	Julie Hagerty
Casino Manager	Garry Marshall
Employment Agent	Art Frankel
Paul Dunn	Michael Greene

Quote 'I've seen the future. It's a bald-headed man from New York!'

Psst! The final scene is one of the most blatant 'You Can Always Park In The Movies' scenes in film history. A mobile home? In the middle of Manhattan? In the middle of the day? Right outside the very building you want? ✦ Casino manager Marshall is the director of films like *Pretty Woman*.

Love at Large • [1990]

Director: Alan Rudolph
Screenplay: Alan Rudolph

A private eye on a case is himself followed by a female dick. What could have been a charming, witty take on love and deception is instead coy, smug and rather irritating. **[97m/15]**

Harry Dobbs	Tom Berenger
Stella Wynkowski	Elizabeth Perkins
Miss Dolan	Anne Archer
Ellen McGraw	Kate Capshaw
Mrs. King	Annette O'Toole

The Love Child •• [1987]

Director: **Robert Smith**
Screenplay: **Gordon Hann**

Life on the wry side on a South London council estate, with Capaldi the good lad, orphaned, who falls in with a bad lot before everything turns out all right again. Unexceptional, small-screen stuff. **[102m/15]**

Edith	Sheila Hancock
Dillon	Peter Capaldi
Maurice	Percy Herbert
The Voices	Alexei Sayle

Love Crimes • [1992]

Director: **Lizzie Borden**
Screenplay: **Allan Moyle**

Unbelievably bad thriller (ha!) has barmy DA Young trying to trap womaniser Bergin. He's been pretending to be a top photographer to get women to pose and then sleep with him. The risible story, with Young both fascinated and repelled by him, makes little sense but is an excuse for a lot of nudity and even a urination scene. Amazing to realise that this drivel comes from one of the top feminist directors. **[90m/18]**

Dana Greenway	Sean Young
David Hanover	Patrick Bergin
Maria Johnson	Arnetia Walker

Psst! The credits include: 'Color polaroids by Patrick Bergin'. As every one is of a naked woman, this must rank up there among the top star perks of all time • According to the director, the studio insisted on cutting out a 20-minute sequence which not only had the usual censor-baiting Young love scene, but also the explanation of the entire plot!

Love Hurts •• [1990]

Director: **Bud Yorkin**
Screenplay: **Ron Nyswaner**

Divorced Daniels turns up for his sister's wedding, only to find his ex and kids there. Yet another of those innumerable bitter-sweet dramas about the effects of divorce. **[101m/15]**

Paul Weaver	Jeff Daniels
Nancy Weaver	Cynthia Sikes
Susan Volcheck	Judith Ivey
Boomer	John Mahoney
Ruth Weaver	Cloris Leachman
Karen Weaver	Amy Wright

Quote 'What is the difference between marriage and prison?' – 'In prison somebody else does the cooking.'

Love Letters ••• [1984]

Director: **Amy Holden Jones**
Screenplay: **Amy Holden Jones**

Curtis discovers her mother's old letters to a secret lover, only to follow in her mom's footsteps by having an obsessive affair herself with a married man. Though marketed as smut, this is intelligent low – budget fare. The passion is often quite brutal and no easy answers or cosy morals are offered. If only Curtis could find other demanding roles like this. **[94m/18]**

Anna	Jamie Lee Curtis
Oliver	James Keach
Wendy	Amy Madigan
Danny	Bud Cort

Also: Matt Clark, Bonnie Bartlett, Rance Howard, Sally Kirkland
Showing *From Here to Eternity.*

The Lover • [1992]

Director: **Jean-Jacques Annaud**
Screenplay: **Jean-Jacques Annaud &**
Gérard Brach

The publicity campaign, centring on whether the 17-year-old 'Sinner from Pinner' had done *IT* on screen was brilliant. Unfortunately, the film is dreadful.

The language in this tale of a schoolgirl's affair with a wealthy young Chinaman in 20's Vietnam has obviously been translated word-for-word from a cheap phrase book. The acting is so bad you pray for them to get on with the bonking. But this is so tedious that you're soon praying for them to do a bit of acting again. Bored me rigid. **[117m/18]**

Young Girl	Jane March
Chinaman	Tony Leung
Voiceover	Jeanne Moreau
Mother	Frédérique Meininger

OOPS! As the boat pulls away at the end of the film, there's a ship in the background with a modern radar system.

Psst! An unknown French actress, Cécile Fleury, later claimed that she had doubled for March in the sex scenes.

Loverboy ••   [1989]

Director: **Joan Micklin Silver**
Screenplay: **Robin Schiff, Tom Ropelewski & Leslie Dixon**

Dempsey is the young stud who delivers more than pizzas to the bored wives of Beverly Hills. This farce delivers pretty much what you'd expect. **[98m/15]**

Randy Bodek	Patrick Dempsey
Diane Bodek	Kate Jackson
Joe Bodek	Robert Ginty
Monica Delancy	Carrie Fisher
Alex Barnett	Barbara Carrera
Dr. Joyce Palmer	Kirstie Alley

Lovesick ••   [1983]

Director: **Marshall Brickman**
Screenplay: **Marshall Brickman**

As with all screen shrinks who have patients of the opposite sex, Moore falls in love with patient McGovern while getting advice from Sigmund Freud in the shape of Alec Guinness. Amiable but nothing more: rather a pity considering the talent involved. **[95m/15]**

Saul Benjamin	Dudley Moore
Chloe Allen	Elizabeth McGovern
Sigmund Freud	Alec Guinness
Nymphomaniac	Christine Baranski

Love Streams ••   [1984]

Director: **John Cassavetes**
Screenplay: **John Cassavetes & Ted Allan**

Cassavetes the writer also directs Cassavetes the actor in this film that will largely appeal only to the Cassavetes fan club. He's an author who's researching a book about prostitution by getting to know some of its practitioners. Long, slow and adored by some. **[141m/15]**

Sarah Lawson	Gena Rowlands
Robert Harmon	John Cassavetes
Susan	Diahnne Abbott
Jack Lawson	Seymour Cassel

Lust in the Dust •   [1985]

Director: **Paul Bartel**
Screenplay: **Philip John Taylor**

Despite featuring gargantuan transvestite Divine, this is a far from divine Western spoof, with Hunter searching for some gold, guided only by a map that's been tattooed on a couple of pairs of buttocks. Sadly, after this refined start, it becomes rather cheap and tawdry. **[85m/15]**

Abel	Tab Hunter
Rosie	Divine
Marguerita	Lainie Kazan

Quote 'Freeze hombre, or I'll be wearing your asshole for a garter.'

Mac and Me •   [1988]

Director: **Stewart Raffill**
Screenplay: **Stewart Raffill & Steven Feke**

This breath-takingly bad *E.T.* clone has a wheelchair lad befriending the usual friendly alien. Despite being a kids' pic, it's got some of the most blatant product placement ever, with huge stretches looking more like an ad for Coke and

Macdonald's than a serious movie. The title's presumably no coincidence. [100m/U]

Janet.................................Christine Ebersole
Michael..................................Jonathan Ward
Courtney.............................Katrina Caspary

Mad Dog and Glory ••• [1993]

Director: John McNaughton
Screenplay: Richard Price

When mild police photographer De Niro saves hoodlum Murray's life, he is sent Thurman as a 'present' for a week. Naturally, the withdrawn De Niro falls in love. The third film with a similar subject, after *Honeymoon in Vegas* and *Indecent Proposal*, this one is a slight but charming romance, helmed by the director of *Henry: Portrait of a Serial Killer*. While both De Niro and Thurman are excellent, Murray gives his best performance yet as the gangster who also does stand-up. [96m/18]

Wayne 'Mad Dog' Dobie.....Robert De Niro
Glory.......................................Uma Thurman
Frank Milo...................................Bill Murray
Mike...David Caruso
Harold..Mike Starr
Andrew..Tom Towles
Lee...Kathy Baker

Madame Sousatzka ••• [1988]

Director: John Schlesinger
Screenplay: Ruth Prawer Jhabvala & John Schlesinger

Dotty, bossy piano-teacher MacLaine believes she's found a potential prodigy in a 15-year-old Indian boy. But he's not as easy to bend to her will as some of her other pupils. An immensely pleasing and moving film, even if MacLaine does act without ever taking her foot off the loud pedal. [122m/15]

Madame Sousatzka.............Shirley MacLaine
Lady Emily...............................Peggy Ashcroft
Jenny..Twiggy
Sushila......................................Shabana Azmi
Ronnie Blum...............................Leigh Lawson
Cordle..................................Geoffrey Bayldon

Psst! MacLaine put on 30lb to play the role.

Made in Heaven •• [1987]

Director: Alan Rudolph
Screenplay: Bruce A. Evans & Raynold Gideon

Hutton, falling in love in heaven, has to find his true love again later on earth. An often charming fantasy in the *Ghost* mould muffs it when the violins and harps come out and it goes for the heart, driving an unsubtle stake through it instead of cupid's arrow. [102m/PG]

Mike Shea/Elmo Barnett........Timothy Hutton
Annie Packert/Ally..................Kelly McGillis
Aunt Lisa...........................Maureen Stapleton
Annette Shea......................Ann Wedgeworth

Psst! Cameoing are Ellen Barkin, Neil Young and Debra Winger as a male archangel.

Madhouse • [1990]

Director: Tom Ropelewski
Screenplay: Tom Ropelewski

Totally stupid and rather tasteless comedy about a couple of yuppies whose new home is descended upon by an interminable stream of house guests. Like three very bad sitcoms back to back. [90m/15]

Mark Bannister.....................John Larroquette
Jessie Bannister............................Kirstie Alley
Claudia..................................Alison La Placa

Mad Max Beyond Thunderdome ••• [1985]

Director: George Miller & George Ogilvie
Screenplay: Terry Hayes

Max stumbles into Tina Turner, the ruler of Bartertown, and finds himself in a lethal duelling game in the Thunderdome. An ambitious attempt to broaden, and soften, the Max persona is intriguing, if not wholly successful. A few more gratuitous car smashes wouldn't have gone amiss while Turner comes close to stealing the movie from Mel. [107m/15]

Mad Max	Mel Gibson
Jedediah	Bruce Spence
Jedediah Jr.	Adam Cockburn
Aunty Entity	Tina Turner
The Collector	Frank Thring
The Master	Angelo Rossitto
The Blaster	Paul Larsson

Quote 'When I first spoke to Mel Gibson, I told him what the film's story really was: "Listen mate. It's Jesus in black leather".' [Terry Hayes]

Psst! The credits show one Mel Gibson not only starring in the film, but also as one of the stuntmen

Major League •• [1989]

Director: **David S. Ward**
Screenplay: **David S. Ward**

The rich-bitch new owner of her late husband's baseball team tries to sabotage it by picking the worst team she can. She doesn't realise that in the movies the underdogs always come through at the last minute, no matter how incompetent. There's a reasonable smattering of laughs in this oh-so-predictable comedy.[107m/15]

Jake Taylor	Tom Berenger
Ricky Vaughn	Charlie Sheen
Roger Dorn	Corbin Bernsen
Rachel Phelps	Margaret Whitton

Also: James Gammon, Rene Russo, Wesley Snipes

Blurb A Comedy With Bats And Balls.

OOPS! If baseball isn't your game and you're watching the clock, watch the one in the stadium which stays stuck at 10.40 for a time before changing to 10.20 for a while. In any case, isn't it rather an odd time to be playing?

Making Mr. Right •• [1987]

Director: **Susan Seidelman**
Screenplay: **Floyd Byars & Laurie Frank**

PR person Magnuson falls madly in love with a beautiful, blonde client who just happens to be a robot bearing an uncanny resemblance to its inventor Malkovich. Moderately amusing fluff. [98m/15]

Jeff Peters/Ulysses	John Malkovich
Fankie Stone	Ann Magnuson
Trish	Glenne Headly
Steve Marcus	Ben Masters
Sandy	Laurie Metcalf

Making the Grade •• [1984]

Director: **Dorian Walker**
Screenplay: **Gene Quintano**

Formulaic teen movie about a rich brat hiring a poor kid to attend school for him while he's off enjoying himself. [104m/15]

Eddie	Judd Nelson
Tracey	Jonna Lee
Harriman	Gordon Jump
Coach	Walter Olkewicz
Nicky	Ronald Lacey

Malcolm •• [1986]

Director: **Nadia Tass**
Screenplay: **David Parker**

A mentally defective young man is made redundant, but is able to turn his mechanical skills to robbing banks. This pleasantly offbeat Australian comedy is apparently based on the screenwriter's brother. One wonders if that's how they financed the movie? [86m/15]

Malcolm	Colin Friels
Frank	John Hargreaves
Judith	Lindy Davies
Willy	Chris Haywood

Malcolm X ••• [1992]

Director: **Spike Lee**
Screenplay: **Arnold Perl & Spike Lee**

This spirited and often wonderfully unusual look at the black radical leader goes sadly awry in the final third. Just when Washington, giving an excellent performance as Malcolm, should be stirring up passions with his oratory, Lee, amazingly, pulls his punches. Instead of going for the jugular, he tugs at the tearducts instead. Despite its length (is it coincidence that it's just longer than JFK?), the early life of Malcolm is vibrant enough to compensate. [201m/15]

Malcolm X ....Denzel Washington
Betty Shabazz............................Angela Bassett
Baines..Albert Hall
Elijah Muhammad....................Al Freeman Jr.
West Indian Archie....................Delroy Lindo
Shorty..Spike Lee
Laura......................................Theresa Randle
Sophia..Kate Vernon

Quote 'The only thing I like integrated is my coffee.'

Psst! When the picture went over budget, Lee put in $3m of his own money and got extra backing from Prince, Bill Cosby, Magic Johnson, Janet Jackson and others ✦ Look out for real-life firebrand Al Sharpton. He's the second orator in the street after we see Washington on the soapbox for the first time.

The Mambo Kings ••• [1992]

Director: **Arne Glimcher**
Screenplay: **Cynthia Cidre**

Whether you find this vibrant, scintillating and sexy, probably depends on whether you like the sort of music played by guys with frilly shirt-sleeves. Two Cuban musicians come to New York to cash in on the craze for Mambo. This rousing adaptation of a steamy, Pulitzer prize-winning novel loses its grip towards the close, but is worth watching for their hilarious appearance on *I Love Lucy* alone. [104m/15]

Cesar Castillo ....Armand Assante
Nestor Castillo ....Antonio Banderas
Lanna Lake ....Cathy Moriarty
Delores Fuentes ....Maruschka Detmers
Desi Arnaz Sr. ....Desi Arnaz Jr.
Evalina Montoya............................Celia Cruz

Quote 'He thinks he's the last Coca-Cola in the desert.'

Psst! Desi Arnaz Jr. plays his father, star of *I Love Lucy*.

The Man from Snowy River ••• [1983]

Director: **George Miller**
Screenplay: **John Dixon**

Fine Australian 'family' Western with Burlinson the young man who falls in love with his boss's daughter. Douglas has great fun playing twin roles; a wealthy rancher and his one-legged prospector brother. Great Sunday afternoon entertainment. [104m/PG]

Spur/Harrison............................Kirk Douglas
Clancy ....Jack Thompson
Jim Craig ....Tom Burlinson
Henry Craig ....Terence Donovan
Jessica......................................Sigrid Thornton

Manhunter •••• [1986]

Director: **Michael Mann**
Screenplay: **Michael Mann**

This is the Hannibal Lecter film you should see, a chilling thriller that gets a good grip early on and refuses to let go until the end credits have finished. Petersen is the FBI man who catches serial killers by putting himself in the killers' minds. Here, he risks his sanity by consulting Lecter, the man he put behind bars. It makes *Silence of the Lambs* look like *Blue Peter*. [118m/18]

Will Graham ....William Petersen
Molly Graham................................Kim Greist
Reba..Joan Allen
Dr. Lecktor..Brian Cox
Jack Crawford............................Dennis Farina
Freddie ....Stephen Lang
Francis ....Tom Noonan
Mrs. Sherman ....Patricia Charbonneau

OOPS! When Petersen is talking to his son about evil in the supermarket , the packets of cereal on the shelves behind him suddenly turn into tinned fruit ✦ In the book, Hannibal's name is *Lecter*. Here it's misspelt *Lecktor* both on the end credits and on a pile of newspapers which are being cut open.

Psst! Although based on the Thomas Harris book *Red Dragon*, producer Dino de Laurentiis had just made the flop *Year of the Dragon* and didn't want to tempt fate by using the word 'Dragon' again.

Maniac Cop •• [1988]

Director: **William Lustig**
Screenplay: **Larry Cohen**

Just because a policeman is dead is no reason he can't run round New York topping people. Despite the crass title, the script has some wit and originality, although it's let down by draggy and obvious direction. Still, surely any film with an actor named Robert Z'Dar is worth a try? **[85m/18]**

Det. Frank McCrae	Tom Atkins
Jack Forest	Bruce Campbell
Teresa Mallory	Laurene Landon
Commissioner Pike	Richard Roundtree
Officer Matthew Cordell	Robert Z'Dar

Blurb You Have The Right To Remain Silent...Forever.

Maniac Cop 2 •• [1991]

Director: **William Lustig**
Screenplay: **Larry Cohen**

Although better made than the original, it's still pretty much par for the course in the horror-movie sequel stakes. This time the officers who refuse to believe that Cordell died at the end of the first film are vindicated as he goes on the rampage again. The third in the series went straight to video. **[88m/18]**

Det. Sean McKinney	Robert Davi
Susan Riley	Claudia Christian
Edward Doyle	Michael Lerner

Also: Bruce Campbell, Laurene Landon, Robert Z'Dar

Manifesto • [1988]

Director: **Dusan Makavejev**
Screenplay: **Dusan Makavejev**

A freewheeling girl arrives in a 20's Balkan town and indulges in a spot of bed-hopping and assassination-planning. Respected director Makavejev doubtless thought these shenanigans were revolutionary but, like so many revolutions, it becomes disjointed and incomprehensible at an early stage. **[94m/18]**

Svetlana	Camilla Søeberg
Avanti	Alfred Molina
Hunt	Simon Callow

Also: Eric Stoltz, Lindsay Duncan, Ronald Lacey, Gabrielle Anwar

A Man in Love •• [1987]

Director: **Diane Kurys**
Screenplay: **Diane Kurys**

A slight, overlong, story about married film writer Coyote falling heavily for Scacchi, the star of his movie being filmed in Rome. However, the two lovers do generate the odd combustible spark or two. An English-language, French-Italian co-production. **[110m/18]**

Steve	Peter Coyote
Jane	Greta Scacchi
Michael	Peter Riegert
Julia	Claudia Cardinale

Also: John Berry, Vincent Lindon, Jamie Lee Curtis

The Man in the Moon ••• [1992]

Director: **Robert Mulligan**
Screenplay: **Jenny Wingfield**

Better get out the extra-strength tissues for this lovely coming-of-age yarn. A 14-year-old has a pash for a boy, who in turn falls for her elder sister. The stirrings of adolescent love have rarely been brought to the screen so vividly, or with such beautiful photography. A delight. **[99m/PG]**

Matthew Trant	Sam Waterston
Abigail Trant	Tess Harper
Marie Foster	Gail Strickland
Dani Trant	Reese Witherspoon
Court Foster	Jason London
Maureen Trant	Emily Warfield

Mannequin • [1987]

Director: **Michael Gottlieb**
Screenplay: **Edward Rugoff & Michael Gottlieb**

Window-dresser McCarthy discovers

Cattrall is a mannequin that comes alive. Unfortunately, the movie never does. Dim comedy that is a must-see only for those actually strapped down in front of it.

[90m/PG]

Jonathan Switcher	Andrew McCarthy
Emmy	Kim Cattrall
Claire Timkin	Estelle Getty
Richards	James Spader

Mannequin on the Move • [1991]

Director: **Stewart Raffill**
Screenplay: **Edward Rugoff, David Isaacs, Ken Levine & Betty Israel**

A shop dummy that's been cursed to suffer a deep sleep for 1,000 years comes to life. The curse passes to the audience and they fall into the deep sleep. Almost the same picture as before, only worse.

[93m/PG]

Jessie	Kristy Swanson
Jason/Prince William	William Ragsdale
Hollywood/Doorman	Meshach Taylor

Quote 'You were in the Marines?' — 'Yeh. They were looking for a few good men and so was I.'

Man of Flowers •••• [1984]

Director: **Paul Cox**
Screenplay: **Paul Cox & Bob Ellis**

A wealthy, lonely man pays a model to strip for him. Her increasingly unhappy boyfriend gets the wrong end of the stick. A fascinating, unpredictable psychological drama from one of the most original of Australian directors. With an attractive musical score and rich, atmospheric photography, this is one worth tracking down.

[91m/18]

Charles	Norman Kaye
Lisa	Alyson Best
David	Chris Haywood
Psychiatrist	Bob Ellis

Psst! The German director Werner Herzog appears in a cameo as the father.

Manon des Sources •••• [1987]

Director: **Claude Berri**
Screenplay: **Claude Berri & Gérard Brach**

This sequel to *Jean de Florette* has Depardieu's daughter Beart, now a beautiful shepherdess, discovering the truth behind her father's death and plotting revenge. If at all possible, this is almost better than the earlier film, becoming almost heart-stoppingly unbearable when Montand realises the true enormity of his crime. Also known as *Manon of the Spring*.

[114m/PG]

Cesar Soubeyran	Yves Montand
Ugolin	Daniel Auteuil
Manon	Emmanuelle Beart
Bernard Olivier	Hoppolyte Girardot
Aimee	Elisabeth Depardieu

Psst! Auteuil and Beart are France's equivalent of our Ken and Emma.

Man Trouble • [1992]

Director: **Bob Rafelson**
Screenplay: **Carole Eastman**

How appropriate that Nicholson's a dog-handler, because a dog is just what this picture is. Jack gets it together with glitzy client Barkin, despite the fact that he smokes, is married, penniless, sleazy and appears to have a small ferret stuck to his upper lip. Together they try to find her kidnapped sister. A complete miscalculation, this comedy-thriller-romance is as funny, thrilling and romantic as a trip to the dentist's.

[100m/15]

Harry Bliss	Jack Nicholson
Joan Spruance	Ellen Barkin
Redmond Layls	Harry Dean Stanton
Andy Ellerman	Beverly D'Angelo
Eddy Revere	Michael McKean
Laurence Moncrief	Saul Rubinek

Psst! Nicholson got paid $8m for his part, yet the film took less than half that in the States.

The Man Who Loved Women • [1983]

Director: **Blake Edwards**
Screenplay: **Blake Edwards, Milton Wexler & Geoffrey Edwards**

A desperate remake of Truffaut's 1977 film, with Reynolds the rampantly libidinous sculptor who consults psychiatrist Andrews when he becomes impotent. Ridiculous and wholly uninteresting.

[110m/15]

David	Burt Reynolds
Marianna	Julie Andrews
Louise	Kim Basinger
Agnes	Marilu Henner

Psst! An apparently very funny scene at the end of the movie, with all the women joking and squabbling, was cut, some say because Reynolds was upset at there being a major scene without him ✦ Writer Wexler is Edwards' psychiatrist. Edwards felt he should be credited on this film and the later *That's Life*.

The Man With Two Brains •• [1983]

Director: **Carl Reiner**
Screenplay: **Carl Reiner**

Martin misses more than he hits as Dr. Hfuhruhurr (that's 'Hfuhruhurr') who falls in love with a talking brain in a jar and decides to transplant it into his vicious, gold-digging wife Turner. After that, it gets a little silly. A bit of discipline in the script and performances wouldn't have come amiss.

[93m/15]

Dr. Michael Hfuhruhurr	Steve Martin
Dolores Benedict	Kathleen Turner
Dr. Necessiter	David Warner
Butler	Paul Benedict
Dr. Pasteur	Richard Brestoff
Realtor	James Cromwell
Brain	Sissy Spacek

Quote 'Into the mud, scum queen!'

Man, Woman and Child ••• [1983]

Director: **Dick Richards**
Screenplay: **Erich Segal & David Z. Goodman**

A happily married couple go through a rough patch when Sheen discovers that he has a 10-year-old orphaned son, the result of a fling. Although pretty slushy in places, it's also funny and involving enough to work as entertainment, assuming you can overlook the daft ending.

[100m/PG]

Bob Beckwith	Martin Sheen
Sheila Beckwith	Blythe Danner
Bernie	Craig T. Nelson
Gavin Wilson	David Hemmings
Nicole Guerin	Nathalie Nell

Maria's Lovers ••• [1984]

Director: **Andrei Konchalovsky**
Screenplay: **Gerard Brach**

When Savage returns to Pennsylvania from World War II, he finds he can't consummate his marriage, something of a pity as his wife is Nastassja Kinski. Although occasionally heavy-going, this is nevertheless a richly atmospheric and well-acted film. A solid American debut for Russian director Konchalovsky.

[105m/15]

Maria Bosic	Nastassja Kinski
Ivan Bibic	John Savage
Ivan's Father	Robert Mitchum
Clarence Butts	Keith Carradine

Also: Anita Morris, Bud Cort, Karen Young, Tracy Nelson, John Goodman

Showing *Let There Be Light*.

Marie ••• [1985]

Director: **Roger Donaldson**
Screenplay: **John Briley**

True-life story of Marie Ragghianti, one-time housewife, who got so fed up with corruption in her state of Tennessee that she tried to blow it wide open. You know that unless it turns out the way you think it will, they'd never have bothered turning it into a film but, though slow in parts, Spacek still makes it all eminently watchable. **[112m/15]**

Marie Ragghianti .... Sissy Spacek
Eddie Sisk .... Jeff Daniels
Kevin McCormack .... Keith Szarabajka
Charles Traughber .... Morgan Freeman
Fred Thompson .... Himself

Psst! Fred Thompson is the actual lawyer who acted for Marie Ragghianti ◆ The film, in the spirit of Frank Capra – the man who brought us such delights as *It's a Wonderful Life* – is produced by his son, Frank Capra Jr.

Marked for Death ◆   [1990]
Director: **Dwight H. Little**
Screenplay: **Michael Grais & Mark Victor**

Those poor drug barons must never get a bit of piece and quiet, what with all the cops, agents, pissed-off brothers of dead junkies and the like, dropping in for tea and a spot of violent revenge. This time it's the turn of Seagal, here a cop, in a below-average actioner. **[93m/18]**

John Hatcher .... Steven Seagal
Screwface .... Basil Wallace
Max .... Keith David

Married to the Mob ◆◆   [1988]
Director: **Jonathan Demme**
Screenplay: **Barry Strugatz & Mark R. Burns**

After the death of her Mafia hitman husband, Pfeiffer tries to break away from the mob, only to find that powerful mobster Stockwell fancies her. Although there's curiosity value in seeing Pfeiffer chewing gum and tottering on high heels, this heavy-handed comedy is let down by an uncharismatic performance from Modine and a script about as lively as a guy wearing concrete galoshes. The end credits only serve to show just how many scenes have been cut. **[104m/15]**

Angela De Marco .... Michelle Pfeiffer
Mike Downey .... Matthew Modine
Tony 'The Tiger' Russo .... Dean Stockwell
Connie Russo .... Mercedes Ruehl
'Cucumber' Frank De Marco ..... Alec Baldwin
Regional Director Franklin .... Trey Wilson
Rose .... Joan Cusack
Ed Benitez .... Oliver Platt
Tommy .... Paul Lazar
Theresa .... Ellen Foley

Blurb Angela Always Wanted To Give Marriage A Shot.

Quote 'That bitch! She thinks her shit don't stink!' ◆ 'Oh, there is a difference. The mob is run by murdering, cheating, thieving psychopaths. We work for the President of the United States.'

OOPS! When Stockwell arrives at Pfeiffer's new flat for the first time, he is carrying flowers. But they're far grander in the corridor than when he presents them to her inside.

Psst! If you're wondering where you've seen Uncle Joe before, he's Al Lewis, Grandpa from the TV series *The Munsters.*

The Marrying Man
SEE: Too Hot to Handle

Mask ◆◆◆   [1985]
Director: **Peter Bogdanovich**
Screenplay: **Anna Hamilton Phelan**

This remarkable film, is based on a true story, about a boy with a rare disease that gives him a swollen face and deformed facial features. Trying to ignore the all-too-predictable reactions of others, he still attempts to be a normal teenager. Both Stoltz and Cher, as his less than perfect single mother, give sterling performances in this moving and courageous story, which also makes great cinema. **[120m/15]**

Rusty Dennis .... Cher
Gar .... Sam Elliott
Rocky Dennis .... Eric Stoltz
Evelyn .... Estelle Getty
Abe .... Richard Dysart
Diana .... Laura Dern

Masquerade •• [1988]

Director: Bob Swaim
Screenplay: Dick Wolf

Rob Lowe masquerades as a leading man in this old-fashioned romantic thriller in which a ne'er-do-well falls for the wealthy Tilly. Unfortunately, Lowe doesn't carry enough ballast and threatens to capsize what would otherwise be a highly-entertaining yarn. [91m/18]

Tim Whalan ....Rob Lowe
Olivia Lawrence................................Meg Tilly
Brooke Morrison ....Kim Cattrall
Mike McGill..............................Doug Savant
Tony Gateworth ....John Glover
Anne Briscoe...........................Dana Delaney

Masters of the Universe ••
[1987]

Director: Gary Goddard
Screenplay: David O'Dell

This live-action, feature-length advert for the He-Man toys turns out to be yet another *Star Wars* rip-off without any of that film's merits. Lots of action, but little else. [106m/U]

He-Man ....Dolph Lundgren
Skeletor....................................Frank Langella
Evil-Lyn ....Meg Foster

Mata Hari • [1985]

Director: Curtis Harrington
Screenplay: Joel Ziskin

Sylvia Kristel is Mata Hari. Oh yeh? And I'm Alexander the Great. The woman who put the 'ell into *Emmanuelle* makes the mistake of dropping state secrets as often as her knickers. Despite all the flesh, this travesty of the life of the World War I spy is staggeringly boring but, sadly, not quite bad enough to be funny. [108m/18]

Mata Hari................................Sylvia Kristel
Kart ....Christopher Cazenove
Ladoux ....Oliver Tobias
Fraulein Doktor...........................Gaye Brown

Matewan •••• [1987]

Director: John Sayles
Screenplay: John Sayles

One of the best films ever made about workers struggling for their rights, here the miners fighting the bitter American Coalfield Wars of 1920. Doing wonders on a budget of just $4m, Sayles creates a truly exciting film, full of fascinating detail, characters, and a tense story to match. A remarkably fine, stirring movie which neither preaches not patronises. [132m/15]

Joe...Chris Cooper
Danny...Will Oldham
Elma..................................Mary McDonnell
C.E. Lively....................................Bob Gunton
Few Clothes.................James Earl Jones
Hickey ....Kevin Tighe
Sephus ....Ken Jenkins
Hillard....................................Jace Alexander

Psst! Writer-director Sayles appears, as in all his movies, here playing 'Hardshell' the preacher.

Matinee •• [1993]

Director: Joe Dante
Screenplay: Charlie Haas

A self-publicising film director brings his gimmicky horror film *Mant* to a Florida town threatened by the Cuban missile crisis. Goodman's performance and the excerpts from the film are hilariously accurate. But the rest is depressingly bland. [99m/PG]

Lawrence Woolsey..................John Goodman
Ruth Corday/Carol...............Cathy Moriarty
Gene Loomis..............................Simon Fenton
Stan..Omri Katz

Blurb Half Man. Half Ant. All Terror.

Psst! Dick Miller makes his usual appearance in Joe Dante movies while John Sayles, who wrote Dante's *The Howling* and *Piranha*, also has a cameo. They play the Family Values spokesmen • Appearing in the spoof 60's horror film *Mant* are Kevin McCarthy, Robert Cornthwaite and William Schallert, veterans of such cult favourites.

Maurice • [1987]

Director: **James Ivory**
Screenplay: **Kit Hesketh-Harvey**

A young Edwardian comes to terms with his homosexuality. This is a catalogue of Merchant Ivory productions at their worst; hellishly over long, pretty-pretty costumes and virtually all trace of drama and excitement smothered in gratuitous gloss. A liability to the cause of gay rights.

[140m/15]

Maurice	James Wilby
Clive	Hugh Grant
Alec	Rupert Graves
Dr. Barry	Denholm Elliott

Also: Simon Callow, Billie Whitelaw, Ben Kingsley, Judy Parfitt

Psst! There's a brief cameo from one of Merchant-Ivory's favourite actresses, Helena Bonham Carter.

Maxie • [1985]

Director: **Paul Aaron**
Screenplay: **Patricia Resnick**

Minie, more like. The spirit of a silent movie actress, furious that her death cut her career short, comes back to possess a dully conventional 80's woman. This body-switch film just isn't very funny and before long you wish some dastardly villain would come along and tie Close to the railway tracks.

[98m/PG]

Jan/Maxie	Glenn Close
Nick	Mandy Patinkin
Mrs. Lavin	Ruth Gordon

Max, Mon Amour • [1986]

Director: **Nagisa Oshima**
Screenplay: **Nagisa Oshima & Jean-Claude Carriere**

It's the old, old story. A diplomat's wife falls for a chimpanzee and is astounded at how stuffy and narrow-minded people can be. Certainly the oddest of the several chimp movies of the past few years. Not released until 1990. Also known as *Max, My Love*.

[92m/18]

Margaret Jones	Charlotte Rampling
Peter Jones	Anthony Higgins
Archibald	Bernard-Pierre Donnadieu
Maria	Victoria Abril

Quote 'Difficult acting with a chimp? No, no. the emotions were the same. In a way it was like playing opposite Paul Newman. The chimpanzee reacted differently, that's all.' [Charlotte Rampling]

Maybe Baby • [1988]

Director: **John G. Avildsen**
Screenplay: **Tim Kazurinsky & Denise DeClue**

...Or Maybe Not. A pair of teenagers have to grow up fast when she becomes pregnant. As this dire self-styled comedy comes from *Rocky's* director, you long for one of the nauseating brats to knock seven bells out of the other. Sadly, nothing as interesting as that happens. At times, it's like a pregnancy information video. Also known as *For Keeps*.

[98m/15]

Darcy	Molly Ringwald
Stan	Randall Batinkoff
Mr. Bobrucz	Kenneth Mars

Also: Miriam Flynn, Conchata Ferrell

The Mean Season •• [1985]

Director: **Phillip Borsos**
Screenplay: **Leon Piedmont**

Journalist Russell becomes the conduit for a publicity-seeking serial killer. This involving story gets lost in the strong Miami atmosphere in the second half.

[104m/15]

Malcolm Anderson	Kurt Russell
Christine Connelly	Mariel Hemingway
Alan Delous	Richard Jordan
Bill Nolan	Richard Masur
Andy Porter	Joe Pantoliano
Phil Wilson	Richard Bradford
Ray Martinez	Andy Garcia

Medicine Man ••• [1992]

Director: John McTiernan
Screenplay: Tom Schulman & Sally Robinson

Connery plays the driven pony-tailed scientist working in the South American rain forest who's found a cure for cancer and then mislaid it. Bracco's his new boss, come to see where all the money's going. These two really strike sparks off each other amid the amazing scenery. Much underrated, this fun film from the writer of *Dead Poets Society* rarely puts a foot wrong and is one of the few Hollywood rainforest-message-movies that entertains as well as informs. Bizarre, though, that Bracco – ostensibly one of the world's top biologists – is frightened of creepy-crawlies. [105m/PG]

Dr. Robert Campbell	Sean Connery
Dr. Rae Crane	Lorraine Bracco
Dr. Miguel Ornega	Jose Wilker
Tanaki	Rodolfo De Alexandre
Medicine Man	Angelo Barra Moreira

Psst! Connery was paid $10m, $1m for each week's work. He is the highest-paid British star • The script, originally called *The Stand* was sold for a massive $3m, the same as *Basic Instinct*, with another $1m then spent on rewrites.

Meeting Venus •• [1991]

Director: István Szabó
Screenplay: István Szabó & Michael Hirst

How odd that a movie supposedly celebrating European unity should have an American star, even if she is supposed to be playing a Swede. Opera buffs might get involved in this romantic comedy about the back-stage infighting on a production of *Tannhauser*. But even they might want to shut their eyes and just listen to the music. [120m/12]

Karin Anderson	Glenn Close
Zoltán Szántó	Niels Arestrup
Jorge Picabia	Erland Josephson
Jean Gabor	Moscu Alcalay

Psst! Close's singing is dubbed by Kiri Te Kanawa. Close was once a singer. [See biography]

Meet the Applegates •• [1991]

Director: Michael Lehmann
Screenplay: Michael Lehmann & Redbeard Simmons

Five Brazilian beetles disguise themselves as the average American family, hoping to strike an ecological blow for all beetle-kind, only to fall foul of the usual problems besetting the average American family. Despite a fair degree of invention, the intriguing ideas get wasted in a plot that goes nowhere. Also known as *The Applegates*. [89m/15]

Dick Applegate	Ed Begley Jr.
Jane Applegate	Stockard Channing
Aunt Bea	Dabney Coleman
Johnny Applegate	Bobby Jacoby

Meet the Feebles • [1992]

Director: Peter Jackson
Screenplay: Peter Jackson & Others

Made in 1990, this spoof of the Muppets is in appalling taste. Sex, drugs, violence, defecation, vomit, porn, perverts and social diseases. Despite this, it's *still* not worth watching. The novelty of seeing puppets get up to such disgusting things soon palls, particularly as the jokes are so poor. Although Jackson's reputation for the worst taste in movies (*Braindead, Bad Taste*) remains intact, in this instance Feeble is spot on. [96m/18]

With: Harry the Hare, Heidi the Hippo, Bletch the Walrus

Melancholia • [1989]

Director: Andi Engel
Screenplay: Andi Engel & Lewis Rodia

Melancholy is the feeling you'll get watching this dire Anglo-German thriller about an ex-terrorist art critic who finds his past catching up with him. [88m/15]

David Keller	Jeroen Krabbé
Catherine Franck	Susannah York
Manfred	Ulrich Wildgruber

Memed, My Hawk • [1984]

Director: Peter Ustinov
Screenplay: Peter Ustinov

Goodness knows what Ustinov was aiming for with this tale of brigands and tyrants in the 1920s. That it's set in Turkey is unfortunately all too apt. Embarrassingly acted and woefully unfunny. [103m/15]

Abdi Aga....................................Peter Ustinov
Ali Safa.......................................Herbert Lom
Also: Simon Dutton, Denis Quilley, Michael Elphick

Memoirs of an Invisible Man •• [1992]

Director: John Carpenter
Screenplay: Robert Collector, Dana Olsen & William Goldman

Chase breaks one of the cardinal rules of the movies: never fall asleep in a top-secret experimental laboratory. Easier to see through than usual, he's chased by Government agents who reckon that an invisible Chevy Chase would make a great secret agent, presumably able to embarrass world leaders by looking up their skirts and trouserlegs with impunity. Although instantly forgettable, it's moderately entertaining, with the star for once acting instead of mugging. The effects are staggering. [99m/PG]

Nick Halloway...........................Chevy Chase
Alice Monroe............................Daryl Hannah
David Jenkins....................................Sam Neill
George Talbot.....................Michael McKean
Singleton........................Stephen Tobolowsky

Quote 'Assassination's entirely ethical if you're on the right side.'

OOPS! The effects are wonderful as Chase inhales smoke into his lungs. But how can he be talking at the same time as the smoke travels inwards?

Psst! Hannah refuses to play blonde bimbos straight, instead insisting that the blonde bimbos she plays have fascinating jobs. Despite her character appearing to possess an invisible brain, she claims here, without any evidence, to be an anthropological documentary-maker for the Smithsonian Institute! Believe that and swallowing invisible men is easy.

Memphis Belle •• [1990]

Director: Michael Caton-Jones
Screenplay: Monte Merrick

A young World War II American air-crew, stationed in England, head into the wide blue yonder on their final bombing mission over Germany. Despite the crises on board, team spirit and good old-fashioned pluck win through. Nothing more than Top Gun with a conscience: You know that because the pilots don't punch the air when they make a kill. Despite some excitement, the script is pretty hackneyed and the effects are under par for the 90s. One wonders what audience the film was aimed at. [107m/12]

Dennis Dearborn...............Matthew Modine
Danny Daly.....................................Eric Stoltz
Col. Bruce Derringer..................John Lithgow
Luke Sinclair..............................Tate Donovan
Phil Rosenthal...........................D.B. Sweeney
Val Kozlowski..................................Billy Zane
Richard 'Rascal' Moore..................Sean Astin
Clay Busby.........................Harry Connick Jr.
The commanding officer........David Strathairn
Faith...Jane Horrocks

Psst! Originally producer David Puttnam intended the aircrew to be British. But he could only raise the necessary finance by changing them to Americans.

Men at Work • [1990]

Director: Emilio Estevez
Screenplay: Emilio Estevez

Real-life brothers Estevez and Sheen star as dustmen in this pathetic comedy written and directed by Estevez. If they were trying to emulate Abbott and Costello, they've succeeded only too well. [90m/12]

Carl Taylor...............................Charlie Sheen
James St. James.......................Emilio Estevez
Susan Wilkins...............................Leslie Hope
Louis Fedders.............................Keith David

Men Don't Leave •• [1990]

Director: Paul Brickman
Screenplay: Paul Brickman & Barbara Benedek

...Actually, they might. For this weepy with the odd laugh is much more likely to appeal to the distaff side. Lange's the bereaved widow struggling to come to terms with having to look after her family alone. It's well done, of its type, but hardly one for the six-pack and curry brigade. [113m/15]

Beth Macauley	Jessica Lange
Charles Simon	Arliss Howard
Jody	Joan Cusack
Lisa Coleman	Kathy Bates
John Macauley	Tom Mason
Chris Macauley	Chris O'Donnell
Matt Macauley	Charlie Korsmo

Men of Respect • [1992]

Director: William Reilly
Screenplay: William Reilly

Instead of just the forest of Dunsinane moving, the whole of Macbeth is transplanted to New York and turned into a gangster pic. The actors seem to be enjoying it, but for the rest of us it isn't worth the effort. [113m/18]

Mike Battaglia	John Turturro
Ruthie Battaglia	Katherine Borowitz
Bankie Como	Dennis Farina

Also: Peter Boyle, Stanley Tucci, Rod Steiger

The Men's Club • [1986]

Director: Peter Medak
Screenplay: Leonard Michaels

A group of men sit around a smart brothel talking about sex and occasionally doing it too. Amazingly, this is even more soporific than it sounds. Between them, this talented director and knockout cast don't generate enough electricity to get a glimmer from a 40-watt bulb. [101m/18]

Phillip	David Dukes
Kramer	Richard Jordan
Solly Berliner	Harvey Keitel
Harold Canterbury	Frank Langella

Also: Roy Scheider, Craig Wasson, Treat Williams, Stockard Channing, Cindy Pickett, Jennifer Jason Leigh

Psst! The poster for this film is prominently displayed outside a Soho sex cinema. They must have some fairly disappointed patrons.

Mermaids •• [1991]

Director: Richard Benjamin
Screenplay: June Roberts

Single mother Cher is a constant source of embarrassment to growing daughter Ryder, as well as to us, as she tries diminutive shoe salesman Hoskins on for size. A schmaltzy, mother and daughter bonding movie of the sort the Americans seem to love. [110m/15]

Mrs. Flax	Cher
Lou Landsky	Bob Hoskins
Charlotte Flax	Winona Ryder
Joe	Michael Schoeffling
Kate Flax	Christina Ricci

OOPS! At one point, Cher complains about Astroturf, although it didn't come into use until a couple of years after 1963, when the film is set.

Psst! Ryder and Cher apparently pushed the original director, Frank Oz (*The Muppets, Housesitter*), off the film ◆ Emily Lloyd was originally cast in Ryder's role.

Merry Christmas, Mr. Lawrence •• [1983]

Director: Nagisa Oshima
Screenplay: Nagisa Oshima & Paul Mayersberg

This strange story of life in a Japanese prisoner of war camp and the struggle between head of the camp Sakamoto and British major Bowie is let down by Bowie. Although his performance in the camp's okay, the flashbacks that show him wearing a school uniform generate hoots of derision and send plausibility right out of the window. [124m/15]

Celliers ....David Bowie
Col. John Lawrence ....Tom Conti
Capt. Yonoi ....Ryuichi Sakamoto
Sgt. Hara..Takeshi
Hicksley-Ellis...........................Jack Thompson

Psst! Not only is the head of the British contingent played by a rock star, but so is the Japanese, Sakamoto being a top pop name in Japan as well as the composer of the wonderful music.

Metalstorm: The Destruction of Jared-Syn •   [1983]

Director: **Charles Band**
Screenplay: **Alan J. Adler**

You know how when you stay in hotels, there's always some incomprehensible, sci-fi rubbish on one of the channels that you never see the whole way through? This is probably it.

[83m/PG]

Dogen ....Jeffrey Byron
Jared-Syn....................................Mike Preston
Rhodes ....Tim Thomerson

Metropolitan •••   [1990]

Director: **Whit Stillman**
Screenplay: **Whit Stillman**

A group of unknown actors. An unknown writer-director. A wonderful low-budget comedy of manners amongst the upper classes in New York, as seen from the viewpoint of the distinctly more plebby Clements. Some thought it a modern Jane Austen. Not to everyone's taste, it's like being present at a particularly witty and fascinating dinner party.

[98m/15]

Audrey Rouget.........................Carolyn Farina
Tom Townsend ....Edward Clements
Nick Smith ....Christopher Eigeman
Charlie Black............................Taylor Nichols
Jane Clarke...............Allison Rutledge-Parisi
Sally Fowler ....Dylan Hundley
Serena Slocum.................Elizabeth Thompson

Miami Blues •••   [1990]

Director: **George Armitage**
Screenplay: **George Armitage**

Violent psychopathic criminal Baldwin arrives in Miami where he shacks up with dumb hooker Leigh and annoys cop Ward by stealing his badge and dentures. An uneven, wildly unpredictable, yet sly and rather enjoyable thriller. Its mixture of satire, violence and social comment is fresh and invigorating, providing the perfect antidote to *Miami Vice*.   [97m/18]

Frederick J. Frenger Jr. ....Alec Baldwin
Sgt. Hoke Moseley ....Fred Ward
Susie Waggoner ....Jennifer Jason Leigh
Ellita Sanchez..................................Nora Dunn
St. Bill Henderson ....Charles Napier

Blurb Real Badge. Real Gun. Fake Cop.

Quote 'He had some good qualities. He always ate everything I cooked for him.'

Micki & Maude •••   [1984]

Director: **Blake Edwards**
Screenplay: **Jonathan Reynolds**

TV chat show host Moore gets involved with cellist Irving. When she gets pregnant, he does the decent thing and marries her, even though he's still married to Reinking. When Reinking gets pregnant, Moore's problems really begin. Despite the painting-by-numbers plot, Moore carries this increasingly frenetic farce off with some panache.   [118m/PG]

Rob Salinger ....Dudley Moore
Maude Salinger..............................Amy Irving
Micki Salinger.............................Ann Reinking
Leo Brody.............................Richard Mulligan
Dr. Eugene Glztski................George Gaynes
Dr. Elliot Fibel........................Wallace Shawn

A Midnight Clear •••   [1992]

Director: **Keith Gordon**
Screenplay: **Keith Gordon**

Gripping tale of a group of young American soldiers in the Ardennes at the tail-end of 1944 and the problems that arise when a group of Germans wants to surrender. Notable for some fine acting from its young cast, this is an intelligent and often witty examination of the futility of men being sent to do something they know is idiotic. Although the film got a shamefully limited release in Britain, it's definitely one well worth seeking out.

[107m/15]

Will Knott	Ethan Hawke
Bud Miller	Peter Berg
Mel Avakian	Kevin Dillon
Stan Shutzer	Arye Gross
Vince (Mother) Wilkins	Gary Sinise
Paul (Father) Mundy	Frank Whaley
Major Griffin	John C. McGinley

Quote 'I'm having my usual trouble, noticing how beautiful the world is just when I might be leaving it.'

Psst! The credits include one for 'snow management'.

Midnight Crossing •   [1988]

Director: **Roger Holzberg**
Screenplay: **Roger Holzberg & Doug Weiser**

An enjoyably bad Caribbean treasure-seeking adventure that gets sillier as it progresses. The potty plot makes little sense and there's over-acting galore, but nothing quite matches the fact that Dunaway is a blind eye doctor!   **[95m/18]**

Helen Barton	Faye Dunaway
Morley Barton	Daniel J. Travanti
Lexa Shubb	Kim Cattrall

Also: John Laughlin, Ned Beatty

Midnight Run ••••   [1988]

Director: **Martin Brest**
Screenplay: **George Gallo**

Hilariously funny as a comedy, this is also a tense and exciting thriller. De Niro's the bounty hunter hired to bring in accountant Grodin who's stolen $15m from the mob. But the mob, the FBI and a rival bounty hunter are also after Grodin. The two stars really strike sparks off each other in what is a near-perfect action flick.   **[126m/15]**

Jack Walsh	Robert De Niro
Jonathan Mardukas	Charles Grodin
Alonzo Mosely	Yaphet Kotto
Marvin Dorfler	John Ashton
Jimmy Serrano	Dennis Farina
Eddie Moscone	Joe Pantoliano

Psst! In order to persuade Charles Grodin to throw himself into the freezing white-water rapids, the director did the jump himself first ✦ Dustin Hoffman turned down the film so that he would not miss his chance to be in the delayed *Rain Man* ✦ The video is missing a scene with De Niro picking a door lock, for fear it might be used as an instruction manual.

Midnight Sting ••••   [1992]

Director: **Michael Ritchie**
Screenplay: **Steven McKay**

Despite the really cheeky title change on this side of the pond, this excellent caper-cum-con *is* reminiscent of *The Sting*. On getting out of jail, Woods wants to scam sleazebag Dern, the bigwig in boxing-obsessed Diggstown, and bets that his man can beat ten of theirs in just one day. Often hilariously funny, this brilliant film has such great twists in the plot that by the end you'll be whooping and hollering in the one-and-nines.   **[98m/15]**

Gabriel Caine	James Woods
"Honey" Roy Palmer	Louis Gossett Jr.
John Gillon	Bruce Dern
Fitz	Oliver Platt
Emily Forrester	Heather Graham
Wolf Forrester	Randall "Tex" Cobb
Robby Gillon	Thomas Wilson Brown

Blurb This Much Fun Can Get You Killed.

Psst! Called *Diggstown* in the States, the film opened to ecstatic reviews. But after $14m spent on a bizarre marketing campaign, it grossed only $3.5m in 2 weeks.

The Mighty Quinn ••   [1989]

Director: **Carl Schenkel**
Screenplay: **Hampton Fancher**

It's the old 'schoolfriend chums now on opposite sides of the law' plot, although as it's set on a Caribbean island, at least we get a change of scenery. But while the background's interesting, not even these actors can breathe much life into a moribund story. **[98m/15]**

Xavier Quinn .... Denzel Washington
Elgin .... James Fox
Hadley .... Mimi Rogers
Miller .... M. Emmet Walsh
Lola .... Sheryl Lee Ralph

Psst! A love scene between Washington and Rogers was cut because of objections from audiences, both black and white, at test screenings.

The Milagro Beanfield War ••• **[1988]**

Director: **Robert Redford**
Screenplay: **David S. Ward & John Nichols**

Despite the dreadful title, this is a charming Redford-directed film about a group of New Mexico villagers who decide to stand up to some rapacious land developers. It doesn't always have its feet firmly on the ground, but those who like Capraesque whimsy will be swept up by its good humour and leave with a firm smile on their face. **[118m/15]**

Joe Mondragon .... Chick Vennera
Ruby Archuleta .... Sonia Braga
Sheriff Montoya .... Ruben Blades
Charlie Bloom .... John Heard
Amarante Cordova .... Carlos Riquelme
Kyril Montana .... Christopher Walken
Ladd Devine .... Richard Bradford
Nancy Mondragon .... Julie Carmen
Horsethief Shorty .... James Gammon
Flossie Devine .... Melanie Griffith
Herbie Platt .... Daniel Stern

Miles from Home •• **[1988]**

Director: **Gary Sinise**
Screenplay: **Chris Gerolmo**

Yet another group of Iowan farmers face foreclosure. But Gere and Anderson don't take their fate lying down. Torching the place, they turn outlaw and become instant heroes to the folk thereabouts. Like the brothers, the film doesn't really have anywhere to go. **[112m/15]**

Frank Roberts .... Richard Gere
Terry Roberts .... Kevin Anderson
Frank Roberts Sr. .... Brian Dennehy
Also: Penelope Ann Miller, Helen Hunt, Judith Ivey, Laurie Metcalf, John Malkovich

Millennium • **[1989]**

Director: **Michael Anderson**
Screenplay: **John Varley**

Passengers on crashing planes are being hijacked wholesale to the future so that they can help repopulate the world. Kristofferson is on to them. Nothing like as thrilling as it sounds. **[108m/PG]**

Bill Smith .... Kris Kristofferson
Louise Baltimore .... Cheryl Ladd
Arnold Mayer .... Daniel J. Travanti

Miller's Crossing •••• **[1990]**

Director: **Joel Coen**
Screenplay: **Ethan Coen & Joel Coen**

Stylish, moody, wonderfully atmospheric 30's gangster picture from the extraordinary Coen Brothers. Byrne's the bright mobster who opts for the transfer from Finney's side to Polito's lot. Or does he? Little is what it seems in this complex, witty and hypnotically mesmerising cinematic tour-de-force. Superb performances and tough, if slightly cartoonish, action make this one of the greatest gangster movies ever. **[115m/18]**

Tom Reagan .... Gabriel Byrne
Verna .... Marcia Gay Harden
Bernie Bernbaum .... John Turturro
Johnny Caspar .... Jon Polito
Eddie Dane .... J.E. Freeman
Leo .... Albert Finney
Mink .... Steve Buscemi
Frankie .... Mike Starr

Quote 'What's the rumpus?'

OOPS! In the scene where Finney decks Byrne, his drink first changes colour then vanishes completely.

Psst! The film's distributors were so worried that British audiences might not understand the slang [despite years of exposure to American films] that, at some cinemas, they gave out sheets translating phrases into English ✦ Despite her superb performance in such a critically-acclaimed movie, Marcia Gay Harden was forced back to waitressing for a full year afterwards! This despite the fact that she's also a skilled dancer, juggler, trapeze artist and tightrope walker ✦ Horror director Sam Raimi appears briefly as 'snickering gunman' in the police shootout. The Coens and he co-wrote his film *Crime Wave* ✦ In addition to writing, producing and directing their films, the Coens also edit them, using the pseudonym of Roderick Jaynes. Jaynes has been quoted on occasion complaining about the difficulties of working with the Coens!

The Miracle •• [1991]

Director: Neil Jordan
Screenplay: Neil Jordan

Two Irish teenagers speculate on the real people behind the strangers they observe. But when a beautiful American woman turns up, their guesses prove less interesting than the reality. A flimsy structure is built on a premise that can't support it so that, even at 95 minutes, it still seems too long. [95m/15]

Renee Baker	Beverly D'Angelo
Sam	Donal McCann
Jimmy	Nial Byrne
Rose	Lorraine Pilkington

Miracle Mile ••• [1989]

Director: Steve DeJarnatt
Screenplay: Steve DeJarnatt

It's terrible what you can pick up from a public phone. When musician Edwards answers one he picks up early warning of a nuclear attack! From a quiet opening, national chaos gradually ensues as Edwards tries to find his girlfriend. Perhaps arriving too late after the Cold War to engender the right level of panic, this was a little seen but rather effective anti-nuclear thriller. [87m/15]

Harry Washello	Anthony Edwards
Julie Peters	Mare Winningham
Landa	Denise Crosby
Ivan Peters	John Agar
Lucy Peters	Lou Hancock

Psst! Denise Crosby is Bing's granddaughter.

Miracles • [1986]

Director: Jim Kouf
Screenplay: Jim Kouf

The miracle is that this turkey ever got made. Newly-divorced Conti and Garr are kidnapped. But for every awful thing that happens to them, a miracle happens to somebody else. Although one prays for even more miracles, far too few awful things befall this unfunny, tiresome couple. [97m/PG]

Roger	Tom Conti
Jean	Teri Garr
Juan	Paul Rodriguez
Harry	Christopher Lloyd

Quote 'I'm a doctor. I know an arsehole when I see one.'

The Misadventures of Mr. Wilt
SEE: Wilt

Misery •••• [1990]

Director: Rob Reiner
Screenplay: William Goldman

Terrifically tense thriller. Novelist Caan crashes in a blizzard and is rescued by his 'greatest fan', the mentally unstable Bates. When she discovers his plans for her favourite character, she persuades him to stay and do a little rewriting. And she can be *very* persuasive. Edge-of-the-seat stuff, you'll have your hand in your mouth, not your popcorn carton, begging them to switch away from that bedroom so you can breathe again. [107m/18]

Paul Sheldon	James Caan
Annie Wilkes	Kathy Bates

Buster ....Richard Farnsworth
Virginia ....Frances Sternhagen
Marcia Sindell ....Lauren Bacall
Oscars Kathy Bates

Blurb Paul Sheldon Used To Write For A Living...Now He's Writing To Stay Alive.

OOPS! Bates' car mysteriously reappears outside the house after she has driven it away ✦ The Post-It notes on the sheriff's board keep changing position ✦ The curtain is still alight after Caan's put it out.

Psst! Originally, Warren Beatty and Bette Midler were to be the stars.

Miss Firecracker ••• [1989]

Director: **Thomas Schlamme**
Screenplay: **Beth Henley**

Recreating the part she made her own on stage, Hunter's the lovelorn woman determined to win this year's Miss Firecracker Contest in Yazoo City. This gentle comedy, filled with Southern eccentrics, is driven by Hunter's energetic performance. **[103m/PG]**

Carnelle Scott ....Holly Hunter
Elain Rutledge ....Mary Steenburgen
Delmount Williams ....Tim Robbins
Popeye Jackson ....Alfre Woodard
Mac Sam ....Scott Glenn

Psst! Christine Lahti appears in a cameo. The baby she's holding is hers and that of her husband, director Schlamme

Missing in Action • [1984]

Director: **Joseph Zito**
Screenplay: **James Bruner**

Chuck Norris is the Vietnam vet, convinced there are still GIs in Vietnam, who sets off to rescue them. At least he's softening the Viet Cong up for John Rambo, who trod much the same ground soon afterwards. **[101m/15]**

Braddock ....Chuck Norris
Tuck ....M. Emmet Walsh
Senator ....David Tress

Psst! Among the stuntmen listed is one J. Claude Van Damme.

The Mission •• [1986]

Director: **Roland Joffé**
Screenplay: **Robert Bolt**

Beautiful-looking but hollow-centred story of Jesuit priest Irons and his work in the mid-18th century among the South American Indians. Joined there by former slave-trader De Niro, the two men have differing reactions to the decision to close the mission. Despite the excellence of the acting, the script never fleshes out the characters enough to make us care. Lovely waterfalls, though. **[125m/PG]**

Mendoza ....Robert De Niro
Gabriel ....Jeremy Irons
Altamirano ....Ray McAnally
Felipe ....Aidan Quinn
Also: Cherie Lunghi, Ronald Pickup, Chuck Low, Liam Neeson

Psst! De Niro learnt to fence to competition standard for the film ✦ Keep watching the credits to the end.

The Missionary •••• [1982]

Director: **Richard Loncraine**
Screenplay: **Michael Palin**

In this utterly delightful British comedy, Palin is the Victorian missionary returning home after years in Africa, only to be posted to an East End mission for fallen women. There he adopts an unconventional hands-on solution to the problem. Seemingly low-key, the film just gets funnier and funnier. **[86m/15]**

Rev. Charles Fortescue ....Michael Palin
Lady Ames ....Maggie Smith
Lord Ames ....Trevor Howard
The Bishop ....Denholm Elliott
Slatterthwaite ....Michael Hordern
Rev. Fitzbanks ....Graham Crowden
Deborah ....Phoebe Nicholls
McEvoy ....Peter Vaughan
Lord Fermly ....Roland Culver
Corbett ....David Suchet
Parswell ....Timothy Spall

Blurb He Gave His Body To Save Their Souls.

Mississippi Burning •• [1988]

Director: **Alan Parker**
Screenplay: **Chris Gerolmo**

Based on real-life events, Hackman and Dafoe are the FBI agents sent to Mississippi to investigate the deaths in 1964 of three civil rights workers. Even though it deals with straight black and white problems, a few subtle shades of grey wouldn't have gone amiss. There's still some excitement but no-one could call the film sophisticated in its approach.
[127m/18]

Anderson	Gene Hackman
Ward	Willem Dafoe
Mrs. Pell	Frances McDormand
Deputy Pell	Brad Dourif
Mayor Tilman	R. Lee Emery
Sheriff Stuckley	Gailard Sartain
Townley	Stephen Tobolowsky
Bailey	Michael Rooker

Quote 'It's the only game [baseball] where a black man can wave a stick at a white man without starting a riot.'

Psst! The film was attacked at the time by the National Association for the Advancement of Colored People for depicting blacks as 'cowed, submissive and blank-faced.' ✦ In France, a video company promoted the movie with free Ku Klux Klan masks!

Mississippi Masala ••• [1992]

Director: **Mira Nair**
Screenplay: **Sooni Taraporevala**

A charming and fascinating love-story with Washington and Choudhury fighting against racism. Set in America's deep south, the bigotry doesn't come from the whites. He's negro and she's Asian and it's their own people who are trying to keep them apart. Although slow-paced, this is a perceptive, witty and charming film.
[114m/15]

Demetrius	Denzel Washington
Mina	Sarita Choudhury
Jay	Roshan Seth
Kinnu	Sharmila Tagore

Tyrone	Charles S. Dutton
Williben	Joe Seneca

Psst! The scenes in Uganda were the first to be filmed there since *The African Queen.*

Mister Johnson •• [1991]

Director: **Bruce Beresford**
Screenplay: **William Boyd**

In 1920's West Africa, a well-educated black encounters hostility when he acts as a go-between the British and the natives. Despite a wry strain of humour and an excellent debut performance from Eziashi, the film is sadly lacking in life. [102m/12]

Mister Johnson	Maynard Eziashi
Harry Rudbeck	Pierce Brosnan
Sargy Gollup	Edward Woodward
Celia Rudbeck	Beatie Edney
Bulteen	Denis Quilley

Mixed Blood •• [1985]

Director: **Paul Morrissey**
Screenplay: **Paul Morrissey**

A group of New York teenage drug-pushers under the care of Brazilian Pera, gets involved in a war with a rival gang. In amidst all the graphic violence, there's quite a bit of black comedy. It's a peculiar mix that won't strike everyone as funny.
[97m/18]

Rita La Punta	Marilla Pera
Thiago	Richard Ulacia
Toni	Geraldine Smith
Jose	Rodney Harvey

Mo' Better Blues •• [1990]

Director: **Spike Lee**
Screenplay: **Spike Lee**

Lee's story of self-destructive jazz trumpeter Washington, to whom nothing is more important than his music, is interesting but far too long and indulgent. Marred by too many tricksy camera shots, it's actually at its best when Lee, no mean comic actor, is on screen. [129m/15]

Bleek Gilliam	Denzel Washington

Giant	Spike Lee
Shadow Henderson	Wesley Snipes
Left Hand Lacey	Giancarlo Esposito
Moe Flatbush	John Turturro
Big Stop Gilliam	Dick Anthony Williams
Lillian Gilliam	Abbey Lincoln

Psst! The music is by Spike's father Bill.

Mobsters: The Evil Empire • [1992]

Director: **Michael Karbelnikoff**
Screenplay: **Michael Mahern & Nicholas Kazan**

Nicknamed *Young Buns with Tommy Guns*, this tale of the early days of gangsters Bugsy Siegel and Lucky Luciano is risible. Despite graphic violence, the film's less realistic than *Bugsy Malone*. The pretty leads, as menacing as a bag of jelly babies, look as if they should be packing hair-dryers, not machine-guns. Watching them act against real actors like Quinn and Gambon is as painful as watching a fight that should have been stopped two rounds earlier. The ones who get taken for a ride are the viewers. **[121m/18]**

Charlie "Lucky" Luciano	Christian Slater
Meyer Lansky	Patrick Dempsey
Bugsy Siegel	Richard Grieco
Frank Costello	Costas Mandylor

Also: F. Murray Abraham, Lara Flynn Boyle, Michael Gambon, Christopher Penn, Anthony Quinn

OOPS! In the steam bath scene, why is nobody sweating?

The Moderns ••• [1988]

Director: **Alan Rudolph**
Screenplay: **Alan Rudolph & Jon Bradshaw**

In 1920's Paris, an American painter loses his wife to a Chinese art dealer, himself caught up in a scam over faked paintings. Rudolph's sly satire on the art world, convincingly recreating Paris in a studio, is refreshingly different to the average Hollywood movie. **[126m/15]**

Nick Hart	Keith Carradine
Rachel Stone	Linda Fiorentino
Oiseau	Wallace Shawn
Libby Valentin	Genevieve Bujold
Nathalie de Ville	Geraldine Chaplin
Hemingway	Kevin J. O'Connor
Bertram Stone	John Lone

Psst! It took ten years to get this made. According to writer-director Rudolph, Esquire wanted to publish it as the most rejected script in Hollywood. He told them: 'I don't want to end up a Trivial Pursuits question. The movie *is* going to be made one day'.

Mo' Money ••• [1992]

Director: **Peter MacDonald**
Screenplay: **Damon Wayans**

This comedy thriller has Wayans as the con-man who goes straight to win delectable Dash's heart, only to get caught up in a credit card fraud. The two Wayans brothers make a great comedy team and, derivative and episodic though the plot may be, it culminates in a great chase and finale in a salt-processing plant. One wonders, though, if a white comedian could get away with such Politically Incorrect jokes mocking gays, the disabled, women and the like? **[90m/15]**

Johnny Stewart	Damon Wayans
Seymour Stewart	Marlon Wayans
Amber Evans	Stacey Dash
Lt. Raymond Walsh	Joe Santos
Keith Heading	John Diehl
Tom Dilton	Harry J. Lennix

Quote 'I'm so against working, I wouldn't even take a blow job.' [Lyrics]

Mona Lisa ••• [1986]

Director: **Neil Jordan**
Screenplay: **David Leland & Neil Jordan**

When Hoskins emerges from seven years inside, crime boss Caine gives him a job chauffeuring hooker Tyson. Gradually he is drawn into her search for a lost friend, discovering that much has changed in the underworld since he's been away. The air of menace hanging over this powerful human drama gets steadily heavier until it is brought to a head by the superbly menacing Caine. **[104m/18]**

George	Bob Hoskins
Simone	Cathy Tyson
Mortwell	Michael Caine
Thomas	Robbie Coltrane
Anderson	Clarke Peters
Cathy	Kate Hardie
Jeannie	Zoe Nathenson
Max	Sammi Davis

The Money Pit • [1986]

Director: **Richard Benjamin**
Screenplay: **David Giler**

A yuppie couple find their dream house turning into a nightmare. This comedy starts in the basement and tunnels its way down from there. The running time may not sound much, but Long isn't half an appropriate name for that woman to have. [See Rose's Rule #3] **[91m/PG]**

Walter Fielding	Tom Hanks
Anna Crowley	Shelley Long
Max Beissart	Alexander Godunov

Monkey Grip •• [1983]

Director: **Ken Cameron**
Screenplay: **Ken Cameron & Helen Garner**

Hazelhurst is the single mother embroiled with bad egg junkie actor Friels in this Australian drama set in the artistic community of Melbourne. Well-made and acted, with an interesting background, but the main story's never terribly involving. **[102m/18]**

Nora	Noni Hazelhurst
Javo	Colin Friels
Gracie	Alice Garner
Willie	Harold Hopkins

Monkey Shines •••• [1989]

Director: **George A. Romero**
Screenplay: **George A. Romero**

A wheelchair-bound young man gets a trained monkey to carry out household chores but it turns from an ally to a threat as a result of human, rather than animal, bestiality. This intelligent horror flick takes time establishing convincing characters before ringing many new changes to a familiar story. The chills, when they come, are a knockout. The film also says more about the plight of the disabled than most Issue-of-the-Week TV movies. **[113m/18]**

Allan Mann	Jason Beghe
Geoffrey Fisher	John Pankow
Melanie Parker	Kate McNeil
Dorothy Mann	Joyce Van Patten
Dr. John Wiseman	Stanley Tucci

Psst! The studio insisted on the ending after test audiences disliked Romero's far darker vision of an army of killer monkeys.

Monsignor • [1982]

Director: **Frank Perry**
Screenplay: **Abraham Polonsky & Wendell Mayes**

Those who relish *Mommie Dearest* as an exercise in high camp will be delighted with this howl of a movie from the same director and producer. Reeves is the ambitious Catholic priest, one of the best-dressed chaps in the profession, who rises within the Vatican after World War II through his dealings on the black market. He is something of a drinker and not averse to a spot of hanky-panky with a nun. Take it all seriously, and you've got a very bad, very dull film. In the right mood, it's absolutely hilarious. **[122m/15]**

Flaherty	Christopher Reeve
Clara	Genevieve Bujold
Santoni	Fernando Rey

The Monster Squad •• [1987]

Director: **Fred Dekker**
Screenplay: **Shane Black & Fred Dekker**

A group of young horror fans discover that Dracula, Frankenstein and their mates have turned up in town. It's not clear what age group this spoof of all the old horror movies is aimed at, although it passes the time. **[82m/15]**

Sean ....Andre Gower
Patrick ....Robby Kiger
Del ....Stephen Macht
Count Dracula........................Duncan Regehr
Frankenstein................................Tom Noonan

A Month in the Country •• [1987]

Director: Pat O'Connor
Screenplay: Simon Gray

A slender story about two young men in the aftermath of World War I. One is working on restoring a mural in a parish church, the other is excavating a grave. A calm and pleasing film, its slow pace will no doubt infuriate many. [96m/PG]

Tom Birkin ....Colin Firth
John Moon............................Kenneth Branagh
Mrs. Keach ....Natasha Richardson
Rev. Keach...........................Patrick Malahide
Also: Tony Haygarth, Jim Carter, Richard Vernon

Monty Python's The Meaning of Life •• [1983]

Director: Terry Jones
Screenplay: Graham Chapman, John Cleese, Terry Gilliam, Eric Idle, Terry Jones & Michael Palin

John Cleese wasn't joking [see below]. As with *And Now For Something Completely Different*, the Python's give us a series of skits. One or two are funny, but they're obviously more interested in testing the bounds of bad taste than in trying to make us laugh. It's still Python, for which we should be thankful, but it's far from vintage stuff. Just for reference, yes, this *is* the one with the exploding Mr. Creosote. [107m/18]

With: Graham Chapman, John Cleese, Terry Gilliam, Eric Idle, Terry Jones, Michael Palin

Quote 'The whole *Meaning of Life* thing is a cheap, last-minute rag-bag of unconnected sketches, if you want the truth.' [John Cleese]

Psst! The film won the Jury award for best film at Cannes. Accepting, Terry Jones

said: 'Thank you. Your money's behind the washbasin.' ✦ With this film Michael Palin set a record for the number of roles credited to one actor in a feature film, 15, including his performances as 'Rear End', 'Debbie' and 'Sixth Fish'.

Moon Over Parador •• [1988]

Director: Paul Mazursky
Screenplay: Leon Capetanos & Paul Mazursky

This variation on *The Prisoner of Zenda* has Dreyfuss as a terrible actor agreeing to impersonate the dead ruler of a tinpot Caribbean country. Despite being fitfully amusing, that feeling of déjà vu is never far away. [104m/15]

Jack Noah............................Richard Dreyfuss
Roberto Strausmann ....Raul Julia
Madonna..Sonia Briggs
Ralph......................................Jonathan Winters
Also: Fernando Rey, Michael Greene, Polly Holliday, Marianne Sägebrecht

Psst! There are cameos from the likes of Sammy Davis Jr., Dick Cavett and, as in all of his films, director Mazursky. Here he goes overboard playing 'Momma', though the credits list him as Carlotta Gerson.

Moonstruck •••• [1987]

Director: Norman Jewison
Screenplay: John Patrick Shanley

An utter charmer of a movie about an Italian–American family in Brooklyn and, in particular, the nearly-Fortysomething widow Cher. She falls for Cage, the estranged brother of her fiancée Aiello. Wit and wisdom shine out from this beautifully written and acted tale of love and family as the characters, so we're to believe, are driven by the influence of the moon. [102m/PG]

Loretta ....Cher
Ronny Cammareri ....Nicolas Cage
Cosmo Castorini.................Vincent Gardenia
Rose Castorini ....Olympia Dukakis
Mr. Johnny Cammareri..............Danny Aiello

Rita Cappomaggi..........................Julie Bovasso
Perry..John Mahoney
Raymond Cappomaggi ....Louis Guss
Old man..............................Feodor Chaliapin
Mona..Anita Gillette
Shy waiter ....Joe Grifasi
Barbara ....Robin Bartlett
Lotte...Helen Hanft

Oscars Cher, Olympia Dukakis, Best Screenplay

Quote 'No matter where you go or what you do, you're gonna die.' [Rose to errant husband Cosmo]

Psst! The script was originally about a Jewish family but was changed at the studio's insistence.

The Morning After • [1986]

Director: **Sidney Lumet**
Screenplay: **James Hicks**

Unsuccessful actress Fonda wakes up with a hangover and a dead man in the bed beside her. Thus begins a tiresome, boring *Jagged Edge* rip-off. Sitting through one of her fitness videos is more scintillating than this tripe. **[103m/15]**

Alex Sternbergen............................Jane Fonda
Turner Kendall................................Jeff Bridges
Joaquin Manero.................................Raul Julia

OOPS! Keep an eye on the level of wine in the bottle as it bobs up and down.

Psst! Kathy Bates has a tiny part as 'woman on Mateo Street'.

Morons from Outer Space • [1985]

Director: **Mike Hodges**
Screenplay: **Mel Smith & Griff Rhys Jones**

They said it! Griff Rhys Jones and Mel Smith are less amusing than Cannon and Ball in this pathetic tale of aliens on holiday from their home planet of Blob. **[87m/PG]**

Bernard...Mel Smith
Graham..................................Griff Rhys Jones
Sandra.......................................Joanne Pearce
Desmond.......................................Jimmy Nail

Mortal Thoughts •• [1991]

Director: **Alan Rudolph**
Screenplay: **William Reilly & Claude Kerven**

Bruce Willis, trying yet again to shrug off his macho image, is a lout of a husband who gets murdered. The police have some trouble finding out exactly what happened. Rudolph's eccentric style brings some interest to a fairly routine story. Although Moore has a credible stab at the heroine, it's Headly who steals the show. **[102m/15]**

Cynthia Kellogg..........................Demi Moore
Joyce Urbanski..........................Glenne Headly
James Urbanski ....Bruce Willis
Arthur Kellogg............................John Pankow
Detective John Woods...............Harvey Keitel

Psst! Moore, Mrs Willis, co-produced ◆ Director Rudolph was brought in at the very last minute.

Moscow on the Hudson ••• [1984]

Director: **Paul Mazursky**
Screenplay: **Paul Mazursky & Leon Capetanos**

Williams is excellent in this gently amusing tale of a Russian circus saxophonist who decides, in the middle of Bloomingdales, to defect to the West. The charm, and occasional corn, comes as he tries to adjust to the oddities and privations of life in the West, helped by his new girlfriend. **[115m/15]**

Vladimir Ivanoff ....Robin Williams
Lucia Lombardo........Maria Conchita Alonso
Lionel Witherspoon ....Cleavant Derricks
Orlando Ramirez......................Alejandro Rey

Showing *An Unmarried Woman* [one of Mazursky's previous films]

The Mosquito Coast •• [1986]

Director: **Peter Weir**
Screenplay: **Paul Schrader**

Eccentric inventor Ford, disillusioned with so-called civilised life in America, ups sticks and whisks his family off to Central America. But his un-American dream starts falling to pieces and so does he. Ford's character is so unsympathetic that it's hard to get totally involved in what happens to the family.

[119m/PG]

Allie Fox	Harrison Ford
Mother	Helen Mirren
Charlie	River Phoenix
Jerry	Jadrien Steele
April	Hilary Gordon
Clover	Rebecca Gordon

Blurb How Far Should A Man Go To Follow His Dream? Allie Fox Went To The Mosquito Coast. He Went Too Far.

Psst! The original actor offered the part was Jack Nicholson.

Mountains of the Moon •••• [1990]

Director: **Bob Rafelson**
Screenplay: **William Harrison & Bob Rafelson**

The true story of the Victorian explorer Richard Burton's quest for the source of the Nile. He's accompanied by Speke, a friend who later becomes a bitter enemy. A striking film with sumptuous photography, it was rather swamped on release by the likes of *Total Recall*. Yet it's pretty exciting and streets ahead of most historical costume pics.

[135m/15]

Richard Burton	Patrick Bergin
John Hanning Speke	Iain Glen
Oliphant	Richard E. Grant
Isabel	Fiona Shaw
Lord Oliphant	James Villiers
Lord Houghton	Peter Vaughan
Dr. Livingstone	Bernard Hill

Also: Delroy Lindo, Roshan Seth, Anna Massey, Leslie Phillips, Roger Rees, Omar Sharif

Mr. and Mrs. Bridge ••• [1990]

Director: **James Ivory**
Screenplay: **Ruth Prawer Jhabvala**

Another typical Merchant-Ivory production with domineering Newman and cowed Woodward the conservative 40's couple whose ways are fixed, even though the world is changing around them. Although more a series of episodes than straight narrative, the fine observation and superb acting are a joy to behold.

[124m/PG]

Walter Bridge	Paul Newman
India Bridge	Joanne Woodward
Grace Barron	Blythe Danner
Dr. Alex Sauer	Simon Callow
Ruth Bridge	Kyra Sedgwick

Also: Robert Sean Leonard, Margaret Walsh, Austin Pendleton

OOPS! In the Paris hotel bedroom they swap sides a couple of times while in bed.

Psst! Newman and Woodward have been married in real life for over 35 years • Senator Robert Dole is credited as 'Shakespearean tutor to Mr. Newman'. Newman needed the lines read by a Texan for the scene where he coaches his daughter on *Romeo and Juliet*.

Mr. Love ••• [1986]

Director: **Roy Battersby**
Screenplay: **Kenneth Eastaugh**

A whimsical little British comedy about how a legend of sexual prowess grew around a rather timid Southport gardener. The story is undoubtedly slight, but it's all done with great charm and a nice eye for the eccentric. There's also one out-and-out hilarious bit when the projector breaks down during a screening of *Casablanca*.

[91m/15]

Donald Lovelace	Barry Jackson
Theo	Maurice Denham
Pink lady	Margaret Tyzack
Barbara	Linda Marlowe

Mr. Mom
SEE: Mr. Mum

Mr. Mum •• [1983]

Director: Stan Dragoti
Screenplay: John Hughes

Although not a supernatural movie, that doesn't stop a strange, spooky feeling tak-ing grip, a feeling of...déjà vu. Out of work Keaton stays at home and has the usual hassles coping with the kids while mom Garr goes back to work. Pleasant enough, but surely we've seen it all before? **[91m/PG]**

Jack..Michael Keaton
Caroline ....Teri Garr
Ron ....Martin Mull
Also: Ann Jillian, Jeffrey Tambor

Psst! Hughes was still learning his craft on this film, presumably why it took him all of a week to write it. He was faster on *Weird Science* two years later • An American magazine report on product placement found that companies had paid for appearance plugs for the following products: McDonald's, Jack Daniel's, Tide, Borax, Folger's coffee, Domino's Pizza, Terminix exterminators, Lite beer, Van Camp's chili, Clorox 2, Downy fabric softener and Ban deodorant.

Mr. Nanny • [1993]

Director: Michael Gottlieb
Screenplay: Edward Rugoff & Michael Gottlieb

A film with little of the wit, character or subtlety of Hogan's earlier film, *Suburban Commando*. Here the balding, peroxide blonde wrestler bodyguards a couple of spoilt rich kids. Even Hogan clad in a purple tutu and leotard doesn't raise a laugh. Almost worth watching the open-ing, though, for the worst example ever of an 'actor' pretending to be asleep. **[84m/PG]**

Sean Armstrong...........................Hulk Hogan
Burt Wilson.......................Sherman Hemsley
Alex Mason Sr.....................Austin Pendleton
Also: Robert Gorman, Madeline Zima

Psst! This movie has one of the most extraordinary credits ever: Bodyguard to Mr. Hogan!

Mr. North •• [1988]

Director: Danny Huston
Screenplay: Janet Roach, John Huston & James Costigan

A young tutor in Rhode Island in the 20s becomes something of a celebrity with the local gentry thanks to the electrical charge he carries about with him. This pleasant tale, although beautiful to look at, is so slightly directed by John Huston's son that a breath of wind would carry it away. **[93m/PG]**

Theophilus North ....Anthony Edwards
James McHenry Bosworth ....Robert Mitchum
Mrs. Amelia Cranston...............Lauren Bacall
Henry Simmons..............Harry Dean Stanton
Persis ....Anjelica Huston
Also: Mary Stuart Masterson, Virginia Madsen, Tammy Grimes, David Warner

Psst! John Huston co-wrote the film and helped to produce it. He was prevented from playing the Mitchum part by ill health.

Mr. Saturday Night •• [1992]

Director: Billy Crystal
Screenplay: Billy Crystal, Lowell Ganz & Babaloo Mandel

Billy Crystal gives the big-screen treat-ment to his *Saturday Night Live* comedian Buddy Young Jr., the man who never uses a wisecrack when an unwise one will do. We see far too little of Crystal doing his wonderful standup and far too much of heavily-latexed wrinklies discussing where their lives have gone wrong. And as for slush, oy, don't get me started on that! **[119m/15]**

Buddy Young Jr. ....Billy Crystal
Stan Yankelman.......................David Paymer
Elaine ....Julie Warner
Annie...Helen Hunt
Also: Mary Mara, Jerry Orbach, Ron Silver

Psst! It took six hours for Crystal to get his make-up on each day, and two hours to get it off again [See Rose's Rule #5] • Jerry Lewis has a brief cameo.

Mrs. Soffel •• [1984]

Director: Gillian Armstrong
Screenplay: Ron Nyswaner

At the turn of the century, the wife of a Pittsburgh prison warder, Keaton, falls for condemned prisoner Gibson and gives up everything to help him escape. Despite the stars, it's a gloomy and curiously uninvolving tale

[110m/PG]

Kate Soffel.................................Diane Keaton
Ed Biddle...Mel Gibson
Jack Biddle ....Matthew Modine
Peter Soffel.........................Edward Herrmann
Irene Soffel................................Trini Alvarado

Quote 'Money's the only thing that ever saves you.'

Much Ado About Nothing ••• [1993]

Director: Kenneth Branagh
Screenplay: William Shakespeare

This splendid Shakespeare adaptation is both hilarious and moving and, remarkably, extremely accessible to modern audiences, be they Bard groupie or not. Maybe the plot's a bit creaky, but it *is* a few hundred years old. Forget the mixture of American and British accents and revel in Ken and Emma's superb comic performances. Only the uncomfortable Reeves and Branagh's over-fussy direction, particularly clumsy in the crowd scenes, let down this otherwise superb comedy.

[110m]

Benedick.................................Kenneth Branagh
Dogberry................................Michael Keaton
Claudio ....Robert Sean Leonard
Don John ....Keanu Reeves
Beatrice ....Emma Thompson
Don Pedro ....Denzel Washington
Also: Richard Briers, Kate Beckinsale, Brian Blessed, Ben Elton, Phyllida Law, Imelda Staunton.

The Muppet Christmas Carol •• [1992]

Director: Brian Henson
Screenplay: Jerry Juhl

Too much Scrooge and not enough Muppets make this a disappointing outing for Kermit, Miss Piggy and pals, the first time they've played roles rather than themselves. Fozzie Bear gets shamefully little to do while some upstart called Caine hogs the limelight and even – a mistake – sings a bit. The music's bland while the jokes are feeble and well past their sell-by date. Saying this is sentimental is like saying Barbara Cartland likes wearing pink. [85m/U]

Scrooge.....................................Michael Caine
Also: Dave Goetz, Steve Whitmire, Jerry Nelson, Frank Oz, David Rudman

Psst! Look out for a couple of in-jokes in the final scenes on Christmas Day. One shop is called 'Micklewhite', the real name of Michael Caine, and another is 'Stadtler and Waldorf', the real names of the actors playing Jacob and Robert Marley.

The Muppets Take Manhattan ••• [1984]

Director: Frank Oz
Screenplay: Frank Oz & Jay Tarses

Flushed with the success of their college show, our hand-operated friends head for the bright lights of Broadway. As so often, the talents of Fozzie Bear are shamelessly hidden behind the caperings of the camera-hogging pig and frog. Still, the songs are great and the gags are well up to scratch too. Great fun. [94m/U]

With: Jim Henson, Frank Oz, Dave Goetz, Steve Whitmire, Jerry Nelson, Lonny Price, Dabney Coleman, John Landis, Joan Rivers, Gregory Hines, James Coco, Art Carney, Linda Lavin, Liza Minnelli

Psst! Along with other assorted celebrities the then-mayor of New York, Ed Koch, appears in a cameo.

Murphy's Law • [1986]

Director: J. Lee Thompson
Screenplay: Gail Morgan Hickman

Bronson's a cop who is being framed by a psycho he once put away. Much shooting and shouting. Little entertainment or excitement. [100m/18]

Jack Murphy.........................Charles Bronson
Arabella McGee................Kathleen Wilhoite
Joan Freeman......................Carrie Snodgress

Murphy's Romance ••• [1985]

Director: Martin Ritt
Screenplay: Harriet Frank Jr. & Irving Ravetch

Delightfully old-fashioned and pleasing romantic comedy. Field is the divorcée from the big city who arrives in a one-horse town in Arizona aiming to increase that number by breeding more horses. Just when she and twinkly-eyed Garner look as if they might get it together, her ex turns up to complicate things. [107m/15]

Emma Moriarty ....Sally Field
Murphy Jones ....James Garner
Bobby Jack Moriarty.................Brian Kerwin
Jake Moriarty...............................Corey Haim
Freeman Coverly ....Dennis Burkley
Margaret ....Georgann Johnson

Music Box ••• [1989]

Director: Costa-Gavras
Screenplay: Joe Eszterhas

Tough, emotional drama about lawyer Lange defending her Hungarian immigrant father Mueller-Stahl when he faces deportation on war crimes charges. A challenging film which poses many uncomfortable questions, it is perhaps the best work of Joe Eszterhas, the writer who also gave us *Basic Instinct* and *Jagged Edge.* [126m/15]

Ann Talbot ....Jessica Lange
Mike Laszlo ....Armin Mueller-Stahl
Jack Burke..............................Frederic Forrest
Harry Talbot............................Donald Moffat
Mikey Talbot................................Lukas Haas

Psst! Lange received her fifth Oscar nomination for the film. She lost out to Jessica Tandy for *Driving Miss Daisy.*

My Beautiful Laundrette ••• [1985]

Director: Stephen Frears
Screenplay: Hanif Kureishi

A young Pakistani entrepreneur runs an advanced laundrette with the help of an ex-skinhead. Social, racial and class tensions in South London don't help business. Despite a couple of weakish performances and, perhaps, the raising of too many unresolved issues, this remains an original, unpredictable and thought-provoking drama which cleverly tapped into the mood of mid-80's Britain. [97m/15]

Johnny...............................Daniel Day-Lewis
Nasser ....Saeed Jaffrey
Pap...Roshan Seth
Omar ....Gordon Warnecke
Rachel...............................Shirley Anne Field

My Blue Heaven •• [1990]

Director: Herbert Ross
Screenplay: Nora Ephron

This tale of Mafia stoolie Martin going into the Witness Protection Program under the eagle eye of Moranis is light on jokes and plot. As always, though, Martin is amiable as the gangster who finds it hard to give up altogether while Cusack strikes a few sparks as a local DA. Almost worth it just for Martin and Moranis dancing the Maranga. [96m/PG]

Vinnie Antonelli..........................Steve Martin
Barney Coopersmith...................Rick Moranis
Hannah Stubbs ....Joan Cusack
Crystal Rybak ....Melanie Mayron
Also: Bill Irwin, Carol Kane, William Hickey, Deborah Rush, Daniel Stern

Psst! Warners wasn't above a little subliminal advertising. The cinema is showing *White Hunter, Black Heart,* a film the company was to release in a few months' time. Odd, though, how it still seems to be showing near the end of the film.

My Cousin Vinny •••• [1992]

Director: **Jonathan Lynn**
Screenplay: **Dale Launer**

Uproariously funny tale of incompetent Brooklyn lawyer Pesci turning up in Wahzoo, Alabama, in leather jacket and cowboy boots to defend a young cousin and his friend on a murder rap. Not only has Pesci never won a case; he's never had one before. As if that wasn't bad enough, he has to contend with by-the-book hostility of the judge, the wonderful Fred Gwynne. Although the film's a mite draggy in a couple of places, Pesci is brilliant in his first leading role. Despite this, he's almost acted off the screen by Tomei as his fiery, gum-chewing, wise-cracking girlfriend in one of the most electrifying comedy performances in years. **[119m/15]**

Vinny	Joe Pesci
Bill Gambini	Ralph Macchio
Mona Lisa Vito	Marisa Tomei
Stan Rothenstein	Mitchell Whitfield
Judge Haller	Fred Gwynne
Jim Trotter	Lane Smith
John Gibbons	Austin Pendleton

Oscars Marisa Tomei

OOPS! The tapes used to pull Pesci's skin upwards on his face and make him look younger can occasionally be spotted.

Psst! If it's bugging you where you've seen the judge before, it's probably from his long-running TV role as Hermann Munster.

My Favourite Year •••• [1982]

Director: **Richard Benjamin**
Screenplay: **Norman Steinberg & Dennis Palumbo**

...and My Favourite Film. Well, one of them. Linn-Baker's the young writer on a 50's TV show given the unwanted task of looking after swashbuckling film star O'Toole, a renowned lush, womaniser and hell-raiser. The film delights on all levels. Not only is it an astonishingly funny, fast-paced comedy with some incredible lines, a few thrills and a little romance thrown in, but it also gives us a remarkable view of the early days of live television. Ninety-two minutes of pure, cinematic joy. **[92m/PG]**

Alan Swann	Peter O'Toole
Benjy Stone	Mark Linn-Baker
K.C. Downing	Jessica Harper
King Kaiser	Joseph Bologna
Sy Benson	Bill Macy
Belle Carroca	Lainie Kazan
Alice Miller	Anne DeSalvo
Uncle Morty	Lou Jacobi

Quote 'Live? I can't go on *live*! I'm a movie star, not an actor!' ♦ 'This is for ladies only!' [Woman in lavatory] — 'So is this, madam. But every now and again I have to run some water through it.'

Psst! Made by Mel Brooks' company, the basis for the story was the occasion when Brooks, a writer on Sid Caesar's TV show, had to look after guest Errol Flynn ♦ As well as Brooks, the programme, 'The Show of Shows', had writers such as Woody Allen and Larry Gelbart (*M*A*S*H*), as well as writer-performer Carl Reiner, later a top director and father of Rob.

My First Forty Years • [1989]

Director: **Carlo Vanzina**
Screenplay: **Carlo Vanzina & Enrico Vanzina**

An ineptly-dubbed, badly-acted, unerotic Italian airport-blockbuster of a movie. One of the better arguments against closer European integration. **[107m/18]**

Marina	Carol Alt
Nino Ranuzzi	Elliott Gould
Prince Riccio	Jean Rochefort
Count	Pierre Cosso

Psst! Alt uses a body double, Carmen Stowe, in all the rather more interesting bits.

My First Wife •• [1985]

Director: Paul Cox
Screenplay: Paul Cox & Bob Ellis

A composer hits the minor chords when his wife leaves him. A powerful, well-performed drama, it gets bogged down in an increasing degree of talk. Australian director Paul Cox isn't firing on all cylinders here, perhaps because it's apparently autobiographical. [97m/15]

John	John Hargreaves
Helen	Wendy Hughes
Lucy	Lucy Angwin
Tom	David Cameron

My Girl • [1992]

Director: Howard Zieff
Screenplay: Laurice Elehwany

Those who dislike Culkin probably *should* watch this ham-fisted weepie just to see the lad come a cropper, out-acted by Chlumsky. She's mortician Aykroyd's daughter and doesn't take kindly to his romance with corpse make-up artist Curtis. Her best friend Culkin has an aversion to bee stings and, well, you can fill in the plot without even seeing it. Don't bother with sweet popcorn. You'll get all the sugar you want from the screen. [102m/PG]

Harry Sultenfuss	Dan Aykroyd
Shelly DeVoto	Jamie Lee Curtis
Thomas J. Sennett	Macaulay Culkin
Vada Sultenfuss	Anna Chlumsky

Also: Richard Masur, Griffin Dunne

OOPS! Culkin's not the greatest actor when he's alive. When he plays dead, you can still see him breathing.

My Left Foot •••• [1989]

Director: Jim Sheridan
Screenplay: Shane Connaughton & Jim Sheridan

The remarkable story of Christy Brown, the best-selling writer who suffered from cerebral palsy from birth and was able to control his left foot and nothing else. While the idea might sound depressing, this turns out to be a remarkably joyous and witty film, superbly acted by the entire cast. It has its sentimental moments, to be sure, but the overall experience is wonderfully uplifting. [98m/PG]

Christy Brown	Daniel Day-Lewis
Mrs. Brown	Brenda Fricker
Mr. Brown	Ray McAnally
Mary	Ruth McCabe
Dr. Eileen Cole	Fiona Shaw
Lord Castlewelland	Cyril Cusack
Peter	Adrian Dunbar

Oscars Daniel Day-Lewis, Brenda Fricker

Psst! Although it only cost £1m to make, writer Connaughton told everyone in Hollywood it cost £5m, fearing they wouldn't take him seriously if they knew the truth • Brown was one of 13 surviving children out of a total of 22 born.

My Life as a Dog •••• [1987]

Director: Lasse Hallström
Screenplay: Lasse Hallström, Reidar Jönsson, Brasse Brännstrom & Per Berglund

Just when you think you've had enough coming-of-age movies, one comes along that knocks the others into a cocked hat. In this delightful little Swedish film, a mischievous 12-year-old is sent to the country for the summer when his mother falls ill. Full of oddball humour, the impish Glanzelius convinces as a real human being having to grow up all too quickly. Made in 1984 but not released in Britain or America until 1987. [101m/PG]

Ingemar	Anton Glanzelius
Uncle Gunnar	Tomas von Bromseen
Mother	Anki Liden
Saga	Malinda Kinnaman

Psst! Unusually for a foreign film it received two Oscar nominations in the main – rather than foreign – categories, for director and screenplay.

My Little Girl ••• [1987]

Director: Connie Kaiserman
Screenplay: Connie Kaiserman

The idea of a privileged girl deciding to spend the summer holidays working at an inner-city shelter for children sounds absolutely ghastly. In fact, it turns out to be a story free of schmaltz, full of insight, and well-acted. [117m/15]

Franny Bettinger ....Mary Stuart Masterson
Ike Bailey ....James Earl Jones
Grandmother Molly.................Geraldine Page
Mrs. Bettinger ....Pamela Payton-Wright
Mr. Bettinger..................Peter Michael Goetz
Kai ....Peter Gallagher

My Little Pony •• [1986]

Director: Michael Joens
Screenplay: George Arthur Bloom

Once upon a time, toys were toys and films were films. These days no toy's a success unless it's also got its own movie. This one's exactly what you expect. Can it be long before we see a Little Pony hoof-print in the cement outside Grauman's Chinese Theatre in Hollywood? [89m/U]

With: Danny DeVito, Madeline Kahn, Cloris Leachman, Rhea Perlman

Mystic Pizza ••• [1988]

Director: Donald Petrie
Screenplay: Amy Holden Jones, Perry Howze & Alfred Uhry

A nice little film about the romantic complications suffered by three girls working in Mystic, Connecticut's pizza parlour. Despite a wisp of a plot, it's warm, humorous and very much alive. Although everyone's good, Roberts is particularly so in this, her first starring role. [104m/15]

Daisy Araujo..............................Julia Roberts
Kat Araujo ....Annabeth Gish
Jojo Barboza ....Lili Taylor
Bill Montijo ....Vincent D'Onofrio
Tim Travers....:.................William R. Moses
Charles Gordon Winsor ....Adam Storke
Leona Valsouano ....Conchata Ferrell

My Own Private Idaho •• [1992]

Director: Gus Van Sant
Screenplay: Gus Van Sant

An oddly made film about two young gay hustlers and the Falstaffian ruffian they fall in with. Peppered with bizarre directorial tricks, it never seems to know where it's headed and distractingly and pretentiously turns into a Shakespearian spoof at half-time. Phoenix suffers from narcolepsy and keeps falling asleep. He's only giving the audience ideas. [105m/18]

Mike Waters...........................River Phoenix
Scott Favor ....Keanu Reeves
Richard Waters...........................James Russo
Bob Pigeon ....William Richert

Psst! The film's title was inspired by the B-52 song 'Private Idaho' • Behind Reeves and Phoenix at one point is a statue of early settlers bearing the inscription 'The Coming of the White Man'.

My Stepmother is an Alien •• [1988]

Director: Richard Benjamin
Screenplay: Jerico Weingrod, Herschel Weingrod, Timothy Harris & Jonathan Reynolds

Basinger's no comedienne, but there are some nice touches in this tale of a gorgeous alien getting hitched to Aykroyd so that she can save her planet from his invention and, along the way, learn all about love, sex and sneezing. [107m/15]

Dr. Steve Mills ....Dan Aykroyd
Celeste...Kim Basinger
Ron Mills ....Jon Lovitz
Dr. Lucas Budlong ....Joseph Maher

Psst! This is the film debut of Juliette Lewis as Lexie • Shelley Michelle, the body double used for Julia Roberts in *Pretty Woman* was used in this film to stand in for Kim Basinger's legs as she pulls her stocking on while weightless.

Mystery Train •• [1989]

Director: **Jim Jarmusch**
Screenplay: **Jim Jarmusch**

A sleazy Memphis hotel seems only to cater for guests obsessed with Elvis. Jarmusch's usual quirky, slice-of-life epics are either an inspiration or the cause of much gritting of teeth. Those who like this sort of thing probably will. **[111m/15]**

Mitzuko	Youki Kudoh
Jun	Masatoshi Nagase
Luisa	Nicoletta Braschi
DeeDee	Elizabeth Bracco

My Tutor •• [1983]

Director: **George Bowers**
Screenplay: **Joe Roberts**

Wealthy Lattanzi gets a French tutor, the more mature Kaye, who teaches him more than just the French language. An amiable teen sex comedy so predictable, you can practically recite the lines with the actors. **[97m/18]**

Terry	Caren Kaye
Bobby	Matt Lattanzi
Chrystal	Kevin McCarthy
Billy	Clark Brandon

Nadine •• [1987]

Director: **Robert Benton**
Screenplay: **Robert Benton**

Basinger's the hairdresser who witnesses a murder while trying to recover compromising photographs and is forced to ask sleazeball separated husband Bridges for help. This supposed screwball comedy is flat and terribly unfunny. Someone should tell Basinger that she really can't do comedy. It's plain embarrassing watching her try. **[83m/PG]**

Vernon Hightower	Jeff Bridges
Nadine Hightower	Kim Basinger
Buford Pope	Rip Torn
Vera	Gwen Verdon
Renee	Glenne Headly

The Naked Face •• [1984]

Director: **Bryan Forbes**
Screenplay: **Bryan Forbes**

Roger Moore's a psychiatrist. One of his patients dies and the police think it might not have been through boredom. Under suspicion himself, he and Carney have to find the real killer, but they look as confused as we are by the complicated plot. **[105m/18]**

Dr. Judd Stevens	Roger Moore
Lt. McGreavy	Rod Steiger
Angeli	Elliott Gould
Morgens	Art Carney
Ann Blake	Anne Archer

The Naked Gun: From the Films of Police Squad! ••• [1988]

Director: **David Zucker**
Screenplay: **Jim Abrahams, David Zucker, Jerry Zucker & Pat Proft**

Yet another triumph from the team that brought the world *Airplane* and *Kentucky Fried Movie*. Former straight actor Nielsen is incompetent cop Frank Drebin, out to foil an assassination attempt on the Queen during a visit to LA. Pratfalls, slapstick, gags old and even older, jostle for position in this zany, fast-paced comedy. The jokes come so thick and fast, it's almost impossible to catch them all the first time through. **[85m/15]**

Frank Drebin	Leslie Nielsen
Jane Spence	Priscilla Presley
Vincent Ludwig	Ricardo Montalban
Ed Hocken	George Kennedy
Nordberg	O.J. Simpson

Quote 'You don't know real heat until you've spent several hours inside a giant condom.' [Priscilla Presley]

Psst! Keep an eye on the closing credits, as you should in all ZAZ films. They include the line: 'In Case Of Tornado... Southwest Corner Of Basement' ✦ The film is based on, and many of the jokes are taken from, a sadly discontinued television series in the same vein called *Police Squad*. Only 6 episodes were ever made.

Naked Gun 2½ – The Smell of Fear •• [1991]

Director: **David Zucker**
Screenplay: **David Zucker & Pat Proft**

Frank Drebin foils a plot by the power companies to squash the Government's new energy policy. Although nothing like as funny as the original, there are still plenty of good gags. Nielsen is immensely watchable, even if his *Naked Gun* persona means that all his old, serious, films now seem hysterical.

[81m/12]

Lieut. Frank Drebin	Leslie Nielsen
Jane Spencer	Priscilla Presley
Ed Hocken	George Kennedy
Nordberg	O.J. Simpson
Quentin Hapsburg	Robert Goulet
Dr. Meinheimer	Richard Griffiths

Quote 'Nice party. A lot of familiar facelifts.' ✦ 'Is this some kind of a bust?'

OOPS! Lieutenant Frank Drebin was promoted to Captain at the end of the first film. So why is he still a Lieutenant here?

Psst! The wonderful spoof of the potter's wheel scene in *Ghost* – directed by David Zucker's brother Jerry – was filmed for a trailer before shooting even started on the movie. They liked it so much, they kept it in ✦ Look out for cameos from the likes of Mel Tormé and Zsa Zsa Gabor
✦ David Zucker appears as Davy Crockett.

Naked Lunch • [1991]

Director: **David Cronenberg**
Screenplay: **David Cronenberg**

They said it was unfilmable. They were right. This adaptation of Burrough's infamous semi-autobiographical novel about the weird imaginings of a writer so stoned his feet never touch the ground, is a mess. The visuals are impressive, particularly the sex-obsessed, bug-like talking typewriter. But they're far more interesting than the human actors, who look as if they've strayed from a bad zombie flick. Distasteful it may be, but it's too dull to become a cult. [115m/18]

William Lee	Peter Weller
Joan Frost/Joan Lee	Judy Davis
Tom Frost	Ian Holm
Yves Cloquet	Julian Sands
Dr. Benway	Roy Scheider

Blurb Exterminate All Rational Thought.

Quote 'It's a Kafka high. You feel like a bug.'

Psst! The book tie-in in the US is said to have taken more than the film! ✦ An Australian cinema offered a special screening for those who turned up nude. It had to be cancelled for lack of interest.

Naked Tango • [1990]

Director: **Leonard Schrader**
Screenplay: **Leonard Schrader**

Buenos Aires. 1924. Young bride. Brothel. Tango. Sex. Broken glass. Bad acting. Madonna probably found it inspirational, but nobody else did. *Strictly Ballroom* this is not. Strictly bullshit would be more like it. You'll know you've been tangoed after this rubbish. [92m/18]

Cholo	Vincent D'Onofrio
Alba/Stephanie	Mathilda May
Zico Borenstein	Esai Morales
Judge Torres	Fernando Rey
Bertoni	Josh Mostel

Showing *The Four Horsemen of the Apocalypse*.

Psst! Leonard Schrader is Paul's brother.

The Name of the Rose •••• [1986]

Director: Jean-Jacques Annaud
Screenplay: Andrew Birkin, Gérard Brach, Howard Franklin & Alain Godard

Take what might be a conventional detective yarn, set it in a 14th-century Italian abbey where the power of life and death lies with the Inquisition, make the private eye a less-than-reverential English monk, and you have one of the most remarkable films of recent years. Connery is superb as William of Baskerville, who becomes the bloodhound of the Baskervilles, accompanied by his novice Slater as they try to prove that a series of murders are not the work of the Devil. This gripping and fascinating film oozes atmosphere so thick you can practically drink it. Once seen, never forgotten. **[131m/18]**

William of Baskerville	Sean Connery
Bernardo Gui	F. Murray Abraham
Adso of Melk	Christian Slater
Severinus	Elya Baskin
Jorge de Burgos	Feodor Chaliapin
Ubertino de Casale	William Hickey
The Abbot	Michel Lonsdale
Salvatore	Ron Perlman

Psst! After looking at over three hundred monasteries around Europe, filming eventually took place at Klöster Eberbach near Frankfurt, where time has stood still since the 12th century • The exterior was built on a hill near Rome, the largest exterior set Europe has seen since the making of *Cleopatra*.

Narrow Margin •• [1990]

Director: Peter Hyams
Screenplay: Peter Hyams

In this remake of a 1952 film, DA Hackman escorts witness Archer to give evidence while the baddies try to silence her. Despite the quality of the stars and some great photography as the train hurtles through the Rockies, it's disappointingly predictable stuff and the adrenalin never really gets going. Isn't it about time the talented Archer played something other than a loyal wife? **[97m/15]**

Robert Caulfield	Gene Hackman
Carol Hunnicut	Anne Archer
Nelson	James B. Sikking
Michael Tarlow	J.T. Walsh
Sgt. Dominick Benti	M. Emmet Walsh

Nate and Hayes
SEE: Savage Islands

National Lampoon's Christmas Vacation •• [1989]

Director: Jeremiah Chechik
Screenplay: John Hughes

Presumably there's somebody out there who likes Chevy Chase, otherwise they wouldn't let him keep making films. There are others who will look at Chase as Santa on the poster and light a Yuletide fire in the grate immediately. Marginally better than some in the series, it's almost worth a peek just to see Juliette Lewis in an early role. Also known as *National Lampoon's Winter Holiday*. **[97m/PG]**

Clark Griswold	Chevy Chase
Ellen Griswold	Beverly D'Angelo
Audrey Griswold	Juliette Lewis
Rusty Griswold	Johnny Galecki

Also: John Randolph, Diane Ladd, E.G. Marshall, Randy Quaid

Blurb Yule Crack Up!

National Lampoon's Class Reunion • [1982]

Director: Michael Miller
Screenplay: John Hughes

It's pretty easy to dismiss this class. An excruciating horror spoof. **[84m/15]**

Bob	Gerrit Graham
Dr. Young	Michael Lerner
Gary	Fred McCarren

National Lampoon's European Vacation •• [1985]

Director: Amy Heckerling
Screenplay: John Hughes & Robert Klane

The Griswolds invade Europe, producing about as many laughs as when A. Hitler did it. At least he had a silly moustache. Marginally funnier than the bog-standard *Vacation*, which isn't saying much. [95m/15]

Clark W. Griswold ....Chevy Chase
Ellen Griswold ....Beverly D'Angelo
Audrey Griswold............................Dana Hill
Rusty Griswold............................Jason Lively
Also: John Astin, Paul Bartel, Mel Smith

National Lampoon's Loaded Weapon 1 •• [1993]

Director: Gene Quintano
Screenplay: Don Holley & Gene Quintano

One of those rare comedies with fewer jokes than the poster. How can you spoof the *Lethal Weapon* films when they're already spoofs? Most of the jokes fired here are blanks. Simply referring to other movies is not enough to make an audience laugh, not unless it's Leslie Nielsen doing it. [83m/PG]

Jack Colt....................................Emilio Estevez
Wes Luger............................Samuel L. Jackson
Becker..Jon Lovitz
Also: Tim Curry, Kathy Ireland, Frank McRae, William Shatner, Whoopi Goldberg, F. Murray Abraham

Blurb See It Before They Make The Sequel.

Psst! There are cameos from Charlie Sheen and Bruce Willis.

National Lampoon's Vacation • [1983]

Director: Harold Ramis
Screenplay: John Hughes

Chevy Chase and his family have various mishaps, unfortunately none of them fatal, on their way to 'Walley World'. In a fairer world, Walley World would up stumps and head for the Griswolds. A screamingly unfunny movie, the only smile it raises is when those longed-for words 'The End' appear. [98m/15]

Clark Griswold ....Chevy Chase
Ellen Griswold ....Beverly D'Angelo
Aunt Edna................................Imogene Coca
Cousin Eddie.............................Randy Quaid

Psst! Hughes took four days to write the script. Who knows why it took so long?
♦ Eddie Bracken and John Candy appear in cameos.

National Lampoon's Winter Holiday SEE: National Lampoon's Christmas Vacation

The Natural •• [1984]

Director: Barry Levinson
Screenplay: Roger Towne & Phil Dusenberry

The rise and fall of a baseball star with an attractive cast, gorgeous cinematography and Levinson's usual failure to knock a story into proper shape. The mythic underpinnings to this film make it very much a matter of taste. [134m/PG]

Roy Hobbs..............................Robert Redford
Max Mercy...............................Robert Duvall
Iris ....Glenn Close
Memo Paris ....Kim Basinger
Pop Fisher ....Wilford Brimley
Harriet Bird..........................Barbara Hershey
Judge ....Robert Prosky
Red Blow ....Richard Farnsworth
The Whammer........................Joe Don Baker

Quote 'I believe we live two lives: the lives we learn with and the lives we live with after that.'

The Nature of the Beast • [1988]

Director: Franco Rosso
Screenplay: Janni Howker

Up North there's a mysterious animal killing chickens and sheep. A typical 80's British film, depressingly set in a depressed Lancashire textile town full of depressed people. It ends up depressing the audience without saying anything worthwhile. **[95m/PG]**

Bill Coward............................Lynton Dearden
Mick..Paul Simpson
Granddad.................................Tony Melody

The Navigator: A Medieval Odyssey ••• [1989]

Director: **Vincent Ward**
Screenplay: **Vincent Ward, Kely Lyons & Geoff Chapple**

A group of medieval Cumbrians flee the plague by burrowing through the earth, emerging in 20th-century New Zealand. Although a thinnish script prevents this from being a masterpiece, the original storyline, clever historical parallels and stunning imagery are compelling. Well worth a look. **[92m/U]**

Connor ....Bruce Lyons
Arno....................................Chris Haywood
Griffin.............................Hamish McFarlane
Searle ....Marshall Napier

Navy SEALS • [1990]

Director: **Lewis Teague**
Screenplay: **Chuck Pfarrer & Gary Goldman**

The desperate search to find another branch of the services to undergo a *Top Gun* Treatment settles on naval commandos. America's response to Middle Eastern terrorism is to send this bunch of lager louts in, knowing that whichever side ends up dead, the world will be a better place. **[113m/15]**

Lt. Dale Hawkins......................Charlie Sheen
Lt. James Curran ....Michael Biehn
Claire Verens ....Joanne Whalley-Kilmer
Also: Rick Rossovich, Dennis Haysbert, Bill Paxton

Near Dark •• [1987]

Director: **Kathryn Bigelow**
Screenplay: **Eric Red & Kathryn Bigelow**

Bitten by a pale but interesting girl, a cowboy finds himself among a group of modern-day vampires touring the West. This stylish, incredibly bloodthirsty, film brought Bigelow to the directorial fore, but the poor characterisations prevent the film itself from being particularly good. **[95m/18]**

Caleb..Adrian Pasdar
Mae..Jenny Wright
Jesse.....................................Lance Henriksen
Severen ....Bill Paxton
Diamondback.......................Jenette Goldstein
Quote 'You haven't met any girls like me.'

Necessary Roughness • [1992]

Director: **Stan Dragoti**
Screenplay: **Rick Natkin & David Fuller**

Philosophical question. We feel fine. We watch a movie about a college with a terrible football team. The team gets better. So why do we feel worse? Answers on one side of the paper only. **[108m/12]**

Paul Blake ....Scott Bakula
Coach Gennero......................Hector Elizondo
Coach Rig.................................Robert Loggia
Also: Harley Jane Kozak, Larry Miller

Neil Simon's Broadway Bound
SEE: **Broadway Bound**

Never Cry Wolf ••• [1983]

Director: **Carroll Ballard**
Screenplay: **Curtis Hanson, Sam Hamm & Richard Kletter**

Stirring true-life story of an inadequately-prepared scientist journeying to the Arctic to study wolves, only to discover that he first has to ensure his own survival. It isn't only species of animals that are dying out. Splendid old-time family films like this are almost extinct too. Grab this one when you get the chance. **[105m/PG]**

Tyler ....Charles Martin Smith
Rosie..Brian Dennehy
Ootek...........................Zachary Ittimangnaq

The Neverending Story •• [1984]

Director: Wolfgang Petersen
Screenplay: Wolfgang Petersen & Herman Weigel

Okay German children's fantasy about a boy who borrows a book and finds himself drawn into the story. While the tale of the land of Fantasia, under threat from the fast-encroaching Nothing, is wonderful to look at and should keep kids enthralled, adults are likely to find the title all too true.
[94m/U]

Bastian	Barret Oliver
Bastian's Father	Gerald McRaney
Atreyu	Noah Hathaway

The Neverending Story II: The Next Chapter •• [1990]

Director: George Miller
Screenplay: Karin Howard

This return to the land of Fantasia has a lamentably thin plot. But there's still plenty for kids to enjoy as good triumphs over evil with the aid of some furry creatures and the odd special effect.
[90m/U]

Bastian Balthazar Bux	Jonathan Brandis
Atreyu	Kenny Morrison
Xayide	Clarissa Burt

Never Say Never Again •• [1983]

Director: Irvin Kershner
Screenplay: Lorenzo Semple Jr.

Although it's great to see Connery back as Bond after an absence of twelve years, it's something of a pity that the film should really just be *Thunderball* all over again with a different name. Despite the stunts, the girls and the wisecracks, it's just a little bit too thin to be completely satisfying.
[134m/PG]

James Bond	Sean Connery
Largo	Klaus Maria Brandauer
Blofeld	Max Von Sydow
Fatima	Barbara Carrera
Domino	Kim Basinger

Also: Bernie Casey, Alec McGowen, Edward Fox, Rowan Atkinson

Psst! The title is a dig at Connery, who had said after *Diamonds are Forever* that he would 'never again' do another Bond film. Presumably the $5m, the most ever paid to a British star at the time, helped cushion the blow.

New Jack City ••• [1991]

Director: Mario Van Peebles
Screenplay: Thomas Lee Wright & Barry Michael Cooper

A New York policeman and his colleagues take on the black mafia and the bullets fly. Although the film pretends to have a serious anti-drug message, it is actually just an excuse for tons of well-executed sex and violence. It is thus considerably more entertaining than most of the more critically-acclaimed recent African-American films.
[101m/18]

Nino Brown	Wesley Snipes
Scotty Appleton	Ice T
Gee Money	Allen Payne
Pookie	Chris Rock
Stone	Mario Van Peebles
Selina	Michael Michele
Duh Duh Duh Man	Bill Nunn

Showing *Scarface* [1983]

The News Boys ••• [1992]

Director: Kenny Ortega
Screenplay: Bob Tzudiker & Noni White

A rare, old-style musical based on the true story of a newspaper vendor's strike at the turn of the century. Cliché-ridden and unoriginal it may be, but this cross between *Oliver* and *Les Miserables* is nonetheless pretty enjoyable for those who like this sort of thing. There are far worse shows packing them in in the West End. Also known as *Newsies*.
[121m/PG]

Jack Kelly/Francis Sullivan	Christian Bale
David Jacobs	David Moscow
Les Jacobs	Luke Edwards
Joseph Pulitzer	Robert Duvall
Bryan Denton	Bill Pullman
Medda Larkson	Ann-Margret
Weasel	Michael Lerner
Racetrack	Max Casella

Newsies
SEE: The News Boys

New York Stories •• [1989]
Director: **Martin Scorsese, Francis Ford Coppola & Woody Allen**
Screenplay: **Richard Price, Francis Ford Coppola, Sofia Coppola & Woody Allen**

When teacher sets the three top boys the essay 'My story about New York', what did they come up with? Marty produced a leaden comedy about painter Nolte's obsession with young Arquette. Out of his hat Francis pulled not a rabbit, but a turkey of a children's story starring 'The Relative Who Would Kill Godfather III'. Then young Woody came up with a hilarious and delightful gem of a fantasy of a man haunted by his mother. Fast forward to Woody and see who got the gold star. **[125m/15]**

Life Lessons

Lionel Dobie	Nick Nolte
Phillip Fowler	Patrick O'Neal
Paulette	Rosanna Arquette
Gregory Stark	Steve Buscemi

Life without Zoe

Charlotte	Talia Shire
Claudio	Giancarlo Giannini
Zoe	Heather McComb

Oedipus Wrecks

Sheldon	Woody Allen
Lisa	Mia Farrow
Treva	Julie Kavner
Mother	Mae Questel

Blurb One City. Three Stories Tall.

Psst! Woody Allen originally wanted his co-directors to be his idols Ingmar Bergman and Federico Fellini
♦ Debbie Harry cameos in *Life Lessons* as 'Girl at Blind Alley' while Peter Gabriel appears as himself ♦ In the credits are 'stunt diners' ♦ The 'street musician' in *Life Without Zoe* is Carmine Coppola
♦ In *Oedipus Wrecks*, Mayor Ed Koch plays himself.

Next of Kin •• [1989]
Director: **John Irvin**
Screenplay: **Michael Jenning**

Fairly routine action pic has Swayze as the country cop who moves to Chicago with his younger brother Paxton, only for bro to be offed by the Mob. This creates a problem. Swayze can't act on his own as every buddy-cop-revenge movie has to have two people. So the third brother, Neeson, ups stumps and joins in. **[109m/15]**

Truman Gates	Patrick Swayze
Briar Gates	Liam Neeson
Joey Rosselini	Adam Baldwin
Jessie Gates	Helen Hunt

Also: Andreas Katsulas, Bill Paxton, Ben Stiller, Michael J. Pollard

Nicky and Gino •• [1988]
Director: **Robert M. Young**
Screenplay: **Alvin Sargent & Corey Blechman**

Hyper-sentimental story of two brothers. Liotta's a medical student who looks after his retarded twin Hulce but has been offered a residency in another town. There's a curiosity value in seeing Liotta in such an angelic role, but if you don't like people playing tunes on your heart strings, keep clear. Also known as *Dominick and Eugene*. **[109m/15]**

Eugene Luciano	Ray Liotta
Dominick Luciano	Tom Hulce
Jennifer Reston	Jamie Lee Curtis
Dr. Levinson	Robert Levine

Nico •• [1988]
Director: **Andrew Davis**
Screenplay: **Andrew Davis, Steven Pressfield & Ronald Shusett**

In this inauspicious debut for Seagal, he's a Chicago cop who uncovers a conspiracy massive enough to excite Oliver Stone. Although there's plenty of violent action, there's little of the humour that makes these films bearable. The wooden Seagal doesn't look as if he's going to be collect-

ing a Best Actor Oscar for some time yet.
Also known as *Above the Law*. **[99m/18]**

Nico Tosacani	Steven Seagal
Delores Jackson	Pam Grier
Zagon	Henry Silva

Also: Ron Dean, Daniel Faraldo, Sharon Stone

OOPS! Near the end of the pic, Seagal's black boots change to trainers as he leaps through the store window.

Night and the City •• [1992]

Director: **Irwin Winkler**
Screenplay: **Richard Price**

This disappointingly flat remake of the 1950 film has De Niro as a sleazy lawyer, so unsuccessful he has given up chasing ambulances in favour of the easier prospect of hearses. Inexplicably, he decides not to decamp to Florida with barmaid Lange but instead to stay around and risk having bits of his body slowly broken off for daring to set up a boxing match against the wishes of a big-time promoter. **[98m/15]**

Harry Fabian	Robert De Niro
Helen Nasseros	Jessica Lange
Phil Nasseros	Cliff Gorman
Boom Boom Grossman	Alan King
Al Grossman	Jack Warden
Peck	Eli Wallach

OOPS! If he's so poor, how come he has all that money to pay into the bank in the opening scene?

Psst! Screenwriter Price imagined the film set in the bar he used to frequent years earlier in New York. Coincidentally, before she was a successful actress, Lange was a waitress there and knew the person Price based her character on.

Nightbreed • [1990]

Director: **Clive Barker**
Screenplay: **Clive Barker**

A young man comes across a race of shape-shifting monsters able, with little effort, to transform themselves into a convincing impression of a dog's break-fast. **[102m/18]**

Aaron Boone	Craig Sheffer
Lori Winston	Anne Bobby
Dr. Decker	David Cronenberg

Quote 'Don't hold your breath till Oscar night.' [Cronenberg, on his performance.]

Psst! Desperate rejigging of the film after it was made meant that instead of having a starring role, Suzi Quatro was omitted from the movie entirely!

A Night in the Life of Jimmy Reardon

SEE: Jimmy Reardon

A Nightmare on Elm Street ••• [1984]

Director: **Wes Craven**
Screenplay: **Wes Craven**

A group of teens find they are being attacked in their dreams. Only young Nancy can save them, assuming she can stay awake. An ingenious new concept for a horror movie (then), with Freddy Krueger a genuinely sinister figure. The dream/reality trick is cunningly exploited, but the surprise ending fooled nobody. **[91m/18]**

Freddy Krueger	Robert Englund
Lt. Thompson	John Saxon
Nancy Thompson	Heather Langenkamp
Tina Grey	Amanda Wyss
Rod Lane	Nick Corri
Marge Thompson	Ronee Blakley
Glen Lantz	Johnny Depp

Quote 'God! I look 20 years old.'

Psst! This was Johnny Depp's screen debut.

A Nightmare on Elm Street Part 2: Freddy's Revenge • [1985]

Director: **Jack Sholder**
Screenplay: **David Chaskin**

Five years on, the man who never cuts his nails is back, haunting the dreams of another young teen, male this time. This sloppily plotted sequel sorely misses Wes Craven's touch.   [85m/18]

Freddy Krueger	Robert Englund
Jesse Walsh	Mark Patton
Lisa Poletti	Kim Myers
Grady	Robert Rusler

A Nightmare on Elm Street 3: Dream Warriors •• [1987]

Director: Chuck Russell
Screenplay: Wes Craven & Bruce Wagner

Nancy, now a shrink, comes back to help the Elm Street kids pool their dreams and take on Mr. K. Although better than the second thanks to Craven's script input, coherence is abandoned in favour of impressive special effects.

[97m/18]

Nancy Thompson	Heather Langenkamp
Kristen Parker	Patricia Arquette
Max	Larry Fishburne
Dr. Elizabeth Simms	Priscilla Pointer
Dr. Neil Goldman	Craig Wasson
Freddy Krueger	Robert Englund

Psst! Look out for cameo appearances from Zsa Zsa Gabor and Dick Cavett.

A Nightmare on Elm Street 4: The Dream Master •• [1988]

Director: Renny Harlin
Screenplay: Brian Helgeland & William Kotzwinkle

Mr. K, the Ever-Freddy batterer, lays into the unfortunate friends of his previous victims. All this kerfuffle can't be doing much for property values on Elm Street. Director Harlin, soon to move on to *Die Hard 2*, keeps it all moving briskly along.

[93m/18]

Freddy Krueger	Robert Englund
Joey	Rodney Eastman
Danny	Danny Hassel

A Nightmare on Elm Street 5: The Dream Child • [1989]

Director: Stephen Hopkins
Screenplay: Leslie Bohem

Freddy, bless his cotton socks, wants a child to carry on in his footsteps when daddy dies. If only he would. The sixth in the series is *Freddy's Dead: The Final Nightmare*. [90m/18]

Freddie Krueger	Robert Englund
Alice	Lisa Wilcox
Dan	Danny Hassel

The Night of the Comet ••• [1984]

Director: Thom Eberhardt
Screenplay: Thom Eberhardt

A couple of feather-brained California girls are all that's left after a comet wipes out the earth's population, if you don't count all those cannibal zombies roaming around. A very funny, low-budget, tongue-in-cheek, sci-fi movie. [95m/PG]

Regina	Catherine Mary Stewart
Samantha	Kelli Maroney
Hector	Robert Beltran
Carter	Geoffrey Lewis

Night of the Creeps •• [1986]

Director: Fred Dekker
Screenplay: Fred Dekker

A veteran policeman helps college students fight lethal zombies. A horror movie which manages slyly to parody the genre while also delivering the goods.

[88m/18]

Chris Romero	Jason Lively
J.C. Hooper	Steve Marshall
Cynthia Cronenberg	Jill Whitlow
Ray Cameron	Tom Atkins
Det. Landis	Wally Taylor

Quote 'I've good news and bad news, girls. The good news is your dates are here. The bad news is they're dead.'

Psst! The main characters' surnames are named after famous horror directors.

Night of the Living Dead •• [1990]

Director: **Tom Savini**
Screenplay: **George A. Romero**

A competent remake of George A. Romero's 1968 classic zombie chiller. It's in colour and has better effects but there's a whiff of putrefaction in the air. **[96m/18]**

Ben	Tony Todd
Barbara	Patricia Tallman
Harry	Tom Towles

Psst! It wasn't remade for artistic reasons but because the rights of the original were about to lapse and this was the only way Romero could regain control.

Night on Earth •• [1992]

Director: **Jim Jarmusch**
Screenplay: **Jim Jarmusch**

Had this Jarmusch bloke – never 'eard of 'im meself – in the back of me cab. Made a film about five taxi-rides in different countries. Saw it. Couple were funny, if you like that arthouse stuff, but the others bored me socks off. Anyway, where's London in all this, that's what I'd like to know? Best cabbies in the world, London. Get out the way, you gormless nurk! **[129m/15]**

Corky	Winona Ryder
Victoria Snelling	Gena Rowlands
Yo Yo	Giancarlo Esposito
Helmut	Armin Mueller-Stahl
Angela	Rosie Perez
Paris driver	Isaach De Bankolé
Blind woman	Béatrice Dalle

A Night on the Town

SEE: Adventures in Babysitting

Night Shift •• [1982]

Director: **Ron Howard**
Screenplay: **Lowell Ganz & Babaloo Mandel**

Shy, reserved Winkler gets a quiet night job at the morgue, only to find himself bamboozled by motormouth Keaton into setting up a prostitution business there. Although moderately entertaining, the excess of sentiment and paucity of the gags keep the laughter in check. It's also way, way too tasteful. **[106m/15]**

Chuck	Henry Winkler
Bill	Michael Keaton
Belinda	Shelley Long
Charlotte	Gina Hecht

Quote 'Is this a great country or what?'

Psst! This was Keaton's first film ◆ Keep your eyes peeled in the morgue party scene. There, playing the one-line part of 'Frat Boy #1', is a very young Kevin Costner ◆ The girl braining Winkler with the cookies is none other than the now infamous Shannen Doherty of *Beverly Hills 90210* fame.

The Night We Never Met ••• [1993]

Director: **Warren Leight**
Screenplay: **Warren Leight**

In this gentle and pleasing romantic comedy, Sciorra, Broderick and Anderson time-share an apartment in Greenwich village. Although never meeting, Sciorra falls for Broderick but a mix-up over days means that she throws herself at Anderson instead. **[99m]**

Sam Lester	Matthew Broderick
Ellen Holder	Annabella Sciorra
Brian McVeigh	Kevin Anderson
Pastel	Jeanne Tripplehorn

Psst! The patient in the chair obsessed with Sciorra is comic Garry Shandling, while Naomi Campbell crops up as a customer of Broderick's.

Nikita •• [1990]

Director: **Luc Besson**
Screenplay: **Luc Besson**

After being involved in a violent robbery, punky junkie Parillaud is turned into a Government hitperson. Initially very exciting, the movie goes nowhere, uncertain if it's an art film or a shoot-'em-up. The mini-skirted Parillaud is tremendous, but you might as well look at the wonderful poster for a couple of hours. Also known as *La Femme Nikita*. Remade as *Assassin*. [116m/18]

Nikita	Anne Parillaud
Marco	Jean-Hugues Anglade
Bob	Tcheky Karyo
Amande	Jeanne Moreau

9¹/₂ Weeks •• [1986]

Director: Adrian Lyne
Screenplay: Patricia Louisianna Knop, Zalman King & Sarah Kernochan

It only *seems* that long. Even in the sexier European version, this examination of an obsessive relationship between Basinger and Rourke is tiresome stuff. For once 'all mouth and no trousers' is a perfectly apt description. Style is everything, with the hi-fi equipment getting more attention from the camera than Basinger. Some of the much-touted sex scenes raise nothing more than a snigger. Surprisingly, perhaps, the film appears more popular with women than men. [116m/18]

John	Mickey Rourke
Elizabeth	Kim Basinger
Molly	Margaret Whitton
Harvey	David Margulies

Quote 'I became an actress in my own eyes...I was electrically disturbed after it was over; marbles were rolling off the table.' [Basinger]

OOPS! After Rourke buys her a scarf in the market, it vanishes from her shoulders as they walk, as does the shopping bag.

Psst! Basinger and Rourke didn't get on. He didn't think she was sexy enough for the part and she thought necking him was like kissing an ashtray ✦ Cut by the American distributor for being too steamy, it was far more popular abroad, where it was shown complete ✦ Worthing Council wouldn't let the film be shown until the councillors had a private screening to check if it was decent. In its place was offered *Body Lust, Best Bit of Crumpet in Denmark* ✦ The credits include a 'physical fitness consultant'.

976-EVIL •• [1988]

Director: Robert Englund
Screenplay: Rhet Topham & Brian Helgeland

Even the Devil's got a freephone number now. A teen dials it and rather wishes he hadn't. Robert Englund, better known as Freddie Krueger, does a reasonable directorial job, but perhaps shouldn't give up the day job just yet. [97m/18]

"Hoax" Arthur Wilmoth	Stephen Geoffreys
Aunt Lucy	Sandy Dennis
Spike	Patrick O'Bryan
Marty	Jim Metzler

1984 •• [1984]

Director: Michael Radford
Screenplay: Michael Radford

This workmanlike but uninspiring transfer of Orwell's book came out in the same year as the title. Despite, or perhaps because of, the gruesome scenes with Burton as the torturer, you end up feeling every bit as miserable and cowed as the citizens of Oceania under Big Brother. [120m/15]

Winston Smith	John Hurt
O'Brien	Richard Burton
Julia	Suzanna Hamilton
Carrington	Cyril Cusack

Blurb The Film Of The Year.

OOPS! Watch Hurt's mouth when Burton is torturing him. Almost straight after a tooth's pulled out, it magically regrows.

Psst! This was Richard Burton's last film.

19/19 • [1985]

Director: Hugh Brody
Screenplay: Hugh Brody & Michael Ignatieff

The last two living patients of Freud meet in 1970 and chew the fat. Don't be fooled. It's nothing like as interesting as it sounds! [99m/15]

Alexander	Paul Scofield
Sophie	Maria Schell
Voice of Sigmund Freud	Frank Finlay

1969 •• [1988]

Director: Ernest Thompson
Screenplay: Ernest Thompson

Downey and Sutherland are a couple of teenagers trying to stay out of the Army and get laid while Richard Nixon is being made President and men are landing on the moon. The usual rebellious teenager stuff is smothered in a layer of unconvincing 60's nostalgia. **[96m/15]**

Ralph	Robert Downey Jr.
Scott	Kiefer Sutherland
Cliff	Bruce Dern
Jessie	Mariette Hartley
Beth	Winona Ryder
Ev	Joanna Cassidy

Ninja III – The Domination •• [1984]

Director: Sam Firstenberg
Screenplay: James R. Silke

If you've made it through *Ninja I & II*, perhaps you're in the right mood for the third, in which Dickey is occasionally taken over by the spirit of a dead ninja. **[95m/18]**

Christie	Lucinda Dickey
Secord	Jordan Bennett
Yamada	Sho Kosugi

Nobody's Fool •• [1986]

Director: Evelyn Purcell
Screenplay: Beth Henley

Arquette's a wacky waitress who – shock horror – is an unmarried mother. When a troupe of strolling players comes to town, she thinks she's found Mr. Right in Roberts. An odd, but generally pleasing, romantic comedy. **[107m/15]**

Cassie	Rosanna Arquette
Riley	Eric Roberts
Pat	Mare Winningham

Also: Jim Youngs, Louise Fletcher, Gwen Welles, Stephen Tobolowsky

No Holds Barred • [1989]

Director: Thomas J. Wright
Screenplay: Dennis Hackin

This is a pretty weak vehicle for the incredible Hulk, but he still has trouble holding it up. Unfortunately, although it's about wrestling, it actually requires him to act. Hogan moved onto much safer ground when he embraced comedy, squeezing the life out of that instead. **[90m/15]**

Rip	Hulk Hogan
Brell	Kurt Fuller
Samantha Moore	Joan Severance

Noises Off ••• [1992]

Director: Peter Bogdanovich
Screenplay: Marty Kaplan

A remarkably funny adaptation of Michael Frayn's hilarious farce about the ructions within a second-rate touring company. Despite the artificiality of seeing theatre jokes on screen and a trite Hollywood ending, there are plenty of belly laughs to be had as this splendid ensemble cast go through their paces. As with all comedies, best not watched alone. **[104m/15]**

Dotty Otley/Mrs. Clackett	Carol Burnett
Lloyd Fellowes	Michael Caine
Selsdon Mowbray/Burglar	Denholm Elliott
Poppy Taylor	Julie Hagerty
Belinda Blair/Flavia Brent	Marilu Henner
Tim Allgood	Mark Linn-Baker
Frederick Dallas/Philip	Christopher Reeve
Brooke Ashton/Vicki	Nicollette Sheridan

Quote 'Is there anything wrong with your seat?' – 'Yes, it's facing the stage.'

No Man's Land •• [1987]

Director: Peter Werner
Screenplay: Dick Wolf

Once again an undercover cop finds a life of crime more attractive than pounding the beat, with Sweeney's head turned by car thief Sheen and his lifestyle. Middle of the road stuff. **[105m/15]**

Benjy Taylor	D.B. Sweeney
Ted Varrick	Charlie Sheen
Ann Varrick	Lara Harris
Lieut. Vincent Bracey	Randy Quaid

Also: Bill Duke, R.D. Call, Arlen Dean Snyder, M. Emmet Walsh

No Mercy •• [1986]

Director: **Richard Pearce**
Screenplay: **James Carabatsos**

Chicago policeman Gere heads for Louisiana to track down his partner's killer. There he falls in love with Basinger, who's the property of the villain. Basinger pouts, Gere smoulders, the bayous steam. You'd find more passion on a wet January night in Penge. In this unexciting thriller, it's the viewer who's given no mercy. **[108m/18]**

Eddie Jillette	Richard Gere
Michel Duval	Kim Basinger
Losado	Jeroen Krabbé
Capt. Stemkowski	George Dzundza

OOPS! Keep an eye on Basinger's face when she gets it dirty. Now you see it, now you don't. Now you see it, now you don't.

The North
SEE: El Norte

No Surrender •• [1986]

Director: **Peter Smith**
Screenplay: **Alan Bleasdale**

Catholics and Protestants don't always see eye to eye when a double booking crams them together in a Liverpool nightclub to welcome in the New Year. This allegory about Northern Ireland is far too draggy and self-conscious to be either very entertaining or illuminating. As always, the much-missed McAnally steals the show. **[100m/15]**

Paddy Burke	James Ellis
Billy McRacken	Ray McAnally
Bernard	Bernard Hill
Cheryl	Joanne Whalley-Kilmer

Psst! Elvis Costello appears in a cameo.

Not for Publication •• [1984]

Director: **Paul Bartel**
Screenplay: **John Meyer & Paul Bartel**

Oddball comedy from Bartel, responsible for *Eating Raoul*, has Allen as a reporter on a tabloid scandal paper moonlighting as the Mayor's assistant at election time. Great off-the-wall stuff for those who know and love Bartel's oeuvre. **[87m/15]**

Lois	Nancy Allen
Barry	David Naughton
Mayor Franklyn	Laurence Luckinbill

Nothing But Trouble • [1991]

Director: **Dan Aykroyd**
Screenplay: **Dan Aykroyd**

It should be a criminal offence to inflict movies like this on the public. Candy, Chase, Moore and Aykroyd are at their very worst in this lamentable Aykroyd-directed clunker about a Gothic town where the penalty for speeding is death at the hands of over-made-up corpses. The entire quartet should be locked in a screening-room for 24 hours and forced to watch this tripe again and again. **[94m/12]**

Chris Thorne	Chevy Chase
J.P. Valkenheiser/Bobo	Dan Aykroyd
Sheriff Purda/Eldona	John Candy
Diane Lightson	Demi Moore

Nothing in Common •• [1986]

Director: **Garry Marshall**
Screenplay: **Rick Podell & Michael Preminger**

Although initially a pretty funny satire on the ad business, when adman Hanks is forced to care for his sick father Gleason, the laughs dry up. The serious stuff isn't as sentimental as it might be, but it doesn't half slow everything down. **[118m/15]**

David Basner	Tom Hanks
Max Basner	Jackie Gleason
Lorraine Basner	Eva Marie Saint
Charlie Gargas	Hector Elizondo

Psst! This was the last film role for Jackie Gleason, most famous for the TV sitcom *The Honeymooners*.

Not Quite Jerusalem •• [1985]

Director: **Lewis Gilbert**
Screenplay: **Paul Kember**

American Robards falls for Israeli Pacula while working on a kibbutz. There's nothing more to it than that really, bar a highly silly Arab attack to inject a bit of drama and stop the audience falling asleep. Also known, sensibly, as *Not Quite Paradise*. [114m/15]

Mike	Sam Robards
Gila	Joanna Pacula
Rothwell T. Schwarz	Todd Graff
Pete	Kevin McNally

Not Quite Paradise

SEE: **Not Quite Jerusalem**

Not Without My Daughter ••
[1991]

Director: **Brian Gilbert**
Screenplay: **David W. Rintels**

Iranian doctor Molina takes his American wife and child with him back to Iran and then announces that he'd rather live in a primitive, fundamentalist, isolated nation than with Sally Field in the West. Although his attitude's understandable, we have to follow the over-powering Field in this true-life story as she plans an escape with her daughter. In the dark, we plan our own escape. [115m/12]

Betty Mahmoody	Sally Field
Moody	Alfred Molina
Mahtob	Sheila Rosenthal
Houssein	Roshan Seth

No Way Out ••• [1987]

Director: **Roger Donaldson**
Screenplay: **Robert Garland**

Tense and racy thriller has Pentagon naval officer Costner sharing lover Young with Secretary of Defence Hackman, even in the back of his limousine. When Hackman kills her in a fit of jealousy, Costner is put in charge of the investigation. Like all good thrillers, the tension is steadily racked up notch by notch. Although not always entirely plausible, Young is excellent compensation, never sexier than here. Others hated the ending. I think it's great. [114m/15]

Tom Farrell	Kevin Costner
David Brice	Gene Hackman
Susan Atwell	Sean Young
Scott Pritchard	Will Patton
Senator Duvall	Howard Duff
Sam Hesselman	George Dzundza
Major Donovan	Jason Bernard
Nina Beka	Iman

Psst! The project was in 'turnaround', indicating nobody wanted to make it, when Costner came across it and championed its cause ♦ The movie is a remake, although not a very close one, of the 1948 *The Big Clock*, starring Charles Laughton ♦ Apparently limousine hire companies saw a noticeable pick-up in business after the film!

Nuns on the Run •• [1990]

Director: **Jonathan Lynn**
Screenplay: **Jonathan Lynn**

...Or *Some Like It Lukewarm*. Two crooks on the run from their boss get into the abbey habit, taking refuge in a convent where there's plenty of flogging of stereotypes. It's hard not to find Coltrane in drag funny, but this amiable film's little more than a timewaster. [95m/12]

Brian Hope	Eric Idle
Charlie McManus	Robbie Coltrane
Faith	Camille Coduri
Sister Superior	Janet Suzman

Nuts •• [1987]

Director: **Martin Ritt**
Screenplay: **Tom Topor, Darryl Ponicsan & Alvin Sargent**

...And Nuts to you. High-class hooker Streisand is arrested for murdering a client. She wants to stand trial even though everyone else thinks she's barking mad and should be put in the nuthouse. Dreyfuss is the poor sod who not only has to defend her, but also gets the full force of nearly two hours of Streisand's near-hysterical over-acting. Credibility isn't helped by the fact that the dead guy is Leslie Nielsen in his last straight film part before *Naked Gun*.

[116m/18]

Claudia Draper	Barbra Streisand
Aaron Levinsky	Richard Dreyfuss
Rose Kirk	Maureen Stapleton
Arthur Kirk	Karl Malden
Dr. Herbert A. Morrison	Eli Wallach

Psst! To research her role, Streisand paid a visit to a brothel in LA. Apparently one businessman said to the madam: 'Okay, so how much do you want for the Barbra Streisand lookalike?' Excuses were made ♦ With *Nuts* Streisand became the first woman paid $5m for a film.

O

The Object of Beauty •• [1991]

Director: Michael Lindsay-Hogg
Screenplay: Michael Lindsay-Hogg

Malkovich and MacDowell are the couple living beyond their means in a swank London hotel. They decide to sell their Henry Moore figurine, only to discover it's been swiped. This sporadically amusing comedy is made rather irritating by the way in which the actors clearly think they're being very funny.

[103m/15]

Jake Bartholomew	John Malkovich
Tina Leslie Barth. Oates	Andie MacDowell
Mr. Mercer	Joss Ackland
Joan	Lolita Davidovich

Also: Rudi Davies, Bill Paterson, Ricci Harnett, Peter Riegert, Roger Lloyd Pack

Octopussy ••• [1983]

Director: John Glen
Screenplay: George Macdonald Fraser

The plot's ludicrous, all about a Russian general trying to start World War III by himself, but who cares? It's still a pretty droll, action-packed outing for Bond, culminating in one of those wonderful disarming-the-device races in which the clock gets slower and slower as zero approaches, much like the train indicators on the London Underground. **[130m/PG]**

James Bond	Roger Moore
Octopussy	Maud Adams
Kamal	Louis Jourdan
Magda	Kristina Wayborn
Gobinda	Kabir Bedi
Orlov	Steven Berkoff
Q	Desmond Llewelyn
M	Robert Brown
Gogol	Walter Gotell
Minister of Defence	Geoffrey Keen

Psst! The film was in competition with the rival *Never Say Never Again* starring Connery ♦ Tennis star Vijay Amritraj appears as himself ♦ Maud Adams, here a villain, was the love interest 9 years earlier in *The Man With the Golden Gun*.

Off and Running • [1992]

Director: Edward Bianchi
Screenplay: Mitch Glazer

Cyndi Lauper has another go at becoming a movie star with this silly caper movie. There are fish with more talent in their fingers... **[90m/12]**

Cyd Morse	Cyndi Lauper
Jack Cornett	David Keith
Pompey	Johnny Pinto

An Officer and a Gentleman •• [1982]

Director: Taylor Hackford
Screenplay: Douglas Day Stewart

An officer, maybe. But a *gentleman?* Gere's the lad from the slums who wants to be a naval cadet. But first he has to endure training under bully Gossett. Mild consolation comes from local girl Winger. The plot is as old as the Hollywood sign itself and there's something rather disquieting about Winger's only means of escape being on Gere's coat-tails. Still, there are compensations, not least of them Gossett and his wonderful performance as the martinet.

[124m/15]

Zack Mayo	Richard Gere
Paula Pokrifki	Debra Winger
Sgt. Emil Foley	Louis Gossett Jr.
Sid Worley	David Keith
Lynette Pomeroy	Lisa Blount
Byron Mayo	Robert Loggia
Casey	Lisa Eilbacher
Emiliano Serra	Tony Plana
Topper Daniels	David Caruso
Esther Pokrifki	Grace Zabriskie

Oscars Louis Gossett Jr.

Blurb It'll Lift You Up Where You Belong.

Quote 'So there I am, on top of him, with tears coming out of my eyes and people thinking it's because I'm so moved, when actually I'm really crying because I'm so unhappy.' [Winger]

Psst! The studio had little faith in the movie and spent very little promoting it. Word of mouth made it into a hit ◆ The smouldering looks between Gere and Winger are not the result of off-screen attraction. They are said to have loathed each other [see above] ◆ Richard Gere's role was apparently written with John Denver in mind ◆ Writer Stewart had been through the school himself, and survived ◆ 'On the sand [says the script] Lynette's fingers work at the gold buttons on Sid's tunic while Sid's fingers grope for the zipper that would unlock all the mysteries...'

Off Limits
SEE: Saigon

Of Mice and Men ••• [1992]

Director: **Gary Sinise**
Screenplay: **Horton Foote**

Sinise does Steinbeck proud with this remake, himself playing George, the farm labourer encumbered in the Depression by his retarded and occasionally violent friend Lenny. We just know that tragedy is in the offing when bored, sultry Fenn starts getting Lenny hot under the collar, but it's no less shocking when it arrives. This is a well-crafted and beautifully photographed film.

[110m/PG]

Lennie	John Malkovich
George	Gary Sinise
Candy	Ray Walston
Curley	Casey Siemaszko
Curley's wife	Sherilyn Fenn

Quote 'He's a nice fellow. A guy don't need no sense to be a nice fellow.'

Psst! Malkovich wore platforms while filming to give him the necessary height ◆ Steinbeck might be horrified to discover that wheat fields where he set his novel are now areas growing aubergines and miniature artichokes ◆ Isn't it odd that freightcars always have their doors conveniently open so that people can hop on and off with impunity?

Old Gringo •• [1989]

Director: **Luis Puenzo**
Screenplay: **Aida Bortnik & Luis Puenzo**

No wonder Fonda gave up films after striving so long to drag this disappointing Mexican epic to the screen. She plays a spinster who gets caught up with Pancho Villa's revolution and discovers her own sexuality along the way. It's a pretty dull revolution, hardly worth waking Gregory Peck up for.

[119m/15]

Harriet Winslow	Jane Fonda
Ambrose Bierce	Gregory Peck
Tomas Arroyo	Jimmy Smits
Col. Frutos Garcia	Patricio Contreras

Oliver and Company •• [1988]

Director: George Scribner
Screenplay: Jim Cox & Others

This updating of *Oliver Twist*, with cats and dogs in modern New York, is middle of the road Disney. Passable, but hardly a classic. **[74m/U]**

Oliver	Joey Lawrence
Dodger	Billy Joel
Tito	Cheech Marin
Einstein	Richard Mulligan
Rita	Sheryl Lee Ralph
Fagin	Dom DeLuise
Bill Sykes	Robert Loggia
Georgette	Bette Midler

Omen IV: The Awakening • [1991]

Director: Jorge Montesi & Dominique Othenin-Gerard
Screenplay: Brian Taggert

A couple adopt a little girl who turns out to be possessed. Major root canal work would be preferable to this tired sequel of a sequel of a sequel. **[89m/15]**

Karen York	Faye Grant
Gene York	Michael Woods
Earl Knight	Michael Lerner

Once upon a Crime • [1992]

Director: Eugene Levy
Screenplay: Charles Shyer, Nancy Myers & Steve Kluger

The word 'abysmal' doesn't even begin to describe the sheer awfulness and vacuity of this designed-by-committee Euro-comedy starring four actors known more for their ability to choose the wrong movies than anything else. [See Rose's Rule #2] **[94m/PG]**

Augie Morosco	John Candy
Neil Schwary	James Belushi
Marilyn Schwary	Cybill Shepherd
Phoebe	Sean Young

Once Upon a Time in America •••• [1984]

Director: Sergio Leone
Screenplay: Sergio Leone, Leonardo Benvenuti, Piero De Bernardi, Enrico Medioli, Franco Arcalli & Franco Ferrini

The story of a group of Jewish gangsters, known as the Kosher Nostra, in 20's and 30's New York. Leone's best film is a corrective to the sentimentality of *The Godfather*. Brutal, ambitious, even affectionate, it's shot through with Hollywood-fed fantasies of the American Dream and its betrayal by Prohibition's institutionalisation of crime. Although the plot isn't always plausible, the mood and action is terrific, as is the acting. Avoid any of the truncated versions of the film that are around. **[228m/18]**

Noodles	Robert De Niro
Max	James Woods
Deborah	Elizabeth McGovern
Jimmy O'Donnell	Treat Williams
Carol	Tuesday Weld
Joe	Burt Young
Frankie	Joe Pesci
Police Chief Aiello	Danny Aiello
Cockeye	William Forsythe
Young Deborah	Jennifer Connelly

Quote 'Age cannot wither me, Noodles.'

One False Move ••• [1992]

Director: Carl Franklin
Screenplay: Billy Bob Thornton & Tom Epperson

Despite a nastily violent and untypical opening sequence, this is a splendid, low-budget thriller. Paxton's small-town sheriff eager as a puppy when he learns that a trio of tough LA murderers is headed his way. Reminiscent of many Westerns, the characters are wonderfully fleshed out. It's one of those movies that draws you in, bit by bit, like a hooked fish. **[105m/18]**

Dale 'Hurricane' Dixon	Bill Paxton
Fantasia/Lila	Cynda Williams

Ray Malcolm	Billy Bob Thornton
Pluto	Michael Beach
Dud Cole	Jim Metzler
McFeely	Earl Billings

Psst! During filming Williams and Thornton fell in love, marrying shortly afterwards.

One from the Heart •• [1982]

Director: **Francis Ford Coppola**
Screenplay: **Armyan Bernstein & Francis Ford Coppola**

Certainly one from Coppola's heart. But strip away the extraordinary style and lavish sets he brought to the project and you're left with just another romantic comedy with a couple splitting up, seeing other people and then getting back together again. Brave, but foolhardy. **[101m/15]**

Hank	Frederic Forrest
Frannie	Teri Garr
Ray	Raul Julia
Leila	Nastassja Kinski
Maggie	Lainie Kazan
Moe	Harry Dean Stanton

Psst! This was the first film for Coppola's Zoetrope studios, his $20m–plus attempt to break away from the Hollywood studios with his own outfit. It was not a success and his new studio had to put out the For Sale sign • Look out for Rebecca DeMornay making her screen debut in the restaurant with the memorable line: 'Excuse me, I think those are my waffles.' • As always, there are a few other Coppolas around. Carmine, the composer, and Italia are the 'couple in elevator'.

One Woman or Two • [1985]

Director: **Daniel Vigne**
Screenplay: **Daniel Vigne & Elisabeth Rappeneau**

...Frankly, if the two women are Sigourney Weaver and sexologist Dr. Ruth Westheimer, then just the one, please. Depardieu is the obsessed palaeontologist trying to find France's first woman. Let's make no bones about it, this unfunny rubbish smells and should be

re-buried fast. Worth watching only for the bizarre voices used to dub Weaver and Depardieu. **[97m/PG]**

Julien Chayssac	Gérard Depardieu
Jessica Fitzgerald	Sigourney Weaver
Mrs. Heffner	Dr. Ruth Westheimer

Only the Lonely ••• [1991]

Director: **Chris Columbus**
Screenplay: **Chris Columbus**

Lonely Candy falls in love with Sheedy. The only problem is, he's still living with his mother. This sentimental comedy from *Home Alone* director Columbus shows Candy to be a surprisingly good actor. Old hat maybe, but nonetheless charmingly done. **[104m/12]**

Danny Muldoon	John Candy
Rose Muldoon	Maureen O'Hara
Theresa Luna	Ally Sheedy
Nick	Anthony Quinn
Sal	James Belushi
Patrick Muldoon	Kevin Dunn
Doyle	Milo O'Shea
Spats	Bert Remsen

Psst! Macaulay Culkin pops in for a quick cameo as Billy. A cameo? Aged 11? Good grief • This was Maureen O'Hara's first film in almost twenty years.

Ordeal by Innocence • [1985]

Director: **Desmond Davis**
Screenplay: **Alexander Stuart**

...And the verdict of this court is that you be taken from here to a place of entertainment and that you there be forced to watch bad Agatha Christie adaptations. Sutherland's the man returning to Britain and realising that he could have stopped an innocent man being hanged. The chap probably would have strung himself up if he'd had to sit through this deathly whodunnit. **[87m/15]**

Arthur Calgary	Donald Sutherland
Rachel Calgary	Faye Dunaway
Leo Argyle	Christopher Plummer

Also: Sarah Miles, Ian McShane, Diana Quick, Annette Crosbie

Order of Death • [1983]

Director: Roberto Faenza
Screenplay: Ennio De Concini, Roberto Faenza & Hugh Fleetwood

Completely weird, English-language, Italian psychological thriller with Keitel the New York cop with a peculiar relationship with the weird Lydon and on the hunt for a killer. Almost bad enough to be compulsive. Also known as *Corrupt*.

[101m/18]

Lt. Fred O'Connor ....Harvey Keitel
Leo Smith..John Lydon
Margaret Smith..........................Sylvia Sidney

Psst! Lydon was better known as Johnny Rotten of the Sex Pistols.

Orlando ••• [1993]

Director: Sally Potter
Screenplay: Sally Potter

Virginia Woolf's fantasy of an Elizabethan nobleman who crosses oceans, centuries – even gender – in pursuit of love and identity. An occasionally awkward, but generally intriguing art movie with the usual ravishing visuals and rather more wit and pace than usual. [93m/PG]

Orlando.....................................Tilda Swinton
Shelmerdine ....Billy Zane
Archduke Harry ....John Wood
The Khan................................Lothaire Bluteau

Quote 'She had lived for 400 years and scarcely aged a day. Because this was England, everyone pretended not to notice.'

Psst! Among the faces popping up are those of Ned Sherrin, Quentin *Naked Civil Servant* Crisp (as Queen Elizabeth I) and Jimmy Somerville (as a singing angel).

Orphans ••• [1987]

Director: Alan J. Pakula
Screenplay: Lyle Kessler

Sneak thief Modine picks the wrong person when he brings wealthy drunk Finney home to his brother Anderson, hoping to hold him for ransom. It isn't long before the tables are turned and Finney's telling the boys what to do. Finney is mesmerising in this stagey but wonderful version of Kessler's play. [115m/15]

Harold ....Albert Finney
Treat....................................Matthew Modine
Phillip ....Kevin Anderson
Barney...John Kellogg

Oscar •• [1991]

Director: John Landis
Screenplay: Michael Barrie & Jim Mulholland

A real curiosity. A combination of Damon Runyon and French farce, this broad comedy has slamming doors, matching bags, mistaken identities and all the other essential elements of farce. Stallone's surprisingly good as the gangster trying to go straight, as is the future star Tomei as his daughter. But despite the odd wonderful laugh, it's ultimately disappointing. [110m/PG]

Angelo "Snaps" Provolone ..Sylvester Stallone
Sofia Provolone...........................Ornella Muti
Father Clemente..........................Don Ameche
Aldo ....Peter Riegert
Anthony Rossano.....................Vincent Spano
Dr. Poole..Tim Curry
Also: Chazz Palminteri, Richard Romanus, Kurtwood Smith, Joycelyn O'Brien, Marisa Tomei

Psst! Although he usually has other directors do guest cameos in his films, Landis seems just as keen to tell us those who aren't in. Here the 'Face on the cutting room floor' is Joe Dante, while in *Coming to America* it was Jim Abrahams • The unconvincing death-bed scene at the opening is played by Kirk Douglas as Stallone's dad. His aunt is Yvonne de Carlo, Lily Munster from the TV series. Eddie Bracken also cameos. Oscar is played by writer Mulholland • The set was destroyed in a big fire at Universal at the end of 1990. Also burnt in the blaze were thoses for *Back to the Future* and *The Sting* • The credits include two pigeon wranglers.

The Osterman Weekend •• [1983]

Director: Sam Peckinpah
Screenplay: Alan Sharp

A chatshow host has a group of friends round for the weekend but the CIA has its own plans for the party. Being a Peckinpah movie, it isn't long before we're into slow-motion violence. The story was pretty hackneyed even ten years ago and the suspicion lurks that Sam's sending the whole thing up. When the talk stops and the mayhem begins, it becomes exciting enough to regret that this was his last film. [102m/18]

Tanner	Rutger Hauer
Fassett	John Hurt
Osterman	Craig T. Nelson
Tremayne	Dennis Hopper
Cardone	Chris Sarandon
Danforth	Burt Lancaster

Quote 'I'm getting so fond of the characters in this story, I'd like to keep them alive.' [Peckinpah]

Other People's Money •• [1991]

Director: Norman Jewison
Screenplay: Alvin Sargent

DeVito is on good form as Larry the Liquidator, a corporate raider targeting a sleepy New England firm run by Peck. Luckily, Peck's daughter, the gorgeous Miller, just happens to be a top-notch lawyer, too. A slightly soft satire on the greed of the 80s has been softened still further. Despite a few laughs, it doesn't really get going and its trite message, affirming old-style values, seems rather dated already. [101m/15]

Lawrence Garfield	Danny DeVito
Andrew Jorgenson	Gregory Peck
Kate Sullivan	Penelope Ann Miller
Bea Sullivan	Piper Laurie

Quote 'I take from the rich and I give to the middle-class...well, the upper middle-class.'

Psst! Peck got cross that the ending was toned down in response to test screenings: 'It absolutely takes the backbone out of everything. You get pictures that aren't going to make anybody mad, certainly not challenge anybody's intelligence...They've tried to turn motion picture-making into an industry like making shoes and sausage.'

Out Cold •• [1989]

Director: Malcolm Mowbray
Screenplay: Leonard Glasser & George Malko

Butcher Lithgow panics on discovering his partner in the freezer, and tries, with Garr's help, to dispose of the body. Unfortunately, somebody left the script of this black comedy in the freezer along with the corpse and it still hasn't defrosted by the time the end credits come up. [89m/15]

Dave Geary	John Lithgow
Sunny Cannald	Teri Garr
Lester Atlas	Randy Quaid
Ernie Cannald	Bruce McGill

Out for Justice •• [1991]

Director: John Flynn
Screenplay: David Lee Henry

Brooklyn cop Seagal discovers that the local crime boss is his old mate from the school playground. At least the action is slick and fast-paced enough to prevent too close an examination of Seagal's acting or screen charisma. [91m/18]

Gino Felino	Steven Seagal
Richie	William Forsythe
Ronnie	Jerry Orbach
Vicky	Jo Champa

Out of Africa ••• [1985]

Director: Sydney Pollack
Screenplay: Kurt Luedtke

'I haard a faaarm in Aaafreekar.' Overlong and slight of plot, this story of writer Karen Blixen tiring of boorish husband Brandauer and falling for dashing hunter Redford is still exquisitely shot and acted. A little imagination is needed to believe that Redford is English, but perhaps it's better than him trying an accent and getting it wrong.   **[161m/PG]**

Karen...Meryl Streep
Denys ....Robert Redford
Bror...........................Klaus Maria Brandauer
Berkeley ....Michael Kitchen
Farah.......................................Malick Bowens
Kamanto ....Joseph Thiaka
Also: Suzanna Hamilton, Rachel Kempson, Michael Gough, Graham Crowden, Leslie Phillips, Shane Rimmer

Oscars Best Picture, Best Director, Best Screenplay

Quote 'You should have asked permission.' – 'I did. She said yes.' [Bror and Denys arguing over Karen] ✦ 'Robert Redford's the very best kisser I ever met.' [Streep]

OOPS! If you're getting just the teensiest bit bored, try counting the fluctuating oranges when they're having a picnic.

Psst! The film-makers had to cope with restrictions making it illegal to touch or interfere with any wild animal. Five trained lions were imported from California, as there were none in Africa ✦ In the view of the coffee plantation flowering, the blooms are actually dollops of shaving foam.

Out of the Dark ••   [1989]

Director: **Michael Schroeder**
Screenplay: **J. Gregory de Felice & Zane W. Levitt**

The girls working for a Hollywood phone sex company are being cut down systematically by a vicious murderer in a clown's mask. This rather steamy, violent thriller does have some flashes of dark humour to relieve the gloom.   **[89m/18]**

Kevin.......................................Cameron Dye
Ruth ....Karen Black
Stringer..Bud Cort
Also: Lynn Danielson, Karen Witter, Starr Andreeff, Tracey Walter, Geoffrey Lewis, Paul Bartel, Tab Hunter, Divine

Psst! This was heavily cut by the censor, with a good deal of violence taken out as well as most of the conversation of the phone sex girls.

Outrageous Fortune ••   [1987]

Director: **Arthur Hiller**
Screenplay: **Leslie Dixon**

Prissy Long and foul-mouthed Midler discover they have some things in common: they don't like each other, they both shared the same foreign-spy lover and they're both unfunny. Just because two women, rather than two men, have been paired in a bad buddy comedy is no reason to think it's amusing. Some people will love Midler and Long together in a film. For others it will be their worst nightmare come true.   **[100m/15]**

Sandy ....Bette Midler
Lauren ....Shelley Long
Michael.......................................Peter Coyote
Stanislov Korzenowski..............Robert Prosky

OOPS! When the money is thrown to the winds at the end, it's gathered up by the local Indians. Yet some of them seem to have money sprouting from their pockets even before it's thrown, presumably from an earlier take.

The Outsiders ••   [1983]

Director: **Francis Ford Coppola**
Screenplay: **Kathleen Knutson Rowell**

Coppola's attempt to do an arty teen-flick, all about the gang rivalry between the high-born 'Socs' and the low-born greasers. Pretty pictures can't disguise the fact that we've seen it umpteen times before. What can't be faulted is Coppola's extraordinary ability to pick so many actors who would become such big names over the next few years.   **[91m/PG]**

Dallas Winston ....Matt Dillon
Johnny Cade............................Ralph Macchio
Ponyboy Curtis.................C. Thomas Howell
Darrel Curtis ....Patrick Swayze
Sodapop Curtis ....Rob Lowe
Two-Bit Matthews...................Emilio Estevez
Steve Randle.................................Tom Cruise
Also: Diane Lane, Darren Dalton, Michelle Meyrink, Gailard Sartain, Tom Waits

Psst! To get into his part, Cruise barely washed during the nine weeks of filming, something that didn't endear him to his fellow actors ♦ The novel was the first written by Susie Hinton, then aged 17. She appears in a cameo as a nurse.

Overboard •••   [1987]

Director: **Garry Marshall**
Screenplay: **Leslie Dixon**

Hawn is an heiress suffering from amnesia who is taken advantage of by blue-collar single father Russell, who uses her to help keep his mob of kids in order. Despite its predictability, it's good-natured fun along *Taming of the Shrew* lines, with Hawn a good deal less painful than usual.   **[112m/PG]**

Joanna/Annie	Goldie Hawn
Dean Proffitt	Kurt Russell
Grant Stayton III	Edward Herrmann
Edith Mintz	Katherine Helmond
Billy Pratt	Michael Hagerty
Andrew	Roddy McDowall

Psst! Russell and Hawn are long-standing partners in real-life ♦ There are cameos from director Garry Marshall and Hector Elizondo, the hotel manager in Marshall's *Pretty Woman*, here captaining a rubbish barge.

Over Her Dead Body ••   [1991]

Director: **Maurice Phillips**
Screenplay: **Maurice Phillips**

A woman who accidentally kills her sister has trouble disposing of the body. One of a slew of body-disposal comedies that came out in quick succession, this is no funnier than the others, despite the efforts star and director made to get it away from the studio and cut it the way *they* wanted. Also known as *Enid is Sleeping*.   **[101m/15]**

June	Elizabeth Perkins
Harry	Judge Reinhold
Floyd	Jeffrey Jones

Also: Maureen Mueller, Rhea Perlman, Brion James, Michael J. Pollard

Psst! Rhea Perlman, Carla from *Cheers*, appears as Mavis.

Over the Brooklyn Bridge •   [1984]

Director: **Menahem Golan**
Screenplay: **Arnold Somkin**

Dull romantic comedy with Gould the Jewish owner of a café in Brooklyn who wants to open a restaurant in Manhattan. Throughout, you get the impression that they belatedly discovered a film which should have been released in the 60s.

[107m/15]

Alby	Elliott Gould
Elizabeth	Margot Hemingway
Uncle Ben	Sid Caesar

Also: Burt Young, Shelley Winters

Over the Top •   [1987]

Director: **Menahem Golan**
Screenplay: **Stirling Silliphant & Sylvester Stallone**

Probably the best movie ever made about arm wrestling. Probably the *only* movie ever made about arm wrestling. And for good reason. Sly tries to mix the 'tender father fighting horrible daddy-in-law for custody' routine with the violent stuff. But he can't overcome Rose's Rule #8. **[93m/PG]**

Lincoln Hawk	Sylvester Stallone
Jason Cutler	Robert Loggia
Christina Hawk	Susan Blakely

Psst! Stallone received $12m to write and star.

Oxford Blues ••   [1984]

Director: **Robert Boris**
Screenplay: **Robert Boris**

This unremarkable remake of the 1938 *Yank at Oxford* has rower Lowe having to come to terms with such anachronistic British ideas as sportsmanship and fair play. Not released in the UK until 1986.

[97m/15]

Nick	Rob Lowe
Rona	Ally Sheedy
Lady Victoria	Amanda Pays
Colin	Julian Sands

P

Johnny Gallagher.....................Gene Hackman
Eileen Gallagher ....Joanna Cassidy
Thomas Boyette ....Tommy Lee Jones
Col. Glen Whitacre ....John Heard

Pale Rider •••   [1985]

Director: **Clint Eastwood**
Screenplay: **Michael Butler & Dennis Shryack**

Eastwood's first Western since *The Outlaw Josey Wales* has its pretentious, mystical moments of embarrassment. But its story of lone drifter Eastwood round-ing up a group of gold-miners and herding them into action against the evil Dysart is still pretty exciting.

[115m/15]

Preacher ....Clint Eastwood
Mull Barret ....Michael Moriarty
Sarah Wheeler ....Carrie Snodgress
Josh La Hood ....Christopher Penn
Coy La Hood ....Richard Dysart
Megan Wheeler ....Sydney Penny
Club..Richard Kiel

Pacific Heights ••   [1990]

Director: **John Schlesinger**
Screenplay: **Daniel Pyne**

The Tenant From Hell. Weirdo Keaton rents a room from the ideal yuppie couple and proceeds to turn their life into a nightmare. Although competently put together, it's just a little too silly in places to really scale the heights, while the use of a cat scaring us at the moment of highest tension is surely a little passé these days.

[102m/15]

Patty Palmer...........................Melanie Griffith
Drake Goodman..................Matthew Modine
Carter Hayes...........................Michael Keaton
Toshio Watanabe......................................Mako
Mira Watanabe ....Nobu McCarthy
Stephanie MacDonald..............Laurie Metcalf
Also: Tippi Hedren, Sheila McCarthy, Jerry Hardin, Beverly D'Angelo, Dan Hedaya, Miriam Margolyes
Blurb They Were The Perfect Couple, Buying The Perfect House. Until A Perfect Stranger Moved Into Their Lives.
OOPS! Griffith's character is misspelt 'Parker' on the end credits.
Psst! Tippi Hedren, star of Hitchcock's *The Birds* is Griffith's mother •
Apparently the script grew out of Pyne's own experiences with a lodger.

Paperhouse ••   [1989]

Director: **Bernard Rose**
Screenplay: **Matthew Jacobs**

During various blackouts, a young girl approaching puberty finds that through her drawings, she has created a sinister world which begins to take her, and oth-ers, over. An original, atmospheric British horror story that doesn't quite come off, but deserves points for trying.

[94m/15]

Anna ....Charlotte Burke
Marc ....Elliott Spiers
Kate ....Glenne Headly
Dad..Ben Cross

The Package ••   [1989]

Director: **Andrew Davis**
Screenplay: **John Bishop**

This conspiracy thriller seemed dated even when it came out, with Hackman caught up in a plot on Gorbachev's life. No movie with Hackman in is ever *com-pletely* dull, but it's pretty routine stuff.

[108m/15]

Paper Mask •••   [1990]

Director: **Christopher Morahan**
Screenplay: **John Collee**

An unqualified hospital worker imper-sonates a dead doctor and gets all the usual perks, like romping with nurse Amanda Donohoe. This original, and alarmingly convincing, British thriller unfortunately botches the ending. **[103m/15]**

Matthew Harris/Hennessey .... Paul McGann
Christine Taylor .... Amanda Donohoe
Dr. Mumford .... Frederick Treves
Dr. Thorn .... Tom Wilkinson
Alec Moran .... Jimmy Yuill
Celia Mumford .... Barbara Leigh-Hunt

Psst! Worryingly, the film was written by a former doctor.

Paradise •••• **[1992]**

Director: **Mary Agnes Donoghue**
Screenplay: **Mary Agnes Donoghue**

Mel and Don starring together for the first time in a remake of the magical French childhood tale *Le Grand Chemin*? Surprisingly enough, it works brilliantly. A young lad is foisted upon his mother's friend for the summer and, taken up by the town's tomboy, has a summer he'll never forget. The beautiful South Carolina scenery complements perfectly this funny, touching and gently sentimental tale. A real gem. **[111m/12]**

Lily Reed .... Melanie Griffith
Ben Reed .... Don Johnson
Willard Young .... Elijah Wood
Billie Pike .... Thora Birch
Sally Pike .... Sheila McCarthy
Rosemary .... Eve Gordon
Catherine Reston Lee .... Louise Latham

Parenthood ••• **[1989]**

Director: **Ron Howard**
Screenplay: **Lowell Ganz & Babaloo Mandel**

A massive starry cast give us four generations of a large family practising just about every method of parenting yet devised, from Dr. Spock to Mr. Spock. Although occasionally mushy, the film is warm-hearted and funny enough to carry it off. A really pleasing couple of hours, with the scene where Steenburgen tries to 'relax' husband Martin a particular delight. One of the few 'family' films aimed at the adults, rather than the kids. **[124m/15]**

Gil .... Steve Martin
Karen .... Mary Steenburgen
Helen .... Dianne Wiest
Frank .... Jason Robards
Nathan .... Rick Moranis
Larry .... Tom Hulce
Julie .... Martha Plimpton
Tod .... Keanu Reeves
Susan .... Harley Jane Kozak
David Brodsky .... Dennis Dugan
Gary .... Leaf Phoenix
Marilyn .... Eileen Ryan
Grandma .... Helen Shaw
Kevin .... Jasen Fisher

Blurb It Could Happen To You.

Quote 'I can't be a grandmother. I was at Woodstock!' • 'Would you like to see me make strange animals with balloons?'

Psst! Rance Howard, Ron's dad, regularly crops up in his movies. Here he's the 'Dean at college'.

Parents • **[1989]**

Director: **Bob Balaban**
Screenplay: **Christopher Hawthorne**

A small boy in 50's suburbia isn't too happy about his parents' continual diet of red meat. He becomes still less happy when he sees what's in the cellar. This attempt to out-Lynch David lacks his surreal atmosphere and sly wit, so that all the carefully kitsch production values lead nowhere slowly. **[82m/18]**

Nick Laemle .... Randy Quaid
Lily Laemle .... Mary Beth Hurt
Millie Dew .... Sandy Dennis

Quote 'We've been having leftovers every day since we came here. I'd like to know what they were before they were leftovers.'

Paris by Night • **[1989]**

Director: **David Hare**
Screenplay: **David Hare**

MEP Rampling, tough as hobnail boots, does away with a man she thinks is blackmailing her. Hare makes his hastily-written thriller so convoluted and obtuse that, despite Rampling, we are about as interested in what goes on as we are in the proceedings of the European Parliament itself. **[101m/15]**

Clara Paige	Charlotte Rampling
Gerald Paige	Michael Gambon
Adam Gillvray	Robert Hardy
Also: Iain Glen, Jane Asher	

Paris, Texas •• [1984]

Director: **Wim Wenders**
Screenplay: **Sam Shepard**

Stanton turns up, dumb after four years in the desert, and is helped reconnect with his wife and child by his brother. Wenders is not everybody's glass of lager and this highly rated existential allegory on the current state of the American nuclear family can seem a bit of a haul. However, the acting and camerawork are faultless, while the extraordinary reunion with Kinski stays in the mind long afterwards. **[150m/15]**

Travis	Harry Dean Stanton
Walt	Dean Stockwell
Anne	Aurore Clement
Hunter	Hunter Carson
Jane	Nastassja Kinski

Quote 'I hear your voice all the time. Every man has your voice.'

Paris Trout •• [1991]

Director: **Stephen Gyllenhaal**
Screenplay: **Pete Dexter**

Hopper is Trout, a racist maniac in 50's Georgia, shooting a black woman who owed him money and abusing wife Hershey with a coke bottle. Although it's well-acted and Hopper's well at home with this sort of forceful drama, it's pretty bleak and unpleasant.

[100m/18]

Paris Trout	Dennis Hopper
Hanna Trout	Barbara Hershey
Harry Seagraves	Ed Harris
Carol Bonner	Ray McKinnon

Parker ••• [1985]

Director: **Jim Goddard**
Screenplay: **Trevor Preston**

An intriguing and gripping British thriller about a businessman kidnapped in Berlin. When released, he's determined to get to the bottom of what's been going on. Plenty of twists, murder and tension. **[97m/15]**

Parker	Bryan Brown
Jenny	Cherie Lunghi
Insp. Haag	Kurt Raab
Rohl	Bob Peck

Pascali's Island •• [1988]

Director: **James Dearden**
Screenplay: **James Dearden**

A beautifully-filmed tale of cross and double-cross set in the Aegean in 1908. Kingsley is a Turkish spy who forms an alliance with the dapper Dance. Although written and directed by Dearden, scripter of *Fatal Attraction*, there's little excitement here. **[103m/15]**

Basil Pascali	Ben Kingsley
Anthony Bowles	Charles Dance
Lydia Neuman	Helen Mirren
Herr Gesing	George Murcell

A Passage to India ••• [1984]

Director: **David Lean**
Screenplay: **David Lean**

Despite its unnecessary length, there's much to admire in this E.M. Forster tale of the clash of cultures revolving around early friendship and then recriminations between British woman Davis and Indian doctor Banerjee. Acting, photography, atmosphere, period all are top-hole. But it's still way too long. **[163m/PG]**

Adela Quested	Judy Davis
Dr. Aziz	Victor Banerjee
Mrs. Moore	Peggy Ashcroft
Richard Fielding	James Fox
Godbole	Alec Guinness
Ronny Heaslop	Nigel Havers
Turton	Richard Wilson
Mahmoud Ali	Art Malik

Hamidullah ....Saeed Jaffrey
Maj. Callendar................................Clive Swift
Amritrao..Roshan Seth

Oscars Peggy Ashcroft

Psst! This was David Lean's first film for 14 years. It was also his last.

Passenger 57 •• [1992]

Director: **Kevin Hooks**
Screenplay: **David Loughery & Dan Gordon**

In this hare-brained thriller, Snipes is the airline security guy who just happens to be on board a passenger jet when the world's top hijacker is being taken to court – BY AIR!!! – by a paltry pair of FBI men. One of the most ludicrous action pics in years, with extraordinarily unnecessary twists in the plot, the fact that they've paid as much attention to detail as *Airplane* and peppered it with B-movie dialogue becomes endearing after a while. Utterly daft, but still entertaining.

[84m/15]

John Cutter ....Wesley Snipes
Charles Rane................................Bruce Payne
Sly Delvecchio ....Tom Sizemore
Marti Slayton ....Alex Datcher

Quote 'Always bet on the black.'

OOPS! 'This is a jumbo jet,' says stewardess Datcher, seemingly ignorant of the fact that she works on an L-1011 ♦ The same passenger leaves the plane three times! A blonde wearing a pink top and mini-skirt gets off with the first batch of hostages, then the next lot and then once again as reporters are thronging the plane ♦ If the plane can only just land at Lake Lucille airport, it almost certainly wouldn't be able to take off again with a full load ♦ Snipes gets into the plane by clambering into the nose-wheel, emerging in the cockpit (which the terrorists have mysteriously left vacant) through a sign saying 'Access to nosegear'. Impossible. The plane is pressurised and any access to a jet from its landing gear could be disastrous ♦ Any shot would be catastrophic in the pressurised environment of a jet, yet there are umpteen shootings before the skin finally tears apart with the inevitable consequences.

Psst! Robert Hooks, playing 'Dwight Henderson', is the director's father.

Patriot Games •••• [1992]

Director: **Phillip Noyce**
Screenplay: **W. Peter Iliff & Donald Stewart**

Armed with only a five-film contract to ensure that he survives, Ford debuts as Jack Ryan, the Bond for the 90s, foiling the dastardly plots of IRA terrorists from Rent-A-Villain. Yes, the dialogue's trite and the plot's wildly implausible (particularly wife Archer as the eye surgeon who still picks the kiddies up from school). But that applied to Bond, too, and the action sequences are so good at getting the adrenalin pumping everything else is forgiven.

[117m/15]

Jack Ryan ....Harrison Ford
Cathy Ryan....................................Anne Archer
Kevin O'Donnell.......................Patrick Bergin
Sean Miller ....Sean Bean
Sally Ryan.....................................Thora Birch
Lord Holmes ....James Fox
Robby ....Samuel L. Jackson
Annette ....Polly Walker
Marty Cantor ..............................J.E. Freeman
Admiral Greet........................James Earl Jones
Paddy O'Neil............................Richard Harris

Blurb Not For Honour. Not For Country. For His Wife And Child.

OOPS! Look carefully at the copy of *The Independent* in Bean's cell. Although the photo is of Jack Ryan, the surrounding words concern the air–sea search for Robert Maxwell! ♦ The film-makers' grip on geography's a little lax. Running from Piccadilly to Aldwych tube is but the work of a moment, while it's hard to see why a prisoner sent from Southwark to the Isle of Wight should pass through Kent ♦ Bean's trial must surely be the quickest in English legal history.

Psst! This was the first movie allowed to film inside CIA headquarters ✦ Alec Baldwin, who played Jack Ryan in *Hunt for Red October*, wouldn't accept the $4m offered. Ford ended up getting $9m. After the pic came out, he signed for a record $50m to play Ryan in five more movies ✦ When Ford is attacked after leaving the Naval Academy, the street's called Hanover Street, the name of one of his earlier films.

Patti Rocks •• [1988]

Director: **David Burton Morris**
Screenplay: **David Burton Morris, Chris Mulkey, John Jenkins & Karen Landry**

Two men on a long drive to see the pregnant mistress of one, have a competition to see who can bore the other one to sleep. They both lose, because it's the audience that nods off first. So low-budget, it's a wonder they didn't run out of petrol. **[87m/18]**

Billy...Chris Mulkey
Eddie..John Jenkins
Patti...Karen Landry

Psst! Credits include a 'spiritual adviser'.

Patty Hearst •• [1988]

Director: **Paul Schrader**
Screenplay: **Nicholas Kazan**

This attempt to dramatise the kidnap and subsequent indoctrination of heiress Patty Hearst by the Symbionese Liberation Army is surprisingly intelligent but also uninvolving. Richardson, however, is magnificent. **[104m/18]**

Patricia Hearst.................Natasha Richardson
Teko ....William Forsythe
Cinque...Ving Rhames
Yolanda ....Frances Fisher

Pee-Wee's Big Adventure •• [1985]

Director: **Tim Burton**
Screenplay: **Phil Hartman**

You either love Pee-Wee Herman or hate him. A sort of surrealistic combination of Jerry Lewis and Norman Wisdom, this bizarre but incredibly stylish movie revolves around Pee-Wee's search for his red bike. Former Disney animator Burton here gives us a cartoon with human beings...and Herman. Occasionally very funny, but a little Pee-Wee goes an awfully long way. **[92m/U]**

Pee-Wee Herman ....Paul Reubens
Dottie...E.G. Daily
Francis ....Mark Holton
Simone.......................................Diane Salinger

Quote 'I know you are, but what am I?'

Psst! This was Burton's first feature film. He also introduced Danny Elfman's music, going on to use him most famously with the *Batman* films.

Peggy Sue Got Married ••• [1986]

Director: **Francis Ford Coppola**
Screenplay: **Jerry Leichtling & Arlene Sarner**

Middle-aged mother Turner, on the point of divorce, passes out at her high school reunion and is transported back in time to 1960. A more serious trip to *Back to the Future* territory, questioning whether we handle life's major choices better with foresight. An interesting and sometimes delightful film, although asking us to believe Turner is 17 is a bit much. **[103m/15]**

Peggy Sue ....Kathleen Turner
Charlie Bodell ....Nicolas Cage
Richard Norvik...........................Barry Miller
Carol Heath...........................Catherine Hicks
Maddy Nagle...............................Joan Allen
Michael Fitzsimmons........Kevin J. O'Connor
Walter Getz ....Jim Carrey
Delores Dodge.....................Lisa Jane Persky
Rosalie Testa ....Lucinda Jenney
Evelyn Kelcher..........................Barbara Harris
Nancy Kelcher ....Sofia Coppola
Elizabeth Alvorg.............Maureen O'Sullivan
Barney Alvorg...............................Leon Ames
Beth Bodell.....................................Helen Hunt

Quote 'Peggy. You know what a penis is? Stay away from it.'

Pelle the Conqueror •••• [1988]

Director: **Bille August**
Screenplay: **Bille August**

Young Pelle is a Swedish worker on a Danish farm who, through a close relationship with his widowed father, learns to become his own man. One of those rare Foreign Oscar-winners that actually deserves the award, this moving, beautifully detailed epic is well worth tracking down. **[155m/15]**

Lasse Karlsson	Max Von Sydow
Pelle Karlsson	Pelle Hvenegaard
Manager	Erik Paaske
Anna	Kristina Tornqvists

Psst! The parents of Pelle Hvenegaard had actually named him after the hero of the novel on which the film was based.

The People Under the Stairs •• [1991]

Director: **Wes Craven**
Screenplay: **Wes Craven**

A young boy attempting to save his mother from eviction ends up ensnared in a bizarre asylum run by a murderous pair of landlords. There's clearly an allegory of the Reagan years underlying this uneven horror-comedy, which marks Craven's partial return to form. **[102m/18]**

Poindexter Williams	Brandon Adams
Man	Everett McGill
Woman	Wendy Robie
Alice	A.J. Langer

Psst! McGill and Robie were Ed and Nadine in *Twin Peaks* ◆ Adams is the boy in Michael Jackson's *Moonwalker*.

Perfect • [1985]

Director: **James Bridges**
Screenplay: **Aaron Latham & James Bridges**

Great poster. Shame about the film. Travolta's a *Rolling Stone* journalist about to blow the cover on the aerobics business when he falls for fitness instructor Curtis. Watergate, it isn't. There's an awful lot of aerobics here. Unfortunately not quite enough to edge Travolta out of the picture completely. **[120m/15]**

Adam	John Travolta
Jessie	Jamie Lee Curtis
Frankie	Anne De Salvo

Quote 'I've worked so hard to find my identity. Now all they want to know is where I got my body.' [Jamie Lee Curtis]

Psst! Curtis underwent a rigorous regime for several months to get her body into shape, taking up aerobics, weight-lifting and swimming ◆ It's Carly Simon who comes into the restaurant and throws the drink in Travolta's face.

Perfectly Normal •• [1991]

Director: **Yves Simoneau**
Screenplay: **Eugene Lipinsky & Paul Quarrington**

It's nothing of the sort of course, but a peculiar Canadian comedy about Coltrane opening a restaurant with opera-singing waiters. Although quaintly eccentric, it isn't particularly funny. **[105m/15]**

Alonzo Turner	Robbie Coltrane
Renzo Parachi	Michael Riley
Denise	Deborah Duchene
'Hopeless'	Eugene Lipinsky

Psst! The production company is called 'Bialystock & Bloom', named after the Zero Mostel and Gene Wilder characters in Mel Brooks' *The Producers*.

Personal Services •• [1987]

Director: **Terry Jones**
Screenplay: **David Leland**

The story of what is clearly madam Cynthia Payne, through to her setting up her Sex for Luncheon Vouchers brothel in suburbia, catering for those of advanced years. Despite Walters' excellent performance and a surfeit of eccentric characters, it's appallingly coy and nothing like as funny as it should be. **[105m/18]**

Christine Painter	Julie Walters
Wing Commander Morton	Alec McCowen
Shirley	Shirley Stelfox
Dolly	Danny Schiller

Peter's Friends ••• [1992]

Director: **Kenneth Branagh**
Screenplay: **Rita Rudner & Martin Bergman**

This reunion of a college revue troupe one New Year has been compared to *The Big Chill*. But despite similarities in plot and in the use of music, this is much more straightforwardly entertaining. Less a feature film than a series of witty sketches strung together, it is packed with enough splendid retorts and one-liners to keep you chortling, even if Fry's let's-put-a-dampener-on-the-party revelation does come too late in the proceedings not to throw the film off balance. **[101m/15]**

Andrew ....Kenneth Branagh
Sarah ....Alphonsia Emmanuel
Peter ....Stephen Fry
Roger ....Hugh Laurie
Vera ....Phyllida Law
Paul ....Alex Lowe
Carol ....Rita Rudner
Brian ....Tony Slattery
Mary ....Imelda Staunton
Maggie ....Emma Thompson

Quote 'If there is a God, he takes extremely long lunches.'

Psst! Phyllida Law, who plays Vera, is Emma Thompson's mum and, come to that, Ken's mother-in-law.

Pet Sematary • [1989]

Director: **Mary Lambert**
Screenplay: **Stephen King**

A family moves into their new house, bordered on one side by a juggernaut-infested highway and on the other by a pet graveyard built on an old Indian burial ground. Presumably, they managed to knock a few quid off the asking price. The only truly horrific things here are the dialogue and acting. **[102m/18]**

Dr. Louis Creed ....Dale Midkiff
Jud Crandall ....Fred Gwynne
Rachel Creed ....Denise Crosby

Blurb Sometimes Dead Is Better.

OOPS! Watch the flowers behind Dr.

Creed, as he sits by his son's grave, change from purple to yellow.

Psst! This is the first Stephen King novel that he adapted for the cinema himself ♦ He appears in a cameo as the minister.

Phantasm II • [1988]

Director: **Don Coscarelli**
Screenplay: **Don Coscarelli**

The Tall Man stalks teenagers again in this uneagerly awaited sequel to a largely forgotten cult film a decade earlier. The effects are fairly gruesome, though. **[97m/18]**

Mike ....James Le Gros
Reggie ....Reggie Bannister
The Tall Man ....Angus Scrimm

Showing *Phantasm*.

The Phantom of the Opera • [1989]

Director: **Dwight H. Little**
Screenplay: **Duke Sandefur**

Nightmare on Oxford Street. The actor best known as Freddy Krueger has a different costume, but is still being beastly to people in this remake, oddly relocated to London (in reality Budapest). Both effects and film are pretty gruesome. **[92m/18]**

Erik Destler (The phantom) ....Robert Englund
Christine Day ....Jill Schoelen
Richard ....Alex Hyde–White

Phar Lap ••• [1984]

Director: **Simon Wincer**
Screenplay: **David Williamson**

The moving and often exciting true-life story of Australia's version of Red Rum, from its discovery in New Zealand, to the bonding with stable lad Burlinson that started it winning races, through to its end in 1932. Along the way, we get some fascinating insights into Australia of the time. Whip-cracking entertainment. **[107m/PG]**

Tommy Woodcock ....Tom Burlinson
Dave Davis ....Ron Leibman
Harry Telford ....Martin Vaughan
Bea Davis ....Judy Morris

The Philadelphia Experiment ••• [1984]

Director: **Stewart Raffill**
Screenplay: **William Gray & Michael Janover**

In this wildly implausible sci-fi tale, a couple of sailors from 1943 fall through a hole in the plot, ending up in the middle of the Nevada Desert in 1984. Although you have to swallow a lot to believe in any of it, it's still great fun, like one big episode of *The Twilight Zone*. **[101m/PG]**

David	Michael Pare
Allison	Nancy Allen
Longstreet	Eric Christmas
Jim	Bobby Di Cicco

Physical Evidence • [1989]

Director: **Michael Crichton**
Screenplay: **Bill Phillips**

Terrible thriller with Russell the lawyer defending cop Reynolds on a murder charge. Russell is miscast and wildly out of her depth. It isn't often you wish Reynolds had *more* screen time, but that's the case with this moribund *Jagged Edge* rip-off. **[99m/18]**

Joe Paris	Burt Reynolds
Jenny Hudson	Theresa Russell
James Nicks	Ned Beatty

The Pick-up Artist • [1987]

Director: **James Toback**
Screenplay: **James Toback**

Ladies' man Downey puts the make on gutsy Ringwald with lines Cleopatra would have recognised. Downey displays as much charisma as a pot plant and would have trouble picking up a cold. Proof positive that it's possible to have Aiello, Hopper and Keitel in a film and for it *still* to be unbearably tedious. **[81m/PG]**

Randy Jensen	Molly Ringwald
Jack Jericho	Robert Downey Jr.
Flash	Dennis Hopper
Phil	Danny Aiello
Alonzo	Harvey Keitel

Pinocchio and the Emperor of the Night • [1987]

Director: **Hal Sutherland**
Screenplay: **Various**

Just what you've been waiting for – Pinocchio: The Sequel. This follow-up to the wooden lad's wanderings only serves to show how good the original Disney effort was. Dull animation and a flat story are served up with bucketfuls of gooey sentiment. Yuk! **[87m/U]**

With: Ed Asner, Tom Bosley, Lana Beeson, James Earl Jones

Pirates •• [1986]

Director: **Roman Polanski**
Screenplay: **Gérard Brach & Roman Polanski**

Behind a beard of massive proportions, Matthau hams it up outrageously as a pirate of old in what is presumably meant to be a spoof of those old pirate pics. Despite its visual splendour, the script is holed below the waterline and the enterprise soon runs aground. Interesting only if you fancy the sight of someone flushing 30 million dollars straight down the drain. **[124m/PG]**

Capt. Red	Walter Matthau
The Frog	Cris Campion
Don Alfonso	Damien Thomas
Boomako	Olu Jacobs

Psst! The film was the 9th biggest flop in movie history ✦ The galleon is the most expensive prop ever made. Costing £7m, it took 2,000 Maltese shipyard workers an entire year to build.

The Pirates of Penzance ••• [1983]

Director: **Wilford Leach**
Screenplay: **Wilford Leach**

Though rather an uninspiring adaptation of the successful Broadway and West End productions, there's plenty of fun left in this modernised Gilbert & Sullivan classic. Kline is superb recreating his role as the Pirate King. **[112m/U]**

Pirate King.....................................Kevin Kline
Ruth...Angela Lansbury
Mabel...Linda Ronstadt
Major-General.............................George Rose
Frederic...Rex Smith

Psst! This was the first movie to be pre-miered simultaneously in the cinema and on cable TV in America.

Places in the Heart ••• [1984]

Director: **Robert Benton**
Screenplay: **Robert Benton**

Is widowed Field going to roll over and play dead when the bank wants to fore-close on her property in the midst of the Great Depression? Come on, this is Sally Field we're talking about. She doesn't play those sort of parts. She plays gutsy, 'lets do something with the cotton field out back' roles as she does here in this sur-prisingly well-written, warm and pleasing movie. **[111m/PG]**

Edna Spaling ....Sally Field
Margaret Lomax ....Lindsay Crouse
Wayne Lomax ....Ed Harris
Viola Kelsey ....Amy Madigan
Mr. Will ....John Malkovich
Moze ....Danny Glover

Oscars Sally Field, Best Screenplay

Psst! Writer-director Benton set the film in Waxahachie, Texas, where his family has lived for over a hundred years. *Tender Mercies* also filmed there ◆ Fields won her second Oscar for the part. Recollection of her 'You like me!' accep-tance speech has the same effect on many people as the scraping of nails across a blackboard.

Planes, Trains and Automobiles ••• [1987]

Director: **John Hughes**
Screenplay: **John Hughes**

This fun comedy has yuppie Martin try-ing desperately to get home to his family for a snowy Thanksgiving, but finding

himself lumbered with overbearing slob of a shower-curtain ring salesman Candy every step of the way. The gags don't always sit well with the more sentimental aspects of the tale, but there's plenty to enjoy, with both stars giving excellent performances. **[93m/15]**

Neal Page.....................................Steve Martin
Del Griffith.......................................John Candy
Susan Page ....Laila Robbins
State Trooper.......................Michael McKean
Taxi Racer ....Kevin Bacon
Owen...Dylan Baker
Joey...Carol Bruce
Motel clerk.............................Martin Ferrero

Showing *She's Having a Baby* [another Hughes film].

Psst! As no transport business would co-operate in having themselves sent up, the film-makers had to build an airport ter-minal, create a fictitious car-hire firm and rent twenty miles of train track on which they could run their train ◆ The film was called *Better To Be Alone Than In Bad Company* in Spain.

Platoon ••• [1986]

Director: **Oliver Stone**
Screenplay: **Oliver Stone**

It's Vietnam. It's war. It's hell. Stone's version is more hellish than most with Sheen the volunteer – like Stone himself – who finds that his new platoon is divid-ed between those who follow the more compassionate Dafoe and those who go for Berenger's brutal approach. In its portrayal of life as a soldier on the ground in 'Nam, this semi-autobiographical film is realistic, fascinating and harrowing. Whether you'd want to watch it twice is another matter. **[120m/15]**

Sgt. Barnes...............................Tom Berenger
Sgt. Elias ....Willem Dafoe
Chris ....Charlie Sheen
Big Harold.............................Forest Whitaker
Rhah....................................Francesco Quinn
Sgt. O'Neill.......................John C. McGinley
Sal...Richard Edison
Bunny...Kevin Dillon

Junior...Reggie Johnson
King...Keith David
Lerner ....Johnny Depp
Tex ....David Neidorf
Lt. Wolfe ....Mark Moses

Oscars Best Picture, Best Director

Quote 'We did not fight the enemy. We fought ourselvs and the enemy was in us.'

Psst! Stone spent over ten years trying to get the film made, which he said he wrote inspired by acid and Jim Morrison ◆ Little was expected of the film. But it grossed well over $100m, despite costing only $6m, and was probably the biggest word-of-mouth hit since *Easy Rider* ◆ Stone appears briefly near the close as an officer in the command bunker that's blown up ◆ The cast underwent a gruelling fortnight training session in the Philippine jungles before filming, led by an ex-Marine Captain. Stone started filming immediately afterwards to capture their discomfort ◆ Although military equipment came from the Philippine government, the US Defence Department wouldn't cooperate in any way on the film ◆ Johnny Depp's helmet has *Sherilyn* on it. At the time, he was engaged to Sherilyn Fenn ◆ Listen out for the real Adrian Cronauer, the Williams character in *Good Morning, Vietnam* calling out his famous catchphrase ◆ Mickey Rooney felt the film was so disturbing that women should be banned from seeing it.

The Playboys ••••   [1992]

Director: Gillies MacKinnon
Screenplay: Shane Connaughton & Kerry Crabbe

A sleepy 50's Irish village, scandalised by unmarried mum Wright, comes alive when a disreputable troupe of actors pitches its tent. Penned by half of the writing team that gave us *My Left Foot*, this is a delightful, old-fashioned, quality film. Witty and charming, occasionally black, it boasts some superb performances from leads and support alike.

[108m/12]

Constable Hegarty....................Albert Finney
Tom ....Aidan Quinn
Tara...Robin Wright
Freddie ....Milo O'Shea
Malone...Alan Devlin
Brigid..Niamh Cusack
Cassidy ....Ian McElhinney
Mick ....Adrian Dunbar

Showing *Wuthering Heights, The Westerner, Wonder Man.*

Psst! Annette Bening was to play Wright's part, but dropped out just before filming started.

The Player ••••   [1992]

Director: Robert Altman
Screenplay: Michael Tolkin

This wickedly delicious satire on Hollywood tells us more about the industry than any documentary ever could. A pressured studio executive overreacts in a big way to a series of threatening postcards. It's almost impossible to concentrate on the slender thriller plot because of the countless stars who pop in and out of the picture for a few seconds at a time. Full of delicious in-jokes, it doesn't hold up too well to a second viewing, but is a must at least once.

[124m/15]

Griffin Mill ....Tim Robbins
June Gudmundsdottir ....Greta Scacchi
Walter Stuckel...............................Fred Ward
Det. Avery ....Whoopi Goldberg
Larry Levy ....Peter Gallagher
Joel Levison ....Brion James
Bonnie Sherow..................Cynthia Stevenson
David Kahane ....Vincent D'Onofrio
Andy Civella...........................Dean Stockwell
Tom Oakley ....Richard E. Grant
Dick Mellen............................Sydney Pollack
Det. DeLongpre............................Lyle Lovett
Also: Steve Allen, Richard Anderson, Rene Auberjonois, Harry Belafonte, Shari Belafonte, Karen Black, Michael Bowen, Gary Busey, Robert Carradine, Charles Champlin, Cher, James Coburn, Cathy Lee Crosby, John Cusack, Brad Davis, Paul Dooley, Thereza Ellis, Peter Falk, Felicia Farr, Kasia Figura, Louise Fletcher, Dennis

Franz, Teri Garr, Leeza Gibbons, Scott Glenn, Jeff Goldblum, Elliott Gould, Joel Grey, David Alan Grier, Buck Henry, Anjelica Huston, Kathy Ireland, Steve James, Maxine John-James, Sally Kellerman, Sally Kirkland, Jack Lemmon, Marlee Matlin, Andie MacDowell, Malcolm McDowell, Jayne Meadows, Martin Mull, Jennifer Nash, Nick Nolte, Alexandra Powers, Bert Remsen, Guy Remsen, Patricia Resnick, Burt Reynolds, Jack Riley, Julia Roberts, Mimi Rogers, Annie Ross, Alan Rudolph, Jill St. John, Susan Sarandon, Adam Simon, Rod Steiger, Joan Tewkesbury, Brian Tochi, Lily Tomlin, Robert Wagner, Ray Walston, Bruce Willis, Marvin Young

Quote 'Traffic was a bitch.' ◆ 'Rumours are always true. You know that.'

Psst! 65 stars agreed to take part for next to nothing. If they'd been paid their usual rate, the wages bill would have come to over $100m ◆ For film buffs, the opening scene is one continuous take lasting 8 minutes ◆ The lead was nearly played by Chevy Chase until he was talked out of it ◆ Patrick Swayze's part was left on the cutting-room floor, while Warren Beatty was apparently furious that, because he didn't return Altman's calls, he wasn't in it ◆ Scripter Michael Tolkin is the right-hand one of the pair of writers who land a deal with Mill.

Playing Away ●● [1987]

Director: **Horace Ové**
Screenplay: **Caryl Phillips**

All the problems of Britain, neatly tied up in one cricket match. That, at least, must have been the idea of pitching a village cricket team against the visitors from Brixton. This uninspiring TV-financed project headed to its natural home pretty quickly. [98m/15]

Willie-Boy	Norman Beaton
Godfrey	Robert Urquhart
Marjorie	Helen Lindsay
Derek	Nicholas Farrell

Playing for Keeps ●● [1986]

Director: **Bob Weinstein & Harvey Weinstein**
Screenplay: **Bob Weinstein, Harvey Weinstein & Jeremy Leven**

Were it not for the presence in the cast list of Tomei, on her way to becoming the greatest actress Hollywood has seen for a generation, this otherwise unremarkable formulaic teen movie about youngsters doing up an old hotel to dance in, would have passed, forgotten, into the mists of time. [106m/15]

Danny	Daniel Jordana
Spikes	Matthew Penn
Silk	Leon W. Grant
Chloe	Mary B. Ward
Tracy	Marisa Tomei

Psst! Bob and Harvey Weinstein, the directors, producers and writers, run Miramax, the American independent distribution company that has been responsible for the US success of many a British film, including *The Crying Game*.

The Pleasure Principle ● [1992]

Director: **David Cohen**
Screenplay: **David Cohen**

In this laughably unlaughable British comedy, Firth, subtly called 'Dick', is something of a swordsman with the ladies. Sadly, this is no *Alfie*, Firth is no Caine and it's never clear why anyone should want to sleep with this lying philanderer. Even the fiercest chauvinists are likely to be embarrassed. [96m/18]

Dick	Peter Firth
Sammy	Lynsey Baxter
Judith	Haydn Gwynne
Charlotte	Lysette Anthony

Psst! The £200,000 to make the film came, surprisingly, from Cohen's local bank.

Plenty •• [1985]

Director: Fred Schepisi
Screenplay: David Hare

A neurotic woman finds love and meaning as a wartime resistance fighter in France and then cracks up in post-war Britain. Hare's fine play loses plenty in being opened up for the cinema and Streep, giving her English accent a second run for our money, becomes glacially tiresome. Gielgud, inevitably, is splendid. [124m/15]

Susan	Meryl Streep
Lazar	Sam Neill
Raymond Brock	Charles Dance
Sir Leonard Darwin	John Gielgud

Also: Tracey Ullman, Sting, Ian McKellen, Andre Maranne

The Plot Against Harry ••• [1990]

Director: Michael Roemer
Screenplay: Michael Roemer

From the moment a Jewish crook gets out of prison, he finds things going wrong in this splendid little zippy farce. Just when he thinks things can't get worse for him, they do. Full of wonderfully etched and lively characters, it's also fascinating for its glimpse at life in the late 60s. [81m/PG]

Harry Plotnick	Martin Priest
Leo Perlmutter	Ben Lang
Kay Plotnick	Maxine Woods
Max	Henry Nemo

Psst! Made in 1969, this black-and-white film wasn't released until 21 years later because a distributor couldn't be found at the time. It cost only $700,000 to make.

The Ploughman's Lunch •• [1983]

Director: Richard Eyre
Screenplay: Ian McEwan

A British journalist climbs up the greasy pole by rewriting history. This okay political drama, loved by the left and fortunate in coinciding with the Falklands War, was still too talky and preachy to really work as cinema. [100m/15]

James Penfield	Jonathan Pryce
Jeremy Hancock	Tim Curry
Susan Barrington	Charlie Dore

Also: Rosemary Harris, Frank Finlay, Bill Paterson

Point Break •• [1991]

Director: Kathryn Bigelow
Screenplay: W. Peter Iliff

Some fantastic action sequences on land, sea and in the air aren't quite enough to overcome the silly and tiresome plot, which has FBI man Reeves infiltrating a gang of surfers to investigate a series of bank robberies. Whatever happens to the romance started in the first half? [120m/15]

Bodhi	Patrick Swayze
Johnny Utah	Keanu Reeves
Angelo Pappas	Gary Busey
Tyler	Lori Petty

Psst! The credits include a 'tattoo specialist', a 'surf forecaster' and an 'aerial hairstylist' ✦ The video's an '18' and has scenes not seen in the cinema.

Point of No Return
SEE: Assassin

Police Academy •• [1984]

Director: Hugh Wilson
Screenplay: Neal Israel, Pat Proft & Hugh Wilson

You might imagine that any film spawning five sequels would be pretty hot stuff. But this raucous comedy about a bunch of unlikely recruits at a Police training school is really just *The Dozen Stooges* with uniforms on. [95m/18]

Carey	Steve Guttenberg
Karen	Kim Cattrall
Lt. Harris	G.W. Bailey
Moses	Bubba Smith
Leslie	Donovan Scott
Commandant Lassard	George Gaynes
Tackleberry	David Graf
Sgt. Callahan	Leslie Easterbrook

Police Academy 2: Their First Assignment • [1985]

Director: Jerry Paris
Screenplay: Barry W. Blaustein & David Sheffield

Suddenly the first one doesn't look quite so bad. Police trainees fire off jokes indiscriminately in all directions. Almost none of them hit their target. In case you care, this is the one where they go after the local thugs. [87m/PG]

With: Steve Guttenberg, Bubba Smith, David Graf, Michael Winslow, Bruce Mahler, Marion Ramsey, Colleen Camp

Police Academy 3: Back in Training •• [1986]

Director: Jerry Paris
Screenplay: Gene Quintano

Horrible though it sounds, there's more than one Police Academy, and our lot are involved in a contest with the other. Marginally better than #2. [82m/PG]

With: Steve Guttenberg, Bubba Smith, David Graf, Michael Winslow, Marion Ramsey, Leslie Easterbrook

Police Academy 4: Citizens on Patrol • [1987]

Director: Jim Drake
Screenplay: Gene Quintano

The Police try to save money by getting the local citizenry to participate in policing. Why don't the *Police Academy* makers save money by only printing up new posters and showing the old films again. Who would notice? This one's most noticeable for having Sharon Stone in a role that will no doubt now make her squirm to think of. [87m/PG]

With: Steve Guttenberg, Bubba Smith, Michael Winslow, David Graf, Tim Kazurinsky, Sharon Stone

Police Academy 5: Assignment Miami Beach • [1988]

Director: Alan Myerson
Screenplay: S.J. Kurwick

Officer, those appalling people are back. You know, the ones who keep doing totally stupid things very loudly. I keep telling them they're not funny, but they won't listen. Still, as the first four made $450m around the world, perhaps it's our fault rather than theirs? [90m/PG]

With: Bubba Smith, David Graf, Michael Winslow, Leslie Easterbrook

Police Academy 6: City Under Siege • [1989]

Director: Peter Bonerz
Screenplay: Stephen J. Curwick

Don't come near me, officer. Unless those awful *Police Academy* people stop making those terrible movies, I'm definitely going to throw myself off. I mean it. I'm not trying to be funny. If they don't, why should I? [83m/PG]

With: Bubba Smith, David Graf, Michael Winslow, Leslie Easterbrook

Police Story ••• [1987]

Director: Jackie Chan
Screenplay: Edward Tang

If you don't mind kung-fu movies, then this is one of the best of the bunch. Chan's the cop with St. Vitus's dance in a fast-moving and action-packed actioner, which redeems itself by having a reasonable sense of humour. Also known as *Jackie Chan's Police Story*. [98m/18]

Kevin Chan ....Jackie Chan
May...Maggie Cheung
Frankie ....Kenneth Tony

Poltergeist II: The Other Side • [1986]

Director: Brian Gibson
Screenplay: Mark Victor & Michael Grais

Little Heather O'Rourke gets kidnapped by those loveable furniture movers. It's not half as scary as its predecessor and the mystical mumbo-jumbo gets pretty tiresome. **[91m/15]**

Diane Freeling ....JoBeth Williams
Steve Freeling ....Craig T. Nelson
Carol Ann Freeling ....Heather O'Rourke
Also: Oliver Robins, Zelda Rubinstein, Will Sampson, Julian Beck

Quote 'They're ba-a-ack.'

Psst! The series was dogged by bad luck. Dominique Dunne died after the first film, while Beck and Sampson died soon after completing this one. [See *Poltergeist III*] ◆ Noble Craig's c.v. must look wonderful. Here he plays the 'Vomit Creature'.

Poltergeist III ◆ [1988]

Director: **Gary Sherman**
Screenplay: **Gary Sherman & Brian Taggert**

A cheapo third spin on the story. By this time, the tragic events surrounding the series had made the on-screen action pale in comparison. **[98m/15]**

Bruce Gardner............................Tom Skerritt
Patricia Gardner.........................Nancy Allen
Carol Anne ....Heather O'Rourke

Psst! The bad luck, which saw at least one major actor dying after each instalment, continued. This time it was 12-year-old Heather O'Rourke, killed by ruptured intestines before the movie came out. It was dedicated to her.

The Pope Must Die ◆◆ [1991]

Director: **Peter Richardson**
Screenplay: **Pete Richens**

Thanks to a computer error, a cherubic, rather hip, priest becomes the new Pope and proceeds to expose corruption in high places. Not even the substantial bulk of Coltrane can hide the threadbare nature of this farce. A few laughs, but only a few. **[97m/15]**

Dave Albinizi ....Robbie Coltrane
Veronica Dante..................Beverly D'Angelo
Vittorio Corelli ....Herbert Lom
Also: Alex Rocco, Balthazar Getty, William Hootkins, Robert Stephens, Annette Crosbie, John Sessions, Peter Richardson, Adrian Edmondson

Psst! So worried were the American distributors about the reaction of religious groups to the title that they changed it. Copying a piece of graffiti in London, they amended it to *The Pope Must Diet* ◆ Getty's attempt at an English accent wasn't too successful, so his voice was dubbed ◆ Jeff Beck appears as a postman.

The Pope Must Diet
SEE: The Pope Must Die

The Pope of Greenwich Village ◆◆ [1984]

Director: **Stuart Rosenberg**
Screenplay: **Vincent Patrick**

Rourke and Roberts mumble their way through another *Mean Streets* lookalike as Italian-American hustlers in New York who get involved with a robbery that goes wrong. At times, these two make Marlon Brando sound as if he's a BBC announcer enunciating the best Queen's English. **[120m/15]**

Paulie ....Eric Roberts
Charlie.....................................Mickey Rourke
Diane ....Daryl Hannah
Mrs. Ritter ....Geraldine Page
Also: Kenneth McMillan, Tony Musante, M. Emmet Walsh, Burt Young

Porky's II: The Next Day ◆ [1983]

Director: **Bob Clark**
Screenplay: **Roger E. Swaybill, Alan Ormsby & Bob Clark**

Porky's was a lousy comedy with the odd sexy moment. This has little sex and even fewer laughs. **[95m/18]**

PeeWee...................................Dan Monahan
Tommy.......................................Wyatt Knight
Billy ....Mark Herrier

Porky's Revenge • [1985]

Director: James Komack
Screenplay: Ziggy Steinberg

Need you ask? [91m/18]

Pee Wee.................................Dan Monahan
Tommy.......................................Wyatt Knight
Meat..Tony Ganio

Posse ••• [1993]

Director: Mario Van Peebles
Screenplay: Sy Richardson & Dario
Scardapane

Although confusingly directed and full of wild implausibilities, this story of a group of black deserters – and one white – becoming Western outlaws is still both fascinating and exciting stuff. [109m]

Jessie Lee..........................Mario Van Peebles
Little J.....................................Stephen Baldwin
Weezie..Charles Lane
Obobo..Tiny Lister Jr.
Father Time...........................Big Daddy Kane
Col. Graham.....................................Billy Zane

Psst! According to the film-makers, one in three cowboys were, in fact, black.

Postcards from the Edge •••• [1990]

Director: Mike Nichols
Screenplay: Carrie Fisher

An excellent, consistently amusing, satire about the wacky world of Hollywood. It is told from the viewpoint of Streep, the drug-taking actress daughter of showbiz mom MacLaine, always trying to upstage her daughter. Mercifully unsentimental, it's funny and sharp and an excellent glimpse of Tinseltown at work. Even Streep's a joy in this.

[104m/15]

Suzanne Vale..............................Meryl Streep
Doris Mann.......................Shirley MacLaine
Jack Falkner...............................Dennis Quaid
Lowell....................................Gene Hackman
Dr. Frankenthal..................Richard Dreyfuss
Joe Pierce..Rob Reiner
Grandma...................................Mary Wickes

Grandpa.......................................Conrad Bain
Evelyn Ames............................Annette Bening
Simon Asquith ....Simon Callow
Aretha.......................................Robin Bartlett
George Lazan ....Anthony Heald
Wardrobe mistress..........................Dana Ivey
Neil Bleene ....Oliver Platt
Robert Munch.....................Michael Ontkean

Blurb Having A Wonderful Time, Wish I Were Here.

Psst! Although not strictly autobiographical, Carrie Fisher's novel, on which this is based, bears some close resemblances to her relationship with her own showbiz mother, Debbie Reynolds ♦ Rob Reiner, director of When Harry Met Sally, appears as Joe Pierce.

P.O.W. The Escape • [1986]

Director: Gideon Amir
Screenplay: Jeremy Lipp, James Bruner, Malcolm Barbour & John Langley

This yarn of GI prisoners of war making a bid for freedom just before the final whistle is mere Cannon fodder, fairly typical of the shoddy output of the ill-fated teaming of producers Menahem Golan and Yoram Globus. [90m/15]

Col. Cooper.........................David Carradine
Sparks...................................Charles R. Floyd
Capt. Vinh...Mako

Power •• [1986]

Director: Sidney Lumet
Screenplay: David Himmelstein

A behind-the-scenes look at an American presidential election, with Gere the slick and slippery image consultant who suddenly wakes up to the fact that it's all a sham, much like the film.

[111m/15]

Pete St. John...............................Richard Gere
Ellen Freeman............................Julie Christie
Wilfred Buckley......................Gene Hackman
Sydney Betterman.....................Kate Capshaw
Also: Denzel Washington, E.G. Marshall, Beatrice Straight, J.T. Walsh

The Power of One •• [1992]

Director: **John G. Avildsen**
Screenplay: **Robert Mark Kamen**

Horrified by apartheid in 30's and 40's South Africa, a nice white boy fights for an essential point of principle: the right to box blacks. Director Avildsen also helmed *Karate Kid* – so we get plenty of advice on life from Mueller-Stahl à la Pat Morita – and *Rocky* – so we get lots of gruesome boxing. The distinctions between black and white are simply too black and white to stop tedium setting in. [127m/12]

P.K. ....Stephen Dorff
Doc ....Armin Mueller-Stahl
Geel Piet ....Morgan Freeman
Headmaster St. John ....John Gielgud
Maria Marais ....Fay Masterson

Powwow Highway ••• [1989]

Director: **Jonathan Wacks**
Screenplay: **Janet Heaney & Jean Stawarz**

Rather likeable road movie with a pair of Cheyenne Indians heading off the reservation for New Mexico and encountering many laughs and truths about racial prejudice along the way. [91m/15]

Buddy Red Bow...............................A. Martinez
Philbert Bono ....Gary Farmer
Rabbit Layton...........................Amanda Wyss
Bonnie Red Bow ....Joanelle Nadine Romero

A Prayer for the Dying •• [1987]

Director: **Mike Hodges**
Screenplay: **Edmund Ward & Martin Lynch**

IRA terrorist Rourke blows up the wrong people and goes on a massive guilt trip in London, only to have his former colleagues arrive to hunt him down. This hilariously bad thriller, trying to ape Graham Greene, is rife with ludicrous performances and ripe in symbolism, even down to the blind girl Rourke falls for. Almost worth it for Hoskins as a priest beating someone over the head with a dustbin lid! [108m/15]

Martin Fallon..........................Mickey Rourke
Jack Meehan....................................Alan Bates
Father DaCosta..........................Bob Hoskins
Also: Sammi Davis, Christopher Fulford, Liam Neeson, Alison Doody, Camille Coduri

Psst! Rourke and director Hodges disowned the film after it was re-cut by the producer.

Prayer of the Roller Boys •• [1991]

Director: **Rick King**
Screenplay: **W. Peter Iliff**

In the 21st century, where law and order have broken down completely, Haim infiltrates a roller-skating gang of drug-pushing neo-Fascists. However, as you can still get a pizza delivered, civilisation obviously hasn't vanished completely. Daft, derivative dross. [90m/15]

Griffin...Corey Haim
Gasey ....Patricia Arquette
Gary Lee ....Christopher Collet
Speedbagger................................Julius Harris

Predator •• [1987]

Director: **John McTiernan**
Screenplay: **Jim Thomas & John Thomas**

Arnie and the boys are on a rescue mission in the South American jungle when they encounter a shape-shifting alien with an attitude problem. Violent, but some good effects. [107m/18]

Dutch ....Arnold Schwarzenegger
Dillon..Carl Weathers
Anna ....Elpidia Carrillo
Mac..Bill Duke
Blain...Jesse Ventura
Billy.......................................Sonny Landham
Poncho ....Richard Chaves
Gen. Phillips..........................R.G. Armstrong
Hawkins ....Shane Black
The Predator........................Kevin Peter Hall

Quote 'Stick around.'

Psst! Shane Black, writer of *Lethal Weapon* and *The Last Boy Scout* appears briefly as Hawkins. Part of the deal when selling a script to producer Joel Silver was that he could be in an action movie ✦ Kevin Peter Hall, playing the alien, is 7 feet 2 inches tall.

Predator 2 •• [1990]

Director: Stephen Hopkins
Screenplay: Jim Thomas & John Thomas

The shifty one from Outer Space drops in on the urban jungle of futuristic L A. No Arnie this time, but there's Danny Glover and a lot of firepower. [107m/18]

Det–Lieut. Mike Harrigan	Danny Glover
Keyes	Gary Busey
Danny	Ruben Blades
Leona	Maria Conchita Alonso
Jerry	Bill Paxton
Heinemann	Robert Davi
Garber	Adam Baldwin
Anna	Elpidia Carrillo

Blurb He's In Town With A Few Days To Kill.

OOPS! The underground train is supposed to be in Los Angeles but it's marked 'BART', the name of San Francisco's system.

Psst! Probably the first mainstream movie in which a black has saved the world from alien domination. Despite Joel Silver being a *bête noire* of the liberals, he seems more willing than most to put black heroes in his films.

The Presidio •• [1988]

Director: Peter Hyams
Screenplay: Larry Ferguson

If Sean Connery hated your guts, would *you* dare make a play for his daughter? San Francisco cop Harmon does while investigating a murder on Connery's military base. As usual Connery wipes the floor in the acting stakes and is virtually the only reason to see this slick but inane and predictable thriller. [98m/15]

Lt. Col. Alan Caldwell	Sean Connery
Jay Austin	Mark Harmon
Donna Caldwell	Meg Ryan
Sgt. Mjr. Ross Maclure	Jack Warden

Presumed Innocent ••• [1990]

Director: Alan J. Pakula
Screenplay: Frank Pierson & Alan J. Pakula

A prosecutor has to investigate the murder of his former mistress, a crime of which he is soon himself accused. Although lacking some of the subtlety and tension of the bestseller on which it's based, this is still a stylish and intelligent thriller with Scacchi particularly fine as the independent murdered woman. Somebody should have run another investigation, though, into who allowed Ford on screen with that haircut! [126m/15]

Rusty Sabich	Harrison Ford
Raymond Horgan	Brian Dennehy
Sandy Stern	Raul Julia
Barbara Sabich	Bonnie Bedelia
Judge Larren Lyttle	Paul Winfield
Carolyn Polhemus	Greta Scacchi

Quote 'They're so close, you can see Molto's nose sticking out of Nico's belly button.'

OOPS! One of my favourite fluffs of all comes as Ford and Bedelia leave the court. As reporters jostle them for their comments, notice the microcassette recorder with no tape in it!

Pretty in Pink •• [1986]

Director: Howard Deutch
Screenplay: John Hughes

Ringwald is the girl from the wrong side of the tracks (but she still has her own car) at a high school mainly attended by high-born snobs, of whom only McCarthy will give her the time of day. But will he ask her to the Prom? Okay, by-the-numbers stuff. If you've seen one Hughes' teen-pic... [96m/15]

Andie	Molly Ringwald
Jack	Harry Dean Stanton
Duckie	Jon Cryer
Iona	Annie Potts
Steff	James Spader
Blane	Andrew McCarthy

Pretty Woman ••• [1990]

Director: **Garry Marshall**
Screenplay: **J.F. Lawton**

Morally dubious but otherwise highly entertaining modern fairy tale. Roberts is the street hooker lucky enough to proposition tycoon Gere just when he needs a companion for the week. No prizes for guessing what happens next, but it happens in such a manipulatively enjoyable manner that the predictability's part of the fun. Roberts is so divine in the part, it's hard to imagine anybody else bringing it off as well. All credit to Elizondo, too, for his delightful portrayal of the hotel manager. If only more films had decent supporting roles like this. **[120m/15]**

Edward Lewis	Richard Gere
Vivian Ward	Julia Roberts
James Morse	Ralph Bellamy
Philip Stuckey	Jason Alexander
Kit De Luca	Laura San Giacomo
Hotel manager	Hector Elizondo

Also: Alex Hyde-White, Amy Yasbeck, Elinor Donahue, Judith Baldwin, Larry Miller

Quote 'Listen, I appreciate this whole seduction scene you've got going, but let me give you a tip. I'm a sure thing, okay?' ♦ 'Pick one. I got red, I got green, I got yellow. I'm out of purple.'

Showing *Charade.*

OOPS! A delight for those spotting boo-boos. Gere's tie pops back on after Roberts first removes it ♦ At breakfast the next morning, her croissant changes to a pancake ♦ A man watching Gere play the piano vanishes ♦ Gere's shoes and socks are on again in the park just after she's taken them off ♦ At the polo match, we see sticking plaster on her toes. It's gone when she's back at the hotel ♦ At the sprauncy restaurant, the dessert dishes in front of Gere and Bellamy vanish then reappear ♦ In some versions, as the usher seats them at the opera, he appears to call Vivian 'Miss Roberts'.

Psst! The opening dressing scene isn't Roberts at all, but body double Shelley Michelle. She got just $750 a day, about the same rate Vivian charges in the film. Model Donna Scoggins stood in for Roberts on the famous poster, with the star's face superimposed on her body. Some claim the man on the poster isn't Gere either ♦ Until late on, the film was to be called *Three Thousand*, Roberts' fee for the week. The real-life hotel room costs more than that each night ♦ Before being given the Disney treatment, the script was darker and ended with her walking out on him ♦ The beautiful music Gere is making at the piano, prior to making beautiful music on top of it with Roberts, is a little thing of his own. It's him playing it too.

Prick Up Your Ears ••• [1987]

Director: **Stephen Frears**
Screenplay: **Alan Bennett**

This entertaining but gritty film penned by Alan Bennett is stronger and more interesting when concentrating on the details of Joe Orton's private life and what it meant to be a homosexual in Britain in the 50s and 60s than when focussing on Orton's theatrical career. Full of great lines, it is also wonderfully acted by Oldman and Molina. **[110m/18]**

Joe Orton	Gary Oldman
Kenneth Halliwell	Alfred Molina
Peggy Ramsey	Vanessa Redgrave
John Lahr	Wallace Shawn
Anthea Lahr	Lindsay Duncan
Elsie Orton	Julie Walters

Psst! When reviewing the biography of Orton, also called *Prick Up Your Ears*, the Spectator headed the article: 'No thanks'.

Prince of Darkness •• [1987]

Director: **John Carpenter**
Screenplay: **John Carpenter**

The Devil is holed up in a canister of green slime, confronted by Pleasence and a group of teens. Carpenter's direction of this low-budget venture is close to his best. Unfortunately, his script lacks the wit or originality of *Assault on Precinct 13*.

[101m/18]

Priest	Donald Pleasence
Brian	Jameson Parker
Birack	Victor Wong
Catherine	Lisa Blount

Psst! Although Carpenter wrote the script, the credit said 'Martin Quatermass', the lead character in the great British film *Quatermass and the Pit*.

The Prince of Pennsylvania •• [1988]

Director: **Ron Nyswaner**
Screenplay: **Ron Nyswaner**

In this appropriately black comedy set in a Pennsylvania coal town, Reeves kidnaps his father to raise some cash. Although full of oddball characters, the film doesn't seem to know what to do with them, while Reeves does his damnedest to make sure we don't care a jot about him. [93m/15]

Gary Marshetta	Fred Ward
Rupert Marshetta	Keanu Reeves
Pam Marshetta	Bonnie Bedelia
Carla Headlee	Amy Madigan

The Prince of Tides •• [1991]

Director: **Barbra Streisand**
Screenplay: **Pat Conroy & Becky Johnston**

Psychiatrist Streisand decides the best way to treat Nolte's sister is to put him on the couch, from where they progress to the bed. Along the way, he unburdens himself of some terrible childhood memories and has a good cry. Although it looks good, the story's pretentious and sentimental and takes forever unfolding. The camera dwells at extraordinary lengths on Streisand's nails, probably the fault of the director, who was Streisand.

[131m/15]

Tom Wingo	Nick Nolte
Susan Lowenstein	Barbra Streisand
Sally Wingo	Blythe Danner
Lila Wingo Newbury	Kate Nelligan
Herbert Woodruff	Jeroen Krabbé

Savannah Wingo	Melinda Dillon
Eddie Detreville	George Carlin
Bernard Woodruff	Jason Gould
Henry Wingo	Brad Sullivan

Quote 'I don't know when my parents began their war against each other, but I do know the only prisoners they took were their children.'

OOPS! With almost 12,000 taxis in New York City, isn't it amazing that Cab Number 6X24 should appear on three separate occasions? First, it ferries Nolte to his sister's, then Gould to the station and then it reappears once more to pick Nolte and Streisand up after the turbulent dinner party ✦ There can't be much crime where Streisand has her other house. When she and Nolte turn up, every window is wide open.

Psst! Streisand was paid $6m ✦ Jason Gould is Streisand's son.

The Princess and the Goblin ••• [1992]

Director: **Jozsef Gemes**
Screenplay: **Robin Lyons**

Pleasing animated fairy tale about, well, about a princess and a goblin, with the former ordered to marry the latter. Writer Lyons is the chap behind *SuperTed*, so that should give you an idea of what to expect. [82m/U]

With: Joss Ackland, Claire Bloom, Rik Mayall, Peggy Mount, Molly Sugden, Roy Kinnear, Victor Spinetti, William Hootkins

The Princess Bride •• [1987]

Director: **Rob Reiner**
Screenplay: **William Goldman**

This tongue-in-cheek Ruritanian swash-buckling romance is nowhere near as good as its reputation. Despite some lively, oddball humour, the invention and the jokes quickly pall. Daft disguised cameos from the likes of Billy Crystal simply destroy the illusion, leaving us with a piece of mildly diverting hokum. The kids should love it, though. [98m/PG]

Westley ....Cary Elwes
Inigo Montaya ....Mandy Patinkin
Prince Humperdinck ....Chris Sarandon
Count Rugen ....Christopher Guest
Vizzini ....Wallace Shawn

Quote 'I've got my country's 500th anniversary to plan, my wedding to arrange, my wife to murder and Gilda to frame for it. I'm swamped.'

Prison ••• [1988]

Director: **Renny Harlin**
Screenplay: **C. Courtney Joyner**

A tough prison is haunted by the ghost of a prisoner executed 20 years earlier, which is seeking revenge on the warden. An enjoyable blend of the horror and prison-movie genres which never takes itself too seriously and is energised by Harlin's all-stops-out direction. **[103m/18]**

Sharpe ....Lane Smith
Burke..................................Viggo Mortensen
Katherine ....Chelsea Field
Sandor ....Andre De Shields
Cresus ....Lincoln Kilpatrick

Psst! Filmed in a real Wyoming prison.

A Private Function ••• [1985]

Director: **Malcolm Mowbray**
Screenplay: **Alan Bennett**

In ration-bound 1947 Britain, snobby Smith persuades timid chiropodist hubby Palin to steal a pig being fattened up by the town's top brass for the impending royal nuptials. Bennett's first feature film script brings home the bacon in a big way. Wonderfully observed, with his usual incredible ear for eccentric dialogue, it is also hugely funny. **[94m/15]**

Gilbert Chilvers ....Michael Palin
Joyce Chilvers ....Maggie Smith
Betty the Pig..Himself
Dr. Swaby ....Denholm Elliott
Allardyce..............................Richard Griffiths
Also: Tony Haygarth, Bill Paterson, Liz Smith, Alison Steadman, Jim Carter

Psst! Probably the first movie in which a pig gets third billing.

A Private Life ••• [1989]

Director: **Francis Gerard**
Screenplay: **Andrew Davies**

A remarkable, well-told, true story of the thirty-year tragedy befalling a South African woman wrongly labelled by the authorities as black and the terrible effect it has upon her family. **[95m/15]**

Stella...Jana Cilliers
Jack...Bill Flynn
Paul ....Kevin Smith
Sgt. Smit..Ian Roberts

Privates on Parade •• [1983]

Director: **Michael Blakemore**
Screenplay: **Peter Nichols**

The jokey story of a British military theatrical troupe during wartime Singapore. It transfers uneasily from the stage, losing much of the humour, while its authenticity isn't helped by being so obviously filmed in England. **[112m/15]**

Maj. Giles Flack...........................John Cleese
Acting Capt. Terri ....Denis Quilley
Sgt. Maj. Reg Drummond......Michael Elphick
Acting Lt. Sylvia Morgan ....Nicola Pagett

Psst! Julian Sands crops up as a sailor.

Prizzi's Honour •• [1985]

Director: **John Huston**
Screenplay: **Richard Condon**

Wildly overrated Huston-directed black comedy. Nicholson's the dim mob hitman who falls for Turner only to discover she's in the same line of business. A potentially hilarious idea is taken at the pace of a funeral procession with about as many laughs. The characters and the acting are splendid but, black though it is, it simply isn't very funny. **[129m/15]**

Charley Partanna....................Jack Nicholson
Irene Walker.........................Kathleen Turner
Eduardo Prizzi ....Robert Loggia
Angelo 'Pop' Partanna ....John Randolph
Don Corrado Prizzi ....William Hickey
Dominic Prizzi.......................Lee Richardson
Filargi 'Finlay' ....Michael Lombard
Maerose Prizzi.......................Anjelica Huston

Oscars Anjelica Huston

Quote 'Come on, Charley. You wanna do it? Let's do it, right here on the Oriental.' ✦ 'Do I ice her or marry her?'

Psst! When Anjelica Huston won her Best Supporting Oscar, the Hustons became the first family with three generations to win the coveted statuettes, with father John and grandfather Walter before her ✦ Huston and Nicholson were a long-standing couple when the film was made ✦ Nicholson gained 30 lb for the part.

Problem Child ●   [1990]

Director: **Dennis Dugan**
Screenplay: **Scott Alexander & Larry Karaszewski**

The Child From Hell in The Movie From Hell. A little monster goes on the rampage when a couple is foolish enough to adopt him. Witless, tasteless and violent rubbish. Oliver is so extraordinarily repulsive in the title role, you'll find yourself begging for a nice Macaulay Culkin movie. **[80m/12]**

Ben Healy	John Ritter
Big Ben Healy	Jack Warden
Junior	Michael Oliver

Problem Child 2 ●   [1992]

Director: **Brian Levant**
Screenplay: **Scott Alexander & Larry Karaszewski**

In a moment of madness that should surely get them committed, the Healy's adopt *another* little monster. More moronic, tasteless drivel along the same lines. **[90m/PG]**

Ben Healy	John Ritter
Junior Healy	Michael Oliver
"Big" Ben Healy	Jack Warden

Quote 'They'd have to wheel my corpse in to do *Problem Child 3*.' [John Ritter]

Psst! The day before filming Michael Oliver's manager and mother insisted that he be paid, not the agreed $80,000, but $500,000. A year later, the courts insisted that $175,000 of it be paid back.

Promised Land ●●   [1988]

Director: **Michael Hoffman**
Screenplay: **Michael Hoffman**

A teen-pic that struggles to be a little more and doesn't really manage it. Hancock's the basketball star who turns cop when he doesn't make enough hoops. Sutherland's the drop-out who returns to his home town with psychotic, tattooed Ryan as his bride. Are these people going to settle down happily ever after and raise kids? Somehow we don't think so. **[101m/15]**

Hancock	Jason Gedrick
Danny	Kiefer Sutherland
Bev	Meg Ryan
Mary	Tracy Pollan

Proof ●●●●   [1991]

Director: **Jocelyn Moorhouse**
Screenplay: **Jocelyn Moorhouse**

A blind photographer has to contend with his lusting housekeeper and the arrival of a young dishwasher who sets the cat among the pigeons. A bizarre but superb drama on the emotional games people play, wittily and perceptively captured by novice writer-director Moorhouse and acted with total conviction and sympathy. The kind of incisive, low-budget Aussie drama that's worth a dozen bloated Hollywood weepies. **[90m/15]**

Martin	Hugo Weaving
Celia	Genevieve Picot
Andy	Russell Crowe
Mother	Heather Mitchell

Prospero's Books ●●●   [1991]

Director: **Peter Greenaway**
Screenplay: **Peter Greenaway & William Shakespeare**

This No Holds Bard version of Shakespeare's *The Tempest* is one of Greenaway's best films. He's helped by the fact that he's starting off with a decent script from Bill the Quill and has the infallible Gielgud as lead actor. Some of the directorial tricks still irritate but the visual beauty and technical trickery is very impressive. There's an amazing amount of bare flesh, too. **[120m/15]**

Prospero	John Gielgud
Caliban	Michael Clark
Alonso	Michel Blanc
Gonzalo	Roland Josephson
Miranda	Isabelle Pasco
Antonio	Tom Bell
Sebastian	Kenneth Cranham

The Protector •• [1986]

Director: James Glickenhaus
Screenplay: James Glickenhaus

Standard Jackie Chan actioner. Here he tangles with a drugs empire. **[95m/18]**

Insp. Billy Wong	Jackie Chan
Danny Garoni	Danny Aiello
Gang leader	Sandy Alexander
Police Captain	Victor Arnold

Protocol •• [1984]

Director: Herbert Ross
Screenplay: Buck Henry

One moment Goldie's serving people as a cocktail waitress, the next she's serving the People as a diplomat. It's easy enough swallowing the drinks, but a little trickier going along with her getting involved in top-level politics. Has there ever been an American film of this sort that *doesn't* end up with the hero/heroine reciting bits of the Declaration of Independence? Not Hawn's finest hour. **[95m/PG]**

Sunny	Goldie Hawn
Michael Ransome	Chris Sarandon
Emir	Richard Romanus

Psycho II •• [1983]

Director: Richard Franklin
Screenplay: Tom Holland

Bates is unwisely released from the asylum and goes back home to Mother. But Vera Miles still remembers what happened and goes after him. Although this unnecessary sequel to Hitchcock's classic is pretty well done, it's clever rather than frightening and breaks no new ground. Colour doesn't help either. **[113m/15]**

Norman Bates	Anthony Perkins
Lila	Vera Miles
Mary	Meg Tilly
Dr. Raymond	Robert Loggia

Blurb It's 22 Years later, And Norman Bates Is Coming Home.

Psycho III • [1986]

Director: Anthony Perkins
Screenplay: Charles Edward Pogue

A nun who's a dead ringer for Janet Leigh flees a bell-tower death at her convent. Guess where she checks in to recover? Norman gets all twitchy again, but she doesn't seem to notice. This generally tiresome retread, directed by Perkins, has its moments. But it's a shame to see it all reduced to the level of *Friday the 13th*. **[93m/18]**

Norman Bates	Anthony Perkins
Maureen	Diana Scarwid
Duane	Jeff Fahey

The Public Eye ••• [1992]

Director: Howard Franklin
Screenplay: Howard Franklin

Pesci is The Great Bernzini, a brilliant 40's crime photographer who can't relate emotionally to anyone who doesn't have a chalk silhouette drawn around them. His head is turned when glamorous nightclub owner Hershey asks him for a small favour which soon threatens to make him the subject of one of his competitors' photos. Not only is the background to Pesci's trade fascinating, but this bitter-sweet Frog and Princess story has about it an air of film noir that makes it look like the Bogart picture Bogie never made. Riveting stuff. **[99m/15]**

Leon "Bernzy" Bernstein	Joe Pesci
Kay Levitz	Barbara Hershey
Sal Minetto	Stanley Tucci
Arthur Nabler	Jerry Adler
Danny the Doorman	Jared Harris
Conklin	Gerry Becker

Pump Up the Volume ••• [1990]

Director: Allan Moyle
Screenplay: Allan Moyle

Shy high school student by day, at night Slater slips behind the mike and becomes Happy Harry Hard-On, dispensing philosophy, advice and music over the airwaves in a style that's all the rage with kids but enrages the adults. Splendid acting and an intriguing plot make this an interesting slant on the problems and desires of teenagers.   [102m/15]

Mark Hunter...........................Christian Slater
Loretta Creswood..........................Annie Ross
Nora Diniro.........................Samantha Mathis
Jan Emerson ....Ellen Greene
Brian Hunter ....Scott Paulin
Marta Hunter.........................Mimi Kennedy
Quote 'So be it.'

Punchline ••• [1988]

Director: David Seltzer
Screenplay: David Seltzer

This examination of the world of the stand-up comic centres on self-destructive but brilliant Hanks and housewife Field, who wants more out of life than kitchen drudgery. Although over sentimental when revealing Field's domestic life to us, the stand-up stuff is wonderful, showing us what it's really like trying to survive by making people laugh.

[122m/15]

Lilah Krytsick ....Sally Field
Steven Gold ....Tom Hanks
John Krytsick............................John Goodman
Romeo ....Mark Rydell
Madeline Urie................................Kim Greist
Blurb Dying Is Easy. Comedy Is Hard.
Quote 'I don't think I want to be intimate with anything that has "Panasonic" written on it.' ◆ 'Adam and Eve are in the Garden of Eden...and he says: "Stand back! I don't know how big this thing gets".'
Psst! Arnold, the chap selling jokes in the café in the opening scene, is director Paul Mazursky ◆ Look out for Damon Wayans as Percy, one of the comics.

The Punisher •• [1990]

Director: Mark Goldblatt
Screenplay: Boaz Yakin

A comic book character is turned into a comic book film, with Lundgren the avenging cop whose efforts to do away with criminals sends the crime wave statistics soaring. Can we please have a moratorium on torture scenes in which, after our hero is stretched on a rack and suffers sundry other indignities, he is still able to escape and do a three-minute mile?

[88m/18]

Frank Castle..........................Dolph Lundgren
Det. Jake Berkowitz ....Louis Gossett Jr.
Gianni Franco...........................Jeroen Krabbé
Lady Tanaka..................................Kim Miyori

Purple Haze • [1983]

Director: David Burton Morris
Screenplay: Victoria Wozniak

Yet another return to 60's America with lots of music but also lots of angst about the Draft. Unremarkable stuff. The film wasn't released in Britain until 1986.

[97m/18]

Matt..Peter Nelson
Jeff..Chuck McQuary
Derek.....................................Bernard Baldan

Purple Rain • [1984]

Director: Albert Magnoli
Screenplay: Albert Magnoli & William Blinn

Some people prance around preening themselves in front of the mirror. Others make films about themselves. Prince's film debut is an obviously autobiographical tale serving as an excuse for lots of his music. For his fans only.

[111m/15]

The Kid...Prince
Apollonia ....Apollonia Kotero
Morris ....Morris Day

The Purple Rose of Cairo •• [1985]

Director: **Woody Allen**
Screenplay: **Woody Allen**

So besotted is unhappy small-town housewife Farrow with the movies that the hero of her favourite film steps out of the screen and begins romancing her. This intriguing idea begins well but, despite its short running time, runs out of wit and invention long before the film runs out of the projector. It's plain curmudgeonly giving us a fantasy and then denying us an upbeat ending.

[82m/PG]

Cecilia ....Mia Farrow
Tom Baxter/Gil Shepherd ....Jeff Daniels
Monk ....Danny Aiello
Emma ....Dianne Wiest

Quote 'I met a wonderful man. He's fictional, but you can't have everything.'
Showing *Top Hat.*

Psst! Michael Keaton, as the lead, was booted off the pic after a week after creative differences with Allen and Farrow.

Q & A •• [1990]

Director: **Sidney Lumet**
Screenplay: **Sidney Lumet**

Director Lumet obviously hadn't had enough of New York police corruption with *Serpico* and *Prince of the City.* Back he is again with this painting-by-numbers tale of young Hutton investigating cop Nolte's killing of a drug dealer. Starting slowly, it gets slower. **[132m/18]**

Mike Brennan................................Nick Nolte
Al Reilly................................Timothy Hutton
Bobby Texador ....Armand Assante
Kevin Quinn............................Patrick O'Neal

Q – The Winged Serpent •• [1982]

Director: **Larry Cohen**
Screenplay: **Larry Cohen**

Quetzalcoatl, an ancient Aztec flying serpent god, is alive and well and living on top of the Chrysler Building. Unwary New York sunbathers find themselves taken for a free, but brief, aerial tour of the city. Typical trashy Cohen fare, delivering a monster movie complete with satirical asides and movie references aplenty but little plot. **[92m/18]**

Jimmy..................................Michael Moriarty
Joan ....Candy Clark
Shepard................................David Carradine
Powell ....Richard Roundtree

Queen of Hearts •••• [1989]

Director: **Jon Amiel**
Screenplay: **Tony Grisoni**

Enchanting little film about an Italian immigrant family settling in London and setting up a cafe, only to lose it in a card game. The director of *The Singing Detective* has fashioned a unique blend of comedy, whimsy, romance and magic into a delightful, unforgettable whole. Shamefully overlooked. **[112m/PG]**

Nonno ....Vittorio Duse
Danilo...Joseph Long
Rosa ....Anita Zagaria
Mamma Sibilla..............................Eileen Way
Barbariccia ....Vittorio Amandola

Blurb A Story Of Love, Revenge And Cappuccino.

Quick Change •• [1990]

Director: **Howard Franklin & Bill Murray**
Screenplay: **Howard Franklin**

After an audacious New York bank robbery, a trio of thieves can't find their way to the airport. Although the heist's one of the cleverest yet put on film, the movie then gets as lost as the thieves with gags being scattered aimlessly everywhere.

They needed better directions, particularly from behind the director's chair, occupied by Murray for the first time.

[89m/15]

Grimm .... Bill Murray
Phyllis .... Geena Davis
Loomis .... Randy Quaid
Chief Rotzinger .... Jason Robards
Also: Richard Joseph Paul, Tony Shalhoub, Victor Argo, Philip Bosco, Kurtwood Smith, Jack Gilpin

The Quiet Earth •• [1985]

Director: Geoff Murphy
Screenplay: Bill Baer, Bruno Lawrence & Sam Pillsbury

'Woke up this morning, Everyone else on earth was gone.' Boffin Lawrence gets the blues in a big way in this New Zealand sci-fi pic. Sadly, a great idea isn't wholly successfully sustained.

[91m/15]

Zac Hobson .... Bruno Lawrence
Joanne .... Alison Routledge
Api .... Peter Smith

Quigley Down Under ••• [1990]

Director: Simon Wincer
Screenplay: John Hill

This entertaining Australian set Western has marksman Selleck locking antlers with wealthy landowner Rickman, whose idea of sport is culling Aborigines.

[120m/12]

Matthew Quigley .... Tom Selleck
Crazy Cora .... Laura San Giacomo
Elliott Marston .... Alan Rickman
Maj. Ashley Pitt .... Chris Haywood
Quote 'God created all men, but Sam Colt made them equal.'

The Rachel Papers • [1989]

Director: Damian Harris
Screenplay: Damian Harris

Fletcher logs his girlfriends' details on a computer as an aid to his seductions. However, his determination to bed older Rachel before going to university meets with stiffer than usual resistance. A silly compromise of Martin Amis' enjoyably unpleasant novel, set in the wrong era, softened and with an American actress plonked in the middle.

[95m/18]

Charles Highway .... Dexter Fletcher
Rachel Noyce .... Ione Skye
Norman .... Jonathan Pryce
Also: James Spader, Bill Paterson, Shirley Anne Field, Jared Harris, Michael Gambon
OOPS! The title made sense in the pre-tech 70s when it was a novel. Now that Charles keeps all his records on a computer, it's completely nonsensical.
Psst! The director is Richard Harris' son.

Racing with the Moon ••• [1984]

Director: Richard Benjamin
Screenplay: Steve Kloves

Two small-town lads are about to join the forces in World War II. One falls in love and the other has to cope with his girlfriend's pregnancy. The commonplace material is deftly and entertainingly handled by one-time actor Benjamin. Several scenes are also a visual joy, particularly the old-fashioned bowling alley and the moment when the boys play 'Boogie-Woogie Bugle Boy' to a first-aid rehearsal and get the make-believe corpses jiving.

[108m/15]

Henry 'Hopper' Nash .... Sean Penn
Caddie Winger .... Elizabeth McGovern
Nicky .... Nicolas Cage
Mr. Nash .... John Karlen
Mrs. Nash .... Rutanya Alda
Mr. Arthur .... Max Showalter
Gatsby Boy .... Crispin Glover
Frank .... Michael Madsen
Baby Face .... Dana Carvey

Psst! Dana Garvey, Garth of *Wayne's World*, has a bit part as 'Baby Face.'

R

Radio Days ••• [1987]

Director: Woody Allen
Screenplay: Woody Allen

Woody's tribute to the time when families gathered round their wireless sets will probably best be enjoyed by those who remember those nostalgic days of valves, dance bands and cats' whiskers. But there's still a good deal of pleasure in the picture of Jewish family life, even if it is presented in a series of sketches, rather than melded into a coherent whole.

[85m/PG]

Narrator ....Woody Allen
Sally White....................................Mia Farrow
Little Joe ....Seth Green
Mother...Julie Kavner
Father ....Michael Tucker
Aunt Bea ....Dianne Wiest
Uncle Abe.....................................Josh Mostel
Masked Avenger....................Wallace Shawn
Rabbi Baumel...........................Kenneth Mars
Rocco..Danny Aiello
Biff Baxter ....Jeff Daniels
Ad man..................................Mercedes Ruehl
Sy ....Richard Portnow
'Silver Dollar' M.C..................Tony Roberts
New Year's singer ....Diane Keaton

A Rage in Harlem ••• [1991]

Director: Bill Duke
Screenplay: Bobby Crawford

Fast-paced comedy caper with Givens the gangster's moll on the run with stolen gold, who bewitches open-mouthed wimp Whitaker into sheltering her. Great fun, with plenty of action and laughs. The former Mrs. Mike Tyson is superbly sassy, as well as incredibly sexy, in dresses she was apparently sewn into.

[110m/18]

Jackson ....Forest Whitaker
Goldy ....Gregory Hines
Imabelle......................................Robin Givens
Bith Kathy....................................Zakes Mokae
Easy Money..............................Danny Glover

The Raggedy Rawney ••• [1989]

Director: Bob Hoskins
Screenplay: Bob Hoskins & Nicole De Wilde

A deserter takes refuge with a band of gypsies, who discover that he has strange powers. In his debut behind the camera, Hoskins fashions a mystical, magical, humorous tale which has a strange, other-wordly feel to it. [102m/15]

Darky ....Bob Hoskins
Tom ....Dexter Fletcher
Jessie...Zoe Nathenson
Lamb ....Dave Hill
Weasel..Ian Dury
Elle ....Zoe Wanamaker

Quote 'Being a director is like being pecked to death by a thousand pigeons. Everybody's got questions. You get out of the car in the morning. All you want is a bacon sandwich and there they are: "What do you want me to do about this? How are we going to do that?" It even got to the point when I'd go to the loo they'd be banging on the door.' [Hoskins]

The Rainbow •• [1989]

Director: Ken Russell
Screenplay: Vivian Russell & Ken Russell

Ken Russell does D.H. Lawrence again, giving us a prequel to *Women in Love* twenty years on. But with a '15' certificate, we know his heart can't be in it. A surprisingly straight and un-Russell-like adaptation of the story of a girl's sexual awakening, helped along the way by gym teacher Donohoe and soldier McGann.

[104m/15]

Ursula Brangwen ....Sammi Davis
Anton Skrebensky......................Paul McGann
Winifred Inger....................Amanda Donohoe
Also: Christopher Gable, David Hemmings, Glenda Jackson, Dudley Sutton, Jim Carter

Psst! Glenda Jackson here plays the mother of the character she played in *Women in Love*, made in 1970.

Rain Man •••• [1988]

Director: **Barry Levinson**
Screenplay: **Ronald Bass & Barry Morrow**

How rare to find an 'issue' movie that is so immensely enjoyable. Cruise is the self-centred hotshot, furious to discover that his father's money has been left to an unknown autistic brother. Cruise nabs him from the asylum in the hope he can con him out of the money but as they drive, his character begins to change. Tacky though it might sound, the movie is not only a moving insight into the world of the *idiot savant*, but also an incredibly funny buddy movie. Hoffman naturally relishes his part, but Cruise, with no autistic acting props to fall back on, is also remarkably good.   **[133m/15]**

Raymond Babbitt	Dustin Hoffman
Charles Babbitt	Tom Cruise
Susanna	Valeria Golino
Dr. Bruner	Gerald R. Molen
John Mooney	Jack Murdock
Vern	Michael D. Roberts
Lanny	Ralph Seymour
Iris	Lucinda Jenney
Sally Dibbs	Bonnie Hunt

Oscars Best Picture, Dustin Hoffman, Best Director, Best Screenplay

Quote 'K-Mart sucks!'

Psst! In the restaurant, the last two names memorised by Hoffman are Marsha and William Gottsegen, his real in-laws ✦ Hoffman received a total of around $20m ✦ He was originally offered the Cruise part but preferred to be Raymond. He was the one who suggested that the disability be switched from simple retardation to autism ✦ Every airline in the world bar one cut the scene where Raymond's afraid to fly. Only Quantas showed it, as Raymond quoted statistics that it was the only airline never to have had a fatal crash. Quantas had every reason to be grateful. Ticket sales rose after the film came out ✦ This is said to be Princess Diana's favourite film ✦ Among the directors associated with the project before Levinson were Martin Brest, Steven Spielberg and Sydney Pollack, who quarrelled with Hoffman as he had done on *Tootsie* ✦ Spielberg turned down $5m to direct it. Levinson said later that among the Spielberg ideas he jettisoned were some wacky chase scenes ✦ Levinson appears in a cameo as the psychiatrist near the end of the film.

Raising Arizona •••• [1987]

Director: **Joel Coen**
Screenplay: **Ethan Coen & Joel Coen**

Thief Cage has his mugshot taken so many times by cop Hunter that they get hitched. When they can't have a child, they decide that a millionaire with quintuplets wouldn't miss just one. Things are further complicated by a couple of Cage's old buddies showing up uninvited. A hilarious way-out comedy from those fabulous Coen boys, full of great acting, gags, chases and photography.   **[94m/15]**

H.I.	Nicolas Cage
Ed	Holly Hunter
Nathan Arizona Sr.	Trey Wilson
Gale	John Goodman
Evelle	William Forsythe
Glen	Sam McMurray
Dot	Frances McDormand
Leonard Smalls	Randall "Tex" Cobb
Machine shop earbender	M. Emmet Walsh

Quote 'I'll be taking these Huggies and, er, whatever cash you got.'

Raising Cain •• [1992]

Director: **Brian De Palma**
Screenplay: **Brian De Palma**

Silly De Palma thriller has Lithgow as a child psychologist with a split personality who starts kidnapping children to experiment upon. Although the visuals are interesting, it's incredibly confusing stuff with reality and dreams mixed so much we're in danger of going as mad as Cain. It ends up inspiring laughs rather than shocks. Steadicam buffs will love the long walk in the hi-tech police station.

[92m/15]

Carter/Cain/Nix/Josh/Margo.....John Lithgow
Jenny ....Lolita Davidovich
Jack...Steven Bauer
Dr. Waldheim..................Frances Sternhagen

OOPS! As he enters the baby's bedroom late in the movie to check on a noise, the light switch changes positions in consecutive shots.

Rambling Rose •••• [1991]

Director: **Martha Coolidge**
Screenplay: **Calder Willingham**

A naive but sexually uninhibited girl arrives in an old-fashioned Southern household and soon has all the men in the family, indeed in the town, in a tizzy. This unusual coming-of-age movie is charming, warm, witty and full of delightful suprises. [112m/15]

Rose..Laura Dern
Daddy ....Robert Duvall
Mother...Diane Ladd
Buddy Hillyer................................Lukas Haas
Willcox Hillyer ....John Heard
Dr. Martinson ....Kevin Conway
Dave Wilkie ....Robert Burke

Psst! Dern and Ladd were both nominated for Oscars, the first time it has ever happened to a mother and daughter for the same film.

Rambo: First Blood Part II •• [1985]

Director: **George Pan Cosmatos**
Screenplay: **Sylvester Stallone & James Cameron**

This daft, macho, gung-ho tale has one-man-army Rambo popping into Cambodia to rescue soldiers reported missing in action. Despite occasional excitement, credibility is strained considerably by Rambo's invincibility. At least Superman can be brought down by Kryptonite. The sequel to *First Blood*. [96m/15]

John Rambo........................Sylvester Stallone
Major Trautman ....Richard Crenna
Murdock...............................Charles Napier

Co Bao......................................Julia Nickson
Podovsky ....Steven Berkoff

Quote 'This time do we get to win?'

Psst! After 39 Americans, who had been kidnapped in Lebanon, were released in June 1985, President Reagan said: 'Boy, I saw *Rambo* last night. I know what to do the next time this happens.' • At test screenings, half the audience voted that Rambo should die at the end • The National Coalition of Television Violence clocked up 161 violent acts an hour, while *The Sun* recorded 44 killings, 5 by knife, 14 by bow and arrow, 3 by explosions, 2 from helicopters, 15 from guns and 2 by strangulation.

Rambo III • [1988]

Director: **Peter MacDonald**
Screenplay: **Sylvester Stallone & Sheldon Lettich**

Rambo leaves his nice, quiet monastery to tackle the Russians in Afghanistan. No wonder they got out soon afterwards. Leave any idea of plausibility behind. The violent action moves far faster than the script. [100m/18]

John Rambo........................Sylvester Stallone
Col. Trautman........................Richard Crenna
Zaysen......................................Marc De Jonge
Griggs..................................Kurtwood Smith

Quote 'God will have mercy. He won't.'

OOPS! Why has the Russian helicopter that Rambo steals got an American flag on it?

Psst! With a budget said to have reached $63m — of which Stallone got $19.5m — this was then the most expensive film in movie history. It was also made it into the list of top ten flops, with $30m lost • Filmgoers got plenty for their money, though, with around 130 killings in the film, more than one a minute • During the making of the movie, Stallone had to fire an arrow towards a camera 75 yards away. The nearer he got it, the better-looking the shot. The arrow hit and smashed the lens • The original ending had Rambo turning back and joining the rebels.

Rapid Fire •• [1992]

Director: Dwight H. Little
Screenplay: Alan McElroy

Some of us go for weeks without attending one drinks party where a machine gun fight breaks out. Not so Brandon Lee, son of the famous Bruce, who takes his bow as a pacifist student forced to help a cop break up a heroin operation after the wine and canapés are so rudely interrupted. The late Lee can handle himself in a fight but has rather more trouble chopping his way through the banal dialogue. [95m/18]

Jake Lo ....Brandon Lee
Mace Ryan ....Powers Boothe
Antonio Serrano.......................Nick Mancuso
Agent Stuart.......................Raymond J. Barry
Blurb Unarmed And Extremely Dangerous.
Psst! The fight on the elevated railway was almost as dangerous as it looks. In order to bring the train in, the current couldn't be turned off. So the rail is live throughout. The only safety device was a buzzer to alert the doctor if an actor touched the rail • Like his father, Lee was killed on the film set when, during the making of his next film, a real .44 bullet hit him instead of a blank.

Rappin' • [1985]

Director: Joel Silberg
Screenplay: Robert Litz & Adam Friedman

Rappin' can solve all the world's problems, so we're led to believe. Here it helps ex-con Van Peebles clear out the bad guys from a Pittsburgh ghetto area. Pretty much along the lines of *Breakdance*. [92m/PG]

John Hood ....Mario Van Peebles
Dixie...Tasia Valenza
Duane...Charles Flohe

The Rapture • [1992]

Director: Michael Tolkin
Screenplay: Michael Tolkin

A telephone operator into sex of the most casual sort gets God in a big way and prepares for the Apocalypse. Despite being from the writer of *The Player*, this is a tedious, confusing and ultimately pointless satire on religion. [100m/18]

Sharon ....Mimi Rogers
Randy...................................David Duchovny
Vic...Patrick Bauchau
Mary ....Kimberly Cullum

Ratboy •• [1986]

Director: Sondra Locke
Screenplay: Rob Thompson

If you think you've seen this tale of a creature that's half-rat and half-man before, that's probably because it's so similar to *The Elephant Man*. Here, window dresser Locke hopes to cash in on the freak value, but sentiment and better nature intrude. [104m/15]

Nikki Morrison.........................Sondra Locke
Manny ....Robert Townsend
Acting coach....................Christopher Hewett
Jewell..Larry Hankin
aaa...Jon Lovitz
Psst! This was Locke's directorial debut. She was then Clint Eastwood's partner. They split up in 1989 with a $30m palimony settlement.

Raw Deal • [1986]

Director: John Irvin
Screenplay: Gary DeVore & Norman Wexler

Arnie takes on the Mafia and before you know it organised crime in the United States is at an end. Rather draggy vehicle for the pneumatic one, with some unwise attempts at injecting romance and human feeling when what's needed is extra steroids. Arnie in a dinner jacket has some amusement value, though. [106m/18]

Kaminski ....Arnold Schwarzenegger
Monique ....Kathryn Harrold
Patrovita..............................Sam Wanamaker
Also: Paul Shenar, Robert Davi, Ed Lauter
Quote 'One should not drink and bake.'

Razorback • [1985]

Director: Russell Mulcahy
Screenplay: Everette De Roche

The continent of Australia is threatened by a giant, man-eating ... pig? This boar is a bore. Short of making a horror pic about a man-eating canary, it's hard to see how they could have chosen a less frightening animal to terrorise the countryside. [95m/18]

Carl	Gregory Harrison
Sarah	Arkie Whiteley
Jake	Bill Kerr

Real Genius ••• [1985]

Director: Martha Coolidge
Screenplay: Neal Israel, Pat Proft & Peter Torokvei

This above-average teen comedy has a group of college boffins discovering that the laser they're building for their prof is destined for the military, who probably aren't planning on curing cataracts with it. It is refreshing to find real wit in such a film, which is briskly put together and decently acted. [104m/15]

Chris	Val Kilmer
Mitch	Gabe Jarret
Kent	Robert Prescott
Prof. Hathaway	William Atherton
CIA man Decker	Ed Lauter
Sherry	Patti D'Arbanville

Re-Animator •••• [1985]

Director: Stuart Gordon
Screenplay: Dennis Paoli, William J. Norris & Stuart Gordon

Potty scientist Combs develops a serum that brings a dead cat back to life. Before long, lethal corpses are rampaging. An absolutely splendid horror movie, combining sick humour with genuine scares and wasting not a second of screen time. Be warned, though. It is *very* gory. [86m/18]

Herbert West	Jeffrey Combs
Dan Cain	Bruce Abbott
Megan Halsey	Barbara Crampton

Dr. Carl Hill	David Gale
Dean Halsey	Robert Sampson

Blurb Death Is Just The Beginning.

Psst! Probably the first movie in which someone is murdered by a rampaging human intestine ✦ The credits include characters such as 'Failed Operation' and 'Motorcycle Accident'.

Rebecca's Daughters ••• [1992]

Director: Karl Francis
Screenplay: Guy Jenkin

The story of the Welsh revolt against English tollgates in the mid-19th century, when the men dressed up as women, is transformed into a rollicking, tongue-in-cheek farce. O'Toole, at one point dressed as a cigar-smoking Elizabeth I, hams it up so outrageously you could start a pig farm. Great fun. [90m/12]

Lord Sarn	Peter O'Toole
Anthony Raine	Paul Rhys
Rhiannon	Joely Richardson
Davy	Keith Allen
Capt. Marsden	Simon Dormandy

Quote 'No man's dressed up in my underclothes since the day my late husband died.'

Psst! Although rejigged, the original screenplay by Dylan Thomas was written in 1948. The 44-year gap in bringing it to the screen is a record, beating the previous title-holder, *The Doctor and the Devils*, also written by Dylan Thomas.

Rebel •• [1986]

Director: Michael Jenkins
Screenplay: Michael Jenkins & Bob Herbert

An American deserter in World War II falls for a nightclub singer in this Australian drama with music. Dillon should have deserted the film. He does it no favours. [91m/15]

Rebel	Matt Dillon
Kathy	Debbie Byrne
Tiger	Bryan Brown
Browning	Bill Hunter

Red Dawn • [1984]

Director: **John Milius**
Screenplay: **Kevin Reynolds & John Milius**

The eminently believable idea that the Russians and Cubans would invade the States by parachute was rendered slightly less plausible by the sight of acne-ridden American high school kids taking to the hills and there holding down the might of the Soviet War machine. **[114m/15]**

Jed...Patrick Swayze
Robert..............................C. Thomas Howell
Erica...Lea Thompson
Also: Charlie Sheen, Darren Dalton, Jennifer Grey, Harry Dean Stanton

Psst! The studio had to apologise to the Senator from Alaska because of the publicity saying that: 'In our time, no foreign army has ever occupied American soil. Until now.' He had to remind them that the Aleutians were occupied in World War II. The studio continued with the campaign, though, with the studio claiming that 'in our time' did not stretch back that far.

Red Heat •• [1988]

Director: **Walter Hill**
Screenplay: **Harry Kleiner, Walter Hill & Troy Kennedy Martin**

For once Der Arnold gets a chance to use his accent, even if it is anachronistically as a Russian cop on the trail of a drug pusher. Teaming up with Chicago cop Belushi, he nearly manages to shove the Cold War back into the freezer. Despite *48 HRS* director Hill and *Edge of Darkness* scripter Martin as co-writer, it's a rather draggy and witless thriller. **[104m/18]**

Ivan Danko...............Arnold Schwarzenegger
Art Ridzik ....James Belushi
Lou Donnelly ....Peter Boyle
Viktor Rostavili..............................Ed O'Ross
Lieut. Stobbs..........................Larry Fishburne

Psst! This was the first American movie allowed to film in Moscow's Red Square.

Red Rock West ••• [1993]

Director: **John Dahl**
Screenplay: **John Dahl & Rick Dahl**

Splendid, often amusing, thriller has Cage down to his last five dollars in hick town Red Rock West in Wyoming. Mistaken for a hitman, he agrees to take on the contract but complications arise when the real gunman, the ever-brilliant Hopper, arrives. It's exciting stuff, despite being partly tongue-in-cheek, and the multi-layered plot is full of satisfying twists and turns. Boyle is wonderful in the sort of part Mary Astor used to make her own. **[98m/15]**

Michael Williams.......................Nicolas Cage
Lyle...Dennis Hopper
Suzanne Brown.....................Lara Flynn Boyle
Wayne Brown.................................J.T. Walsh
Deputy Greytack ....Timothy Carhart
Deputy Bowman ....Dan Shor

Red Sonja • [1985]

Director: **Richard Fleischer**
Screenplay: **Clive Exton & George Macdonald Fraser**

The only interest here is in a sword and sorcery epic having a female lead. As Nielsen is too wooden to display any emotions, it's hard to tell if she's cheesed off at discovering that her leading man has a bigger chest than her. **[89m/PG]**

Kalifor ....Arnold Schwarzenegger
Red Sonja.................................Brigitte Nielsen
Queen Gedren......................Sandahl Bergman
Quote 'In life, all is not swordplay.'

OOPS! When Sonja's sister is shot, you can clearly see that she is wearing a square object under her costume, out of which is sticking the arrow.

Reefer and the Model ••• [1989]

Director: **Joe Comerford**
Screenplay: **Joe Comerford**

Try and catch this entertaining Irish thriller if it comes on the box. Although a low-budget production with unknown actors, the tale of a quartet who turn to bank robbery is funny, off-beat and beautifully put together.

[90m/15]

Reefer	Ian McElhinney
Mother	Eve Watkinson
The model	Carol Scanlon
Spider	Sean Lawlor

The Reflecting Skin • [1990]

Director: **Philip Ridley**
Screenplay: **Philip Ridley**

Set in 50's Idaho, this oddball British pic is a surreal slice of Americana, full of eccentrics. A youngster worries that a vampire lives next door. Dire. Feels like David Lynch with constipation.

[95m/15]

Cameron Dove	Viggo Mortensen
Dolphin Blue	Lindsay Duncan
Seth	Jeremy Cooper

Psst! Probably the first movie to have an exploding frog in the first reel.

Regarding Henry •• [1991]

Director: **Mike Nichols**
Screenplay: **Jeffrey Abrams**

Harrison Ford gets whacked on the head, loses his memory and completely forgets that he's supposed to be good at picking decent scripts. Athough coming out just as everyone said goodbye to 80s greed and hello to the caring 90s, few were daft enough to fall for this crassly unsubtle and melodramatic tale of a scheming, cheating lawyer who suddenly begins his life afresh as New Man, all caring, wonderful and honest. A real wash-your-mouth-out-with-soap opera.

[107m/12]

Henry Turner	Harrison Ford
Sarah Turner	Annette Bening
Bradley	Bill Nunn
Rachel Turner	Mikki Allen
Charlie	Donald Moffat

Remo — Unarmed and Dangerous •• [1985]

Director: **Guy Hamilton**
Screenplay: **Christopher Wood**

A rather lacklustre spoof of James Bond — at least I *think* it's a spoof — in which Ward is signed up for undercover work and given the *Karate Kid* makeover by mentor Grey. Also known as *Remo Williams: The Adventure Begins.* **[121m/15]**

Remo Williams	Fred Ward
Chium	Joel Grey
Harold Smith	Wilford Brimley
Conn MacCleary	J.A. Preston

Remo Williams: The Adventure Begins

SEE: Remo — Unarmed and Dangerous

Renegades •• [1989]

Director: **Jack Sholder**
Screenplay: **David Rich**

Aren't policemen getting young? Few look quite as wet behind the ears as Sutherland in this virtually plotless but fast-moving buddy action thriller set in Philadelphia. Okay hokum. **[105m/18]**

Buster McHenry	Kiefer Sutherland
Hank	Lou Diamond Phillips
Barbara	Jami Gertz

Repo Man •• [1984]

Director: **Alex Cox**
Screenplay: **Alex Cox**

Another of those independent movies whose reputation far exceeds what's on offer. Estevez gets involved in the car repossession business with Stanton. There's a man with something malevolent glowing in his car boot, the odd car chase and some sort of government conspiracy. Whenever Cox — that irritating man who annoys us before *Moviedrome* films — runs out of ideas, he throws a new genre in. The sort of disjointed film that gives 'cult' a bad name. **[92m/18]**

Bud	Harry Dean Stanton
Otto	Emilio Estevez
Miller	Tracey Walter
Leila	Olivia Barash

Repossessed •   [1990]

Director: Bob Logan
Screenplay: Bob Logan

Proof that not every *Airplane*-style comedy with Leslie Nielsen is funny. This spoof of horror movies certainly won't rise again, despite Nielsen's best efforts as an eccentric exorcist.

[85m/15]

Nancy Aglet	Linda Blair
Ernest Weller	Ned Beatty
Father Jedidiah Mayii	Leslie Nielsen

Psst! The split pea soup Blair serves her family is an in-joke referring back to her role in *The Exorcist*. In the famous vomit sequence, it was actually split pea soup that came out of her mouth.

The Rescue
SEE: Let's Get Harry

The Rescuers Down Under •••   [1991]

Director: Hendel Butoy & Mike Gabriel
Screenplay: Jim Cox, Joe Ranft & Others

A little odd to be doing this sequel 13 years after the original, but definitely a sign that the resurgence of Disney cartoons was truly on the way. The mice travel to Australia on a rescue mission, taking along several suitcases of gags and some pretty nifty animation.

[77m/U]

Bernard	Bob Newhart
Miss Bianca	Eva Gabor
Wilbur	John Candy

Also: Tristan Rogers, Adam Ryen, George C. Scott, Douglas Seale, Frank Welker, Peter Firth

Reservoir Dogs ••••   [1992]

Director: Quentin Tarantino
Screenplay: Quentin Tarantino

Startlingly good debut by writer-director Tarantino, depicting in real time the aftermath of a bungled jewel robbery. Be warned that one scene is horrifically violent. The acting and dialogue fairly fizz with wit and energy. If only film-makers didn't forget how to make tight little thrillers like this once they're given big bucks to spend.   **[105m/18]**

Mr. White	Harvey Keitel
Mr. Orange	Tim Roth
Nice Guy Eddie	Christopher Penn
Mr. Pink	Steve Buscemi
Joe Cabot	Lawrence Tierney
Mr. Blonde	Michael Madsen
Mr. Brown	Quentin Tarantino
Mr. Blue	Eddie Bunker

Blurb Let's Get To Work.

Psst! Tarantino was working as a videostore manager when he wrote the script. To add to his credibility, he claimed to have acted in Jean-Luc Godard's *King Lear*, on the pretty safe assumption that no-one in Hollywood would actually have seen it ✦ Eddie Bunker, playing Mr. Blue, was at 17 the youngest prisoner in San Quentin, serving several sentences over the year for forgery and armed robbery before turning to writing and acting ✦ Madsen's role as the psycho was so convincing that his sister Virginia was subsequently able to ward off unwanted advances by simply mentioning who her brother was ✦ This wasn't the first crime movie where the principals used colours for names, as those who remember the wonderful *The Taking of Pelham, One, Two, Three* recalled.

Restless Natives •   [1985]

Director: Michael Hoffman
Screenplay: Ninian Dunnett

In this dreadfully pale imitation of Bill Forsyth whimsy, a couple of lads become modern highwaymen, robbing tourist coaches on motorbikes, only to find that the tourists love it. **[89m/PG]**

Will..Vincent Friell
Ronnie...Joe Mullaney
Mr. Bryce.....................................Bernard Hill
Also: Ann Scott-Jones, Ned Beatty

Resurrected •• [1989]

Director: **Paul Greengrass**
Screenplay: **Martin Allen**

A dead Falklands 'hero' causes problems for himself and everyone else when he turns up seven weeks after he was reported missing. A rather downbeat true tale. **[96m/15]**

Mr. Deakin.......................................Tom Bell
Mrs. Deakin..........................Rita Tushingham
Kevin Deakin..........................David Thewlis
Gregory Deakin.......................Michael Pollitt
Showing *Reach For The Sky.*

Retribution • [1988]

Director: **Guy Magar**
Screenplay: **Guy Magar & Lee Wasserman**

Taken over by the soul of a murder victim, an artist is forced to seek the bad guys who did him in. A stylish but still rather tiresome horror pic. **[108m/18]**

George Miller.....................Dennis Lipscomb
Jennifer Curtis..............................Leslie Wing
Angel.......................................Suzanne Snyder
Psst! Probably the first movie to have a villain placed inside a pig and sent through an abattoir.

The Return of Captain Invincible •• [1983]

Director: **Philippe Mora**
Screenplay: **Steven E. de Souza & Andrew Gaty**

Bet you didn't even know he'd been away. The poor old Cap's now a drunk in the back streets, hauled out of retirement to save the world just one more time. This Aussie *Superman* spoof is enjoyable, if a little lacking in inspiration. **[100m/PG]**

Capt. Invincible...........................Alan Arkin
Mr. Midnight.......................Christopher Lee
Patty.......................................Kate Fitzpatrick
Tupper...Bill Hunter

The Return of Swamp Thing • [1989]

Director: **Jim Wynorski**
Screenplay: **Derek Spenser & Grant Morris**

Not a patch on the original tale of the friendly human vegetable, which itself wasn't a patch on almost anything else. **[88m/12]**

Dr. Anton Arcane.....................Louis Jourdan
Abby Arcane.......................Heather Locklear
Dr. Lana Zurrell.....................Sarah Douglas
Swamp Thing............................Dick Durock
Psst! At one point Jourdan spouts to a parrot the lyrics of a song from *Gigi*, the musical he was in thirty years earlier.

Return of the Jedi ••• [1983]

Director: **Richard Marquand**
Screenplay: **Lawrence Kasdan & George Lucas**

A near-clone of *Star Wars*, this third in the series has some great effects, Vader building an unbeatable new Death Star (ha!), Luke going off to play with daddy and Leia getting some unwanted sexual harrassment. But it also has Yoda and the Ewoks and some pretty icky sentimental stuff along the way. That's not to say it's not great entertainment. It's just not quite as good as the others. **[133m/PG]**

Luke Skywalker...........................Mark Hamill
Han Solo..................................Harrison Ford
Princess Leia..............................Carrie Fisher
Lando Calrissian..............Billy Dee Williams
Yoda...Frank Oz
C-3PO...............................Anthony Daniels
Chewbacca...............................Peter Mayhew
Anakin Skywalker..................Sebastian Shaw
Emperor.................................Ian McDiarmid
Darth Vader............................David Prowse
Voice of Darth Vader...........James Earl Jones
Ben (Obi-Wan) Kenobi..........Alec Guinness
R2-D2..Kenny Baker

Psst! Even after some of the posters were printed, it was still called *Revenge of the Jedi*. Then they decided that noble Jedi didn't go in for revenge. Those few posters are now worth a few bob ✦ Although by this stage Princess Leia was wearing very little, for *Star Wars* itself Carrie Fisher had to have her breasts taped down, as producer George Lucas had decided that there were 'no breasts in space'. She claimed she toyed with the idea of setting up a lottery to see who could rip the tape off at the end of each day's filming ✦ Mark Hamill was once the voice of *Flipper* and of Jeannie in the *I Dream of Jeannie* cartoon TV series ✦ In theory this is the third film in the middle of three trilogies, *Star Wars* being No. 4.

The Return of the Living Dead ••• [1985]

Director: **Dan O'Bannon**
Screenplay: **Dan O'Bannon**

A lethal gas escapes from a military depot and makes the local graveyard a livelier than usual spot to be of an evening. Entertaining piss-take on George Romero's zombie trilogy, with a kinky subtext on the eroticism of death. The laughs and chills are somewhat clumsily integrated, though. **[91m/18]**

Burt	Clu Gulager
Frank	James Karen
Ernie	Don Calfa
Freddy	Thom Mathews

Quote 'More brainsssss!'

The Return of the Living Dead: Part II • [1988]

Director: **Ken Wiederhorn**
Screenplay: **Ken Wiederhorn**

Same old gas, same old corpses. But all the life's been drained out of the party. **[90m/18]**

Ed	James Karen
Joey	Thom Mathews
Tom Essex	Dana Ashbrook

The Return of the Musketeers •• [1989]

Director: **Richard Lester**
Screenplay: **George Macdonald Fraser**

The musketeers, whose maths is so bad they get stuck at three when there are really four of them, decide that there's money in the sequel business and get together again for a reunion. This third Lester Musketeer film looks much like the first all over again, with lots of roustabout bawdy humour and sword fights. **[100m/PG]**

D'Artagnan	Michael York
Athos	Oliver Reed
Porthos	Frank Finlay
Aramis	Richard Chamberlain
Athos's son	C. Thomas Howell

Psst! Roy Kinnear was killed during the making of the film.

Return of the Soldier •• [1983]

Director: **Alan Bridges**
Screenplay: **Hugh Whitemore**

Bates is the shell-shocked officer returning home after World War I with no memory. Despite the splendid acting from all concerned, particularly Bates as the man who doesn't want to remember, we've been through the amnesia trip just once too often. **[101m/12]**

Chris	Alan Bates
Margaret	Glenda Jackson
Kitty	Julie Christie
Jenny	Ann-Margret

Return to Oz • [1985]

Director: **Walter Murch**
Screenplay: **Walter Murch & Gill Dennis**

Any time you think you might be tiring of *The Wizard of Oz*, just try this desperate sequel, as full of *joie de vivre* as a cadaver. A truly depressing story that will make you long to get back to Kansas. **[110m/U]**

Dr. Worley/Nome King	Nicol Williamson
Nurse Wilson/Princess Mombi	Jean Marsh
Dorothy	Fairuza Balk
Aunt Em	Piper Laurie

Return to the Blue Lagoon •   [1991]

Director: William A. Graham
Screenplay: Leslie Stevens

One of the least welcome sequels ever. The son of the original castaways gets cast away himself on yet another tropical island with a pretty girl and her mom. Soon the chaperone isn't feeling too well and it's time to learn about sex all over again. If only that bally shark were just a little quicker.   [98m/PG]

The girl	Milla Jovovich
The boy	Brian Krause
Sarah Hargrave	Lisa Pelikan

Reuben, Reuben ••   [1983]

Director: Robert Ellis Miller
Screenplay: Julius J. Epstein

A Scottish poet indulges in much drinking and chasing of women, until he finds himself in love for the first time with a young student. Only Conti's charm can make this palatable.   [100m/15]

Gowan McGland	Tom Conti
Geneva Spofford	Kelly McGillis
Frank Spofford	Roberts Blossom
Bobby Springer	Cynthia Harris

Psst! This was McGillis' debut.

Reunion •••   [1990]

Director: Jerry Schatzberg
Screenplay: Harold Pinter

Elderly Jewish businessman Robards travels back to his home town in Germany. There, he recalls his childhood friendship with a local aristocrat when Nazism was in the ascendent. A well-written and atmospheric film, with wonderful acting from the young leads, this is a coming-of-age story with a difference.   [110m/12]

Henry Strauss	Jason Robards
Hans Strauss	Christien Anholt
Konradin von Lohenburg	Samuel West
Grafin von Lohenburg	Françoise Fabian

Revenge ••   [1990]

Director: Tony Scott
Screenplay: Jim Harrison & Jeffrey Fiskin

Flier Costner falls for Stowe, Quinn's comely young wife. This isn't Surbiton, where wife-swapping's the order of the day. It's Mexico, where they take these things seriously, *very* seriously. For two-thirds of the way, this is an underrated romantic thriller, with strong atmosphere and a sense of doom. It does take a siesta before the end, though.   [124m/18]

Jay Cochran	Kevin Costner
Tiburon	Anthony Quinn
Miryea	Madeleine Stowe

Also: Tomas Milian, James Gammon, Jesse Corti, Sally Kirkland, Miguel Ferrer

Revenge of the Nerds ••   [1984]

Director: Jeff Kanew
Screenplay: Steve Zacharias & Jeff Buhai

The nerds on campus (i.e. those who want an education) form their own fraternity and fight back against the bullying of the football-playing jocks. Despite the fact that more of the audience can probably identify with the heroes here than in other teen pics, it's not really all that different, except that the ones we're rooting for wear glasses.   [90m/18]

Lewis	Robert Carradine
Gilbert	Anthony Edwards
Poindexter	Timothy Busfield
Coach Harris	John Goodman
Stan	Ted McGinley

Revenge of the Ninja ••   [1983]

Director: Sam Firstenberg
Screenplay: James R. Silke

The sequel to *Enter the Ninja* and the one before *Ninja III*. It moves fast enough but it's unlikely to convert any martial arts haters to the genre.   [88m/18]

Cho	Sho Kosugi
Dave	Keith Vitali
Lt. Dime	Virgil Frye

Reversal of Fortune •••• [1990]

Director: **Barbet Schroeder**
Screenplay: **Nicholas Kazan**

The comatose Sunny von Bulow reflects on her insulin overdose and the case for murder brought against her husband. A brilliantly original approach to the stuff of TV docudramas, pitting European decadence against American naivety. A devastating exposé of the seductions and corruptions of the ultra-rich, with the show stolen by Irons as the charming, enigmatic Claus. [111m/15]

Sunny Von Bulow........................Glenn Close
Claus Von Bulow........................Jeremy Irons
Alan Dershowitz.............................Ron Silver
Sarah ....Annabella Sciorra
Maria...Uta Hagen
David Marriott ....Fisher Stevens
Peter Macintosh..............................Jack Gilpin
Andrea Reynolds ....Christine Baranski
Elon Dershowitz......................Stephen Mailer
Alexandra....................................Julie Hagerty

Oscars Jeremy Irons

Revolution • [1985]

Director: **Hugh Hudson**
Screenplay: **Robert Dillon**

At last, the real reason Britain lost America. We bored them so much they couldn't stand it any more. Words can hardly describe the sheer scale of this monumental turkey, enough for Thanksgiving for the entire rebel army. Confusing battle scenes, terrible acting and a staggeringly dull script spelt doom, not only for the audience, but also for the great white hope of British film production, Goldcrest, which was brought to its knees by this disaster.

[125m/PG]

Tom Dobb ....Al Pacino
Sgt. Maj. Peasy..................Donald Sutherland
Daisy ....Nastassja Kinski
Also: Joan Plowright, Dave King, Steven Berkoff

Rich In Love •• [1993]

Director: **Bruce Beresford**
Screenplay: **Alfred Uhry**

When mum Clayburgh leaves home and the demanding Finney, a young girl has to try to hold the family together. One expects great things from the talent involved, particularly as these are the film-makers who brought us *Driving Miss Daisy*. Unfortunately, having a meandering storyline is one thing, but there's a big difference between languid and lethargic.

[105m/PG]

Warren Odom ....Albert Finney
Helen Odom ....Jill Clayburgh
Lucille Odom ....Kathryn Erbe
Billy McQueen....................Kyle MacLachlan
Also: Piper Laurie, Ethan Hawke, Suzy Amis, Alfre Woodard

Ricochet ••• [1991]

Director: **Russell Mulcahy**
Screenplay: **Steven E. de Souza**

Psycho Lithgow escapes from prison, determined to revenge himself on the Assistant DA, Washington, who's soon the victim of a frame the Mona Lisa would be proud of. Despite the gratuitous violence and some holes in the plot big enough to drive a juggernaut through, this is another gritty and exciting action pic from producer Joel Silver.

[110m/18]

Nick Styles........................Denzel Washington
Blake ....John Lithgow
Odessa ....Ice T
Larry...Kevin Pollak
Brimleigh..................................Lindsay Wagner
Alice.......................................Victoria Dillard

Blurb This Is One Case That's Going To Be Settled Out Of Court.

Riders of the Storm
SEE: **The American Way**

Riff-Raff •• [1991]

Director: **Ken Loach**
Screenplay: **Bill Jesse**

Made for TV, this dour, low-budget picture of life on a London building site proved immensely popular on the Continent, but not with British audiences. If you're feeling too happy, you could always try it as a depressant. [95m/15]

Stevie	Robert Carlyle
Susan	Emer McCourt
Shem	Jimmy Coleman
Mo	George Moss

Psst! Because of the dialects, the film was subtitled for the American and Australian markets.

The Right Stuff •••• [1983]

Director: **Philip Kaufman**
Screenplay: **Philip Kaufman**

Long but often exhilarating account of the early days of America's space pro-gramme, largely centred around the story of test pilot Chuck Yeager. Based on the book by Tom Wolfe, it's nothing like the straightforward documentary you'd expect, but has some sharp and funny satire mixed in with the exciting aerial footage. Despite its length, *The Right Stuff* is just that. [193m/15]

Chuck Yeager	Sam Shepard
Glennis Yeager	Barbara Hershey
Alan Shepard	Scott Glenn
John Glenn	Ed Harris
Gordon Cooper	Dennis Quaid
Gus Grissom	Fred Ward
Pancho Barnes	Kim Stanley
Betty Grissom	Veronica Cartwright
Trudy Cooper	Pamela Reed
Deke Slayton	Scott Paulin
Scott Carpenter	Charles Frank
Wally Schirra	Lance Henriksen
Lyndon Johnson	Donald Moffat
Sally Rand	Peggy Davis
Government recruiter	Jeff Goldblum
Louise Shepard	Kathy Baker

Psst! Brigadier General Chuck Yeager, played in the film by Sam Shepard, has a small part as Fred, the barman • A stuntman was killed filming the scene where an ejecting pilot doesn't pull his ripcord in time • The space suit material was left over from some silver costumes that had been made for Cher!

Rising Sun [1993]

Director: **Philip Kaufman**
Screenplay: **Philip Kaufman**

This controversial murder mystery set in Los Angeles touched a raw nerve in Hollywood because of its background of competition between American and Japanese big business. Detectives Connery and Snipes are investigating a woman's murder in the offices of a Japanese company.

With: Sean Connery, Wesley Snipes, Tia Carrere, Harvey Keitel, Kevin Anderson, Ray Wise

Psst! As with another Summer '93 block-buster, *Jurassic Park*, this is based on a novel by Michael Crichton, once a director of films like *Coma*. However, because of Japanese investment in Hollywood, the anti-Jap sentiment of the book was sharply toned down • This is the first film in which Shelley Michelle's face has been seen. Her body, however, has been seen in films like *Pretty Woman* and *My Stepmother Is An Alien*, doubling for the shy stars.

Risky Business •• [1983]

Director: **Paul Brickman**
Screenplay: **Paul Brickman**

Every parent's nightmare brought to life. As soon as young puppy Cruise's folks go away, he starts dallying with delightful hooker De Mornay, only to find things going seriously wrong when she pushes him into a money-making scheme. There are some things Yellow Pages *can't* put right before your parents get home. Despite the film's high reputation, it's only slightly better than the average 'first time' teen sex comedy, although interest-ing to see two stars just starting out. It's a crime it took De Mornay almost another ten years to make it after this. Worth checking out that famous subway ride...

[98m/18]

Joel Goodsen	Tom Cruise
Lana	Rebecca De Mornay
Guido	Joe Pantoliano
Rutherford	Richard Masur
Barry	Bronson Pinchot

OOPS! Keep your eye on the van taking away the furniture from the house and watch the furniture vanish.

Psst! The film originally ended with Cruise losing De Mornay and failing to get into college. But when only 38% of a test audience said they 'would recommend' the movie to friends, the studio hurriedly filmed two extra minutes. This time 70% said they 'would recommend' the film ◆ Cruise dieted to lose a stone in a month for the movie, then gave up on exercise to put on 'a little layer of baby fat.' ◆ He also did Ray-Ban something of a favour. Their Wayfarers, designed in the early 50s, were shifting only 18,000 a year until *Risky Business*. The following year 360,000 were sold. It's now up to four million a year. *Top Gun* had the same effect with another Ray-Ban model. The company now pays to put its glasses in a couple of hundred movies and TV shows each year.

Rita, Sue and Bob Too ••• [1987]

Director: **Alan Clarke**
Screenplay: **Andrea Dunbar**

Rita and Sue babysit for a middle-class couple in the evening, then bonk husband Bob on the way home in the car. A raucous, energetic comedy of Northern urban life, giving a more vivid insight than some fastidious critics would care to admit about moral values and attitudes north of Watford Gap. More laughs than *Distant Voices* too. **[93m/18]**

Bob	George Costigan
Rita	Siobhan Finneran
Sue	Michelle Holmes
Michelle	Lesley Sharp

The River •• [1984]

Director: **Mark Rydell**
Screenplay: **Robert Dillon & Julian Barry**

Oh dear. Mel and Spacek are farmers having all the problems farmers have in movies: the bank about to foreclose, the river threatening to overflow, the crop failing and the cows giving birth to three-toed sloths. Oh, and there's that pesky wealthy neighbour planning to flood the valley by building a dam. All so tiresome, predictable and deathly slow that you want to wade in there and help with the dam yourself. **[124m/PG]**

Tom Garvey	Mel Gibson
Mae Garvey	Sissy Spacek
Lewis Garvey	Shane Bailey
Beth Garvey	Becky Jo Lynch
Joe Wade	Scott Glenn

Psst! The cow is called Jessica. Is it pure coincidence that Jessica Lange pulled out to make *Country* instead?

A River Runs Through It •• [1992]

Director: **Robert Redford**
Screenplay: **Richard Friedenberg**

J.R. Hartley: The Movie. And every bit as exciting as you'd expect. Sheffer and Pitt are the sons of fishing-mad clergyman Skerritt. The good one studies. The bad one becomes a drinking, womanising, gambling newspaperman. Only when they are fishing together on the Big Blackfoot are they together as a family (except for mum, who only gets to gut and cook their catch). Although the scenery's magnificent, relatively little happens in two hours. It's also mighty confusing that while Redford narrates, the Redford-lookalike Pitt is supposed to be not him but the other brother. **[123m/PG]**

Norman Maclean	Craig Sheffer
Paul Maclean	Brad Pitt
Rev. Maclean	Tom Skerritt
Mrs. Maclean	Brenda Blethyn
Jessie Burns	Emily Lloyd

Quote 'In our family, there was no clear line between religion and fly-fishing.'

Psst! The credits say that 'no fish were killed or injured during the making' of the film. If only one could say the same about the buffet at the Hollywood premiere, where salmon was served!
• So keen were they not to harm fish that they used a mechanical one for some shots and where real fish were used, they had a line tied through their lower jaw where there are no nerves. No hooks were used at all • Craig Sheffer was for a time valet to Count Basie.

River's Edge •••• [1987]

Director: **Tim Hunter**
Screenplay: **Neal Jimenez**

When a teenager murders his girlfriend, his friends decide not to let on. A black comic study of teenage alienation and moral vacuity, with Glover splendidly OTT and Hopper doing another of his 60's burn-outs. A welcome antidote to the John Hughes' cycle of wholesome teen comedies and, what's more, based on a real incident.

[99m/18]

Layne	Crispin Glover
Matt	Keanu Reeves
Clarissa	Ione Skye
Samson	Daniel Roebuck
Feck	Dennis Hopper
Tim	Joshua Miller

The Road Home •• [1989]

Director: **Hugh Hudson**
Screenplay: **Michael Weller**

Despite a strong debut performance from Adam Horovitz of The Beastie Boys, there's little we haven't seen before in this run-of-the-mill tale of a psychiatric clinic for troubled teenagers. Also known as *Lost Angels*.

[116m/15]

Dr. Charles Loftis	Donald Sutherland
Tim Doolan	Adam Horovitz
Cheryl Anderson	Amy Locane
Andy Doolan	Don Bloomfield

Road House •• [1989]

Director: **Rowdy Herrington**
Screenplay: **David Lee Henry & Hilary Henkin**

Swayze's a bouncer who likes nothing better than to get his teeth into a meaty philosphy book. Hired to clean up 'the kind of place where they sweep up the eyeballs after closing', he still finds time to take on local bad guy Gazzara and to show doctor Lynch that he has a mind to go with his body. Entertaining for a time, it's derailed by an excess of violence. [114m/18]

Dalton	Patrick Swayze
Elizabeth Clay	Kelly Lynch
Wade Garrett	Sam Elliott
Brad Wesley	Ben Gazzara

Quote 'I thought you'd be bigger.'

Robin Hood •• [1991]

Director: **John Irvin**
Screenplay: **Mark Allen Smith & John McGrath**

This rival to the Costner version is nothing like as bad as its reputation, but still shows signs of being rushed terribly to be first to the starting gate. Telling it straight, but with the tongue occasionally in the cheek, this one's historically on far surer ground than Kev; the Normans even sound as though they originated in France! Moderately entertaining – even though Robin's merry men are a pretty miserable bunch – it also contains some of worst rhubarbing from extras in many a year. [104m/PG]

"Robin Hood"	Patrick Bergin
Maid Marian	Uma Thurman
Sir Miles Folcanet	Jurgen Prochnow
Prince John	Edward Fox

Quote 'Baron, sometimes you are so wet one could shoot snipe off you.'

OOPS! After Robin wins the shooting contest with Will, he claims the secret's in the middle finger and makes a gesture with it that might be familiar to Americans, but certainly wouldn't be to the earthy Anglo-Saxons.

Robin Hood: Prince of Thieves ••• [1991]

Director: **Kevin Reynolds**
Screenplay: **Pen Densham & John Watson**

Deservedly the more successful of the two 1991 Robin Hoods. Although it starts sluggishly, once the film-makers forget this was supposed to be Politically Correct, it all becomes rollicking good fun, full of spectacle and great gags. Costner makes a likeable Hood, although his West Coast of Nottingham accent takes some getting used to. Although Costner's the outlaw, Rickman's the one who steals the picture as the hysterically funny, yet never less than evil, Sheriff of Nottingham. **[143m/PG]**

Robin of Locksley	Kevin Costner
Azeem	Morgan Freeman
Sheriff of Nottingham	Alan Rickman
Marian	Mary Elizabeth Mastrantonio
Will Scarlett	Christian Slater
King Richard	Sean Connery
Mortianna	Geraldine McEwan
Friar Tuck	Michael McShane
Lord Locksley	Brian Blessed
Guy of Gisborne	Michael Wincott
Little John	Nick Brimble
Fanny	Soo Drouet
Bull	Daniel Peacock

Quote 'Cancel the kitchen scraps for lepers and orphans. No more merciful behead-ings. And call off Christmas.' ♦ 'You! My room. 10.30 tonight...You! 10.45. And bring a friend.'

OOPS! Some say the use of gunpowder and a telescope wouldn't have been possible in the twelfth century. My old history professor claims it's feasible a Moor might have known about these, if a little unlikely ♦ However, printing definitely wasn't invented for another 200 years, so where do the 'Wanted' posters come from? ♦ The Sheriff's codpiece is well ahead of its time, as is his use of '10.30' to make assignations ♦ Even in the twelfth century, Hadrian's Wall wasn't anywhere near Nottingham, yet they're on it just before they arrive.

Psst! That isn't Costner's bottom in the bathing scene. A body double was used, not apparently because Costner was shy, but because the water was so cold! ♦ Sean Connery was paid $500,000 for his cameo turn, not a bad return for one day's work and one minute's screen time. He donated his fee to charity ♦ Several scenes with Rickman were cut when it seemed he was in danger of run-ning away with the movie. Amongst the bits lost is the revelation that the Sheriff is the witch's son ♦ The video has 30 further seconds gone, particularly noticeable when the Sheriff is trying to consummate his 'marriage', but the cut-ting off of a prisoner's hand is also gone, as is the hanging of the boy, while price-less dialogue like 'I've never seen the breasts of a noblewoman' and 'Bugger me' have vanished ♦ Look out for Jack Wild, star of the film musical *Oliver* as Much, one of Robin's men.

Robocop ••• [1987]

Director: **Paul Verhoeven**
Screenplay: **Edward Neumeier & Michael Miner**

Weller's the cop in ultra-violent future Detroit killed in the line of duty. Soon he's back as a rebuilt super-cyborg, the per-fect policeman. Then his human memory returns and he realises that OCP isn't such a philanthropic company after all. Great action-sci-fi that's more stylish, grittier and violent than most of its ilk, yet still has plenty of wit to dispense. Such a shame that ED209's effects have dated so quickly. **[103m/18]**

Murphy/RoboCop	Peter Weller
Lewis	Nancy Allen
Jones	Ronny Cox
Clarence Boddiker	Kurtwood Smith
Morton	Miguel Ferrer
Sgt. Reed	Robert DoQui
The Old Man	Dan O'Herlihy
TV Anchorwoman	Leeza Gibbons
Leon	Ray Wise
Johnson	Felton Perry

Blurb Part Man. Part Machine. All Cop.

Quote 'I'd buy that for a dollar!' ✦ 'Your move, creep!'

Psst! The TV anchorwoman who says 'You give us three minutes and we'll give you the world' is Leeza Gibbons, the reporter for the popular American TV show *Entertainment Tonight*. As well as the sequel, she pops up in *Maxie*, *Soapdish* and *The Player* ✦ 36 seconds of violence were cut from the cinema release while a further four seconds, showing how to break into a car, disappeared from the video.

Robocop 2 ✦   [1990]

Director: Irvin Kershner
Screenplay: Frank Miller & Walon Green

Despite one of the greatest cinema trailers of the decade, this was a pathetic sequel with plenty of nasty violence but little in the way of plot or humour.   [116m/18]

Robocop	Peter Weller
Anne Lewis	Nancy Allen
Donald Johnson	Felton Perry

Rock-a-Doodle ✦✦   [1991]

Director: Don Bluth
Screenplay: David N. Weiss

Excellent Bluth animation is, as usual, accompanied by a confused story. A ridiculed rooster heads to the big city, only for the animals on the farm to discover that the sun doesn't rise any more.
[74m/U]

With: Phil Harris, Glen Campbell

The Rocketeer ✦✦   [1991]

Director: Joe Johnston
Screenplay: Danny Bilson, Paul De Meo & William Dear

This tale of a pilot in the 30s who finds a top secret rocket-pack quickly runs out of fuel and plummets to earth. The characters are flimsy, the plot insubstantial and, worst of all, the flying sequences are incredibly jerky and unbelievable, as is the airship. What should have been great fun sadly isn't, although there are several neat in-jokes about Howard Hughes and his Spruce Goose project and wonderful walk-on parts for W.C. Fields and Clark Gable.   [120m/PG]

Cliff Secord	Bill Campbell
Peevy	Alan Arkin
Neville Sinclair	Timothy Dalton
Jenny	Jennifer Connelly
Eddie Valentine	Paul Sorvino

Quote 'How do I look?' – 'Like a hood ornament.' ✦ 'Congratulations, gentlemen. Thanks to the vigilance of the FBI, this particular vacuum cleaner won't fall into enemy hands.'

OOPS! The evening of Campbell's daring first stunt with the rocket-pack, Connelly has a date with Dalton. How come Campbell's derring-do is plastered over the Los Angeles Times in between? It's a morning paper ✦ Though Deutschmarks are used in the film, Germany's currency was the Reichsmark until 1948.

Psst! To understand the in-joke near the end, you should know that the famous sign was set up to sell property in the area and used to read 'Hollywoodland' ✦ A stuntman was killed after being thrown into a tree during filming.

Rocky IV ✦✦   [1985]

Director: Sylvester Stallone
Screenplay: Sylvester Stallone

Rocky dons the Stars and Stripes to whop seven bells out of the Russkie who did for his mate. The featherweight script has none of the agility or punch of the original and is topped off by a sick-making 'let's change the world for the better' speech by Sly to the Politburo.   [91m/PG]

Rocky Balboa	Sylvester Stallone
Drago	Dolph Lundgren
Apollo Creed	Carl Weathers

Also: Talia Shire, Burt Young, Brigitte Nielsen

Psst! This is where Stallone met Brigitte Nielsen, resulting in a short, tumultuous marriage and even more tumultuous divorce ✦ Stallone got $16m for acting, writing and directing it.

Rocky V •• [1990]

Director: John G. Avildsen
Screenplay: Sylvester Stallone

A gentler, kinder, brain-damaged Rocky loses everything and starts out again. Strictly formula stuff. The umpire should have counted Rocky out long ago. [104m/PG]

Rocky Balboa	Sylvester Stallone
Adrian Balboa	Talia Shire
Paulie	Burt Young
Rocky Balboa Jr.	Sage Stallone
Mickey Goldmill	Burgess Meredith

Psst! Stallone's remuneration was said to be $27.5m − over a quarter of a million dollars for each minute of screen time − plus 35% of the profits • Stallone's girlfriend Jennifer Flavin is one of the 'delivery girls', together with Tricia Flavin and Julie Flavin • Sly Jr. plays Rocky Jr.

Roger & Me •••• [1989]

Director: Michael Moore
Screenplay: Michael Moore

If you see only one documentary in your life, make it this one. Genial Moore's film is about the killing of Flint, Michigan by the closure of General Motors' plant there. Moore decides to track down GM's boss Roger Smith and ask him a few pertinent questions. The indifference to the personal tragedies by company officials is shocking, but what could have been so dull turns out instead to be lively and frequently hysterically funny. Much of the pleasure comes from knowing that this documentary was so startlingly successful that it will take GM years to recover from the public relations disaster. [91m/15]

With: The citizens of Flint, Michigan

Quote 'I was having a hard time finding my business card because I don't have any business cards. So I gave Mr. Slaughter my discount pass to Chucky Cheese.'

Psst! The one town in America where you couldn't see *Roger & Me* was Flint, Michigan. The cinema had closed down! • Moore sold his home and most of his

possessions to finance the film. He ran bingo games in Flint to raise cash and even collected empty drinks bottles for the refundable deposits!

Roger Corman's Frankenstein Unbound • [1990]

Director: Roger Corman
Screenplay: Roger Corman, F.X. Feeney & Edward Neumeier

After 19 years, low-budget quickie king Corman went behind the camera again. But this tale of a futuristic scientist going back to the early 19th century to meet Mary Shelley, author of Frankenstein, is a distinct disappointment. Also known as *Frankenstein Unbound*. [86m/18]

Dr. Joe Buchanan	John Hurt
Dr. Frankenstein	Raul Julia
Mary Godwin Shelley	Bridget Fonda

Also: Nick Brimble, Jason Patric

Romancing the Stone ••• [1984]

Director: Robert Zemeckis
Screenplay: Diane Thomas

Shy romantic novelist Turner travels to Colombia when her sister's in trouble, falling into big doo-doos herself and finding only the reluctant Douglas to help her. Splendid tongue-in-cheek old-fashioned adventure, with lots of gags, plenty of top-notch action and superb hate-each-other chemistry between the two stars. DeVito also scores as a slimy villain. [105m/PG]

Jack Colton	Michael Douglas
Joan Wilder	Kathleen Turner
Ralph	Danny DeVito
Ira	Zack Norman
Juan	Alfonso Arau
Zolo	Manuel Ojeda

OOPS! Although Douglas gives Turner a pretty necklace, what she takes in the next shot is completely different and looks rather crummy • Douglas must be putting on weight. As he swings on a rope into a rockface, it moves.

Romantic Comedy •• [1983]

Director: **Arthur Hiller**
Screenplay: **Bernard Slade**

A playwright falls in love with his writing partner, but finds romance easier to get right on the page than in real life. They could at least have blown the dust off this one after taking it off the shelf. **[103m/PG]**

Jason	Dudley Moore
Phoebe	Mary Steenburgen
Blanche	Frances Sternhagen

Romero ••• [1989]

Director: **John Duigan**
Screenplay: **John Sacret Young**

The church goes into the film business, starting with this gripping true-life tale of the Salvadoran archbishop, chosen for his meekness, who decides to stand up against the military government. Hardly classic film-making, but thanks to Julia it's powerful stuff. **[106m/15]**

Archbishop Oscar Romero	Raul Julia
Father Rutilio Grande	Richard Jordan
Arista Zelada	Ana Alicia
Lt. Columa	Eddie Velez

Psst! Probably the first movie produced by a Roman Catholic Priest. A branch of the Los Angeles Archdiocese set up the production company to make 'features about human values'.

Romper Stomper • [1993]

Director: **Geoffrey Wright**
Screenplay: **Geoffrey Wright**

Forgot those who garlanded this tale of Aussie skinheads with praise, claiming it was another *Clockwork Orange*. Like the characters it portrays, it's vicious, nasty and utterly pointless. **[94m/18]**

Hando	Russell Crowe
Davey	Daniel Pollock
Gabe	Jacqueline McKenzie
Martin	Alex Scott

Psst! Pollock, a heroin addict, killed himself by standing in front of a commuter train.

Rooftops • [1989]

Director: **Robert Wise**
Screenplay: **Terence Brennan**

Dire 'modern' musical set among the drifters and drug pushers on the Lower East Side of New York. Formulaic drivel from the 76-year-old director of *West Side Story*. **[95m/15]**

T	Jason Gedrick
Elana	Troy Beyer
Lobo	Eddie Velez

The Rookie • [1990]

Director: **Clint Eastwood**
Screenplay: **Boaz Yakin & Scott Spiegel**

A disappointing Eastwood cop pic that doesn't really gel. This despite the usual action and wisecracks and the bizarre sight of Braga raping the bound Clint while he tries not to do what a man's gotta do. **[115m/18]**

Nick Pulovski	Clint Eastwood
David Ackerman	Charlie Sheen
Strom	Raul Julia

OOPS! In the confusion, as Sheen's wife struggles with the villains, look out for a glimpse of a member of the crew.

Psst! There were more stuntmen than actors on the film, 87 against 37.

A Room With a View •••• [1986]

Director: **James Ivory**
Screenplay: **Ruth Prawer Jhabvala**

It's another Merchant-Ivory film of an E.M. Forster novel, this time set in Italy in 1907. Everyone is scandalised when young Bonham Carter gets a peck from Sands and bags are packed. This beautifully photographed and acted comedy of manners may be predictable, but it's also utterly delightful. There are times when it seems a pity that the only decent English films are costume dramas, but at least we do do them terribly, terribly well.

[115m/PG]

Charlotte Bartlett	Maggie Smith
Lucy Honeychurch	Helena Bonham Carter

Mr. Emerson	Denholm Elliott
George Emerson	Julian Sands
Cecil Vyse	Daniel Day-Lewis
Reverend Beebe	Simon Callow
Miss Lavish	Judi Dench
Freddy Honeychurch	Rupert Graves
Mrs. Honeychurch	Rosemary Leach

Oscars Best Screenplay (adapted)

Rosalie Goes Shopping •• [1990]

Director: Percy Adlon
Screenplay: Percy Adlon, Eleonore Adlon & Christopher Doherty

A third pic from the combination of Adlon and the chubby charms of Sägebrecht. Here she plays an ex-GI bride from Germany who spends, spends, spends. Without a pools win to help out, she resorts to a little embezzlement. And then to a big embezzlement. Sadly, the laughs are much thinner on the ground than she is. **[93m/15]**

Rosalie Greenspace	Marianne Sägebrecht
Ray Greenspace	Brad Davis
Priest	Judge Reinhold
Rosalie's father	William Harlander

The Rose and the Sword
SEE: Flesh Blood

Rosencrantz and Guildenstern Are Dead •• [1990]

Director: Tom Stoppard
Screenplay: Tom Stoppard

Hamlet as seen from the point of view of a couple of courtiers, who rapidly discover that they aren't in control of events. Playwright Stoppard does rather a good job in his directorial debut, adding plenty of nice sight gags to his play. The endless word games have become rather aggravating, though. **[117m/PG]**

Rosencrantz	Gary Oldman
Guildenstern	Tim Roth
The player	Richard Dreyfuss
Ophelia	Joanna Roth
Prince Hamlet	Iain Glen

'Round Midnight ••• [1986]

Director: Bertrand Tavernier
Screenplay: David Rayfiel & Bertrand Tavernier

A jazz musician, down on his luck in 50's Paris, is helped to recover his self-esteem by an admiring fan. An essential movie for jazz fans, its incisive portrait of a troubled artist will also be appreciated by others. **[131m/15]**

Dale Turner	Dexter Gordon
Francis Borier	Francois Cluzet
Berangere	Gabrielle Haker
Buttercup	Sandra Reaves-Phillips

Psst! Herbie Hancock and Martin Scorsese appear in cameos.

Roxanne •••• [1987]

Director: Fred Schepisi
Screenplay: Steve Martin

Steve Martin is the big-nosed, big-hearted chief of an incompetent crew of firemen. In this modern version of Cyrano de Bergerac he helps Rossovich woo astronomer Hannah, despite being in love with her himself. Martin wrote this brilliant romantic comedy, the straightest yet funniest and most satisfying of all his films. If only it weren't for the odd bit of mistimed slapstick, it would be perfect. **[107m/PG]**

C.D. Bales	Steve Martin
Roxanne	Daryl Hannah
Chris	Rick Rossovich
Dixie	Shelley Duvall
Chuck	John Kapelos
Mayor Deebs	Fred Willard
Dean	Max Alexander
Andy	Michael J. Pollard
Jerry	Damon Wayans

Quote 'Laugh and the world laughs with you. Sneeze and it's "Goodbye Seattle".'

Psst! Hannah's penchant for insisting that she always be given a career to go with her looks doesn't disappoint here.

Ruby •• [1992]

Director: John Mackenzie
Screenplay: Stephen Davis

Miss one picture about the topping of JFK and another one will be along in a minute. This one's told from Jack Ruby's viewpoint, whose business picks up when stripper Fenn arrives. Before long, Ruby's chums are serving her up to JFK on a platter, a part of the conspiracy that Stone forgot about. Strong acting can't make up for an otherwise dull and uninvolving storyline. The fact that Fenn's character is completely fictitious doesn't help, great stripper though she is.

[111m/15]

Jack Ruby ....Danny Aiello
Candy Cane..............................Sherilyn Fenn
Maxwell...................................Arliss Howard
David Ferrie ....Tobin Bell
Officer Tippit.......................David Duchovny

Psst! The credits include a 'massage therapist' for Ms. Fenn.

Rude Awakening • [1989]

Director: Aaron Russo & David Greenwalt
Screenplay: Neil Levy & Richard LaGravenese

Cheech Marin and Roberts are dire as hippies returning to New York after 20 years on a commune, to find that people aren't quite as loose as they were. So bad, it *almost* manages to make Cheech and Chong together look funny.

[101m/15]

Hesus..Cheech Marin
Red Wouk...................................Eric Roberts
Petra...Julie Hagerty
Also: Robert Carradine, Buck Henry, Louise Lasser

Psst! Lloyd is played by Buck Henry, who wrote *The Graduate* ◆ Dr. Timothy Leary, guru of the drugs culture, has a cameo eating at the 'Nouveau Woodstock' restaurant.

Rumble Fish ••• [1983]

Director: Francis Ford Coppola
Screenplay: S.E. Hinton & Francis Ford Coppola

The second of Coppola's Hinton adaptations, this is better than *The Outsiders*, although still occasionally pretentious. Centring on a pair of brothers, Dillon and Rourke, it helped to launch the careers of several bratpackers. Check out the black & white photography (one of the characters is colour-blind) and that clock symbolism! [94m/18]

Rusty–James................................Matt Dillon
Motorcycle Boy.......................Mickey Rourke
Patty..Diane Lane
Father.....................................Dennis Hopper
Cassandra...............................Diana Scarwid
Steve ....Vincent Spano
Smokey ....Nicolas Cage
B.J.......................................Christopher Penn
Midget ....Larry Fishburne
Benny..Tom Waits

Runaway •• [1984]

Director: Michael Crichton
Screenplay: Michael Crichton

In the future, cop Selleck tracks down robots that have gone bad. Although the story and leads are depressingly bland, there's a tense, vertiginous finale, while the acid-squirting, exploding electric spiders are a creepy touch of genius.

[100m/15]

Ramsay..Tom Selleck
Karen ....Cynthia Rhodes
Luther....................................Gene Simmons
Jackie..Kirstie Alley

Runaway Train ••• [1985]

Director: Andrei Konchalovsky
Screenplay: Djordje Milicevic, Paul Zindel & Edward Bunker

Making their break from an horrifically violent Alaskan prison, Voight and Roberts jump a train, only to discover that it's out of control. Although no attempt is made to make the pair sympathetic, the scenes with the uncontrollable train hurtling through the icy wastes are heart-stoppingly exciting. The ending, however, is a trifle weird. [111m/18]

Manny	Jon Voight
Buck	Eric Roberts
Sara	Rebecca De Mornay
Frank Barstow	Kyle T. Heffner
Warden Ranken	John P. Ryan

Psst! If you thought it must be dangerous filming the train going through all those tunnels, you'd be right. One of the helicopter pilots died in a crash.

Running Brave •• [1983]

Director: D.S. Everett
Screenplay: Henry Bean & Shirl Hendryx

Okay Canadian tale of Billy Mills, the Sioux Indian who won the 10,000 metres Gold at Tokyo in 1964. [102m/PG]

Billy Mills	Robby Benson
Coach Easton	Pat Hingle
Pat Mills	Claudia Cron
Dennis	Jeff McCraken

Psst! The film was financed by a group of Cree Indians using their oil revenues.

Running Hot
SEE: Highway to Hell

The Running Man •• [1987]

Director: Paul Michael Glaser
Screenplay: Steven E. de Souza

In the future, the top game show is a gladatorial-style contest in which convicted criminals are hunted down in the streets. Nobody has ever survived. But then Arnie hasn't played before. Derivative of several other films, but efficient entertainment nonetheless. [101m/18]

Ben Richards	Arnold Schwarzenegger
Amber Mendez	Maria Conchita Alonso
Laughlin	Yaphet Kotto
Fireball	Jim Brown

Quote 'He had to split.'

Running on Empty ••• [1988]

Director: Sidney Lumet
Screenplay: Naomi Foner

Young Phoenix's music teacher says he's a good enough musician to attend the Julliard School. There's a slight complication. Mom and Pop were 60's student activists and they've been on the run for the past 15 years. An intelligent family melodrama is driven home with Lumet's usual power, even if he is directing from a soapbox. [117m/15]

Annie Pope	Christine Lahti
Danny Pope	River Phoenix
Arthur Pope	Judd Hirsch
Harry Pope	Jonas Abry
Lorna Phillips	Martha Plimpton
Mr. Phillips	Ed Crowley

Running Scared •• [1986]

Director: Peter Hyams
Screenplay: Gary DeVore & Jimmy Huston

Crystal and Hines make a decent cop pairing in this 'last case before retirement' comedy thriller. We've seen it all before, but it's still reasonably entertaining. [107m/15]

Ray Hughes	Gregory Hines
Danny Costanzo	Billy Crystal
Frank	Steven Bauer
Anna Costanzo	Darlanne Fluegel
Snake	Joe Pantoliano

Psst! Jimmy Smits made his film debut here in a small role.

Rush • [1991]

Director: Lili Fini Zanuck
Screenplay: Pete Dexter

Two narcotics cops go undercover and, indeed, under the covers together, when they are drawn too deeply into the world they're supposed to be cracking open. Dour, depressing and downright dull, it's also frequently implausible, particularly in the latter stages. Still, as few will still be awake then, perhaps it doesn't matter that two important cops in danger of their lives are billeted in a caravan with no phone.   **[120m/18]**

Jim Raynor.....................................Jason Patric
Kristen Cates..................Jennifer Jason Leigh
Larry Dodd....................................Sam Elliott
Walker...Max Perlich

Psst! Powdered vitamin B was snorted on set instead of cocaine. According to Leigh, 'It burned like a son of a bitch.' ◆ Producer Richard Zanuck paid $1m for the almost-true-story book, a near record for a first novel, before it was even finished.

The Russia House •• [1990]

Director: **Fred Schepisi**
Screenplay: **Tom Stoppard**

British publisher Connery gets caught up in glasnost espionage when visiting a Russian bookfair. Love, of course, complicates matters. Casting that well-known Muscovite, Michelle Pfeiffer, as his lover is just one example of the misuse of a host of talented people in a dullish story. Ken Russell has fun, though, as a camp British intelligence officer.   **[123m/15]**

Barley Blair...............................Sean Connery
Katya.....................................Michelle Pfeiffer
Russell...Roy Scheider
Ned...James Fox
Also: Klaus Maria Brandauer, John Mahoney, Michael Kitchen, J.T. Walsh, Ken Russell, David Threlfall

Psst! Connery received $10m as his fee.

Russicum • [1989]

Director: **Pasquale Squitieri**
Screenplay: **Valerio Riva, Robert Balchus & Pasquale Squitieri**

Hideously bad Italian thriller revolving around a planned visit by the Pope to Russia. If they export many more like this, it could be grounds for war. Also known as *The Third Solution*.   **[111m/15]**

Father Carafa.................F. Murray Abraham
Mark Hendrix.......................Treat Williams
George Sherman.........................Danny Aiello

Ruthless People •••• [1986]

Director: **Jim Abrahams, David Zucker & Jerry Zucker**
Screenplay: **Dale Launer**

One of the very best comedies of the 80s. Reinhold and Slater kidnap the awful Midler, holding her to ransom. Little do they know that her still more obnoxious hubbie DeVito had been planning to murder her and has no wish to see her back. Although from the *Airplane* guys, it's more realistic than their other films, with a fiendishly clever plot. But it's still hysterically, manically, blackly and deliciously funny.   **[94m/18]**

Sam Stone................................Danny DeVito
Barbara Stone ....Bette Midler
Ken Kessler..............................Judge Reinhold
Sandy Kessler...............................Helen Slater
Carol...Anita Morris
Earl ....Bill Pullman
Police Commissioner......William G. Schilling

Quote 'I'm being marked down? I've been kidnapped by K-Mart!'

Psst! At one point, writer Launer was told that Madonna was to play Midler's part. But even though the plot hinges on it, she wasn't willing to be seen as someone fat.

S

Sahara • [1984]

Director: **Andrew V. McLaglen**
Screenplay: **James R. Silke**

Shields agrees to her late father's request to drive his car in a 1927 race across the Sahara, even though she's got to disguise herself as a man and face kidnapping by a Sheikh to do it. Even in the desert, the radiator never gets warm.   **[104m/PG]**

Dale ....Brooke Shields
Jaffar...Lambert Wilson
Also: Horst Buchholz, John Rhys-Davies, Ronald Lacey, John Mills

Saigon •• [1988]

Director: **Christopher Crowe**
Screenplay: **Christopher Crowe & Jack Thibeau**

That old, old story of the one white, one black, seen-it-all cops on the trail of a serial killer, given a new twist by being set in Saigon in 1968. But aside from the change of background, a little extra violence and a little less originality in the plot, everything else is the same. Also known as *Off Limits*. **[102m/18]**

Buck McGriff	Willem Dafoe
Albaby Perkins	Gregory Hines
Dix	Fred Ward
Nicole	Amanda Pays
Lime Green	Kay Tong Lim
Col. Armstrong	Scott Glenn

Salaam Bombay! ••• [1988]

Director: **Mira Nair**
Screenplay: **Sooni Taraporevala**

As far from the E.M. Forster vision of India as you can get, this semi-documentary shows us the squalor endured by the children who survive, just, on the streets of Bombay. Although a horrific tale, it's still full of life and fascinating characters. A remarkable debut by Nair. **[113m/15]**

Krishna/Chaipau	Shafiq Syed
Chillum	Raghubir Yadav
Rekha	Aneeta Kanwar
Baba	Nana Patekar

Salome's Last Dance •• [1988]

Director: **Ken Russell**
Screenplay: **Ken Russell**

Oscar Wilde's banned play of *Salome* is given a private performance in a brothel. Given that all the action takes place in one room, it's surprising how interesting the various camp excesses from Our Ken are. **[90m/18]**

Herodias/Lady Alice	Glenda Jackson
Herod/Alfred Taylor	Stratford Johns
Oscar Wilde	Nickolas Grace
John the Baptist/Bosie	Douglas Hodge
Salome/Rose	Imogen Millais-Scott

Salsa • [1988]

Director: **Boaz Davidson**
Screenplay: **Boaz Davidson, Tomas Benitez & Shepard Goldman**

Saturday Night Fever goes Latin as Rosa aims for fame with his salsa dancing. Apart from the vibrancy of the dance scenes, there's no plot that you would notice. **[99m/PG]**

Rico	Robby Rosa
Ken	Rodney Harvey
Margrita	Magali Alvarado

Salute of the Jugger • [1990]

Director: **David Webb Peoples**
Screenplay: **David Webb Peoples**

Daft, belated, futuristic *Rollerball* clone, with teams of gladiator-sportsmen roaming the countryside challenging teams to play the vicious game of juggers. A blood-splattered blot on the copybook of the man who wrote *Unforgiven* and *Blade Runner*. Also known as *The Blood of Heroes*. **[92m/18]**

Sallow	Rutger Hauer
Kidda	Joan Chen
Young Gar	Vincent D'Onofrio

Psst! The script was originally written in 1977.

Salvador •••• [1986]

Director: **Oliver Stone**
Screenplay: **Richard Boyle & Oliver Stone**

Seedy journalist Woods tricks his DJ friend Belushi into going to El Salvador for some easy drinks, drugs and women. Instead, they are thrown into the horrors of the Salvadorean revolution. After a scrappy start, Stone's best movie brilliantly combines a personal and political story with terrifying scenes of a country falling apart. This is also Woods' finest role yet, energising the true narrative with wit, compassion and his hyper-kinetic drive. **[123m/18]**

Richard Boyle	James Woods
Dr. Rock	James Belushi

Ambassador Kelly	Michael Murphy
Maria	Elpidia Carrillo
John Cassady	John Savage
Major Max	Tony Plana
Jack Morgan	Colby Chester
Cathy Moore	Cynthia Gibb

Quote 'If God gave me this woman, then there must be a God.'

Psst! A one-time extreme right-winger, it was while making *Salvador* that Stone did a volte-face, emerging as Hollywood's most aggressive liberal.

Salvation! • [1987]

Director: Beth B
Screenplay: Beth B & Tom Robinson

A TV evangelist, sex scandal, blackmail, boredom. This dispiriting satire has them all. But then so do the newspapers. [80m/18]

Rev. Edward Randall	Stephen McHattie
Lenore Finley	Dominique Davalos
Rhonda Stample	Exene Cervenka

Sammy and Rosie Get Laid • [1987]

Director: Stephen Frears
Screenplay: Hanif Kureishi

...And the Audience Get Conned. This tiresome diatribe against Thatcherite Britain centres around the return to England of Kapoor after thirty years. The sexy come-on of the title is little more than an excuse to tempt in punters so they can be bludgeoned about the head with blunt placards. [100m/18]

Rafi	Shashi Kapoor
Rosie	Frances Barber
Alice	Claire Bloom

Santa Claus: The Movie • [1985]

Director: Jeannot Szwarc
Screenplay: David Newman

So ghastly is this comic fantasy about St. Nick that you start wondering if it isn't all some diabolical conspiracy to put the world's children off Christmas altogether.

Moore's grinning elf has all the appeal of a mooning garden gnome. Heaven 'elf us. [108m/U]

Patch	Dudley Moore
B.Z.	John Lithgow
Claus	David Huddleston
Ancient elf	Burgess Meredith

Psst! The film achieved the sixth biggest loss in film history, with Santa and his little helpers pulling in $37m less than they cost.

Sarafina ••• [1992]

Director: Darrell James Roodt
Screenplay: William Nicholson & Mbongeni Ngema

A musical about life in the township of Soweto during a widespread protest against apartheid by schoolchildren shouldn't work but does. The zippy Broadway-style song-and-dance numbers heighten the feeling of revulsion at the poverty and the appalling scenes of brutality and torture. An oddity, with variable acting, the film nonetheless has extraordinary power. Goldberg seems like an afterthought, but Khumalo is astonishly good. [116m/15]

Sarafina	Leleti Khumalo
Mary Masombuka	Whoopi Goldberg
Angelina	Miriam Makeba
Crocodile	Dumisani Dlamini

Savage Islands •• [1983]

Director: Ferdinand Fairfax
Screenplay: John Hughes & David Odell

A swashbuckling New Zealand pic about piracy and derring-do in the South Pacific last century, with Jones helping missionary O'Keefe get his fiancée back from a shiver-me-timbers pirate. All very fast and furious but it rides a little low in the water to get too excited about. Also known as *Nate and Hayes*. [99m/PG]

Capt. Bully Hayes	Tommy Lee Jones
Nate Williamson	Michael O'Keefe
Ben	Max Phipps
Sophie	Jenny Seagrove

Saving Grace • [1986]

Director: **Robert M. Young**
Screenplay: **Joaquin Montana**

De Holy Fadder, de Pope himaself, he escape-a de Vattican and go outta da meeta da peeples. Anda da village wherea he goes, watta joy he-a bring, even dough dey notta know dat he's-a de Pope. Chico Marx, he-a sounda more like-a da Pope dan dis Conti fella. Dis-a one Pope gonna have a lotta trouble finding an audience.

[112m/PG]

Pope Leo XIV................................Tom Conti
Abalardi ....Giancarlo Giannini
Also: Erland Josephson, Fernando Rey, Patricia Mauceri, Edward James Olmos

Scandal •• [1989]

Director: **Michael Caton-Jones**
Screenplay: **Michael Thomas**

Christine Keeler was the good-time gal taken up by Stephen Ward in a 60's Britain not quite ready to swing. Her affair with the War Minister precipitated disaster. This okay reconstruction of a fascinating episode is rather tame in the sleaze department and a touch sluggish. McKellan's hairpiece, which turns John Profumo into the Last of the Mohicans, is almost as big a mistake as the affair.

[114m/18]

Stephen Ward..................................John Hurt
Christine Keeler.......Joanne Whalley-Kilmer
Mandy Rice-Davies ....Bridget Fonda
John Profumo............................Ian McKellen
Lord Astor................................Leslie Phillips
Also: Britt Ekland, Jeroen Krabbé, Jean Alexander, Ken Campbell

Psst! The film was cut, particularly in the orgy scene, for the United States, where censors had threatened to give it the 'X' rating, the kiss of death to serious movies • John Profumo was married to British vintage film actress Valerie Hobson, star of movies like *Q Planes*, *Kind Hearts and Coronets* and *Great Expectations*.

Scandalous • [1984]

Director: **Rob Cohen**
Screenplay: **Rob Cohen & John Byrum**

Sir John Gielgud as a punk rocker? Just one of the bizarre sights in this dreadful farrago with Gielgud and Stephenson rummaging through the dressing-up cupboard as a couple of con men clashing with a reporter trying to clear himself of a murder charge.

[94m/15]

Uncle Willie...............................John Gielgud
Fiona ....Pamela Stephenson
Also: Robert Hays, M. Emmet Walsh, Jim Dale

Scarface •• [1983]

Director: **Brian De Palma**
Screenplay: **Oliver Stone**

A Cuban refugee arrives in Miami and sets about taking, rather than making, his fortune. This remake of the 30's Hawks gangster classic looks better than when it opened, thanks to De Palma's stylised direction, Pacino's energy and a smart pair of early appearances by Pfeiffer and Mastrantonio. It's very violent and the chainsaw sequence still chills, even in the...er...cut version. But it's way too long and offers nothing new.

[170m/18]

Tony Montana..................................Al Pacino
Manny Ray ....Steven Bauer
Elvira....................................Michelle Pfeiffer
Gina................Mary Elizabeth Mastrantonio
Frank Lopez...............................Robert Loggia
Omar.............................F. Murray Abraham

Quote 'The only thing that gives orders in this world is balls.'

Psst! Until the arrival of *Goodfellas*, this film held the record for the most uses of the F-word, notching up 206 of them.

Scenes from a Mall •• [1991]

Director: **Paul Mazursky**
Screenplay: **Paul Mazursky & Roger L. Simon**

Shopping as a couple is always stressful, but here it leads to the breakdown of the marriage as Woody and Bette choose the mall to confess all. Rare though it is for Woody to be in anybody else's movie, it still emerges as pretty unengaging and unamusing.   **[88m/15]**

Deborah Fifer	Bette Midler
Nick Fifer	Woody Allen
Mime	Bill Irwin
Sam	Daren Firestone

Showing *Salaam Bombay!*

Psst! Allen's contract included the demand that Mia Farrow and the entire family be flown to Disneyland and shown around by Disney head Jeffrey Katzenberg personally ✦ Writer–producer–director Paul Mazursky appears as Dr. Hans Clava.

Scenes from the Class Struggle in Beverly Hills • [1989]

Director: **Paul Bartel**
Screenplay: **Bruce Wagner**

A brainless and astonishly unamusing sex farce played out at a furious pace among the rampantly randy rich of Beverly Hills and their servants. Bisset's got talent and looks. Why can't she *ever* be in a good film? [See Rose's Rule #1]

[104m/18]

Clare Lipkin	Jacqueline Bisset
Frank	Ray Sharkey
Juan	Robert Beltran

Also: Mary Woronov, Ed Begley Jr., Wallace Shawn, Rebecca Schaeffer

Psst! Paul Bartel and Paul Mazursky appear in cameos ✦ Rebecca Schaeffer's character loses her virginity in the film. Robert Bardo, an obsessed fan convinced that he would marry her, shot her dead in disgust in 1989.

Scent of a Woman ••• [1992]

Director: **Martin Brest**
Screenplay: **Bo Goldman**

Pacino gives an astonishingly good performance as the crotchety, blind ex-officer who virtually kidnaps schoolboy minder O'Donnell for a wild weekend in New York. Pacino, as the man who may not have an eye for the women, but certainly has a nose for them, is amazing. Poor O'Donnell is given little to do, other than muddle through a boring subplot about possible expulsion from school. The restaurant tango scene with the delectable Anwar is one of the most sublime moments in the movies. Such a shame that the whole thing ends in such a suffocating wave of slush.   **[156m/15]**

Lt. Col. Frank Slade	Al Pacino
Charlie Simms	Chris O'Donnell
Mr. Trask	James Rebhorn
Donna	Gabrielle Anwar
George Willis Jr.	Philip S. Hoffman
W.R. Slade	Richard Venture
Randy	Bradley Whitford

Oscars Al Pacino

Quote 'Hoo–ha!' ✦ 'The day we stop looking is the day we die.' ✦ 'He may be Jack to you, but when you've known him as long as I have...'

OOPS! Keep an eye on the liquid rising and falling in Pacino's glass when he first meets O'Donnell. The cigarette, too, appears to smoke and unsmoke itself a few times.

Psst! With Pacino's usual dedication, he covered his head with a dark hood for long periods to experience what it was like to be blind. At the end of shooting, he was so into it that he told O'Donnell: 'I didn't see it, but I hear you gave a great performance' ✦ The extraordinary tango scene was done in just one take ✦ The director left the mad walk across the path of speeding traffic until last, only convincing Pacino it was feasible by doing it himself first, as he had done with Charles Grodin on *Midnight Run*.

School Daze •• [1988]

Director: **Spike Lee**
Screenplay: **Spike Lee**

This weak second film from Lee about life on a black university campus in the South revolves around the difference between those who want to fit in and those who want to keep their identity. It's all done with such a straight face and lack of fun that it's mostly a bore. (120m/18)

Dap Dunlap	Larry Fishburne
Julian Eaves	Giancarlo Esposito
Jane Toussaint	Tisha Campbell
Rachel Meadows	Kyme

Psst! Lee appears as 'Half-Pint'.

School Ties •• [1992]

Director: **Robert Mandel**
Screenplay: **Dick Wolf & Darryl Ponicsan**

Fraser is the Jewish boy winning a scholarship to a posh WASP-ish school in the 50's, largely thanks to his talents at football. In the face of obvious anti-semitism, he hides his roots. Although a nicely-acted and well-made film, it cops out by making Fraser such an excellent football player, able to win people round with his talents on the field. (107m/12)

David Greene	Brendan Fraser
Charlie Dillon	Matt Damon
Chris Reece	Chris O'Donnell
Rip Van Kelt	Randall Batinkoff
McGivern	Andrew Lowery

Scorchers • [1992]

Director: **David Beaird**
Screenplay: **David Beaird**

Wrong title. Dismal transfer of a talky play about a bride reluctant to take anything more than a good book into the bridal bed on her wedding night. If only it was half as funny as the cast list. (88m/18)

Splendid, the virgin	Emily Lloyd
Talbot, the jilted wife	Jennifer Tilly
Jumper, the narrator	Leland Crooke
Thais, the whore	Faye Dunaway
Bear, the barman	James Earl Jones
Howler, the drunk	Denholm Elliott

Scream for Help • [1984]

Director: **Michael Winner**
Screenplay: **Tom Holland**

A teenager is having trouble making anyone believe her stepfather is about to top her mum. When it happens, she sets off to do what a girl has to do in a Michael Winner film. One of those all round extraordinarily awful films that, in the right mood, could be screamingly funny. (89m/18)

Christie	Rachael Kelly
Karen	Marie Masters
Paul	David Brooks

Screwballs • [1983]

Director: **Rafal Zielinski**
Screenplay: **Linda Shayne & Jim Wynorski**

Unbelievably pathetic Canadian teen sex comedy about nothing more than some wildy, wacky, wonderful guys plotting to get a glimpse of a girl's breasts. No doubt Orson Welles is up there somewhere, cursing that he never thought of that one. (79m/18)

Rick	Peter Keleghan
Bootsie	Linda Shayne
Howie	Alan Deveau

Scrooged •• [1988]

Director: **Richard Donner**
Screenplay: **Mitch Glazer & Michael Donoghue**

An updating of *Christmas Carol*, with Murray the Scrooge-like head of a TV company. It starts off well enough but ruins it all by becoming even more sentimental than the original. The jokes just aren't good enough to overcome the schmaltz. (101m/PG)

Frank Cross	Bill Murray
Claire Phillips	Karen Allen
Lew Hayward	John Forsythe
Brice Cummings	John Glover

Also: Bobcat Goldthwait, David Johansen, Carol Kane, Robert Mitchum, Michael J. Pollard, Alfre Woodard

Psst! Donner fired the cast and crew on Christmas Eve, then rehired them in January. It was the only way he could let them go home for Christmas when the studio, in *Scrooged* mode, wouldn't give them the holidays off.

Sea of Love ••• [1989]

Director: Harold Becker
Screenplay: Richard Price

Cracking thriller with cop Pacino investigating the murders of lonely hearts advertisers by placing an ad himself. Although she's soon the lead suspect, it isn't long before he's bonkin' Barkin. Is she the killer or not? The plot's not the greatest ever, but what really grabs is the raw sensuality, the wonderful characterisation and dialogue and the fantastic observation of the singles scene. If only more erotic thrillers aped this rather than *Basic Instinct*, what a wonderful world it would be. [113m/18]

Frank Keller	Al Pacino
Helen Cruger	Ellen Barkin
Sherman Touhy	John Goodman
Terry	Michael Rooker
Frank Sr.	William Hickey
Gruber	Richard Jenkins

OOPS! Look carefully when Pacino is getting dressed after making love with Barkin the first time and, as he puts on his briefs, you can see that he's already wearing a pair.

Psst! There's another, longer, version around that also has Lorraine Bracco in it as Pacino's ex-wife • The original script had a far more ambiguous ending with the person who's the killer in the released film committing suicide, leaving us unsure who's the guilty one.

Secret Admirer •• [1985]

Director: David Greenwalt
Screenplay: Jim Kouf & David Greenwalt

Howell gets the wrong end of the stick when he finds a love letter, assuming they're from someone different. A teen comedy with little in the way of comedy or originality, although the actors look pretty enough. [98m/15]

Michael Ryan	C. Thomas Howell
Toni	Lori Loughlin
Debora	Kelly Preston

Also: Dee Wallace Stone, Cliff De Young, Fred Ward

Secret Friends • [1992]

Director: Dennis Potter
Screenplay: Dennis Potter

Everyday Potter tale of madness, hookers, murder and watercolour artists. Totally potty and indecipherable rubbish from a man supposedly one of the most talented of British writers. Heaven help us. [97m/15]

John	Alan Bates
Helen	Gina Bellman
Angela	Frances Barber

Secret Honor •• [1984]

Director: Robert Altman
Screenplay: Donald Freed & Arnold M. Stone

Something of a curio, this Altman film is a rerun of Hall's one-man play about Nixon in full paranoid flow. If you happen to be interested in that, it's brilliant. Otherwise, forget it. [90m/15]

Richard M. Nixon	Philip Baker Hall

The Secret of My Success •• [1987]

Director: Herbert Ross
Screenplay: Jim Cash & Jack Epps Jr.

Unwilling to wait for his turn for the next rung of the corporate ladder, ambitious Fox takes some complicated short-cuts. Despite the unoriginality of the plot, Fox is so likeable it's difficult to dislike this over-long comedy. [110m/PG]

Brantley Foster	Michael J. Fox
Christy Wills	Helen Slater
Howard Prescott	Richard Jordan
Vera Prescott	Margaret Whitton

Also: John Pankow, Christopher Murney, Gerry Bamman, Mercedes Ruehl

Secret Places •• [1984]

Director: Zelda Barron
Screenplay: Zelda Barron

In wartime Britain, a German refugee at a girls' school strikes up a friendship with one of the few girls not doing Hitler jokes. An occasionally moving story, although it doesn't move anything like fast enough. [96m/15]

Laura Meister	Marie-Thérès Relin
Patience MacKenzie	Tara MacGowran
Sophie Meister	Claudine Auger
Miss Lowrie	Jenny Agutter

See No Evil, Hear No Evil ••• [1989]

Director: Arthur Hiller
Screenplay: Earl Barret, Arne Sultan, Andrew Kurtzman, Eliot Wald & Gene Wilder

Pryor is blind, Wilder is deaf. Useless on their own, they're even worse together. Nothing like as tasteless as it sounds, this is one of the funniest films starring this pair, full of great verbal and sight gags. Here they're innocent murder suspects trying to clear their names and coming up against the gloriously wicked and sexy Severance. [107m/15]

Dave Lyons	Gene Wilder
Wally Karew	Richard Pryor
Eve	Joan Severance
Kirgo	Kevin Spacey
Braddock	Alan North
Sutherland	Anthony Zerbe

Quote 'Does Dad know?' [Pryor, on being told he is black]

OOPS! During the attempted rescue of Pryor's sister, Pryor asks the deaf Wilder a question and receives an answer, even though Wilder is not actually looking at his lips.

See You in the Morning •• [1989]

Director: Alan J. Pakula
Screenplay: Alan J. Pakula

Over-sentimental and earnest story of Bridges and Krige, divorced and widowed respectively, having to get to know not only each other, but also their new partner's children. Macaulay Culkin crops up as one of Bridges' brood. [118m/12]

Larry Livingston	Jeff Bridges
Beth Goodwin	Alice Krige
Jo Livingston	Farrah Fawcett
Cathy Goodwin	Drew Barrymore

Also: David Dukes, Frances Sternhagen, Macaulay Culkin

September • [1987]

Director: Woody Allen
Screenplay: Woody Allen

Allen lets his admiration for Bergman take over completely with this unbelievably dour and depressing tale of six people moaning at each other interminably. Somewhere Ingmar Bergman is saying: 'Why doesn't Woody Allen make funny movies any more?' [83m/PG]

Howard	Denholm Elliott
Stephanie	Dianne Wiest
Lane	Mia Farrow

Also: Elaine Stritch, Sam Waterston, Jack Warden

OOPS! In a scene with Warden, Waterston's tie keeps doing itself up and then untying itself.

Psst! This was one of the nails in the coffin of Orion which collapsed, despite making *Silence of the Lambs* and *Dances with Wolves*. Allen shot the movie once and then decided he didn't like it. He fired Charles Durning, Sam Shepard and Maureen O'Sullivan, Mia Farrow's mother, and started all over again. Afterwards he claimed that he would have liked to have shot it a third time.

The Serpent and the Rainbow ••• [1988]

Director: Wes Craven
Screenplay: Richard Maxwell & A.R. Simoun

An American anthropologist in Haiti discovers that there's a political dimension to all the voodoo and black magic. A typically intelligent and partially factual Craven shocker with an original plot line, it has one of the surprisingly few nail-hammered-through-scrotum scenes in the movies. It still suffers from trying to cram in too many ideas on a limited budget.

[98m/18]

Dennis Alan.................................Bill Pullman
Marielle Celine ....Cathy Tyson
Dargent Peytraud ....Zakes Mokae
Lucien Celine..............................Paul Winfield
Also: Brent Jennings, Badja Djola, Michael Gough, Paul Guilfoyle

The Seventh Sign • [1988]

Director: Carl Schultz
Screenplay: Clifford Green & Ellen Green

Demi Moore fears that her lodger Prochnow intends to use her unborn child to bring about the end of the world. What should she do? Save the earth, or try to get on as many magazine covers as possible before the Apocalypse? An unbelievably pretentious load of cods-wallop.

[97m/PG]

Abby Quinn ....Demi Moore
Russell Quinn ....Michael Biehn
The Border...........................Jurgen Prochnow

Psst! On the credits, the writers changed their names to W.W. Wicket and George Kaplan. Kaplan is the name of the character Cary Grant was mistaken for in *North by Northwest*. [See *Hudson Hawk*]

sex, lies, and videotape ••• [1989]

Director: Steven Soderbergh
Screenplay: Steven Soderbergh

This remarkable debut from writer-director Soderbergh has Spader as the old college friend visiting the repressed MacDowell while hubby Gallagher is cheating with her sister San Giacomo. Spader's a teensy bit weird, getting his kicks from taping women talking intimately about sex, a pastime that has dramatic consequences. More talk than action, this is a timely reminder that the sexiest films don't have to feature much of the act at all. Intelligent and witty, it's a beautifully-constructed film that draws you deeper and deeper into these people's lives. [100m/18]

Graham Dalton ....James Spader
Ann Millaney ....Andie MacDowell
John Millaney..........................Peter Gallagher
Cynthia Bishop ....Laura San Giacomo
Therapist ..:....................................Ron Vawter

Quote 'It's all downhill from here.' [The all-too-prescient Soderbergh on winning the Palme d'Or at Cannes]

OOPS! Watch for the vanishing necklace as MacDowell tackles Gallagher on whether he's having an affair or not.

Psst! At Cannes, the Rob Lowe video scandal broke, helping the film considerably.

Shadey • [1986]

Director: Philip Saville
Screenplay: Snoo Wilson

A strong candidate for the worst British movie of the decade. Sher is able to put his thoughts onto film, a talent that has escaped the director. Shadey's also looking for a sex change. The audience is looking for the exit sign. [106m/15]

Oliver Shadey..............................Antony Sher
Dr. Cloud...............................Billie Whitelaw
Sir Cyril Landau....................Patrick Macnee
Carol Landau.................................Leslie Ash

Shadow Makers •• [1989]

Director: Roland Joffé
Screenplay: Bruce Robinson & Roland Joffé

...Or How I Built The Bomb. The tale of the Manhattan Project, with Newman the blinkered Army general overseeing the project, and Schultz as Oppenheimer the head boffin. Despite the magnitude of what they did, it makes for a dense, talkative and rather dull film. **[127m/PG]**

Gen. Leslie R. Groves ....Paul Newman
J. Robert Oppenheimer ....Dwight Schultz
Kitty Oppenheimer ....Bonnie Bedelia
Michael Merriman ....John Cusack
Kathleen Robinson ....Laura Dern
Also: Ron Frazier, John C. McGinley, Natasha Richardson, Ron Vawter

Psst! The film originally had the title *Fat Man and Little Boy*, but audiences thought it was a slapstick comedy.

Shadows and Fog ••• [1992]

Director: Woody Allen
Screenplay: Woody Allen

Proof that Woody *can* still be funny. This black and white tale of vigilante groups on the hunt for a murderer in pre-war Europe mixes the look of German expressionism with the sort of gags that cropped up in his early films. Peppered with star cameos (blink, and you'll miss Madonna), this is a weird but very amusing film. **[86m/15]**

Kleinman ....Woody Allen
Irmy ....Mia Farrow
Clown ....John Malkovich
Also: Madonna, Donald Pleasence, Lily Tomlin, Jodie Foster, Kathy Bates, John Cusack, Kate Nelligan, Fred Gwynne, Julie Kavner, Kenneth Mars

Quote 'I've never paid for sex in my life.' – 'You just think you haven't.'

Psst! Release was delayed when *Husbands and Wives* was rushed out to capitalise on Woody and Mia's real-life problems ♦ Donald Pleasence's name is spelt wrongly on the credits.

Shag •• [1988]

Director: Zelda Barron
Screenplay: Robin Swicord, Lanier Laney & Terry Sweeney

Presumably 'shag' doesn't have the same slang meaning in the States as it does in Britain. Here it's a dance, apparently. Four high school students head for the beach for one last fling. Though intended as a spoof of teen beach movies, it comes across as yet another in a never-ending line of them. **[98m/15]**

Carson ....Phoebe Cates
Chip ....Scott Coffey
Melaina ....Bridget Fonda
Also: Annabeth Gish, Page Hannah, Robert Rusler, Tyrone Power Jr.

Psst! Page Hannah is Daryl's sister.

Shakedown

SEE: Blue Jean Cop

Shaking the Tree •• [1991]

Director: Duane Clark
Screenplay: Duane Clark & Steven Wilde

A group of friends suffer terrible angst, so worried are they about the prospect of becoming adults. Sound familiar? **[107m/15]**

Barry ....Arye Gross
Sully ....Gale Hansen
Michael ....Doug Savant
Duke ....Steven Wilde

Shame •• [1987]

Director: Steve Jodrell
Screenplay: Beverley Blankenship & Michael Brindley

An Australian film with a feminist slant on the revenge movie. A woman barrister visiting a hick outback town persuades a young raped girl to bring charges against her attackers. As formulaic and violent as its macho counterparts, but well enough made. **[92m/15]**

Asta Cadell ....Deborra-Lee Furness
Tim Curtis ....Tony Barry
Lizzie Curtis ....Simone Buchanan
Tina Farrel ....Gillian Jones

Shanghai Surprise • [1986]

Director: Jim Goddard
Screenplay: John Kohn & Robert Bentley

As soon as you're told Madonna is a missionary, you know this film's in trouble. Add Penn as a tie salesman and we're talking big, big doo-doos. This Eastern-set screwball comedy about a madcap search for medicinal opium makes you long for something lighter and wittier such as a documentary on the Khmer Rouge. **[97m/15]**

Glendon Wasey	Sean Penn
Gloria Tatlock	Madonna
Walter Faraday	Paul Freeman
Willis Tuttle	Richard Griffiths

Psst! Penn and Madonna were married at the time ◆ George Harrison turns up briefly in a cameo. His company, Handmade Films, produced the movie.

Shattered •• [1991]

Director: Wolfgang Petersen
Screenplay: Wolfgang Petersen

Berenger wakes from a car crash, his face restored by plastic surgery, his memory a complete blank. He vaguely recalls he was once an actor, but worries that if he digs too deep, he'll remember that he was so bad at it he nearly sank a movie called *Shattered*. Although the intriguing, twisting plot is wildly implausible in places, it's still pretty entertaining if you can overlook the awfulness of Berenger and Scacchi's acting. **[106m/15]**

Dan Merrick	Tom Berenger
Gus Klein	Bob Hoskins
Judith Merrick	Greta Scacchi
Jenny Scott	Joanne Whalley-Kilmer

She-Devil • [1989]

Director: Susan Seidelman
Screenplay: Barry Strugatz & Mark R. Burns

A dismally unfunny rendering of Fay Weldon's novel of a wife taking revenge on her departed husband and his lover. Truss it up, shove some stuffing inside it, and you're ready for next Thanksgiving or Christmas. **[99m/15]**

Mary Fisher	Meryl Streep
Ruth Patchett	Roseanne Arnold
Bob Patchett	Ed Begley Jr.
Hooper	Linda Hunt
Mrs. Fisher	Sylvia Miles

Blurb The Story Of The Greatest Evil Ever Known To Man...His Ex-Wife.

Psst! Director Seidelman was ill during filming with what she thought was stomach cancer. It turned out she was seven months pregnant ◆ Briton Robin Leach, host of America's TV programme *Lives of the Rich and Famous*, turns up as himself.

Sheena • [1984]

Director: John Guillermin
Screenplay: David Newman & Lorenzo Semple Jr.

Silly jungle adventure in the company of a female Tarzan. Roberts' ample endowments do not include acting ability. **[115m/PG]**

Sheena	Tanya Roberts
Vic	Ted Wass
Fletcher	Donovan Scott

She'll Be Wearing Pink Pyjamas •• [1985]

Director: John Goldschmidt
Screenplay: Eva Hardy

Walters dominates this film about a group of women on an Outward Bound survival course. It's the audience which should be congratulated on surviving an hour and a half of 'men, can't live with them, can't live without them' gabbing. **[90m/15]**

Fran	Julie Walters
Tom	Anthony Higgins
Catherine	Jane Evers
Lucy	Janet Henfrey

She's Been Away •• [1989]

Director: **Peter Hall**
Screenplay: **Stephen Poliakoff**

After over half a century in a mental home, Ashcroft comes to stay with her nephew in a household where it's hard to know who's maddest. A little daft and unfathomable in places, it's nonetheless beautifully acted by Ashcroft. [103m/PG]

Lillian Huckle ....Peggy Ashcroft
Harriet Ambrose ....Geraldine James
Hugh Ambrose ....James Fox
Psst! The story was inspired in part by the extraordinary tale of the Queen Mother's long-lost cousin.

She's Gotta Have It •• [1986]

Director: **Spike Lee**
Screenplay: **Spike Lee**

Johns is an independent free-spirited woman unwilling to be tied to the three men trying to gain exclusive rights. Lee's directorial debut was overrated on release, but the film does contain energy, charm and some shrewd observations about black life in the 80s. [85m/18]

Nola Darling ....Tracy Camila Johns
Jamie Overstreet ......Tommy Redmond Hicks
Greer Childs ....John Canada Terrell
Mars Blackmon ....Spike Lee
Quote 'Please, baby, please, baby, baby, baby, please...'
Psst! The movie was made on 16mm film in just a fortnight on a budget of $175,000 • Lee's father wrote the music, as he did for Mo' Better Blues.

She's Out of Control • [1989]

Director: **Stan Dragoti**
Screenplay: **Seth Winston & Michael J. Nathanson**

It's dad Danza who's out of control, unable to cope with the fact that boys are getting interested in his little girl. There are sitcoms transmitted at three in the morning better than this hyperactive rubbish. [94m/12]

Doug Simpson ....Tony Danza
Janet Pearson ....Catherine Hicks
Also: Wallace Shawn, Dick O'Neill, Ami Dolenz, Dana Ashbrook
Psst! Ami Dolenz is the daughter of Micky Dolenz, formerly of The Monkees.

The Sheltering Sky • [1990]

Director: **Bernardo Bertolucci**
Screenplay: **Bernardo Bertolucci & Mark Peploe**

An American couple with marital problems arrive in 1940's North Africa. Just what the world needs; another couple discovering themselves at inordinate length in an exotic clime. There's precious little humour or insight and only the odd sex scene to keep you awake. Africa's pretty, though. If only they'd taken Alan Whicker with them. [138m/18]

Kit Moresby ....Debra Winger
Port Moresby ....John Malkovich
Also: Campbell Scott, Jill Bennett, Timothy Spall
Psst! The narrator is Paul Bowles, author of the novel. He also appears in a Tangiers café watching Malkovich and Winger • There's a bit of male nudity when Malkovich gets out of bed at one point • To make the costumes look suitably threadbare, the art director went round Morocco offering new jellabahs in return for old ones.

Shining Through •• [1992]

Director: **David Seltzer**
Screenplay: **David Seltzer & Laurie Frank**

One of the funniest bad movies ever. Despite superb prôduction values, the script is so silly and the dialogue so priceless that audiences were shrieking with laughter. Secretary Griffith convinces Douglas she can be a spy by baking him apple strüdel and is sent into Nazi Germany as a nanny-cum-secret agent. There she takes her charges – children of a top Nazi – to look for the hiding place of her Jewish relatives, photographs some documents with the important bits conveniently circled in red and makes her escape in a full-length ballgown. Douglas meanwhile pops in and out of Germany as if it were his club, despite speaking not a word of the lingo. All this is framed by a hilarious BBC documentary with Griffith in terrible old-age makeup yet talking in the same little-girl voice. Hugely entertaining, for *all* the wrong reasons. [132m/15]

Ed Leland	Michael Douglas
Linda Voss	Melanie Griffith
Franze-Otto Dietrich	Liam Neeson
Margrete	Joely Richardson
Sunflower	John Gielgud

Quote 'I knew it was on a Friday that Ed and I said goodbye because the next day was Saturday.' ◆ 'Mein Gott, you've got guts.' ◆ 'There would be no symphonies for me and Ed.' ◆ 'By late October of '41 London was reeling under a hailstorm of German bombs called The Blitz, and life in America was energised with the knowledge of what was inevitable.'

Showing *The Mortal Storm.*

OOPS! When she escapes, she's dressed in a white ballgown and runs from Potsdam to Berlin, no mean feat as it's 15 miles.

Shirley Valentine ••• [1989]

Director: **Lewis Gilbert**
Screenplay: **Willy Russell**

Willy Russell's play about the discontented Liverpudlian housewife who's driven to talk to the wall but finds happiness on a Greek holiday. The screen version is sentimentalised and rendered slightly risible by Conti's extraordinary accent. But Collins is so good, and Russell's one-liners so screamingly funny that it's unfair to quibble. [109m/15]

Shirley Valentine	Pauline Collins
Costas	Tom Conti
Gillian	Julia McKenzie
Jane	Alison Steadman
Marjorie	Joanna Lumley
Headmistress	Sylvia Syms
Joe	Bernard Hill

Quote 'Marriage is like the Middle East, isn't it? There's no solution.'

Shocker •• [1989]

Director: **Wes Craven**
Screenplay: **Wes Craven**

An electrocuted killer is able to take people over through the unwilling mind of a policeman's son. Craven is holding himself back here and, although the film has its moments, the dream/reality/possession gimmick was done to death in his own *Elm Street.* [110m/18]

Lt. Don Parker	Michael Murphy
Horace Pinker	Mitch Pileggi
Jonathan Parker	Peter Berg

Showing *Frankenstein.*

Psst! Dr. Timothy Leary, guru to users of hallucinogenic drugs, appears in a cameo as the TV evangelist.

A Shock to the System •• [1990]

Director: **Jan Egelson**
Screenplay: **Andrew Klavan**

Tasteless but occasionally amusing comedy with adman Caine discovering that a few well-chosen murders help enormously in the promotion stakes. [87m/15]

Graham Marshall	Michael Caine
Stella Anderson	Elizabeth McGovern
Robert Benham	Peter Riegert
Leslie Marshall	Swoosie Kurtz

The Shooting Party ••• [1985]

Director: **Alan Bridges**
Screenplay: **Julian Bond**

A group of Edwardian upper-crusters gather for the weekend to shoot pheasants – and the occasional peasant. Although this tale of the old aristocracy at play is slightly stagey in places, there are still wonderful performances and period detail to revel in. [96m/15]

Sir Randolph Nettleby	James Mason
Lady Minnie Nettleby	Dorothy Tutin
Lord Gilbert Hartlip	Edward Fox
Lady Aline Hartlip	Cheryl Campbell
Cornelius Cardew	John Gielgud
Tom Harker	Gordon Jackson

Psst! This was James Mason's last film.

Shoot to Kill
SEE: Deadly Pursuit

Short Circuit •• [1986]
Director: John Badham
Screenplay: S.S. Wilson & Brent Maddock

A Government robot gets struck by a lightning bolt and does a bunk, turning into yet another savvy, wise-cracking, alien pal for Sheedy. Youngsters will like it but the rest will be reaching for a screwdriver to dismantle him. [99m/PG]

Stephanie Speck..............................Ally Sheedy
Newton Crosby ....Steve Guttenberg
Ben Jabituya..............................Fisher Stevens
Howard Marner...................Austin Pendleton

Short Circuit 2 • [1988]
Director: Kenneth Johnson
Screenplay: S.S. Wilson & Brent Maddock

Johnny Five is back, not a five-pack of protectives, but the infuriating robot with all the wit and personality of Bob Monkhouse. Undemanding kids might like this sequel, with the robot foiling bank robbers, but for the rest of us a trip to the junkyard is called for. [110m/PG]

Ben Jahrvi..............................Fisher Stevens
Fred Ritter............................Michael McKean
Sandy Banatoni..........................Cynthia Gibb
Oscar Baldwin;..........................Jack Weston

Short Time •• [1990]
Director: Gregg Champion
Screenplay: John Blumenthal & Michael Berry

When cop Coleman discovers he's dying, he tries to get himself killed in the line of duty so that his family will be well provided for. Coleman is superb in this implausible, but reasonably entertaining, action-comedy marred, as so often, by a dollop too much of syrup. [97m/12]

Burt Simpson......................Dabney Coleman
Ernie Dills....................................Matt Frewer
Carolyn Simpson............................Teri Garr
Captain.......................................Barry Corbin

Shy People •• [1987]
Director: Andrei Konchalovsky
Screenplay: Gérard Brach, Marjorie David & Andrei Konchalovsky

Reporter Clayburgh drags her horrible daughter with her into the backward bayous for a Cosmo piece on a distant branch of her family. It's another world, where nothing much happens. Sadly, director Konchalovsky conveys that all too well. Both melodramatic and implausible, Hershey's as watchable as always. [119m/15]

Diana...Jill Clayburgh
Ruth......................................Barbara Hershey
Grace....................................Martha Plimpton
Mike.......................................Merritt Butrick

Sibling Rivalry •• [1990]
Director: Carl Reiner
Screenplay: Martha Goldhirsch

Bored Alley has an affair with a stranger who dies on her. Then he turns out to be related. Although Alley's surprisingly good, this intriguing idea for a farce is never given full rein and, at the end, plunges into corn as high as an elephant's eye. [88m/15]

Marjorie Turner ....Kirstie Alley
Nicholas Meany............................Bill Pullman
Iris Turner-Hunter....................Carrie Fisher
Keanine ....Jami Gertz
Harry Turner ....Scott Bakula
Rose Turner ....Frances Sternhagen

Quote 'You had sex with your brother-in-law?' – 'It was not sex. It was good.' ✦ 'I gave Carl a fish and he gave me three turtles.' [Alley exchanging tokens of affection with her director]

The Sicilian •• [1987]
Director: Michael Cimino
Screenplay: Steve Shagan

A view through rose-tinted spectacles of Sicilian bandit Salvatore Guiliano, trying to liberate Sicily in the 40s. While the full director's cut has some moments of Cimino's directorial flair, it also has

Lambert giving his impression of a petrified olive tree. There's less of him in the two-hour version but that version makes no sense dramatically.

[146m/15]

Salvatore Giuliano.........Christopher Lambert
Prince Borsa...........................Terence Stamp
Don Masino Croce.....................Joss Ackland
Also: John Turturro, Barbara Sukowa, Ray McAnally

Psst! This could well be the only film to give a credit to the designer of a wound!

Sid and Nancy ••   [1986]

Director: **Alex Cox**
Screenplay: **Alex Cox & Abbe Wool**

Sid Vicious of the Sex Pistols has an affair with American groupie Nancy Spungen. It ends horribly. A useful reminder of how hideous the 70s were, this Romeo and Juliet tale with razor blades is not for all tastes, though Oldman is as compelling as ever in the first of his true-life portrayals.   **[111m/18]**

Sid Vicious...............................Gary Oldman
Nancy Spungen............................Chloe Webb
Johnny Rotten..........................Drew Schofield
Malcolm McLaren.................David Hayman

Psst! Oldman suffered from malnutrition after starving himself for the part.

Side Out •   [1990]

Director: **Peter Israelson**
Screenplay: **David Thoreau**

Yet another sport brought to the cinema screen – beach volleyball. Oh, there've been minor volleyball scenes in other movies. But never a mainstream film almost entirely dedicated to the sport. *Almost* as gripping as you would expect.

[100m/12]

Monroe Clark.................C. Thomas Howell
Zack Barnes.................................Peter Horton
Samantha.................Courtney Thorne-Smith

Siesta •   [1987]

Director: **Mary Lambert**
Screenplay: **Patricia Louisianna Knop**

Barkin's a skydiver who falls out of a plane and survives. Travelling round Spain to explain it involves bonking Byrne and repelling cabbie Sayle. You'd think it impossible that any film with Barkin throwing her togs to the winds in the first minute would be a dog. But this is a real chihuahua. Don't be fooled by the cast. This one's so bad that it's dreadful. **[97m/18]**

Claire..Ellen Barkin
Augustine.................................Gabriel Byrne
Kit...Julian Sands
Also: Isabella Rossellini, Martin Sheen, Alexei Sayle, Grace Jones, Jodie Foster

Quote 'Some people think it's the greatest film they ever saw. Of course most of them are medicated.' [Gabriel Byrne]

Psst! It's only Bronze for Barkin in the Disrobing Stakes. Although the clothes are off soon after the opening credits, she loses out to her competitors in *Diamond Skulls* and *Zandalee*.

The Silence of the Lambs •••   [1991]

Director: **Jonathan Demme**
Screenplay: **Ted Tally**

Overrated chiller with FBI trainee Foster deputed to seek help from 'Hannibal the Cannibal' Hopkins in tracking down a serial killer. The scenes with the brilliant but dangerous Hopkins burrowing into Foster's mind are compulsive and deeply disturbing. But when Hopkins disappears half-way through, the pic turns into a daft and implausible thriller. If you want to be *really* frightened, try the other Hannibal movie, *Manhunter*.   **[119m/18]**

Clarice Starling............................Jodie Foster
Dr. Hannibal Lecter..........Anthony Hopkins
Jack Crawford................................Scott Glenn
Jame Gumb....................................Ted Levine
Dr. Frederick Chilton.............Anthony Heald
Catherine Martin.......................Brooke Smith
Senator Ruth Martin....................Diane Baker

Oscars Best Picture, Best Director, Jodie Foster, Anthony Hopkins, Best Screenplay (adapted)

Quote 'A census taker once tried to test me. I ate his liver with some fava beans and a nice Chianti.' ◆ 'I have to go now. I'm having an old friend for dinner.'

Psst! This was only the third film to win the top five Oscars, after *It Happened One Night* (1934) and *One Flew Over the Cuckoo's Nest* (1975) ◆ As a sick joke, they opened it in America on Valentine's Day ◆ Look out for horror director Roger Corman as FBI director Burke ◆ The magazine Hopkins reads in his temporary cell is *Bon Appetit!* ◆ The death's head at the centre of the moth on the ads is actually made up of 6 naked women ◆ When the film came to Britain, Hopkins apparently delighted in waiting for the first scream, then turning round and smiling devilishly at the person behind him ◆ He claimed to have based his character on a combination of Katharine Hepburn, Truman Capote and HAL, the computer in *2001* ◆ This was to have been Gene Hackman's first film as director, but he decided it was too violent ◆ Among those working on the film was a 'Moth Wrangler/Stylist'.

Silent Voice ●● [1987]

Director: **Mike Newell**
Screenplay: **David Field**

Even for a nation that thinks the world revolves around baseball, this is going some. A lad gives up the game until the nuclear threat has vanished, only to be joined first by top American athletes and then by the Russians. The two nations' leaders are brought to their knees and the lad's aim is achieved. Whimsical to the point of pain. Also known as *Amazing Grace and Chuck*. [115m/PG]

Lynn Taylor	Jamie Lee Curtis
Amazing Grace Smith	Alex English
President	Gregory Peck
Russell	William Petersen

Silkwood ●●● [1983]

Director: **Mike Nichols**
Screenplay: **Nora Ephron & Alice Arlen**

Karen Silkwood, a nuclear power worker, died mysteriously in 1974 on her way to hand over proof of safety violations. This slow-paced, rather sudsy treatment of the story is redeemed by the excellent performances, although Streep could have made Karen a mite more sympathetic. [131m/15]

Karen Silkwood	Meryl Streep
Drew Stephens	Kurt Russell
Dolly Pelliker	Cher
Winston	Craig T. Nelson
Angela	Diana Scarwid
Morgan	Fred Ward
Paul Stone	Ron Silver

Also: Charles Hallahan, Josef Sommer, Sudie Bond, E. Katherine Kerr, David Strathairn, J.C. Quinn, M. Emmet Walsh

OOPS! After Cher is questioned in Streep's house, she's driven away. But you can see her back in the house again afterwards in the background.

Silverado ●●● [1985]

Director: **Lawrence Kasdan**
Screenplay: **Lawrence Kasdan & Mark Kasdan**

Four less-than-likely lads help a town beat off the baddies. This startlingly original idea is matched by a saddle-sore plot so implausible in places it makes *The Lone Ranger* look like a documentary. Who cares? There's plenty of entertaining action, a few laughs, and none of the ludicrous revisionism that mars other modern Westerns. [133m/PG]

Paden	Kevin Kline
Emmett	Scott Glenn
Jake	Kevin Costner
Mal	Danny Glover
Cobb	Brian Dennehy
Stella	Linda Hunt
Slick	Jeff Goldblum
Hannah	Rosanna Arquette
Sheriff Langston	John Cleese

Quote 'I'm Sheriff John Langston and, as you may have guessed, I'm not from these parts.'

Psst! The credits include a 'livestock ramrod'.

Silver Bullet • [1985]

Director: **Daniel Attias**
Screenplay: **Stephen King**

A werewolf is terrorising the inhabitants of a small town, sensibly picking a place where the residents act with all the intelligence of Wile E. Coyote. A daft, far-fetched adaptation of a Stephen King novel. **[95m/18]**

Uncle Red	Gary Busey
Rev. Lowe	Everett McGill
Marty Coslaw	Corey Haim

Silver City •• [1985]

Director: **Sophia Turkiewicz**
Screenplay: **Sophia Turkiewicz & Thomas Keaneally**

Love among the Polish immigrant community in Australia in the 40s. It's a slightly uncomfortable and soapy rendering of what presumably is a semi-autobiographical tale. **[110m/15]**

Nina	Gosia Dobrowolska
Julian	Ivar Kants
Anna	Anna Jemison
Viktor	Steve Bisley

Simple Men •• [1992]

Director: **Hal Hartley**
Screenplay: **Hal Hartley**

A pair of brothers, one into computer fraud, the other a student, go looking for their anarchist father. Another weird slice of everyday American life from Hartley, who really should stick to fly fishing. **[105m/15]**

Bill McCabe	Robert Burke
Dennis McCabe	William Sage
Kate	Karen Sillas

Sing • [1989]

Director: **Richard Baskin**
Screenplay: **Dean Pitchford**

Sub-*Fame* drivel set in a Brooklyn high school where 'the show must go on'. Not while there's an off button, it mustn't. **[98m/PG]**

Miss Lombardo	Lorraine Bracco
Dominic	Peter Dobson
Hanna	Jessica Steen

Singles •••• [1992]

Director: **Cameron Crowe**
Screenplay: **Cameron Crowe**

Wonderfully funny romantic comedy, following the wiggly course of love, true or otherwise, for half a dozen Twenty-somethings in Seattle. Spot-on in its examination of dating rituals, particularly the use of the telephone, this film from former rock journalist Crowe has been compared to Woody Allen. However, it's a true original and more pertinent to the life of the average moviegoer than Allen's New York middle-class, middle-aged, angst. The pull-back ending, showing an ever-widening circle of people going through exactly the same problems is particularly memorable. **[99m/12]**

Janet Livermore	Bridget Fonda
Steve Dunne	Campbell Scott
Linda Powell	Kyra Sedgwick
Debbie Hunt	Sheila Kelley
David Bailey	Jim True
Cliff Poncier	Matt Dillon
Dr. Jamison	Bill Pullman
Andy	James Le Gros
Ruth	Devon Raymond
Luiz	Camilo Gallardo
Pam	Ally Walker
Mime	Eric Stoltz

Psst! Look out for *Batman* director Tim Burton in a brief cameo as the chap picking up twenty bucks to direct Debbie's dating video ✦ Underneath the mime's makeup is Eric Stoltz, an actor who seems to spend most of his movie career in disguise (see *Mask* and *The Fly II*).

Single White Female •• [1992]

Director: **Barbet Schroeder**
Screenplay: **Don Roos**

This initially intriguing psychological thriller has Fonda taking on Leigh as her flatmate, only to find her borrowing her clothes and her hairstyle and looking set to borrow her life as well. Unfortunately, halfway through all credibility is thrown out of the window as it suddenly turns into The Flatmate From Hell, a silly copycat thriller. Any movie that relies on conversations heard through air vents and a shoebox full of the psycho's press clippings in the wardrobe deserves what it gets which, when I saw it, was derisive laughter. **[108m/18]**

Allison Jones	Bridget Fonda
Hedra Carlson	Jennifer Jason Leigh
Sam Rawson	Steven Weber
Graham Knox	Peter Friedman
Myerson	Stephen Tobolowsky

Psst! Winner of our award for the Most Gratuitous Misuse of a Stiletto Heel in a Movie.

Sister Act •• [1992]

Director: **Emile Ardolino**
Screenplay: **Joseph Howard**

Goldberg is the gangster's moll who goes into hiding when she sees him giving an employee a terminal P 45. She's hidden by the Police in a convent where she clashes with Mother Superior Smith and helps the nuns with the sound of their music. Despite the odd funny scene and some great music from the revamped choir, the plot's got whiskers down to the ground and much of it is terribly corny. **[100m/PG]**

Deloris	Whoopi Goldberg
Mother Superior	Maggie Smith
Mary Patrick	Kathy Najimy
Mary Robert	Wendy Makkena
Mary Lazarus	Mary Wickes
Vince LaRocca	Harvey Keitel
Eddie Souther	Bill Nunn
Joey	Robert Miranda
Willy	Richard Portnow

Blurb No Sex. No Booze. No Men. No Way.

Quote 'If this turns into a nuns' bar, I'm out of here.'

Psst! Goldberg hated working for Disney and had T-shirts printed bearing a black Mickey Mouse saying 'Niggerteer' ✦ To encourage her to make the sequel, Disney bought and released *Sarafina*, despite knowing they were likely to lose their shirts ✦ The part was originally intended for Bette Midler ✦ Among those uncredited writers working on the script was Carrie Fisher.

Sisters •• [1988]

Director: **Michael Hoffman**
Screenplay: **Rupert Walters**

Dempsey goes to Quebec for Christmas with girlfriend Connelly's eccentric family. This peculiarly plotless comedy has some charm, unlike Dempsey himself. Also known as *Some Girls*. **[94m/15]**

Michael	Patrick Dempsey
Gabriella	Jennifer Connelly
Irenka	Sheila Kelley
Nick	Lance Edwards

'68 • [1988]

Director: **Steven Kovacs**
Screenplay: **Steven Kovacs**

A Hungarian family escape to San Francisco after the uprising of '68, a time when politics and sex were going through revolutions of their own. Heavy, man. **[98m/15]**

Peter Szabo	Eric Larson
Sandy Szabo	Robert Kocke
Zoltan Szabo	Sandor Tecsi

Six Weeks •• [1982]

Director: **Tony Bill**
Screenplay: **David Seltzer**

An out-and-out tearjerker with MTM a cosmetics tycoon with a dying daughter meeting up with politician Moore. Although the film's only for devotees of the Kleenex genre, the surprising thing is that Moore (Dudley rather than Mary) is so good in a straight part. But if ever there was a man bad at picking the films to be good in, it's him.   [107m/PG]

Patrick Dalton	Dudley Moore
Charlotte Dreyfus	Mary Tyler Moore
Nicole Dreyfus	Katherine Healy
Peg	Shannon Wilcox

Skin Deep • [1989]

Director: **Blake Edwards**
Screenplay: **Blake Edwards**

Despite a few funny scenes, particularly the one with the luminous condoms, this tale of the woman-obsessed, angst-ridden novelist is typical Blake Edwards at his least inspired.   [101m/18]

Zach Hutton	John Ritter
Barnie, the bartender	Vincent Gardenia
Alex	Alyson Reed

Ski Patrol • [1990]

Director: **Richard Correll**
Screenplay: **Steven Long Mitchell & Craig W. Van Sickle**

The producers of *Police Academy* have effectively come up with *Police Academy on Skis*, only nothing like as witty. Sadly, the hoped-for avalanche doesn't arrive.
                    [91m/PG]

Jerry	Roger Rose
Ellen	Yvette Nipar
Iceman	T.K. Carter
Pops	Ray Walston

Slacker • [1991]

Director: **Richard Linklater**
Screenplay: **Richard Linklater**

You know the sort of conversation you have when trying to sober up at three in the morning? This entire film's like that as we follow one student type after another, leaving each just as they say anything interesting. A cult hit on American campuses.   [97m/15]

With: Richard Linklater, Others

Quote 'I may live badly, but at least I don't have to work to do it.'

Psst! Made for just $23,000 with amateur actors, this debut became a hit at festivals ◆ Among the characters on the credits are 'Been on the Moon Since the 50s', 'Scooby Doo Philosopher' and 'Should Have Stayed at the Bus Station', the latter played by the writer-director.

Slamdance •• [1987]

Director: **Wayne Wang**
Screenplay: **Don Opper**

No sooner has Cartoonist Hulce shown femme fatale Madsen his etchings than he's being framed for her murder. An oddball film which, despite some quirky charm and good performances, is really just another conveyor-belt designer thriller.   [100m/15]

C.C. Drood	Tom Hulce
Helen Drood	Mary Elizabeth Mastrantonio
Jim	Adam Ant

Also: Judith Barsi, Don Opper, John Doe, Harry Dean Stanton, Robert Beltran, Virginia Madsen

Psst! Political Correctness was obviously the order of the day here. The credits have, not the usual 'Best Boy', but an 'Electrical Best Person'.

Slate, Wyn and Me •• [1987]

Director: **Don McLennan**
Screenplay: **Don McLennan**

A couple of brothers rob a bank, kill a policeman and kidnap a pretty witness who is soon sowing seeds of discord between them. This is a slow-moving Australian road movie that gets a flat fairly early on and doesn't seem to have a spare.
                    [90m/18]

Blanche McBride	Sigrid Thornton
Wyn Jackson	Simon Burke
Slate Jackson	Martin Sacks
Morgan	Tommy Lewis

Slaves of New York •• [1989]

Director: James Ivory
Screenplay: Tama Janowitz

An occasionally amusing adaptation of the successful book about a group of Bohemian characters, eccentric even by New York standards. Lacking anything you'd call a story, it's an unusual film for Ivory to have chosen to direct. [125m/15]

Eleanor .... Bernadette Peters
Victor Okrent .... Chris Sarandon
Ginger Booth .... Mary Beth Hurt
Also: Madeleine Potter, Nick Corri, Mercedes Ruehl, Steve Buscemi
Showing *Holiday.*
Psst! Author of the original book Tama Janowitz appears as 'Abby'.

Slayground • [1984]

Director: Terry Bedford
Screenplay: Trevor Preston

If you were making a taut crime thriller, would *you* shift the action from New York to Southport? That's where Coyote, on the run from a hired assassin, heads. As if things weren't bad enough, he runs into Mel Smith. One of the very few films that *is* worse than a wet weekend in Southport. [89m/18]

Stone .... Peter Coyote
Abbatt .... Mel Smith
Madge .... Billie Whitelaw

Sleeping With the Enemy • [1991]

Director: Joseph Ruben
Screenplay: Ronald Bass

Hell, I'll sleep with anybody – even the writer – not to have to watch this melodramatic load of tosh again. Bergin's the ultimate anal retentive who beats up on wife Roberts. Faking her death she escapes, finding romance with drippy drama teacher Anderson. Unfortunately Anderson hasn't given Roberts any lessons before hubby turns up, a mite peeved. Beautiful she may be, convincing damsel in distress she's not. [100m/15]

Sara Waters/Laura Burney .... Julia Roberts
Martin Burney .... Patrick Bergin
Ben Woodward .... Kevin Anderson
Chloe .... Elizabeth Lawrence
Psst! New York model Shelley Sinclair body doubled for Roberts.

Sleepwalkers • [1992]

Director: Mick Garris
Screenplay: Stephen King

If you were a shape-changing creature needing a supply of virgins to survive, would you choose America to live? Incestuous mom and son Brady do, targeting delicious Amick as the next Brady brunch. Despite steamy Oedipal sex scenes, this is a silly, illogical and badly-made horror pic. Audiences were sleepwalking out of cinemas. [89m/18]

Charles Brady .... Brian Krause
Tanya Robertson .... Mädchen Amick
Mary Brady .... Alice Krige
Quote 'Just try to think of yourself as lunch.'
OOPS! If a cat can see them early in the pic, why can't any of the moggies spot them later? • The front door reappears magically on its hinges shortly after being broken down.
Psst! The house featured in the film is that used in the TV series *The Waltons.*

Slipstream • [1989]

Director: Steven M. Lisberger
Screenplay: Tony Kayden

This British-made sci-fi plodder never gets up enough speed to generate a slipstream. It's the future. The weather's gone mad. So have the people. Bounty hunter Paxton has nabbed android Peck. Hamill chases after them, wondering whether he'll ever get a part in a film that *doesn't* look like *Star Wars.* [102m/PG]

Tasker .... Mark Hamill
Byron .... Bob Peck
Matt Owens .... Bill Paxton
Also: Kitty Aldridge, Eleanor David, Ben Kingsley, F. Murray Abraham, Robbie Coltrane, Roshan Seth

Sliver [1993]

Director: **Phillip Noyce**
Screenplay: **Joe Eszterhas**

From one *Basic Instinct* to an even baser one – voyeurism. Stone's the literary editor who moves into a new apartment building. She begins to think somebody is watching her which, considering the amount of clothing she's wearing is a pretty safe bet. **[18]**

Carly Norris...............................Sharon Stone
Zeke Hawkins.......................William Baldwin
Jack Lansford...........................Tom Berenger

Blurb You Like To Watch. Don't You.

Psst! Stone's pay, which had been only $300,000 on *Basic Instinct* jumped to $2.5m plus a percentage of profits ✦ She agreed to full frontal nudity only if Baldwin endured the same. She was furious when his scenes were cut. Much of the raunchiness was too strong for the American censor, forcing hasty reshooting ✦ Film cameraman Mike Benson was trapped for 2 days in a Hawaiian volcano before being rescued, only to find the Hollywood studios fighting over his story.

The Slumber Party Massacre • [1982]

Director: **Amy Holden Jones**
Screenplay: **Rita Mae Brown**

Er, it's about a slumber party. Lot's of pretty girls have nothing much on. There's a massacre. And that's it. Although it's from one of the top feminist writers and filmed by an all-women crew, it looks exactly like every other power-drill splatter movie you've ever seen. What *did* serial killers do before power tools were invented?

[78m/18]

Trish...................................Michele Michaelis
Valerie...Robin Stille
Russ..Michael Villela

Smash Palace •• [1982]

Director: **Roger Donaldson**
Screenplay: **Roger Donaldson, Peter Hansard & Bruno Lawrence**

The manager of a car wreck dump fails to notice the wreck of his own marriage. When his wife leaves him, he falls apart. This key film in the emergence of Kiwi cinema is no classic, but a powerful melodrama which escapes the Good Taste trap of so many films of the period from Down Under. **[108m/18]**

Al Shaw..............................Bruno Lawrence
Jacqui Shaw...............................Anna Jemison
Georgie Shaw...........................Greer Robson
Ray Foley................................Keith Aberdein

Smithereens ••• [1982]

Director: **Susan Seidelman**
Screenplay: **Susan Seidelman**

An amazingly assured low-budget debut for Seidelman, later to go on to make *Desperately Seeking Susan*. Essentially just a romantic triangle set in a seedy part of New York, it's tough, wryly observant and has the ring of truth about it.

[93m/15]

Wren..Susan Berman
Paul...Brad Rinn
Eric..Richard Hell
Cecile.................................Nada Despotovich

Smooth Talk ••• [1985]

Director: **Joyce Chopra**
Screenplay: **Tom Cole**

A rebellious teenage girl on the verge of womanhood encounters a sinister stranger. This little seen but highly accomplished portrayal of the fears and pressures of adolescence boasts a fine star performance from Dern. **[92m/15]**

Arnold Friend.........................Treat Williams
Connie...Laura Dern
Katherine...............................Mary Kay Place
June.....................................Elizabeth Berridge
Harry..Levon Helm

Sneakers ••• [1992]

Director: **Phil Alden Robinson**
Screenplay: **Phil Alden Robinson, Walter F. Parkes & Lawrence Lasker**

The return of the comedy-spy-buddy-caper movie Hollywood was so fond of in the 70s. A group of misfits who advise banks on computer security are drawn into a plot concerning a code-breaking box that threatens the fate of the Western world. Although losing credibility completely in the final stages, the writers of *WarGames* have come up with a fast-paced, witty and highly enjoyable movie.

[125m/12]

Martin Bishop	Robert Redford
Mother	Dan Aykroyd
Cosmo	Ben Kingsley
Liz	Mary McDonnell
Carl	River Phoenix
Crease	Sidney Poitier
Whistler	David Strathairn
Dick Gordon	Timothy Busfield
Gregor	George Hearn
Buddy Wallace	Eddie Jones
Dr. Gunter Janek	Donal Logue
Dr. Elena Rhyzkov	Lee Garlington
Dr. Brandes	Stephen Tobolowsky

Blurb We Could Tell You What It's About. But Then, Of Course, We Would Have To Kill You.

Quote 'I want peace on earth and goodwill towards men.' – 'We're the US Government. We don't go in for that sort of thing.'

OOPS! In the scene where Redford speaks to James Earl Jones via satellite links, he is using a speakerphone, not a handset. Yet the others are shouting how close the call is to being traced, even though Jones would be able to hear them.

Psst! One of the consultants on the film was the infamous 'Captain Crunch', a hacker who made his name in the 70s when he discovered that you could make a payphone work without money using the toy whistle in a 'Cap'n Crunch' cereal box ♦ The film was originally called *Raiders of the Lost Computer*.

Sniper •• [1993]

Director: **Luis Llosa**
Screenplay: **Michael Frost Beckner & Crash Leyland**

Top army sniper Berenger has inexperienced Zane foisted on him on a jungle mission to cut off a rebel leader's mandate. More intelligent and less gung-ho than you might expect, there are some splendid action sequences which work by putting you firmly behind the sniper's gunsight. However, the film's deadened by the lack of fire between the two main characters.

[98m/15]

Thomas Beckett	Tom Berenger
Richard Miller	Billy Zane
Chester Van Damme	J.T. Walsh
Doug Papich	Aden Young

Soapdish • [1991]

Director: **David Seltzer**
Screenplay: **David Seltzer**

Shenanigans behind the scenes of a TV soap *can* be funny, as *Tootsie* demonstrated. But not here. The proceedings aren't helped by the actors, worst of whom is Field, not knowing whether to play it straight or for laughs. The final scene is nothing short of outright plagiarism. The makers of *Tootsie* should have sued.

[96m/12]

Celeste Talbert	Sally Field
Jeffrey Anderson	Kevin Kline
David Barnes	Robert Downey Jr.
Montana Moorehead	Cathy Moriarty

Also: Whoopi Goldberg, Elisabeth Shue, Kathy Najimy, Garry Marshall, Carrie Fisher

OOPS! Although the doorman says that Kline lives in flat 2D, it's 2A that we see on the door.

Psst! Edwards, the head of the TV station, is played by Garry Marshall, the director of *Pretty Woman* and *Frankie & Johnny*.

Society • [1990]

Director: **Brian Yuzna**
Screenplay: **Woody Keith & Rick Fry**

A young man is puzzled by the shape-shifting antics of his family and finds that arse-crawling to powerful figures is being taken too literally. An unwise attempt to combine social comment with splatter-horror. The totally disgusting effects are fairly impressive when they finally arrive, but by that stage you don't care. [99m/18]

Billy Whitney	Billy Warlock
Clarisa	Devin DeVasquez
Milo	Evan Richards

Blurb The Rich Have Always Fed Off The Poor. This Time It's For Real.

Psst! The credits include the line: 'Make-up effects by Screaming Mad George'.

Soft Top, Hard Shoulder •• [1993]

Director: **Stefan Schwartz**
Screenplay: **Peter Capaldi**

That rare thing, a British road movie. Capaldi has to get himself and his open-top Triumph Herald from London to Glasgow in time for his dad's 60th birthday party if he's to inherit his share of the family's ice-cream fortune. Along the way he very reluctantly picks up a hitch-hiker. Although it has its moments, it's all rather slow and is spoiled by Capaldi writing himself as such an extraordinarily unsympathetic character. [95m/15]

Gavin Bellini	Peter Capaldi
Yvonne	Elaine Collins
Uncle Salvatore	Richard Wilson

Psst! Collins is married to Capaldi.

A Soldier's Story ••• [1984]

Director: **Norman Jewison**
Screenplay: **Charles Fuller**

When a soldier is murdered in 1944 at a blacks-only army camp in the deep south, there's some surprise that a black captain,

Rollins, is sent to investigate. Clearly derived from a play, this is still a cracking good detective yarn with a fascinating background. [101m/15]

Capt. Davenport	Howard E. Rollins Jr.
Sgt. Waters	Adolph Caesar
Pte. Wilkie	Art Evans
Corp. Cobb	David Alan Grier
Capt. Taylor	Dennis Lipscomb
Corp. Ellis	Robert Townsend
PFC Peterson	Denzel Washington

Some Girls

SEE: Sisters

Someone to Watch Over Me •••• [1987]

Director: **Ridley Scott**
Screenplay: **Howard Franklin**

Cop Berenger is assigned to protect wealthy Manhattan murder witness Rogers. He falls in love with her, endangering himself and his family. A superb romantic thriller fashioned from a thinnish story. New York has seldom looked so glamorous and Scott here revealed for the first time that there's a heart underneath those dazzling visuals. None of this swamps the excellent acting and the sharp observations about class. [106m/15]

Mike Keegan	Tom Berenger
Claire Gregory	Mimi Rogers
Ellie Keegan	Lorraine Bracco
Lt. Garber	Jerry Orbach
Neil Steinhart	John Rubinstein
Joey Venza	Andreas Katsulas
T.J.	Tony Di Benedetto

OOPS! Berenger must be something of a slow reader. He's still on the same newspaper, with the same headline, days after he first started.

Something Wicked This Way Comes •• [1983]

Director: **Jack Clayton**
Screenplay: **Ray Bradbury**

A creepy carnival arrives at a small

American town at the start of the century. But despite offering people their deepest desires, things begin to go wrong. Despite the accomplished work all round, this fantasy effort is rather disappointing and blander than had been hoped. **[95m/PG]**

Charles Halloway	Jason Robards
Mr. Dark	Jonathan Pryce
Mrs. Nightshade	Diane Ladd
Dust Witch	Pam Grier

Psst! This was a project much cherished by Sam Peckinpah.

Something Wild ••• [1986]

Director: **Jonathan Demme**
Screenplay: E. Max Frye

Meek pencil-pusher Daniels is virtually kidnapped by the anarchic, totally OTT, Griffith and dragged along on a wild trip that involves that famous handcuff scene and attending her high school reunion. The film switches abruptly from farce to something darker when violent ex Liotta turns up. Constantly confounding your expectations of where it's going, possibly because it doesn't know itself, this is still a highly entertaining and blackly amusing film. Griffith is just wonderful. **[113m/18]**

Charles Driggs	Jeff Daniels
Audrey Hankel	Melanie Griffith
Ray Sinclair	Ray Liotta
Irene	Margaret Colin
The Country Squire	Tracey Walter
Peaches	Dana Preu
Larry Dillman	Jack Gilpin

Sommersby •••• [1993]

Director: **Jon Amiel**
Screenplay: **Nicholas Meyer & Sarah Kernochan**

After seven years away Southern gentlewoman Foster's husband returns from the Civil War a much changed man. The question is, is he the same man at all? Foster and Gere are both superb in this fascinating period love story. This is old-fashioned film-making at its finest, with a story that keeps you guessing up to the final minute. How rare to find a film that

really is about love, rather than lust. Yet despite the tameness of the sex scenes, this pair's passion practically burns a hole in the screen. A shame that Gere's character has to be quite such a 90's liberal, but you can't have everything. **[112m/12]**

Jack Sommersby	Richard Gere
Laurel Sommersby	Jodie Foster
Judge Isaacs	James Earl Jones
Orin Meecham	Bill Pullman
Lawyer Dawson	Maury Chaykin
Buck	Lanny Flaherty
Travis	Wendell Wellman

Psst! The cow is called Clarice, presumably a reference to Foster's part in *Silence of the Lambs* ✦ Some apparently hot love scenes filmed between Gere and Foster never made it to the screen. According to Gere, they took a heavy toll: 'If the day is filled with explicit sex scenes I seldom feel like even more sex at night' ✦ The film is based on the 1982 French film *The Return of Martin Guerre*.

Sophie's Choice •• [1982]

Director: **Alan J. Pakula**
Screenplay: **Alan J. Pakula**

A Polish woman's disintegration in post-war New York is revealed to have been caused by her suffering in a concentration camp. The revelation of the awful Choice Sophie has to make is devastatingly chilling. But the incredible time it takes for us to discover what it is and the irritating mannerisms of Meryl in Polish mode make the whole film's handling of its subject matter exploitative and disasteful. **[151m/15]**

Sophie	Meryl Streep
Nathan	Kevin Kline
Stingo	Peter MacNicol
Narrator	Josef Sommer

Oscars Meryl Streep

Psst! William Stryon, who wrote the novel, said he always visualised Ursula Andress in the lead, while Pakula originally wanted Liv Ullmann ✦ Streep lost 25 pounds (and shaved her head) for the scenes in Auschwitz.

Soul Man ••• [1986]

Director: **Steve Miner**
Screenplay: **Carol Black**

After his father cuts off financial support, Howell blacks up to qualify for the only scholarship going at the Harvard Law School. Less patronising than it sounds, this surprisingly funny comedy is also quite perceptive. **[102m/PG]**

Mark Watson ....C. Thomas Howell
Gordon Bloomfeld.......................Arye Gross
Sarah Walker....................Rae Dawn Chong
Prof. Banks...........................James Earl Jones
Whitney Dunbar....................Melora Hardin
Mr. Dunbar.............................Leslie Nielsen

Soursweet •• [1989]

Director: **Mike Newell**
Screenplay: **Ian McEwan**

An otherwise realistic and fascinating picture of life for Chinese immigrants setting up a takeaway business in London amidst their more violent compatriots is let down by a real bird's nest mess of a script. **[110m/15]**

Lily..Sylvia Chang
Husband ....Danny Dun
Mui...Jodi Long

South Central •• [1992]

Director: **Steve Anderson**
Screenplay: **Steve Anderson**

A gang leader only wakes up to the effects of drugs and violence on the young when he becomes a father himself. Despite the depressing topic, this is an interesting insight into another world, providing a much-needed antidote to those films still glamorising the gang culture. **[99m/15]**

Bobby Johnson........................Glenn Plummer
Ray Ray...........................Byron Keith Minns
Bear ....Lexie D. Bigham
Loco ....Vincent Craig Dupree

Souvenir •• [1989]

Director: **Geoffrey Reeve**
Screenplay: **Paul Wheeler**

An elderly German returns to the France he had such a great time occupying to search for his old girlfriend. But what was his involvement in a wartime massacre? A serious topic is given all the reverence and care of an Australian daytime soap, with the ending of the novel changed completely. **[93m/15]**

Ernst Kestner..............Christopher Plummer
Tina ....Catherine Hicks
Xavier Lorion.......................Michel Lonsdale
William Root ....Christopher Cazenove

Spaceballs •• [1987]

Director: **Mel Brooks**
Screenplay: **Mel Brooks, Thomas Meehan & Ronny Graham**

Mel Brooks lampooning *Star Wars* should have been great fun, even so long after the event, but isn't. Despite the odd smattering of good gags, it's all far too tasteful and uninventive. **[96m/PG]**

Pres. Skroob/Yogurt ....Mel Brooks
Barf..John Candy
Dark Helmut..............................Rick Moranis
Lone Starr.....................................Bill Pullman
Princess Vespa ....Daphne Zuniga
Colonel Sandurz.....................George Wyner
Radar technician ....Michael Winslow
Dot Matrix....................................Joan Rivers
Pizza the Hut............................Dom DeLuise
Captain of the guard ......Stephen Tobolowsky

Space Camp •• [1986]

Director: **Harry Winer**
Screenplay: **W.W. Wicket & Casey D. Mitchell**

NASA get careless and accidentally shoot a bunch of sightseeing kids into orbit in the space shuttle. Are they in trouble? With all the computer games they've played? So-so. **[107m/PG]**

Andie...Kate Capshaw
Kathryn ....Lea Thompson
Tish...Kelly Preston
Also: Larry B. Scott, Leaf Phoenix, Tate Donovan, Tom Skerritt

Psst! Leaf is River Phoenix's brother.

Spaced Invaders • [1990]

Director: **Patrick Read Johnson**
Screenplay: **Patrick Read Johnson & Scott Alexander**

Martians picking up a broadcast of *War of the Worlds* believe it's the real thing and head for earth as the spearhead of the invading force. Witless, derivative and interminable. [100m/PG]

Sam Hoxley ....Douglas Barr
Wrenchmuller ....Royal Dano
Kathy Hoxly............................Ariana Richards

Spacehunter: Adventures in the Forbidden Zone • [1983]

Director: **Lamont Johnson**
Screenplay: **Edith Rey, David Preston, Dan Goldberg & Len Blum**

Even 3-D can't save this desperate sci-fi plodder about Strauss rescuing three ladies in distress, their distress presum-ably caused by their agents getting them parts in rubbish like this. [90m/PG]

Wolff...Peter Strauss
Niki.......................................Molly Ringwald
Washington ....Ernie Hudson

Spies Like Us •• [1985]

Director: **John Landis**
Screenplay: **Dan Aykroyd, Lowell Ganz & Babaloo Mandel**

A rather disappointing rendition of the old Bob Hope, Bing Crosby *Road* movies, with Chase and Aykroyd as a couple of agents sent on a secret government mis-sion behind the Iron Curtain, not knowing that they are expected to fail. Even the talking camel in *Road to Morocco* got more laughs. [102m/PG]

Emmet Fitz-Hume.......................Chevy Chase
Austin Millbarge.......................Dan Aykroyd
Jerry Hadley ....Charles McKeown
Karen Boyer.............................Donna Dixon

Psst! As with so many John Landis films, there are cameos galore, particularly from other directors. They include Frank Oz, Ray Harryhausen, Joel Coen, Sam

Raimi, Michael Apted, Costa-Gavros, Martin Brest, Bob Swaim and Terry Gilliam • There's also an amusing cameo from Bob Hope • Donna Dixon is Mrs. Aykroyd • Matt Frewer, later to find fame as Max Headroom, appears in a bit part as a soldier.

Spinal Tap
SEE: This Is Spinal Tap

Splash •••• [1984]

Director: **Ron Howard**
Screenplay: **Lowell Ganz, Babaloo Mandel & Bruce Jay Friedman**

This superb comic fantasy has Hannah as the mermaid emerging onto dry land and Hanks as the gawky young man who falls for her, unaware that there's something fishy about her story. Their sweet romance is complicated by the interest shown in Hannah by the usual sinister scientist types. Perfect casting, a witty and inventive script and reasonably brisk direction make this a wholly delightful, if a trifle whimsical, movie. [110m/PG]

Allen Bauer ....Tom Hanks
Madison...................................Daryl Hannah
Walter Kornbluth.......................Eugene Levy
Freddie Bauer................................John Candy
Mrs. Simler ....Dody Goodman
Dr. Ross ....Richard B. Shull
Jerry..Bobby DiCicco
Dr. Zidell ....Howard Morris

Blurb She Was The Woman Of Allen's Dreams. She Had Large Dark Eyes, A Beautiful Smile And A Great Pair Of Fins.

OOPS! Keep an eye out for the boom mike which appears on several occasions.

Psst! This was the first Disney movie to feature bare breasts. Some Disney employees held a prayer meeting to protest about it. The studio originally tried out devices to cover up Hannah's nipples, until somebody pointed out that, without nipples, the audiences were even *more* likely to stare at her breasts

• Hanks claims he got the part after almost everybody else turned it down. Those who were up for it include Michael Keaton, Chevy Chase, Dudley Moore, Bill Murray and John Travolta • Ron Howard's dad Rance here plays 'McCullough', while the writers Ganz and Mandel (who later wrote *City Slickers* and *League of Their Own*) can be seen as 'Stan' and 'Rudy'.

Split Second •• [1992]

Director: Tony Maylam
Screenplay: Gary Scott Thompson

In a rather wet future London, something's ripping people to pieces. Hauer's the cop shooting off bullets and wisecracks at anything that moves. Hopelessly derivative, there are still a few laughs and thrills to be had from this British pic.

[91m/18]

Harley Stone	Rutger Hauer
Michelle	Kim Cattrall
Dick Durkin	Neil Duncan

Also: Michael J. Pollard, Alun Armstrong, Pete Postlethwaite, Ian Dury

Quote 'The only thing we know for sure is that he's not a vegetarian.'

OOPS! Cannon Street station doesn't have a lift to street level. As the film-makers are British, there's really no excuse.

Psst! The credits include a 'rat/pigeon wrangler'.

Splitting Heirs • [1993]

Director: Robert Young
Screenplay: Eric Idle

A Turkey Called Eric. In Idle's dire British comedy he's the heir to a dukedom but was left in a restaurant as a baby. Years later, he plots to get his estate back. Production values are terrible, the jokes are all growing mould and the acting, from everyone bar the glorious Hershey as the nymphomaniac duchess, is execrable. What a pity somebody didn't leave the script in a restaurant. [86m/12]

Henry	Rick Moranis
Tommy Patel	Eric Idle
Duchess Lucinda	Barbara Hershey
Kitty	Catherine Zeta Jones
Raoul P. Shadgrind	John Cleese
Angela	Sadie Frost
Butler	Stratford Johns
Mrs. Bullock	Brenda Bruce
Doorman	Eric Sykes

Quote 'You remind me of my late husband. Of course, I haven't seen you naked.'

Psst! If you're still with it, look out for Mr. and Mrs. Gary Lineker in a restaurant near the close • Although Hershey is playing Idle's mother, at 45 she's actually five years younger than him – and looks it.

Spotswood ••• [1992]

Director: Mark Joffe
Screenplay: Max Dann & Andrew Knight

Hopkins is the clinical and friendless 60's Australian efficiency expert giving the once-over to an archaic moccasin factory stuffed with eccentrics one sausage short of a barbie. Lacking a soul, he decides he wants to see the last of the moccasins. Gradually, however, he gets drawn into the lives of the workers and begins to live. Although the plot contains few surprises, the characters are reminiscent of films like *Gregory's Girl* and this odd, rather charming film wiles away the time nicely. [95m/PG]

Wallace	Anthony Hopkins
Carey	Ben Mendelsohn
Wendy	Toni Collette
Mr. Ball	Alwyn Kurts
Fletcher	Dan Wyllie

Spring Break • [1983]

Director: Sean S. Cunningham
Screenplay: David Smilow

Another one of those silly 'students off for a vacation of sun, sea and sex' films.

[101m/15]

Nelson	David Knell
Adam	Perry Lang
Stu	Paul Land

Square Dance •• [1987]

Director: Daniel Petrie
Screenplay: Alan Hines

Another coming-of-age movie, notable mainly for Lowe playing a retarded boy and an early appearance of Ryder, here a 13-year-old leaving grandpa behind and going to live with her promiscuous mother in the city. Well-acted but nothing special. **[112m/15]**

Dillard	Jason Robards
Juanelle	Jane Alexander
Gemma	Winona Ryder
Rory	Rob Lowe

The Squeeze • [1987]

Director: Roger Young
Screenplay: Daniel Taplitz

Dreadful action-comedy with Keaton a con man involved in uncovering a sweepstake scam. You've more chance of your ticket coming up in the lottery than laughing at this. **[102m/15]**

Harry Berg	Michael Keaton
Rachel Dobs	Rae Dawn Chong
Norman	Joe Pantoliano

Stakeout ••• [1987]

Director: John Badham
Screenplay: Jim Kouf

Estevez and Dreyfuss are cops watching Stowe's house in case her escaped convict boyfriend shows up. Dreyfuss, however, gets rather more heavily involved with the object of their surveillance than police regulations usually permit. Part romance, part comedy and part thriller, the ingredients make for a highly entertaining movie. **[117m/12]**

Chris Lecce	Richard Dreyfuss
Bil Reimers	Emilio Estevez
Maria McGuire	Madeleine Stowe
Richard "Stick" Montgomery	Aidan Quinn
Phil Goldshank	Dan Lauria
Jack Pismo	Forest Whitaker

Psst! During the stakeout, when they're throwing each other Trivial Pursuit type questions, Estevez asks who said: 'This was no boating accident!'. The line actually comes from *Jaws*, in which Dreyfuss starred, although the plot intervenes before he gets a chance to answer.

Stand and Deliver ••• [1988]

Director: Ramon Menendez
Screenplay: Ramon Menendez & Tom Musca

A remarkable true-life story of idiosyncratic teacher Olmos who galvanises the dead-end Hispanic kids he teaches. Not only do they start coming to class but they sit an advanced calculus exam, only to face appalling prejudice and racism. An intelligent, hope-inspiring movie. **[104m/15]**

Jaime Escalante	Edward James Olmos
Angel	Lou Diamond Phillips
Fabiola Escalante	Rosana De Soto
Ramirez	Andy Garcia

Blurb In 1982, A New Troublemaker Hit Garfield High...He Was Tough. He Was Wild. He Was Willing To Fight. He Was the New Maths Teacher.

Stand by Me •• [1986]

Director: Rob Reiner
Screenplay: Bruce A. Evans & Raynold Gideon

Despite its extraordinary reputation, this is a pleasant but run-of-the-mill coming-of-age story. Told in flashback by Dreyfuss, four friends set off on a trek to see a real body left in the woods. The performances are great, as is the music, but in some places time doesn't half hang heavy while you're waiting for something to happen. The pie-eating contest is the undoubted highlight. **[87m/15]**

Gordie Lachance	Wil Wheaton
Chris Chambers	River Phoenix
Teddy Dechamp	Corey Feldman
Vern Dechamp	Jerry O'Connell
Ace Merrill	Kiefer Sutherland
The Writer	Richard Dreyfuss
Billy Tessio	Casey Siemaszko

Psst! Look out for an early appearance of

John Cusack as Denny Lachance ✦ The town is called Castle Rock, the name that Carl Reiner later used for his very successful production company.

Stanley & Iris •• [1990]

Director: **Martin Ritt**
Screenplay: **Harriet Frank Jr. & Irving Ravetch**

Two big stars try to pretend to be ordinary, mundane people with ordinary, totally mundane problems. They've got an ordinary, mundane script to help them, but they're still Fonda and De Niro, feeling their way towards a relationship as she teaches him to read. Perhaps no other film has ever so completely ignored its source material. [104m/15]

Iris King...Jane Fonda
Stanley Cox.............................Robert De Niro
Sharon Fuller ....Swoosie Kurtz
Kelly ....Martha Plimpton

Psst! Pat Barker's original novel was about 7 women in poverty-stricken conditions in the north of England. Iris was a fat chip-butty-eating 50-year-old cleaner. Six of the women disappeared in the transfer to the screen, with Iris becoming the keep-fit figure of Fonda living on the West Coast.

The Star Chamber •• [1983]

Director: **Peter Hyams**
Screenplay: **Roderick Taylor & Peter Hyams**

A clever play on the widely-held view that too many criminals exploit the law to escape justice. A group of judges have their own secret club that metes out its own sentences and Douglas is invited to join. An intriguing idea is weighed down by an elephantine script that gives you a headache just trying to follow it. [109m/15]

Steven Hardin.......................Michael Douglas
Benamin Caulfield....................Hal Holbrook
Det. Harry Lowes.......................Yaphet Kotto
Emily Hardin ....Sharon Gless

Psst! This was Sharon Gless's film debut.

Star 80 •• [1983]

Director: **Bob Fosse**
Screenplay: **Bob Fosse**

Dorothy Stratten's slimy husband Paul Snider promotes her as a Playboy centre-fold and actress but then becomes murderously jealous of her success. Although technically slick, this is a fairly vacuous account of a sordid true story. [103m/18]

Dorothy ....Mariel Hemingway
Paul..Eric Roberts
Hugh Hefner...........................Cliff Robertson
Dorothy's mother......................Carroll Baker
Also: Roger Rees, David Clennon, Josh Mostel, Keenen Ivory Wayans

Psst! Mariel Hemingway had silicone breast implants before playing the role ✦ Look out for Keenen Ivory Wayans as the club comic ✦ This was Bob Fosse's last film.

Starlight Hotel ••• [1988]

Director: **Sam Pillsbury**
Screenplay: **Grant Hinden Miller**

A beautifully observed, charming New Zealand film, set in the Depression era, which has a teenager in search of her father linking up with a traumatised World War I veteran on the run. [93m/PG]

Kate Marshall..........................Greer Robson
Patrick ....Peter Phelps
Det. Wallace........................Marshall Napier
Spooner...The Wizard

Starman ••• [1984]

Director: **John Carpenter**
Screenplay: **Bruce A. Evans & Raynold Gideon**

Alien Bridges pops down to earth for a quick 'Greetings, Earthmen' visit, taking the form of Allen's dead husband. He gets her to take him to where he's hitching a lift back but, wouldn't you know it, a bunch of pesky scientists want to study him (don't those guys ever watch movies?). At times less sci-fi than straight romance, it is made by Bridges' amazingly convincing performance. An extremely entertaining yet sadly 'undiscovered' film.

[115m/PG]

Starman	Jeff Bridges
Jenny Hayden	Karen Allen
Mark Shermin	Charles Martin Smith
George Fox	Richard Jaeckel
Maj. Bell	Robert Phalen
Sgt. Lemon	Tony Edwards

Psst! This is the film that Columbia decided to make instead of *E.T.*, which they turned down.

Stars and Bars • [1988]

Director: Pat O'Connor
Screenplay: William Boyd

This monstrously unfunny Englishman-in-America comedy has stereotypical Day-Lewis trying to get a group of silly Southern oddball characters to sell him a picture. So bad that you wonder whether Boyd the scriptwriter actually bothered to read the book by Boyd the novelist.

[94m/15]

Henderson Dores	Daniel Day-Lewis
Loomis Gage	Harry Dean Stanton
Freeborn	Maury Chaykin
Irene	Joan Cusack

Also: Keith David, Spalding Gray, Glenne Headly, Laurie Metcalf

Starstruck ••• [1982]

Director: Gillian Armstrong
Screenplay: Stephen MacLean

This uncharacteristic film from Australian director Armstrong (*My Brilliant Career*) is an engaging rendering of the familiar tale about a teen wannabe singer helped in her ambition by her 14-year-old cousin. Taking the mickey out of these sort of films, it also beats them at their own game. Good fun.

[95m/PG]

Jackie	Jo Kennedy
Angus	Ross O'Donovan
Pearl	Margo Lee
Reg	Max Cullen

Star Trek III: The Search for Spock •• [1984]

Director: Leonard Nimoy
Screenplay: Harve Bennett

Although emphatically killed in the previous film, Kirk and his buddies think they hear Spock's voice and so trek halfway across the galaxy to find him. If their eyesight wasn't failing, they'd see him standing behind the camera, directing this disappointing outing to places people have boldly gone too often before. Too much talk, bad acting and Vulcan mysticism. Not enough action, humour or plot.

[105m/PG]

Kirk	William Shatner
Spock	Leonard Nimoy
McCoy	DeForest Kelley
Scotty	James Doohan
Sulu	George Takei
Chekov	Walter Koenig
Uhura	Nichelle Nichols
Sarek	Mark Lenard

Star Trek IV — The Voyage Home •••• [1986]

Director: Leonard Nimoy
Screenplay: Harve Bennett, Steve Meerson, Peter Krikes & Nicholas Meyer

Our gallant lads (lads!) have to fetch a pair of future-extinct whales from 20th-century earth if 23rd-century earth isn't to be wiped out. Played largely for the fish-out-of-water laughs, and getting them, this is an immensely entertaining outing for the Enterprise and all who sail in her.

[119m/PG]

Kirk	William Shatner
Spock	Leonard Nimoy
McCoy	DeForest Kelley
Scotty	James Doohan
Sulu	George Takei
Chekov	Walter Koenig
Uhura	Nichelle Nichols
Amanda	Jane Wyatt
Gillian	Catherine Hicks

Star Trek V: The Final Frontier •   [1989]

Director: **William Shatner**
Screenplay: **David Loughery**

If you thought Shatner was a bad actor, wait till you see him direct this dull, sentimental, tiresome film. Trek is right. Thank heavens there was another. It would have been too bad if this had been their swansong.   **[102m/PG]**

Capt. James T. Kirk .... William Shatner
Mr. Spock .... Leonard Nimoy
'Bones' McCoy .... DeForest Kelley
Also: James Doohan, Walter Koenig, Nichelle Nichols, George Takei, David Warner

Quote This Time, Have They Gone Too Far?

OOPS! Kirk's jacket changes colour from blue to black as he falls from the mountain • Watch the lift indicator and see them pass the same floor twice.

Psst! The credits include a *Klingon Dialogue Consultant*. In the States, apparently, someone has invented a Klingon language and it is not only spoken by more people than Esperanto, but also taught in some American universities.

Star Trek VI: The Undiscovered Country ••••   [1991]

Director: **Nicholas Meyer**
Screenplay: **Nicholas Meyer & Denny Martin Flinn**

The crew of the Enterprise boldly push their Zimmer frames where no man has pushed them before. Despite looking as if they should be travelling on senior citizen passes, this is one of the best of the bunch, with Kirk framed by the Klingons and deported to a prison planet. A rattling good yarn is enlivened by plenty of thrills, lots of cod Shakespearian references and some delightful deadpan humour. It closes, however, with the corniest of end credits, as they all literally sign off.   **[109m/PG]**

Captain James T. Kirk .... William Shatner
Spock .... Leonard Nimoy
Dr. McCoy .... DeForest Kelley
Scotty .... James Doohan
Chekov .... Walter Koenig
Uhuru .... Nichelle Nichols
Captain Sulu .... George Takei
Lt. Valeris .... Kim Cattrall
Chancellor Gorkon .... David Warner
Chang .... Christopher Plummer

Quote 'You've not discovered Shakespeare until you've read him in the original Klingon.' • 'Once again, we have saved civilisation as we know it.'

OOPS! Under attack, Sulu drops a cup which shatters. Obviously there's some incredible cleaning system available in the future, because the bits disappear incredibly quickly • Surely Romulan ale was blue in Star Trek II? These bally breweries; always tinkering with the formula • They don't know their Shakespeare as well as they pretend. The 'Undiscovered Country' is actually death!

Psst! This is where we finally learn that the 'T' of James T. Kirk is short for 'Tiberius' • The film is dedicated to Gene Roddenberry, creator of the TV series, who died just before the film opened • Christian Slater appears in a doorway of the *Excelsior* receiving orders from Sulu, a cameo so short he doesn't even have time to whip his shirt off. His mum, a devoted Trekkie, was casting director and wanted nothing more than for her boy to appear in a Star Trek pic • The video has a couple of minutes not seen in the cinema.

State of Grace •••   [1990]

Director: **Phil Joanou**
Screenplay: **Dennis McIntyre**

Despite some strong acting, this 70's gangster film – inspired by the real Irish–American 'Westies' – is overlong. However, there is plenty of tension and the film fully earns its '18' rating.   **[134m/18]**

Terry Noonan	Sean Penn
Frankie Flannery	Ed Harris
Jackie Flannery	Gary Oldman
Kathleen Flannery	Robin Wright
Nick	John Turturro
Stevie	John C. Reilly
Nicholson	R.D. Call
Finn	Burgess Meredith

Psst! When the blood didn't look dramatic enough in the final gun-battle, the director had the exploding blood capsules placed in condoms, a technique which gives a more vicious squirt of liquid.

Static •• [1986]

Director: **Mark Romanek**
Screenplay: **Keith Gordon & Mark Romanek**

A very peculiar satire about an inventor who has built a television set that receives pictures from Heaven. He, however, is the only one who sees a picture. Often amusing, but just as often tiresome.

[93m/15]

Ernie	Keith Gordon
Julia	Amanda Plummer
Frank	Bob Gunton

Staying Alive •• [1983]

Director: **Sylvester Stallone**
Screenplay: **Sylvester Stallone & Norman Wexler**

The idea of Stallone writing and directing the sequel to *Saturday Night Fever* makes the mind boggle. Unfortunately, the film doesn't. Travolta finally gets his big break but the magic has gone, largely because of Stallone's belief that he's directing another *Rocky* pic.

[96m/PG]

Tony Manero	John Travolta
Jackie	Cynthia Rhodes
Laura	Finola Hughes
Jesse	Steve Inwood

Psst! Director, co-producer and co-writer Sylvester Stallone pops up briefly in a cameo. His brother Frank wrote those numbers that didn't come from the Bee Gees.

Staying Together •• [1989]

Director: **Lee Grant**
Screenplay: **Monte Merrick**

The sentimental trials and tribulations of three brothers who are gob-smacked when daddy sells the family business out from under them. Unoriginal but pleasant enough.

[91m/15]

Duncan McDermott	Sean Astin
Nancy Trainer	Stockard Channing
Eileen McDermott	Melinda Dillon
Jack McDermott	Jim Haynie

Stay Tuned ••• [1992]

Director: **Peter Hyams**
Screenplay: **Tom S. Parker & Jim Jennewein**

A shamefully over-looked knockabout satire on TV. Jones is the agent of the devil offering couch-potato Ritter a 666-channel TV system, the sort of thing he'd give his soul for. Before you can say 'Mephistopheles', he and wife Dawber are fighting for their lives in a nightmare world of TV shows like *Dwayne's Underworld* and *Three Men and Rosemary's Baby*. Packed with brilliant black humour and the sort of wacky inventiveness that made *Back to the Future* so enjoyable, this is great fun for those who love childish humour.

[89m/PG]

Roy Knable	John Ritter
Helen Knable	Pam Dawber
Spike	Jeffrey Jones
Darryl Knable	David Tom
Diane Knable	Heather McComb

Showing *The Maltese Falcon.*

Psst! The brilliant sequence where they turn into cartoon mice was supervised by Warners' famous animator Chuck Jones, one of the head animators of Loony Tunes.

Stealing Heaven •• [1989]

Director: **Clive Donner**
Screenplay: **Chris Bryant**

The true, ill-starred story of Abelard and

Heloise, told with all the subtlety and intelligence of an airport blockbuster. He's supposed to be celibate, but what's a chap supposed to do when faced with such temptation? Back then it took balls to defy the church. In Abelard's case, the Church took them back. **[115m/15]**

Abelard	Derek de Lint
Heloise	Kim Thomson
Fulbert	Denholm Elliott
Bishop Martin	Bernard Hepton

Steaming •• [1986]

Director: **Joseph Losey**
Screenplay: **Patricia Losey**

In being translated to the screen, this play about a group of women fighting to keep their local Turkish bath open has lost most of its bite and wit. Despite the talent on display, there's little they can do to stiffen a limp script which must have been left in the steam for too long. **[95m/18]**

Nancy	Vanessa Redgrave
Sarah	Sarah Miles
Violet	Diana Dors
Josie	Patti Love
Mrs. Meadows	Brenda Bruce

Psst! This was Joseph Losey's last film.

Steel Magnolias •• [1989]

Director: **Herbert Ross**
Screenplay: **Robert Harling**

A group of Southern women get together in Dolly's beauty salon to chew the cud knowing that, as this is one of those women's weepies, one of them is bound to get a fatal disease pretty soon. The sort of film that is so nearly exactly what you expect, you know beforehand whether you're going to enjoy it or not. **[117m/15]**

M'Lynn Eatenton	Sally Field
Truvy Jones	Dolly Parton
Ouiser Boudreaux	Shirley MacLaine
Annelle Dupuy Desoto	Daryl Hannah
Clairee Belcher	Olympia Dukakis
Shelby Eatenton Latcherie	Julia Roberts
Drum Eatenton	Tom Skerritt
Spud Jones	Sam Shepard

OOPS! For those finding their eyelids drooping, keep an eye on Field's young sons, the only teenagers in existence to change not a jot over a three year period. **Psst!** Filming at the wrong time of year to catch the magnolia trees flowering, they had the blooms flown in and attached with wire ✦ For the scene with Dukakis in the school changing room, the lads got paid a basic $100 a day, increased to $150 if they'd do it without the jock-strap.

Stella • [1990]

Director: **John Erman**
Screenplay: **Robert Getchell**

A needless remake of the 1937 Barbara Stanwyck weepie of the mother who gives up everything for her daughter. Apart from curiosity about what they've done to a good film, most people need know nothing more than the fact that Midler is at her most Midleresque in this. **[114m/15]**

Stella Claire	Bette Midler
Ed Munn	John Goodman
Jenny Claire	Trini Alvarado

Also: Stephen Collins, Marsha Mason, Eileen Brennan, Linda Hart

St. Elmo's Fire • [1985]

Director: **Joel Schumacher**
Screenplay: **Joel Schumacher & Carl Kurlander**

This younger version of *The Big Chill* involves little more than a group of youngsters sitting round yapping about what it will mean to be an adult. Despite the cast, it's not a patch on *Diner*. **[108m/15]**

Kirbo	Emilio Estevez
Billy	Rob Lowe
Kevin	Andrew McCarthy
Jules	Demi Moore

Also: Judd Nelson, Ally Sheedy, Mare Winningham, Martin Balsam, Andie MacDowell

OOPS! Keep an eye on Moore's earrings while she and Lowe are getting it to-gether in the jeep.

The Stepfather ••• [1987]

Director: **Joseph Ruben**
Screenplay: **Donald E. Westlake**

A man has an obsession to find the perfect family. Woe betide any which turn out to be less than perfect. This intelligent thriller, taking a few sly swipes at some American sacred cows, boasts a splendidly manic performance from O'Quinn. The mayhem at the finale is a bit of a sop to the slasher crowd, but otherwise this is superior entertainment. [98m/18]

Jerry Blake	Terry O'Quinn
Stephanie Maine	Jill Schoelen
Susan Blake	Shelley Hack
Jim Ogilvie	Stephen Shellen
Dr. Bondurant	Charles Lanyer

Blurb Jerry Blake Likes To Look After The Family – *Any* Family

Stepfather 2: Make Room for Daddy • [1989]

Director: **Jeff Burr**
Screenplay: **John Auerbach**

Don't bother Making Room. Uninspired sequel, with another to follow on video. [88m/18]

Dr. Gene Clifford	Terry O'Quinn
Carol Grayland	Meg Foster
Matty Crimmin	Caroline Williams

Stephen King's Graveyard Shift

SEE: **Graveyard Shift**

Stepkids • [1992]

Director: **Joan Micklin Silver**
Screenplay: **Frank Mugavero**

A monotonous comedy about a young girl fed up of being part of a modern dysfunctional family in which everybody is related to everybody else, but never for very long. Mercifully, it ends long before you've managed to work out who's who. Also known as *Big Girls Don't Cry...They Get Even.* [104m/PG]

David	Griffin Dunne
Keith	David Strathairn
Melinda	Margaret Whitton

Stepping Out •• [1991]

Director: **Lewis Gilbert**
Screenplay: **Richard Harris**

Minnelli's a tap teacher struggling with a class of nitwits who keep tripping over their stereotypical characters. In adapting the play, the cringe factor has been turned up to full while their final transformation from clodhoppers to the sort of dancers West End audiences pay good money for is totally ludicrous. Even a keen tapper like myself found it dull. [105m/PG]

Mavis Turner	Liza Minnelli
Mrs. Fraser	Shelley Winters
Geoffrey	Bill Irwin
Maxine	Ellen Greene
Vera	Julie Walters

Sticky Fingers • [1988]

Director: **Catlin Adams**
Screenplay: **Melanie Mayron & Catlin Adams**

Two unbelievably silly women musicians find the temptation of a bag of drug money too much to resist and spend it wildly. An attempt at a screwball comedy that falls flat on its face. [88m/15]

Hattie	Helen Slater
Lolly	Melanie Mayron
Stella	Eileen Brennan

Still of the Night •• [1982]

Director: **Robert Benton**
Screenplay: **Robert Benton**

Psychiatrist Scheider falls for patient Streep, despite her irritating habit of playing with her blonde hair. Is she really a killer? Do we give a toss? Streep totally lacks the fire beneath the ice required of a Hitchcock-style heroine. [90m/15]

Sam Rice	Roy Scheider
Brooke Reynolds	Meryl Streep
Grace Rice	Jessica Tandy
Joseph Vitucci	Joe Grifasi

The Sting II • [1983]

Director: Jeremy Kagan
Screenplay: David S. Ward

The Film That Should Not Have Been. Making this lacklustre, uninspiring, pathetic sequel to a great movie practically amounts to blasphemy. All concerned should have been excommunicated. [102m/PG]

Gondorff...................................Jackie Gleason
Hooker...Mac Davis
Veronica..Teri Garr
Macalinski.................................Karl Malden
Lonnegan......................................Oliver Reed

Stockade •• [1990]

Director: Martin Sheen
Screenplay: Dennis Schyrack & Martin Sheen

Martin Sheen wrote and directed this drab pic of a rebellious young man who gets the choice of jail or the army and chooses the army. Before long, though, he's in the army *and* jail. Also known as *Count a Lonely Cadence*. [98m/12]

Franklin Bean Jr.........................Charlie Sheen
Sgt. Otis V. McKinney.............Martin Sheen
Garcia.............................F. Murray Abraham
Also: Larry Fishburne, Blu Mankuma, Michael Beach, James Marshall

Stone Cold •• [1992]

Director: Craig R. Baxley
Screenplay: Walter Doniger

One of America's most successful American football players, 'The Boz', stars in this formulaic story of a cop blackmailed into infiltrating a gang of evil bikers known as The Brotherhood. Boz is personable enough but interest is only kept alive by Henriksen's great villain and a couple of neat, loud and violent action scenes. [92m/18]

Joe Huff/John Stone................Brian Bosworth
Chains Cooper ....Lance Henriksen
Ice..William Forsythe
Nancy....................................Arabella Holzbog

Stop! Or My Mom Will Shoot • [1992]

Director: Roger Spottiswoode
Screenplay: Blake Snyder, William Osborne & William Davies

No buddy team on film has managed to misfire quite so badly as Getty and Stallone in this schmaltzy supposed comedy. He's the LA cop. She's his New Jersey mom turning his life upside-down when she visits and witnesses a murder. If he shot her to shut her up, no jury on earth would convict. [87m/PG]

Joe Bomowski......................Sylvester Stallone
Tutti..Estelle Getty
Gwen Harper ....JoBeth Williams
Parnell..Roger Rees

Stormy Monday • [1988]

Director: Mike Figgis
Screenplay: Mike Figgis

Jones is an American buying up Newcastle but finding club-owner Sting reluctant to sell. Despite the thriller tag, this is a tedious exercise in style that isn't lifted by its uncharismatic leads. What is it with these Geordie directors? Figgis, Tony Scott and brother Ridley. All flash and no pan. [93m/15]

Kate ....Melanie Griffith
Cosmo ....Tommy Lee Jones
Finney...Sting
Brendan ....Sean Bean

Storyville • [1992]

Director: Mark Frost
Screenplay: Mark Frost & Lee Reynolds

Spader's being groomed for Congress but gets involved in a ludicrous murder plot. Mark Frost, co-creator of *Twin Peaks* produces an atmospheric New Orleans, but tries to cram so much into the story that it collapses under the weight. [110m/15]

Cray Fowler...............................James Spader
Natalie Tate ....Joanne Whalley-Kilmer
Clifford Fowler..........................Jason Robards
Lee ....Charlotte Lewis

Straight Out of Brooklyn •• [1991]

Director: **Matty Rich**
Screenplay: **Matty Rich**

A bleak look at life in one of the most depressed areas of Brooklyn. Although it's amazing what such a young talent has produced, if you ignore his age you're left with a slightly amateurish drama that's bitten off more than it can chew. **[83m/15]**

Ray Brown	George T. Odom
Frankie Brown	Ann D. Sanders
Dennis Brown	Lawrence Gillard Jr.
Carolyn Brown	Barbara Sanon
Larry Love	Matty Rich

Psst! Rich was 19 when he wrote, produced, directed and acted in this, his first film ✦ $16,000 of the budget came from his mother's and sister's credit cards.

Straight Talk ••• [1992]

Director: **Barnet Kellman**
Screenplay: **Craig Bolotin & Patricia Resnick**

Newly arrived in the Windy City, Parton begins work at a radio station. Before you can say 'Bob's your sex-change Auntie', she's the station's agony aunt, dispensing home-spun wisdom to Chicago. Woods is the reporter on her trail who falls for her in one of the unlikeliest romances yet. Although the plot's ludicrous, the film is frequently funny. True, it's so corny Kelloggs could turn it into a cereal, but it's still hard not to stop the tears welling up at the end. Those who loathe Parton's music should steer well clear. **[91m/PG]**

Dr. Shirlee Kenyon	Dolly Parton
Jack Russell	James Woods
Alan Riegert	Griffin Dunne
Steve Labell	Michael Madsen
Lily	Deirdre O'Connell
Guy Girardi	John Sayles
Janice	Teri Hatcher
Dr. Erdman	Spalding Gray
Milo Jacoby	Jerry Orbach

Quote 'Get down off your cross, honey. Someone needs the wood.'

Straight to Hell • [1987]

Director: **Alex Cox**
Screenplay: **Dick Rude & Alex Cox**

Straight to Video, more like. A pathetic and wholly unfunny British spoof of the Spaghetti Western that surely proves, once and for all, that *Repo Man* was a fluke for Cox. **[86m/15]**

Norwood	Sy Richardson
Simms	Joe Strummer

Also: Dick Rude, Courtney Love, Jim Jarmusch, Dennis Hopper, Grace Jones, Elvis Costello

Strange Invaders ••• [1983]

Director: **Michael Laughlin**
Screenplay: **Bill Condon & Michael Laughlin**

A wonderful spoof of those 1950's aliens–are–coming sci-fi pics. Here the aliens assume human form under an agreement with the American government. But when they go home, LeMat's not too pleased that his family are going back with them. Bright, witty, oddball and gently scary, this is a little gem of a film. **[93m/PG]**

Charles	Paul LeMat
Betty	Nancy Allen
Margaret	Diana Scarwid
Willie	Michael Lerner
Mrs. Benjamin	Louise Fletcher
Earl	Wallace Shawn

Strangers Kiss •• [1984]

Director: **Matthew Chapman**
Screenplay: **Blaine Novak & Matthew Chapman**

Two actors working on a low-budget 50's thriller find their offscreen lives reflect their onscreen actions. This is an oddball charmer with an interesting background whose quirkiness makes up for its variable quality. **[94m/15]**

Director	Peter Coyote
Carol/Betty	Victoria Tennant
Stevie/Billy	Blaine Novak
Farris/Producer	Dan Shor

Stranger Than Paradise •• [1984]

Director: Jim Jarmusch
Screenplay: Jim Jarmusch

Despite the critical plaudits, this small, comic road movie about a trio of Hungarian immigrants heading from New York to Miami has long, flat patches as well as moments of inspired comedy.

[90m/15]

Willie	John Lurie
Eva	Eszter Balint
Eddie	Richard Edson
Aunt Lottie	Cecilia Stark

Strapless • [1990]

Director: David Hare
Screenplay: David Hare

Pointless. An American doctor's middle-aged crisis is brought to a head by a visit from her younger sister and an affair with a mysterious foreign businessman. A good cast do their best with the theme of the importance of true emotion, but it's all rather a heavy dose. [99m/15]

Lilian Hempel	Blair Brown
Raymond Forbes	Bruno Ganz
Amy Hempel	Bridget Fonda

Also: Alan Howard, Hugh Laurie

Streamers •• [1983]

Director: Robert Altman
Screenplay: David Rabe

Four draftees are confined to barracks just before being sent to Vietnam. Altman does little to open out the stage play, concentrating almost entirely on these four squabbling squaddies as tensions build to a head. Great acting, but an awful lot of talking going on. [118m/18]

Billy	Matthew Modine
Carlyle	Michael Wright
Richie	Mitchell Lichtenstein
Roger	David Alan Grier

Psst! A 'streamer', in Army parlance, is a paratrooper whose parachute hasn't opened.

Street Fleet •• [1983]

Director: Joel Schumacher
Screenplay: Joel Schumacher

Mildly amusing comedy about the cabbies of a decrepit Washington taxi outfit pulling together when the going gets tough. All rather silly. Also known as *D.C.Cab.* [99m/15]

Hrold	Max Gail
Albert	Adam Baldwin
Samson	Mr. T
Tyrone	Charlie Barnett
Dell	Gary Busey

Streets of Fire • [1984]

Director: Walter Hill
Screenplay: Walter Hill & Larry Gross

A bike gang kidnap a pop singer but boyfriend Pare sets out to rescue her. An odd attempt at a rock urban fable is dripping with style, but has nowhere to go. Madigan provides some welcome relief from the endless machismo. [94m/15]

Tom	Michael Pare
Ellen	Diane Lane
Billy	Rick Moranis
McCoy	Amy Madigan

Also: Willem Dafoe, Deborah Van Valkenburgh, Rick Rossovich, Bill Paxton, Robert Townsend, Ed Begley Jr.

Streets of Gold •• [1986]

Director: Joe Roth
Screenplay: Heywood Gould, Richard Price & Tom Cole

Brandauer used to be a Russian boxing champion until it was discovered he was Jewish. Now in America and washing dishes, he seizes the opportunity to train a couple of lads to whop the Russkies. Unremarkable, but watchable.

[95m/12]

Alek Neuman	Klaus Maria Brandauer
Timmy Boyle	Adrian Pasdar
Roland Jenkins	Wesley Snipes
Elena Gitman	Angela Molina

Strictly Ballroom •••• [1992]

Director: Baz Luhrmann
Screenplay: Baz Luhrmann & Craig Pearce

The ideal pick-me-up picture. Mercurio wants to do his own steps in the forth-coming dancing championships but no-one will partner him except ugly duckling Morice. The time-honoured storyline of youth rebelling against authority conceals one of the freshest, funniest and happiest films to hit the cinema in years. A joy from start to finish. No wonder it received a fifteen-minute standing ovation at Cannes.

[94m/PG]

Scott Hastings	Paul Mercurio
Fran	Tara Morice
Barry Fife	Bill Hunter
Doug Hastings	Barry Otto
Shirley Hastings	Pat Thompson
Liz Holt	Gia Carides
Les Kendall	Peter Whitford

Psst! The film was originally a $50 student theatrical production that grew like Topsy. Nicknamed *Dirty Dancing Down Under*, the film swept Australia like wildfire. There were even ballroom dancers performing at half time during the national rugby championships.

The Stuff •• [1985]

Director: Larry Cohen
Screenplay: Larry Cohen

A heavily marketed brand of pudding has unpleasant side effects. One expects Cohen's mixture of horror, comedy and satire to be scrappy and uneven, but even by his standards this is pushing it. There's some fun, nonetheless.

[87m/15]

David	Michael Moriarty
Nicole	Andrea Marcovicci
Chocolate Charlie	Garrett Morris
Col. Spears	Paul Sorvino
Vickers	Danny Aiello

Suburban Commando ••• [1991]

Director: Burt Kennedy
Screenplay: Frank Cappello

Childish but droll outing for balding, blonde wrestling star Hulk Hogan, a man who acts better in the ring than out of it. This routine tale of an alien chased by bounty hunters who crashlands on earth is a variant on *Crocodile Dundee*. But, although it strains the bounds of credibility at times, it's enlivened by some very funny gags. The sort of film that shouldn't work, but does. [90m/PG]

Shep Ramsey	Hulk Hogan
Charlie Wilcox	Christopher Lloyd
Jenny Wilcox	Shelley Duvall
General Suitor	William Ball
Adrian Beltz	Larry Miller

Suburbia • [1984]

Director: Penelope Spheeris
Screenplay: Penelope Spheeris

A group of Punks try to form their own community in abandoned homes. A tiresome, rather repellent, rebellious youth flick, with no real story to keep our interest alive. [99m/18]

Jack	Chris Pederson
Evan	Bill Coyne
Sheila	Jennifer Clay

Subway •• [1985]

Director: Luc Besson
Screenplay: Luc Besson & Various

Stylish burglar Lambert joins a weird community living in the Metro where Adjani finds him irresistible. Initially, this drop-dead stylish Gallic nonsense is intoxicating. By the end, you just wish it would drop dead. [104m/15]

Helena	Isabelle Adjani
Fred	Christopher Lambert
The Florist	Richard Bohringer
Insp. Gesberg	Michel Galabru

Sudden Impact •• [1983]

Director: Clint Eastwood
Screenplay: Joseph C. Stinson

Dirty Harry meets Dirty Harriet. Eastwood's back for the fourth time as the man who gives community policing a bad name, encountering a woman whose violent revenge on the men who raped her meets with his approval. It's okay, but Clint's definitely treading water. [117m/18]

Harry Callahan	Clint Eastwood
Jennifer Spencer	Sondra Locke
Chief Jannings	Pat Hingle
Capt. Briggs	Bradford Dillman

Quote 'Go ahead. Make my day.'

Psst! The role of Callahan was turned down by Paul Newman, Frank Sinatra and John Wayne.

Summer Lovers • [1982]

Director: Randal Kleiser
Screenplay: Randal Kleiser

This daft tale of an American couple on holiday in Greece entering into a ménage-à-trois with a French archaeologist is yet another attempt from the director of *Blue Lagoon* to produce mainstream soft-porn. In this case, it's so soft you could put your head on it and go to sleep. At least you could if it wasn't for the incredibly loud soundtrack. [98m/15]

Michael	Peter Gallagher
Cathy	Daryl Hannah
Lina	Valerie Quennessen

Summer Story •• [1988]

Director: Piers Haggard
Screenplay: Penelope Mortimer

A turn of the century British romance set in rural Devon between Wilby and Stubbs. He's posh. She's not. Can their love survive the difference in class? Can we be bothered to find out? [97m/15]

Megan	Imogen Stubbs
Frank Ashton	James Wilby
Jim	Ken Colley
Stella	Sophie Ward
Mrs. Narracombe	Susannah York

Sunset • [1988]

Director: Blake Edwards
Screenplay: Blake Edwards

The intriguing premise is that in 20's Hollywood, real-life gunman Wyatt Earp gets together with king of the movie cowboys Tom Mix to solve a crime. Unfortunately, it's written and directed by Blake Edwards, and the miscast Willis seems to be doing an impersonation of one of those old wooden Indians. [107m/15]

Tom Mix	Bruce Willis
Wyatt Earp	James Garner
Alfie Alperin	Malcolm McDowell
Cheryl King	Mariel Hemingway

Also: Kathleen Quinlan, Jennifer Edwards, Patricia Hodge, Richard Bradford, M. Emmet Walsh

OOPS! The sunset itself is in the wrong place. At the end, Garner heads towards the setting sun, but he's going east!

Supergirl • [1984]

Director: Jeannot Szwarc
Screenplay: David Odell

Superman's cousin turns up, and disappears again pretty quickly. Although Dunaway makes a wonderfully campy villainess, Slater's more like a soppy Bunty girl than a superheroine. Now if only *Superman* and *Supergirl* had been kissing cousins, maybe they'd have had something. [114m/PG]

Selena	Faye Dunaway
Supergirl/Linda Lee	Helen Slater
Zeitar	Peter O'Toole

Also: Mia Farrow, Brenda Vaccaro, Peter Cook, Simon Ward

Supergrass •• [1985]

Director: Peter Richardson
Screenplay: Peter Richardson & Pete Richens

The Comic Strip's first feature is a rather lacklustre, hit-and-miss comedy with Edmondson boasting of his criminal empire to his girlfriend, only for the cops to take him seriously. Despite their best efforts to usher in some bad taste, it's a lot closer to the old-fashioned British comedies than they'd probably admit. **[105m/15]**

Dennis ....Adrian Edmondson
WPC Lesley Reynolds.........Jennifer Saunders
Sgt. Harvey Duncan.............Peter Richardson
Also: Dawn French, Keith Allen, Nigel Planer, Robbie Coltrane, Alexei Sayle

Superman III •• [1983]

Director: **Richard Lester**
Screenplay: **David Newman & Leslie Newman**

Superman splits in two as he fights Robert Vaughn's super-computer. This patchy outing for the man in tights is played for laughs and has too little of Lois Lane and too much of Richard Pryor. Supe may be able to save the world, but he's no comedian. An interesting compilation of early 80's paranoias, though. **[120m/PG]**

Superman/Clark Kent ....Christopher Reeve
Gus Gorman...........................Richard Pryor
Perry White..............................Jackie Cooper
Russ Webster..........................Robert Vaughn
Also: Margot Kidder, Annette O'Toole, Annie Ross, Pamela Stephenson

Psst! When Nick Nolte was originally offered the part of *Superman*, he said: 'I'll do it if I can play him as a schizophrenic'.

Superman IV: The Quest for Peace • [1987]

Director: **Sidney J. Furie**
Screenplay: **Lawrence Kohner & Mark Rosenthal**

You'll believe a superhero can bellyflop. Superman here does his bit for CND (apparently at Reeves' insistence) by reducing the world's stock of nuclear weapons. He should stop wearing his underpants outside his trousers; they're beginning to wear out. Next thing you know he'll be turning them into dusters and showing us that a superhero can do the housework just like any New Man.
[90m/PG]

Superman/Clark Kent ....Christopher Reeve
Lex Luthor...............................Gene Hackman
Perry White..............................Jackie Cooper
Also: Marc McClure, Jon Cryer, Sam Wanamaker, Mark Pillow, Mariel Hemingway, Margot Kidder

OOPS! Why does the front of the tube train say 'Cockfosters' when it's supposed to be Metropolis? London's Piccadilly Line doesn't go that far ♦ How does Mariel Hemingway breathe when she's kidnapped and taken into deep space?
Psst! Milton Keynes stood in for Metropolis.

Super Mario Bros. [1993]

Director: **Rocky Morton & Annabel Jankel**
Screenplay: **Barry Morrow & Edward Solomon**

A massive budget big screen version of the Nintendo video game. Brooklyn plumbers Mario and Luigi have to rescue Daisy from the evil King Koopa and save the planet while they're at it. Mind you, they can't do it till next Thursday, guv, and there's a massive call-out charge.

With: Bob Hoskins, John Leguizamo, Samantha Mathis, Dennis Hopper
Blurb This Ain't No Game.
Quote 'I got a feeling we're not in Brooklyn no more.'
Psst! Husband and wife directors Morton and Jankel created the original *Max Headroom* TV series.

The Sure Thing ••• [1985]

Director: **Rob Reiner**
Screenplay: **Steven L. Bloom & Jonathan Roberts**

Cusack's the student who flunks so badly with girls, he's willing to head out to California for a certainty. Zuniga's the uptight, Cusack-hating one who travels with him. This road movie from the superb Rob Reiner is made with wit and compassion and is far superior to most teen romantic comedies. **[94m/15]**

Walter 'Gib' Gibson....................John Cusack
Alison Bradbury......................Daphne Zuniga
Lance.................................Anthony Edwards
Jason.................................Boyd Gaines
Gary Cooper..............................Tim Robbins
Mary Ann Webster..............Lisa Jane Persky
Prof. Taub............................Viveca Lindfors
The Sure Thing................Nicollette Sheridan

Psst! Look out for the poster for *Spinal Tap*, another Rob Reiner film, in Cusack's room.

Surf II • [1984]

Director: **R.M. Badat**
Screenplay: **R.M. Badat**

Cheeky! There never was a *Surf I* but they reckoned more people would go to a sequel than an original. A mild spoof on beach movies and horror pics, there are enough topless babes and zombified surfers for you to have trouble telling the difference from the real thing.   **[91m/18]**

Menlo.......................................Eddie Deezen
Sparkel...................................Linda Kerridge
Daddy......................................Cleavon Little
Chuck...Eric Stoltz

Surrender ••• [1987]

Director: **Jerry Belson**
Screenplay: **Jerry Belson**

A breezily lightweight comedy with Caine the best-selling novelist weighed down with alimony payments and worried that new love Field might want to add her name to the list. Hardly original, but pleasing enough if you can take Field playing 'quirky'.   **[95m/PG]**

Daisy.................................Sally Field
Sean...................................Michael Caine
Marty..................................Steve Guttenberg
Jay.....................................Peter Boyle
Ace....................................Jackie Cooper
Ronnie...............................Julie Kavner
Joyce...................................Louise Lasser
Hedy..Iman

Quote 'I make it a policy never to have sex before the first date.'

Suspect •• [1987]

Director: **Peter Yates**
Screenplay: **Eric Roth**

Public defender Cher, never too harrassed or busy to attend to her make-up and clothes, defends murder suspect Neeson with the help of one of the jurors, a Washington lobbyist. Not only is Neeson deaf and a derelict, but he's also an ex-Vietnam vet with an impeccable record, so it isn't too hard to guess how this will all turn out. Wildly implausible, with some incredibly dull courtroom scenes, there is some decent suspense if you can wait long enough.   **[121m/15]**

Kathleen Riley...........................Cher
Eddie Sanger..............................Dennis Quaid
Carl Wayne Anderson...............Liam Neeson
Judge Matthew Helms..............John Mahoney
Charlie Stella.............................Joe Mantegna
Paul Gray....................................Philip Bosco

OOPS! The boom mike appears in Quaid's first inside scene.

Sweet Dreams •• [1985]

Director: **Karel Reisz**
Screenplay: **Robert Getchell**

Lange is Patsy Cline in this pleasant but uninspired biopic of the country singer. As usual, Lange gives her all but there's nothing particularly special for her to get her teeth into.   **[114m/15]**

Patsy Cline................................Jessica Lange
Charlie Dick..................................Ed Harris
Hilda Hensley....................Ann Wedgeworth
Also: David Clennon, James Staley, Gary Basaraba, John Goodman

Psst! Lange is miming to Cline's original recordings ◆ Boxcar Willie appears as 'old man in jail'.

Sweet Hearts Dance •• [1988]

Director: **Robert Greenwald**
Screenplay: **Ernest Thompson**

A couple of one-time childhood sweethearts, Johnson and Sarandon are in a marriage that is going to the dogs. A little slow and predictable at times, it's amiable enough and does have some amusing moments. **[101m/15]**

Wiley Boon	Don Johnson
Sandra Boon	Susan Sarandon
Sam Manners	Jeff Daniels
Adie Nims	Elizabeth Perkins

OOPS! When they're on holiday on the hotel balcony, a second camera and crew are clearly visible.

Sweetie •• [1990]

Director: **Jane Campion**
Screenplay: **Gerard Lee & Jane Campion**

This bizarre Australian family drama centres on two unhappy sisters and their parents. At first, the film's weirdness is exciting and fresh. But the novelty seems to be going nowhere and ultimately leaves a sense of exasperation. **[90m/15]**

Sweetie	Genevieve Lemon
Kay	Karen Colston
Louis	Tom Lycos
Gordon	Jon Darling

Sweet Liberty •• [1986]

Director: **Alan Alda**
Screenplay: **Alan Alda**

A film crew arrives to make a movie of history teacher Alda's book on the American Revolution in his own town. Although one of the best depictions yet of what it's actually like to make a film, the comedy is very uneven. Some parts are superb, others drag. Unusually, it's Caine who lets things down, looking rather lost and out of place throughout. **[107m/PG]**

Michael Burgess	Alan Alda
Elliott James	Michael Caine
Faith Healy	Michelle Pfeiffer
Stanley Gould	Bob Hoskins

Also: Lise Hilboldt, Lillian Gish, Saul Rubinek, Lois Chiles

Quote 'It's the wonderful way they smell. I told my wife I would never look at another woman if I could cut off my nose.' – 'What did she say?' – 'She said I was aiming too high.'

Sweet Lorraine ••• [1987]

Director: **Steve Gomer**
Screenplay: **Michael Zettler & Shelly Altman**

Alvarado goes to work for the summer at grandmother Stapleton's failing hotel in the Catskills. A slow, gentle and very pleasing little film, full of atmosphere and character. Treat it like a good hot bath; just lie back, relax, and let it put you in a good mood. **[91m/PG]**

Lillian	Maureen Stapleton
Molly	Trini Alvarado
Sam	Lee Richardson
Jack	John Bedford-Lloyd
Phil Allen	Giancarlo Esposito
Leonard	Todd Graff

Switch •• [1991]

Director: **Blake Edwards**
Screenplay: **Blake Edwards**

A murdered chauvinist returns to earth inside Ellen Barkin's body, somewhere he would no doubt have been delighted to be as his former self. Barkin struggles manfully, if that's the word, with her role but the jokes just don't click. **[103m/15]**

Amanda Brooks	Ellen Barkin
Walter Stone	Jimmy Smits
Margo Brofman	JoBeth Williams
Sheila Faxton	Lorraine Bracco

Also: Tony Roberts, Perry King, Bruce Payne, Lysette Anthony

Switching Channels • [1988]

Director: **Ted Kotcheff**
Screenplay: **Jonathan Reynolds**

You couldn't switch channels in the cinema, but you certainly can if this drivel comes on the box. This updating of *The Front Page* has Turner the TV reporter trying to escape boss and ex-hubby Reynolds to marry the vacuous Reeves. **[105m/PG]**

Christy Colleran	Kathleen Turner
John L. Sullivan IV	Burt Reynolds
Blaine Bingham	Christopher Reeve

Also: Ned Beatty, Henry Gibson

Sylvia •• [1985]

Director: Michael Firth
Screenplay: Michael Quill, Ferdinand
Fairfax & Michael Firth

David is splendid in this true-life New
Zealand tale of educationalist Sylvia
Ashton-Warner, who ran foul of the
education authorities with her 'different'
methods of teaching Maori children. Its
fascination, however, lies more at the
documentary level than that of real drama.
[98m/PG]

Sylvia Henderson .... Eleanor David
Aden Morris .... Nigel Terry
Keith Henderson .... Tom Wilkinson
Opal Saunders .... Mary Regan

Table for Five •• [1983]

Director: Robert Lieberman
Screenplay: David Seltzer

Get your table by the door so you can
make a quick exit. Divorced Voight has a
guilt trip and takes his three kids on a
cruise, only for Mommy to have a terrible car crash. That this sentimental
twaddle was picked for the 1983 Royal
Film Performance probably explains a lot
about the current state of the Royal
Family. It would be an ideal movie to
watch on a plane – at least they provide
free sick bags.
[121m/PG]

J.P. Tannen .... Jon Voight
Mitchell .... Richard Crenna
Marie .... Marie Christine Barrault
Kathleen .... Millie Perkins

Psst! Keep your eyes skinned for Kevin
Costner in the dining room on the cruise
ship. He plays a newly-married man
getting drinks.

Taffin • [1988]

Director: Francis Megahy
Screenplay: David Ambrose

A monotonous thriller, set in Ireland,
with Brosnan a debt collector – obviously
not making enough to buy razor blades –
getting involved in a battle over a planned
new chemical plant.
[96m/18]

Mark Taffin .... Pierce Brosnan
O'Rourke .... Ray McAnally
Charlotte .... Alison Doody

Psst! Brosnan took this part after being
pipped by Dalton as the new James
Bond.

Take It Easy • [1986]

Director: Albert Magnoli
Screenplay: Evan Archerd & Jeff Benjamin

...Take It Away. Piffling tosh about a boy
who escapes his horrid family to train as
an athlete. Gaylord may be an Olympic
gold medallist, but the nearest he's going
to get to an Oscar statuette is if he eats at
Planet Hollywood. Also known as
American Anthem.
[101m/PG]

Steve Tevere .... Mitch Gaylord
Julie Lloyd .... Janet Jones
Linda Tevere .... Michelle Phillips

Taking Care of Business
SEE: Filofax

Tale of a Vampire • [1992]

Director: Shimako Sato
Screenplay: Shimako Sato & Jane Corbett

Boring Gothic vampire movie set in
London where student Sands, a vampire,
finds a librarian reminds him of his long
dead love. There's lots of fog and smoke
swirling round, but the story has less
blood to it than the vampire's victims.
[102m/18]

Alex .... Julian Sands
Anne/Virginia .... Suzanna Hamilton
Edgar .... Kenneth Cranham

Tales from the Darkside: The Movie ••• [1991]

Director: John Harrison
Screenplay: Michael McDowell & George A. Romero

Sweet Debbie Harry is here a cannibal, waiting to eat a young boy once he has told her three stories. A nicely gruesome set of horror stories, well-packaged. [93m/18]

The Wraparound Story

Betty	Deborah Harry
Timmy	Matthew Lawrence

Lot 249

Andy Smith	Christian Slater
Edward Bellingham	Steve Buscemi
Lee	Robert Sedgwick
Susan Smith	Julianne Moore

Cat from Hell

Halston	David Johansen
Drogan	William Hickey

Lover's Vow

Preston	James Remar
Carola	Rae Dawn Chong
Wyatt	Robert Klein

Talk Radio •••• [1988]

Director: Oliver Stone
Screenplay: Eric Bogosian & Oliver Stone

An outspoken talk-show radio presenter fans the flames by encouraging outrageous views over the airwaves. Further proof that Stone works best on smaller budgets, this powerfully written and acted true-life drama, adapted from a play, really gains from the claustrophobia of its radio station setting and some superbly sinuous camera work. [108m/18]

Barry Champlain	Eric Bogosian
Ellen	Ellen Greene
Laura	Leslie Hope
Stu	John C. McGinley
Dan	Alec Baldwin
Dietz	John Pankow
Kent	Michael Wincott

Blurb The Last Neighborhood In America.

Quote 'Sticks and stones may break my bones, but words cause permanent damage.'

Psst! The film was based on real-life Dallas DJ Alan Berg, murdered in 1984 ◆ Although Stone doesn't actually appear in the film, a copy of Playboy in the radio station features an interview with him!

The Tall Guy •• [1989]

Director: Mel Smith
Screenplay: Richard Curtis

Goldblum is an American actor in London, suffering as straight guy to obnoxious comic Atkinson. He finds compensations when he falls for Nurse Thompson. Although it might be hilarious if you're up with West End gossip, this is otherwise a patchy romantic comedy. The room demolished-by-sex scene is an instant classic, but the casting of the excellent Goldblum in the lead makes a nonsense of some of the plot. [90m/15]

Dexter King	Jeff Goldblum
Kate Lemon	Emma Thompson
Ron Anderson	Rowan Atkinson
Gavin	Peter Kelly

Quote 'There is an old man expecting my hand up his bottom and one doesn't like to disappoint the old folks.' ◆ 'I spent two days naked with Jeff Goldblum and enjoyed it very much. It was so freeing. I would recommend it to anybody.' [Emma Thompson]

Psst! Melvyn Bragg cameos as himself.

Tampopo •• [1987]

Director: Juzo Itami
Screenplay: Juzo Itami

Bizarre and occasionally funny Japanese series of sketches on the subject of food, spun round a central story of a widow trying to perfect her recipe for noodles. Sound weird? It is. One of a kind. [117m/18]

Goro	Tsutomu Yamazaki
Tampopo (Dandelion)	Nobuko Miyamoto
Man in white suit	Koji Yakusho
Gun	Ken Watanabe

Tango and Cash ••• [1989]

Director: Andrei Konchalovsky
Screenplay: Randy Feldman

A smart Stallone and scruffy Russell take on Jack Palance. Framed, they're thrown in jug with the very thugs they've put there. Although ludicrous, it's thoroughly enjoyable buddy-cop nonsense, with one of the finest prison breaks on film. Sadly, director Konchalovsky was removed during filming over arguments about the ending and the final scenes are a bit of a let down. [104m/15]

Ray Tango	Sylvester Stallone
Gabe Cash	Kurt Russell
Kiki	Teri Hatcher
Yves Perret	Jack Palance
Courier/Requin	Brion James
Quan	James Hong
Owen	Michael J. Pollard

Quote 'Rambo is a pussy.' [Stallone]
Psst! In Britain, the film's violence was toned down to get a '15' certificate
♦ Kurt's dad, Bing, plays the 'van driver'.

Tank •• [1984]

Director: Marvin J. Chomsky
Screenplay: Dan Gordon

When soldier Garner's son is wrongly imprisoned by a bigoted sheriff, he decides to argue his case with the help of a borrowed Sherman tank. Passable. [113m/PG]

Zack	James Garner
LaDonna	Shirley Jones
Billy	C. Thomas Howell
Elliott	Mark Herrier

Tank Malling • [1989]

Director: James Marcus
Screenplay: James Marcus & Mick Southworth

Believe it or not, the title is the name of a London journalist. Amanda Donohoe plays the hooker in this totally predictable and shoddy thriller. If you want an explanation of the demise of the British film industry, here it is. [108m/18]

Tank	Ray Winstone
Sir Robert Knights	Peter Wyngarde
Dunboyne	Jason Connery
Helen	Amanda Donohoe

Tap •• [1989]

Director: Nick Castle
Screenplay: Nick Castle

Out of prison for burglary, Hines tries getting it together with Douglas. He haunts the dance studio where she works, a place that just happens to have some of the greatest tap dancers the world has ever known hanging around. Will Hines go back to crime or dancing? The clichéd plot's too thin and, despite a couple of joyous dance scenes, the film seems too scared that modern audiences won't accept conventional tap routines. As a result, the dance is 'modernised' and all the fun evaporates. Fast forward to Hines' duel with the old-timers, including Sammy Davis Jr., and have a ball. [110m/PG]

Max Washington	Gregory Hines
Amy	Suzzanne Douglas
Little Mo	Sammy Davis Jr.
Louis	Savion Glover

Target •• [1985]

Director: Arthur Penn
Screenplay: Howard Berk & Don Petersen

When mom's kidnapped in Paris, dad and junior are plunged into a tiresome, convoluted and unbelievable spy thriller. [118m/15]

Walter Lloyd	Gene Hackman
Chris Lloyd	Matt Dillon
Donna Lloyd	Gayle Hunnicutt
Lise	Victoria Fyodorova

Teachers •• [1984]

Director: Arthur Hiller
Screenplay: W.R. McKinney

This satire on American high schools doesn't really hit the spot, despite its wonderful cast. Madcap humour is all very well, but only if you've got some decent jokes hidden in your desk.   [106m/15]

Alex...Nick Nolte
Lisa...JoBeth Williams
Roger...Judd Hirsch
Also: Ralph Macchio, Allen Garfield, Lee Grant

Psst! Look out for Laura Dern, Morgan Freeman and Crispin Glover in bit parts • Richard Mulligan was Burt in *Soap*.

Teenage Mutant Ninja Turtles •• [1990]

Director: Steve Barron
Screenplay: Todd W. Langen & Bobby Herbeck

A quartet of crime-busters bust crime, making a lot of noise and wisecracks as they do so. If it weren't for the fact that they were mutated turtles named after Italian painters, with a rat as their mentor, there'd be nothing to distinguish this from hundreds of other martial arts pics.

[93m/PG]

April O'Neil ....Judith Hoag
Casey Jones ....Elias Koteas
Raphael..Josh Pais
Michaelangelo...........................Michelan Sisti
Donatello ....Leif Tilden
Leonardo....................................David Forman

Psst! New Line paid around $2m for the movie. It grossed $135m in America alone, making it the most successful ever independent film • Hard to believe, but there's probably no other film in British film history that's been played around with as much by the censors, mainly because Michaelangelo has a couple of chainsticks. Being illegal weapons, they can't be seen on screen. Some scenes had to be filmed again for Britain, others were cut, while occasionally Michaelangelo is electronically removed from the picture.

Teenage Mutant Ninja Turtles II: The Secret of the Ooze •• [1991]

Director: Michael Pressman
Screenplay: Todd W. Langen

More of the same for those whose brains have mutated into cabbages.   [87m/PG]

April O'Neil................................Paige Turco
Prof. Jordan Perry....................David Warner
Keno ....Ernie Reyes Jr.

Psst! Further chops were made on this one. Ten seconds of Michaelangelo were cut because he was waving a meancing string of sausages about. The censor felt they looked a little like chain-sticks.

Teenage Mutant Ninja Turtles III: The Turtles Are Back...In Time • [1993]

Director: Stuart Gillard
Screenplay: Stuart Gillard

The turtles travel back in time to feudal Japan to rescue April. Isn't turtle soup a delicacy in Japan? With any luck, they won't be back.   [95m/PG]

Casey Jones/Whit.........................Elias Koteas
April O'Neil................................Paige Turco
Walker ....Stuart Wilson

Teen Agent •• [1991]

Director: William Dear
Screenplay: Darren Star

Grieco's in Paris with his high school class, doing the usual things. Seeing the Eiffel Tower, wandering by the Seine, being mistaken for a CIA agent and getting caught up in a dastardly plot to destabilise Europe's money supply. So-so hokum. Also known as *If Looks Could Kill*.   [89m/PG]

Michael Corben ....Richard Grieco
Ilsa Grunt ....Linda Hunt
Augustus Steranko.........................Roger Rees
Mrs. Grober.............................Robin Bartlett
Mariska................................Gabrielle Anwar

Teen Wolf •• [1985]

Director: Rod Daniel
Screenplay: Joseph Loeb III & Matthew Weisman

A 24-year-old actor can transform himself into a teenager at will but discovers, to his horror, that he gets stuck and can't switch back to being an adult. Here the ever-teen Fox finds himself turning into a werewolf. As werewolves are amazingly good at basketball and wooing girls, he has a great time. It's innocuous and occasionally mildly amusing. **[92m/PG]**

Scott Howard	Michael J. Fox
Harold Howard	James Hampton
Lisa 'Boof' Marconi	Susan Ursitti
Rupert 'Stiles' Stilinsky	Jerry Levine

Teen Wolf Too • [1987]

Director: Christopher Leitch
Screenplay: R. Timothy Kring

From the darkness comes a howling, like an animal in pain. It's the audience, trying to get away from this pathetic sequel, which hasn't even got Fox. **[94m/PG]**

Todd Howard	Jason Batemen
Prof. Brooks	Kim Darby
Dean Dunn	John Astin

Tempest •• [1982]

Director: Paul Mazursky
Screenplay: Paul Mazursky & Leon Capetanos

This peculiarly handled comedy has architect Cassavetes abandoning New York and his wife and haring off to a Greek island to have his mid-life crisis. There are some splendid moments, but overall it's all a bit contrived and draggy. Shakespeare's agent needn't lose any sleep just yet. **[141m/15]**

Phillip	John Cassavetes
Antonia	Gena Rowlands
Aretha	Susan Sarandon

Also: Vittorio Gassman, Raul Julia, Molly Ringwald

Tender Mercies ••• [1983]

Director: Bruce Beresford
Screenplay: Horton Foote

A pleasingly old-fashioned tale of country singer Duvall down on his luck, finding life worth warbling about again when he meets up with the hyper-religious Harper. A nice story, well-acted and well-told. **[90m/PG]**

Mac Sledge	Robert Duvall
Rosa Lee	Tess Harper
Dixie	Betty Buckley
Harry	Wilford Brimley
Sue Anne	Ellen Barkin

Oscars Robert Duvall, Best Screenplay

Quote 'I never trust happiness. I never did. I never will.'

Psst! Duvall wrote and sang all eight of the songs. When researching his role, he performed for a while in a country bar ♦ *Places in the Heart* was also filmed in the same location of Waxahachie, Texas.

10 to Midnight •• [1983]

Director: J. Lee Thompson
Screenplay: William Roberts

Although it's not a *Death Wish* film, it might as well be, with Bronson the cop kicked off the force for falsifying evidence against a murderer. Well, what's a reasonable, law-abiding guy to do other than go after him, ensuring as many people get killed along the way as possible? **[102m/18]**

Leo Kessler	Charles Bronson
Laurie Kessler	Lisa Eilbacher
Paul McAnn	Andrew Stevens
Warren Stacey	Gene Davis

Tequila Sunrise • [1988]

Director: Robert Towne
Screenplay: Robert Towne

Drug dealer Gibson and tough cop Russell were once childhood chums, but are now competing in business and boudoir. Although Pfeiffer's terrific as the tough cookie restaurant owner they're both after, this is otherwise a curiously

unthrilling thriller. If we're talking cock-
tails, this one's a Zombie.

[115m/15]

McKussic	Mel Gibson
Jo Ann	Michelle Pfeiffer
Frescia	Kurt Russell
Carlos/Escalante	Raul Julia
Maguire	J.T. Walsh

Psst! Pfeiffer says she won't ever watch
the film. The director 'said I was the
worst actress he'd ever worked with.'

The Terminator •••• [1984]

Director: James Cameron
Screenplay: Gale Anne Hurd & James
Cameron

Highly influential sci-fi thriller with
Arnie in pre-superstar days as an evil
cyborg, sent back from the future to stop a
future rebel leader being born to a bewildered Linda Hamilton. One of those rare
films in which the splendid action
sequences are complemented by an intelligent and witty script. It holds up
brilliantly no matter how many times you
watch it. [108m/18]

Terminator	Arnold Schwarzenegger
Kyle Reese	Michael Biehn
Sarah Connor	Linda Hamilton
Traxler	Paul Winfield
Vukovich	Lance Henriksen
Matt	Rick Rossovich
Ginger	Bess Motta
Silberman	Earl Boen

Quote 'I'll be back.'

OOPS! When Arnie makes his famous
return to the police station, there's the
dazzle of headlights. But the car that
crashes into the station doesn't have its
lights on ◆ Arnie finds three addresses
for Sarah Connor in the phone book.
The first house he pays a housecall on
is numbered 14239, which wasn't one
of them.

Psst! Harlan Ellison successfully sued,
claiming that the plot was taken from an
Outer Limits TV episode he wrote.

Terminator 2: Judgment Day ••• [1991]

Director: James Cameron
Screenplay: James Cameron & William
Wisher

Now that Arnie's a superstar, he's the
good guy, even if he does look exactly the
same as the baddie in the first film. He's
sent back from the future to save the
future leader of the rebels fighting the
machines. The script's nothing like as
clever or witty as the original, but the
effects are out of this world. You can tell
Arnie's the goody because he only shoots
people in the leg, not anywhere it'll hurt!

[136m/15]

Terminator T-800	Arnold Schwarzenegger
Sarah Connor	Linda Hamilton
John Connor	Edward Furlong
Terminator T-1000	Robert Patrick
Dr. Silberman	Earl Boen
Miles Dyson	Joe Morton
Tarissa Dyson	S. Epatha Merkerson

Blurb It's Nothing Personal.

Quote 'Hasta la vista, baby.' ◆ 'Who sent
you?' — 'You did, 35 years from now.'

OOPS! As the truck dives off the bridge, the
glass in the cab shatters. Yet it's back for
the evil Terminator to smash soon after ◆
As the evil Terminator flies the helicopter, he reloads his gun using both
hands. So whose is the other hand we
see flying the helicopter? ◆ When Linda
Hamilton runs through the hospital barefoot, the noise is of someone wearing
shoes ◆ If we're quibbling, the boy
should actually only be six or seven to fit
with the first film ◆ They've also conveniently forgotten that we learnt in the
earlier film that all the records had been
wiped out.

Psst! The most expensive film ever made,
with a cost reckoned to be in the order of
$100m, with the studio spending another
$20m on publicity ◆ Schwarzenegger is
said to have been given a Gulfstream G-
III jet as part of his $15m fee ◆ You could
argue that his rate of pay was lower than

on the first *Terminator*. Then he was eventually paid $6m for the 133 words he uttered, $45,000 a word. In the sequel he had 474 words, which works out at just $31,500 each.

Terms of Endearment ••• [1983]

Director: James L. Brooks
Screenplay: James L. Brooks

This highly emotional Oscar-winner is TV soap opera played at Gale Force Ten, yet is still worth watching for the acting. MacLaine's the overbearing mother who drives daughter Winger into an unsuitable marriage while being wooed by wise-cracking ex-astronaut Nicholson. Kleenex sales must have soared when it came out. [132m/15]

Aurora Greenway	Shirley MacLaine
Emma Greenway Horton	Debra Winger
Garrett Breedlove	Jack Nicholson
Flap Horton	Jeff Daniels
Vernon Dahlart	Danny DeVito
Sam Burns	John Lithgow

Oscars Best Picture, Best Director, Shirley MacLaine, Jack Nicholson, Best Screenplay (adapted)

Blurb Come To Laugh, Come To Cry, Come To Care, Come To Terms.

Quote 'I like the lights *on*.' – 'Then go home and turn them on.' • 'It sure would be nice to have a mother that somebody liked.'

Psst! It took writer-director Brooks four years to find a studio that would back the project • Winger went to some lengths to get into her part, wearing a fake pregnancy prosthetic for three months, even in bed, although she's only seen very briefly in that state in the film. She also insisted that MacLaine call her by her character's name whenever they spoke • Winger and MacLaine did not see eye to eye and, to the delight of the public, carried their quarrels over into the media • Collecting her Oscar, MacLaine said: 'I really deserve this'.

Testament ••• [1983]

Director: Lynne Littman
Screenplay: John Sacret Young

A chilling and credible tale of one family's efforts to survive the aftermath of a nuclear holocaust. It's rendered much more effective by concentrating on one typical American family, showing their increasing isolation. [90m/PG]

Carol Wetherly	Jane Alexander
Tom Wetherly	William Devane
Brad Wetherly	Ross Harris
Mary Liz Wetherly	Roxana Zal
Scottie Wetherly	Lukas Haas

Also: Philip Anglim, Lilia Skala, Leon Ames

Psst! Look out for Rebecca De Mornay and Kevin Costner in small parts as the married Pitkins.

Testimony • [1988]

Director: Tony Palmer
Screenplay: Tony Palmer & David Rudkin

Strange to say, this unbelievably lengthy British biography of the Russian composer Shostakovich didn't set the box office alight. Despite Kingsley, you've got to be *very* interested in the subject to sit through this one. [157m/PG]

Dimitri Shostakovich	Ben Kingsley
Nina Shostakovich	Sherry Baines
Stalin	Terence Rigby
Tukhachevsky	Ronald Pickup

A Test of Love

SEE: Annie's Coming Out

Texasville •• [1990]

Director: Peter Bogdanovich
Screenplay: Peter Bogdanovich

The Texan youngsters of *The Last Picture Show* have grown older, but not necessarily wiser. Their children are now the rebellious teens they once were. The freshness and originality had evaporated before this long-delayed sequel was made. [126m/15]

Duane Jackson.................................Jeff Bridges
Jacy Farrow............................Cybill Shepherd
Karla Jackson ....Annie Potts
Sonny Crawford..................Timothy Bottoms
Also: Cloris Leachman, Randy Quaid,
Eileen Brennan

That Championship Season •• [1983]

Director: Jason Miller
Screenplay: Jason Miller

Miller's play about the annual reunion of
college basketball team, still wittering on
about their big victory a quarter of a century before, won him the Pulitzer Prize.
Whatever it had on stage hasn't translated
well to the screen, where it comes over as
rather dull and pointless.   [109m/15]

George Sikowski............................Bruce Dern
James Daley...................................Stacy Keach
Coach Delaney......................Robert Mitchum
Tom Daley...................................Martin Sheen
Phil Romano ....Paul Sorvino

That's Dancing •• [1985]

Director: Jack Haley Jr.
Screenplay: Jack Haley Jr.

A dance equivalent of MGM's *That's
Entertainment* and its sequel, this has some
wonderful moments, but looks as though
far less attention has been paid to the
selection of clips or the links.   [104m/U]

With: Mikhail Baryshnikov, Ray Bolger,
Sammy Davis Jr., Gene Kelly, Liza
Minnelli

That's Life •• [1986]

Director: Blake Edwards
Screenplay: Milton Wexler & Blake
Edwards

Esther Rantzen would be preferable.
Edwards' most autobiographical film has
most of Lemmon's family either hypo-
chondriacs or seriously sick. No less
interesting than hearing anybody whinge
about their illnesses for a couple of hours.
[102m/15]

Harvey Fairchild.........................Jack Lemmon
Gillian Fairchild.......................Julie Andrews
Holly Parrish...........................Sally Kellerman
Father Baragone.........................Robert Loggia

Psst! Perhaps the most nepotistic film ever.
Edwards cast his wife Andrews, his
daughter Jennifer, Julie's daughter
EmmaWalton, Jack Lemmon's son Chris
and his wife Felicia Farr. He even,
apparently, put one of his pets in it and
filmed it at his own house in Malibu
Beach, presumably so that they didn't
have too far to travel to work each day.

That Summer of White Roses • [1990]

Director: Rajko Grlic
Screenplay: Borislav Pekic, Rajko Grlic &
Simon MacCorkindale

Aimless Anglo-Yugoslav co-production
with Conti an incompetent Yugo bodyguard in the last year of the Second World
War giving us a bewildering tour of
accents of the world. Quite what he and
Steiger are doing in this, we shall probably never know. Yugo to it if you want. I
won't.   [104m/15]

Andrija Gavrilovic...........................Tom Conti
Ana ....Susan George
Martin ....Rod Steiger

That Was Then... This Is Now •• [1985]

Director: Christopher Cain
Screenplay: Emilio Estevez

Yet more teenage angst. Starring and
written by Estevez, he's the kid who
won't take life seriously and whose nose
is put out of joint when best pal Sheffer
starts seeing – gasp! – a woman.
Depressingly familiar stuff.   [101m/15]

Mark Jennings ....Emilio Estevez
Bryon Douglas............................Craig Sheffer
Terry Jones.................................Larry B. Scott
Curly Shepard......................Matthew Dudley
Angela Shepard............................Jill Schoelen
Cathy...Kim Delaney
Charlie..................................Morgan Freeman

Thelma & Louise •••• [1991]

Director: **Ridley Scott**
Screenplay: **Callie Khouri**

Waitress Sarandon gets meek housewife Davis away from her sexist husband for the weekend. But things go wrong when a rape attempt forces them to go on the run. Although widely acclaimed as a feminist film, this is really just another buddy road movie (with a relatively well-worn tread on the script) where the genders have been switched. However, the two women are so good in their gutsy, often very funny roles, and the photography is so stylish that we get carried along for the ride with them. A hugely enjoyable movie, whichever sex you are. **[130m/15]**

Thelma Dickinson	Geena Davis
Louise Sawyer	Susan Sarandon
Hal	Harvey Keitel
Jimmy	Michael Madsen
Darryl	Christopher McDonald
Max	Stephen Tobolowsky
J.D.	Brad Pitt

Oscars Best Screenplay

Quote 'He's got a cute butt. Not like Darryl. You could park a car in the shadow of his ass.'

OOPS! In the country and western bar, Sarandon's marguerita is in one of those magical movie glasses where the drink level keeps bobbing around.

Psst! Incredible though it may seem, the original ending had the two landing their car safely at the bottom of the Grand Canyon and driving away free as birds. For some reason, someone thought this a little implausible. Despite the actual ending, in the wake of the film's success one executive still suggested to Sarandon the possibility of a sequel.

They Live •• [1988]

Director: **John Carpenter**
Screenplay: **John Carpenter**

A wanderer in LA tries on a pair of special sunglasses and discovers that there is a sinister consumerist conspiracy afoot. An unhappy attempt to mix an action movie with anti-Reagan satire. The film's budget is too low for its ambitions, while the once-great Carpenter seems sadly to have lost the knack of witty, suspenseful action. **[95m/18]**

Nada	Roddy Piper
Frank	Keith David
Holly	Meg Foster
Drifter	George 'Buck' Blower

Quote 'I'm here to chew bubble gum and kick ass. And I'm right out of bubble gum.'

Psst! Although the credits show Frank Armitage as the writer, it's a pseudonym for Carpenter.

Thief of Hearts • [1984]

Director: **Douglas Day Stewart**
Screenplay: **Douglas Day Stewart**

A burglar armed with all the latest designer labels swipes Williams' diary and, after reading all her erotic secrets, sets about seducing her. The plot is completely swamped by tiresome early-80's movie clichés and a horrendously intrusive score. **[100m/18]**

Scott Muller	Steven Bauer
Mickey Davis	Barbara Williams
Ray Davis	John Getz

The Thin Blue Line •••• [1988]

Director: **Errol Morris**

This investigation into the murder of a Dallas policeman in the mid-70s is compelling stuff, an object lesson in how to make documentaries interesting, with boldly stylised recreations and chilly Philip Glass music. The film exonerated the original man convicted and condemned another. It created such a stink that the case was reopened and, several years later, innocent Randall Adams was released from prison. **[101m/15]**

Psst! Despite this film being the main reason Adams got out of jail, he sued Morris for using his story.

Things Change ••• [1988]

Director: David Mamet
Screenplay: David Mamet & Shel
Silverstein

Elderly cobbler Ameche agrees to take the
rap for a Mafia guy but is taken for a last
night on the tiles by minder Mantegna. A
winning little comedy of character that is
wholly delightful, as Ameche reveals hidden depths beneath his seemingly naive
exterior. How wonderful for Ameche,
once one of Hollywood's top stars, to
have a lead role again after so many years.
[100m/PG]

Gino	Don Ameche
Jerry	Joe Mantegna
Joseph Vincent	Robert Prosky
Frankie	J.J. Johnston
Mr. Silver	Ricky Jay
Mr. Green	Mike Nussbaum
Repair shop owner	Jack Wallace

Quote 'The Sicilian people say: A big man
knows the value of a small coin.'

Psst! For a while, after his film *The Story of
Alexander Graham Bell* came out in 1939,
the telephone was known in America as
'The Ameche'.

The Third Solution

SEE: Russicum

This is My Life • [1992]

Director: Nora Ephron
Screenplay: Nora Ephron & Delia Ephron

Imagine having your dullest relatives
come to visit and then show no signs of
ever leaving. That's what this tale of part-
time comic Kavner making good feels like,
with interminable yak–yak–yaking as she
tries to reconcile career with the demands
of her two daughters. A deathly directorial debut from the writer of *When Harry
Met Sally*. [94m/12]

Dottie Ingels	Julie Kavner
Erica Ingels	Samantha Mathis
Opal Ingels	Gaby Hoffman
Claudia Curtis	Carrie Fisher
Arnold Moss	Dan Aykroyd

This is Spinal Tap •••• [1984]

Director: Rob Reiner
Screenplay: Christopher Guest, Michael
McKean, Harry Shearer & Rob Reiner

A beautifully observed and often hilarious
satire on the rock scene, following a
declining heavy–metal band as they make
a steadily less successful tour of America,
followed by a documentary film team. It is
amazing how well these guys ape the real
thing, the only problem being that they are
so bad, they would surely be more successful. Catch those great speakers with
knobs going all the way to 11. Also known
as *Spinal Tap*. [82m/15]

David St. Hubbins	Michael McKean
Nigel Tufnel	Christopher Guest
Derek Smalls	Harry Shearer
Mick Shrimpton	R.J. Parnell
Marti DiBerti	Rob Reiner
Tommy Pischedda	Bruno Kirby

Psst! Many of the scenes were improvised
on the basic script ✦ There are cameos
from Anjelica Huston, Patrick Macnee
and Billy Crystal, with Reiner himself
playing the director of the documentary ✦
In the film the band decide to seek their
fortune in Japan because their 'Smell the
Glove' album was doing so well there.
Oddly enough, in Japan the spoof *Spinal
Tap* album became a big hit ✦ Guest, the
lead guitarist and husband of Jamie–Lee
Curtis, is in line to inherit a seat in the
House of Lords and the title Baron.

¡Three Amigos! • [1986]

Director: John Landis
Screenplay: Steve Martin, Lorne Michaels
& Randy Newman

Three failing silent–movie cowboy stars
discover too late that their appearance as
hired guns defending a Mexican village
threatened by bandits is for real. Martin,
Short and Chase here achieve the impossible – making The Three Stooges look
funny by comparison. Any movie that
resorts to a talking tortoise has serious
problems. Amiable though the three are,
it's a one–joke comedy. Unfortunately,

somebody forgot to include the joke. 'Wherever there's suffering, we'll be there,' they sing repeatedly. They're not wrong. [105m/PG]

Dusty Bottoms............................Chevy Chase
Lucky Day ....Steve Martin
Ned Nederlander ....Martin Short
Also: Patrice Martinez, Alfonso Arau, Tony Plana, Joe Mantegna, Jon Lovitz

Psst! Not only does Randy Newman play 'The singing bush', he also co-wrote the script.

Three Fugitives •• [1989]

Director: Francis Veber
Screenplay: Francis Veber

Yet another rip-off of a French film, this time a frenetic farce with Short robbing a bank to support his autistic daughter and taking an ex-con hostage by mistake. Although the film's written and directed by the man responsible for the French version, it's only fitfully funny and alarmingly mawkish in places. [97m/PG]

Daniel Lucas ....Nick Nolte
Ned Perry ....Martin Short
Meg Perry.................Sarah Rowland Doroff
Det. Dugan ....James Earl Jones

Psst! Nolte had himself wheeled to the set for every take lying on a hospital trolley.

Three Men and a Baby •• [1987]

Director: Leonard Nimoy
Screenplay: James Orr & Jim Cruickshank

Immensely popular remake of a French comedy about three bachelors who have a baby foisted upon them. The plot, thinner than Danson's hair, is wholly unrealistic. These chaps endure sleepless nights, nappy changings, feeding, bathtime, urinations and yet, despite their wealth, never contemplate paid help? Come on! The jokes are pathetic, the sentiment is slapped on with a trowel and the daft drugs subplot is a miscalculation. The baby's pretty sweet, though.
[102m/PG]

Peter ....Tom Selleck

Michael................................Steve Guttenberg
Jack..Ted Danson
Sylvia ....Nancy Travis
Rebecca....................................Margaret Colin
Detective Melkowitz ....Philip Bosco

Quote 'I'll give you a thousand dollars if you'll do it.'

Psst! Watch closely as Celeste Holm, Danson's mum, picks up the baby and moves out of the room. In the background, you can see the outline of what looks like a little boy peering through the window. The Disney switchboard was swamped for months as people claimed to have seen a ghost. Rumours said it was a boy who had died in the house where filming took place. The studio claims it's a cutout of Danson in a fez and that in any case the scene was shot on a Toronto soundstage where no-one has ever died. Have a look for yourself • In the interests of in-depth research Guttenberg, Selleck and Danson apparently spent as much time as they could investigating the singles life in Toronto!

Three Men and a Little Lady • [1990]

Director: Emile Ardolino
Screenplay: Charlie Peters

This truly dreadful follow-up to *Three Men and a Baby* has the moppet's mom wanting to marry Englishman Cazenove. But our three gay bachelors don't think he's good enough for their little girl. Unfunny and slushy, it's almost worth watching for its extraordinary depiction of England, seemingly derived from a combination of watching old Ealing comedies and re-creating the pictures on biscuit tins. An English theatre director living in a castle? Into the dungeons with the writers. [104m/PG]

Peter Mitchell ....Tom Selleck
Michael Kellam....................Steve Guttenberg
Jack Holden ....Ted Danson
Sylvia ....Nancy Travis

OOPS! Sylvia covers her efforts at baking a cake with icing which then vanishes.

Three of Hearts • [1993]

Director: Mario Van Peebles
Screenplay: Sy Richardson & Dario Scardapane

Dire, supposedly daring tale, with Lynch trying to use gigolo Baldwin to win Fenn, her ex-girlfriend, back. Terribly acted and directed, you never believe in the story for a minute, despite the butchness of Lynch's leather jacket.

Joe...William Baldwin
Connie ....Kelly Lynch
Ellen.......................................Sherilyn Fenn
Mickey ....Joe Pantoliano

Blurb Just Your Average Girl Meets Girl. Girl Loses Girl. Girl Hires Boy To Get Girl Back Story. With A Twist.

Throw Momma from the Train ••• [1987]

Director: Danny DeVito
Screenplay: Stu Silver

This delicious black comedy, de Vito's debut as a director, has him as a 40-year-old still under the tyrannical thumb of his hideous mother, Ramsey. When he discovers blocked writer Crystal harbours a grudge against his ex-wife, DeVito offers to 'swap' murders. Stuffed with Hitchcockian references, it takes its plot line from *Strangers on a Train* but twists it wonderfully to its own purpose. The humour may be black, but it's brilliant. **[88m/15]**

Owen..Danny DeVito
Larry...Billy Crystal
Beth...Kim Greist
Momma....................................Anne Ramsey
Margaret..................................Kate Mulgrew
Lester ....Brandford Marsalis
Joel..Rob Reiner
Det. DeBenedetto ....Bruce Kirby
Mrs. Hazeltine..............................Annie Ross
Herself....................................Oprah Winfrey

Showing *Strangers on a Train*

Psst! Although Ramsey plays DeVito's mother, she was only 58 against his 43.

Thunder Alley •• [1985]

Director: J.S. Cardone
Screenplay: J.S. Cardone & William R. Ewing

The story of a teen rock band making it. Not actually bad, but wholly unoriginal and undistinguished. **[111m/PG]**

Richie...Roger Wilson
Beth..Jill Schoelen
Donnie ....Scott McGinnis
Lorraine ....Cynthia Eilbacher

Thunderheart •••• [1992]

Director: Michael Apted
Screenplay: John Fusco

A detective movie with a difference. Kilmer's the FBI man of Indian descent sent to the Navajo reservation in the 70s to investigate a murder at a time of political unrest. A superb thriller on one level, the depiction of third-world life in a first-world nation is also fascinating. If you think you've seen Indian territory on film before, wait till you see this. The story grips throughout while the performances are wonderful, particularly from Greene as the Indian cop who makes Sherlock Holmes look thick. The ending turns the Western genre completely on its head. Highly recommended. **[119m/15]**

Ray Levoi ....Val Kilmer
Walter Crow Horse..............Graham Greene
Frank "Cooch" Coutelle ....Sam Shepard
Maggie Eagle Bear....................Sheila Tousey
Grandpa Sam Reaches......Chief Ted Thin Elk
Jack Milton.....................................Fred Ward
Jimmy Looks Twice ....John Trudell
Dawes ....Fred Dalton Thompson

Tie Me Up, Tie Me Down ••• [1990]

Director: Pedro Almodovar
Screenplay: Pedro Almodovar

Although far from his weirdest or most outrageous, this is perhaps the best of Almodovar's pics. Banderas kidnaps and fetters porn-star Abril in the hope that she will fall for him. Although this comedy – yes, comedy – takes a while to get going, the wonderful Abril is gloriously sexy and the scene with the toy diver in the bath is defnitely going in my *Desert Island Filmclips*. [102m/18]

Marina	Victoria Abril
Ricky	Antonio Banderas
Maximo Espejo	Francisco Rabal
Lola	Loles Leon

Blurb A Love Story...With Strings Attached.

A Tiger's Tale • [1988]

Director: Peter Douglas
Screenplay: Peter Douglas

It's the Old Boy Meets Girl's Mother story, the twist being that Patrick Dempsey isn't in it. Instead, we've got the unbelievable romantic combination of Howell and Ann-Margret. [97m/15]

Rose Butts	Ann-Margret
Bubber Drumm	C. Thomas Howell
Charlie Drumm	Charles Durning
Shirley Butts	Kelly Preston

Psst! The writer, producer and director is Kirk Douglas's son, making his first film.

Tiger Warsaw • [1988]

Director: Amin Q. Chaudhri
Screenplay: Roy London

Swayze is the ex-junkie returning home after 15 years to say 'Hi' to his family. As he shot his father before he left, there's obviously a little reconciliation to be done. Melodramatic drivel. [92m/15]

Chuck 'Tiger' Warsaw	Patrick Swayze
Frances Warsaw	Piper Laurie
Mitchell Warsaw	Lee Richardson
Paula Warsaw	Mary McDonnell

Tightrope •• [1984]

Director: Richard Tuggle
Screenplay: Richard Tuggle

Clint is a New Orleans cop who fears he may have a few things in common with the kinky killer he's hunting. Although it's interesting to see Alison Eastwood steal a scene or two from her dad, this has all been much better done by *Manhunter*. [114m/18]

Wes Block	Clint Eastwood
Beryl Thibodeax	Genevieve Bujold
Det. Molinari	Dan Hedaya
Amanda Block	Alison Eastwood

Till There Was You • [1992]

Director: John Seale
Screenplay: Michael Thomas

Described as an Australian *Romancing the Stone*, but only by those who've seen neither film, Harmon's a sax player summoned by his brother from New York to a South Sea Island. Despite pretty scenery, murder and bungee jumping, the pic's a stiff, as is the acting. The Easter Island statues could do better. [95m/PG]

Frank Flynn	Mark Harmon
Anna	Deborah Unger
Viv	Jeroen Krabbé

Time of Destiny •• [1988]

Director: Gregory Nava
Screenplay: Anna Thomas

A wartime soap with Hurt the soldier out to do away with his brother-in-law for causing the death of his dear dad. Despite moments of silliness, you get swept up in it all, particularly the dramatic climax. [118m/15]

Martin Larraneta	William Hurt
Jack	Timothy Hutton
Josie	Melissa Leo
Jorge	Francisco Rabal
Margaret	Stockard Channing

Tin Men ••• [1987]

Director: Barry Levinson
Screenplay: Barry Levinson

Levinson returns to home town Baltimore for another of his extraordinary, fascinating, slice-of-life films. Two aluminium window salesmen get involved in an escalating tit-for-tat quarrel which culminates in Dreyfuss deciding to seduce

DeVito's wife Hershey. Not only do we get funny, realistic dialogue and fine attention to period detail, but we also learn the secrets of some of the salesmen's remarkable scams. Odd, though, how Dreyfuss never once refers to DeVito's size in their arguments.   [112m/15]

Bill "BB" Babowsky.............Richard Dreyfuss
Ernie Tilley...............................Danny DeVito
Nora Tilley............................Barbara Hershey
Moe...John Mahoney
Sam..Jackie Gayle
Gil...Stanley Brock
Cheese.....................................Seymour Cassel
Mouse...Bruno Kirby
Wing..J.T. Walsh
Carly.....................................Richard Portnow

Quote 'My car's got a sixteenth of a mile on the clock and it's already been hit.'

To Be or Not to Be •• [1983]

Director: Alan Johnson
Screenplay: Thomas Meehan & Ronny Graham

A group of Jewish actors help the Polish Underground after the Nazis invade. A close remake of Lubitsch's superb 1942 black comedy with Brooks in the Jack Benny part as the vain ham and Bancroft as his less than faithful wife. Although there are some decent laughs, it lacks the inspiration of the original. The superb Sweet Georgia Brown sequence in Polish is well worth a look, though. Try the original. It is one of the best comedies ever made.   [108m/PG]

Frederick Bronski..........................Mel Brooks
Anna Bronski............................Anne Bancroft
Lt. Andre Sobinski...................Tim Matheson
Col. Erhardt.........................Charles Durning
Prof. Siletski.....................................Jose Ferrer
Capt. Schultz......................Christopher Lloyd

Quote 'What he did to Shakespeare, we are doing now to Poland.' ✦ 'So, they call me Concentration Camp Erhardt?'

Psst! Mel Brooks and Anne Bancroft are, of course, also married in real life. This is the only time they have starred together.

To Kill a Priest • [1988]

Director: Agnieszka Holland
Screenplay: Agnieszka Holland

A demonstration of just how ghastly international co-productions can be. This multi-accented, one-dimensional tale of a Polish priest falling foul of the secret police manages to turn the true, tragic story of Father Popieluszko into banal pap.   [113m/15]

Father Alek...................Christopher Lambert
Stefan...Ed Harris
Colonel..Joss Ackland
Also: Tim Roth, Timothy Spall, Pete Postlethwaite, Cherie Lunghi, Joanne Whalley-Kilmer

To Live and Die in L.A. •• [1985]

Director: William Friedkin
Screenplay: William Friedkin & Gerald Petievich

A tough LA policeman goes after a counterfeiter, but doesn't always stick to the rulebook. Full of *Miami Vice* vices, with pastel colours and pounding rock soundtrack, this stylishly brutal thriller doesn't concentrate too much on plot or characterisation.   [116m/18]

Richard Chance...................William Petersen
Eric Masters.............................Willem Dafoe
John Vukovich.............................John Pankow
Also: Debra Feuer, John Turturro, Darlanne Fluegel, Dean Stockwell, Robert Downey Jr.

Psst! Probably the first movie with a car chase the wrong way down a Los Angeles freeway.

Too Hot to Handle •• [1991]

Director: Jerry Rees
Screenplay: Neil Simon

Despite being one of the most famously troubled productions of recent years, this romantic comedy still has quite a few gags. Baldwin is the guy who falls for

Bugsy Siegel's mistress and ends up marrying her four times. Neil Simon disowned the picture, which turned out to be the biggest flop of his career. Also known as *The Marrying Man*.

[117m/15]

Vicki Rosemary Anderson	Kim Basinger
Charley Raymond Pearl	Alec Baldwin
Lew Horner	Robert Loggia
Adele Horner	Elisabeth Shue
Bugsy Siegel	Armand Assante

Psst! Baldwin and Basinger became an item during filming, with technicians delighted when Basinger once described what she intended doing with Baldwin that night while miked up ✦ They were less delighted when filming was repeatedly held up by 'conferences' between her and Baldwin in their trailer ✦ Basinger's dislike for the sun on her skin meant that not only had someone to keep her covered with an umbrella, but that one scene in the desert had the pair driving in a convertible with the top up! ✦ Her demands grew steadily more outrageous, from having Evian water to wash her hair in to announcing that she was off to Brazil to consult a psychic – until the studio said she'd have to pay $85,000 a day for the cost of the stalled film ✦ Temper tantrums included Baldwin attacking a Disney executive's cellular phone and Basinger screaming at Pulitzer-winning playwright Neil Simon: 'Whoever wrote this doesn't understand comedy'.

Tootsie ••••   [1982]

Director: **Sydney Pollack**
Screenplay: **Larry Gelbart & Murray Schisgal**

Unemployable actor Hoffman puts on a frock and high heels and promptly lands a leading role in a soap. A constantly entertaining, frequently hilarious, movie which also reveals many truths about the behaviour of the sexes towards each other. A witty script is complemented by a raft of excellent performances from leads and supports alike.   [116m/PG]

Michael Dorsey/Dorothy	Dustin Hoffman
Julie	Jessica Lange
Sandy	Teri Garr
Ron	Dabney Coleman
Les	Charles Durning
Jeff	Bill Murray
George Fields	Sydney Pollack
John Van Horn	George Gaynes
April	Geena Davis

Oscars Jessica Lange

Quote [Director to cameraman]'The only reason you're still living is that I never kissed you.' ✦ 'I'd like to make her a little more attractive . How far back can you go?' – 'How about Cleveland?'

Psst! Being a method actor, Hoffman insisted on testing out his character in real life. Not content with a visit to his daughter's school, where he wasn't recognised, he propositioned actor José Ferrer in a lift. However, Ferrer politely declined the offer ✦ Asked if he would do a sequel, Hoffman said it was a possibility only if he could push the character still further, perhaps by giving birth ✦ The make-up gave him terrible acne and a constant watch had to be kept on set for signs of a five o'clock shadow ✦ Director Pollack appears as Hoffman's agent. He and Hoffman often had furious rows during filming, similar in nature to the one in the agent's office in the movie ✦ With eight writers involved in the troubled gestation of the project, the Writer's Guild had to arbitrate the fight over which of the writers was to be credited. Barry Levinson was one of the wriers who lost out ✦ When the script was originally bought, the producer thought it would be a great role for George Hamilton ✦ It was then called *Would I Lie To You?* Hoffman suggested the new title. It had been a nickname he used to have when he was a child ✦ This was Geena Davis's first film ✦ Estelle Getty, Sophia from *The Golden Girls* has a bit part as a 'middle-aged woman'.

Top Gun •• [1986]

Director: Tony Scott
Screenplay: Jim Cash & Jack Epps Jr.

To help him remember his characterisation, maverick pilot Cruise is called Maverick. He's got a problem with authority, is a whizz in a plane, has a guilt trip over his father and is irresistible to his teacher. Fortunately, she's a woman. Although it's fantastic while in the air, albeit a little confusing at times, it's rather more leaden on the ground. McGillis is perhaps not the most convincing flying instructor in the history of the movies.

[110m/15]

Maverick .... Tom Cruise
Charlie .... Kelly McGillis
Ice .... Val Kilmer
Goose .... Anthony Edwards
Viper .... Tom Skerritt
Jester .... Michael Ironside
Cougar .... John Stockwell
Wolfman .... Barry Tubb
Slider .... Rick Rossovich
Merlin .... Tim Robbins
Sundown .... Clarence Gilyard
Hollywood .... Whip Hubley
Stinger .... James Tolkan
Carole .... Meg Ryan
Chipper .... Adrian Pasdar

Quote 'I feel the need...the need for speed!'

OOPS! Cruise miraculously changes planes in mid-air in the concluding battle. Just watch the number on his tail.

Psst! The inspiration for the film was a 1983 magazine article titled Top Guns • In preparation for the film Cruise attended classes at the Miramar Naval Air Station and flew with Navy pilots. He also drank with them and was sick over Anthony Edwards's BMW! • Cruise couldn't have been a pilot, even if he'd wanted. They insist their chaps be at least 5 feet 10, an inch taller than Cruise • Although the Navy gave the film-makers an amazing degree of cooperation, they also gave them a bill for over $1m. When the film came out, levels of recruitment soared • Sales of Ray-Ban Aviators, sported by Cruise in the movie, also soared [see Risky Business] • Initial tests screenings weren't good enough, so 6 months after filming ended the actors had to return for some additional scenes, including some extra steam between Cruise and McGillis. Unfortunately, she no longer had blonde hair and had had it cut for another film, so had to wear a cap in one scene in a lift • Admiral T.J. Cassidy plays himself.

Top Secret! •• [1984]

Director: Jim Abrahams, David Zucker & Jerry Zucker
Screenplay: Jim Abrahams, David Zucker, Jerry Zucker & Martyn Burke

The Airplane team tackle spy movies. Kilmer's an American rock 'n' roller caught up in espionage activities during a tour of Eastern Europe. The usual barrage of jokes are a little below par while the plot meanders all over the place before being forgotten entirely. [90m/15]

Nick Rivers .... Val Kilmer
Hillary Flammond .... Lucy Gutteridge
Nigel .... Christopher Villiers
Also: Omar Sharif, Peter Cushing, Jeremy Kemp, Michael Gough

Psst! As in all ZAZ films, you should keep a close eye on the closing credits. They include fake jobs like 'Focus Loader', 'Clapper Puller', 'Puller Clapper' and 'Flipper Flapper' as well as 'Hey Diddle Diddle...The Cat And The Fiddle', 'Foreez...A Jolly Good Fellow' and 'This Space For Rent'.

Torch Song Trilogy ••• [1988]

Director: Paul Bogart
Screenplay: Harvey Fierstein

The life and loves of a drag queen, as adapted from the Broadway smash. A pretty decent account of a topic Hollywood is still all too often scared to touch. The humour prevents matters becoming too self-pitying and the acting, particularly from Bancroft, is a treat.

[119m/15]

Arnold	Harvey Fierstein
Ma	Anne Bancroft
Alan	Matthew Broderick
Ed	Brian Kerwin
Laurel	Karen Young

Quote 'When I started in this business I looked like a young Joan Crawford. Ten years later – Marjorie Main.'

Psst! Fierstein lost 63 pounds for the role.

To Sleep with Anger ••• [1990]

Director: **Charles Burnett**
Screenplay: **Charles Burnett**

A couple, now living in LA, get a visit from Glover, an old friend from the days when they lived in the south as children. Although initially overjoyed to see him, he gradually gets his feet further and further under the table. An excellent, hard-edged family drama with Glover superb as the slightly devilish visitor.

[102m/12]

Gideon	Paul Butler
Suzie	Mary Alice
Sunny	DeVaughn Nixon
Linda	Sheryl Lee Ralph
Harry Mention	Danny Glover
Babe Brother	Richard Brooks

Psst! Glover agreed to work for a small fee and also served as executive producer, helping to raise funding for the pic.

Total Recall ••• [1990]

Director: **Paul Verhoeven**
Screenplay: **Ronald Shusett, Dan O'Bannon & Gary Goldman**

In the future, Arnie's a mere construction worker who dreams of being a secret agent and travelling to Mars on a mission. Then he remembers that he *is* a secret agent and suddenly everything he thinks is real in his life turns out not to be. A constantly intriguing and often amusing sci-fi actioner is needlessly violent and nothing like as clever as the Philip K. Dick short story on which it's based. But the effects are astounding and the action's highly entertaining.

[109m/18]

Doug Quaid	Arnold Schwarzenegger
Melina	Rachel Ticotin
Lori	Sharon Stone
Cohaagen	Ronny Cox
Richter	Michael Ironside
George/Juato	Marshall Bell
Benny	Mel Johnson Jr.
Helm	Roy Brocksmith

Blurb They Stole His Mind, Now He Wants It Back.

Quote 'Consider this a divorce.'

OOPS! Although Arnie shoots the psychiatrist who has tried to convince him that he's just having a very vivid dream, we see the chap again later prior to the reprogramming treatment.

Psst! It took writer Shusett fifteen years to get the film made. At one time Matthew Broderick was the projected star ✦ One watchdog group counted 110 acts of violence an hour and 35 slayings, 18 of them by Arnie.

Toto the Hero •••• [1991]

Director: **Jaco van Dormael**
Screenplay: **Jaco van Dormael**

A film so unique it's difficult to explain why it's so wonderful. In old age, Bouquet, still blaming his wealthy next-door neighbour for stealing his life after a mix-up in the maternity ward, vows revenge. This Belgian film is movie story-telling at its very best, with flashbacks to youth and middle-age fleshing out the compelling yarn. Extraordinarily witty and inventive and utterly spellbinding, it's hard to believe that this is Dormael's first film, or that he was once a circus clown! Be warned, the song *Boum* is one of the catchiest ever used in a movie.

[90m/15]

Thomas van Hasebroeck	Michael Bouquet
Thomas (as young man)	Jo De Backer
Thomas (as child)	Thomas Godet
Evelyne	Gisela Uhlen
Evelyn (as young woman)	Mireille Perrier
Alice	Sandrine Blancke
Alfred	Peter Böhlke

Tough Guys •• [1986]

Director: Jeff Kanew
Screenplay: James Orr & Jim Cruickshank

The last train-robbers in America, Lancaster and Douglas, emerge from jail after a quarter of a century and decide to go back into business. Although both leads are a delight to look at throughout, the script is pretty feeble in places and downright silly near the end. **[103m/15]**

Harry Doyle ....:....Burt Lancaster
Archie Long ....Kirk Douglas
Deke Yablonski ....Charles Durning
Also: Alexis Smith, Dana Carvey, Darlanne Fluegel, Eli Wallach

Psst! Called *Archie and Harry, They Can't Do It* in Germany.

Tough Guys Don't Dance • [1987]

Director: Norman Mailer
Screenplay: Norman Mailer

Are there two Norman Mailers? Surely the well-known novelist couldn't be responsible for writing and directing this black comedy, in which Ryan O'Neal is merely the biggest of many mistakes. What we end up with is black alright, but black as in dense and impenetrable, not black as in funny. **[108m/18]**

Tim Madden ....Ryan O'Neal
Madeleine............................Isabella Rossellini
Patty Lareine ....Debra Sandlund
Regency ....Wings Hauser

The Toy • [1982]

Director: Richard Donner
Screenplay: Carol Sobieski

This one seems to have its batteries missing. A pathetic and rather nauseating comedy about a wealthy tycoon 'buying' employee Pryor for his appalling son as a present. Insulting drivel. **[102m/PG]**

Jack Brown ....Richard Pryor
U.S. Bates ....Jackie Gleason
Mr. Morehouse..............................Ned Beatty

Toys •• [1992]

Director: Barry Levinson
Screenplay: Valerie Curtin & Barry Levinson

It took Levinson over ten years to get this ambitious project onto the screen and what an infuriating film it is. Williams is the manic (what else?) son of a toy factory owner taken over by his General uncle Gambon on his father's death. Visually brilliant, flashes of extraordinary wit occasionally bubble to the surface, enough for film buffs to enjoy. But for others, this disjointed, rambling mess of a movie will be a big turn-off, especially considering its simplistic message that toys you wind up are better than ones that rely on batteries and make a lot of noise. Not even Williams, here given too much free rein, can save this one. **[121m/PG]**

Leslie Zevo.............................Robin Williams
The General........................Michael Gambon
Alsatia Zevo ....Joan Cusack
Gwen ....Robin Wright
Patrick ....LL Cool J

Quote 'You're as big a fool as your father ever was.' – 'You really think so? Thank you.'

Psst! Donald O'Connor, from *Singing in the Rain*, appears in a cameo as Williams' father.

Toy Soldiers •• [1991]

Director: Daniel Petrie Jr.
Screenplay: Daniel Petrie Jr. & David Koepp

Terrorists make the mistake of taking over a school for wealthy misfit kids. Trying to be a combination of *Die Hard* and *Dead Poets Society*, the film manages neither. **[112m/15]**

Billy Tepper.....................................Sean Astin
Joey Trotta ....Wil Wheaton
Snuffy Bradberry........................Keith Coogan
Also: Andrew Divoff, R. Lee Ermey, Mason Adams, Denholm Elliott, Louis Gossett Jr., Jerry Orbach

Traces of Red ••• [1992]

Director: Andy Wolk
Screenplay: Jim Piddock

Palm Beach cop Belushi gets into deep water when investigating the murder of a waitress he had a fling with. His long-standing wealthy girlfriend Bracco is involved, if only he can work out how. Although indifferently made and acted, the plot has more twists than a ride at Alton Towers and, unlike so many slick modern thrillers, keeps confounding expectations and providing fresh surprises. Highly entertaining drivel. [104m/15]

Jack Dobson	James Belushi
Ellen Schofield	Lorraine Bracco
Steve Frayn	Tony Goldwyn
Michael Dobson	William Russ

Track 29 • [1988]

Director: Nicolas Roeg
Screenplay: Dennis Potter

An American woman gets a visit from a young Englishman who could be her long lost son. Her husband, however, is more interested in playing with his train set. You might expect an incendiary experience from Roeg, Potter, Oldman and Russell. Unfortunately, sitting under a tree waiting for the autumn leaves to fall would be more interesting. [90m/15]

Linda Henry	Theresa Russell
Martin	Gary Oldman
Henry	Christopher Lloyd

Trading Places •••• [1983]

Director: John Landis
Screenplay: Timothy Harris & Herschel Weingrod

Near perfect comedy about a couple of crusty old buffers switching the life of pompous, wealthy commodity trader Aykroyd with that of sassy beggar Murphy for the sake of a bet. Murphy's never been better and there's excellent support from Curtis and Elliott. A total delight which is eminently rewatchable. [116m/15]

Louis Winthorpe III	Dan Aykroyd
Billy Ray Valentine	Eddie Murphy
Coleman	Denholm Elliott
Randolph Duke	Ralph Bellamy
Mortimer Duke	Don Ameche
Ophelia	Jamie Lee Curtis
Penelope Witherspoon	Kristin Holby
Attendant	Robert Earl Jones
Clarence Beeks	Paul Gleason
Corrupt Cop	Frank Oz
Pawnbroker	Bo Diddley
Harvey	James Belushi
Doctor	Philip Bosco

Quote 'When I was growing up and we wanted a Jacuzzi, we had to fart in the tub.'

Psst! For years John Landis put the words 'See you next Wednesday' in every film. Here it's on a poster in Curtis's room. He stopped around the time of ¡*Three Amigos!* when he realised audiences had spotted it ♦ On discovering that Bellamy had made 99 films and Ameche 49, Murphy said, 'That means between the three of us, we've made 150 movies!'.

The Trail of the Pink Panther • [1982]

Director: Blake Edwards
Screenplay: Franz Waldman & Tom Waldman

This distasteful bit of cinematic necrophilia has the dead Sellers starring in yet another Clouseau film! Edwards used out-takes and scenes from the earlier movies, framing them with a documentary about the great man. Such a gross idea that, even where it is marginally funny, it can't raise a laugh. [96m/PG]

Insp. Clouseau	Peter Sellers
Sir Charles Litton	David Niven
Dreyfus	Herbert Lom

Psst! Probably the first movie which began filming *after* its main star had died. A lookalike was used to get round the fact that Sellers himself couldn't appear in front of the camera ♦ Lynne Frederick sued for violation of late husband Sellers' rights and won $1.7m from United Artists, plus costs.

Transformers-The Movie • [1986]

Director: **Nelson Shin**
Screenplay: **Ron Friedman**

Possibly the longest advert for toys ever put on screen (if you exclude Top Gun), with the shape-changing Transformers saving the Universe from the Decepticons. Why anyone should acquire such a top-notch cast and then disguise their voices electronically is one of the great mysteries of our time.   [85m/U]

Wreck Gar ....Eric Idle
Hot Rod/Rodimus Prime...............Judd Nelson
Galvatron ....Leonard Nimoy
Ultra Magnus ....Robert Stack
Unicorn ....Orson Welles

Psst! This was the very last film role for cinema's *enfant terrible* Orson Welles. Even the sherry ads would have been a better epitaph than this.

Transylvania 6-5000 • [1985]

Director: **Rudy De Luca**
Screenplay: **Rudy De Luca**

A stupid vampire spoof whose title shows how off target the film is. How many of the youngsters the movie is aimed at will understand the joke, if joke isn't putting it too strongly?   [94m/PG]

Jack Harrison ....Jeff Goldblum
Dr. Malavaqua........................Joseph Bologna
Gil Turner..................................Ed Begley Jr.
Also: Jeffrey Jones, Geena Davis

Travelling North ••• [1988]

Director: **Carl Schultz**
Screenplay: **David Williamson**

Taking a break from Rumpole, McKern is wonderful in this lovely Australian film as a cantankerous old buffer falling in love and doing his best to retire peacefully. A witty and often moving film with a great actor at the peak of his form.   [98m/15]

Frank..Leo McKern
Francis ....Julia Blake
Freddie................................Graham Kennedy
Saul...Henri Szeps

Treasure Island ••• [1990]

Director: **Fraser Heston**
Screenplay: **Fraser Heston**

This is a pretty entertaining outing for Stevenson's timeless tale, full of action, gorgeous scenery and lots of well-known actors hamming it up so much the film was probably banned in Israel. The film was written, produced and directed by Charlton Heston Jr.   [132m/PG]

Long John Silver....................Charlton Heston
Jim Hawkins..............................Christian Bale
Capt. Billy Bones.........................Oliver Reed
Blind Pew...............................Christopher Lee
Dr. Livesey.................................Julian Glover

Tree of Hands •• [1989]

Director: **Giles Foster**
Screenplay: **Gordon Williams**

Shaver is an American novelist living in Hampstead, distraught at the death of her son. Luckily mum Bacall's around to lend a helping hand, kidnapping somebody else's boy to cheer her up. A stilted but still occasionally gripping adaptation of a Ruth Rendell novel.   [90m/18]

Benet Archdale ....Helen Shaver
Marsha.......................................Lauren Bacall
Terence...Peter Firth
Barry..Paul McGann
Carol ....Kate Hardie

Tremors ••• [1990]

Director: **Ron Underwood**
Screenplay: **Brent Maddock & S.S. Wilson**

Giant earthworms are burrowing through the desert and snacking on unwary campers. Witty, fast and highly enjoyable, this delivers the thrills while at the same time parodying the monster genre. Note, too, the ingenious way in which the Politically Correct 90's heroine is still separated from her jeans.   [95m/15]

Valentine McKee........................Kevin Bacon
Earl Basset......................................Fred Ward
Rhonda LeBeck.............................Finn Carter
Burt Gummer ....Michael Gross

Heather Gummer......................Reba McEntire
Melvin Plug................................Bobby Jacoby

Psst! The credits include a 'dirt' wrangler and a 'sage' wrangler.

Trespass ••• [1992]

Director: **Walter Hill**
Screenplay: **Bob Gale & Robert Zemeckis**

A pair of firemen searching for loot hidden in a warehouse discover they've strayed into the territory of a vicious black gang. Improbably written by the *Back to the Future* and *Roger Rabbit* team, this violent thriller suffers from poor characterisation and an uninspiring plot. But veteran action man Hill gives us enough shots of adrenalin to make it worthwhile. **[101m/18]**

Vince..Bill Paxton
King James.....................................Ice T
Don..William Sadler
Savon...Ice Cube
Bradlee..Art Evans
Lucky..................................De'voreaux White

Psst! Formerly called *Looters*, the film's release was delayed in the aftermath of the LA riots, emerging later with some alterations and a title change ◆ Although almost unrecognisable, Sadler brilliantly portrayed the Grim Reaper in *Bill & Ted's Bogus Journey*

Trick or Treat •• [1986]

Director: **Charles Martin Smith**
Screenplay: **Michael S. Murphey, Joel Soisson & Rhet Topham**

A much derided teenager is able to summon up the soul of a dead rock star by playing a record backwards, revenging himself on those who mocked him. This nice idea is well handled by actor–director Smith, the nerdy accountant from *The Untouchables*. **[97m/18]**

Eddie Weinbauer..........................Marc Price
Sammi Curr....................................Tony Fields
Leslie Graham...........................Lisa Orgolini
Tim Hainey.................................Doug Savant

The Trip to Bountiful ••• [1985]

Director: **Peter Masterson**
Screenplay: **Horton Foote**

Old woman Page lives with her wimpish son and his shrew of a wife and dreams of her earlier life in Bountiful. Finally, she can stand it no more and sneaks off home. Page is superb in this Oscar–winning role which really warms the heart. True, it's something of an eye–moistener, but then everybody needs a little cry from time to time. **[106m/U]**

Mrs. Watts.............................Geraldine Page
Ludie Watts..................................John Heard
Jessie Mae..................................Carlin Glynn
Sheriff....................................Richard Bradford
Thelma...........................Rebecca De Mornay
Roy...Kevin Cooney

Oscars Geraldine Page

OOPS! The boom mike appears when Page is in the cornfield.

Triumph of the Spirit •• [1989]

Director: **Robert M. Young**
Screenplay: **Andrzej Krakowski & Laurence Heath**

Dafoe plays a Greek–Jewish boxer deported to Auschwitz in World War II who was forced to box other inmates to survive. Despite being based on a true story and being reasonably made, we endure a harrowing two hours to little purpose. **[120m/15]**

Salamo Arouch.........................Willem Dafoe
Gypsy............................Edward James Olmos
Poppa..Robert Loggia
Allegra.....................................Wendy Gazelle

Psst! Filming took place at Auschwitz itself, the first movie allowed through the gates ◆ Dafoe lost 20 pounds before filming began ◆ Extraordinarily, Dafoe revealed recently that Madonna very nearly starred in the film!

Triumphs of a Man Called Horse •• [1983]

Director: John Hough
Screenplay: Ken Blackwell & Carlos Aured

A Man Called Horse seemed to have got something stuck in its hoof by this third in the series. Beck, Horse's son, does his best to keep white settlers off Sioux land. Despite being seen from the other side, it's still pretty routine cowboys and Indians stuff. [85m/15]

Man Called Horse	Richard Harris
Koda	Michael Beck
Redwing	Ana DeSade
Capt. Cummings	Vaughn Armstrong

Psst! John Cleese claims that it was A Man Called Horse that inspired the title A Fish Called Wanda

Troll • [1986]

Director: John Buechler
Screenplay: Ed Naha

Trolls are taking over an apartment building. As the city is San Francisco, will anyone notice anything out of the ordinary? Sonny Bono spends a lot of time mulling over the fact that if he and Cher hadn't split, he'd probably be in a better class of rubbish altogether. [86m/15]

Harry Porter Jr.	Noah Hathaway
Mr. Potter	Michael Moriarty
Mrs. Potter	Shelley Hack
Peter Dickenson	Sonny Bono

Troop Beverly Hills •• [1989]

Director: Jeff Kanew
Screenplay: Pamela Norris & Margaret Grieco Oberman

A stinking-rich Beverly Hills housewife takes her daughter's troop of obnoxious girl guides off on a caring, sharing trip. Unfortunately, they return. [105m/PG]

Phyllis Nefler	Shelley Long
Freddy Nefler	Craig T. Nelson
Velda Plendor	Betty Thomas
Annie Herman	Mary Gross
Vicki Sprantz	Stephanie Beacham

Trouble in Mind •• [1985]

Director: Alan Rudolph
Screenplay: Alan Rudolph

Kristofferson is a futuristic ex-cop who befriends a crook new in town but knows that whatever he does, his character's name 'Hawk' dooms the film to mediocrity [See Rose's Rule #8]. Director Alan Rudolph is one of those mannered, quirky birds who loves style over substance. If you're in the mood to play, try it, but not perhaps after a heavy session in the pub. [111m/15]

Hawk	Kris Kristofferson
Coop	Keith Carradine
Georgia	Lori Singer
Wanda	Genevieve Bujold
Solo	Joe Morton
Hilly Blue	Divine

Psst! As well as starring in the movie, Kristofferson wrote the title song.

True Identity •• [1991]

Director: Charles Lane
Screenplay: Andy Breckman

In his Hollywood debut, Henry's an actor who finds a Mafia man confessing all when they're about to die in a plane crash. When the plane lands safely, he has to go on the run. Some splendid impersonations from Henry can't overcome the feebleness of the script. [95m/15]

Miles Pope	Lenny Henry
Frank Luchino	Frank Langella
Duane	Charles Lane
Craig Houston	J.T. Walsh

Also: Anne-Marie Johnson, Andreas Katsulas, Michael McKean, Peggy Lipton

True Love •• [1989]

Director: Nancy Savoca
Screenplay: Nancy Savoca & Richard Guay

A pleasing comedy about a less than perfect Italian couple from the Bronx getting married. Well-crafted and slyly observant, but all a little insubstantial. [104m/15]

Donna.................................Annabella Sciorra
Michael...Ron Eldard
Grace..Aida Turturro
Dom..Roger Rignack

True Stories •• [1986]

Director: **David Byrne**
Screenplay: **Stephen Tobolowsky, Beth Henley & David Byrne**

David Byrne of Talking Heads wanders around Texas, meeting lots of weird people and giving Jonathan Ross a great idea for a series. This rather patronising pseudo-documentary suffers from the problem that any film which sets out to be a cult almost inevitably fails in its aim. **[89m/PG]**

Narrator......................................David Byrne
Louis Fyne...............................John Goodman
Kay Culver............................Annie McEnroe
The Lying Woman ....Jo Harvey Allen
Earl Culver ....Spalding Gray
The Lazy Woman ....Swoosie Kurtz

Truly, Madly, Deeply •• [1990]

Director: **Anthony Minghella**
Screenplay: **Anthony Minghella**

The love of two Highgate trendies is so strong that even after he dies, he still hangs around her place with a bunch of his spectral mates. This is one of those films that splits the sexes, with the distaff side generally thinking it witty, romantic and deserving of a good weep while many males reckon it sloppy tripe. Whichever camp you're in, there are some splendid moments to treasure in this British version of *Ghost*, which looks better on the small screen for which it was originally intended. **[106m/PG]**

Nina ....Juliet Stevenson
Jamie..Alan Rickman
Sandy ....Bill Paterson
Mark....................................Michael Maloney

Showing *Brief Encounter*, *The Lavender Hill Mob*, *Easy Street*.

Psst! Originally, the film was known simply as *Cello*.

Trust •• [1991]

Director: **Hal Hartley**
Screenplay: **Hal Hartley**

Hartley's second film is full of the same sort of oddball characters and humour as *The Unbelievable Truth*. Shelly and Donovan are two teenagers at odds with their families. She's pregnant, he carries a hand grenade around in case he decides to top himself. After an hour of relentless quirkiness, you begin to hope that the pin will fall out. **[106m/15]**

Maria Coughlin ....Adrienne Shelly
Matthew Slaughter ....Martin Donovan
Jean Coughlin ....Merritt Nelson
Jim Slaughter..............................John MacKay

Truth or Dare
SEE: **In Bed With Madonna**

Tucker: The Man and His Dream ••• [1988]

Director: **Francis Ford Coppola**
Screenplay: **Arnold Schulman & David Seidler**

Preston Tucker designed a brilliant new car in the 40s but fell foul of the vested interests of the less-advanced, more conventional auto manufacturers, who ran him out of town. Stylishly designed and movingly performed, unfortunately this fascinating story ultimately proves a hollow exercise, despite the director's clear identification with the hero. **[111m/PG]**

Preston Tucker ....Jeff Bridges
Vera...Joan Allen
Abe ....Martin Landau
Eddie.....................................Frederic Forrest
Jimmy...Mako
Alex ....Elias Koteas
Junior....................................Christian Slater
Marilyn Lee ....Nina Siemaszko
Howard Hughes ....Dean Stockwell
Senator Ferguson ....Lloyd Bridges

Psst! Some 50 Tuckers were built. Amazingly, all but 4 are still in use.

Tuff Turf • [1985]

Director: Fritz Kiersch
Screenplay: Jette Rinck

Spader has trouble settling in at his new school when the family move West and he finds himself tangling with the local gang of yobbos. Spader fans might do well to steer clear of this early embarrassment. **[112m/18]**

Morgan Hiller ....James Spader
Frankie Croyden ....Kim Richards
Also: Paul Mones, Matt Clark, Claudette Nevins, Robert Downey Jr.

Tune in Tomorrow

SEE: Aunt Julia and the Scriptwriter

Turkey Shoot • [1981]

Director: Brian Trenchard-Smith
Screenplay: Jon George & Neill Hicks

A rather brutal and sadistic Australian flick visualising an unpleasant future. Those deviating from society's rules end up in a vicious prison where the warder's idea of fun is letting prisoners loose and then hunting them down. Not released in Britain until 1983. Also known as *Escape 2000.* **[88m/18]**

Paul ....Steve Railsback
Chris ....Olivia Hussey
Mallory ....Noel Ferrier

Turk 182! •• [1985]

Director: Bob Clark
Screenplay: James Gregory Kingston, Dennis Hamill & John Hamill

When the City won't give Hutton's fire-man brother a pension because he got hurt being brave while off duty, he lowers his head and does battle with the powers that be. Frank Capra sneezing was more cre-ative than this low-grade tosh. **[98m/15]**

Jimmy Lynch ....Timothy Hutton
Terry Lynch ....Robert Urich
Danny Boudreau ....Kim Cattrall
Mayor Tyler ....Robert Culp

Turner and Hooch •• [1989]

Director: Roger Spottiswoode
Screenplay: **Dennis Shryack, Michael Blodgett, Daniel Petrie Jr., Jim Cash & Jack Epps Jr.**

You wouldn't think that a film pairing a cop with a dog could possibly be pre-dictable, but this one manages it. Hanks, the only tidy and punctilious cop in the movies, does his best with the slobbering, ever-hungry murder witness, but the comedy never gets let off the lead. **[99m/PG]**

Scott Turner ....Tom Hanks
Emily Carson....................Mare Winningham
Chief Hyde ....Craig T. Nelson
David Sutton ....Reginald Veljohnson

Psst! In the original version of the script, Hooch survived.

Turtle Beach • [1992]

Director: **Stephen Wallace**
Screenplay: **Ann Turner**

Don't shell out your money on this plod-ding Australian thriller, set against what should have been the fascinating back-ground of the Vietnamese boat people in Malaysia. Even the sex scenes with Scacchi are dull. **[88m/15]**

Judith..Greta Scacchi
Lady Minou Hobday........................Joan Chen
Ralph Hamilton ....Jack Thompson
Kanan..Art Malik

Turtle Diary •••• [1985]

Director: **John Irvin**
Screenplay: **Harold Pinter**

A shy British couple discover that they have a mutual interest in helping turtles to escape from the zoo. In summary it may sound awful, but this little-known British comedy is handled with great flair, under-stated wit and charm. Those who don't care for the turtles' genetically-chal-lenged, kick-boxing cousins should love it. **[96m/PG]**

Neaera Duncan......................Glenda Jackson
William Snow............................Ben Kingsley

Mr. Johnson	Richard Johnson
George Fairbairn	Michael Gambon
Mrs. Inchcliff	Rosemary Leach
Miss Neap	Eleanor Bron
Harriet	Harriet Walter
Sandor	Jeroen Krabbé

Psst! Writer Harold Pinter appears as a customer in the bookshop.

Twenty-One •   [1991]

Director: Don Boyd
Screenplay: Zoe Heller & Don Boyd

It's no fun being young, pretty and single in Britain, so Kensit heads for America. Virtually a monologue, this tiresome film delivers neither the smut nor the sharp observation which would hold the interest. It also fails to convince that Kensit – who started her career by putting her finger in her mouth to make a popping sound for a Bird's Eye peas commercial – has advanced very far in the acting stakes since then.   **[101m/15]**

Katie	Patsy Kensit
Kenneth	Jack Shepherd
Jack	Patrick Ryecart

Twice in a Lifetime •••   [1985]

Director: Bud Yorkin
Screenplay: Colin Welland

An excellent drama with Hackman taking up with another woman when he turns fifty, causing considerable grief to his family. Although the outline could be one of a hundred movies, Welland has scripted a realistic, moving and engrossing tale.
[117m/15]

Harry	Gene Hackman
Audrey	Ann-Margret
Kate	Ellen Burstyn
Sunny	Amy Madigan
Helen	Ally Sheedy

Also: Stephen Lang, Darrell Larson, Brian Dennehy

Psst! The TV play on which it was based was set in Manchester, rather than Seattle, as here.

Twilight Zone – The Movie ••   [1983]

Director: John Landis, Steven Spielberg, Joe Dante & George Miller
Screenplay: John Landis, George Clayton Johnson, Richard Matheson & Josh Rogan

This is a somewhat disappointing big screen version of the cult TV series, split into a prologue and four stories. Three are remakes of TV episodes. Best is the last, with Lithgow a passenger convinced his plane is about to crash.   **[101m/15]**

Segment One & Prologue

Passenger	Dan Aykroyd
Driver	Albert Brooks
Bill	Vic Morrow

Segment Two

Bloom	Scatman Crothers

Segment Three

Helen	Kathleen Quinlan
Anthony	Jeremy Licht

Segment Four

Valentine	John Lithgow

Psst! When a helicopter went out of control during filming at night, actor Vic Morrow and two children were killed. Director Landis and four others were acquitted, five years later, of manslaughter charges brought against them.

Twin Peaks: Fire Walk With Me •   [1992]

Director: David Lynch
Screenplay: David Lynch & Robert Engels

Desperately disappointing feature film prequel to the events of the TV series, following events leading up to Laura Palmer's death. Whereas the series was fresh, original, funny and quirky, this is obscure, confusing and frequently downright nasty. Lacking many of the familiar actors, the film's more explicit yet far less erotic, while the violence is gross. Coop almost disappears part-way through as well.   **[134m/18]**

Laura Palmer ....Sheryl Lee
Donna Hayward ....Moira Kelly
Phillip Jeffries ....David Bowie
Chester Desmond ....Chris Isaak
Carl Rodd.......................Harry Dean Stanton
Leland Palmer...................................Ray Wise
Dale Cooper.......................Kyle MacLachlan
Bobby Briggs ....Dana Ashbrook
Sam Stanley ....Kiefer Sutherland
Norma Jennings.............................Peggy Lipton
James Hurley...........................James Marshall
Sarah Palmer ....Grace Zabriskie
Teresa Banks ....Pamela Gidley
Gordon Cole ....David Lynch
Shelly Johnson ....Mädchen Amick
Albert Rosenfeld.........................Miguel Ferrer
Annie Blackburn ....Heather Graham
Woodsman ....Jurgen Prochnow
Sheriff Cable ....Gary Bullock

Psst! The incomprehensible scene with the girls in the bar had subtitles in the US, but were absent from the UK version.

Twins •• [1988]

Director: **Ivan Reitman**
Screenplay: **William Davies, William Osborne, Timothy Harris & Herschel Weingrod**

Twins DeVito and Schwarzenegger, part of a genetic experiment, are split at birth. Reunited in their 30s, they go in search of their mother but are diverted by a silly hoodlum subplot. A great idea is never truly developed. Nor is it explained why, if bright twin Arnie has indeed learnt to speak twelve languages, English is not one of them. **[112m/PG]**

Julius Benedict...........Arnold Schwarzenegger
Vincent Benedict ....Danny DeVito
Marnie Mason............................Kelly Preston
Linda Mason ....Chloe Webb
Mary Ann Benedict..................Bonnie Bartlett

Blurb Only Their Mother Can Tell Them Apart.

Quote 'Actually, I hate violence.' — 'But you're so good at it.'

OOPS! Watch the bottle of beer in the bar's loo jump from left-hand towel dispenser to the one on the right as they throw

their towels in the bin.

Psst! Look out for Arnie comparing his muscles with a poster of Rambo ✦ Schwarzenegger received something like $25m as a fee and share of the profits. The basic fee alone works out at over $200,000 for each minute of the film.

The Two Jakes •••• [1991]

Director: **Jack Nicholson**
Screenplay: **Robert Towne**

The sequel to *Chinatown* may have had its share of problems in production, but emerges as a wonderfully stylish, atmospheric 40's detective pic in the same mould as its predecessor, with an amazingly strong sense of time and place. The plot, involving investigations into infidelities and shenanigans over oil deposits, is well-nigh incomprehensible, but no more so than *Chinatown*. Nicholson, who also directed, gives a superlative performance, as does Keitel as the other Jake. Slagged off almost universally by critics, this is a treasure just waiting to be discovered. **[137m/15]**

Jake Gittes................................Jack Nicholson
Jake Berman..............................Harvey Keitel
Kitty Berman ....Meg Tilly
Lillian Bodine ....Madeleine Stowe
Cotton Weinberger.......................Eli Wallach
Mickey Nice ....Ruben Blades
Chuck Newty.........................Frederic Forrest
Loach Jnr ....David Keith
Earl Rawley ....Richard Farnsworth
Tyrone Otley............................Tracey Walter
Captain Lou Escobar....................Perry Lopez

Quote 'I suppose it's fair to say that infidelity has made me what I am today.' ✦ 'In this town, I'm the leper with the most fingers.'

OOPS! As Nicholson wanders into a beauty parlour, an ATM cash machine is clearly visible in the cinema. Cramming the wider screen onto video means it's barely visible at the right of the frame.

Psst! Credits include a 'golf adviser' ✦ Look out for Tom Waits in a cameo as a policeman.

Two Moon Junction • [1988]

Director: **Zalman King**
Screenplay: **Zalman King**

A rich Southern girl gets the hots for a carnival worker. A classic example of the Zalman King recipe at work: glitzy camerawork, camp performances, blatant Freudian symbolism and just enough plot to reassure viewers they're not watching out-and-out porn. Deadly. [104m/18]

April Delongpre..........................Sherilyn Fenn
Perry..Richard Tyson
Belle..Louise Fletcher
Sheriff Earl Hawkins..........................Burl Ives

Two of a Kind • [1983]

Director: **John Herzfeld**
Screenplay: **John Herzfeld**

God's had enough and wants to destroy the world. But He's giving just two humans a chance to redeem us all. Who's He picked to save the human race? John Travolta and Olivia Newton-John. Heaven help us! This may be their first time together since *Grease* but that's once too often judging by this dismal heap of mush. [87m/PG]

Zack...John Travolta
Debbie..Olivia Newton-John
Charlie ....Charles Durning
Also: Beatrice Straight, Scatman Crothers, Oliver Reed, Kathy Bates

2010 •• [1984]

Director: **Peter Hyams**
Screenplay: **Peter Hyams**

The Russians and Americans unite to discover what went wrong on the Discovery nine years earlier. This over-explicit and unnecessary sequel merely points up how brilliant the original was, replacing its play on myth and mystery with banality and over-explicitness. It looks good and Mirren is outstanding as usual, but that's it. [116m/PG]

Heywood Floyd............................Roy Scheider
Walter Curnow..........................John Lithgow

Tanya Kirbuk............................Helen Mirren
R. Chandra...................................Bob Balaban
Dave Bowman..............................Keir Dullea
Psst! Look out for author Arthur C. Clarke. He's the chap feeding the pigeons outside the White House and is also on the cover of *Time* magazine as the American president • The face of the USSR leader is director Stanley Kubrick.

U

The Ultimate Solution of Grace Quigley •• [1984]

Director: **Anthony Harvey**
Screenplay: **A. Martin Zweibach**

In a twist on the euthenasia theme, Hepburn is the elderly woman who hires hit man Nolte to kill those of her acquaintance who would rather be dead. It has its humorous moments. [95m/15]

Grace Quigley.................Katharine Hepburn
Seymour Flint ....Nick Nolte
Emily Watkins.....................Elizabeth Wilson
Psst! There are several versions of this around, one shorter and one longer. This 'writer's cut' is the best of the trio.

The Umbrella Woman
SEE: The Good Wife

The Unbearable Lightness of Being • [1988]

Director: **Philip Kaufman**
Screenplay: **Philip Kaufman & Jean-Claude Carriere**

At the time of the Russian invasion in the '68, a Czech doctor has one of those terrible choices medical men are all too often confronted with, this time whether to favour Juliette Binoche or Lena Olin.

Unbearable's the word for this elephantine but much-praised adaptation of
Kundera's short novel. Despite the
impeccable acting, it goes on for so long
the Russians could get their invasion over
and done with before the end credits roll.

[172m/18]

Tomas	Daniel Day-Lewis
Tereza	Juliette Binoche
Sabina	Lena Olin

The Unbelievable Truth •• [1990]

Director: Hal Hartley
Screenplay: Hal Hartley

There's a tendency to lavish praise on any
movie costing less than $1m. As this only
cost $200,000 and was filmed in eleven
days, the critics went wild. An ex-con
comes back to his home town, a place so
full of eccentrics they should just fence it
off and call it an asylum. Oddball is funny
for a while. But if there's nothing else, it
just becomes tiresome. [90m/15]

Audry Hugo	Adrienne Shelly
Josh Hutton	Robert Burke
Vic Hugo	Christopher Cooke
Pearl	Julia McNeal

Uncle Buck •• [1989]

Director: John Hughes
Screenplay: John Hughes

Candy tries hard as The Babysitter From
Hell who ends up the good uncle. But this
is Hughes cooking on auto-pilot, a dash of
sentiment here, a spot of kids teaching
adults about life there, here a joke, there a
pratfall. Yes, it's funny in places. But if
only it weren't so darned calculated.

[100m/12]

Uncle Buck Russell	John Candy
Tia Russell	Jean Louisa Kelly
Maizy Russell	Gaby Hoffman
Miles Russell	Macaulay Culkin
Chanice Kobolowski	Amy Madigan

Also: Elaine Bromka, Garrett M. Brown,
Laurie Metcalf

Uncommon Valor •• [1983]

Director: Ted Kotcheff
Screenplay: Joe Gayton

If the movies are anything to go by,
Vietnam must once have been full of
Americans blundering round trying to
find soldiers that got left behind. In this
routine actioner, it's the turn of a misfit
bunch led by Hackman, searching for his
MIA son. [105m/18]

Col. Rhodes	Gene Hackman
MacGregor	Robert Stack
Wilkes	Fred Ward
Blaster	Reb Brown
Sailor	Randall "Tex" Cobb
Scott	Patrick Swayze

Under Fire •••• [1983]

Director: Roger Spottiswoode
Screenplay: Ron Shelton & Clayton
Frohman

American journalists get caught up in the
Nicaraguan revolution in the late 70s.
Though subsequently eclipsed by Oliver
Stone's *Salvador*, this great action thriller,
which also has plenty to say about the
responsibilities of the press, remains
Spottiswoode's best movie. [128m/15]

Russell Price	Nick Nolte
Oates	Ed Harris
Alex	Gene Hackman
Claire	Joanna Cassidy
Isela	Alma Martinez
Jazy	Jean-Louis Trintignant
Hub	Richard Masur

Quote 'You're gonna love this war: good
guys, bad buys and cheap shrimp!'

Under Siege ••• [1992]

Director: Andrew Davis
Screenplay: J.F. Lawton

Terrorists hijack the nuclear-armed battleship USS Missouri and threaten to
nuke Honolulu; presumably because of an
unhappy package holiday. But cook Seagal
was once an ex-Special Services agent
and he's soon making a few extra-meaty

shish-kebabs. Although lacking much of the wit and logic of the *Die Hard* films, the action scenes are fantastic. After so much recent Political Correctness, it's almost refreshing to see Eleniak in a 'bimbo popping topless out of the cake' role. **[103m/15]**

Casey Ryback .... Steven Seagal
William Strannix .... Tommy Lee Jones
Commander Krill .... Gary Busey
Also: Erika Eleniak, Patrick O'Neal, Nick Mancuso, Andy Romano

Quote 'He's in a gunfight right now. I'm going to have to take a message.'

OOPS! Okay, so Eleniak's not too bright here. But surely she'd have noticed *something* when a group of terrorists hijacked the helicopter she was in? And wouldn't they have noticed her?

Psst! Eleniak is not only a former Playboy model and cast member of *Baywatch*, but was first seen on screen in *E.T.*, as the girl Elliott kisses when the frogs are hopping around ♦ The USS Alabama, the ship used for filming, is moored permanently in Mobile. The film-makers had to use a massive blackout cloth on a barge to stop us seeing the lights of the surrounding city.

Under Suspicion ••• [1991]

Director: **Simon Moore**
Screenplay: **Simon Moore**

Pleasing little thriller set in the 50s. Neeson's a private eye facilitating divorces by arranging the taking of compromising photos. When his wife is murdered, he finds himself the prime suspect. A nicely twisting story, well handled and with great period detail, it builds to a nail-biting, if somewhat ludicrous, finale. **[95m/18]**

Tony Aaron .... Liam Neeson
Angeline .... Laura San Giacomo
Frank .... Kenneth Cranham
Selina .... Alphonsia Emmanuel
Hazel Aaron .... Maggie O'Neill
Stasio .... Michael Almaz
Roscoe .... Stephen Moore

Under the Cherry Moon • [1986]

Director: **Prince**
Screenplay: **Becky Johnston**

Once you could find booths where you could record your own records. It looks as if Prince has found one that lets you film your own films. This supremely narcissistic, egocentric drivel has him as a gigolo in the South of France. There's not even much music. **[98m/15]**

Christopher Tracy .... Prince
Also: Jerome Benton, Kristin Scott Thomas, Steven Berkoff, Francesca Annis

Psst! Mary Lambert was to direct it, but Prince fired her and had a go himself ♦ Although made in colour, Prince insisted that it be released in black and white.

Under the Volcano ••• [1984]

Director: **John Huston**
Screenplay: **Guy Gallo**

During festivities for the Day of the Dead in a Mexican town, former British consul Finney does his bit for the old country by drinking to the health of Generals Gordon and Booth. This harrowing portrayal of a man right at the bottom of the slippery slope is superbly acted by Finney, a sorry sight amidst the visual splendour of the festivities. **[112m/15]**

Geoffrey Firmin .... Albert Finney
Yvonne Firmin .... Jacqueline Bisset
Hugh Firmin .... Anthony Andrews
Dr. Vigil .... Ignacio Lopez Tarso
Senora Gregoria .... Katy Jurado
Brit .... James Villiers

Unfaithfully Yours ••• [1984]

Director: **Howard Zieff**
Screenplay: **Valerie Curtin, Barry Levinson & Robert Klane**

Forget what they say about this remake of Preston Sturges' 1948 comedy with Rex Harrison not being a patch on the original. The original has dated terribly badly and raises very few laughs. This is no masterpiece, but the story of conductor

Moore plotting terrible revenge when he thinks wife Kinski has been conducting herself improperly is very funny in places. What's more, musician Moore looks as though he's actually leading the orchestra, rather than miming painting a wall like Harrison. [96m/15]

Claude Eastman	Dudley Moore
Daniella Eastman	Nastassja Kinski
Maxmillian Stein	Armand Assante
Norman Robbins	Albert Brooks
Carla Robbins	Cassie Yates

Unforgiven ••• [1992]

Director: **Clint Eastwood**
Screenplay: **David Webb Peoples**

A group of prostitutes offer a reward for the murder of the man who cut one of them up. Hog-farmer Eastwood saddles up one more time and sets off to do what a man's got to do. This Eastwood-directed Western is good, but nothing like as brilliant or unconventional as the critics maintained. There are several over-indulgent scenes of Clint riding through fields of swirling corn, while its supposed message preaching against violence is not particularly clear. But Hackman's superb as the psychotic sheriff and Harris and Rubineck are delightful as the Royalist killer and his biographer sidekick. [131m/15]

Bill Munny	Clint Eastwood
Little Bill Daggett	Gene Hackman
Ned Logan	Morgan Freeman
English Bob	Richard Harris
The "Schofield Kid"	Jaimz Woolvett
W.W.Beauchamp	Saul Rubinek
Strawberry Alice	Frances Fisher
Delilah Fitzgerald	Anna Thomson
Quick Mike	David Mucci
Davey Bunting	Rob Campbell
Skinny Dubois	Anthony James

Oscars Best Picture, Best Director, Gene Hackman

Quote 'I ain't like that no more.'

OOPS! Although English Bob shoots at pheasants from the train, they weren't introduced into America until 1882, the year after the film is set.

Psst! The film is dedicated to 'Sergio and Don', Sergio Leone and Don Siegel respectively ◆ Frances Fisher, playing 'Strawberry Alice', is Eastwood's partner ◆ Despite his association with Westerns, Eastwood is allergic to horses.

The Unholy • [1988]

Director: **Camilio Vila**
Screenplay: **Philip Yordan & Fernando Fonsea**

Father Ben Cross takes over at a New Orleans church, but the Devil is furious that he wasn't consulted in the selection process. Trevor Howard looks as lost as the audience, although even a saint could be led off the straight and narrow by the demonic Nicole Fortier. [100m/18]

Father Michael	Ben Cross
Archbishop Mosely	Hal Holbrook
Millie	Jill Carroll

Also: William Russ, Trevor Howard, Claudia Robinson, Ned Beatty, Nicole Fortier

Blurb You Haven't Got A Prayer.

Psst! This was Trevor Howard's last film.

Universal Soldier ••• [1992]

Director: **Roland Emmerich**
Screenplay: **Richard Rothstein, Christopher Leitch & Dean Devlin**

Dying GIs are brought back from Vietnam and turned into superhuman robotic soldiers for $250,000 a throw, a snip compared to the six million dollars such men used to cost. Van Damme rebels and goes on the lam, chased by Lundgren. Wham-bang action pic for the boys, keeping tongue nicely in cheek. Bizarre, though, that these guys can shoot through a telephone line but still miss an escaping car. [103m/18]

Luc	Jean-Claude Van Damme
Scott	Dolph Lundgren
Veronica	Ally Walker
Col. Perry	Ed O'Ross
Dr. Gregor	Jerry Orbach

Blurb The Future Has A Bad Attitude.

Unlawful Entry ••• [1992]

Director: Jonathan Kaplan
Screenplay: Lewis Colick

The Cop From Hell. After Russell and Stowe are burgled, they are delighted by solicitous cop Liotta. But when he develops the hots for Stowe, it's clear that he's at least one stripe short of a promotion and should be bundled out of uniform and into a strait jacket. Clear, that is, to everyone except Stowe's underwritten character. Occasionally ridiculous in its plotting and with a daft *Fatal Attraction*-type ending, this is still a pretty tense and exciting thriller. [111m/18]

Michael Carr	Kurt Russell
Officer Pete Davis	Ray Liotta
Karen Carr	Madeleine Stowe
Officer Roy Cole	Roger E. Mosley
Roger Graham	Ken Lerner
Penny	Deborah Offner

Untamed Heart ••• [1993]

Director: Tony Bill
Screenplay: Tom Sierchio

Waitress Tomei is saved from thugs by Slater, the taciturn guy who works in the kitchens. Despite a slender, and occasionally silly, thread of a plot, this is an innocent love story providing plenty of opportunities for a sob as well as a few laughs. It's the acting here that's so delightful, not only from the wonderful Tomei – proving that *My Cousin Vinny* was no flash in the pan – but also from Perez in another of her sassy, wise-cracking roles and even from Slater, who plays it all down nicely, even if he does take his shirt off yet again. [102m/15]

Adam	Christian Slater
Caroline	Marisa Tomei
Cindy	Rosie Perez
Howard	Kyle Secor
Patsy	Willie Garson

Quote 'My life is like watching The Three Stooges in Spanish.'

OOPS! When she comes with the cookies, his chin is fresh-shaven one moment and stubbled-bound the next.

Psst! Originally called *Baboon Heart* ◆ Madonna coveted the role that went to Tomei, but refused to take a screen test.

Until the End of the World ◆ [1992]

Director: Wim Wenders
Screenplay: Wim Wenders & Peter Carey

Watching this, you'll feel that the end of the world could come before the end credits. In 1999, Hurt is Wendering around the world and encounters a scientist with a device that lets blind people see. Interminable. [158m/15]

Trevor McPhee	William Hurt
Claire	Solveig Dommartin

Also: Sam Neill, Max Von Sydow, Rudiger Vogler, Jeanne Moreau

Psst! The film was originally six hours long and was filmed in 7 different countries in 15 cities.

The Untouchables •••• [1987]

Director: Brian de Palma
Screenplay: David Mamet

In the midst of Prohibition in Chicago, Treasury agent Eliot Ness decides to get tough with Al Capone, helped by gnarled cop Connery and a group of incorruptable colleagues. Although a little slow to start and rather confusing in the shoot-out scene with the horses, this is a taut, exciting gangster picture taken to a higher level by some excellent acting and occasionally inspired direction. Never mind that Ness really had nothing to do with convicting Capone. Just sit back and enjoy. [119m/15]

Eliot Ness	Kevin Costner
Jim Malone	Sean Connery
Oscar Wallace	Charles Martin Smith
George Stone	Andy Garcia
Al Capone	Robert De Niro
Mike	Richard Bradford
Payne	Jack Kehoe
George	Brad Sullivan
Nitti	Billy Drago

Oscars Sean Connery

Quote 'He's in the car.'

OOPS! In a warehouse raid, the crates have Canada's maple leaf symbol on them, thirty years before it was first used ✦ The amazing station steps sequence only lasts three minutes (even in slow motion), yet the clock shows that ten minutes passes ✦ The camera and crew can be seen in the reflection from a window in Connery's flat.

Psst! The final shoot out on the station steps, arguably the film's finest scene (albeit a rip-off of Eisenstein's *Battleship Potemkin*) was improvised by De Palma in a matter of hours when he was told that there was no money for the period train he wanted. The money, $200,000, went to pay off Bob Hoskins when Robert De Niro became available to play Al Capone. De Niro not only shoved plugs up his nose and, as usual, added weight, but also wore silk underwear from the firm that had supplied Capone.

Used People •• [1992]

Director: **Beeban Kidron**
Screenplay: **Todd Graff**

After 23 years worshipping her from afar, Mastroianni asks MacLaine out at her husband's wake. Despite this promising start, the film never really comes alive. Mastroianni is harder to understand in English than he is with subtitles while MacLaine looks shamefully younger than both her screen and real age. So many eccentric characters are crammed in, you long for somebody ordinary to appear. The most memorable scene is a view of the rooftops of Queens, chock-a-block with people looking through telescopes, on the night when the first men landed on the moon. [115m/15]

Pearl Berman	Shirley MacLaine
Bibby	Kathy Bates
Freida	Jessica Tandy
Joe Meledandri	Marcello Mastroianni
Norma	Marcia Gay Harden
Becky	Sylvia Sidney

Showing *The Graduate.*

V

Valley Girl ••• [1983]

Director: **Martha Coolidge**
Screenplay: **Wayne Crawford & Andrew Lane**

The routine plot has valley girl Foreman going out with wrong-trackside Cage, to the jeers of her peers. When she bows to pressure and drops him for the prom, he has to win her back. Despite the triteness of the storyline, it's so enjoyably put together that it carries you along. It's a little peculiar, though, seeing the young Nicolas Cage in something so mild and unsensational. [95m/15]

Randy	Nicolas Cage
Julie	Deborah Foreman
Loryn	E.G. Daily
Tommy	Michael Bowen
Fred	Cameron Dye
Suzie	Michelle Meyrink
Sarah	Colleen Camp
Steve	Frederic Forrest

Valmont ••• [1991]

Director: **Milos Forman**
Screenplay: **Jean-Claude Carriere**

This version of *Dangerous Liaisons* was delayed for almost three years to let people forget about the other one filmed at the same time. Although criticised for being softer than the source material, that actually makes it much more enjoyable while, largely thanks to Bening, this is also the sexier of the two by far. [137m/15]

Vicomte de Valmont	Colin Firth
Marquise de Merteuil	Annette Bening
Madame de Tourvel	Meg Tilly
Cecile de Volanges	Fairuza Balk
Madame de Volanges	Sian Phillips
Gercourt	Jeffrey Jones
Danceny	Henry Thomas

Madame de Rosemonde ....Fabia Drake
Baron ....T.P. McKenna
José ....Ronald Lacey
Jean ....Vincent Schiavelli

Vamp • [1986]

Director: **Richard Wenk**
Screenplay: **Richard Wenk**

Students on the look-out for a stripper for a college party stumble onto something far more sinister. Grace Jones' bump 'n' grind routine is the highlight of this wearisome, jokey horror spoof, which seriously overdoes the purple and green lighting. **[93m/18]**

Keith ....Chris Makepeace
Vic ....Sandy Baron
Also: Robert Rusler, Dedee Pfeiffer, Gedde Watanabe, Grace Jones

Vampire's Kiss ••• [1989]

Director: **Robert Bierman**
Screenplay: **Joseph Minion**

A truly peculiar black comedy with Cage as the yuppie who thinks that he's been bitten by a vampire and is turning into one himself. As the fangs aren't coming through yet, he has to buy them in a joke shop. If you hate Cage, you'll hate this, but his scintillating performance is pretty unforgettable. **[103m/18]**

Peter Loew ....Nicolas Cage
Alva Restrepo ....Maria Conchita Alonso
Rachel ....Jennifer Beals
Dr. Dorothy Glaser..............Elizabeth Ashley
Jackie...Kasi Lemmons
Emilio ....Bob Lujan

Psst! Cage swallowed a *real* cockroach to add veracity to one scene. He said, 'I wanted there to be a special moment in the film which would really shock...When I eventually saw *Vampire's Kiss* with an audience and heard their reaction, I knew it had been worth it'. Apparently, it took six takes to get it satisfactorily captured on film!

The Vanishing •• [1990]

Director: **George Sluizer**
Screenplay: **Tim Krabbé**

Although critics said that this Dutch thriller was in the Hitchcockian vein, the master would never have waited until the final minutes of a film before injecting any tension or excitement. A boy spends three years trying to find out what happened to his girlfriend, who went missing on a trip to France. The way he eventually discovers her fate is deeply disturbing and stays in the memory long afterwards. Despite this, in many ways the Hollywood remake is a little better. **[107m/12]**

Raymond ....Bernard-Pierre Donnadieu
Rex ....Gene Bervoets
Saskia...............................Johanna Ter Steege

The Vanishing •• [1993]

Director: **George Sluizer**
Screenplay: **Todd Graff**

An American remake by the original Dutch director, this version adds some ingenious plot twists to the scenario, but then blows everything in the ludicrous finale. Bridges is on top creepy form. **[110m/15]**

Barney ....Jeff Bridges
Jeff..Kiefer Sutherland
Rita ....Nancy Travis
Also: Sandra Bullock, Park Overall, Maggie Linderman, Lisa Eichhorn

The Verdict •••• [1982]

Director: **Sidney Lumet**
Screenplay: **David Mamet**

Lawyer Newman is so far gone that he resorts to touting for business at funerals. But, in taking up a malpractice case, he begins to claw back some self-respect. One of the very best of courtroom dramas, both Newman and opposing lawyer Mason are at the very peak of their form. **[128m/15]**

Frank Galvin ....Paul Newman
Laura Fischer ....Charlotte Rampling

Mickey Morrissey ....Jack Warden
Ed Concannon ....James Mason
Judge Hoyle ....Milo O'Shea
Kaitlin Costello Price ....Lindsay Crouse
Bishop Brophy............................Edward Binns
Maureen Brophy.........................Julie Bovasso
Sally Doneghy ....Roxanne Hart

Blurb Frank Galvin Has One Last Chance To Do Something Right.

Vice Versa ••   [1988]

Director: **Brian Gilbert**
Screenplay: **Dick Clement & Ian La Frenais**

Yet another body-swap flick, with father and son Reinhold and Savage picking up a few laughs. It's still not a patch on *Big*, though.   **[98m/PG]**

Marshall....................................Judge Reinhold
Charlie..Fred Savage
Sam ....Corinne Bohrer
Tina...Swoosie Kurtz

Videodrome •••   [1983]

Director: **David Cronenberg**
Screenplay: **David Cronenberg**

A porno TV manager becomes obsessed with a pirate S&M channel which has unusual side-effects on those who watch it. This is a highly original and creepy portrayal of our media-saturated age, with James Woods on top twitchy form and Debbie Harry as Nicki Brand, a human ashtray. Too many competing ideas make the last reel incomprehensible, but it remains haunting.   **[89m/18]**

Max Renn ....James Woods
Bianca..Sonja Smits
Nicki......................................Deborah Harry
Harlan.......................................Peter Dvorsky

Quote 'It's not that difficult to lie around naked on top of Debbie Harry all day, you know what I mean? Certain instincts take over after a while and make the scene really play.' [James Woods]

Psst! Over a minute was cut by the censors in Britain.

A View to a Kill ••   [1985]

Director: **John Glen**
Screenplay: **Richard Maibaum & Michael G. Wilson**

Roger Moore said goodbye to Bond with something of a whimper in this overlong and rather tired tale of baddie Walken planning to wipe out Silicon Valley. There's far too much boring talk and not enough action, although the airship scene above the Golden Gate Bridge is stirring and shaking stuff.

[131m/PG]

James Bond................................Roger Moore
Max Zorin......................Christopher Walken
Stacey Sutton ....Tanya Roberts
May Day......................................Grace Jones
Also: Patrick Macnee, Patrick Bauchau, Fiona Fullerton, Alison Doody, Desmond Llewelyn, Robert Brown, Lois Maxwell

Psst! Look out for Dolph Lundgren in a bit part ✦ The film was known in Hong Kong as *The Indestructible Iron Man Fights Against the Electronic Gang* ✦ On every picture, Moore insists on being given an unlimited supply of Montecristo havanas. The bill on one Bond film was over $3,000.

Vincent and Theo •••   [1990]

Director: **Robert Altman**
Screenplay: **Julian Mitchell**

The sad later life of Vincent Van G., focussing on his hard, neglected years and the efforts of his brother to get him recognised, although with one ear you'd have thought him easy to recognise. Yet another Van Gogh biopic, but arguably the finest, lifted by the unusual direction of Altman and the intense acting of Roth as the man himself.

[140m/15]

Vincent Van Gogh ....Tim Roth
Theo Van Gogh...............................Paul Rhys
Jo Bonger ....Johanna Ter Steege
Paul Gauguin.................Wladimir Yordanoff

V.I. Warshawski •• [1992]

Director: **Jeff Kanew**
Screenplay: **Edward Taylor, David Aaron Cohen & Nick Thiel**

Turner as a tough-boiled, leggy, private eye sounds like a casting-director's dream. But a dreadful script and direction ruin this story of the unmaternal V.I. hired by a 13-year-old girl to find her father's killer. Despite her use of nut-crackers in a rather literal sense, the pic's mostly far too soft-hearted. [89m/15]

Victoria I. Warshawski .... Kathleen Turner
Murray Ryerson .... Jay O. Sanders
Lieutenant Mallory .... Charles Durning
Kat Grafalk .... Angela Goethals

Quote 'You know how hard it is to get blood out of cashmere?' • 'Likes her drinks hard and her men too.' [American film reviewer]

Volunteers • [1985]

Director: **Nicholas Meyer**
Screenplay: **Ken Levine & David Isaacs**

Take one step backwards if someone suggests this one. Hanks is a rich kid who mistakenly joins the Peace Corps and ends up building a bridge in Thailand. Hard to know what it was aiming to be. If it was a comedy, it's missed by a mile. [107m/15]

Lawrence Bourne III .... Tom Hanks
Tom Tuttle .... John Candy
Beth Wexler .... Rita Wilson

Voyager ••• [1992]

Director: **Volker Schlondorff**
Screenplay: **Volker Schlondorff & Rudy Wurlitzer**

Shepard is a rootless, roaming engineer who refuses to get tied down until he's caught up in a spiral of coincidences. When he finds himself unusually attracted to Delpy, he's probably the only one who can't guess what's coming next. A surprisingly entertaining and fascinating film. [117m/15]

Walter Faber .... Sam Shepard
Sabeth .... Julie Delpy
Hannah .... Barbara Sukowa
Herbert Henke .... Dieter Kirchlechner

Waiting for the Light ••• [1990]

Director: **Christopher Monger**
Screenplay: **Christopher Monger**

A heart-warming fable set at the time of the Cuban missile crisis. Garr is the single mother having to cope not only with a couple of mischievous kids, but also a troublesome aunt MacLaine. She's at her eccentric best in this slight, but wholly charming comedy. [102m/PG]

Aunt Zena .... Shirley MacLaine
Kay Harris .... Teri Garr
Joe .... Clancy Brown
Mullins .... Vincent Schiavelli
Emily .... Hillary Wolf
Eddie .... Colin Baumgartner

Walker • [1987]

Director: **Alex Cox**
Screenplay: **Rudy Wurlitzer**

In the mid-19th century an American soldier of fortune took over Nicaragua for a couple of years. That history lesson out of the way, there's no earthly reason to watch this leaden attempt to turn the story into a condemnation of America's recent misadventures in the region. [95m/18]

William Walker .... Ed Harris
Ephraim Squier .... Richard Masur
Maj. Henningson .... Rene Auberjonois

OOPS! Apparently Marlee Martin says something pretty rude in sign language at one point.

Walls of Glass •• [1985]

Director: Scott Goldstein
Screenplay: Edmond Collins & Scott Goldstein

Bosco is an actor who dreams of being a Shakespearian actor. We just want to be taken to the end of the film in a straight line, but instead we're taken all round the houses while the meter's running. Also known as *Flanagan*. [86m/15]

James Flanagan	Philip Bosco
Mama	Geraldine Page
Andrea	Linda Thorson
Papa	William Hickey
Mary	Olympia Dukakis

Wall Street ••• [1987]

Director: Oliver Stone
Screenplay: Stanley Weiser & Oliver Stone

This tale of an Ivan Boesky-like corporate raider is now almost as fascinating as a picture of a bygone era as it is a rattling good yarn. Sheen is excellent as the young broker so eager to get in with Douglas that he'll do almost anything. But it's Douglas's compelling performance as the lord of all he surveys that makes the picture so riveting even if, as so often with Stone, things are rather too black and white to be wholly convincing. [124m/15]

Gordon Gekko	Michael Douglas
Bud Fox	Charlie Sheen
Carl Fox	Martin Sheen
Darien Taylor	Daryl Hannah
Sir Larry Wildman	Terence Stamp
Kate Gekko	Sean Young
Realtor	Sylvia Miles
Roger Barnes	James Spader
Marvin	John C. McGinley
Lou Mannheim	Hal Holbrook
Cromwell	Richard Dysart
Harold Salt	Saul Rubinek
Muffie Livingston	Annie McEnroe
Stone Livingston	Paul Guilfoyle

Oscars Michael Douglas

Quote 'Greed is good. Greed is right. Greed works. Greed will save the USA!' • 'Lunch is for wimps!'

Psst! The movie was originally called *Greed* • It is dedicated to Louis, Oliver's stockbroker father • Stone appears very briefly during a split-screen Wall Street sequence • Martin and Charlie Sheen are, of course, father and son • Young was fired during filming, only finding out when she discovered Hannah delivering one of her lines. The story that when she was tasked leaving the studio with a costume on, she simply stripped off all her clothes is, it appears, another of those legends with little basis in fact.

Wanted: Dead or Alive •• [1987]

Director: Gary Sherman
Screenplay: Michael Patrick Goodman, Brian Taggert & Gary Sherman

Actioner with Hauer an ex-CIA operative who's now in the bounty hunter business. There's some pretty good, though violent, action sequences, but little else. [104m/18]

Nick Randall	Rutger Hauer
Malak Al Rahim	Gene Simmons
Philmore Walker	Robert Guillaume
Terry	Mel Harris

WarGames •••• [1983]

Director: John Badham
Screenplay: Lawrence Lasker & Walter F. Parkes

Computer whizzkid Broderick hacks into a computer and starts playing a game called Thermonuclear War, only to discover that the game's for real. An invigoratingly entertaining and nail-biting thriller, with plenty of laughs, a little romance and just the teeniest bit of preaching. Surprisingly re-watchable, too. [113m/PG]

David Lightman	Matthew Broderick
Jennifer	Ally Sheedy
McKittrick	Dabney Coleman
Falken	John Wood
General Berringer	Barry Corbin
Pat Healy	Juanin Clay
Cabot	Kent Williams
Watson	Dennis Lipscomb

Quote 'Goddamn it. I'd piss on a spark plug if I thought it would do any good!'

Psst! Originally a 'message' film, when market research showed how little the public wanted a film about nuclear war, director Martin Brest (*Beverly Hills Cop*) was fired, the film was pepped up and the original ending, which had the Biggest Bang of all, was junked ✦ MGM head honcho Freddie Fields was dissuaded from including one more shot showing Broderick and Sheedy walking into the sunset ✦ This is the movie Costner left *after* filming had begun, in order to be in *The Big Chill*, only to have his part dropped almost entirely ✦ Said to be one of Ronald Reagan's favourite films.

Warlock •• [1989]

Director: **Steve Miner**
Screenplay: **David Twohy**

Jumping in time from 1691 to 1991, an evil warlock sets off to find the scattered pages of the Grand Grimoire (all of which are in America for some inexplicable reason) and thus end the world. The special effects are a mite ropey but the thrills are delivered with a touch of eccentric humour.

[100m/15]

Giles Redferne	Richard E. Grant
Warlock	Julian Sands
Kassandra	Lori Singer
Chas	Kevin O'Brien

The War of the Roses •• [1989]

Director: **Danny DeVito**
Screenplay: **Michael Leeson**

Even black comedies are supposed to be funny. And while there are incidental delights in this tale of the dream marriage that turns into the ultimate nightmare, all we are really witnessing is a tit-for-tat battle of the sort that Laurel and Hardy did so much better many years before. In its latter stages, it achieves a level of silliness even Stan and Ollie wouldn't have dared attempt but, without a sympathetic character to latch onto, it leaves us detached from the proceedings. [111m/15]

Oliver Rose	Michael Douglas
Barbara Rose	Kathleen Turner
Gavin D'Amato	Danny DeVito
Susan	Marianne Sägebrecht

Blurb Once In A Lifetime Comes A Motion Picture That Makes You Feel Like Falling In Love All Over Again. This Is Not That Movie.

Quote 'When I watch you eat, when I see you sleep, when I look at you lately, I just want to smash your face in.'

OOPS! When Douglas and DeVito are in the latter's office discussing splitting the house, Douglas calls DeVito by his real name at one point.

Psst! The original ending had the Roses murdering each other ✦ The film-makers bottled out in other areas, too. That shot of the dog *after* the paté scene was inserted at the last moment.

War Party •• [1989]

Director: **Franc Roddam**
Screenplay: **Spencer Eastman**

During a reconstruction of a famous Cowboys and Indians battle, a white man is killed and a group of Indians have to take to the hills, pursued by a mob. An intriguing way of updating the Western is frittered away. [96m/18]

Sonny Crowkiller	Billy Wirth
Skitty Harris	Kevin Dillon
Warren Cutfoot	Tim Sampson
Jay Stivic	Jimmie Ray Weeks

War Zone • [1987]

Director: **Nathaniel Gutman**
Screenplay: **Hanan Peled**

Tedious thriller with Walken a TV journalist in Beirut waking up to the horrors of war, just as we drift gently off to sleep. Also known as *Deadline*.

[99m/15]

Don Stevens	Christopher Walken
Linda Larson	Marita Marschall
Mike Jessop	Hywel Bennett

Watchers • [1988]

Director: **Jon Hess**
Screenplay: **Bill Freed & Damian Lee**

A couple of genetically-engineered animals escape from the government laboratory where they've been created and run amok. This horror-splatter flick is a real dog – crossed with a bit of a monkey, a bear and an alligator. **[92m/18]**

Travis	Corey Haim
Nora	Barbara Williams
Lem	Michael Ironside

Water • [1985]

Director: **Dick Clement**
Screenplay: **Dick Clement, Ian La Frenais & Bill Persky**

A British commonwealth island is discovered to have a source of mineral water. Unfortunately, this *Water* turns out to be flat rather than sparkling. It's even more unfunny for pretending to be a Falklands' allegory. **[95m/15]**

Baxter	Michael Caine
Pamela	Valerie Perrine
Bianca	Brenda Vaccaro

Also: Billy Connolly, Leonard Rossiter, Maureen Lipman, Dennis Dugan, Fulton Mackay, Fred Gwynne

The Waterdance •••• [1992]

Director: **Neal Jimenez & Michael Steinberg**
Screenplay: **Neal Jimenez**

Don't be put off by the subject matter. Far from being depressing, this story of a group of paraplegics in a hospital ward coming to terms with their lot, is a life-enhancing, often downright hilarious, tale of the triumph of the human spirit. We are caught up from the word go as Stoltz tries to cope with his fragile and now unconsummated relationship with married Hunt. A superlative piece of story-telling, with excellent performances from everyone, but particularly Forsythe as the racist biker, and Snipes as the lippy erstwhile ladies' man. **[107m/15]**

Joel	Eric Stoltz
Anna	Helen Hunt
Bloss	William Forsythe
Ray	Wesley Snipes
Rosa	Elizabeth Pena

Psst! The story is based on the personal experiences of writer Jimenez, wheelchair-bound after a similar accident.

Waterland ••• [1992]

Director: **Stephen Gyllenhaal**
Screenplay: **Peter Prince**

An English history teacher in Philadelphia tells his pupils of his extraordinary childhood in the Fen country during World War II. Although disappointing devotees of Graham Swift's novel, the gradually unfolding tragedy is utterly absorbing. An intelligent film, marred only by the daftness of the present-day subplot about a stolen baby. **[95m/15]**

Tom Crick	Jeremy Irons
Mathew Price	Ethan Hawke
Mary Crick	Sinead Cusack
Lewis Scott	John Heard
Judy Dobson	Cara Buono
Young Tom	Grant Warnock
Young Mary	Lena Headey

Waxwork •• [1988]

Director: **Anthony Hickox**
Screenplay: **Anthony Hickox**

Reasonably entertaining horror flick, with a group of teenagers in their local macabre museum getting caught up in a fight with the real counterparts of the exhibits. **[97m/18]**

Mark	Zach Galligan
Sarah Brightman	Deborah Foreman
Mr. Lincoln	David Warner
China	Michelle Johnson

Wayne's World •••• [1992]

Director: **Penelope Spheeris**
Screenplay: **Mike Myers, Bonnie Turner & Terry Turner**

A pair of dweebish teenagers running a public-access cable show from their mum's basement get a shot at the big-time. This comedy, full of references to 60's TV shows and heavy metal is infantile, silly, pointless and thus hysterically funny to those who love childish humour. On top of that, the babes are great, with Carrere particularly babelicious. Deep philosophy question, NOT! Which came first? Wayne and Garth or Bill and Ted? Who knows? Who cares? Love 'em all. For those of mature years, this should be essential viewing for its perceptive insights into youth culture. **[95m/PG]**

Wayne Campbell	Mike Myers
Garth Algar	Dana Carvey
Benjamin Oliver	Rob Lowe
Cassandra	Tia Carrere
Noah Vanderhoff	Brian Doyle-Murray
Stacy	Lara Flynn Boyle
Russell	Kurt Fuller
Mrs. Vanderhoff	Colleen Camp

Blurb You'll Laugh. You'll Cry. You'll Hurl.

Quote 'Party on.' ✦ 'Excellent.' ✦ 'NOT!' ✦ 'And monkeys might fly out my butt.'

Psst! There are plenty of cameos. Alice Cooper's easy to spot, that's Meat Loaf as a bouncer, Ione Skye as Lowe's suspiciously underage-looking girlfriend and Donna Dixon (Dan Aykroyd's wife) as Garth's dream girl.

Weekend at Bernie's •• [1989]

Director: Ted Kotcheff
Screenplay: Robert Klane

A film dies in its first few minutes, but a group of actors prop it up and spend another hour and a half pretending it's still alive. With a smattering of laughs along the way, this comedy has McCarthy and Silverman doing everything they can to convince people that their murdered boss is still in the land of the living. The best performance on screen is from Terry Kiser as the corpse, a role he is set to reprise in the sequel! **[99m/12]**

Larry Wilson	Andrew McCarthy
Richard Parker	Jonathan Silverman
Gwen Saunders	Catherine Mary Stewart

Weird Science • [1985]

Director: John Hughes
Screenplay: John Hughes

A couple of nerds who have trouble with girls invent one of their own, managing to conjure up Kelly LeBrock. Not bad for their first go. Hughes at his most infantile and least amusing. **[94m/15]**

Gary	Anthony Michael Hall
Lisa	Kelly LeBrock
Wyatt	Ilan Mitchell-Smith

Psst! John Hughes established a Hollywood record with this film, completing the script in just two days.

Welcome Home • [1989]

Director: Franklin J. Schaffner
Screenplay: Maggie Kleinman

Yet another returning Vietnam vet. The twist is that he's taken 17 years to get home, though that doesn't stop him being surprised that people have gone on with their lives. All the excitement of watching ditch water stagnate. **[92m/15]**

Jake Robbins	Kris Kristofferson
Sarah	JoBeth Williams
Woody	Sam Waterston

Welcome Home, Roxy Carmichael ••• [1990]

Director: Jim Abrahams
Screenplay: Karen Leigh Hopkins

Quirky comedy about a town galvanised by the forthcoming homecoming of its only famous citizen, with Ryder a little more excited than everyone else. A charming and quite delightful little film. **[95m/12]**

Dinky Bossetti	Winona Ryder
Denton Webb	Jeff Daniels
Elizabeth Zaks	Laila Robins
Gerald Howells	Thomas Wilson Brown
Barbara Webb	Joan McMurtrey
Les Bossetti	Graham Beckel

Also: Sachi Parker, Frances Fisher, Robby Kiger, Dinah Manoff, Stephen Tobolowsky

Wendy Cracked a Walnut • [1991]

Director: **Michael Pattison**
Screenplay: **Suzanne Hawley**

...But We Don't Crack A Smile. This pathetic comedy limped into release in the UK and disappeared immediately. Arquette's a bored housewife who has a succession of uninspired and uninspiring fantasies.   [87m/PG]

Wendy ....Rosanna Arquette
Ronnie...Bruce Spence
Jake...Hugo Weaving

We of the Never Never ••• [1983]

Director: **Igor Auzins**
Screenplay: **Peter Schreck**

A fascinating true tale of one of the first white women to venture into untamed Australia. This story of her struggle to be accepted as an equal and then to survive on her own when her husband dies is a mite slow and overlong. It's all beautiful to look at but a little lacking in the drama department. Some shearing of the wooliness before release wouldn't have hurt.

[134m/U]

Jeannie....................Angela Punch McGregor
Aenus Gunn ....Arthur Dignam
Mac..Tony Barry
Jackeroo....................................Tommy Lewis
Jack....................................Lewis Fitz-Gerald
Dan.......................................Martin Vaughan

We're No Angels • [1989]

Director: **Neil Jordan**
Screenplay: **David Mamet**

...And This Is No Comedy. As if *High Spirits* wasn't bad enough, Jordan now brings his comic touch to this remake of the 1955 Bogart pic that wasn't too funny to begin with. Penn and De Niro are escaped convicts who disguise themselves as priests. Now if only they'd donned nuns' habits, they might have had something.   [106m/15]

Ned......................................Robert De Niro
Jim...Sean Penn
Molly..Demi Moore
Also: Hoyt Axton, Bruno Kirby, Ray McAnally, James Russo, Wallace Shawn
Quote 'Sentiment has no cash value.'

Wetherby •• [1985]

Director: **David Hare**
Screenplay: **David Hare**

School teacher Redgrave meets a nice but intense young man who promptly blows his brains out in front of her. Hare is a great playwright and TV director. But his feature films, of which this is the first, incline towards the glacial and ponderous.
[102m/15]

Jean Travers.......................Vanessa Redgrave
Stanley Pilborough..............................Ian Holm
Marcia Pilborough ....Judi Dench
Verity Braithwaite ....Marjorie Yates

We Think the World of You •• [1988]

Director: **Colin Gregg**
Screenplay: **Hugh Stoddart**

With his lover Oldman in prison, Bates has to look after his dog and becomes obsessed with it. Despite the nicely weird premise, it's a bit depressing and slow.
[91m/PG]

Frank Meadows ....Alan Bates
Johnny....................................Gary Oldman
Megan ....Frances Barber
Millie..Liz Smith

The Whales of August ••• [1987]

Director: **Lindsay Anderson**
Screenplay: **David Berry**

If you want to see what real old fashioned film-acting was all about, look no further than this tale of two elderly spinster sisters spending the summer of 1954 in Maine. Davis is the blind crabby one, while Gish is the kind one who's looked after her for over a decade. As they squabble about whether to put in a window to see the whales that don't come anymore, the elegant Price flatters them. The script's a little flat, but what a joy it is to see the three principals strutting their stuff. **[91m/U]**

Libby Strong	Bette Davis
Sarah Webber	Lillian Gish
Mr. Maranov	Vincent Price
Tisha Doughty	Ann Southern
Joshua Brackett	Harry Carey Jr.
Young Sarah	Mary Steenburgen

Psst! Aged 94, this was the last film role for Lillian Gish. She had the longest-ever film career, beginning in 1912 at the age of 19 in *An Unseen Enemy*. She died in 1993 ✦ Although Gish rarely spoke ill of anybody, even she confessed to finding Davis tough going, saying she could understand why her co-stars so often retired from the profession after working with her.

What About Bob? ●●● [1991]

Director: **Frank Oz**
Screenplay: **Tom Schulman**

When shrink Dreyfuss goes on holiday, Bob, a totally dependent patient, shows up. This enjoyable satire on the therapy business has a sharper edge than most Disney products and less ingratiating performances than one would expect. **[110m/PG]**

Bob Wiley	Bill Murray
Dr. Leo Marvin	Richard Dreyfuss
Fay Marvin	Julie Hagerty
Siggy Marvin	Charlie Korsmo
Anna Marvin	Kathryn Erbe
Mr. Guttman	Tom Aldredge

Quote 'Roses are red, Violets are Blue. I'm a schizophrenic, And so am I.'

Psst! One of those movies where the off-screen antics were almost as much fun. Clashes between Murray and producer Laura Ziskin led him, at one point, to a screaming match during which he tore her glasses off and broke them in two.

When Harry Met Sally ●●●● [1989]

Director: **Rob Reiner**
Screenplay: **Nora Ephron**

Hilarious examination of the age-old question: Can men and women be friends as well as lovers? Extraordinarily witty and wise, everything about this movie is spot on. The actors are perfect for their roles, the direction is unobtrusive and the mix between humour, sentiment and plot is just right. Unlike so many other comedies, it also works well on repeated viewings. **[95m/15]**

Harry Burns	Billy Crystal
Sally Albright	Meg Ryan
Marie	Carrie Fisher
Jess	Bruno Kirby
Joe	Steven Ford
Alice	Lisa Jane Persky
Amanda	Michelle Nicastro
Helen	Harley Jane Kozak

Quote 'I'll have what she's having.' ✦ 'Women need a reason to have sex. Men need a place.' ✦ 'You made a woman miaow?'

Showing *Casablanca.*

Psst! At the end of the justly-famous restaurant episode, Meg Ryan was presented with a salami by the crew ✦ The famous reaction line to Ryan's performance is said by Estelle Reiner, the director's mother ✦ The film was to have been called *It Had To Be You*, but another film in development already had that name. Another rejected name was *Boy Meets Girl* ✦ For the New Year's Eve scene, 200 bulbs in the Empire State Building were changed to a seasonal red and green for three days. It appears in the background for only 20 seconds.

When I Fall in Love ●● [1988]

Director: **Taylor Hackford**
Screenplay: **Tom Rickman**

A quarter of a century in the company of one-time football star Quaid and his former beauty queen wife Lange. If Mills and

Boon did stories about American foot-
ballers, this would be one. So soapy you
could wash with it, it's saved only by
some good acting, particularly from the
ever-reliable Lange. Also known as
Everybody's All-American.

[127m/15]

Babs Rogers	Jessica Lange
Gavin Grey	Dennis Quaid
Donnie 'Cake'	Timothy Hutton
Lawrence	John Goodman

Psst! So worried were the distributors
about the prospects for this film in
Britain that they released it on video first
and then, when it did well, put it into the
cinemas ✦ Quaid put on forty pounds for
the part.

When the Whales Came •• [1989]

Director: Clive Rees
Screenplay: Michael Morpurgo

A couple of children on the Scilly Isles in
1914 befriend hermit Scofield. Together
they save a school of whales. A surprisingly dour and lifeless tale. [100m/U]

The Birdman	Paul Scofield
Gracie Jenkins	Helen Pearce
Daniel Pender	Max Rennie
Jack Jenkins	David Threlfall
Clemmie Jenkins	Helen Mirren

When the Wind Blows •• [1987]

Director: Jimmy T. Murakami
Screenplay: Raymond Briggs

How odd that one of the most effective
depictions of the horror of nuclear war
should be a cartoon, with Mills and
Ashcroft voicing the slightly simple couple who make the mistake of following
those nice government leaflets to the letter. Overlong and occasionally a little
silly, it's still pretty powerful at times.

[84m/PG]

Hilda Bloggs	Peggy Ashcroft
James Bloggs	John Mills

Where Angels Fear to Tread •• [1991]

Director: Charles Sturridge
Screenplay: Derek Granger, Charles
Sturridge & Tim Sullivan

British widow Mirren falls for an Italian,
a liaison of which her family strongly dis-
approve. This okay Brit Lit adaptation is
as pretty and well acted as one would
expect, but turns out to be less Merchant
Ivory than Grocer Bakelite. [113m/PG]

Caroline Abbott	Helena Bonham Carter
Harriet Herriton	Judy Davis
Philip Herriton	Rupert Graves
Gino Carella	Giovanni Guidelli
Mrs. Herriton	Barbara Jefford
Lilia Herriton	Helen Mirren

Quote 'Some people are born not to do
things, and I am one of them.'

Where the Boys Are '84 • [1984]

Director: Hy Auerbach
Screenplay: Stu Krieger & Jeff Burkhart

If there *was* a reason for remaking a 1960
beach movie about a group of randy girls
on holiday, it must have been forgotten by
the time the cameras rolled. About as
enjoyable as getting damp sand in your
underwear. [97m/15]

Jennie	Lisa Hartman
Scott	Russell Todd
Carole	Lorna Luft

Where the Heart Is • [1990]

Director: John Boorman
Screenplay: Telsche Boorman & John
Boorman

A desperate attempt at comedy from people who obviously don't know that it's
supposed to make you laugh. Fed up of his
maturing kids sponging off him, Coleman
instals them in a slum building to fend for
themselves. Like the building, this film
should be condemned. [107m/15]

Stewart McBain	Dabney Coleman
Daphne McBain	Uma Thurman
Jean McBain	Joanna Cassidy

The Whistle Blower •• [1987]

Director: **Simon Langton**
Screenplay: **Julian Bond**

When no-questions-asked patriot Caine discovers that his son's death might be related to his stirring up trouble at his top secret GCHQ job, he does some digging of his own. What he finds threatens to undermine all he holds dear. Despite its topicality upon release, it was never an exciting thriller and seems a little slow and dated now.   **[104m/PG]**

Frank Jones	Michael Caine
Lord	James Fox
Bob Jones	Nigel Havers
Cynthia Goodburn	Felicity Dean
Sir Adrian Chapple	John Gielgud

White Dog •• [1982]

Director: **Sam Fuller**
Screenplay: **Sam Fuller & Curtis Hanson**

This tale of actress McNichol taking in a dog trained to attack blacks raised such a storm in the States that it was never released in cinemas. The fuss was ludicrous because the film attacks racism, not celebrates it. Unfortunately, while the dog might have a tight grip, the movie doesn't.   **[90m/18]**

Julie Sawyer	Kristy McNichol
Keys	Paul Winfield
Carruthers	Burl Ives
Roland Gray	James Parker

Psst! In the film, the dog is a killer that McNichol tries to have retrained, but when it turned up on American TV the studio had erased any mention of the dog's homicidal tendencies ◆ Director Fuller appears in a small cameo as Julie's agent.

White Fang ••• [1990]

Director: **Randal Kleiser**
Screenplay: **Jeanne Rosenberg, Nick Thiel & David Fallon**

A young lad, in Alaska to pick up a little of the yellow stuff during the Gold Rush, makes friends with a wolf, thus standing him in good stead for a future career in Hollywood. A well-made version of the famous Jack London book.   **[108m/PG]**

Alex Larson	Klaus Maria Brandauer
Jack Conroy	Ethan Hawke
Skunker	Seymour Cassel
Belinda	Susan Hogan
Beauty Smith	James Remar
Luke	Bill Moseley

Psst! Animal rights activists demanded that the film-makers remove a scene in which a wolf attacks a man, describing it as 'an anti-wolf statement'. At their insistence, the film carries the message that: 'There is no documented case in North America of a healthy wolf or pack of wolves attacking a human'.
◆ Around 50 people were on hand to look after the dogs and wolves, one of whose jobs involved a shovel!
◆ The snow caused problems. Normally potato flakes are used to simulate it, but they discovered that the dogs simply ate it.

White Hunter, Black Heart •• [1990]

Director: **Clint Eastwood**
Screenplay: **Peter Viertel, James Bridges & Burt Kennedy**

A film director shooting a movie in Africa is more intent on shooting animals instead. In this fictionalised account of John Huston at work and play on *The African Queen*, Clint gives one of his richest and least typical performances. Unfortunately the script, left lying around in the sun for too long, has definitely gone off.

[112m/PG]

John Wilson	Clint Eastwood
Pete Verrill	Jeff Fahey
Paul Landers	George Dzundza
Ralph Lockhart	Alun Armstrong
Kay Gibson	Marisa Berenson
Hodkins	Timothy Spall

White Men Can't Jump •••• [1992]

Director: Ron Shelton
Screenplay: Ron Shelton

A vastly entertaining mismatched buddy pic from the creator of *Bull Durham*. This time the sport is basketball, with Harrelson making a living capitalising on blacks' belief that no white man can play the sport properly. It's screamingly funny, on and off the court, with Perez a particular stand-out as Harrelson's quiz-show obsessed girlfriend. Great fun whether you're interested in basketball or not.   [112m/15]

Sidney Deane ....Wesley Snipes
Billy Hoyle ....Woody Harrelson
Gloria Clemente ....Rosie Perez
Rhonda Deane ....Tyra Ferrell
Robert..Cylk Cozart
Junior..................................Kadeem Hardison
George.................................Ernest Harden Jr.
Walter.............................John Marshall Jones
Blurb It Ain't Easy Being This Good.
Quote 'Your mother's an astronaut.'

White Mischief •• [1988]

Director: Michael Radford
Screenplay: Michael Radford & Jonathan Gems

Wartime life in the British Happy Valley colony in Kenya is enlivened by the arrival of a playboy, and positively galvanised when he is shot. Although it's a true story, they're a dreary and unlikeable bunch of people. Only odd moments like Charles Dance in a dress and Sarah Miles' masturbation scene hold any morbid interest.   [106m/18]

Alice de Janze...............................Sarah Miles
Sir 'Jock' Broughton.....................Joss Ackland
Gilbert Colvile....................................John Hurt
Diana Broughton........................Greta Scacchi
Earl of Errol............................Charles Dance
Also: Geraldine Chaplin, Trevor Howard, Alan Dobie, Hugh Grant, Ray McAnally
Quote 'Oh God, not another fucking beautiful day.'

White Nights •• [1985]

Director: Taylor Hackford
Screenplay: James Goldman & Eric Hughes

A Russian ballet star who defected to the West finds himself a prisoner when his plane crash lands in the Soviet Union. Although there are some good dance sequences if you're into that sort of thing, they're surrounded by a pathetic and over-complicated thriller plot that's got two left feet.   [135m/PG]

Nikolai Rodchenko.........Mikhail Baryshnikov
Raymond Greenwood..............Gregory Hines
Col. Chaiko ....Jerzy Skolimowski
Galina Ivanova ....Helen Mirren
Psst! This was Isabella Rossellini's first film.

White of the Eye ••• [1987]

Director: Donald Cammell
Screenplay: China Cammell & Donald Cammell

Designer murders are being committed on women in Arizona. Moriarty can't decide if her husband or ex-lover is responsible. Forget the Indian mumbo-jumbo; this is a highly sophisticated slasher flick with an intelligent heroine well to the fore and some sour observations on American machismo. The opening kitchen murder is a dazzling piece of cinematic virtuosity.   [111m/18]

Paul White ....David Keith
Joan White ....Cathy Moriarty
Mike Desantos........................Alan Rosenberg
Mendoza ....Art Evans

White Palace ••• [1990]

Director: Luis Mandoki
Screenplay: Ted Tally & Alvin Sargent

Young yuppie Spader is feeling down until he's picked up by sexy older Sarandon. Can their relationship survive the difference in their social and ethnic backgrounds? Although a little unbelievable in places, the superb performances from the leads sweep us along in this often sexy love story with a difference.

[105m/18]

Nora Baker	Susan Sarandon
Max Baron	James Spader
Neil	Jason Alexander
Rosemary	Kathy Bates
Judy	Eileen Brennan
Sol Horowitz	Steven Hill

Blurb The Story Of A Younger Man And A Bolder Woman.

OOPS! Although the electricity is off, the little light in the fridge still comes on when the door is opened.

Psst! Sarandon added 20 lb for the part.

White Sands ••• [1992]

Director: **Roger Donaldson**
Screenplay: **Daniel Pyne**

This constantly entertaining thriller has Dafoe as the small-town cop who worries away at a murder investigation, falling foul of an FBI arms-busting operation. Although the plot makes little sense in places, it's stylish, atmospheric and intriguing throughout, while the New Mexico scenery is wonderful. The acting's excellent, even from Mickey Rourke as a psychotic arms dealer. [101m/15]

Ray Dolezal	Willem Dafoe
Lane Bodine	Mary Elizabeth Mastrantonio
Gorman Lennox	Mickey Rourke
Greg Meeker	Samuel L. Jackson
Bert Gibson	M. Emmet Walsh
Flynn	James Rebhorn

Psst! Mimi Rogers makes an uncredited appearance early on as Dafoe's wife. Her far bigger part was cut to ribbons in the editing.

Who Framed Roger Rabbit? ••• [1988]

Director: **Robert Zemeckis**
Screenplay: **Jeffrey Price & Peter S. Seaman**

...Or *Who Rogered Jessica Rabbit*, as some wags had it. In 40's Los Angeles, cartoon characters exist alongside humans. When Roger is accused of murder, he turns to private eye Hoskins for help. Despite the presence of the sexiest cartoon character ever in Jessica Rabbit, it's mainly worth watching to admire the technical achievement, rather than the lacklustre story. You never really get involved in what's going on, although Hoskins does his best when you consider that he was acting against thin air for much of the time.

[103m/PG]

Eddie Valiant	Bob Hoskins
Judge Doom	Christopher Lloyd
Dolores	Joanna Cassidy
Marvin Acme	Stubby Kaye
R. K. Maroon	Alan Tilvern
Raoul, the director	Joel Silver
Roger	Charles Fleischer
Jessica (speaking)	Kathleen Turner
Jessica (singing)	Amy Irving
Baby Herman	Lou Hirsch
Daffy Duck	Mel Blanc
Singing Sword	Frank Sinatra

Quote 'I'm not bad. I'm just drawn that way.'

Psst! The book's title was *Who Censored Roger Rabbit?*, appropriately perhaps as a momentary flash of her boobs by Betty Boop was excised by the studio from the video version. However, slow down the moment early on when Baby Herman storms off the set and through a woman's legs and you'll see something else the studio probably wishes it had cut ♦ Felix and Popeye refused to appear, claiming that the $5,000 on offer wasn't enough ♦ To help Hoskins, Fleischer wore a rabbit costume for the four months he did Roger's voice ♦ Seven hundred and forty-three people were credited on the film, a record ♦ In Golders Green, a storm changed the title at one cinema to *Who Framed Roger Rabbi?* ♦ The exterior of the Acme factory is actually London Transport's Shepherd's Bush bus depot ♦ The director of the film at the beginning is Joel Silver, producer of some of the best action pictures of the past decade.

Whoops Apocalypse •• [1987]

Director: **Tom Bussmann**
Screenplay: **Andrew Marshall & David Renwick**

Although less disciplined and funny than the British TV series from which it was adapted, there are still plenty of laughs in this fast-paced comedy about the countdown to nuclear Armageddon, which comes about in the unlikeliest way. Don't forget: Wear Your Mushroom With Pride. **[91m/15]**

President Adams	Loretta Swit
Sir Mortimer Chris	Peter Cook
Lacrobat	Michael Richards
Specialist Catering Commander	Rik Mayall

Also: Ian Richardson, Alexei Sayle, Herbert Lom

Whore • [1991]

Director: **Ken Russell**
Screenplay: **Ken Russell & Deborah Dalton**

The life and slime in the career of an LA hooker. Putting the two Russells, Ken and Theresa, together should have been a dream team in this antidote to *Pretty Woman*, but we get *Shitty Woman* instead, dull, tame, squalid and predictable. **[81m/18]**

Liz	Theresa Russell
Blake	Benjamin Mouton
Rasta	Antonio Fargas

Quote 'I've lost track of how many I've had. Must be miles.'

Psst! The play on which it was based was written by a King's Cross cabbie.

Who's Harry Crumb? • [1989]

Director: **Paul Flaherty**
Screenplay: **Robert Conte & Peter Martin Wortmann**

Candy tries to out-Chase Chevy Chase in this pathetically unfunny comedy, with Candy a bungling private detective who is jack of all disguises, master of none. Just imagine how bad it *could* be. It's worse. **[95m/PG]**

Harry Crumb	John Candy
Eliot Draisen	Jeffrey Jones
Helen Downing	Annie Potts

Psst! James Belushi appears in a cameo as a bus passenger.

Who's That Girl? • [1987]

Director: **James Foley**
Screenplay: **Andrew Smith & Ken Finkleman**

Unfortunately that girl is Madonna, trying yet again to be a movie star and falling flat on her face. A quick look at the characters' names gives you an idea of the level of humour in this deathly derivative farce that steals from everywhere, without coming up with an idea of its own. Poor John Mills. **[92m/15]**

| Nikki Finn | Madonna |
| Loudon Troff | Griffin Dunne |

Also: Haviland Morris, John McMartin, Bibi Besch, John Mills

Psst! At one point the director had to kiss Madonna's feet in order to persuade her to redub a line of dialogue • Four Rolls Royces were destroyed in the making of this film • The title had been *Slammer*, but was changed to cash in on Madonna's song 'Who's That Girl?'

Why Me? •• [1990]

Director: **Gene Quintano**
Screenplay: **Donald E. Westlake & Leonard Maas Jr.**

International jewel thief Lambert steals a ruby, prompting the world and his dog to target him as Public Enemy Number One. One of those slapstick caper pics Hollywood was so fond of twenty years ago. There's a distinct feeling of déjà vu about the whole enterprise. **[87m/15]**

Gus Cardinale	Christopher Lambert
June Daley	Kim Greist
Bruno Daley	Christopher Lloyd
Francis Mahoney	J.T. Walsh
Ralph	Michael J. Pollard

The Wicked Lady •• [1983]

Director: **Michael Winner**
Screenplay: **Leslie Arliss & Michael Winner**

In this toothless remake of the 1935 Gainsborough pic the lady highwayman is less wicked than just a touch naughty, with Dunaway giving one of the campest performances of her career. Despite the furore at the time, the actors seem to be having a far better time than the audience, thanks to the leaden hand of Winner cracking the whip. **[98m/18]**

Lady Barbara Skelton ....Faye Dunaway
Capt. Jerry Jackson...........................Alan Bates
Hogarth ....John Gielgud
Sir Ralph Skelton ....Denholm Elliott
Also: Prunella Scales, Oliver Tobias, Glynis Barber, Joan Hickson

Psst! When the censor said that the scene with Dunaway and Sirtis fighting with whips had to be cut, Winner was able to get the likes of John Schlesinger, Kingsley Amis and Lindsay Anderson to object. In the face of such opposition to this attempt to tamper with this major masterpiece of British cinema, the censor relented ✦ The original had its own problems. Many scenes had to be reshot for the American market because Margaret Lockwood was displaying a slight cleavage! ✦ In the seduction scene with Tobias, Barber uses a body double.

Wild at Heart • [1990]

Director: **David Lynch**
Screenplay: **David Lynch**

Cage and Dern go on the lam in the deep South, to the consternation of her crazed mother who goes to considerable lengths to get them back. As you'd expect from Lynch, it's stuffed with violence, sex and out-and-out weirdness. Visually, it has more flair than Carnaby Street in the 60s [radio joke], but much of it makes no sense and is just plain pretentious and tedious. Don't look too hard for the plot or you'll strain your eyes. Naturally it won the Palme D'Or at Cannes. **[127m/18]**

Sailor Ripley ....Nicolas Cage
Lula Pace Fortune..........................Laura Dern
Marietta Fortune ....Diane Ladd
Bobby Peru...............................Willem Dafoe
Perdita Durango..................Isabella Rossellini
Quote 'This whole world's wild at heart and weird on top. I wish I was some-where over the rainbow.'
Psst! Dern and Ladd are also real-life mother and daughter ✦ Dern and Cage became lovers during filming ✦ That's Sherilyn Fenn from *Twin Peaks* in the road accident, while the angel is Sheryl Lee, later to make her name shrouded in plastic as Laura Palmer.

Wild Geese II • [1985]

Director: **Peter Hunt**
Screenplay: **Reginald Rose**

A Wild Goose chase. In this sequel, a TV station desperate to get guests for their chatshow, hire some mercenaries to spring Rudolph Hess from Spandau prison, presumably hoping he'll be doing the cheery morning weather forecasts before long. The phrase 'wild horses' springs to mind. **[125m/15]**

John Haddad..................................Scott Glenn
Kathy Lukas ....Barbara Carrera
Alex Faulkner...............................Edward Fox
Rudolf Hess..........................Laurence Olivier

Wild Orchid • [1990]

Director: **Zalman King**
Screenplay: **Zalman King & Patricia Louisianna Knop**

Lawyer Otis goes to work with Bisset in Rio de Janeiro and becomes distracted by the carnival and by Mickey Rourke. During the decades between the rather boring bonking you might try this quiz. Whoever told Otis she could act? Why is Rourke such a deep shade of orange? And when was the last time Bisset was in a decent film? **[112m/18]**

James Wheeler........................Mickey Rourke
Claudia Lirones.....................Jacqueline Bisset
Emily Reed.......................................Carre Otis

Psst! Those love scenes are as realistic as they look. There have been several notable instances where actors got carried away, such as in *Don't Look Now*, the Nicholson version of *The Postman Always Rings Twice* and *Betty Blue*, but this is probably the first time it was done deliberately just to garner publicity for the film ◆ Otis and Rourke married after making the film. Presumably, Rourke changed his mind after once saying: 'I don't care about sex any more. It's years since I made love. Nowadays I so much prefer motorcycles'.

Wild West ••• [1993]

Director: David Attwood
Screenplay: Harwant Bains

One of the most exhilirating British comedies in years, concerning a group of young Pakistani tearaways and their country band, the *Honky Tonk Cowboys*. Their ambitions are complicated when Andrews falls in love with the unhappily married Choudhury. Anarchic, free-wheeling, observant and hysterically funny, it's as if Bill Forsyth has been crossed with Spike Lee. Great fun. Great music. [85m/15]

Zaf......................................Naveen Andrews
Rifat.....................................Sarita Choudhury
Kay...Ronny Jhutti
Ali..Ravi Kapoor

Quote 'Zafir, there are no Pakistani cowboys.'

Willow •• [1988]

Director: Ron Howard
Screenplay: Bob Dolman

All the inspiration in this George Lucas fantasy has gone into the sets and special effects. Wonderful though they are, the tale of an elf protecting the baby that can put an end to the evil queen's reign is trite, clichéd and leaden. [125m/PG]

Madmartigan................................Val Kilmer
Sorsha....................Joanne Whalley-Kilmer
Willow Ufgood.....................Warwick Davis
Queen Bavmorda..........................Jean Marsh

Raziel..Patricia Hayes
High Aldwin..................................Billy Barty
Gen. Kael..Pat Roach

Psst! 'Gen. Kael' is a dig at American film critic Pauline Kael. The two-headed monster was nicknamed Ebersisk, after TV film critics Siskel and Ebert. When the film came out, there was plenty of opportunity for all three to get their own back ◆ This is where Kilmer and Whalley met, he subsequently gaining a wife and she a hyphen.

Wilt ••• [1989]

Director: Michael Tuchner
Screenplay: Andrew Marshall & David Renwick

An often hilarious adaptation of Tom Sharpe's novel. Smith is the dense policeman convinced that lecturer Jones has murdered his obnoxious wife. Although it gets bogged down between the comic set-pieces, just thinking about the tartan dildo joke *still* makes me laugh. Also known as *The Misadventures of Mr. Wilt*. [91m/15]

Henry Wilt...........................Griff Rhys Jones
Insp. Russell Flint............................Mel Smith
Eva Wilt...............................Alison Steadman
Sally...Diana Quick
Also: Jeremy Clyde, David Ryall

Quote 'Look here, if anyone's going to murder my wife, it'll be me.'

Wind • [1992]

Director: Carroll Ballard
Screenplay: Rudy Wurlitzer & Mac Gudgeon

In this yachting drama, Modine blames himself for losing the America's Cup and determines to win it, and former love Grey, back. The sailing sequences are quite exciting, but the cardboard characters get soggy with all that water around. [125m/PG]

Will Parker.........................Matthew Modine
Kate Bass..................................Jennifer Grey
Joe Heiser............................Stellan Skarsgard
Also: Rebecca Miller, Ned Vaughn, Cliff Robertson

Wings of Fame •• [1991]

Director: **Otakar Votocek**
Screenplay: **Otakar Votocek & Herman Koch**

A murdered film star finds himself in a heavenly hotel for celebrities, where the quality of the rooms depends upon your reputation back on earth. Once you're ejected from the basement, the lights are turned out for good. Very little of it makes much sense, but O'Toole is as watchable as ever. **[109m/15]**

Cesar Valentin	Peter O'Toole
Brian Smith	Colin Firth

Also: Marie Trintignant, Maria Becker, Walter Gotell, Ken Campbell, Robert Stephens

Quote 'What do you think of British cinema?' – 'Oh, that would be a very good idea.'

Wings of the Apache • [1990]

Director: **David Green**
Screenplay: **Nick Thiel & Paul F. Edwards**

This dismal clone of *Top Gun*, with helicopters instead of jets, is so lacking in energy, it barely gets off the ground before crashing to earth again. Also known as *Firebirds*. **[89m/15]**

Jake Preston	Nicolas Cage
Brad Little	Tommy Lee Jones
Billie Lee Guthrie	Sean Young

Winter People •• [1989]

Director: **Ted Kotcheff**
Screenplay: **Carol Sobieski**

An old-fashioned tale of Depression-era feuding in the farming communities of Appalachia, with Russell and his daughter caught up in the middle with local lass McGillis. **[111m/15]**

Wayland Jackson	Kurt Russell
Collie Wright	Kelly McGillis
William Wright	Lloyd Bridges
Drury Campbell	Mitchell Ryan

Wired • [1989]

Director: **Larry Peerce**
Screenplay: **Earl Mac Rauch**

Although ostensibly based on Bob Woodwards' biography of the doomed John Belushi, the moment you see Belushi unzip his body bag to be taken on a guide through his life, you just know that we're in trouble. While the story's grotesque in the extreme, it's not helped by the fact that Chiklis not for one minute convinces that he's Belushi. **[100m/18]**

John Belushi	Michael Chiklis
Angel Velasquez	Ray Sharkey
Bob Woodward	J.T. Walsh
Cathy Smith	Patti D'Arbanville
Judy Belushi	Lucinda Jenney
Dan Aykroyd	Gary Groomes

Psst! A rather sick in-joke occurs on *The Blues Brothers* set when the director is in view. The noise of helicopters is a reference to the flying disaster during the making of *The Twilight Zone*, another John Landis movie ✦ The $12m budget came from Lion Breweries of New Zealand ✦ Chiklis put on 30 lb for the part.

Wish You Were Here ••• [1987]

Director: **David Leland**
Screenplay: **David Leland**

In the morally-repressive Britain of the 50s, troubled teenager Lloyd gives vent to her frustrations in sexual and verbal abandon. Lloyd is everything here, giving an hilariously funny and poignant performance. Although she's unforgettable, the film surrounding her is slight and rather miserable. **[92m/15]**

Lynda	Emily Lloyd
Mrs. Parfitt	Clare Clifford
Valerie	Barbara Durkin
Hubert	Geoffrey Hutchings
Gillian	Charlotte Barker
Eric	Tom Bell
Aunt Millie	Pat Heywood

Psst! Like *Personal Services*, also written by Leland, the central character is based on the madam Cynthia Payne.

The Witches •• [1990]

Director: **Nicolas Roeg**
Screenplay: **Allan Scott**

A small boy discovers a witches' convention at the hotel he's staying at, overhearing a plot to turn all of England's children into mice. Children might enjoy Huston's Mother of All Witches and not notice that most of the action is confined to one building. The direction from Roeg is typically atmospheric. **[92m/PG]**

Miss Ernst	Anjelica Huston
Helga	Mai Zetterling
Luke	Jasen Fisher

Also: Rowan Atkinson, Bill Paterson, Brenda Blethyn, Charlie Potter, Jane Horrocks

Psst! Roeg fought the studio, but failed in his attempt to stick with Roald Dahl's much less gooey ending.

The Witches of Eastwick ••• [1987]

Director: **George Miller**
Screenplay: **Michael Cristofer**

The man with the devilish grin finally gets to play the part that's made for him, conjured up by three sexually-needy women in a small New England town. Much of the film makes little sense and Miller (the *Mad Max* director) practically changes genre with each shot. Yet despite its faults, this battle of the sexes is eminently watchable and in places nicely raunchy. Dominating everything, despite the female talent on screen, is Nicholson, who's enjoying himself so much he doesn't even bother to slice the ham. He just gives us the whole hog in one go. **[118m/18]**

Daryl Van Horne	Jack Nicholson
Alexandra Medford	Cher
Jane Spofford	Susan Sarandon
Sukie Ridgemont	Michelle Pfeiffer
Felicia Alden	Veronica Cartwright
Clyde Alden	Richard Jenkins
Walter Neff	Keith Jochim
Fidel	Carel Struycken

Quote 'Just your average horny little devil.'
Psst! Sarandon had been preparing for the lead role when, at the last minute, it was switched to Cher instead.

Withnail and I •• [1987]

Director: **Bruce Robinson**
Screenplay: **Bruce Robinson**

Two unemployed layabout actors unable to stick life in London in the 60s head for the country, only to find themselves even worse off. Despite its cult status and some fine acting, the relentlessly dour black humour becomes very quickly irritating. **[105m/15]**

Withnail	Richard E. Grant
... & I	Paul McGann
Monty	Richard Griffiths
Danny	Ralph Brown

Psst! Richard Starkey M.B.E., a.k.a. Ringo Starr, is on the credits as a 'Special Production Consultant'. George Harrison's company Handmade produced the film.

Without a Clue • [1988]

Director: **Thom Eberhardt**
Screenplay: **Larry Strawther & Gary Murphy**

This lamentable farce suggests that Dr. Watson invented Sherlock Holmes and was then forced to get an actor to impersonate the famous detective. It was a clever idea getting a robot to impersonate Michael Caine, but it's not in the least bit convincing. **[107m/PG]**

Sherlock Holmes	Michael Caine
Dr. Watson	Ben Kingsley
Insp. Lestrade	Jeffrey Jones
Fake Leslie	Lysette Anthony

Without a Trace • [1983]

Director: **Stanley R. Jaffe**
Screenplay: **Beth Gutcheon**

A tiresome melodramatic story of mother Nelligan discovering that her six-year-old son has gone missing on the way to school. Also missing is a decent plot. The characters are unconvincing and the story ends up being plain daft.

[120m/15]

Susan Selky	Kate Nelligan
Al Menetti	Judd Hirsch
Graham Selky	David Dukes
Jocelyn Norris	Stockard Channing

Witness •••• [1985]

Director: **Peter Weir**
Screenplay: **Earl W. Wallace & William Kelley**

A young boy witnesses a killing and, when cop Ford realises his boss is involved, they take refuge in the boy's Amish community. How refreshing to come across a completely new background for a thriller. Weir spins a superb, steadily-tightening yarn as he contrasts the violent outside world with the peaceful Amish and brings Ford together with McGillis in an obviously doomed romance. Excellent, eminently rewatchable, stuff. [112m/15]

John Book	Harrison Ford
Rachel	Kelly McGillis
Schaeffer	Josef Sommer
Samuel	Lukas Haas
Eli Lapp	Jan Rubes
Daniel Hochleitner	Alexander Godunov
McFee	Danny Glover
Carter	Brent Jennings
Elaine	Patti LuPone
Moses Hochleitner	Viggo Mortensen

OOPS! Odd, isn't it, how the Amish come at the double when the bell rings, but don't notice the gunfire earlier?

Psst! Having Ford work at the carpentry bench is an in-joke. Before making it as an actor, he was a carpenter by trade and it's still his hobby • The Amish community wanted nothing to do with the film. Their religion forbids them either to be photographed or to watch movies • McGillis did live briefly with an Amish family to study the life and the accent, but she was turfed out when they discovered why she was there.

The Wolves of Willoughby Chase • [1989]

Director: **Stuart Orme**
Screenplay: **William N. Akers**

It's worth catching a little of this pathetic kids' film, if only to see the hilarious wolves themselves. Presumably for budgetary reasons, they're only too obviously dogs wearing large-scale toupées. Otherwise it's not worth bothering with this daft British tale of wicked Beacham plotting to get her hands on Willoughby Chase. [93m/PG]

Slighcarp	Stephanie Beacham
Grimshaw	Mel Smith
James	Richard O'Brien

The Woman in Red •• [1984]

Director: **Gene Wilder**
Screenplay: **Gene Wilder**

It's easy to understand why happily-married Wilder's eyes should pop out on the end of stalks when he sees LeBrock doing a Marilyn Monroe impression with her skirt. It's less clear why she wouldn't use her Mace the first time she sees Wilder. A largely unfunny remake of the French film *Pardon Mon Affaire*. [86m/15]

Theodore Pierce	Gene Wilder
Buddy	Charles Grodin
Joe	Joseph Bologna
Didi	Judith Ivey
Michael	Michael Huddleston
Charlotte	Kelly LeBrock
Ms. Miner	Gilda Radner

Women on the Verge of a Nervous Breakdown •• [1988]

Director: **Pedro Almodovar**
Screenplay: **Pedro Almodovar**

An overrated Spanish farce about an actress sent over the edge when her two-timing lover leaves her. Despite the usual wonderfully kooky Almodovar characters, it's marred by a handful of extraordinary coincidences and is nowhere near as funny as it thinks it is. [98m/15]

Pepa Marcos	Carmen Maura
Carlos	Antonio Banderas
Lucia	Julieta Serrano
Candela	Maria Barranco

Wonderland
SEE: The Fruit Machine

The Woo Woo Kid ••• [1987]

Director: **Phil Alden Robinson**
Screenplay: **Phil Alden Robinson**

In 1944, America's papers were full of Sonny Wisecarver, a 15-year-old who had a devastating effect on older women. He ran away with one, married her, got caught and then got involved with another one. A pleasantly amusing telling of the story, with Dempsey the type-cast choice for the role. Also known as *In the Mood*.

[98m/PG]

'Sonny' Wisecarver	Patrick Dempsey
Judy Cusimano	Talia Balsam
Francine Glatt	Beverly D'Angelo
Mr. Wisecarver	Michael Constantine
Mrs. Wisecarver	Betty Jinnette
Mrs. Marver	Kathleen Freeman

Psst! Director Carl Reiner narrates a newsreel sequence in which the real Sonny Wisecarver cameos as a postman.

Working Girl •••• [1988]

Director: **Mike Nichols**
Screenplay: **Kevin Wade**

Griffith is superb as the ambitious secretary who discovers that new boss Weaver has been passing off her ideas as her own. Taking advantage of Weaver's absence, she latches onto banker Ford as her key to doing the deal herself. It's pointless carping that the business machinations aren't realistic. Just sit back and enjoy one of the funniest, sharpest and liveliest fairy tales of the decade. And, while we're at it, three cheers for Cusack in one of the funniest ever supporting performances.

[113m/15]

Tess McGill	Melanie Griffith
Jack Trainer	Harrison Ford
Katharine Parker	Sigourney Weaver
Cyn	Joan Cusack
Mick Dugan	Alec Baldwin
Oren Trask	Philip Bosco
Ginny	Nora Dunn
Lutz	Oliver Platt
Turkel	James Lally
Bob Speck	Kevin Spacey
Ambrister	Robert Easton
Personnel director	Olympia Dukakis

Quote 'I've a head for business and a body for sin.' ✦ 'Sometimes I sing and dance around my house in my underwear. That doesn't make me Madonna.' ✦ 'Can I get you anything? Coffee? Tea? Me?'

Working Girls •• [1986]

Director: **Lizzie Borden**
Screenplay: **Lizzie Borden**

The problem with this drama about life in a small Manhattan brothel is that it's too realistic. Although scripted and acted by professionals – actors, that is – it plays exactly like a documentary. Fascinating though it is seeing how similar the conversations are to those in any job, in the end we get as bored as the girls.

[90m/18]

Molly	Louise Smith
Lucy	Ellen McElduff
Dawn	Amanda Goodwin

The World According to Garp ••• [1982]

Director: **George Roy Hill**
Screenplay: **Steve Tesich**

Following his unusual conception, Garp finds that bizarre events dog his life. John Irving's quirky novels aren't to everybody's taste. This adaptation should satisfy his fans, while the rest will find compensation in Williams giving an early demonstration of his star potential.

[136m/15]

Garp	Robin Williams
Helen Holm	Mary Beth Hurt

Jenny Fields	Glenn Close
Roberta Muldoon	John Lithgow
Mr. Fields	Hume Cronyn
Mrs. Fields	Jessica Tandy
Hooker	Swoosie Kurtz
Ellen James	Amanda Plummer

Psst! Novelist John Irving appears in a cameo as a wrestling referee, while director Hill drops in as a pilot.

A World Apart ••• [1988]

Director: **Chris Menges**
Screenplay: **Shawn Slovo**

Apartheid in South Africa in the 60s, as seen through the eyes of a young girl whose mother is a civil rights campaigner. This intelligent social issue drama is honest enough to view the moral angles from various sides and avoid easy emotionalism.

[110m/PG]

Diane Roth	Barbara Hershey
Molly Roth	Jodhi May
Gus Roth	Jeroen Krabbé
Muller	David Suchet
Kruger	Paul Freeman
Harold	Tim Roth

Psst! The screenplay is semi-autobiographical. Slovo's mother was assassinated by a parcel bomb in Mozambique in 1982. Slovo was present for filming in Zimbabwe, although she dyed her hair and used a false name.

The Wraith • [1986]

Director: **Mike Marvin**
Screenplay: **Mike Marvin**

A group of car thieves are challenged by a mysterious driver in black leather. One of those pseudo-Westerns which invariably fall between two stools. [92m/18]

The Wraith/Jake	Charlie Sheen
Packard	Nick Cassavetes
Keri	Sherilyn Fenn
Loomis	Randy Quaid

Blurb He's Not From Around Here.

Wuthering Heights •• [1992]

Director: **Peter Kosminsky**
Screenplay: **Anne Devlin**

...Or *Wuzzerin' 'Ights* as it was dubbed by those who found that while Binoche looks like a European Julia Roberts, she talks more like Inspector Clouseau. The locations are wonderful but the telling of the tale of doomed love on the moors is sadly lacking in passion. Still, the story's strong enough to overcome many of the film's flaws. Also known as *Emily Brontë's Wuthering Heights*, presumably to distinguish it from Jackie Collins' *Wuthering Heights*. [106m/U]

Cathy/Catherine	Juliette Binoche
Heathcliff	Ralph Fiennes
Ellen Dean	Janet McTeer
Isabella Linton	Sophie Ward

Quote 'Come back and finish your dinner, Hareton.'

Psst! It's Sinead O'Connor at the opening, narrating as Emily Brontë herself.

The Year My Voice Broke ••• [1988]

Director: **John Duigan**
Screenplay: **John Duigan**

Rather different in character to its delightful sequel, *Flirting*, this Australian coming-of-age tale also centres on Danny. Here, he's suffering the pangs of unrequited love in a small town in New South Wales. Despite its languid pace, it turns into an absorbing tale that's well worth sticking with. [104m/15]

Danny	Noah Taylor
Freya	Loene Carmen
Trevor	Ben Mendelsohn
Nils Olson	Graeme Blundell
Anne Olson	Lynette Curran

The Year of Living Dangerously ••• [1983]

Director: Peter Weir
Screenplay: David Williamson, C.J. Koch & Peter Weir

TV journalist Mel becomes involved in the Indonesian civil war and with journalist Weaver, who is supposedly English! The first of the hacks-in-world-troublespots melodramas, director Weir is as strong as ever on the atmospherics, although the mishmash of a story could have used some work. [115m/PG]

Guy Hamilton .... Mel Gibson
Jill Bryant .... Sigourney Weaver
Billy Kwan .... Linda Hunt
Pete Curtis .... Michael Murphy
Colonel Henderson .... Bill Kerr
Wally O'Sullivan .... Noel Ferrier

Oscars Linda Hunt

Quote 'You must look at the shadows, not the puppets.'

Psst! At 4 foot 9 Linda Hunt was the shortest adult actress to win an Oscar, as well as being the only one to win for playing a man. It was only her second film and she was chosen after Weir rejected hundreds of male actors ✦ Although considerably taller than Hunt, Mel is smaller than Weaver and wore built-up shoes for their scenes together, much as Bogart had done years earlier in Casablanca.

Year of the Dragon •••• [1985]

Director: Michael Cimino
Screenplay: Michael Cimino & Oliver Stone

An obsessed Nam veteran, now a cop, takes on the Chinese mafia, determined to reassert America's supremacy at home, having failed in the East. The battleground covers his marriage and the local police department, too. With the exception of the wooden Ariane, this was a much under-rated thriller, provocatively co-written by Stone and pushed into directorial overdrive by Cimino in, arguably, his best film. In between the full-blown set pieces, some awkward questions on race are raised. [134m/18]

Stanley White .... Mickey Rourke
Joey Tai .... John Lone
Tracy Tzu .... Ariane
Angelo Rizzo .... Leonard Termo
Louis .... Raymond J. Barry
Connie .... Caroline Kava

Quote 'If I give up, the system gives up.'

Year of the Gun • [1991]

Director: John Frankenheimer
Screenplay: David Ambrose

It's almost impossible to believe that veteran thriller director Frankenheimer was responsible for this insufferably boring and interminable thriller about a writer and his photographer girlfriend getting caught up in the Red Brigade plot to kidnap Aldo Moro. Even the actors whose first language is English sound as if they're being dubbed. The extraordinarily complicated plot's about as easy to understand as British Rail's fare structure. [111m/15]

David Raybourne .... Andrew McCarthy
Alison King .... Sharon Stone
Lia Spinelli .... Valeria Golino

Yellowbeard • [1983]

Director: Mel Damski
Screenplay: Graham Chapman, Peter Cook & Bernard McKenna

Dismal pirate spoof that buries an amazing array of comic talent and forgets where it put the key. Doesn't shiver *my* timbers. [96m/PG]

Yellowbeard .... Graham Chapman
Moon .... Peter Boyle
El Segundo .... Richard Cheech
El Nebuloso .... Tommy Chong
Also: Peter Cook, Marty Feldman, Martin Hewitt, Michael Hordern, Eric Idle, Madeline Kahn, James Mason, John Cleese, Spike Milligan, Beryl Reid

Psst! This was Marty Feldman's last job. He was discovered dead the day after finishing filming.

Yentl •• [1983]

Director: Barbra Streisand
Screenplay: Jack Rosenthal & Barbra Streisand

The trouble with Streisand's films is that the person who most wants to see her on screen is her. In this ego trip to the Steppes, she writes, produces, sings and directs a tale of a turn-of-the-century Jewish Russian girl who disguises herself as a man in order to be allowed to study the Talmud. Occasionally funny, the fact that she doesn't even allow anyone else to sing with her becomes infuriating. If you like Streisand, fine, but please keep her to yourself. [133m/PG]

Yentl.....................................Barbra Streisand
Avigdor ....Mandy Patinkin
Hadass ....Amy Irving
Papa ....Nehemiah Persoff

Psst! This was the first film a woman produced, directed and starred in. Streisand had owned the rights to the Isaac Bashevis Singer story for 14 years before being able to make it. Singer was said not to be best pleased with the result!

Youngblood • [1986]

Director: Peter Markle
Screenplay: Peter Markle

Rob Lowe's an ice hockey player...Gibb is pretty...she's the boss's daughter. Join up the dots to get the picture of something that looks like a film, only a good deal less interesting. [110m/15]

Dean Youngblood............................Rob Lowe
Jessie Chadwick.........................Cynthia Gibb
Derek Sutton ....Patrick Swayze
Also: Ed Lauter, Jim Youngs, Keanu Reeves

Young Doctors in Love ••• [1982]

Director: Garry Marshall
Screenplay: Michael Elias & Rich Eustis

A great madcap hospital comedy, ostensible a spoof of daytime soaps and featuring cameos from some real-life soap stars.

Although the plot's anorexically thin, the gags come thick and fast, with many good enough to make you weep. [95m/15]

Dr. Simon August...............Michael McKean
Dr. Stephanie Brody......................Sean Young
Dr. Oliver Ludwig.........Harry Dean Stanton
Dr. Jacobs...............................Patrick Macnee
Angelo/Angela ....Hector Elizondo
Dr. Prang............................Dabney Coleman
Norine Sprockett.........................Pamela Reed
Dr. Phil Burns.........................Taylor Negron
Dr. Kurtzman ....Saul Rubinek

Psst! Among the soap stars clocking in and out, most of whom mean nothing to a British audience, are Mr. T, Demi Moore and *Northern Exposure*'s Janine Turner.

Young Einstein •• [1989]

Director: Yahoo Serious
Screenplay: Yahoo Serious & David Roach

As a lad in New Zealand, so we are led to believe, Einstein invented not only relativity, but also the electric guitar and surfing, splitting the atom in his spare time. Out-and-out wackiness is the order of the day in this Serious-produced, written, directed and acted fantasy. [91m/PG]

Albert Einstein ....Yahoo Serious
Marie Curie...........................Odile Le Clezio
Preston Preston...........................John Howard
Mr. Einstein ....Peewee Wilson
Mrs. Einstein.........................Su Cruickshank

Psst! The credits include a 'cockroach wrangler' • Yahoo Serious's real name is Greg Pead.

Young Guns •• [1988]

Director: Christopher Cain
Screenplay: John Fusco

This attempt to 'yoof' the Western works better than *Mobsters* did with gangsters. But its desperation to win over youngsters and its threadbare plot weigh down what is actually quite an intriguing tale of the early days of Billy the Kid. [107m/18]

William H. Bonney....................Emilio Estevez
Doc Scurlock........................Kiefer Sutherland
Chavez Y Chavez.........Lou Diamond Phillips
Dick Brewer.............................Charlie Sheen
Quote 'See? Ya got three or four good pals, why then you got yerself a tribe. There ain't nothin' stronger than that.'

Young Guns II – Blaze of Glory ••

[1990]

Director: Geoff Murphy
Screenplay: John Fusco

More of the same, presented in an attractive package, as the old and new *Young Gunners* head for Mexico with a posse in pursuit. **[104m/12]**

William H. Bonney....................Emilio Estevez
Doc Scurlock........................Kiefer Sutherland
Chavez Y Chavez.........Lou Diamond Phillips
Arkansas Dave........................Christian Slater
Also: William Petersen, Alan Ruck, R.D. Call, James Coburn, Balthazar Getty

Psst! Way down the cast list, playing 'Dove', is Ginger Lynn Allen, leading porn actress and star of what she claims were 69 such films before turning legitimate. She was for a time the girlfriend of Charlie Sheen, Emilio Estevez's brother ♦ Lou Diamond Phillips was dragged by a horse during filming, badly shattering his elbow.

Young Sherlock Holmes ••

[1985]

Director: Barry Levinson
Screenplay: Chris Columbus

Speculating that Holmes met Watson while they were both still schoolboys is a nice idea, but the film is Spielbergised – he executive produced it – with unnecessary special effects and sub–Indiana Jones heroics. **[109m/PG]**

Sherlock Holmes....................Nicholas Rowe
John Watson.....................................Alan Cox
Elizabeth....................................Sophie Ward
Also: Anthony Higgins, Susan Fleetwood, Freddie Jones, Nigel Stock

Young Warriors •

[1983]

Director: Lawrence D. Foldes
Screenplay: Lawrence D. Foldes & Russell W. Colgin

Some high school students turn into Charles Bronson clones after one of their sisters dies after being raped. Exceedingly violent, exploitative and boring to boot. **[103m/18]**

Lt. Bob Carrigan....................Ernest Borgnine
Sgt. John Austin................Richard Roundtree
Beverly..............................Lynda Day George

Z

Zandalee •

[1991]

Director: Sam Pillsbury
Screenplay: Mari Kornhauser

In sultry New Orleans, feisty young wife Anderson tires of her husband and finds abusing a bottle of virgin olive oil with Cage helps pass the time. Despite gratuitous nudity being the film's *raison d'etre*, watching leaves fall would be still more fun than wading through this tripe. **[104m/18]**

Johnny Collins ....Nicolas Cage
Thierry Martin........................Judge Reinhold
Zandalee Martin....................Erika Anderson
Also: Joe Pantoliano, Viveca Lindfors, Marisa Tomei, Zach Galligan, Steve Buscemi

Quote 'I wanna shake you naked and eat you alive, Zandalee.'

Psst! Contains probably the quickest appearance of a birthday suit by a lead – well, let's use 'actress' – in a mainstream movie, beating the previous record held by Amanda Donohoe in the film *Diamond Skulls*.

A Zed and Two Noughts • [1985]

Director: **Peter Greenaway**
Screenplay: **Peter Greenaway**

Twin brothers lose their wives in a car crash with a swan, and seek consolation with a one-legged survivor. The regrettably brief performances from Barber and Ackland are the only merits of this hideously acted and ill-conceived attempt to fool people with artistic whitewash. The title hasn't enough 'Z's. Zzzzzzzzz. [115m/18]

Alba Bewick	Andrea Ferreol
Oswald Deuce	Brian Deacon
Oliver Deuce	Eric Deacon
Venus de Milo	Frances Barber
Van Hoyten	Joss Ackland

Psst! Note for pseuds: Vermeer's pictures were the inspiration behind the lighting of several scenes.

Zelig •• [1983]

Director: **Woody Allen**
Screenplay: **Woody Allen**

An odd little Allen movie about a pre-war, chameleon-like man able to conform perfectly to his surroundings. The idea of mixing Allen in with old newsreels is clever but it's really just one joke over and over again. Although praised for its extraordinary technical achievement, there is another school of thought which says that Allen actually was there at the time, proof of which is the glazed expression on the people's faces around him as he explains yet again why he doesn't want to make funny films any more. [79m/PG]

Leonard Zelig	Woody Allen
Dr. Eudora Fletcher	Mia Farrow
Dr. Sindell	John Buckwalter
Glandular Doctor	Marvin Chatinover

Psst! Because of the technical difficulties involved in matching Allen to old newsreel, he managed to complete both *Midsummer Night's Sex Comedy* and *Broadway Danny Rose* in the time it took to finish this. Allen claimed that, as there is no mechanical way to 'age' film, they had to stamp on it.

Zina •• [1986]

Director: **Ken McMullen**
Screenplay: **Terry James & Ken McMullen**

If you want to know all about the problems of being Trotsky's daughter, this is your film. Well enough made, though who knows why anybody would want to. [93m/15]

Zina Bronstein	Domiziana Giordano
Prof. Kronfeld	Ian McKellen
Trotsky	Philip Madoc

Zone Troopers •• [1986]

Director: **Danny Bilson**
Screenplay: **Danny Bilson & Paul De Meo**

The Americans fighting the Hun in Italy in 1944 did not, it seems, manage to win all on their own. They had the help of a conveniently handy group of aliens. Bizarre. [87m/15]

Sarge	Tim Thomerson
Joey	Timothy Van Patten
Mittens	Art LaFleur
Dolan	Biff Manard

Danny Aiello [b. 1933]

Real name Danny Louis Aiello Jr.

Films *The Godfather, Part II* ♦♦♦♦ *(74)*, *The Front* ♦♦♦♦ *(76)*, *Bloodbrothers* ♦♦♦ *(78)*, *Fingers* ♦♦♦ *(78)*, *Fort Apache – The Bronx* *(81)*, *Once Upon a Time in America* ♦♦♦♦ *(84)*, *The Purple Rose of Cairo* ♦♦ *(85)*, *The Stuff* ♦♦ *(85)*, *The Protector* ♦♦ *(86)*, *Moonstruck* ♦♦♦♦ *(87)*, *Radio Days* ♦♦♦ *(87)*, *The Pick-up Artist* ♦ *(87)*, *Do the Right Thing* ♦♦♦♦ *(89)*, *Harlem Nights* ♦ *(89)*, *Russicum* ♦ *(89)*, *The January Man* ♦ *(89)*, *Jacob's Ladder* ♦♦ *(90)*, *Hudson Hawk* ♦ *(91)*, *Ruby* ♦♦ *(92)*, *Mistress (92)*, *The Pickle (93)*, *The Cemetery Club (93)*

Woody Allen [b. 1935]

Real name Allen Stewart Konigsberg

DIRECTOR. The one-time gag writer and stand-up comic is an actor-director people either love or hate. Even his fans are split into two camps; those who love the funny films and those who love the serious ones. Let's be strictly objective here: if you want to avoid the serious stuff just look for the lowest ratings. He has an amazing talent for putting future stars in bit parts. Sylvester Stallone, Sigourney Weaver and Sharon Stone all appeared in brief, wordless roles in Allen movies.

Quote 'Is sex dirty? Only if it's done right.'

Quote 'A face that convinces you that God is a cartoonist.' [Jack Kroll]

Films *What's New, Pussycat?* ♦♦ *(65; a&s only)*, *What's Up, Tiger Lily?* ♦♦ *(66; s only)*, *Casino Royale* ♦♦ *(67; a only)*, *Take the Money and Run* ♦♦♦♦ *(69; also a&s)*, *Bananas* ♦♦♦♦ *(71; also a&s)*, *Play it Again, Sam* ♦♦♦♦ *(72; a&s only)*, *Everything You Always Wanted To Know About Sex (But Were Afraid To Ask)* ♦♦♦ *(72; also a&s)*, *Sleeper* ♦♦♦♦ *(73; also a&s)*, *Love and Death* ♦♦♦ *(75; also a&s)*, *The Front* ♦♦♦♦ *(76; a only)*, *Annie Hall* ♦♦♦ *(77; also a&s)*, *Interiors* ♦ *(78; also s)*, *Manhattan* ♦♦♦♦ *(79; also a&s)*, *Stardust Memories* ♦ *(80; also a&s)*, *A Midsummer Night's Sex Comedy* ♦♦♦ *(82; also a&s)*, *Zelig* ♦♦ *(83; also a&s)*, *Broadway Danny Rose* ♦♦♦ *(84; also a&s)*, *The Purple Rose of Cairo* ♦♦ *(85; also s)*, *Hannah and Her Sisters* ♦♦♦♦ *(86; also a&s)*, *Radio Days* ♦♦♦ *(87; also a&s)*, *September* ♦ *(87; also s)*, *Another Woman* ♦ *(88; also s)*, *Crimes and Misdemeanors* ♦♦ *(89; also a&s)*, *New York Stories* ♦♦ *(89; also a&s)*, *Alice* ♦♦♦ *(90; also s)*, *Scenes from a Mall* ♦♦ *(91; a only)*, *Shadows and Fog* ♦♦♦ *(92; also a&s)*, *Husbands and Wives* ♦♦♦ *(92; also a&s)*, *Manhattan Murder Mystery (93; also a&s)*

Kirstie Alley [b. 1955]

Best-known as Rebecca from TV sitcom *Cheers*. Alley's quirky off-screen persona is more interesting than most of her films, though that doesn't stop her commanding a cool million dollars a picture, thanks to the success of *Look Who's Talking*. A Scientologist and former cocaine addict, she is obsessed with animals, of which she has over 40. Passionately concerned about the environment, her home has solar heating and a water recycling system. She has also banned anyone wearing perfume in her house, because of its destructive effect on the ozone layer.

Quote 'This [collecting the Emmy for *Cheers*] is the big one and I want to thank the man who has been giving me the Big One for eight years.'

Films *Star Trek II: The Wrath of Khan* ♦♦♦ *(82)*, *Runaway* ♦♦ *(84)*, *Champions* ♦♦ *(84)*, *Blind Date* ♦♦ *(84)*, *Deadly Pursuit* ♦♦♦ *(88)*, *Look Who's Talking* ♦♦♦ *(89)*, *Loverboy* ♦♦ *(89)*, *Look Who's Talking Too* ♦ *(90)*, *Madhouse* ♦ *(90)*, *Sibling Rivalry* ♦♦ *(90)*, *Look Who's Talking 3 (94)*

Mädchen Amick [b. 1971]

One of the trio of *Twin Peaks'* babes, her name's pronounced MAY-chen AH-mick.

Films *Sleepwalkers* ♦ *(92)*, *Twin Peaks: Fire Walk With Me* ♦ *(92)*, *Don't Tell Her It's Me* ♦ *(92)*, *Dream Lover (93)*

Gabrielle Anwar [b. 1970]

How could we not include Anwar after that magical scene in the hotel ballroom in *Scent of a Woman*? Those few minutes alone were worth the price of admission. Obviously a British actress headed for great things. Amazing to think that she and Sadie Frost, the sexy vampire Lucy in *Bram Stoker's Dracula* were both in ITV's *Press Gang*.

Films Manifesto ♦ (88), Teen Agent ♦♦ (91), Scent of a Woman ♦♦♦ (92), For Love or Money (93), Body Snatchers (93), The Three Musketeers (94)

Anne Archer [b. 1947]

Films Paradise Alley ♦ (78), Raise the Titanic ♦ (80), The Naked Face ♦♦ (84), Fatal Attraction ♦♦ (87), Love at Large ♦ (90), Narrow Margin ♦♦ (90), Patriot Games ♦♦♦♦ (92), Body of Evidence ♦ (93), Short Cuts (93), Clear and Present Danger (94)

Rosanna Arquette [b. 1959]

Films S.O.B. ♦♦ (81), Baby, It's You ♦♦♦ (83), After Hours ♦♦ (85), Desperately Seeking Susan ♦♦♦ (85), Silverado ♦♦♦ (85), Nobody's Fool ♦♦ (86), The Big Blue ♦♦ (88), New York Stories ♦♦ (89), Black Rainbow ♦♦♦ (90), Wendy Cracked a Walnut ♦ (91), Nowhere to Run (93)

Dan Aykroyd [b. 1952]

Real name Daniel Edward Aykroyd

Films 1941 ♦♦ (79), The Blues Brothers ♦♦♦♦ (80; also s), Trading Places ♦♦♦♦ (83), Twilight Zone – The Movie ♦♦ (83), Ghostbusters ♦♦♦♦ (84; also s), Indiana Jones and the Temple of Doom ♦♦ (c)(84), Spies Like Us ♦♦ (85; also s), Into the Night ♦♦ (c)(85), Dragnet ♦♦ (87; also s), The Couch Trip ♦ (88), My Stepmother is an Alien ♦♦ (88), Driving Miss Daisy ♦♦♦ (89), Ghostbusters II ♦♦ (89; also s), Nothing But Trouble ♦ (91; also d&s), My Girl ♦ (92), This is My Life ♦ (92), Sneakers ♦♦♦ (92), Chaplin ♦♦ (92), The Coneheads (93; also s)

Kevin Bacon [b. 1958]

One of the few Brat-Packers who can actually act, Bacon's early promise was most glaringly obvious in the original *Friday the 13th* film when he copped an arrow in the neck. Married to Kyra Sedgwick.

Films National Lampoon's Animal House ♦♦♦♦ (78), Friday the 13th ♦♦ (80), Diner ♦♦♦♦ (82), Footloose ♦♦ (84), Planes, Trains and Automobiles ♦♦♦ (87), The Big Picture ♦♦♦ (89), Criminal Law ♦♦ (89), Flatliners ♦ (90), Tremors ♦♦♦ (90), JFK ♦♦♦ (91), A Few Good Men ♦♦♦♦ (92), The Air Up There (93)

Alec Baldwin [b. 1958]

Real name Alexander Rae Baldwin III

The brother of Stephen, Daniel and William, but not Adam.

Quote 'I like to be naked in movies. I've a reputation to uphold.'

Films Working Girl ♦♦♦♦ (88), Talk Radio ♦♦♦♦ (88), Beetlejuice ♦♦ (88), Married to the Mob ♦♦ (88), Great Balls of Fire (89), Alice ♦♦♦ (90), Miami Blues ♦♦♦ (90), The Hunt for Red October ♦♦♦ (90), Too Hot to Handle ♦♦ (91), Glengarry Glen Ross ♦♦♦ (92), Prelude to a Kiss (92), Bodily Harm (93), The Getaway (94)

William Baldwin [b. 1963]

The brother of Alec, Daniel and Stephen, but not Adam.

Films Born on the Fourth of July ♦♦♦♦ (c)(89), Flatliners ♦ (90), Internal Affairs ♦♦ (90), Backdraft ♦♦ (91), Three of Hearts ♦ (93), Sliver (93)

Ellen Barkin [b. 1954]

Married to Gabriel Byrne.

Quote 'If you don't want someone to see your breasts, don't take your shirt off.'

Quote 'It's difficult to be married outside the profession. A lawyer might not understand that going to bed with

Gabriel Byrne for three days is work for me.' [She subsequently married him]

Films Diner ✦✦✦✦ (82), Eddie and the Cruisers ✦✦ (83), Daniel ✦✦ (83), Tender Mercies ✦✦✦ (83), Harry and Son ✦✦ (84), Desert Bloom ✦✦✦ (86), Down by Law ✦✦ (86), The Adventures of Buckaroo Banzai Across the 8th Dimension ✦✦ (87), The Big Easy ✦✦✦✦ (87), Made in Heaven ✦✦ (c)(87), Siesta ✦ (87), Johnny Handsome ✦✦ (89), Sea of Love ✦✦✦ (89), Switch ✦ (91), Man Trouble ✦ (92), Into the West ✦✦✦ (92), This Boy's Life (93)

Kim Basinger [b. 1953]

Real name Kimila Ann Basinger

Often criticised as nothing more than a pout on legs or a bland bombshell, model Basinger's film career only took off after her nude Playboy photos got her the 'Bond Girl' role in *Never Say Never Again*. An accomplished guitarist and pianist, she trained as a ballerina until winning the Georgia Junior Miss beauty pageant. Of Cherokee Indian descent, she is generally reckoned to be one of the most temperamental Hollywood actresses [see *Too Hot to Handle*]. Among the highest-paid female stars, she bought the town of Braselton, Georgia for $20m, apparently a very poor investment. However, her newfound coyness about the nude scenes in *Boxing Helena* cost her $8m in damages forcing her to file for bankruptcy. She suffers from agoraphobia and has remained in her home for months at a time.

Quote 'I bet you haven't seen melons like these in a while, boys.' [Basinger to the policemen who stopped her riding naked along the beach]

Films Hard Country ✦✦ (81), Mother Lode ✦✦ (82), The Man Who Loved Women ✦ (83), Never Say Never Again ✦✦ (83), The Natural ✦✦ (84), Fool for Love ✦✦ (85), No Mercy ✦✦ (86), 9 1/2 Weeks ✦✦ (86), Blind Date ✦ (87), Nadine ✦✦ (87), My Stepmother is an Alien ✦✦ (88), Batman ✦✦ (89), Too Hot to Handle ✦✦ (91), Final Analysis ✦✦ (92), Cool World ✦ (92), The Real McCoy (93), The Getaway (94)

Kathy Bates [b. 1949]

Films Straight Time ✦✦✦ (78), Come Back to the Five and Dime, Jimmy Dean, Jimmy Dean ✦✦✦ (82), Two of a Kind ✦ (b)(83), The Morning After ✦ (b)(86), Arthur 2: On the Rocks ✦✦ (88), Dick Tracy (90), Men Don't Leave ✦✦ (90), Misery ✦✦✦✦ (90), White Palace ✦✦✦ (90), At Play in the Fields of the Lord ✦✦ (91), Shadows and Fog ✦✦✦ (92), Fried Green Tomatoes at the Whistle Stop Cafe ✦✦✦✦ (92), Used People ✦✦ (92), Prelude to a Kiss (92), A Home of our Own (93), North (94)

Warren Beatty [b. 1937]

Real name Henry Warren Beaty

The brother of Shirley MacLaine, he worked variously as rat-catcher, bricklayer, pianist and tunnel-builder to survive during his early acting days. Stardom arrived with *Bonnie and Clyde*, which he also produced, a status he has retained ever since despite making relatively few successful films. For twenty-five years he vied with Jack Nicholson for the reputation as Hollywood's leading bachelor, dating some of the most famous actresses in the world. Ex-lover Carly Simon's song *You're So Vain* is said to be about him. Spy magazine revealed that his chat-up line is 'Make a pass at me'. The film community was astounded when Beatty closed his black book and married Annette Bening, soon after becoming a proud father.

Quote 'If I come back in another life, I want to be Warren Beatty's fingertips.' [Woody Allen]

Quote 'I'd like to do a love scene with him just to see what all the yelling is about.' [Shirley MacLaine, his sister]

Films Bonnie and Clyde ✦✦✦✦ (67), McCabe and Mrs. Miller ✦✦✦✦ (71), The Parallax View ✦✦✦✦ (74), The Fortune ✦✦✦ (75), Shampoo ✦ (75; also s), Heaven Can Wait ✦✦✦ (78; also d&s), Reds ✦✦✦ (81; also d&s), Ishtar ✦ (87), Dick Tracy ✦✦ (90; also d), Bugsy ✦✦ (92), Love Affair (94)

Bonnie Bedelia [b. 1948]

Real name Bonnie Culkin

The aunt of Macaulay Culkin.

Films *They Shoot Horses, Don't They?* ◆◆◆ (69), *Heart Like a Wheel* ◆◆◆ (83), *The Boy Who Could Fly* ◆◆ (86), *Die Hard* ◆◆◆◆ (88), *The Prince of Pennsylvania* ◆◆ (88), *Shadow Makers* ◆◆ (89), *Die Hard 2* ◆◆◆ (90), *Presumed Innocent* ◆◆◆ (90), *Needful Things* (93)

Ed Begley Jr. [b. 1949]

Films *Stay Hungry* ◆◆◆ (76), *Goin' South* ◆◆◆ (78), *Blue Collar* ◆◆◆ (78), *Eating Raoul* ◆◆◆ (82), *Cat People* ◆◆◆◆ (82), *Protocol* ◆◆ (84), *Streets of Fire* ◆ (b)(84), *Transylvania 6-5000* ◆ (85), *The Accidental Tourist* ◆◆◆ (88), *Scenes from the Class Struggle in Beverly Hills* ◆ (89), *She-Devil* ◆ (89), *Meet the Applegates* ◆◆ (91)

James Belushi [b. 1954]

Films *Trading Places* ◆◆◆◆ (83), *Salvador* ◆◆◆◆ (86), *About Last Night...* ◆◆ (86), *Jumpin' Jack Flash* ◆◆ (86), *Little Shop of Horrors* ◆◆ (86), *Red Heat* ◆◆ (88), *K-9* ◆ (89), *Who's Harry Crumb?* ◆ (c)(89), *Filofax* ◆◆ (90), *Curly Sue* ◆ (91), *Only the Lonely* ◆◆◆ (91), *Once upon a Crime* ◆ (92), *Traces of Red* ◆◆◆ (92)

Annette Bening [b. 1958]

Married to Warren Beatty.

Films *The Grifters* ◆◆◆ (90), *Postcards from the Edge* ◆◆◆◆ (90), *Valmont* ◆◆◆ (91), *Regarding Henry* ◆◆ (91), *Guilty by Suspicion* ◆◆ (91), *Bugsy* ◆◆ (92), *Love Affair* (94)

Tom Berenger [b. 1950]

Films *Looking for Mr. Goodbar* ◆◆ (77), *In Praise of Older Women* ◆ (78), *Butch and Sundance: The Early Years* ◆◆◆ (79), *The Dogs of War* ◆◆ (81), *The Big Chill* ◆◆◆ (83), *Eddie and the Cruisers* ◆◆ (83), *Platoon* ◆◆◆ (86), *Someone to Watch*

Over Me ◆◆◆◆ (87), *Betrayed* ◆◆ (88), *Deadly Pursuit* ◆◆◆ (88), *Born on the Fourth of July* ◆◆◆◆ (89), *Major League* ◆◆ (89), *The Field* ◆◆◆ (90), *Love at Large* ◆ (90), *Shattered* ◆◆ (91), *At Play in the Fields of the Lord* ◆◆ (91), *Sniper* ◆◆ (93), *Sliver* (93), *Chasers* (94)

Patrick Bergin [b. 1953]

Films The Courier ◆ (88), *Mountains of the Moon* ◆◆◆◆ (90), *Robin Hood* ◆◆ (91), *Sleeping With the Enemy* ◆ (91), *Love Crimes* ◆ (92), *Patriot Games* ◆◆◆◆ (92), *Map of the Human Heart* (93)

Halle Berry [b. 1968]

Films Jungle Fever ◆◆◆ (91), *The Last Boy Scout* ◆◆◆ (92), *Boomerang* ◆◆ (92), *Desperado* (93), *The Program* (93), *The Flintstones* (94)

Helena Bonham Carter [b. 1966]

Films A Room With a View ◆◆◆◆ (86), *Lady Jane* ◆◆◆ (86), *Maurice* ◆ (c)(87), *Getting It Right* ◆◆◆ (89), *Hamlet* ◆◆◆ (90), *Where Angels Fear to Tread* ◆◆ (91), *Howard's End* ◆◆◆◆ (92)

Philip Bosco [b. 1930]

A wonderful supporting actor who brightens every film he's in.

Films Trading Places ◆◆◆◆ (83), *The Pope of Greenwich Village* ◆◆ (84), *Walls of Glass* ◆◆ (85), *Catholic Boys* ◆◆◆ (85), *Children of a Lesser God* ◆◆◆ (86), *The Money Pit* ◆ (86), *Three Men and a Baby* ◆◆ (87), *Suspect* ◆◆ (87), *Working Girl* ◆◆◆◆ (88), *Another Woman* ◆ (88), *The Dream Team* ◆◆◆◆ (89), *Blue Steel* ◆◆ (90), *Quick Change* ◆◆ (90), *F/X2 – The Deadly Art of Illusion* ◆◆ (91), *Shadows and Fog* ◆◆◆ (92), *Straight Talk* ◆◆◆ (92)

Lara Flynn Boyle [b. 1970]

Quote 'When I audition for things they say, "If Winona Ryder doesn't get it, you will." I used to think I would never work, but there are so many movies, Winona Ryder can't do all of them.'

Films Poltergeist III ◆ (88), Dead Poets Society ◆◆◆◆ (89), The Rookie ◆ (90), Wayne's World ◆◆◆◆ (92), Mobsters: The Evil Empire ◆ (92), Red Rock West ◆◆◆ (93), *The Temp (93), Threesome (93)*

Lorraine Bracco [b. 1955]

Best-known for her gutsy role in *Goodfellas*, Bracco was once a DJ for Radio Luxembourg.

Films Someone to Watch Over Me ◆◆◆◆ (87), The Dream Team ◆◆◆◆ (89), Sing ◆ (89), GoodFellas ◆◆◆◆ (90), Switch ◆◆ (91), Medicine Man ◆◆◆ (92), Traces of Red ◆◆◆ (92)

Kenneth Branagh [b. 1960]

Married to Emma Thompson.

Quote 'I'll get married one day. But first we have to save the earth.'

Films High Season ◆◆ (87), A Month in the Country ◆◆ (87), Henry V ◆◆◆◆ (89; also d&s), Dead Again ◆◆ (91; also d), Peter's Friends ◆◆◆ (92; also d), Much Ado About Nothing ◆◆◆ (93; also d), *Swing Kids (93), Mary Shelley's Frankenstein (94)*

Jeff Bridges [b. 1949]

Quote 'I'm not looking to be any more famous than I already am.'

Films *The Last Picture Show* ◆◆◆◆ *(71)*, *Thunderbolt and Lightfoot* ◆◆ *(74), Stay Hungry* ◆◆◆ *(76), King Kong* ◆◆ *(76), Winter Kills* ◆◆◆◆ *(79), Heaven's Gate* ◆◆◆ *(80), Cutter's Way* ◆◆◆ *(81), Starman* ◆◆◆ *(84),* Against All Odds ◆◆ (84), Jagged Edge ◆◆◆ (85), The Morning After ◆ (86), Nadine ◆◆ (87), Tucker: The Man and His Dream ◆◆◆ (88), The Fabulous Baker Boys ◆◆◆ (89), See You in the Morning ◆◆ (89), Texasville ◆◆ (90), Cold Feet ◆ (c)(90), The Fisher King ◆◆◆ (91), The Vanishing ◆◆ (93), *Fearless (93)*

Matthew Broderick [b. 1962]

Films WarGames ◆◆◆◆ (83), Ladyhawke ◆ (85), Ferris Bueller's Day Off ◆◆ (86), Biloxi Blues ◆◆◆ (88), Torch Song Trilogy ◆◆◆ (88), Family Business ◆◆ (89), Glory ◆◆◆◆ (89), The Freshman ◆◆◆◆ (90), *The Night We Never Met* ◆◆◆ (93)

Albert Brooks [b. 1947]

Real name Albert Einstein

Films *Taxi Driver* ◆◆◆ *(76), Private Benjamin* ◆◆ *(80),* Twilight Zone – The Movie ◆◆ (83), Unfaithfully Yours ◆◆◆ (84), Lost in America ◆◆◆ (85; also d&s), Broadcast News ◆◆◆ (87), Defending Your Life ◆◆ (91; also d&s), *I'll Do Anything (93)*

Bryan Brown [b. 1947]

Married to Rachel Ward.

Films *The Chant of Jimmie Blacksmith* ◆◆◆ *(78), Breaker Morant* ◆◆◆◆ *(80),* Give My Regards to Broad Street ◆◆ (84), Parker ◆◆◆ (85), F/X Murder by Illusion ◆◆ (86), Rebel ◆◆ (86), The Good Wife ◆◆ (87), Cocktail ◆◆ (88), Gorillas in the Mist ◆◆◆ (88), F/X2 – The Deadly Art of Illusion ◆◆ (91), Blood Oath ◆◆ (91), Blame it on the Bellboy ◆◆ (92)

Tim Burton [b. 1960]

DIRECTOR. A former Disney animator, Burton launched Pee-Wee Herman's career. After the success of *Beetlejuice*, at the age of 28 he was given the blockbusting *Batman*. His films are incredibly stylish, with a gothic look to them, often at the expense of a coherent script.

Quote 'The Gulf War had a beginning, middle and end. It's actually much better constructed than most of my movies.'

Films Pee-Wee's Big Adventure ◆◆ (85), Beetlejuice ◆◆ (88), Batman ◆◆ (89), Edward Scissorhands ◆◆ (90), Batman Returns ◆◆◆ (92), Singles ◆◆◆◆ (c)(93), *Ed Wood (94)*

Gary Busey [b. 1944]

Quote 'There are only three things you need to do if you want to make it in Hollywood. Learn how to make your own salad. Learn how to fall in slow motion. And learn how to cry.'

Quote 'Being poor sure sucks, but you know what sucks more? Being poor and famous.'

Films *Thunderbolt and Lightfoot* ◆◆ (74), *A Star is Born* ◆◆ (76), *Straight Time* ◆◆◆ (78), *The Buddy Holly Story* ◆◆◆◆ (78), *Carny* ◆◆◆ (80), *Barbarosa* ◆◆◆ (82), *Street Fleet* ◆◆ (83), *Insignificance* ◆◆ (85), *Silver Bullet* ◆ (85), *Let's Get Harry* ◆ (86), *Lethal Weapon* ◆◆◆ (87), *Bullet Proof* ◆ (87), *Hider in the House* ◆◆ (89), *Predator 2* ◆◆ (90), *Point Break* ◆◆ (91), *The Player* ◆◆◆◆ (c)(92), *Under Siege* ◆◆◆ (92), *Rookie of the Year* (93)

Gabriel Byrne [b. 1950]

Married to Ellen Barkin.

Films *Excalibur* ◆◆◆ (81), *Defence of the Realm* ◆◆◆◆ (86), *Hello Again* ◆◆ (87), *Siesta* ◆ (87), *Gothic* ◆◆ (87), *The Courier* ◆ (88), *Miller's Crossing* ◆◆◆◆ (90), *Diamond Skulls* ◆(90), *Cool World* ◆ (92), *Into the West* ◆◆◆ (92), *Assassin* ◆◆ (93)

Nicolas Cage [b. 1964]

Real name Nicolas Coppola

Renowned almost as much for his off-camera stunts as he is for his roles in front of it, Cage is the nephew of film director Francis Ford Coppola. He junked the family name, turning to acting 'to get laid'. Keen to make his performances as authentic as possible, he had two teeth extracted for his role in *Birdy* and ate a live cockroach on *Vampire's Kiss*.

Quote 'Yeah, my real name is Coppola. But nobody took me seriously.'

Films *Fast Times at Ridgemont High* ◆◆◆ (b)(82), *Valley Girl* ◆◆◆ (83), *Rumble Fish* ◆◆◆ (83), *Birdy* ◆◆ (84), *The Cotton Club* ◆◆ (84), *Racing with the Moon* ◆◆◆ (84), *Peggy Sue Got Married* ◆◆◆ (86), *Moonstruck* ◆◆◆◆ (87), *Raising Arizona* ◆◆◆◆ (87), *Vampire's Kiss* ◆◆◆ (89), *Wild at Heart* ◆ (90), *Wings of the Apache* ◆ (90), *Zandalee* ◆ (91), *Honeymoon in Vegas* ◆◆◆◆ (92), *Red Rock West* ◆◆◆ (93), *Guarding Tess* (93)

Michael Caine [b. 1933]

Real name Maurice Micklewhite

Born in the Elephant and Castle, Caine's the son of a Billingsgate fish porter and a charwoman. He himself worked as a Smithfield meat porter while attending acting classes. He took his surname from the film *The Caine Mutiny* and made his mark with the films *Zulu*, *The Ipcress File* and *Alfie*. The most prolific of Hollywood stars, the many appalling movies he's made don't stop him occasionally shining in the right film. Once one of London's most swinging bachelors, he fell in love with Shakira Baksh when he saw her in a TV commercial and pulled weight to get her phone number. They have been married for over twenty years.

Quote 'I'm not interested in directing. Now producing...! The director has to be there when it starts to rain. I notice on the set when it starts to rain, the only person who goes back to the hotel is the producer.'

Quote 'I was rich from the day I was born, I just didn't have the money.'

Films *Zulu* ◆◆◆ (64), *The Ipcress File* ◆◆◆◆ (65), *Alfie* ◆◆◆ (66), *Funeral in Berlin* ◆◆ (67), *Billion Dollar Brain* ◆◆ (67), *The Italian Job* ◆◆◆ (69), *Battle of Britain* ◆◆ (69), *Get Carter* ◆◆◆ (71), *Sleuth* ◆◆◆ (72), *The Man Who Would Be King* ◆◆◆◆ (75), *The Eagle Has Landed* ◆◆ (76), *A Bridge Too Far* ◆◆ (77), *California Suite* ◆◆◆ (78), *Dressed to Kill* ◆◆◆ (80), *Escape to Victory* ◆ (81), *The Hand* ◆ (81), *Deathtrap* ◆◆ (82), *The Honorary Consul* ◆ (83), *Educating Rita* ◆◆◆ (83), *Blame it on Rio* ◆◆ (84), *The Holcroft Covenant* ◆ (85), *Water* ◆ (85), *Hannah and Her Sisters* ◆◆◆◆ (86), *Mona Lisa* ◆◆◆ (86), *Half Moon Street* ◆ (86), *Sweet Liberty* ◆◆ (86), *Jaws the Revenge* ◆ (87), *Surrender* ◆◆◆ (87), *The Whistle Blower* ◆◆ (87), *The Fourth Protocol* ◆◆ (87), *Dirty Rotten Scoundrels* ◆◆◆◆ (88),

Without a Clue ✦ (88), Bullseye! ✦ (90), A Shock to the System ✦✦ (90), Noises Off ✦✦✦ (92), The Muppet Christmas Carol ✦✦ (92), Blue Ice ✦ (92)

James Cameron [b. 1954]

DIRECTOR. An action specialist whose recent big films appear to have drained some of his invention and energy.

Quote 'For me, actors are just more sophisticated rubber puppets.'

Films *Piranha II: Flying Killers* ✦ *(81; s only)*, The Terminator ✦✦✦✦ (84; also s), Rambo: First Blood Part II ✦✦ (85; s only), Aliens ✦✦✦✦ (86; also s), The Abyss ✦✦ (89; also s), Terminator 2: Judgment Day ✦✦✦(91; also s)

John Candy [b. 1950]

Real name John Franklin Candy

Films *1941* ✦✦ *(79)*, *The Blues Brothers* ✦✦✦✦ *(80)*, *Stripes* ✦✦ *(81)*, National Lampoon's Vacation ✦ (c)(83), Splash ✦✦✦✦ (84), Brewster's Millions ✦ (85), Volunteers ✦ (85), Little Shop of Horrors ✦✦ (86), Planes, Trains and Automobiles ✦✦✦ (87), Spaceballs ✦✦ (87), Uncle Buck ✦✦ (89), Who's Harry Crumb? ✦ (89), Home Alone ✦✦ (c)(90), JFK ✦✦✦ (91), Nothing But Trouble ✦ (91), Only the Lonely ✦✦✦ (91), The Rescuers Down Under ✦✦✦ (v)(91), Once upon a Crime ✦ (92)

Phoebe Cates [b. 1963]

Real name Phoebe Katz
Married to Kevin Kline.

Films *Fast Times at Ridgemont High* ✦✦✦ *(82)*, Gremlins ✦✦✦ (84), Shag ✦✦ (88), Bright Lights, Big City ✦ (88), Gremlins 2: The New Batch ✦✦✦ (90), I Love You to Death ✦ (c)(90), Drop Dead Fred ✦ (91), *Bodies, Rest and Motion (93)*

Kim Cattrall [b. 1956]

Films *Porky's* ✦ *(82)*, Police Academy ✦✦ (84), Turk 182! ✦✦ (85), Big Trouble in Little China ✦ (86), Mannequin ✦ (87), Masquerade ✦✦ (88), Midnight Crossing ✦ (88), The Return of the Musketeers ✦✦

(89), The Bonfire of the Vanities ✦ (90), Star Trek VI: The Undiscovered Country ✦✦✦✦ (91), Split Second ✦✦ (92)

Chevy Chase [b. 1943]

Real name Cornelius Crane Chase

Quote 'I'm interested in pushing the envelope in the Chevy Chase world of acting.'

Quote 'I said that I didn't think Chevy Chase could ad-lib a fart after a baked-bean dinner. I think he took umbrage at that a little bit.' [Johnny Carson]

Films *Foul Play* ✦✦ *(78)*, *Seems Like Old Times* ✦✦✦ *(80)*, *Caddyshack* ✦✦✦(80), National Lampoon's Vacation ✦ (83), Fletch ✦ (85), Spies Like Us ✦✦ (85), National Lampoon's European Vacation ✦✦ (85), ¡Three Amigos! ✦ (86), The Couch Trip ✦ (c)(88), Fletch Lives ✦ (89), National Lampoon's Christmas Vacation ✦✦ (89), Nothing But Trouble ✦ (91), L.A. Story ✦✦✦ (c)(91), Memoirs of an Invisible Man ✦✦ (92), Accidental Hero ✦✦✦✦ (c)(92), *Cops and Robbersons (93)*

Cher [b. 1946]

Real name Cherilyn Sarkisian LaPiere

One of the few singing stars to make it to the Hollywood peak, she's come a long way since the days of Sonny & Cher. Of Armenian, Turkish, French and Cherokee descent, she's said to be a walking advertisement for plastic surgery. She's also a godsend to dress designers, if not fabric manufacturers. Married and divorced twice (with daughter Chastity and son Elijah Blue), she now extols the joys of toyboys. She once had a butterfly and flower tattooed on her bottom, although they could be anywhere by now.

Quote 'Husbands are like fires. They go out when unattended.'

Films *Good Times* ✦✦✦ *(67)*, *Chastity* ✦ *(69)*, Come Back to the Five and Dime, Jimmy Dean, Jimmy Dean ✦✦✦ (82), Silkwood ✦✦✦ (83), Mask ✦✦✦ (85), Moonstruck ✦✦✦✦ (87), Suspect ✦✦ (87), The Witches of Eastwick ✦✦✦ (87), Mermaids ✦✦ (91), The Player ✦✦✦✦ (c)(92)

John Cleese [b. 1939]

Real name John Marwood Cleese

Quote 'Filming is like a long air journey – there's so much hanging around and boredom that they keep giving you food. Food is very important. The other actors don't really matter.'

Films *And Now For Something Completely Different* ◆◆◆◆ (71; also s), *Monty Python and the Holy Grail* ◆◆◆ (75; also s), *Monty Python's Life of Brian* ◆◆ (79; also s), *Time Bandits* ◆◆◆◆ (81), *Great Muppet Caper* ◆◆◆ (c)(81), *Monty Python's The Meaning of Life* ◆◆ (83; also s), *Yellowbeard* ◆ (83), *Privates on Parade* ◆◆ (83), *Silverado* ◆◆◆ (85), *Clockwise* ◆◆◆ (86), *A Fish Called Wanda* ◆◆◆ (88; also s), *The Big Picture* ◆◆◆ (c)(89), *Erik the Viking* ◆ (89), *Bullseye!* ◆ (c)(90), *An American Tail: Fievel Goes West* ◆◆ (v)(91), *Splitting Heirs* ◆ (93).

Glenn Close [b. 1947]

Close comes from one of the oldest families in America, established in Greenwich, Connecticut in 1682. After acting at school, she spent five years as a travelling folksinger with the group 'Up the People'. While every other band was singing protest songs, hers espoused traditional values. She is one of the few Hollywood stars who relishes playing unsympathetic roles. Unlike so many other actors who moan about the business, the only thing she claims to dislike about movie-making is coffee in styrofoam cups.

Quote 'She always looks like she has a secret.' [Michael Douglas]

Films *The World According to Garp* ◆◆◆ (82), *The Big Chill* ◆◆◆ (83), *The Natural* ◆◆ (84), *Greystoke: The Legend of Tarzan, Lord of the Apes* ◆◆◆ (v)(84), *Maxie* ◆ (85), *Jagged Edge* ◆◆◆ (85), *Fatal Attraction* ◆◆ (87), *Dangerous Liaisons* ◆◆◆ (88), *Hamlet* ◆◆◆ (90), *Reversal of Fortune* ◆◆◆◆ (90), *Meeting Venus* ◆◆ (91), *Hook* ◆◆◆ (c)(91), *The House of the Spirits* (93), *Once upon a Forest* (v)(93)

Joel Coen [b. 1955]

DIRECTOR. Along with his brother Ethan, the two Coens have written, produced and directed some of the most stylish, witty and innovative films of the past decade. Immense fun's to be had from working out how they manage to make their camera go boldly where no camera has gone before, even down a plughole. They're also one of the best chatshow double acts in the business.

Films *Spies Like Us* ◆◆ (c)(85; a only), *Blood Simple* ◆◆◆◆ (85; also s), *Crimewave* ◆◆ (86; s only), *Raising Arizona* ◆◆◆◆ (87; also s), *Miller's Crossing* ◆◆◆◆ (90; also s), *Barton Fink* ◆ (92; also s), *The Hudsucker Proxy* (93; also s)

Robbie Coltrane [b. 1950]

Films *Krull* ◆ (83), *Supergrass* ◆◆ (85), *Mona Lisa* ◆◆◆ (86), *Absolute Beginners* ◆◆ (86), *Defence of the Realm* ◆◆◆◆ (86), *Caravaggio* ◆◆◆ (86), *Eat the Rich* ◆ (87), *The Fruit Machine* ◆◆ (88), *Bert Rigby, You're a Fool* ◆ (89), *Danny the Champion of the World* ◆◆ (89), *Henry V* ◆◆◆◆ (89), *Slipstream* ◆ (89), *Nuns on the Run* ◆◆ (90), *Perfectly Normal* ◆◆ (91), *The Pope Must Die* ◆◆ (91), *The Adventures of Huck Finn* (93)

Sean Connery [b. 1930]

Real name Thomas Connery

Dropping out of school at 13, Connery tried many different occupations – coffin polisher, bricklayer, milkman, lifeguard, cement mixer, bodybuilder, even modelling swimming trunks – before joining the chorus of a West End production of *South Pacific*. It's said one of his main attractions as James Bond in *Dr. No* – for which he beat Richard Burton and Roger Moore – was the fact that he only cost £15,000 against the $1m a major star would have asked. Now, 40 films later and having at last escaped Bondage, he earns up to $10m a movie. His amazing array of accents includes Russian –Scottish, Irish–Scottish, Spanish–Scottish, Arabian–

Scottish and English-Scottish.

Quote 'I have always hated that damn James Bond. I'd like to kill him.'

Quote 'With the exception of Lassie, he's the only person I know who's never been spoiled by success.' [Terence Young, director]

Films *Dr. No* ◆◆◆◆ *(62)*, *From Russia With Love* ◆◆◆◆ *(63)*, *Marnie* ◆◆◆◆ *(64)*, *Goldfinger* ◆◆◆◆ *(64)*, *Thunderball* ◆◆ *(65)*, *You Only Live Twice* ◆◆◆ *(67)*, *The Anderson Tapes* ◆◆ *(71)*, *Diamonds Are Forever* ◆◆◆ *(71)*, *The Offence* ◆◆◆ *(73)*, *Murder on the Orient Express* ◆◆ *(74)*, *Zardoz* ◆ *(74)*, *The Man Who Would Be King* ◆◆◆◆ *(75)*, *Robin and Marian* ◆◆ *(76)*, *A Bridge Too Far* ◆◆ *(77)*, *The First Great Train Robbery* ◆◆◆ *(79)*, *Time Bandits* ◆◆◆◆ *(81)*, *Outland* ◆ *(81)*, *The Man with the Deadly Lens* ◆◆ *(82)*, *Never Say Never Again* ◆◆ *(83)*, *Highlander* ◆◆ *(86)*, *The Name of the Rose* ◆◆◆◆ *(86)*, *The Untouchables* ◆◆◆◆ *(87)*, *The Presidio* ◆◆ *(88)*, *Family Business* ◆◆ *(89)*, *Indiana Jones and the Last Crusade* ◆◆◆◆ *(89)*, *Highlander II – the Quickening* ◆ *(90)*, *The Russia House* ◆◆ *(90)*, *The Hunt for Red October* ◆◆◆ *(90)*, *Robin Hood: Prince of Thieves* ◆◆◆ *(c)(91)*, *Medicine Man* ◆◆◆ *(92)*, *Rising Sun* *(93)*, *A Good Man in Africa* *(93)*

Francis Ford Coppola [b. 1939]

DIRECTOR. Reputedly fired five times while making *The Godfather*, Coppola was the first of the movie-brat directors, himself Godfather to new talent like Scorsese, De Palma and Spielberg. He hates the studio system, but every time he sets up on his own he comes a cropper financially and is forced to eat humble pie and make run-of-the-mill films, just so he can get enough money to set up on his own again and tell the studios to get lost once more. His first film, although he seems slightly shy about it now, was *Tonight for Sure*, a mild porn pic.

Quote 'The big studios make films like fast food.'

Films *Dementia 13* ◆◆ *(63; also s)*, *Is Paris Burning?* ◆◆ *(66; s only)*, *This Property is Condemned* ◆◆ *(66; s only)*, *You're a Big Boy Now* ◆◆◆ *(67; also s)*, *Finian's Rainbow* ◆◆ *(68)*, *The Rain People* ◆◆◆ *(69; also s)*, *Patton* ◆◆◆◆ *(70; s only)*, *The Godfather* ◆◆◆ *(72; also s)*, *The Godfather, Part II* ◆◆◆◆ *(74; also s)*, *The Conversation* ◆◆◆◆ *(74; also s)*, *The Great Gatsby* ◆◆◆ *(74; s only)*, *Apocalypse Now* ◆◆◆◆ *(79; also a&s)*, *One from the Heart* ◆◆ *(82; also s)*, *The Outsiders* ◆◆ *(83)*, *Rumble Fish* ◆◆◆ *(83; also s)*, *The Cotton Club* ◆◆ *(84; also s)*, *Peggy Sue Got Married* ◆◆◆ *(86)*, *Gardens of Stone* ◆◆◆ *(87)*, *Tucker: The Man and His Dream* ◆◆◆ *(88)*, *New York Stories* ◆◆ *(89; also s)*, *The Godfather, Part III* ◆◆◆ *(90; also s)*, *Bram Stoker's Dracula* ◆◆◆ *(92)*

Kevin Costner [b. 1955]

For some time, the most unseen actor ever. He left *WarGames* after shooting had begun, so that he could be in *The Big Chill*. However, his ten minutes of screen time were cut. He later turned down leads in *Raising Arizona*, *Platoon* and *Jagged Edge*, until finally breaking through with *The Untouchables*, twelve years after his embarrassing tits'n'ass flick *Sizzle Beach USA*. During this fallow period, wife Cindy (his childhood sweetheart) brought home the bacon by working as Snow White at Disneyland. Has largely made his own career, shrewdly picking up films nobody else wanted to do like *No Way Out* and *Bull Durham* before astounding a sceptical Hollywood with *Dances with Wolves*.

Quote 'They're going to have to stay up nights thinking how to cut me out of this one.' [On learning he was going to be in almost every scene in *Fandango*]

Quote 'When I look at a film of Kevin Costner's I die of boredom.' [Mickey Rourke]

Films *Sizzle Beach, U.S.A.* ◆ *(74)*, *Night Shift* ◆◆ *(b)(82)*, *Frances* ◆◆ *(b)(82)*, *Testament* ◆◆◆ *(83)*, *Table for Five* ◆◆ *(b)(83)*, *The Big Chill* ◆◆◆ *(b)(83)*, *Silverado* ◆◆◆ *(85)*, *Fandango* ◆◆ *(85)*, *The Untouchables* ◆◆◆◆

(87), No Way Out ✦✦✦ (87), Bull Durham ✦✦✦ (88), Field of Dreams ✦✦✦✦ (89), Dances With Wolves ✦✦✦✦ (90; also d), Revenge ✦✦ (90), JFK ✦✦✦ (91), Robin Hood: Prince of Thieves ✦✦✦ (91), The Bodyguard ✦✦ (92), *A Perfect World* (94)

Peter Coyote [b. 1942]

Quote 'As far as I'm concerned, I'm a Zen Buddhist student first – an actor second. If I can't reconcile the two lives I'll stop being an actor. The other is more important – I spend more time off-screen than on.'

Films *Southern Comfort* ✦✦✦✦ (80), E.T. The Extra-Terrestrial ✦✦✦✦ (82), Cross Creek ✦✦ (83), Slayground ✦ (84), Strangers Kiss ✦✦ (84), Heartbreakers ✦✦ (85), Jagged Edge ✦✦✦ (85), The Legend of Billie Jean ✦ (85), A Man in Love ✦✦ (87), Outrageous Fortune ✦✦ (87), Heart of Midnight ✦ (89), Bitter Moon ✦ (92)

David Cronenberg [b. 1943]

DIRECTOR. He's done more to besmirch Canada's squeaky-clean image than anyone else. He graduated from exploitation schlock to mainstream, but still specialises in horror, avoiding the supernatural or mad axe-men in favour of sinister medical conglomerates and graphic displays of flesh at war with the mind. His movies aren't ideal pre-operation relaxation! His diffident persona in interviews only make his films seem the more alarming.

Quote 'It's a small field, venereal horror. But at least I'm king of it.'

Quote 'He goes to that part of the brain that doesn't want to be touched.' [Martin Scorsese]

Films *Shivers* ✦✦✦ (75; also s), Rabid ✦✦ (76; also s), The Brood ✦✦ (79; also s), Scanners ✦✦ (80; also s), The Dead Zone ✦✦✦ (83), Videodrome ✦✦✦ (83; also s), Into the Night ✦✦ (85; a only), The Fly ✦✦✦✦ (86; also a&s), Dead Ringers ✦✦ (88; also s), Nightbreed ✦ (90; a only), Naked Lunch ✦ (91; also s), *M. Butterfly* (93)

Tom Cruise [b. 1962]

Real name Thomas Cruise Mapother IV

A one-time trainee monk who suffered from dyslexia as a child, Cruise took up acting out of boredom when he injured himself wrestling in high school. Initially little more than a smile on legs, he has proved himself capable of quality acting in a series of remarkably accomplished pictures. He was married for three years to Mimi Rogers, 9 years his senior, and now to Nicole Kidman, 2 inches taller. Both devout Scientologists, after failing to produce a child, they very publicly adopted a daughter in 1993.

Quote 'I was taught to treat people well. I don't think you can get away with the star stuff. After a while, it just comes back and eats you.'

Quote 'Tom Cruise is frighteningly polite. He's so nice, he's sick.' [Tony Scott, director]

Films *Endless Love* ✦ (81), Taps ✦✦ (81), Risky Business ✦✦ (83), Losin' It ✦✦ (83), The Outsiders ✦✦ (83), Legend ✦ (85), Top Gun ✦✦ (86), The Color of Money ✦✦✦ (86), Rain Man ✦✦✦✦ (88), Cocktail ✦✦ (88), Born on the Fourth of July ✦✦✦✦ (89), Days of Thunder ✦ (90), Far and Away ✦✦ (92), A Few Good Men ✦✦✦✦ (92), The Firm (93)

Billy Crystal [b. 1947]

Films This is Spinal Tap ✦✦✦✦ (c)(84), Running Scared ✦✦ (86), The Princess Bride ✦✦ (c)(87), Throw Momma from the Train ✦✦✦ (87), When Harry Met Sally ✦✦✦✦ (89), City Slickers ✦✦✦✦ (91), Mr. Saturday Night ✦✦ (92; also d&s), *City Slickers II* (94; also s)

Macaulay Culkin [b. 1980]

Paid just $100,000 for *Home Alone*, Mac can now command $8m a film. This makes him not only the highest-paid child the world has ever seen but also puts him ahead of top actresses like Julia Roberts and Sharon Stone. His career is controlled by his parents with father Kit, himself an actor though rather less successful, said to be one of the toughest negotiators in Hollywood. If you're one of those who are allergic to his cute charms and are longing for the day when his voice breaks, you ought to be warned that there are six other Culkin children. Their aunt is Bonnie Bedelia.

Quote 'There aren't too many stars around whom you can bribe with a Big Mac and fries.' [John Hughes]

Quote 'I don't even get an allowance. Whenever I need money, I just ask my mother and...Bang!'

Films *Rocket Gibraltar* ♦♦ (88), *See You in the Morning* ♦♦ (89), *Uncle Buck* ♦♦ (89), *Jacob's Ladder* ♦♦ (90), *Home Alone* ♦♦ (90), *Only the Lonely* ♦♦♦ (c)(91), *My Girl* ♦ (92), *Home Alone 2: Lost in New York* ♦♦ (92), *The Good Son* (93), *The Pagemaster* (v)(94), *Getting Even With Dad* (94)

Jamie Lee Curtis [b. 1958]

The daughter of stars Tony Curtis and Janet Leigh, she began her screen career as the quintessential 'Scream Queen', menaced by knife-wielding maniacs in a series of slasher movies before graduating to the hooker with a heart in *Trading Places*. Since she is frightened by horror movies, she sleeps 'with a basset hound between my legs...I'm well protected.' It is said she once had a studio cooled to make her breasts stand up. Her husband is actor Christopher Guest, who plays the lead guitarist in *Spinal Tap*. He is due to inherit a baronetcy and a seat in the House of Lords, which will make her Lady Guest.

Quote 'My breasts are beautiful and I gotta tell you, they've gotten a lot of attention for what is relatively short screen time.'

Films *Halloween* ♦♦♦♦ (78), *Prom Night* ♦ (80), *Halloween II* ♦ (81), *The Fog* ♦♦ (81), *Trading Places* ♦♦♦♦ (83), *Love Letters* ♦♦♦ (84), *Perfect* ♦ (85), *A Man in Love* ♦♦ (87), *Silent Voice* ♦♦ (87), *The Adventures of Buckaroo Banzai Across the 8th*

Dimension ♦♦ (c)(87), *A Fish Called Wanda* ♦♦♦ (88), *Nicky and Gino* ♦♦ (88), *Blue Steel* ♦♦ (90), *My Girl* ♦ (92), *Forever Young* ♦♦♦ (92), *Mother's Boys* (93)

Joan Cusack [b. 1962]

Sister of John.

Films *Broadcast News* ♦♦♦ (87), *Working Girl* ♦♦♦♦ (88), *Married to the Mob* ♦♦ (88), *Stars and Bars* ♦ (88), *Men Don't Leave* ♦♦ (90), *My Blue Heaven* ♦♦ (90), *Accidental Hero* ♦♦♦♦ (92), *Toys* ♦♦ (92), *Addams Family Values* (93)

John Cusack [b. 1966]

Brother of Joan.

Films *Class* ♦ (83), *The Journey of Natty Gann* ♦♦♦ (85), *The Sure Thing* ♦♦♦ (85), *Stand by Me* ♦♦ (86), *Broadcast News* ♦♦♦ (c)(87), *Eight Men Out* ♦♦ (88), *Shadow Makers* ♦♦ (89), *The Grifters* ♦♦♦ (90), *Shadows and Fog* ♦♦♦ (92), *The Player* ♦♦♦♦ (c)(92), *Bob Roberts* ♦♦♦ (c)(92), *Joey Coyle* (93)

Beverly D'Angelo [b. 1954]

Films *Annie Hall* ♦♦♦ (b)(77), *Coal Miner's Daughter* (80), *National Lampoon's Vacation* ♦ (83), *Finders Keepers* ♦♦ (84), *National Lampoon's European Vacation* ♦♦ (85), *Aria* ♦ (87), *The Woo Woo Kid* ♦♦♦ (87), *High Spirits* ♦ (88), *National Lampoon's Christmas Vacation* ♦♦ (89), *Daddy's Dying, Who's Got the Will?* ♦♦♦ (90), *Pacific Heights* ♦♦ (90), *The Miracle* ♦♦ (91), *The Pope Must Die* ♦♦ (91), *Man Trouble* ♦ (92)

Willem Dafoe [b. 1955]

Real name William Dafoe

Films *Heaven's Gate* ♦♦♦ (b)(80), *The Hunger* ♦ (b)(83), *Streets of Fire* ♦ (84), *To Live and Die in L.A.* ♦♦ (85), *Platoon* ♦♦♦ (86), *Mississippi Burning* ♦♦ (88), *The Last Temptation of Christ* ♦ (88), *Saigon* ♦♦ (88), *Born on the Fourth of July* ♦♦♦♦ (89), *Triumph of the Spirit* ♦♦ (89), *Wild at Heart* ♦ (90), *Cry-Baby* ♦♦

(c)(91), Light Sleeper ♦ (92), White Sands ♦♦♦ (92), Body of Evidence ♦ (93)

Jeff Daniels [b. 1955]

Films *Ragtime* ♦♦♦ *(81)*, Terms of Endearment ♦♦♦ (83), Marie ♦♦♦ (85), The Purple Rose of Cairo ♦♦ (85), Something Wild ♦♦♦ (86), Heartburn ♦ (86), Radio Days ♦♦♦ (87), The House on Carroll Street ♦♦ (88), Sweet Hearts Dance ♦♦ (88), Checking Out ♦ (89), Welcome Home, Roxy Carmichael ♦♦♦ (90), Arachnophobia ♦♦ (90), Love Hurts ♦♦ (90), The Butcher's Wife ♦♦♦ (92)

Ted Danson [b. 1947]

Real name Edward Bridge Danson III

Quote 'People want to fuck movie stars and hug television stars.'

Films *The Onion Field* ♦♦♦ *(79)*, Body Heat ♦♦♦♦ *(81)*, Creepshow ♦♦ *(82)*, A Fine Mess ♦ (86), Just Between Friends ♦♦ (86), Three Men and a Baby ♦♦ (87), Cousins ♦♦♦ (89), Dad ♦♦ (89), Three Men and a Little Lady ♦ (90), *Made in America (93)*

Lolita Davidovich [b. 1962]

Billed in early roles as Lolita David.

Films Adventures in Babysitting ♦♦ (b)(87), The Big Town ♦♦ (b)(87), Blaze ♦♦ (89), The Inner Circle ♦ (91), The Object of Beauty ♦♦ (91), Raising Cain ♦♦ (92), Leap of Faith ♦♦♦ (92), *Boiling Point (93)*, *Younger and Younger (93), Intersection (94)*

Geena Davis [b. 1957]

Real name Virginia Elizabeth Davis

Quote 'The real me isn't glamorous. The real me stays in, pigs out on big break-fasts and hates glitzy parties.'

Quote 'I have an elbow that bends the wrong way, and [when I was young] I'd do things like stand in an elevator and the doors would close, and I'd pretend that my arm had got caught in it, and then I'd scream, "Ow, ow, put it back!".'

Films Tootsie ♦♦♦♦ (82), Transylvania 6-5000 ♦ (85), Fletch ♦ (85), The Fly ♦♦♦♦ (86), The Accidental Tourist ♦♦♦ (88), Beetlejuice ♦♦ (88), Earth Girls Are Easy ♦ (89), Quick Change ♦♦ (90), Thelma & Louise ♦♦♦♦ (91), A League of their Own ♦♦ (92), Accidental Hero ♦♦♦♦ (92), *Angie, I Says (94)*

Judy Davis [b. 1955]

Films *My Brilliant Career* ♦♦♦♦ *(79)*, Who Dares Win ♦ *(82)*, Heatwave ♦♦♦ *(83)*, A Passage to India ♦♦♦ (84), Kangaroo ♦♦ (86), High Tide ♦♦♦ (87), Alice ♦♦♦ (90), Naked Lunch ♦ (91), Impromptu ♦♦♦ (91), Where Angels Fear to Tread ♦♦ (91), Barton Fink ♦ (92), Husbands and Wives ♦♦♦ (92), *The New Age (93)*

Daniel Day-Lewis [b. 1957]

Films Gandhi ♦♦♦ (b)(82), Bounty ♦♦ (84), My Beautiful Laundrette ♦♦♦ (85), A Room With a View ♦♦♦♦ (86), Stars and Bars ♦ (88), The Unbearable Lightness of Being ♦ (88), My Left Foot ♦♦♦♦ (89), The Last of the Mohicans ♦♦ (92), *The Gerry Conlon Story (93), The Age of Innocence (93), In the Name of the Father (94)*

Rebecca De Mornay [b. 1961]

Films One from the Heart ♦♦ (b)(82), Risky Business ♦♦ (83), Testament ♦♦♦ (83), Runaway Train ♦♦♦ (85), The Trip to Bountiful ♦♦♦ (85), And God Created Woman ♦ (88), Dealers ♦♦ (89), Backdraft ♦♦ (91), The Hand That Rocks the Cradle ♦♦ (92), *Beyond Innocence (93), The Three Musketeers (94)*

Robert De Niro [b. 1943]

Almost more extraordinary than his elec-trifying acting, is the length to which he goes to achieve his performance. He's encouraged scabs to grow on his face to play a junkie, learned to speak Sicilian for *The Godfather*, spent a month driving a taxi for *Taxi Driver*, lived for six weeks in a steel-mining town to understand his character in *The Deer Hunter*, gained 60 pounds gorging on pasta to play *Raging*

Bull and learned Latin to play a priest. Only once has he been defeated, when he tried to get a bus driver's licence for *The Bronx Tale*. He failed the test twice!

Quote 'I only go to Los Angeles when I'm paid for it.'

Quote 'What I've always found remarkable about Bobby is his ability to not only become the person he is playing but to physically change the way he looks.' [Brian de Palma]

Films *Greetings* ♦♦♦ (68), *Bloody Mama* ♦♦ (70), *Hi, Mom!* ♦♦♦ (70), *Mean Streets* ♦♦♦ (73), *Taxi Driver* ♦♦♦ (76), *The Last Tycoon* ♦♦♦ (76), *New York, New York* ♦♦ (77), *1900* ♦♦ (77), *The Deer Hunter* ♦♦♦ (78), *Raging Bull* ♦♦♦ (80), *True Confessions* ♦♦ (81), *The King of Comedy* ♦♦♦♦ (83), *Falling in Love* ♦♦ (84), *Once Upon a Time in America* ♦♦♦♦ (84), *Brazil* ♦♦♦♦ (85), *The Mission* ♦♦ (86), *The Untouchables* ♦♦♦♦ (87), *Angel Heart* ♦♦ (87), *Midnight Run* ♦♦♦♦ (88), *Jacknife* ♦♦ (89), *We're No Angels* ♦ (89), *Awakenings* ♦♦♦ (90), *GoodFellas* ♦♦♦♦ (90), *Stanley & Iris* ♦♦ (90), *Backdraft* ♦♦ (91), *Guilty by Suspicion* ♦♦ (91), *Cape Fear* ♦♦ (92), *Night and the City* ♦♦ (92), *Mad Dog and Glory* ♦♦♦ (93), *A Bronx Tale* (93; also d), *This Boy's Life* (93), *Mary Shelley's Frankenstein* (94)

Dana Delaney [b. 1957]

Films *Almost You* ♦♦ (84), *Masquerade* ♦♦ (88), *Patty Hearst* ♦♦ (88), *Light Sleeper* ♦ (92), *Housesitter* ♦♦ (92)

Patrick Dempsey [b. 1966]

Films *Can't Buy Me Love* ♦♦ (87), *The Woo Woo Kid* ♦♦♦ (87), *Sisters* ♦♦ (88), *Loverboy* ♦♦ (89), *Coupe de Ville* ♦♦♦♦ (92), *Mobsters: The Evil Empire* ♦ (92), *With Honors* (93)

Brian Dennehy [b. 1939]

Any time a director needs a cop and Charles Durning's too busy, Dennehy's brought in. Another scene-stealing sup-porting actor who looks immensely familiar but may be hard to put a name to.

Quote 'An actor friend introduced me to my agent, Susan Smith. We met and had a couple of drinks and she got shit-faced. Really, really, shit-faced! I said to myself: That's the agent for me.'

Films *Looking for Mr. Goodbar* ♦♦ (77), *Semi-Tough* ♦♦♦ (77), *F.I.S.T.* ♦♦♦ (78), *Foul Play* ♦♦ (78), *Butch and Sundance: The Early Years* ♦♦♦ (79), *10* ♦♦ (79), *First Blood* ♦♦ (82), *Never Cry Wolf* ♦♦♦ (83), *Gorky Park* ♦♦ (83), *Finders Keepers* ♦♦ (84), *Cocoon* ♦♦ (85), *Twice in a Lifetime* ♦♦♦ (85), *Silverado* ♦♦♦ (85), *F/X Murder by Illusion* ♦♦ (86), *Legal Eagles* ♦♦♦ (86), *The Belly of an Architect* ♦♦ (87), *Best Seller* ♦♦♦♦ (87), *Miles from Home* ♦♦ (88), *Blue Heat* ♦♦ (90), *Presumed Innocent* ♦♦♦ (90), *F/X2 – The Deadly Art of Illusion* ♦♦ (91), *Gladiator* ♦♦♦ (92)

Johnny Depp [b. 1963]

Real name John Christopher Depp II

Quote 'I'm an old-fashioned guy. I want to have a normal life, I want to get married and have kids. I want to be an old man with a beer belly sitting on a porch, looking at a lake or something.'

Films *A Nightmare on Elm Street* ♦♦♦ (84), *Platoon* ♦♦♦ (86), *Edward Scissorhands* ♦♦ (90), *Cry-Baby* ♦♦ (91), *Freddy's Dead: The Final Nightmare* ♦ (c)(92), *Benny & Joon* ♦♦♦ (93), *Gilbert Grape* (93), *Ed Wood* (94)

Laura Dern [b. 1967]

Films *Foxes* ♦♦ (b)(80), *Teachers* ♦♦ (b)(84), *Mask* ♦♦♦ (85), *Smooth Talk* ♦♦♦ (85), *Blue Velvet* ♦♦ (86), *Haunted Summer* ♦ (88), *Shadow Makers* ♦♦ (89), *Wild at Heart* ♦ (90), *Rambling Rose* ♦♦♦♦ (91), *Jurassic Park* (93)

Danny DeVito [b. 1944]

Five feet nothing, De Vito's the shortest leading man in movies. Trained as a hair-dresser, he worked for a year in his sister's boutique as 'Mr. Danny' before breaking into theatre, achieving fame a decade later as Louie in *Taxi*. A star for several years, he's also achieved considerable success as a director. Married to Rhea Perlman, Carla in *Cheers*, he apparently relaxes by playing the violin and piano.

Quote 'A lot of people don't like to look at themselves on the screen. But I've got an ego you can't fit in this room. So, since I love me so much, I can tolerate even the worst work.'

Films *One Flew Over the Cuckoo's Nest* ✦✦✦✦ (75), *The Van* ✦ (76), *The World's Greatest Lover* ✦✦ (77), *Goin' South* ✦✦✦ (78), *Going Ape* ✦ (81), *Terms of Endearment* ✦✦✦ (83), *Romancing the Stone* ✦✦✦ (84), *Johnny Dangerously* ✦✦ (84), *Jewel of the Nile* ✦✦ (85), *My Little Pony* ✦✦ (v)(86), *Ruthless People* ✦✦✦✦ (86), *Tin Men* ✦✦✦ (87), *Throw Momma from the Train* ✦✦✦ (87; also d), *Twins* ✦✦ (88), *The War of the Roses* ✦✦ (89; also d), *Other People's Money* ✦✦ (91), *Batman Returns* ✦✦✦ (92), *Hoffa* ✦✦ (92; also d), *Jack the Bear* ✦✦ (93)

Matt Dillon [b. 1964]

Quote 'I'm a complicated guy. I don't generally make things easy on myself. I debate a lot. There's a whole fucking Senate Committee in my head.'

Films *Over the Edge* ✦✦✦ (79), *The Outsiders* ✦✦ (83), *Rumble Fish* ✦✦✦ (83), *The Flamingo Kid* ✦✦✦ (84), *Target* ✦✦ (85), *Rebel* ✦✦ (86), *The Big Town* ✦✦ (87), *Kansas* ✦ (88), *Drugstore Cowboy* ✦✦ (89), *A Kiss Before Dying* ✦ (90), *Singles* ✦✦✦✦ (92), *Mr. Wonderful* (93), *Golden Gate* (93)

Amanda Donohoe [b. 1962]

Films *Foreign Body* ✦✦ (86), *Castaway* ✦✦ (87), *The Lair of the White Worm* ✦✦✦ (88), *The Rainbow* ✦✦ (89), *Tank Malling* ✦ (89), *Paper Mask* ✦✦✦ (90), *Diamond Skulls* ✦ (90)

Michael Douglas [b. 1944]

Kirk Douglas's son, he grew up with his mother after their divorce. The producer of *One Flew Over the Cuckoo's Nest*, he turned his father down for a part in what had been his pet project. Long-known as the sidekick in TV's *Streets of San Francisco*, it was *Wall Street*, for which he won an Oscar, that made him a star. After his wife caught him making love to her best friend, he underwent treatment for sex addiction.

Quote 'Believe me, movie sex can be real tough. If you're on top of a woman in a love scene, it's very difficult for the camera to get angles. So you do acrobatics – not for fun, just so the lighting is right. Sorry, love scenes are hard work.'

Films *Coma* ✦✦✦ (78), *Running* ✦ (79), *The China Syndrome* ✦✦✦ (79), *It's My Turn* ✦✦✦ (80), *The Star Chamber* ✦✦ (83), *Romancing the Stone* ✦✦✦ (84), *A Chorus Line* ✦ (85), *Jewel of the Nile* ✦✦ (85), *Wall Street* ✦✦✦ (87), *Fatal Attraction* ✦✦ (87), *Black Rain* ✦ (89), *The War of the Roses* ✦✦ (89), *Shining Through* ✦✦ (92), *Basic Instinct* ✦✦ (92), *Falling Down* ✦✦✦✦ (93)

Brad Dourif [b. 1950]

Films *One Flew Over the Cuckoo's Nest* ✦✦✦✦ (75), *The Eyes of Laura Mars* ✦✦ (78), *Wise Blood* ✦✦✦ (79), *Heaven's Gate* ✦✦✦ (80), *Ragtime* ✦✦✦ (81), *Dune* ✦ (84), *Blue Velvet* ✦✦ (86), *Fatal Beauty* ✦ (87), *Mississippi Burning* ✦✦ (88), *Child's Play* ✦✦ (88), *Child's Play 2* ✦ (v)(90), *The Exorcist III* ✦✦ (90), *Graveyard Shift* ✦ (90), *Hidden Agenda* ✦✦ (90), *Jungle Fever* ✦✦✦ (91), *London Kills Me* ✦ (91)

Robert Downey Jr. [b. 1965]

Son of an underground film-maker, he made his film debut aged five playing a puppy in one of dad's films. After blending into the background so perfectly in several films he's unspottable, he shot to prominence with his bravura performance in the lead of *Chaplin*.

Quote 'A lot of my peer group think I'm an eccentric bisexual, like I may even have an ammonia-filled tentacle or something somewhere on my body. That's okay.'

Films Baby, It's You ✦✦✦ (b)(83), To Live and Die in L.A. ✦✦ (85), Tuff Turf ✦ (85), Weird Science ✦ (85), Back to School ✦ (86), The Pick-up Artist ✦ (87), 1969 ✦✦ (88), Air America ✦✦ (89), Soapdish ✦ (91), Chaplin ✦✦ (92), Hearts and Souls (93), Natural Born Killers (94)

Richard Dreyfuss [b. 1947]

Quote 'The only difference between me and John Belushi is he's dead — and that's just the whim of the gods.'

Films The Graduate ✦✦✦✦ (b)(67), American Graffiti ✦✦✦✦ (73), Jaws ✦✦✦✦ (75), Close Encounters of the Third Kind ✦✦✦✦ (77), The Goodbye Girl ✦✦✦✦ (77), Stand by Me ✦✦ (86), Down and Out in Beverly Hills ✦✦✦ (86), Tin Men ✦✦✦ (87), Nuts ✦✦ (87), Stakeout ✦✦✦ (87), Moon Over Parador ✦✦ (88), Always ✦✦ (89), Postcards from the Edge ✦✦✦✦ (90), Rosencrantz and Guildenstern Are Dead ✦✦ (90), What About Bob? ✦✦✦ (91), Lost in Yonkers (93), Stakeout II (93)

Charles Durning [b. 1923]

One of the busiest of supporting actors, he's most famous for playing Lange's father, falling futilely in love with *Tootsie*. He's played more world-weary cops than there are in the New York Police Department.

Films Hi, Mom! ✦✦✦ (70), The Sting ✦✦✦✦ (73), The Front Page ✦✦✦ (74), Dog Day Afternoon ✦✦✦✦ (75), North Dallas Forty ✦✦✦✦ (79), The Muppet Movie ✦✦✦ (c)(79), True Confessions ✦✦ (81), Tootsie ✦✦✦✦ (82), The Best Little Whorehouse in Texas ✦✦ (82), To Be or Not to Be ✦✦ (83), Two of a Kind ✦ (83), Death of a Salesman ✦✦✦ (85), Tough Guys ✦✦ (86), Far North ✦ (88), Cop ✦✦✦ (88), A Tiger's Tale ✦ (88), Cat Chaser ✦✦✦ (89), Dick Tracy ✦✦ (90), V.I. Warshawski ✦✦ (92), The Hudsucker Proxy (93)

Clint Eastwood [b. 1930]

Real name Clinton Eastwood Jr.

Fired from Universal — who spotted him delivering dirt — for having an adam's apple that was too prominent, Eastwood was stuck in movies like *Revenge of the Creature* and *Tarantula* until he accepted $15,000 to be The Man With No Name in *A Fistful of Dollars*, setting him on the trail to stardom. With his reputation now established, he is reckoned to be worth around $200m, although his fortune was dented by a $25m divorce settlement in 1980 and another $30 in palimony when he split from Sondra Locke in 1989. A fine director as well, he worked for $200 a month as the mayor of Carmel for two years in the mid-80s, enabling decent, honest folk to eat ice cream and wear high heels without being run out of town. He also owns a hamburger joint there, the Hog's Breath Bar. He and William Shatner once paid a group of mercenaries $50,000 to rescue American prisoners left in Cambodia after the Vietnam War; "Operation Lazarus" was a flop. Strangely enough, considering the time he has spent in the saddle, Eastwood is actually allergic to horses. If it wasn't for the tablets he takes, he'd be sneezing and wheezing through all his films.

Quote 'I've always had the ability to say to the audience: Watch this if you like; and if you don't, take a hike.'

Quote 'Clint Eastwood is a man who walks softly and carries a big percentage of the gross.' [Bob Hope]

Films Revenge of the Creature ✦✦ (55), Tarantula ✦ (55), A Fistful of Dollars ✦✦✦ (64), For a Few Dollars More ✦✦✦✦ (65), The Good, The Bad and The Ugly ✦✦✦ (67), Coogan's Bluff ✦✦✦✦ (68), Hang 'Em High ✦✦ (68), Paint Your Wagon ✦✦ (69), Where Eagles Dare ✦✦✦ (69), Two Mules For Sister Sara ✦✦ (70), Kelly's Heroes ✦✦ (70), Dirty Harry ✦✦✦✦ (71), Play Misty for Me ✦✦✦ (71; also d), The Beguiled ✦✦✦✦ (71), Joe Kidd ✦✦ (72), Magnum Force ✦✦✦ (73), High Plains Drifter ✦✦✦ (73; also d), Thunderbolt and

Lightfoot ♦♦ (74), The Eiger Sanction ♦♦ (75; also d), The Enforcer ♦♦ (76), The Outlaw Josey Wales ♦♦♦ (76; also d), The Gauntlet ♦♦♦ (77; also d), Every Which Way But Loose ♦ (78), Escape from Alcatraz ♦♦♦ (79), Any Which Way You Can ♦♦ (80), Bronco Billy ♦♦♦ (80; also d), Honkytonk Man ♦♦ (82; also d), Firefox ♦ (82; also d), Sudden Impact ♦♦ (83; also d), City Heat ♦ (84), Tightrope ♦♦ (84), Pale Rider ♦♦♦ (85; also d), Heartbreak Ridge ♦♦♦ (86; also d), The Dead Pool ♦♦ (88), Bird ♦♦♦ (88; d only), The Rookie ♦ (90; also d), White Hunter, Black Heart ♦♦ (90; also d), Unforgiven ♦♦♦ (92; also d), In the Line of Fire (93), A Perfect World (94; also d)

Cary Elwes [b. 1962]

Films Another Country ♦♦ (84), Oxford Blues ♦♦ (84), The Bride,♦ (85), Lady Jane ♦♦♦ (86), The Princess Bride ♦♦ (87), Glory ♦♦♦♦ (89), Days of Thunder ♦ (90), Hot Shots! ♦♦ (91), Bram Stoker's Dracula ♦♦♦ (92), The Crush (93), Robin Hood: Men in Tights (93)

Emilio Estevez [b. 1962]

Charlie Sheen's brother and son of Martin Sheen.

Films The Outsiders ♦♦ (83), Repo Man ♦♦ (84), The Breakfast Club ♦♦ (85), That Was Then...This Is Now ♦♦ (85; also s), St. Elmo's Fire ♦ (85), Stakeout ♦♦♦ (87), Young Guns ♦♦ (88), Men at Work ♦ (90; also d&s), Young Guns II − Blaze of Glory ♦♦ (90), Freejack ♦ (92), National Lampoon's Loaded Weapon 1 ♦♦ (93), Champions (92), Judgment Night (93), Stakeout II (93)

Joe Eszterhas [b. 1944]

WRITER. The highest-paid screenwriter in Hollywood, he received $3m for his script of Basic Instinct. A man who loves to court controversy both inside and out-side his films, there are those who say that he only has one plot − you think you know who did it, then you're not sure,

then it turns out you were right all along. A pet project of his involves a President of the United States being caught in a compromising position with a cow!

Films F.I.S.T. ♦♦♦ (78), Flashdance ♦♦ (83), Jagged Edge ♦♦♦ (85), Hearts of Fire ♦ (87), Betrayed ♦♦ (88), Checking Out ♦ (89), Music Box ♦♦♦ (89), Basic Instinct ♦♦ (92), Sliver (93), Nowhere to Run (93)

Mia Farrow [b. 1945]

Real name Maria de Lourdes Villiers Farrow

Aged 18, Farrow auditioned for the role of one of the children in The Sound of Music. She didn't get it.

Films Rosemary's Baby ♦♦♦ (68), The Great Gatsby ♦♦♦ (74), A Midsummer Night's Sex Comedy ♦♦♦ (82), Zelig ♦♦ (83), Broadway Danny Rose ♦♦♦ (84), Supergirl ♦ (84), The Purple Rose of Cairo ♦♦ (85), Hannah and Her Sisters ♦♦♦♦ (86), September ♦ (87), Radio Days ♦♦♦ (87), Another Woman ♦ (88), Crimes and Misdemeanors ♦♦ (89), New York Stories ♦♦ (89), Alice ♦♦♦ (90), Shadows and Fog ♦♦♦ (92), Husbands and Wives ♦♦♦ (92)

Sherilyn Fenn [b. 1965]

Films The Wraith ♦ (86), Two Moon Junction ♦ (88), Wild at Heart ♦ (90), Ruby ♦♦ (92), Of Mice and Men ♦♦♦ (92), Three of Hearts ♦♦ (93), Boxing Helena (93), Fatal Instinct (93)

Sally Field [b. 1946]

Quote 'The first time I hardly felt it because it was all so new. But now I feel it. You like me!. You LIKE me! [On clutching her second Oscar]

Films Stay Hungry ♦♦♦ (76), Smokey and the Bandit ♦♦♦ (77), Norma Rae ♦♦♦ (79), Absence of Malice ♦♦♦ (81), Places in the Heart ♦♦♦ (84), Murphy's Romance ♦♦♦ (85), Surrender ♦♦♦ (87), Punchline ♦♦♦ (88), Steel Magnolias ♦♦ (89), Not Without My Daughter ♦♦ (91), Soapdish

✦ (91), Homeward Bound: The Incredible Journey ✦✦✦ (v)(93), *Mrs. Doubtfire (93)*

Carrie Fisher [b. 1956]

Quote 'I was street-smart. But unfortunately the street was Rodeo Drive.'

Films *Shampoo* ✦ (75), *Stars Wars* ✦✦✦✦ (77), *The Empire Strikes Back* ✦✦ (80), *The Blues Brothers* ✦✦✦✦ (80), *Return of the Jedi* ✦✦✦ (83), *Hannah and Her Sisters* ✦✦✦✦ (86), *Appointment with Death* ✦✦ (88), *The 'burbs* ✦✦✦ (89), *Loverboy* ✦✦ (89), *When Harry Met Sally* ✦✦✦✦ (89), *Sibling Rivalry* ✦✦ (90), *Postcards from the Edge* ✦✦✦✦ (90; s only), *Drop Dead Fred* ✦ (91), *Soapdish* ✦ (91), *This is My Life* ✦ (92)

Bridget Fonda [b. 1964]

The daughter of Peter Fonda, niece of Jane Fonda and granddaughter of Henry Fonda.

Quote 'I find that there's something about [the role of] a girl who's free and bad that I love.'

Films *Aria* ✦ (87), *Shag* ✦✦ (88), *Scandal* ✦✦ (89), *The Godfather, Part III* ✦✦✦ (90), *Roger Corman's Frankenstein Unbound* ✦ (90), *Strapless* ✦ (90), *Doc Hollywood* ✦✦ (91), *Drop Dead Fred* ✦ (91), *Iron Maze* ✦ (91), *Single White Female* ✦✦ (92), *Singles* ✦✦✦✦ (92), *Army of Darkness: The Medieval Dead* ✦ (c)(93), *Assassin* ✦✦ (93), *Bodies, Rest and Motion (93)*, *Cop Gives Waitress $2m Tip (93)*

Harrison Ford [b. 1942]

Ford was a favourite with the Hollywood community almost from the moment he arrived in LA – as a carpenter! Although he had short-term contracts as an actor with a couple of studios, it was carpentry that helped him survive. Sally Kellerman has a sign on her sundeck saying: 'This is the deck H.F. Built.' He almost turned *American Graffiti* down because it paid less than carpentry. Despite the promise of *Star Wars*, it wasn't until *Raiders* that he became a star. His deal to be paid $50m for five more Jack Ryan films is the biggest package Hollywood's ever seen. He is obsessed with tidiness. In his workshop, all the tools are arranged by size and category while in his wardrobe, the suits are hung in neat rows strictly according to colour. He hasn't bought any of them. He insists that on each of his film, an extra suit is bought which he takes home when filming's finished.

Quote 'I look dorky in all my films. Mine is not a pretty face. I think I'm ordinary.'

Quote 'You look at Harrison Ford and you *listen*. He looks like he's carrying a gun, even if he isn't.' [Carrie Fisher]

Films *American Graffiti* ✦✦✦✦ (73), *The Conversation* ✦✦✦✦ (74), *Stars Wars* ✦✦✦✦ (77), *Force 10 From Navarone* ✦ (78), *The Frisco Kid* ✦✦ (79), *Hanover Street* ✦ (79), *Apocalypse Now* ✦✦✦✦ (79), *The Empire Strikes Back* ✦✦ (80), *Raiders of the Lost Ark* ✦✦✦✦ (81), *Blade Runner: The Director's Cut* ✦✦✦✦ (82), *Return of the Jedi* ✦✦✦ (83), *Indiana Jones and the Temple of Doom* ✦✦ (84), *Witness* ✦✦✦✦ (85), *The Mosquito Coast* ✦✦ (86), *Working Girl* ✦✦✦✦ (88), *Frantic* ✦✦ (88), *Indiana Jones and the Last Crusade* ✦✦✦✦ (89), *Presumed Innocent* ✦✦✦ (90), *Regarding Henry* ✦✦ (91), *Patriot Games* ✦✦✦✦ (92), *The Fugitive* (93), *Clear and Present Danger (94)*

Jodie Foster [b. 1962]

Real name Alicia Christian Foster

Hard to believe that Jodie Foster was once the Coppertone Girl, pictured on ads worldwide aged 3 with a puppy tugging at her knickers. Her breakthrough role as the 12-year-old hooker in *Taxi Driver* not only won her an Oscar nomination but also the unhealthy interest of would-be Reagan assassinator John Hinckley Jr. Her mother has always managed her career, her parents having divorced before they even knew that Jodie had been conceived. Although she studied literature and creative writing at Yale, she never took acting lessons. Her directorial debut, *Little Man Tate*, promises still greater things to come.

Quote 'I spent four hours with a shrink to prove I was normal enough to play a hooker.' [On *Taxi Driver*]

Films *Alice Doesn't Live Here Anymore* ✦✦✦✦ *(74)*, *Bugsy Malone* ✦✦ *(76)*, *Taxi Driver* ✦✦✦ *(76)*, *Candleshoe* ✦✦ *(77)*, *Foxes* ✦✦ *(80)*, *Carny* ✦✦✦ *(80)*, Hotel New Hampshire ✦ *(84)*, Siesta ✦ *(87)*, The Accused ✦✦ *(88)*, Five Corners ✦✦ *(88)*, Catchfire ✦✦✦ *(91)*, The Silence of the Lambs ✦✦✦ *(91)*, Little Man Tate ✦✦✦ *(92; also d)*, Shadows and Fog ✦✦✦ *(92)*, Sommersby ✦✦✦✦ *(93)*

Michael J. Fox [b. 1961]
Real name Michael Andrew Fox

When Fox began acting, there was already somebody called Michael Fox. He didn't want to encourage the jokes that would stem from using his real middle initial so he chose 'J' after the character actor Michael J. Pollard. Initially a TV star, acting on the box from the age of 14, he was in the successful series *Family Ties* when Eric Stoltz was sacked from *Back to the Future*. Fox stepped in, working on the film and the TV show each day and becoming a star. Despite his age – even then he was 24 playing 17 – his efforts to break away from teen roles haven't been successful. Although only 5 feet 4 inches high, he's pointed out that that's the same as Humphrey Bogart. When he married co-star Tracy Pollan in 1988, he received 5,000 abusive letters.

Quote 'You know what the difference between a short actor and a short star is? The short actor stands on an applecart, and the short star has them dig ditches for everybody else!'

Quote 'Girls think you're so cute when you're short – always want to put me in their pocket. Great, as long as it's their breast pocket.'

Films Class of 1984 ✦✦ *(82)*, Back to the Future ✦✦✦✦ *(85)*, Teen Wolf ✦✦ *(85)*, Light of Day ✦ *(87)*, The Secret of My Success ✦✦ *(87)*, Bright Lights, Big City ✦

(88), Back to the Future, Part II ✦✦ *(89)*, Casualties of War ✦✦✦ *(89)*, Back to the Future, Part III ✦✦✦✦ *(90)*, Doc Hollywood ✦✦ *(91)*, The Hard Way ✦✦✦✦ *(91)*, Homeward Bound: The Incredible Journey ✦✦✦ *(v)(93)*, Life With Mikey *(93)*, For Love or Money *(93)*

Morgan Freeman [b. 1937]
Quote 'When I was younger I wanted to be a star, but now I want to be a force.'

Films *The Janitor* ✦✦ *(81)*, Harry and Son ✦✦ *(84)*, Teachers ✦✦ *(b)(84)*, That Was Then...This Is Now ✦✦ *(85)*, Marie ✦✦✦ *(85)*, Clean and Sober ✦✦✦ *(88)*, Driving Miss Daisy ✦✦✦ *(89)*, Glory ✦✦✦✦ *(89)*, Johnny Handsome ✦✦ *(89)*, The Bonfire of the Vanities ✦ *(90)*, Robin Hood: Prince of Thieves ✦✦✦ *(91)*, The Power of One ✦✦ *(92)*, Unforgiven ✦✦✦ *(92)*, Bopha *(93; d only)*, Rita Hayworth & the Shawshank Redemption *(94)*

Peter Gallagher [b. 1955]
Films Summer Lovers ✦ *(82)*, Dreamchild ✦✦✦ *(85)*, My Little Girl ✦✦✦ *(87)*, High Spirits ✦ *(88)*, sex, lies, and videotape ✦✦✦ *(89)*, Aunt Julia and the Scriptwriter ✦✦ *(c)(91)*, The Player ✦✦✦✦ *(92)*, Late for Dinner ✦✦ *(92)*, Bob Roberts ✦✦✦ *(c)(92)*, Bodily Harm *(93)*

Andy Garcia [b. 1956]
Real name Andres Arturo Garcia Menendez

Cuban-born heart-throb who hit the trail to stardom when he persuaded director Brian de Palma to change his mind about casting him as one of the bad guys in *The Untouchables* and make him a goodie instead. He has virtually cornered the market in cool cop parts.

Quote 'Typecast? I certainly hope so. I spent seven years without working, so if they're making cop movies, I'll play cops. I got two kids to bring up.'

Films The Mean Season ◆◆ (85), The Untouchables ◆◆◆◆ (87), Stand and Deliver ◆◆◆ (88), Black Rain ◆ (89), The Godfather, Part III ◆◆◆ (90), Internal Affairs ◆◆ (90), Dead Again ◆◆ (91), Accidental Hero ◆◆◆◆ (92), Jennifer 8 ◆◆◆ (92), *Significant Other* (94)

Richard Gere   [b. 1949]

Heart-throb whose career almost vanished without trace in the mid-80s, before being resurrected by the success of *Pretty Woman*. A musically-inclined Buddhist (he plays banjo, trumpet, guitar and piano), he's a personal mate of the Dalai Lama. He married supermodel Cindy Crawford in 1991, apparently on a whim.

Quote 'My wife doesn't understand why I'm such a sex symbol. She came out of the screening of a film I did recently and said I didn't look any different from a guy you'd see on the street.'

Films *Looking for Mr. Goodbar* ◆◆ (77), *Days of Heaven* ◆◆◆◆ (78), *Bloodbrothers* ◆◆◆ (78), *Yanks* ◆◆◆◆ (79), *American Gigolo* ◆ (80), An Officer and a Gentleman ◆◆ (82), Breathless ◆ (83), The Honorary Consul ◆ (83), The Cotton Club ◆◆ (84), King David ◆◆ (85), Power ◆◆ (86), No Mercy ◆◆ (86), Miles from Home ◆◆ (88), Internal Affairs ◆◆ (90), Pretty Woman ◆◆◆ (90), *Rhapsody in August* ◆ (91), Final Analysis ◆◆ (92), Sommersby ◆◆◆◆ (93), *Mr. Jones* (93), *Intersection* (94)

Mel Gibson   [b. 1956]

Real name Mel Columcille Gibson

Gibson owes his career to being beaten up in a pub the night before the auditions for *Mad Max*. His battered look won him the title role in the low-budget pic that made $100m. The 6th of eleven children living in native New York, his railwayman father took the family to Australia when Mel was 12, partly to keep Mel's brothers out of the Vietnam draft. Bullied at school because of his accent, at one point he almost became a Catholic priest. Although frequently voted the sexiest

man alive, he's a happily married and devoted father with six children.

Quote 'If I've still got my pants on in the second scene of a film these days I think they've sent me the wrong script.'

Quote 'Money gives you the freedom to really do stupid things with your time.'

Films *Mad Max* ◆◆ (79), *Mad Max 2, The Road Warrior* ◆◆◆◆ (81), *Gallipolli* ◆◆◆ (81), The Year of Living Dangerously ◆◆◆ (83), Mrs. Soffel ◆◆ (84), Bounty ◆◆ (84), The River ◆◆ (84), Mad Max Beyond Thunderdome ◆◆◆ (85), Lethal Weapon ◆◆◆ (87), Tequila Sunrise ◆ (88), Air America ◆◆ (89), Lethal Weapon 2 ◆◆◆ (89), Bird on a Wire ◆◆ (90), Hamlet ◆◆◆ (90), Lethal Weapon 3 ◆◆◆◆ (92), Forever Young ◆◆◆ (92), *The Man Without a Face* (93; also d)

Danny Glover   [b. 1947]

Films *Escape from Alcatraz* ◆◆◆ (b)(79), Places in the Heart ◆◆◆ (84), The Color Purple ◆◆◆ (85), Witness ◆◆◆◆ (85), Silverado ◆◆◆ (85), Lethal Weapon ◆◆◆ (87), BAT 21 ◆◆◆ (88), Lethal Weapon 2 ◆◆◆ (89), Predator 2 ◆◆ (90), To Sleep with Anger ◆◆◆ (90), Grand Canyon ◆◆ (91), A Rage in Harlem ◆◆◆ (91), Lethal Weapon 3 ◆◆◆◆ (92), *Bopha* (93)

Whoopi Goldberg   [b. 1949]

Real name Caryn Johnson

A one-time junkie and teenage single welfare mother, she worked variously as a bricklayer and in a mortuary putting makeup on corpses while acting and doing stand-up. Other actors nicknamed her Whoopi Cushion because of her trouble with flatulence. Director Mike Nichols was so impressed, he took her under his wing. She got an Oscar nomination for her very first film, *The Color Purple*, and then nearly blew it with a succession of dire movies, coming back with *Ghost* and *Sister Act*. The second *Sister Act* movie made her one of the highest-paid actresses in Hollywood. She is a grandmother.

Quote ' I worked in strip joints – but I

never got my clothes off. People were screaming: Don't do it!'

Quote 'People, friends, suddenly treat you differently [when you're a star]. They don't even wait for you to change and become an asshole. They just assume you're going to be one and treat you accordingly.'

Films The Color Purple ◆◆◆ (85), Jumpin' Jack Flash ◆◆ (86), Fatal Beauty ◆ (87), Clara's Heart ◆◆ (88), Ghost ◆◆◆◆ (90), Soapdish ◆ (91), The Player ◆◆◆◆ (92), Sister Act ◆◆ (92), Sarafina ◆◆◆ (92), *Naked in New York (93)*, National Lampoon's Loaded Weapon 1 ◆◆ (c)(93), *Made in America (93)*, *The Pagemaster (v)(94)*, *Sister Act II (94)*, *Corrina, Corrina (94)*

Jeff Goldblum [b. 1952]

Quote 'He's a blue alien, which is a step up from a bug.' [Ex-wife Geena Davis on *Earth Girls*]

Films *Death Wish* ◆◆ (b)(74), Nashville ◆◆◆ (75), Annie Hall ◆◆◆ (b)(77), Invasion of the Bodysnatchers ◆◆◆ (78), The Big Chill ◆◆◆ (83), The Right Stuff ◆◆◆◆ (83), Transylvania 6-5000 ◆ (85), Silverado ◆◆◆ (85), Into the Night ◆◆ (85), The Fly ◆◆◆◆ (86), The Adventures of Buckaroo Banzai Across the 8th Dimension ◆◆ (87), Beyond Therapy ◆ (87), Earth Girls Are Easy ◆ (89), The Tall Guy ◆◆ (89), The Favour, the Watch and the Very Big Fish ◆ (92), The Player ◆◆◆◆ (c)(92), Deep Cover ◆◆◆◆ (92), Jurassic Park (93)

Caroline Goodall [b. 1959]

Up-and-coming ex-Royal Shakespeare Company actress who appears to be a favourite with Steven Spielberg.

Films Every Time We Say Goodbye ◆ (86), Hook ◆◆◆ (91), Cliffhanger (93), *Schindler's List (93)*

John Goodman [b. 1952]

Films Maria's Lovers ◆◆◆ (84), Revenge of the Nerds ◆◆ (84), Sweet Dreams ◆◆ (85), True Stories ◆◆ (86), The Big Easy ◆◆◆◆

(87), Raising Arizona ◆◆◆◆ (87), When I Fall in Love ◆◆ (88), Punchline ◆◆◆ (88), Always ◆◆ (89), Sea of Love ◆◆◆ (89), Arachnophobia ◆◆ (90), Stella ◆ (90), King Ralph ◆◆◆ (91), Barton Fink ◆ (92), Matinee ◆◆ (93), *Born Yesterday (93)*, *We're Back (v)(93)*, *The Flintstones (94)*

Louis Gossett Jr. [b. 1936]

Films *The Deep* ◆ (77), An Officer and a Gentleman ◆◆ (82), Jaws 3-D ◆ (83), Finders Keepers ◆◆ (84), Enemy Mine ◆ (85), Firewalker ◆ (86), Iron Eagle ◆ (86), Iron Eagle II ◆ (88), The Punisher ◆◆ (90), Toy Soldiers ◆◆ (91), Midnight Sting ◆◆◆◆ (92), *A Good Man in Africa (93)*

Richard E. Grant [b. 1957]

Films Withnail and I ◆◆ (87), How to Get Ahead in Advertising ◆◆ (89), Killing Dad ◆ (89), Warlock ◆◆ (89), Henry and June ◆ (90), Mountains of the Moon ◆◆◆◆ (90), Hudson Hawk ◆ (91), L.A. Story ◆◆◆ (91), The Player ◆◆◆◆ (92), Bram Stoker's Dracula ◆◆◆ (92)

Melanie Griffith [b. 1957]

The daughter of Hitchcock actress Tippi Hedren, Griffith was once given a miniature coffin by the great man with a model of her mother in it. She had something of a wild adolescence, imbibing sex, drugs and rock'n'roll in copious quantities. At 16, she moved in with Don Johnson but their marriage ended in divorce. Laying off the booze, she married actor Steven Bauer, but that didn't last either. She and Johnson married again in 1989, a decade after splitting up. She has three children and a ripe pear tattooed on her buttock.

Quote 'You say, "Good morning," and she wants to make love. You say, "Good afternoon," and she wants to make love. You say, "Good night," and she wants to make love".' [Don Johnson]

Films *The Drowning Pool* ◆◆ (75), *Night Moves* ◆◆◆ (75), *Smile* ◆◆◆ (75), Body Double ◆ (84), Something Wild ◆◆◆ (86),

Working Girl ✦✦✦✦ (88), The Milagro Beanfield War ✦✦✦ (88), Stormy Monday ✦ (88), The Bonfire of the Vanities ✦ (90), Pacific Heights ✦✦ (90), Shining Through ✦✦ (92), Paradise ✦✦✦✦ (92), *Close to Eden* (92), *Born Yesterday* (93)

Charles Grodin [b. 1935]

Films *Rosemary's Baby* ✦✦✦ (68), Catch-22 ✦✦✦ (70), King Kong ✦✦ (76), Heaven Can Wait ✦✦✦ (78), It's My Turn ✦✦✦ (80), Seems Like Old Times ✦✦✦ (80), Great Muppet Caper ✦✦✦ (c)(81), The Woman in Red ✦✦ (84), Ishtar ✦ (87), The Couch Trip ✦ (88), Midnight Run ✦✦✦✦ (88), Filofax ✦✦ (90), Beethoven ✦✦✦ (92), Dave ✦✦✦ (93), *Hearts and Souls* (93), *Clifford* (93), *Beethoven's 2nd* (94)

Steve Guttenberg [b. 1958]

Films *The Boys from Brazil* ✦✦ (78), Diner ✦✦✦✦ (82), Police Academy ✦✦ (84), Cocoon ✦✦ (85), Police Academy 2: Their First Assignment ✦ (85), Police Academy 3: Back in Training ✦✦ (86), Short Circuit ✦✦ (86), Three Men and a Baby ✦✦ (87), The Bedroom Window ✦✦ (87), Police Academy 4: Citizens on Patrol ✦ (87), Surrender ✦✦✦ (87), Cocoon: The Return ✦ (88), High Spirits ✦ (88), Three Men and a Little Lady ✦ (90), Don't Tell Her It's Me ✦ (92)

Fred Gwynne [b. 1926]

Best-known for his role as Herman Munster in the long-running TV series, Gwynne is one of those actors who, in a fairer world, would be a great star. The real stars probably hate him, because there's hardly a scene that he doesn't steal, often without saying a word. One of the all-time greats.

Films *On the Waterfront* ✦✦✦✦ (b)(54), The Cotton Club ✦✦ (84), Water ✦ (85), The Boy Who Could Fly ✦✦ (86), Fatal Attraction ✦✦ (87), Ironweed ✦✦ (87), The Secret of My Success ✦✦ (87), Pet Sematary ✦ (89), Shadows and Fog ✦✦✦ (92), My Cousin Vinny ✦✦✦✦ (92)

Gene Hackman [b. 1931]

Real name Eugene Alden Hackman

Quote 'It really costs me a lot emotionally to watch myself on-screen. I think of myself – and feel – like I'm quite young, and then I look at this old man with the baggy chins and the tired eyes and the receding hairline and all that.'

Films *Bonnie and Clyde* ✦✦✦✦ (67), Downhill Racer ✦✦✦ (69), The French Connection ✦✦✦✦ (71), The Poseidon Adventure ✦✦✦ (72), Scarecrow ✦✦✦ (73), The Conversation ✦✦✦✦ (74), Young Frankenstein ✦✦✦✦ (c)(74), Night Moves ✦✦✦ (75), French Connection II ✦✦✦ (75), A Bridge Too Far ✦✦ (77), Superman ✦✦✦ (78), Reds ✦✦✦ (81), Superman II (81), All Night Long ✦✦✦ (81), Uncommon Valor ✦✦ (83), Under Fire ✦✦✦✦ (83), Eureka ✦✦✦✦ (83), Target ✦✦ (85), Twice in a Lifetime ✦✦✦ (85), Power ✦✦ (86), No Way Out ✦✦✦ (87), Superman IV: The Quest for Peace ✦ (87), Best Shot ✦✦✦ (87), Mississippi Burning ✦✦ (88), Another Woman ✦ (88), Full Moon in Blue Water ✦✦ (88), BAT 21 ✦✦✦ (88), The Package ✦✦ (89), Narrow Margin ✦✦ (90), Postcards from the Edge ✦✦✦✦ (90), Class Action ✦✦✦ (91), Unforgiven ✦✦✦ (92), *The Firm* (93)

Julie Hagerty [b. 1954]

Films *Airplane!* (80), A Midsummer Night's Sex Comedy ✦✦✦ (82), Airplane II: The Sequel ✦✦ (82), Lost in America ✦✦✦ (85), Goodbye, New York ✦ (85), Beyond Therapy ✦ (87), Rude Awakening ✦ (89), Reversal of Fortune ✦✦✦✦ (90), What About Bob? ✦✦✦ (91), Noises Off ✦✦✦ (92)

Tom Hanks [b. 1956]

Quote 'Believe me, the three hardest jobs in America are coal-mining, police work and stand-up comedy.'

Films *He Knows You're Alone* ✦ (80), Bachelor Party ✦ (84), Splash ✦✦✦✦ (84), Volunteers ✦ (85), Every Time We Say Goodbye ✦ (86), Nothing in Common ✦✦ (86), The Money Pit ✦ (86), Dragnet ✦✦ (87), Big ✦✦✦✦ (88), Punchline ✦✦✦ (88),

The 'burbs ♦♦♦ (89), Turner and Hooch ♦♦ (89), The Bonfire of the Vanities ♦ (90), Joe Versus the Volcano ♦ (90), A League of their Own ♦♦ (92), *Philadelphia (93), Sleepless in Seattle (93)*

Daryl Hannah [b. 1960]

Films *Hard Country* ♦♦ (81), Summer Lovers ♦ (82), Blade Runner: The Director's Cut ♦♦♦♦ (82), Campsite Massacre ♦ (83), The Pope of Greenwich Village ♦♦ (84), Splash ♦♦♦♦ (84), Legal Eagles ♦♦♦ (86), The Clan of the Cave Bear ♦ (86), Wall Street ♦♦♦ (87), Roxanne ♦♦♦♦ (87), High Spirits ♦ (88), Crimes and Misdemeanors ♦♦ (89), Steel Magnolias ♦♦ (89), Crazy People ♦♦ (90), At Play in the Fields of the Lord ♦♦ (91), Memoirs of an Invisible Man ♦♦ (92), *Grumpy Old Men (93)*

Woody Harrelson [b. 1961]

Real name Woodrow Tracy Harrelson

Quote 'I had pretty much always been promiscuous, but right after I started doing *Cheers*, well, I was going on three dates a day. As a guy, you're raised to get as much as you can. Sex, sex, sex, that's what you're after. But after a while, I realized what I was doing was fool-hardy. Still, it took some time to travel from the brain groinward.'

Films Casualties of War ♦♦♦ (c)(89), Doc Hollywood ♦♦ (91), L.A. Story ♦♦♦ (c)(91), White Men Can't Jump ♦♦♦♦ (92), Indecent Proposal ♦♦♦ (93), *Natural Born Killers (94)*

Rutger Hauer [b. 1944]

All his films are in colour. Strange. Not one in black and white.

Films *Nighthawks* ♦♦♦ (81), Blade Runner: The Director's Cut ♦♦♦♦ (82), Eureka ♦♦♦♦ (83), The Osterman Weekend ♦♦ (83), Flesh + Blood ♦♦♦ (85), Ladyhawke ♦ (85), The Hitcher ♦♦♦ (86), Wanted: Dead or Alive ♦♦ (87), Blind Fury ♦♦♦ (90), The Salute of the Jugger ♦ (90), Split Second ♦♦ (92), Buffy, the Vampire Slayer ♦ (92)

Ethan Hawke [b. 1971]

Films Explorers ♦♦ (85), Dad ♦♦ (89), Dead Poets Society ♦♦♦♦ (89), White Fang ♦♦♦ (90), A Midnight Clear ♦♦♦ (92), Waterland ♦♦♦ (92), Alive ♦♦♦ (93), Rich In Love ♦♦ (93), *Reality Bites (94)*

Goldie Hawn [b. 1945]

Quote 'People have never wanted to see, still less to accept, the darker side of Goldie Hawn.'

Films There's a Girl in My Soup ♦♦ (70), The Sugarland Express ♦♦♦♦ (74), Shampoo ♦ (75), Foul Play ♦♦ (78), Seems Like Old Times ♦♦♦ (80), Private Benjamin ♦♦ (80), Best Friends ♦♦ (82), Protocol ♦♦ (84), Overboard ♦♦♦ (87), Bird on a Wire ♦♦ (90), Deceived ♦♦♦ (92), Housesitter ♦♦ (92), Death Becomes Her ♦♦♦ (92)

John Heard [b. 1946]

There are some actors who always beg the question: What else were *they* in. Heard's one of them, always the support, rarely the lead. But good value..

Films *Heartbeat* ♦♦ (79), Cutter's Way ♦♦♦ (81), Cat People ♦♦♦♦ (82), After Hours ♦♦ (85), Catholic Boys ♦♦♦ (85), The Trip to Bountiful ♦♦♦ (85), Big ♦♦♦♦ (88), Beaches ♦ (88), Betrayed ♦♦ (88), The Milagro Beanfield War ♦♦♦ (88), The Seventh Sign ♦ (88), The Package ♦♦ (89), Awakenings ♦♦♦ (90), Home Alone ♦♦ (90), Rambling Rose ♦♦♦♦ (91), Gladiator ♦♦♦ (92), Deceived ♦♦♦ (92), Waterland ♦♦♦ (92), Home Alone 2: Lost in New York ♦♦ (92)

Barbara Hershey [b. 1948]

Real name Barbara Herzstine

Films *Boxcar Bertha* ♦♦♦ (72), The Stunt Man (80), The Entity ♦ (82), The Right Stuff ♦♦♦♦ (83), The Natural ♦♦ (84), Hannah and Her Sisters ♦♦♦♦ (86), Tin Men ♦♦♦ (87), Shy People ♦♦ (87), Best Shot ♦♦♦ (87), The Last Temptation of Christ ♦ (88), Beaches ♦ (88), A World Apart ♦♦♦ (88), Aunt Julia and the Scriptwriter ♦♦ (91), Paris Trout ♦♦ (91), The Public Eye ♦♦♦ (92), Falling Down ♦♦♦♦ (93), *Swing Kids (93)*

Dustin Hoffman [b. 1937]

Real name Dustin Lee Hoffman

Growing up with the worst acne in his neighbourhood, Hoffman originally wanted to be a concert pianist, studying music for a time. Switching to acting, he slept on Gene Hackman's floor, taking jobs washing dishes, checking coats and selling toys in Macy's. Paid only $17,000 for *The Graduate* he went back on the dole afterwards, as no-one was expecting it to be such an immense success. Reputed to be the biggest (though only 5 foot 6) perfectionist in the business, his character in *Tootsie* is said to be very like the real him. Takes a back-stretching machine with him on set. Known by crews as 'The Humping Machine', he claims it's to keep him supple enough to live up to his younger wife's expectations in bed.

Quote 'I am obsessed with myself. I've always thought about myself. I get on the scale every day. I will look in the mirror. I've never been bored!'

Quote 'You have to throw a little cold water on him every once in a while.' [Meryl Streep]

Films *The Graduate* ◆◆◆◆ (67), *Midnight Cowboy* ◆◆◆◆ (69), *Little Big Man* ◆◆◆◆ (70), *Straw Dogs* ◆◆ (71), *Papillon* ◆◆◆ (73), *Lennie* ◆◆◆ (74), *Marathon Man* ◆◆◆◆ (76), *All the President's Men* ◆◆◆ (76), *Straight Time* ◆◆◆ (78), *Kramer vs. Kramer* ◆◆◆ (79), *Agatha* ◆◆ (79), *Tootsie* ◆◆◆◆ (82), *Death of a Salesman* ◆◆◆ (85), *Ishtar* ◆ (87), *Rain Man* ◆◆◆◆ (88), *Family Business* ◆◆ (89), *Dick Tracy* ◆◆ (90), *Hook* ◆◆◆ (91), *Billy Bathgate* ◆◆ (92), *Accidental Hero* ◆◆◆◆ (92)

Anthony Hopkins [b. 1937]

Films *When Eight Bells Toll* ◆◆ (71), *A Bridge Too Far* ◆◆ (77), *Magic* ◆◆◆ (78), *The Elephant Man* ◆◆◆◆ (80), *Bounty* ◆◆ (84), *The Good Father* ◆◆◆ (86), *84 Charing Cross Road* ◆◆◆ (87), *The Dawning* ◆◆◆ (88), *A Chorus of Disapproval* ◆◆ (89), *Desperate Hours* ◆◆ (90), *The Silence of*

the Lambs ◆◆◆ (91), *Freejack* ◆ (92), *Howard's End* ◆◆◆◆ (92), *Bram Stoker's Dracula* ◆◆◆ (92), *Chaplin* ◆◆ (92), *Spotswood* ◆◆◆ (92), *Remains of the Day* (93), *Shadowlands* (94)

Dennis Hopper [b. 1936]

Quote 'You want to hear about insanity? I was found running naked through the jungles in Mexico. At Mexico City airport I decided I was in the middle of a movie and walked out on the wing on takeoff. My body, my liver, okay, my brain – went.'

Quote 'After everything he did to his body, this man should be dead.' [Haskell Wexler, cameraman]

Films *Rebel Without a Cause* ◆◆◆ (55), *Giant* ◆◆◆ (56), *Cool Hand Luke* ◆◆◆◆ (67), *Easy Rider* ◆◆◆ (69; also d&s), *Apocalypse Now* ◆◆◆◆ (79), *Rumble Fish* ◆◆◆ (83), *The Osterman Weekend* ◆◆ (83), *Blue Velvet* ◆◆ (86), *The American Way* ◆◆ (86), *Black Widow* ◆◆◆ (87), *River's Edge* ◆◆◆◆ (87), *Best Shot* ◆◆◆ (87), *Straight to Hell* ◆ (87), *The Pick-up Artist* ◆ (87), *Colors* ◆◆ (88; d only), *Blood Red* ◆ (89), *Chattahoochee* ◆◆ (90), *The Hot Spot* ◆◆◆ (90; d only), *The Indian Runner* ◆◆ (91), *Paris Trout* ◆◆ (91), *Catchfire* ◆◆◆ (91; also d), *Red Rock West* ◆◆◆ (93), *Super Mario Bros.* (93), *True Romance* (93), *Boiling Point* (93), *Vanished* (94; also d)

Bob Hoskins [b. 1942]

Real name Robert William Hoskins

Quote 'My own mum wouldn't call me pretty.'

Quote 'A testicle with legs.' [Pauline Kael, critic]

Films *The Long Good Friday* ◆◆◆◆ (80), *The Honorary Consul* ◆ (83), *The Cotton Club* ◆◆ (84), *Lassiter* ◆ (84), *Brazil* ◆◆◆◆ (85), *Mona Lisa* ◆◆◆ (86), *Sweet Liberty* ◆◆ (86), *The Lonely Passion of Judith Hearne* ◆◆◆ (87), *A Prayer for the Dying* ◆◆ (87), *Who Framed Roger Rabbit?* ◆◆◆ (88), *The Raggedy Rawney* ◆◆◆ (89; also d&s), Heart Condition ♦♦ (90), Shattered ♦♦ (91), The Inner Circle ♦ (91), Hook ♦♦♦ (91), Mermaids ♦♦ (91), The Favour, the Watch and the Very Big Fish ♦ (92), Blue Ice ♦ (92), Super Mario Bros. (93)

John Hughes [b. 1950]
Real name John Hughes Jr.

DIRECTOR. Brought up in Chicago, the setting of most of his films, Hughes dropped out of college early on, married his childhood sweetheart and went to work as an advertising copywriter. He started more creative writing in his spare time, setting himself a target of one hundred jokes a day before he'd allow himself to go to sleep. He quit his job to become editor of *National Lampoon* magazine. He wrote fifteen screenplays (one a Jaws sequel called *Jaws 3, People o*) before one was finally produced. Since then he has written and directed some of the most popular comedies ever made. Hughes is said to take only days over most of his screenplays. Critics claim it shows. Two days is his record, for the script of *Weird Science*. He is colour-blind.

Films National Lampoon's Class Reunion ♦ (82; s only), Savage Islands ♦♦ (83; s only), Mr. Mum ♦♦ (83; s only), National Lampoon's Vacation ♦ (83; s only), The Breakfast Club ♦♦ (85; also s), Weird Science ♦ (85; also s), National Lampoon's European Vacation ♦♦ (85; s only), Ferris Bueller's Day Off ♦♦ (86; also s), Pretty in Pink ♦♦ (86; s only), Planes, Trains and Automobiles ♦♦♦ (87; also s), Uncle Buck ♦♦ (89; also s), National Lampoon's Christmas Vacation ♦♦ (89; s only), Home Alone ♦♦ (90; s only), Curly Sue ♦ (91; also s), Driving Me Crazy ♦♦♦ (92; s only), Home Alone 2: Lost in New York ♦♦ (92; s only), Dennis (93; s only)

William Hurt [b. 1950]
Quote 'I'd like to die by turbine. See, if you're sucked into a turbine, you get whipped into instantaneous ether.'

Quote 'Sexy? I'm a sexual animal. At times. But I'm also interested in a speck of dust. I don't stare at women's legs all the time.'

Films Altered States ♦♦♦ (80), Body Heat ♦♦♦♦ (81), The Janitor ♦♦ (81), The Big Chill ♦♦♦ (83), Gorky Park ♦♦ (83), Kiss of the Spider Woman ♦♦♦♦ (85), Children of a Lesser God ♦♦♦ (86), Broadcast News ♦♦♦ (87), The Accidental Tourist ♦♦♦ (88), Time of Destiny ♦♦ (88), Alice ♦♦♦ (90), I Love You to Death ♦ (90), The Doctor ♦♦ (92), Until the End of the World ♦ (92)

Anjelica Huston [b. 1951]
Quote 'Of course drugs were fun. And that's what's so stupid about anti-drug campaigns: they don't admit that. I can't say I feel particularly scarred or lessened by my experimentation with drugs. They've gotten a very bad name.'

Films The Last Tycoon ♦♦♦ (76), The Postman Always Rings Twice ♦♦♦ (81), This is Spinal Tap ♦♦♦♦ (c)(84), Prizzi's Honour ♦♦ (85), The Dead ♦♦♦ (87), Gardens of Stone ♦♦♦ (87), Mr. North ♦♦ (88), A Handful of Dust ♦♦♦♦ (88), Crimes and Misdemeanors ♦♦ (89), Enemies, A Love Story ♦♦♦ (89), The Grifters ♦♦♦ (90), The Witches ♦♦ (90), The Addams Family ♦♦♦ (91), The Player ♦♦♦♦ (c)(92), *Manhattan Murder Mystery (93), Addams Family Values (93)*

Jeremy Irons [b. 1948]
Quote 'She [his wife] doesn't get jealous. When she sees me in sex scenes she says to herself "Oh, he is only acting. I know he can't last that long".'

Films The French Lieutenant's Woman ♦♦♦ (81), Moonlighting ♦♦♦ (82), Betrayal ♦♦ (83), The Mission ♦♦ (86), Dead Ringers ♦♦ (88), A Chorus of Disapproval ♦♦ (89), Danny the Champion of the World ♦♦ (89), Reversal of Fortune ♦♦♦♦ (90), Waterland ♦♦♦ (92), Damage ♦♦ (92), *The House of the Spirits (93), M. Butterfly (93)*

Samuel L. Jackson [b. 1949]

Films Betsy's Wedding ✦, Mo' Better Blues ✦✦ (90), GoodFellas ✦✦✦✦ (90), Jungle Fever ✦✦✦ (91), White Sands ✦✦✦ (92), Patriot Games ✦✦✦✦ (92), Jurassic Park (93), National Lampoon's Loaded Weapon 1 ✦✦ (93)

Jeffrey Jones [b. 1947]

Films Amadeus ✦✦✦ (84), Transylvania 6-5000 ✦ (85), Ferris Bueller's Day Off ✦✦ (86), Howard...A New Breed of Hero ✦ (86), Beetlejuice ✦✦ (88), Without a Clue ✦ (88), Who's Harry Crumb? ✦ (89), The Hunt for Red October ✦✦✦ (90), Valmont ✦✦✦ (91), Over Her Dead Body ✦✦ (91), Stay Tuned ✦✦✦ (92)

Tommy Lee Jones [b. 1946]

Real name Tom Lee Jones

Films *Love Story* ✦✦ *(70), The Eyes of Laura Mars* ✦✦ *(78), Coal Miner's Daughter* ✦✦✦ *(80), Savage Islands* ✦✦ *(83),* Black Moon Rising ✦✦ (86), The Big Town ✦✦ (87), The Dead Can't Lie ✦✦✦ (88), Stormy Monday ✦ (88), The Package ✦✦ (89), Wings of the Apache ✦ (90), JFK ✦✦✦ (91), Under Siege ✦✦✦ (92), The Fugitive (93), *Heaven and Earth (93), House of Cards (93), Blue Sky (93), Natural Born Killers (94)*

Raul Julia [b. 1940]

Real name Raul Rafael Carlos Julia Y Arcelos

Films *The Panic in Needle Park* ✦✦✦ *(71), The Eyes of Laura Mars* ✦✦ *(78),* One from the Heart ✦✦ (82), Tempest ✦✦ (82), Kiss of the Spider Woman ✦✦✦✦ (85), Compromising Positions ✦✦ (85), The Morning After ✦ (86), Moon Over Parador ✦✦ (88), Tequila Sunrise ✦ (88), Romero ✦✦✦ (89), Havana ✦ (90), Presumed Innocent ✦✦✦ (90), Roger Corman's Frankenstein Unbound ✦ (90), The Rookie ✦ (90), The Addams Family ✦✦✦ (91), *Addams Family Values (93)*

Lawrence Kasdan [b. 1949]

DIRECTOR. The former scriptwriter of two of the *Star Wars* movies and *Raiders of the Lost Ark*, Kasdan now writes and directs some of the more literate and intelligent films today, although perhaps a little worthy in recent years.

Films *The Empire Strikes Back* ✦✦ *(80; s only), Body Heat* ✦✦✦✦ *(81; also s), Raiders of the Lost Ark* ✦✦✦✦ *(81; s only),* The Big Chill ✦✦✦ (83; also s), Return of the Jedi ✦✦✦ (83; s only), Into the Night ✦✦ (85; a only), Silverado ✦✦✦ (85; also s), The Accidental Tourist ✦✦✦ (88; also s), I Love You to Death ✦ (90; also a), Grand Canyon ✦✦ (91; also s), The Bodyguard ✦✦ (92; s only)

Julie Kavner [b. 1951]

Rhoda's sister from the sitcom of the same name.

Films Hannah and Her Sisters ✦✦✦✦ (86), Surrender ✦✦✦ (87), Radio Days ✦✦✦ (87), New York Stories ✦✦ (89), Awakenings ✦✦✦ (90), Shadows and Fog ✦✦✦ (92), This is My Life ✦ (92), *I'll Do Anything (93)*

Diane Keaton [b. 1946]

Real name Diane Hall

The only cast member of any production of the musical *Hair* in any country in the world to refuse to take their clothes off. She's said to be the one woman Warren Beatty ever proposed to before Annette Bening, but she turned him down.

Films *The Godfather* ✦✦✦✦ *(72), Play it Again, Sam* ✦✦✦✦ *(72), Sleeper* ✦✦✦✦ *(73), The Godfather, Part II* ✦✦✦✦ *(74), Love and Death* ✦✦✦ *(75),* Looking for Mr. Goodbar ✦✦ (77), *Annie Hall* ✦✦✦ *(77), Interiors* ✦ *(78), Manhattan* ✦✦✦✦ *(79), Reds* ✦✦✦ *(81),* Shoot the Moon ✦✦ (82), The Little Drummer Girl ✦✦ (84), Mrs. Soffel ✦✦ (84), Crimes of the Heart ✦✦ (86), Baby Boom ✦✦ (87), Radio Days ✦✦✦ (87), The Good Mother ✦ (88), The Godfather, Part III ✦✦✦ (90), Father of the Bride ✦✦ (91), *Manhattan Murder Mystery (93)*

Michael Keaton [b. 1951]

Real name Michael Douglas

The youngest of 7 children, he began acting and writing comedy at Kent State University where he was a Speech major. To stave off starvation, he drove an ice cream van and a taxi while performing in Pittsburgh coffeehouses with Louis, the Incredible Dancing Chicken. Changing his name to avoid confusion with the other Michael Douglas, he chose his new surname after seeing a picture of Diane Keaton in a newspaper. Although his film debut was in *Night Shift*, he made a career error by turning down *Splash* to do *Johnny Dangerously*. His casting in the lead of *Batman* aroused a storm of protest from Bat-freaks.

Films Night Shift ◆◆ (82), Mr. Mum ◆◆ (83), Johnny Dangerously ◆◆ (84), Gung Ho ◆◆ (86), The Squeeze ◆ (87), Clean and Sober ◆◆◆ (88), Beetlejuice ◆◆ (88), Batman ◆◆ (89), The Dream Team ◆◆◆◆ (89), Pacific Heights ◆◆ (90), Batman Returns ◆◆◆ (92), Much Ado About Nothing ◆◆◆ (93), *My Life (93)*

Harvey Keitel [b. 1939]

Films Who's That Knocking at My Door? ◆◆◆ (68), Mean Streets ◆◆◆ (73), Alice Doesn't Live Here Anymore ◆◆◆◆ (74), Taxi Driver ◆◆◆ (76), The Duellists ◆◆◆ (77), Fingers (78), Blue Collar ◆◆◆ (78), Bad Timing ◆◆◆◆ (80), The Border ◆◆ (82), Exposed ◆ (83), Order of Death ◆ (83), Falling in Love ◆◆ (84), The Men's Club ◆ (86), The Pick-up Artist ◆ (87), The Last Temptation of Christ ◆ (88), The January Man ◆ (89), The Two Jakes ◆◆◆◆ (91), Mortal Thoughts ◆◆ (91), Thelma & Louise ◆◆◆◆ (91), Bugsy ◆◆ (92), Sister Act ◆◆ (92), Reservoir Dogs ◆◆◆◆ (92), Bad Lieutenant ◆ (92), Assassin ◆◆ (93), Rising Sun (93), *Snake Eyes (93),*

Moira Kelly [b. 1968]

Films The Cutting Edge ◆◆◆ (92), Twin Peaks: Fire Walk With Me ◆ (92), Chaplin ◆◆ (92), Billy Bathgate ◆◆ (92), *With Honors (93)*

Nicole Kidman [b. 1967]

Married to Tom Cruise.

Films Dead Calm ◆◆◆◆ (89), Days of Thunder ◆ (90), Flirting ◆◆◆◆ (91), Billy Bathgate ◆◆ (92), Far and Away ◆◆ (92), *Bodily Harm (93), My Life (93)*

Val Kilmer [b. 1959]

Married to Joanne Whalley-Kilmer.

Films Top Secret! ◆◆ (84), Real Genius ◆◆◆ (85), Top Gun ◆◆ (86), Willow ◆◆ (88), Kill Me Again ◆◆◆ (89), The Doors ◆◆ (91), Thunderheart ◆◆◆◆ (92), *True Romance (93), The Real McCoy (93), Tombstone (94)*

Bruno Kirby [b. 1949]

Films The Godfather, Part II ◆◆◆◆ (74), Birdy ◆◆◆ (84), This is Spinal Tap ◆◆◆◆ (84), Flesh + Blood ◆◆◆ (85), Good Morning, Vietnam ◆◆◆ (87), Tin Men ◆◆◆ (87), Bert Rigby, You're a Fool ◆ (89), We're No Angels ◆ (89), When Harry Met Sally ◆◆◆◆ (89), The Freshman ◆◆◆◆ (90), City Slickers ◆◆◆◆ (91)

Kevin Kline [b. 1947]

Married to Phoebe Cates.

Quote 'When I was moved by an acting performance, I'd think, "I'd like to do that for somebody. I'd like to make people feel alive." I love sensation...I'm just a born sensationalist, is what it comes down to.'

Films Sophie's Choice ◆◆ (82), The Big Chill ◆◆◆ (83), The Pirates of Penzance ◆◆◆ (83), Silverado ◆◆◆ (85), Cry Freedom ◆◆ (87), A Fish Called Wanda ◆◆◆ (88), The January Man ◆ (89), I Love You to Death ◆ (90), Grand Canyon ◆◆ (91), Soapdish ◆ (91), Consenting Adults ◆ (92), Chaplin ◆◆ (92), Dave ◆◆◆ (93)

Christopher Lambert [b. 1957]

Real name Christophe Lambert

Films Greystoke: The Legend of Tarzan, Lord of the Apes ◆◆◆ (84), Subway ◆◆ (85), Highlander ◆◆ (86), The Sicilian ◆◆

(87), To Kill a Priest ✦ (88), Highlander II – the Quickening ✦ (90), Why Me? ✦✦ (90), Knight Moves ✦ (92)

Jessica Lange [b. 1949]

Films King Kong ✦✦ *(76)*, The Postman Always Rings Twice ✦✦✦ *(81)*, Tootsie ✦✦✦✦ *(82)*, Frances ✦✦ *(82)*, Country ✦✦✦ *(84)*, Sweet Dreams ✦✦ *(85)*, Crimes of the Heart ✦✦ *(86)*, Far North ✦ *(88)*, When I Fall in Love ✦✦ *(88)*, Music Box ✦✦✦ *(89)*, Men Don't Leave ✦✦ *(90)*, Cape Fear ✦✦ *(92)*, Night and the City ✦✦ *(92)*, *Blue Sky (93)*

Spike Lee [b. 1957]

Real name Shelton Jackson Lee

DIRECTOR. Born in Atlanta, Lee was raised in Brooklyn. He wrote, directed and starred in his first successful feature *She's Gotta Have It*, largely financed on his credit cards. Now able to command massive budgets for his films, he may be America's leading black director but he is arguably no less controversial than he was when starting out.

Quote 'I want people to know that if we don't talk about the problems and deal with them head on, they're going to get much worse.'

Quote 'Marketing is something I'm very proud of. The only artist that does it better than me is Madonna. She's the champ.'

Films She's Gotta Have It ✦✦ (86; also a&s), School Daze ✦✦ (88; also a&s), Do the Right Thing ✦✦✦✦ (89; also a&s), Mo' Better Blues ✦✦ (90; also a&s), Jungle Fever ✦✦✦ (91; also a&s), Malcolm X ✦✦✦ (92; also a&s), *Crooklyn N.Y. (94; also s)*

Jennifer Jason Leigh [b. 1958]

Real name Jennifer Lee Morrow

Quote 'Maybe I'm drawn to strange characters because my life is so boring.'

Quote 'The last time I really let go was eleven years ago. But I remember having a really good time.'

Films Fast Times at Ridgemont High ✦✦✦ *(82)*, The Man with the Deadly Lens ✦✦✦ *(82)*, Flesh + Blood ✦✦✦ *(85)*, The Men's Club ✦ *(86)*, The Hitcher ✦✦✦ *(86)*, The Big Picture ✦✦✦ *(89)*, Heart of Midnight ✦ *(89)*, Miami Blues ✦✦✦ *(90)*, Last Exit to Brooklyn ✦✦ *(90)*, Rush ✦ *(91)*, Backdraft ✦✦ *(91)*, Single White Female ✦✦ *(92)*, *The Hudsucker Proxy (93)*, *Vanished (94)*

Barry Levinson [b. 1942]

DIRECTOR. One of that rare breed of directors who have built their career on stories about their home town, Levinson returns with regularity to Baltimore although he has also made some of the most popular films of the 80s. He began in TV but co-wrote two films for Mel Brooks and can be spotted briefly in both *Silent Movie* and *High Anxiety*.

Films Silent Movie ✦✦✦ *(76; s only)*, High Anxiety ✦✦ *(77; s only)*, ...And Justice for All ✦✦ *(79; s only)*, Diner ✦✦✦✦ *(82; also s)*, Best Friends ✦✦ *(82; s only)*, The Natural ✦✦ *(84)*, Unfaithfully Yours ✦✦✦ *(84; s only)*, Young Sherlock Holmes ✦✦ *(85)*, Good Morning, Vietnam ✦✦✦ *(87)*, Tin Men ✦✦✦ *(87; also s)*, Rain Man ✦✦✦✦ *(88; also a)*, Avalon ✦✦✦ *(90; also s)*, Bugsy ✦✦ *(92)*, Toys ✦✦ *(92; also s)*

Juliette Lewis [b. 1973]

Quote 'I think it's a real ability to be ugly and unattractive. I think I can be beautiful and I can be ugly. Michelle Pfieffer can't be ugly.'

Films My Stepmother is an Alien ✦✦ (88), National Lampoon's Christmas Vacation ✦✦ (89), Cape Fear ✦✦ (92), Husbands and Wives ✦✦✦ (92), *Kalifornia (93)*, *Gilbert Grape (93)*, *That Night (93)*, *Natural Born Killers (94)*

Ray Liotta [b. 1955]

Films The Lonely Lady ✦ (83), Something Wild ✦✦✦ (86), Nicky and Gino ✦✦ (88), Field of Dreams ✦✦✦✦ (89), GoodFellas ✦✦✦✦ (90), Unlawful Entry ✦✦✦ (92), *The Penal Colony (94)*, *Corrina, Corrina (94)*

John Lithgow [b. 1945]

Films The World According to Garp ✦✦✦ (82), Terms of Endearment ✦✦✦ (83), Twilight Zone – The Movie ✦✦ (83), 2010 ✦✦ (84), Footloose ✦✦ (84), Santa Claus: The Movie ✦ (85), The Adventures of Buckaroo Banzai Across the 8th Dimension ✦✦ (87), Bigfoot and the Hendersons ✦✦ (87), Out Cold ✦✦ (89), Memphis Belle ✦✦ (90), At Play in the Fields of the Lord ✦✦ (91), Ricochet ✦✦✦ (91), Raising Cain ✦✦ (92), Cliffhanger (93), *A Good Man in Africa (93)*

Christopher Lloyd [b. 1938]

One of the greatest of screen eccentrics, Lloyd's reputation as Reverend Jim from TV sitcom *Taxi* was eclipsed by his triple performance as Dr. Emmett Brown in the *Back to the Future* films.

Films *One Flew Over the Cuckoo's Nest* ✦✦✦✦ *(75), Goin' South* ✦✦✦ *(78), The Onion Field* ✦✦✦ *(79), The Postman Always Rings Twice* ✦✦✦ *(81),* Mr. Mum ✦✦ (83), To Be or Not to Be ✦✦ (83), Star Trek III: The Search for Spock ✦✦ (84), Back to the Future ✦✦✦✦ (85), Clue ✦ (85), Miracles ✦ (86), The Adventures of Buckaroo Banzai Across the 8th Dimension ✦✦ (87), Who Framed Roger Rabbit? ✦✦✦ (88), Eight Men Out ✦✦ (88), Track 29 ✦ (88), Back to the Future, Part II ✦✦ (89), The Dream Team ✦✦✦✦ (89), Back to the Future, Part III ✦✦✦✦ (90), Why Me? ✦✦ (90), The Addams Family ✦✦✦ (91), Suburban Commando ✦✦✦ (91), *Dennis (93), Addams Family Values (93), The Pagemaster (v)(94)*

Robert Loggia [b. 1930]

One of the best supporting actors around, Loggia's probably best-known as Tom Hanks' boss in *Big*, dancing with him on the giant toystore piano.

Films *S.O.B.* ✦✦ *(81),* An Officer and a Gentleman ✦✦ (82), The Trail of the Pink Panther ✦ (82), The Curse of the Pink Panther ✦ (83), Psycho II ✦✦ (83), Scarface ✦✦ (83), Jagged Edge ✦✦✦ (85), Prizzi's Honour ✦✦ (85), That's Life ✦✦ (86), The

Believers ✦ (87), Gaby – A True Story ✦✦✦ (87), Over the Top ✦ (87), Big ✦✦✦✦ (88), Oliver and Company ✦✦ (v)(88), Triumph of the Spirit ✦✦ (89), Too Hot to Handle ✦✦ (91), Gladiator ✦✦✦ (92), Necessary Roughness ✦ (92), Innocent Blood ✦✦✦ (92), *Taking Liberties (94)*

Shelley Long [b. 1949]

Quote 'I send my kids to Shelley Long movies as punishment. My kids say, "No, mommy, no! Not that woman again!"' [Respondent to Movieline's Most Unwanted Poll, 1992]

Films Night Shift ✦✦ (82), Losin' It ✦✦ (83), Irreconcilable Differences ✦ (84), The Money Pit ✦ (86), Hello Again ✦✦ (87), Outrageous Fortune ✦✦ (87), Troop Beverly Hills ✦✦ (89), Don't Tell Her It's Me ✦ (92)

Jon Lovitz [b. 1957]

A Saturday Night Live alumni, he delighted audiences – and obviously casting directors – with his wonderful small role as the talent scout in *A League of their Own*.

Films Jumpin' Jack Flash ✦✦ (86), ¡Three Amigos! ✦ (86), Ratboy ✦✦ (86), Big ✦✦✦✦ (88), My Stepmother is an Alien ✦✦ (88), The Brave Little Toaster ✦✦ (v)(89), An American Tail: Fievel Goes West ✦✦ (v)(91), A League of their Own ✦✦ (92), National Lampoon's Loaded Weapon 1 ✦✦ (93), *North (94), City Slickers II (94)*

Rob Lowe [b. 1964]

Real name Robert Hepler Lowe

Quote 'Finally, Rob Lowe has made a film that everybody wants to see.' [Arsenio Hall, on the notorious video]

Quote 'You don't go out with your buddy's ex-girlfriend. And you certainly don't marry her. Rob Lowe broke that rule. Then he invited me to the wedding...of course, I went.' [Emilio Estevez]

Films Class ✦ (83), The Outsiders ✦✦ (83), Oxford Blues ✦✦ (84), Hotel New

Hampshire ◆ (84), St. Elmo's Fire ◆ (85), About Last Night... ◆◆ (86), Youngblood ◆ (86), Square Dance ◆◆ (87), Masquerade ◆◆ (88), Bad Influence ◆◆ (90), Wayne's World ◆◆◆◆ (92), *Wayne's World 2 (94)*

Dolph Lundgren   [b. 1959]

One of the few action stars whose brain is as well-developed as his biceps. Stockholm born, Australian-educated, six foot five and sixteen stone, he also speaks five languages, has a master's degree in chemical engineering and won a Fulbright scholarship to the Massachusetts Institute of Technology. After working as a bouncer and bodyguard, he got a bit part in *A View to a Kill* and head-butted his way up from there. Of his films released only on video here, well worth a look is the romp *Showdown in Little Tokyo*.

Quote 'My problem is that people get intimidated by someone big and beautiful like me. They hate to think I can be smart as well.'

Quote 'The biggest man I've ever been with. *Definitely* the biggest.' [Grace Jones]

Films Rocky IV ◆◆ (85), A View to a Kill ◆◆ (b)(85), Masters of the Universe ◆◆ (87), Dark Angel ◆◆ (90), The Punisher ◆◆ (90), Universal Soldier ◆◆◆ (92), *Joshua Tree (93)*

David Lynch   [b. 1946]

DIRECTOR. Best-known not so much for his film work, but for the weird and wonderful *Twin Peaks* TV series, Lynch has been astounding filmgoers for a decade now, uniquely bridging the gap between avant-garde and mainstream cinema. He is as surreal in reality as his imagination is on screen, always dressing in black with a white shirt buttoned right up and no tie. For special occasions he dons his lucky untied shoelace. For years he ate the same food every day, working on napkins at Bob's Big Boy diner and overdosing on sugar, which he calls

'granulated happiness.'

Quote 'Jimmy Stewart from Mars.' [Mel Brooks]

Films *Eraserhead* ◆◆ (78; also s), The Elephant Man ◆◆◆◆ (80; also s), Dune ◆ (84; also s), Blue Velvet ◆◆ (86; also s), Wild at Heart ◆ (90; also s), Twin Peaks: Fire Walk With Me ◆ (92; also a&s)

Kelly Lynch   [b. 1959]

Films Cocktail ◆◆ (88), Bright Lights, Big City ◆ (88), Drugstore Cowboy ◆◆ (89), Road House ◆◆ (89), Desperate Hours ◆◆ (90), Curly Sue ◆ (91), Three of Hearts ◆ (93)

Andie MacDowell   [b. 1958]

Real name Rose Anderson MacDowell

Quote 'I just think of myself as a mother who has a pretty good career acting.'

Quote 'I have always thought that in my next life I'd like to come back as a five-foot-three-inch girl with the best butt and best tits you've ever seen.'

Films Greystoke: The Legend of Tarzan, Lord of the Apes ◆◆◆ (84), St. Elmo's Fire ◆ (85), sex, lies, and videotape ◆◆◆ (89), Green Card ◆◆◆ (90), Hudson Hawk ◆ (91), The Object of Beauty ◆◆ (91), The Player ◆◆◆◆ (c)(92), Groundhog Day ◆◆◆ (93), *Ruby Cairo (93), Short Cuts (93)*

Kyle MacLachlan   [b. 1960]

Films Dune ◆ (84), Blue Velvet ◆◆ (86), The Hidden ◆◆ (87), The Doors ◆◆ (91), Twin Peaks: Fire Walk With Me ◆ (92), Don't Tell Her It's Me ◆ (92), Rich In Love ◆◆ (93)

Amy Madigan   [b. 1957]

Films Love Letters ◆◆◆ (84), Places in the Heart ◆◆◆ (84), Streets of Fire ◆ (84), Twice in a Lifetime ◆◆◆ (85), Alamo Bay ◆◆ (85), The Prince of Pennsylvania ◆◆ (88), Field of Dreams ◆◆◆◆ (89), Uncle Buck ◆◆ (89), *The Dark Half (93)*

Madonna [b. 1958]

Real name Madonna Louise Ciccone

Quote 'I lost my virginity as a career move.'

Quote 'Money can't buy you happiness, but at least you can afford to rent it for the evening.'

Films *A Certain Sacrifice* ◆ (80), Desperately Seeking Susan ◆◆◆ (85), Shanghai Surprise ◆ (86), Who's That Girl? ◆ (87), Dick Tracy ◆◆ (90), Shadows and Fog ◆◆◆ (92), A League of their Own ◆◆ (92), Body of Evidence ◆ (93), *Snake Eyes (93)*

Michael Madsen [b. 1958]

Big brother of Virginia.

Films Racing with the Moon ◆◆◆ (b)(84), Kill Me Again ◆◆◆ (89), Blood Red ◆ (89), Thelma & Louise ◆◆◆◆ (91), The Doors ◆◆ (91), Straight Talk ◆◆◆ (92), Reservoir Dogs ◆◆◆◆ (92), *Free Willy (93), The Getaway (94)*

Virginia Madsen [b. 1963]

Sister of Michael.

Films Class ◆ (83), Dune ◆ (84), Electric Dreams ◆◆ (84), Creator ◆◆ (85), Slamdance ◆◆ (87), The Dead Can't Lie ◆◆◆ (88), Mr. North ◆◆ (88), Highlander II – the Quickening ◆ (90), The Hot Spot ◆◆◆ (90), Candyman ◆◆◆ (92)

John Malkovich [b. 1953]

Quote 'It's like Henry Mencken said, "No one ever went broke underestimating the intelligence of the American people." And that goes worldwide. Look what people go to see. Look what they read. Look what they believe. Look at their leaders...But listen, I am much more likely to go to *Terminator* than I am to one of my films.'

Quote 'I'm a small-town person. I've never used drugs. I don't drink. My idea of fun is to stay home and stain a piece of furniture.'

Films The Killing Fields ◆◆◆ (84), Places in the Heart ◆◆◆ (84), Eleni ◆ (85), Empire of the Sun ◆◆◆ (87), The Glass Menagerie ◆◆◆ (87), Making Mr. Right ◆◆ (87), Dangerous Liaisons ◆◆◆ (88), Miles from Home ◆◆ (88), The Sheltering Sky ◆ (90), The Object of Beauty ◆◆ (91), Shadows and Fog ◆◆◆ (92), Of Mice and Men ◆◆◆ (92), Jennifer 8 ◆◆◆ (92), Alive ◆◆◆ (c)(93), In the Line of Fire (93), *We're Back (v)(93)*

Joe Mantegna [b. 1947]

Quote 'I didn't run around with con men and sleazeballs all my life, but I didn't run around with the polo set either.'

Films Compromising Positions ◆◆ (85), ¡Three Amigos! ◆ (86), The Money Pit ◆ (86), House of Games ◆◆◆ (87), Suspect ◆◆ (87), Things Change ◆◆◆ (88), Alice ◆◆◆ (90), The Godfather, Part III ◆◆◆ (90), Homicide ◆◆◆◆ (91), Bugsy ◆◆ (92), Body of Evidence ◆ (93), *Searching for Bobby Fischer (93)*

James Marshall [b. 1969]

Real name James Greenblatt

James Hurley from TV series *Twin Peaks*, he first changed his name to James Green, then decided to adopt Jimi Hendrix's middle name for his surname.

Films Stockade ◆◆ (90), Gladiator ◆◆◆ (92), Twin Peaks: Fire Walk With Me ◆ (92), A Few Good Men ◆◆◆◆ (92)

Steve Martin [b. 1946]

Born appropriately in Waco, Texas, Martin was a cheerleader at high school. When the family moved to California, Martin started working in his spare time down the road in Disneyland. He spent eight years selling Davy Crockett hats and Mouseketeer ears while teaching himself magic, juggling, the banjo and joke-writing. After a course in Symbolic Logic at Long Beach State University, he became a gag-writer for people like Sonny and Cher and Dick Van Dyke before going in front of the mike himself. He once took an entire audience of 500 people off for a Big Mac in the middle of the show. Saturday Night Live brought him fame and he has combined phenomenally successful comedy tours with his burgeoning movie career, taking on more straight roles in recent years. He's married to Victoria Tennant, whom he met while filming *All of Me*. They live in a house in LA with no windows at the front.

Quote 'I'm just a wild and crazy guy.'

Films *The Muppet Movie* ••• (c)(79), *The Jerk* •• (79), *Pennies from Heaven* ••• (81), *Dead Men Don't Wear Plaid* •• (82; also s), *The Man With Two Brains* •• (83), *All of Me* ••• (84), *Little Shop of Horrors* •• (86), *¡Three Amigos!* • (86; also s), *Planes, Trains and Automobiles* ••• (87), *Roxanne* •••• (87; also s), *Dirty Rotten Scoundrels* •••• (88), *Parenthood* ••• (89), *My Blue Heaven* •• (90), *Grand Canyon* •• (91), *Father of the Bride* • (91), *L.A. Story* ••• (91; also s), *Housesitter* •• (92), *Leap of Faith* ••• (92)

Mary Stuart Masterson [b.1967]

Films *The Stepford Wives* ••• (b)(75), *Catholic Boys* ••• (85), *At Close Range* •• (86), *My Little Girl* ••• (87), *Gardens of Stone* ••• (87), *Mr. North* •• (88), *Fried Green Tomatoes at the Whistle Stop Cafe* •••• (92), *Benny & Joon* ••• (93), *Married to It* (93)

Mary Elizabeth Mastrantonio [b. 1958]

Films *Scarface* •• (83), *The Color of Money* ••• (86), *Slamdance* •• (87), *The Abyss* •• (89), *The January Man* • (89), *Fools of Fortune* • (90), *Robin Hood: Prince of Thieves* ••• (91), *Class Action* ••• (91), *White Sands* ••• (92), *Consenting Adults* • (92)

Andrew McCarthy [b. 1962]

Films *Class* • (83), *Catholic Boys* ••• (85), *St. Elmo's Fire* • (85), *Pretty in Pink* •• (86), *Mannequin* • (87), *Fresh Horses* •• (88), *Kansas* • (88), *Weekend at Bernie's* •• (89), *Year of the Gun* • (91), *Weekend at Bernie's II* (93)

Mary McDonnell [b. 1952]

Films *Matewan* •••• (87), *Tiger Warsaw* • (88), *Dances With Wolves* •••• (90), *Grand Canyon* •• (91), *Sneakers* ••• (92), *Passion Fish* (92)

Frances McDormand [b. 1957]

Films *Blood Simple* •••• (85), *Raising Arizona* •••• (87), *Mississippi Burning* •• (88), *Chattahoochee* •• (90), *Darkman* •• (90), *Hidden Agenda* •• (90), *Miller's Crossing* •••• (c)(90), *The Butcher's Wife* ••• (92)

Kelly McGillis [b. 1957]

Films *Reuben, Reuben* •• (83), *Witness* •••• (85), *Top Gun* •• (86), *Made in Heaven* •• (87), *The Accused* •• (88), *The House on Carroll Street* •• (88), *Cat Chaser* ••• (89), *Winter People* •• (89)

Elizabeth McGovern [b. 1961]

Films *Ordinary People* (80), *Heaven's Gate* ••• (80), *Ragtime* ••• (81), *Lovesick* •• (83), *Once Upon a Time in America* •••• (84), *Racing with the Moon* ••• (84), *The Bedroom Window* •• (87), *Johnny Handsome* •• (89), *The Handmaid's Tale* •• (90), *A Shock to the System* •• (90), *Aunt Julia and the Scriptwriter* •• (c)(91)

Michael McKean [b. 1947]

A busy supporting actor, it's always worth looking out for McKean in movies, just so that you can annoy the person next to you by saying, 'Of course no-one recognises him, but he was David St. Hubbins in *Spinal Tap*, you know'. If they have any sense, they'll change seats. Nobody likes a know-all.

Films *Young Doctors in Love* ••• (82), *This is Spinal Tap* •••• (84; also s), *Clue* • (85), *D.A.R.Y.L.* •• (85), *Jumpin' Jack*

Flash ◆◆ (c)(86), Light of Day ◆ (87), Planes, Trains and Automobiles ◆◆◆ (87), Short Circuit 2 ◆ (88), The Big Picture ◆◆◆ (89; also s), Earth Girls Are Easy ◆ (89), Hider in the House ◆◆ (89), The Book of Love ◆◆◆◆ (91), True Identity ◆◆ (91), Memoirs of an Invisible Man ◆◆ (92), Man Trouble ◆ (92)

Laurie Metcalf [b. 1956]

Wonderful supporting actress, perhaps best-known as Roseanne's sitcom sister.

Films Desperately Seeking Susan ◆◆◆ (85), Making Mr. Right ◆◆ (87), Miles from Home ◆◆ (88), Stars and Bars ◆ (88), Uncle Buck ◆◆ (89), Pacific Heights ◆◆ (90), Internal Affairs ◆◆ (90), JFK ◆◆◆ (91), *Blink (93)*

Bette Midler [b. 1945]

Quote 'I have my standards. They may be low, but I have them.'

Quote 'I'd let my wife, children, and animals starve before I'd subject myself to something like that again.' [Don Siegel, on directing her]

Films *The Rose* ◆◆ (79), Ruthless People ◆◆◆◆ (86), Down and Out in Beverly Hills ◆◆◆ (86), Outrageous Fortune ◆◆ (87), Oliver and Company ◆◆ (v)(88), Beaches ◆ (88), Big Business ◆◆ (88), Stella ◆ (90), Scenes from a Mall ◆◆ (91), For the Boys ◆◆ (92), *Hocus Pocus (93)*

Penelope Ann Miller [b. 1964]

Films Adventures in Babysitting ◆◆ (87), Biloxi Blues ◆◆◆ (88), Miles from Home ◆◆ (88), Dead-Bang ◆◆ (89), Awakenings ◆◆◆ (90), The Freshman ◆◆◆◆ (90), Kindergarten Cop ◆◆ (90), Other People's Money ◆◆ (91), Chaplin ◆◆ (92), *Carlito's Way (93)*

Helen Mirren [b. 1946]

Films O, Lucky Man! ◆◆◆ (73), The Long Good Friday ◆◆◆◆ (80), Caligula ◆ (80), Excalibur ◆◆◆ (81), Cal ◆◆◆ (84), 2010 ◆◆ (84), White Nights ◆◆ (85), The

Mosquito Coast ◆◆ (86), Heavenly Pursuits ◆◆ (87), Pascali's Island ◆◆ (88), The Cook, the Thief, His Wife and Her Lover ◆◆◆ (89), When the Whales Came ◆◆ (89), The Comfort of Strangers ◆ (90), Where Angels Fear to Tread ◆◆ (91)

Matthew Modine [b. 1959]

Films Streamers ◆◆ (83), Baby, It's You ◆◆◆ (83), Mrs. Soffel ◆◆ (84), Birdy ◆◆◆ (84), Hotel New Hampshire ◆ (84), Full Metal Jacket ◆◆◆ (87), Orphans ◆◆◆ (87), Married to the Mob ◆◆ (88), Memphis Belle ◆◆ (90), Pacific Heights ◆◆ (90), Wind ◆ (92)

Alfred Molina [b. 1953]

Films *Raiders of the Lost Ark* ◆◆◆◆ *(81),* Ladyhawke ◆ (85), Letter to Brezhnev ◆◆◆ (85), Prick Up Your Ears ◆◆◆ (87), Manifesto ◆ (88), Enchanted April ◆◆◆◆ (91), American Friends ◆◆◆ (91), Not Without My Daughter ◆◆ (91)

Demi Moore [b. 1962]

Real name Demi Guynes

Beginning her career in the TV soap, *General Hospital*, Moore was getting nowhere slowly until she hit the big time with *Ghost*. Once engaged to Emilio Estevez, she has two daughters with husband Bruce Willis, called Rumer and Scout LaRue. She posed naked when pregnant for Vanity Fair but stopped her 48-year-old mother taking her clothes off for Playboy. In case you happen to bump into her, she pronounces her name De-MEE, not DE-mee. Within the industry, she is nicknamed 'Gimmee' Moore because of her love for perks, apparently always insisting on the best trailer.

Quote 'She's like a beautiful ballerina who can also kickbox and talk dirty.' [Alan Rudolph, director]

Films Young Doctors in Love ◆◆◆ (c)(82), Blame it on Rio ◆◆ (84), St. Elmo's Fire ◆ (85), About Last Night... ◆◆ (86), The Seventh Sign ◆ (88), We're No Angels ◆ (89), Ghost ◆◆◆◆ (90), Mortal Thoughts

◆◆ (91), Nothing But Trouble ◆ (91), The Butcher's Wife ◆◆◆ (92), A Few Good Men ◆◆◆◆ (92), Indecent Proposal ◆◆◆ (93)

Dudley Moore [b. 1935]

Quote 'I've been having a mid-life crisis since I was two weeks old. I went right from a midwife to a mid-life crisis.'

Quote 'Masturbation is always very safe, because there you not only control the person you're with but you can leave when you want to.'

Films *Bedazzled* ◆◆◆ (67), *30 Is a Dangerous Age, Cynthia* ◆◆◆ (68; also s), *Monte Carlo or Bust* ◆◆ (69), *The Bed Sitting-Room* ◆◆◆ (69), *Foul Play* ◆◆ (78), *10* ◆◆ (79), *Arthur* ◆◆◆◆ (81), *Six Weeks* ◆◆ (82), *Lovesick* ◆◆ (83), *Romantic Comedy* ◆◆ (83), *Best Defense* ◆ (84), *Micki & Maude* ◆◆◆ (84), *Unfaithfully Yours* ◆◆◆ (84), *Santa Claus: The Movie* ◆ (85), *Like Father, Like Son* ◆◆ (87), *Arthur 2: On the Rocks* ◆◆ (88), *Crazy People* ◆◆ (90), *Blame it on the Bellboy* ◆◆ (92)

Rick Moranis [b. 1954]

Films *Ghostbusters* ◆◆◆◆ (84), *Streets of Fire* ◆ (84), *Brewster's Millions* ◆ (85), *Little Shop of Horrors* ◆◆ (86), *Spaceballs* ◆◆ (87), *Parenthood* ◆◆◆ (89), *Ghostbusters II* ◆◆ (89), *Honey, I Shrunk the Kids* ◆◆◆ (89), *My Blue Heaven* ◆◆ (90), *L.A. Story* ◆◆◆ (c)(91), *Honey, I Blew Up the Kid* ◆◆ (92), *The Flintstones* (94)

Eddie Murphy [b. 1961]

Murphy was raised in comfortable middle-class Long Island after his father, a New York cop and amateur comedian, died when he was eight. He made a cracking start in movies with *48 HRS.* and *Trading Places*. Unfortunately, his films since then have disappointed, some say because he is now so powerful no-one can hold his ego in check. Said to have had an electric golf car with a Rolls-Royce grill for travelling round the Paramount lot. Has a penchant for women, fast cars and jewellery, once having to take off two

pounds of gold necklaces before he could get through an airport metal detector!

Quote 'Eddie can hear the rustle of nylon stockings at fifty yards.' [Walter Hill, director]

Quote 'A Hollywood negro.' [Spike Lee]

Films *48 HRS.* ◆◆◆ (82), *Trading Places* ◆◆◆◆ (83), *Beverly Hills Cop* ◆◆◆ (84), *Best Defense* ◆ (84), *Beverly Hills Cop II* ◆ (87), *The Golden Child* ◆ (87), *Coming to America* ◆◆ (88), *Harlem Nights* ◆ (89; also d&s), *Another 48 HRS.* ◆◆ (90), *Boomerang* ◆◆ (92), *The Distinguished Gentlemen* ◆◆ (92)

Bill Murray [b. 1950]

Quote 'I'm a nut, but not *just* a nut.'

Films *Meatballs* ◆◆ (79), *Caddyshack* ◆◆ (80), *Stripes* ◆◆ (81), *Tootsie* ◆◆◆◆ (82), *Ghostbusters* ◆◆◆◆ (84), *Little Shop of Horrors* ◆◆ (86), *Scrooged* ◆◆ (88), *Ghostbusters II* ◆◆ (89), *Quick Change* ◆◆ (90; also d), *What About Bob?* ◆◆◆ (91), *Groundhog Day* ◆◆◆ (93), *Mad Dog and Glory* ◆◆◆ (93)

Liam Neeson [b. 1953]

Films *Excalibur* ◆◆◆ (81), *Krull* ◆ (83), *Bounty* ◆◆ (84), *The Innocent* ◆◆ (85), *The Mission* ◆◆ (86), *Lamb* ◆◆ (86), *A Prayer for the Dying* ◆◆ (87), *Suspect* ◆◆ (87), *Duet for One* ◆◆ (87), *The Dead Pool* ◆◆ (88), *The Good Mother* ◆ (88), *High Spirits* ◆ (88), *Next of Kin* ◆◆ (89), *The Big Man* ◆◆ (90), *Darkman* ◆◆ (90), *Under Suspicion* ◆◆◆ (91), *Shining Through* ◆◆ (92), *Husbands and Wives* ◆◆◆ (92), *Leap of Faith* ◆◆◆ (92), *Ruby Cairo* (93), *Schindler's List* (93), *Ethan Frome* (93)

Sam Neill [b. 1948]

Films *My Brilliant Career* ◆◆◆◆ (79), *Enigma* ◆◆ (83), *Plenty* ◆◆ (85), *The Good Wife* ◆◆ (87), *A Cry in the Dark* ◆◆ (88), *Dead Calm* ◆◆◆◆ (89), *The Hunt for Red October* ◆◆◆ (90), *Memoirs of an Invisible Man* ◆◆ (92), *Death in*

Brunswick ♦ (92), Until the End of the World ♦ (92), Jurassic Park (93)

Jack Nicholson [b. 1937]

Nicholson's career took years to get anywhere. He worked as an office boy in the cartoon department of MGM, acted on TV, sold the rights to biker pics at Cannes, wrote and acted for schlockmeister Roger Corman and might never have been heard of had Rip Torn not dropped out of *Easy Rider*. Nicholson, the 32-year-old associate producer, stepped in and the rest, as they say, is history. Although he lives modestly, he is one of the richest actors in the world, apparently earning over $50m from *Batman* and thus easily able to turn down an offer of $10m for half a day's work on a TV ad. He was for many years Anjelica Huston's partner. Only in the 70s did he learn that the woman he thought was his mother was his grandmother and that his supposed sister was in fact his mother, a deception made to conceal his illegitimacy.

Quote 'My best feature's my smile. And smiles – praise heaven – don't get fat.'

Quote 'I was always against authority, hated being told anything by my teachers, by parents, by anyone. At school I created a record by being in detention every day for a year. Today I suppose I'm still in love with what I think. I don't like listening to what other people think.'

Films *Easy Rider* ♦♦♦ (69), *Five Easy Pieces* ♦♦♦♦ (70), *Carnal Knowledge* ♦♦♦ (71), *Drive, He Said* ♦♦ (71; d only), *The King of Marvin Gardens* ♦♦♦ (72), *The Last Detail* ♦♦♦♦ (73), *Chinatown* ♦♦♦♦ (74), *One Flew Over the Cuckoo's Nest* ♦♦♦♦ (75), *The Fortune* ♦♦♦ (75), *The Passenger* ♦♦♦ (75), *Tommy* ♦♦♦ (75), *The Last Tycoon* ♦♦♦ (76), *Missouri Breaks* ♦♦ (76), *Goin' South* ♦♦♦ (78; also d), *The Shining* ♦♦♦♦ (80), *Reds* ♦♦♦ (81), *The Postman Always Rings Twice* ♦♦♦ (81), *The Border* ♦♦ (82), *Terms of Endearment* ♦♦♦ (83), *Prizzi's Honour* ♦♦ (85), *Heartburn* ♦ (86), *Broadcast News* ♦♦♦ (c)(87), *Ironweed* ♦♦ (87), *The*

Witches of Eastwick ♦♦♦ (87), Batman ♦♦ (89), The Two Jakes ♦♦♦♦ (91; also d), Man Trouble ♦ (92), A Few Good Men ♦♦♦♦ (92), Hoffa ♦♦ (92), Wolf (94)

Leslie Nielsen [b. 1926]

Thanks to *Naked Gun*, this Canadian-born actor, best-known for a series of less than remarkable straight roles in mediocre TV series, became a comedy star. With a smile, a twinkle and a whoopie cushion, this one-time disc jockey is now the darling of chat shows the world over. His new comic persona creates something of a problem when watching any of his previous serious films, for you keep expecting him to do something Drebinish at any moment.

Quote 'Audiences love him. And I do mean love. Not just a cheap, one-night stand where they merely use you, never calling again or sending flowers.' [David Zucker]

Films *Forbidden Planet* ♦♦♦♦ (56), *The Poseidon Adventure* ♦♦♦ (72), *Airplane!* (80), *Prom Night* ♦ (80), *The Man with the Deadly Lens* ♦♦♦ (82), *Creepshow* ♦♦ (82), *Soul Man* ♦♦♦ (86), *Nuts* ♦♦ (87), *The Naked Gun: From the Films of Police Squad!* ♦♦♦ (88), *Repossessed* ♦ (90), *All I Want For Christmas* ♦ (91), *Naked Gun 2 1/2 – The Smell of Fear* ♦♦ (91)

Nick Nolte [b. 1942]

Although a top college athlete, Nolte was a rebellious youth, receiving a suspended sentence for selling forged draft cards. While his acting has steadily improved from the days when he was little more than a pretty face and body, his private life has been turbulent. Once renowned as one of the hardest drinkers and drug-users in Hollywood, he loves playing troubled types and prepares assiduously for his roles. When offered the part of *Superman*, he said 'I'll do it if I can play him as a schizophrenic'.

Quote 'He spanked me 22 times on my 22nd birthday. His favourite sex fantasy was to have me dress up and pretend to be the wife of a United States senator.' [Ex-wife Sharyn 'Legs' Haddad]

Films *The Deep* ♦ (77), *Dog Soldiers* ♦♦ (78), *Heartbeat* ♦♦ (79), *North Dallas Forty* ♦♦♦♦ (79), 48 HRS. ♦♦♦ (82), *Under Fire* ♦♦♦♦ (83), The Ultimate Solution of Grace Quigley ♦♦ (84), *Teachers* ♦♦ (84), *Down and Out in Beverly Hills* ♦♦♦ (86), *Extreme Prejudice* ♦ (87), *Farewell to the King* ♦ (89), *New York Stories* ♦♦ (89), *Three Fugitives* ♦♦ (89), Another 48 HRS. ♦♦ (90), *Everybody Wins* ♦ (90), Q & A ♦♦ (90), *The Prince of Tides* ♦♦ (91), *Cape Fear* ♦♦ (92), The Player (c)(92), *Lorenzo's Oil* ♦♦ (92), *I'll Do Anything* (93), *Blue Chip* (94), *I Love Trouble* (94)

Chuck Norris [b. 1939]

Real name Carlos Ray Norris

Films Lone Wolf McQuade ♦♦ (83), Missing in Action ♦ (84), Code of Silence ♦♦ (85), Invasion U.S.A. ♦ (85; also s), Firewalker ♦ (86), The Delta Force ♦♦ (86), Delta Force 2: The Colombian Connection ♦ (90), *Sidekicks* (93)

Chris O'Donnell [b. 1971]

Films Men Don't Leave ♦♦ (90), School Ties (92), Fried Green Tomatoes at the Whistle Stop Cafe ♦♦♦♦ (92), Scent of a Woman ♦♦♦(92), *The Three Musketeers* (94)

Gary Oldman [b. 1958]

Heavily influenced by the film *If...*, he changed his mind about wanting to machine-gun his teachers, deciding he'd like to be like Malcolm MacDowell the actor rather than his character. Born in New Cross, London, his father abandoned the family when Oldman was seven. Married and divorced twice, for the second time from Uma Thurman.

Quote 'I always look for neuroses in the characters I play.'

Films Sid and Nancy ♦♦ (86), Prick Up Your Ears ♦♦♦ (87), We Think the World of You ♦♦ (88), Track 29 ♦ (88), Criminal Law ♦♦ (89), Chattahoochee ♦♦ (90), Rosencrantz and Guildenstern Are Dead ♦♦ (90), State of Grace ♦♦♦ (90), JFK ♦♦♦ (91), Bram Stoker's Dracula ♦♦♦ (92), *Romeo is Bleeding* (93), *True Romance* (93)

Al Pacino [b. 1940]

Real name Alberto Pacino

The career of one of the greatest of all film actors was was almost extinguished by the pitiable *Revolution*, a turkey so big it was several Christmases before Pacino was seen again. Raised by his mother and grandparents, they were so protective that, until he was seven, he was allowed out only to go to school and the cinema. A one-time dancer and stand-up comic, it was *The Godfather* that shot him to stardom. One of those actors who truly immerses himself in his roles, a brief affair four years ago resulted in a daughter, although he's never revealed who the mother is.

Films Me, Natalie ♦♦♦ (69), The Panic in Needle Park ♦♦♦ (71), The Godfather ♦♦♦♦ (72), Serpico ♦♦♦♦ (73), Scarecrow ♦♦♦ (73), The Godfather, Part II ♦♦♦♦ (74), Dog Day Afternoon ♦♦♦♦ (75), Bobby Deerfield ♦ (77), ...And Justice for All ♦♦ (79), Cruising ♦ (80), Author! Author! ♦♦ (82), Scarface ♦♦ (83), Revolution ♦ (85), Sea of Love ♦♦♦ (89), Dick Tracy ♦♦ (90), The Godfather, Part III ♦♦♦ (90), Frankie & Johnny ♦♦♦ (91), Glengarry Glen Ross ♦♦♦ (92), Scent of a Woman ♦♦♦ (92), *Carlito's Way* (93)

Sarah Jessica Parker [b. 1965]

Films Footloose ♦♦ (84), Girls Just Want to Have Fun ♦♦ (85), The Flight of the Navigator ♦♦♦ (86), L.A. Story ♦♦♦ (91), Honeymoon in Vegas ♦♦♦♦ (92), *Striking Distance* (93), *Hocus Pocus* (93)

Dolly Parton [b. 1946]

Quote 'It costs a lot of money to look this cheap.'

Quote 'When women's lib started I was the first to burn my bra and it took three days to put out the fire.'

Films *9 to 5* ◆◆ *(80)*, *The Best Little Whorehouse in Texas* ◆◆ *(82)*, *Steel Magnolias* ◆◆ *(89)*, *Straight Talk* ◆◆◆ *(92)*

Sean Penn [b. 1960]

Quote 'My attitude to the press is a presumption that what the press says my attitude to the press is, is what it is, but that's not to say that it isn't – by and large – negative.'

Films *Taps* ◆◆ *(81)*, *Fast Times at Ridgemont High* ◆◆◆ *(82)*, *The Bad Boys* ◆◆◆ *(83)*, *Crackers* ◆ *(84)*, *Racing with the Moon* ◆◆◆ *(84)*, *The Falcon and the Snowman* ◆◆ *(85)*, *At Close Range* ◆◆ *(86)*, *Shanghai Surprise* ◆ *(86)*, *Judgment in Berlin* ◆◆ *(88)*, *Colors* ◆◆ *(88)*, *Casualties of War* ◆◆◆ *(89)*, *We're No Angels* ◆ *(89)*, *State of Grace* ◆◆◆ *(90)*, *The Indian Runner* ◆◆ *(91; d&s only)*, *Carlito's Way (93)*

Rosie Perez

Films *Do the Right Thing* ◆◆◆◆ *(89)*, *White Men Can't Jump* ◆◆◆◆ *(92)*, *Night on Earth* ◆◆ *(92)*, *Untamed Heart* ◆◆◆ *(93)*, *Fearless (93)*

Elizabeth Perkins [b. 1961]

Real name Elizabeth Pisperikos

Films *About Last Night...* ◆◆ *(86)*, *Big* ◆◆◆◆ *(88)*, *Sweet Hearts Dance* ◆◆ *(88)*, *Avalon* ◆◆ *(90)*, *Love at Large* ◆ *(90)*, *Over Her Dead Body* ◆◆ *(91)*, *The Doctor* ◆◆ *(92)*, *Tamakawa (93)*, *The Flintstones (94)*

Joe Pesci [b. 1943]

Pesci is a former child actor, playing a crippled newspaper boy at five and appearing with Connie Francis on television at ten. In his teens, he wanted to be a singer, abandoning high school for his band Joey Dee and the Starlighters. However, their album *Little Joe Sure Can Sing* didn't set the charts alight. At one time, a ditch digger in Las Vegas, he had a great role in *Raging Bull*, but nothing much came of it. Only with *Lethal Weapon 2* and

GoodFellas has stardom beckoned.

Quote 'When you're Mr. Nobody, people think they can push you around...Now things are different and I am seeing the same people, who once cut me dead, fall all over themselves to keep me sweet. No wonder I hate Hollywood with a vengeance.'

Films *Raging Bull* ◆◆◆ *(80)*, *Eureka* ◆◆◆◆ *(83)*, *Once Upon a Time in America* ◆◆◆◆ *(84)*, *Lethal Weapon 2* ◆◆◆ *(89)*, *Betsy's Wedding* ◆ *(90)*, *GoodFellas* ◆◆◆◆ *(90)*, *Home Alone* ◆◆ *(90)*, *JFK* ◆◆◆ *(91)*, *Catchfire* ◆◆◆ *(91)*, *My Cousin Vinny* ◆◆◆◆ *(92)*, *Lethal Weapon 3* ◆◆◆◆ *(92)*, *The Public Eye* ◆◆◆ *(92)*, *Home Alone 2: Lost in New York* ◆◆ *(92)*, *With Honors (93)*

Michelle Pfeiffer [b. 1958]

Bizarre to think that if you were in the Seven-Items-Or-Less queue in the Vons supermarket in El Toro, California in the late 70s, the blonde check-out girl in the red smock and black polyester trousers would have been Michelle Pfeiffer. Dissatisfied for some reason with retailing as a career, she took up modelling and commercials, winning the Miss Orange County competition but being pipped in the Miss LA contest. It's taken her over ten years to become a star, probably because so many of her early films flopped. Although single, she has adopted a baby daughter.

Quote 'I look like a duck. It's the way my mouth sort of curls up, or my nose tilts up. I should have played "Howard the Duck".'

Quote 'My Christianity would make me think twice about certain roles but it wouldn't stop me leaping into bed with Michelle. I'd love to.' [James Fox]

Films *Charlie Chan and the Curse of the Dragon Queen* ◆ *(81)*, *Grease 2* ◆ *(82)*, *Scarface* ◆◆ *(83)*, *Ladyhawke* ◆ *(85)*, *Into the Night* ◆◆ *(85)*, *Sweet Liberty* ◆◆ *(86)*, *The Witches of Eastwick* ◆◆◆ *(87)*, *Dangerous Liaisons* ◆◆◆ *(88)*, *Married to the Mob* ◆◆ *(88)*, *Tequila Sunrise* ◆ *(88)*,

The Fabulous Baker Boys ••• (89), The Russia House •• (90), Frankie & Johnny •• (91), Batman Returns ••• (92), *Love Field (92), The Age of Innocence (93), Wolf (94)*

Lou Diamond Phillips [b. 1962]

Films La Bamba ••• (87), Stand and Deliver ••• (88), Young Guns •• (88), Renegades •• (89), The First Power • (90), Young Guns II – Blaze of Glory •• (90), The Dark Wind ••• (92)

River Phoenix [b. 1970]

Real name River Jude Phoenix

The son of hippy missionary parents whose other children are Leaf, Rainbow, Liberty and Summer Joy. He, apparently, is named after the River of Life in *Siddhartha* by Hermann Hesse while his parents, Arlyn and John, changed the surname to Phoenix after the mythical bird that rose from the ashes. He has a band called Aleka's Attic and travels everywhere by car or train because he doesn't like flying.

Quote 'I don't wanna sound like a hippy, but love is the guiding power of the Universe.'

Films Explorers •• (85), Stand by Me •• (86), The Mosquito Coast •• (86), Running on Empty ••• (88), Jimmy Reardon •• (88), Indiana Jones and the Last Crusade •••• (89), I Love You to Death • (90), My Own Private Idaho •• (92), Sneakers ••• (92), *The Thing Called Love (93)*

Brad Pitt [b. 1963]

Films Thelma & Louise •••• (91), Cool World • (92), A River Runs Through It •• (92), Johnny Suede ••• (92), *True Romance (93), Kalifornia (93)*

Oliver Platt

Delightful supporting actor, usually playing the funny but dodgy lawyer or best friend. Or both.

Films Working Girl •••• (88), Married to the Mob •• (88), Crusoe ••• (89), Flatliners • (90), Postcards from the Edge •••• (90), Beethoven ••• (92), Midnight Sting •••• (92), Indecent Proposal ••• (93), Benny & Joon ••• (93), *The Temp (93), The Three Musketeers (94)*

Sydney Pollack [b. 1934]

DIRECTOR. Pollack has helmed some of the best and most interesting films of the past twenty years. However, he is also increasingly cropping up as a character actor, mainly in other people's films. His best role, undoubtedly, is as Dustin Hoffman's agent in *Tootsie*.

Films *This Property is Condemned* •• *(66), They Shoot Horses, Don't They?* ••• *(69), Jeremiah Johnson* ••• *(72), The Way We Were* ••• *(73), Three Days of the Condor* •••• *(75), Bobby Deerfield* • *(77), The Electric Horseman* •• *(79), Absence of Malice* ••• *(81),* Tootsie •••• (82; also a), Out of Africa ••• (85), Havana • (90), The Player •••• (92; a only), Husbands and Wives ••• (92; a only), Death Becomes Her ••• (92; a only), The Firm (93)

Richard Portnow

Another of those excellent supporting actors, he seems to be in every film that Stephen Tobolowsky doesn't do.

Films Tin Men ••• (87), Good Morning, Vietnam ••• (87), The Squeeze • (87), Radio Days ••• (87), Chattahoochee •• (90), Havana • (90), Kindergarten Cop •• (90), Aunt Julia and the Scriptwriter •• (91), Sister Act •• (92), For the Boys •• (92)

Bill Pullman [b. 1954]

Films Ruthless People •••• (86), Spaceballs •• (87), The Accidental Tourist ••• (88), The Serpent and the Rainbow ••• (88), Sibling Rivalry •• (90), Cold Feet • (90), Liebestraum ••• (92), The News Boys ••• (92), Singles •••• (92), Sommersby •••• (93), *Sleepless in Seattle (93), Bodily Harm (93)*

Dennis Quaid [b. 1954]

Films *Breaking Away* ✦✦✦✦ *(79)*, *The Long Riders* ✦✦ *(80)*, *All Night Long* ✦✦✦ *(81)*, *The Right Stuff* ✦✦✦✦ *(83)*, *Jaws 3-D* ✦ *(83)*, *Dreamscape* ✦✦✦ *(84)*, *Enemy Mine* ✦ *(85)*, *The Big Easy* ✦✦✦✦ *(87)*, *Innerspace* ✦✦ *(87)*, *Suspect* ✦✦ *(87)*, *When I Fall in Love* ✦✦ *(88)*, *D.O.A. (Dead on Arrival)* ✦✦ *(88)*, *Great Balls of Fire* ✦✦ *(89)*, *Come See the Paradise* ✦✦ *(90)*, *Postcards from the Edge* ✦✦✦✦ *(90)*, *Undercover Blues (93)*, *Flesh and Bone (93)*, *Wilder Napalm (93)*

Aidan Quinn [b. 1959]

Films Desperately Seeking Susan ✦✦✦ *(85)*, The Mission ✦✦ *(86)*, Stakeout ✦✦✦ *(87)*, Crusoe ✦✦✦ *(89)*, Avalon ✦✦ *(90)*, The Handmaid's Tale ✦✦ *(90)*, At Play in the Fields of the Lord ✦✦ *(91)*, The Playboys ✦✦✦✦*(92)*, Benny & Joon ✦✦✦ *(93)*, *Blink (93)*

Robert Redford [b. 1937]

Real name Charles Robert Redford Jr.

Quote 'Robert Redford's the very best kisser I ever met.' [Meryl Streep]

Films *This Property is Condemned* ✦✦ *(66)*, *Barefoot in the Park* ✦✦✦✦ *(67)*, *Downhill Racer* ✦✦✦ *(69)*, *Butch Cassidy and The Sundance Kid* ✦✦✦✦ *(69)*, *Jeremiah Johnson* ✦✦✦ *(72)*, *The Candidate* ✦✦✦✦ *(72)*, *How To Steal a Diamond in Four Uneasy Lessons* ✦✦✦ *(72)*, *The Way We Were* ✦✦✦ *(73)*, *The Sting* ✦✦✦✦ *(73)*, *The Great Gatsby* ✦✦✦ *(74)*, *The Great Waldo Pepper* ✦✦✦ *(75)*, *Three Days of the Condor* ✦✦✦✦ *(75)*, *All the President's Men* ✦✦✦ *(76)*, *A Bridge Too Far* ✦✦ *(77)*, *The Electric Horseman* ✦✦ *(79)*, *Ordinary People (80; d only)*, *The Natural* ✦✦ *(84)*, *Out of Africa* ✦✦✦ *(85)*, *Legal Eagles* ✦✦✦ *(86)*, *The Milagro Beanfield War* ✦✦✦ *(88; d only)*, *Havana* ✦ *(90)*, *Sneakers* ✦✦✦ *(92)*, *A River Runs Through It* ✦✦ *(92; d only)*, *Indecent Proposal* ✦✦✦ *(93)*, *Quiz Show (94; d only)*

Keanu Reeves [b. 1971]

Quote 'Hey, I'm a meathead. I can't help it, man.'

Rob Reiner [b. 1947]

DIRECTOR. A former child actor, who was Meathead in *All in the Family*, America's equivalent of *Till Death Us Do Part*, Reiner has emerged as a director of some of the most entertaining, yet diverse, movies being made today.

Films This is Spinal Tap ✦✦✦✦ *(84; also a&s)*, The Sure Thing ✦✦✦ *(85)*, Stand by Me ✦✦ *(86)*, Throw Momma from the Train ✦✦✦ *(87; a only)*, The Princess Bride ✦✦ *(87)*, When Harry Met Sally ✦✦✦✦ *(89)*, Postcards from the Edge ✦✦✦✦ *(90; a only)*, Misery ✦✦✦✦ *(90)*, A Few Good Men ✦✦✦✦ *(92)*, *Sleepless in Seattle (93; a only)*, *North (94)*

Judge Reinhold [b. 1956]

Real name Edward Ernest Reinhold Jr.

'Judge' was a childhood nickname.

Films Stripes ✦✦ *(81)*, Fast Times at Ridgemont High ✦✦✦ *(82)*, The Lords of Discipline ✦✦✦ *(83)*, Gremlins ✦✦✦ *(84)*, Beverly Hills Cop ✦✦✦ *(84)*, Ruthless People ✦✦✦✦ *(86)*, Beverly Hills Cop II ✦ *(87)*, Vice Versa ✦✦ *(88)*, Daddy's Dying, Who's Got the Will? ✦✦✦ *(90)*, Rosalie Goes Shopping ✦✦ *(90)*, Over Her Dead Body ✦✦ *(91)*, *Zandalee ✦ (91)*

Miranda Richardson [b. 1958]

Films Dance with a Stranger ✦✦✦ *(85)*, Empire of the Sun ✦✦✦ *(87)*, Eat the Rich ✦ *(c)(87)*, Enchanted April ✦✦✦✦ *(91)*, The Fool ✦✦ *(91)*, The Crying Game ✦✦ *(92)*, Damage ✦✦ *(92)*

Alan Rickman [b. 1946]

Films Die Hard ✦✦✦✦ (88), The January Man ✦ (89), Truly, Madly, Deeply ✦✦ (90), Quigley Down Under ✦✦✦ (90), Close My Eyes ✦ (91), Robin Hood: Prince of Thieves ✦✦✦ (91), Bob Roberts ✦✦✦ (c)(92)

Tim Robbins [b. 1959]

Films The Sure Thing ✦✦✦ (85), Top Gun ✦✦ (86), Howard...A New Breed of Hero ✦ (86), Bull Durham ✦✦✦ (88), Five Corners ✦✦ (88), Erik the Viking ✦ (89), Miss Firecracker ✦✦✦ (89), Jacob's Ladder ✦✦ (90), Cadillac Man ✦✦ (90), Jungle Fever ✦✦✦ (91), The Player ✦✦✦✦ (92), Bob Roberts ✦✦✦ (92; also d&s), The Hudsucker Proxy (93), Rita Hayworth & the Shawshank Redemption (94)

Eric Roberts [b. 1956]

Brother of Julia.

Quote 'Basically, I'm a blue-collar redneck who loves his tequila.'

Films King of the Gypsies ✦✦ (78), Star 80 ✦✦ (83), The Pope of Greenwich Village ✦✦ (84), The Coca-Cola Kid ✦✦✦ (85), Runaway Train ✦✦✦ (85), Nobody's Fool ✦✦ (86), Blood Red ✦ (89), Best of the Best ✦ (89), Rude Awakening ✦ (89), Final Analysis ✦✦ (92), Best of the Best 2 ✦ (93)

Julia Roberts [b. 1967]

Sister of the now-eclipsed Eric, her parents ran an actors and writers' workshop in Atlanta, Georgia. She hit the Big Time at only 23 with *Pretty Woman*. Although, as a result, able to command salaries which rival the top male stars, she's done nothing half as good since. Something of a recluse, Roberts cancelled her wedding to Kiefer Sutherland in 1991 at the last minute. As part of the separation deal, she was forced to give back her beloved Vietnamese pot-bellied pig, Fergis.

Films Mystic Pizza ✦✦✦ (88), Blood Red ✦ (89), Steel Magnolias ✦✦ (89), Flatliners ✦ (90), Pretty Woman ✦✦✦ (90), Hook ✦✦✦

(91), Dying Young ✦ (91), Sleeping With the Enemy ✦ (91), The Player ✦✦✦✦ (c)(92), I Love Trouble (94), The Pelican Brief (94)

Mimi Rogers [b. 1956]

Ex-wife of Tom Cruise.

Films Gung Ho ✦✦ (86), Someone to Watch Over Me ✦✦✦✦ (87), Hider in the House ✦✦ (89), The Mighty Quinn ✦✦ (89), Desperate Hours ✦✦ (90), The Doors ✦✦ (c)(91), The Player ✦✦✦✦ (c)(92), White Sands ✦✦✦ (c)(92), The Rapture ✦ (92)

Isabella Rossellini [b. 1952]

Ingrid Bergman's daughter, she came to New York in her late teens and worked for Italian TV as an interviewer. One of her interviewees was Martin Scorsese, whom she then married. At 28, she became one of the highest-paid models in the world, working for Lancôme. 'I was surrounded by these beautiful women,' she said, 'and I felt short and fat. Here I was, already 28, and I thought, "This is crazy".' After divorcing Scorsese, she was for five years the partner of oddball director David Lynch.

Films White Nights ✦✦ (85), Blue Velvet ✦✦ (86), Siesta ✦ (87), Tough Guys Don't Dance ✦ (87), Cousins ✦✦✦ (89), Wild at Heart ✦ (90), Death Becomes Her ✦✦✦ (92), Fearless (93)

Tim Roth [b. 1961]

Films The Hit ✦✦✦ (84), To Kill a Priest ✦ (88), A World Apart ✦✦✦ (88), The Cook, the Thief, His Wife and Her Lover ✦✦✦ (89), Rosencrantz and Guildenstern Are Dead ✦✦ (90), Vincent and Theo ✦✦✦ (90), Reservoir Dogs ✦✦✦✦ (92), Bodies, Rest and Motion (93)

Mickey Rourke [b. 1950]

Quote 'I don't care about sex any more. It's years since I made love. Nowadays I so much prefer motorcycles.'

Films 1941 ✦✦ (b)(79), Fade to Black ✦ (b)(80),

Heaven's Gate ◆◆◆ *(80)*, *Body Heat* ◆◆◆◆ *(81)*, Diner ◆◆◆◆ *(82)*, Rumble Fish ◆◆◆ *(83)*, Eureka ◆◆◆◆ *(85)*, The Pope of Greenwich Village ◆◆ *(84)*, Year of the Dragon ◆◆◆◆ *(85)*, 9 1/2 Weeks ◆◆ *(86)*, Angel Heart ◆◆ *(87)*, Barfly ◆◆◆ *(87)*, A Prayer for the Dying ◆◆ *(87)*, Homeboy ◆◆ *(89)*, Johnny Handsome ◆◆ *(89)*, Desperate Hours ◆◆ *(90)*, Wild Orchid ◆ *(90)*, Harley Davidson and the Marlboro Man ◆ *(91)*, White Sands ◆◆◆ *(92)*

Mercedes Ruehl [b. 1954]

Films Heartburn ◆ (b)*(86)*, 84 Charing Cross Road ◆◆◆ *(87)*, Radio Days ◆◆◆ *(87)*, The Secret of My Success ◆◆ *(87)*, Big ◆◆◆◆ *(88)*, Married to the Mob ◆◆ *(88)*, Slaves of New York ◆◆ *(89)*, Crazy People ◆◆ *(90)*, The Fisher King ◆◆◆ *(91)*, The Last Action Hero *(93)*, *Lost in Yonkers (93)*

Kurt Russell [b. 1951]

Quote 'I basically hate my generation. I never got along with them. They were all bullshit.'

Films *Used Cars* ◆◆ *(80)*, *Escape from New York* ◆◆◆ *(81)*, The Thing ◆◆◆ *(82)*, Silkwood ◆◆◆ *(83)*, The Mean Season ◆◆ *(85)*, Big Trouble in Little China ◆ *(86)*, Overboard ◆◆◆ *(87)*, Tequila Sunrise ◆ *(88)*, Tango and Cash ◆◆◆ *(89)*, Winter People ◆◆ *(89)*, Backdraft ◆◆ *(91)*, Unlawful Entry ◆◆◆ *(92)*, *Captain Ron (92)*, *Tombstone (94)*, *Stargate (94)*

Theresa Russell [b. 1957]

Real name Theresa Paup

Quote 'I've never been flavour-of-the-month. You could say I've cornered the market in loonies.'

Quote 'Before I make a film, I always dream I'm showing up on the set naked and everybody else has clothes on. I don't know what the scene is and it's my cue and I just don't know what the fuck is happening. All I know is I'm there without my clothes on and I don't know why.'

Films The Last Tycoon ◆◆◆ *(76)*, *Straight Time* ◆◆◆ *(78)*, *Bad Timing* ◆◆◆◆ *(80)*, Eureka ◆◆◆◆ *(83)*, Insignificance ◆◆ *(85)*, Aria ◆ *(87)*, Black Widow ◆◆◆ *(87)*, Track 29 ◆ *(88)*, Physical Evidence ◆ *(89)*, Whore ◆ *(91)*

Meg Ryan [b. 1962]

Films Rich and Famous ◆◆ *(82)*, Amityville 3-D ◆ *(83)*, Top Gun ◆◆ *(86)*, Innerspace ◆◆ *(87)*, D.O.A. (Dead on Arrival) ◆◆ *(88)*, The Presidio ◆◆ *(88)*, Promised Land ◆◆ *(88)*, When Harry Met Sally ◆◆◆◆ *(89)*, Joe Versus the Volcano ◆ *(90)*, The Doors ◆◆ *(91)*, *Prelude to a Kiss (92)*, *Sleepless in Seattle (93)*, *Flesh and Bone (93)*, *Significant Other (94)*

Winona Ryder [b. 1971]

Real name Winona Horowitz

Taking her name from her birthplace of Winona, Minnesota, she was brought up by her hippy parents in a California commune where, apparently, she gorged on Vitamin C and was a compulsive liar. A one time fiancée of Johnny Depp, with whom she starred in *Edward Scissorhands*, her biggest press notices came when she departed *Godfather III* rather abruptly. Coppola presumably forgave her by casting her in *Dracula*.

Quote 'The press says, "Why are you always playing teenagers?" And, like, I'm 19. What am I supposed to do – play a judge?'

Films Square Dance ◆◆ *(87)*, Beetlejuice ◆◆ *(88)*, 1969 ◆◆ *(88)*, Great Balls of Fire ◆◆ *(89)*, Heathers ◆◆ *(89)*, Welcome Home, Roxy Carmichael ◆◆◆ *(90)*, Edward Scissorhands ◆◆ *(90)*, Mermaids ◆◆ *(91)*, Night on Earth ◆◆ *(92)*, Bram Stoker's Dracula ◆◆◆ *(92)*, *The Age of Innocence (93)*, *The House of the Spirits (93)*, *Reality Bites (94)*

Laura San Giacomo [b. 1962]

Films sex, lies, and videotape ◆◆◆ *(89)*, Quigley Down Under ◆◆◆ *(90)*, *Pretty Woman* ◆◆◆ *(90)*, Under Suspicion ◆◆◆ *(9*

Julian Sands [b. 1958]

Films Privates on Parade ◆◆ (b)(83), The Killing Fields ◆◆◆ (84), Oxford Blues ◆◆ (84), A Room With a View ◆◆◆◆ (86), The Doctor and the Devils ◆ (86), Siesta ◆ (87), Gothic ◆◆ (87), Warlock ◆◆ (89), Arachnophobia ◆◆ (90), Naked Lunch ◆ (91), Impromptu ◆◆◆ (91), Tale of a Vampire ◆ (92), *Boxing Helena (93)*

Susan Sarandon [b. 1946]

Real name Susan Abigail Tomaling

The eldest of a nine-children Catholic family, she was more interested in ballet than acting and never went to drama class. But the agent of her former husband, Chris Sarandon, pushed her into signing up and she has since become one of the strongest and most sophisticated of Hollywood actresses. A political activist, together with partner Tim Robbins, she is also something of a keen amateur racing driver. And, just to set the record straight, it's not pronounced the way most people do, but Sa–RAN–don.

Quote 'It thrills me that one day my grandchildren may see their grandmother in her little half-slip and bra – seducing a monster.'

Films *The Front Page* ◆◆◆ *(74)*, *The Rocky Horror Picture Show* ◆◆◆ *(75)*, *The Great Waldo Pepper* ◆◆◆ *(75)*, *The Great Smokey Roadblock* ◆◆ *(76)*, *Dragonfly* ◆◆ *(76)*, *The Other Side of Midnight* ◆ *(77)*, *King of the Gypsies* ◆◆ *(78)*, *Pretty Baby* ◆◆ *(78)*, *Loving Couples* ◆◆ *(80)*, *Atlantic City* ◆◆◆◆ *(81)*, Tempest ◆◆ *(82)*, The Hunger ◆ *(83)*, Compromising Positions ◆◆ *(85)*, The Witches of Eastwick ◆◆◆ *(87)*, Bull Durham ◆◆◆ *(88)*, Sweet Hearts Dance ◆◆ *(88)*, A Dry White Season ◆◆ *(89)*, The January Man ◆ *(89)*, White Palace ◆◆◆ *(90)*, Thelma & Louise ◆◆◆◆ *(91)*, Light Sleeper ◆ *(92)*, The Player ◆◆◆◆ c)(92), Bob Roberts ◆◆◆ (c)(92), Lorenzo's Oil ◆◆ *(92)*

Greta Scacchi [b. 1960]

Quote 'When I was about eight years old, I happened to mention to my father that I wanted to be an actress and he gave me a wallop in the face.'

Quote 'I don't see filmed nudity as something scary or obscene. It's not something I am afraid of. I think nudity is easier if there are two of you.'

Films Heat and Dust ◆◆ (83), The Coca-Cola Kid ◆◆◆ (85), Defence of the Realm ◆◆◆◆ (86), A Man in Love ◆◆ (87), Good Morning Babylon ◆◆◆ (87), White Mischief ◆◆ (88), Presumed Innocent ◆◆◆ (90), Shattered ◆◆ (91), The Player ◆◆◆◆ (92), Turtle Beach ◆ (92)

Arnold Schwarzenegger [b. 1947]

The son of an Austrian policeman, he grew up in a house with no phone, fridge or toilet. By the age of 20 he was Mr. Europe, Mr. International and Mr. Universe. After studying business and economics part-time (as well as ballet), he had developed a shrewd business head on his enormous shoulders. While nobody took him seriously as *Hercules in New York*, a series of steadily more popular action pics has made him Hollywood's most bankable star. Apparently a neatness freak with an obsession for vanilla ice cream, he's said to love cooking, cleaning and ironing and drives around in an armoured car. Despite being a leading Republican campaigner, he's succeeded in bringing together the Kennedys and the Republicans by marrying Maria Shriver, the niece of Teddy Kennedy. In partnership with Stallone and Willis, he owns the Planet Hollywood restaurant chain.

Quote 'Money doesn't make you happy. I now have $50 million but I was just as happy when I had $48 million.'

Quote 'I just use my muscles as a conversation piece, like someone walking a cheetah down 42nd Street.'

Films *Hercules in New York* ◆ *(70)*, The Long

Goodbye ♦♦♦♦ (b)(73), Stay Hungry ♦♦♦ (76), Pumping Iron ♦♦♦ (77), The Villain ♦♦ (79), Conan the Barbarian ♦♦ (82), The Terminator ♦♦♦♦ (84), Conan the Destroyer ♦♦ (84), Commando ♦♦ (85), Red Sonja ♦ (85), Raw Deal ♦ (86), The Running Man ♦♦ (87), Predator ♦♦ (87), Twins ♦♦ (88), Red Heat ♦♦ (88), Kindergarten Cop ♦♦ (90), Total Recall ♦♦♦ (90), Terminator 2: Judgment Day ♦♦♦ (91), The Last Action Hero (93)

Annabella Sciorra [b. 1964]

Films True Love ♦♦ (89), Cadillac Man ♦♦ (90), Reversal of Fortune ♦♦♦♦ (90), Internal Affairs ♦♦ (90), Jungle Fever ♦♦♦ (91), The Hard Way ♦♦♦♦ (91), The Hand That Rocks the Cradle ♦♦ (92), The Night We Never Met ♦♦♦ (93), *Whispers in the Dark (92), Mr. Wonderful (93), Romeo is Bleeding (93)*

Martin Scorsese [b. 1942]

DIRECTOR. An unhealthy child, plagued by asthma and other illnesses, Scorsese trained for the priesthood before being thrown out. He stopped attending Mass when a priest claimed that the Vietnam War was a holy cause and turned to film-making, startling the world with *Mean Streets* and *Taxi Driver* and courting controversy ever since. The majority of his films star either Harvey Keitel or Robert De Niro, while his mother is also usually in there somewhere. Married briefly to Isabella Rossellini, he's now on his fourth wife.

Quote 'My friends used to say, "Jeez, Marty, do you really believe all that stuff the priests tell you?" Well I did believe it, every word of it. I wouldn't touch meat on Friday and I believed I would go to hell if I missed Mass on Sunday.'

Films Who's That Knocking at My Door? ♦♦♦ (68), Boxcar Bertha ♦♦♦ (72), Mean Streets ♦♦♦ (73; also s), Alice Doesn't Live Here Anymore ♦♦♦♦ (74), Cannonball ♦♦ (76; a only), Taxi Driver ♦♦♦ (76; also a), New York, New York ♦♦ (77), The Last Waltz

♦♦♦ (78), Raging Bull ♦♦♦ (80), The King of Comedy ♦♦♦♦ (83; also a), After Hours ♦♦ (85; also a), 'Round Midnight ♦♦♦ (86; a only), The Color of Money ♦♦♦ (86), The Last Temptation of Christ ♦ (88), New York Stories ♦♦ (89), GoodFellas ♦♦♦♦ (90; also s), Guilty by Suspicion ♦♦ (91; a only), Cape Fear ♦♦ (92), *The Age of Innocence (93)*

Ridley Scott [b. 1939]

DIRECTOR. The South Shields lad renowned for his sense of filmic style was the only student attending the Royal College of Art in a suit. Graduating from *Hovis* commericals (the one with the big hill), Scott now creates some of the most visually arresting movies there are. He finally seems to have realised that actors are as important as visuals and need to be directed as well, an obvious omission on some of his early films.

Quote 'Ridley likes his smoke. He loves things floating in the air – banners, fabrics – it gives the feeling of movement.' [Ann Mollo, set decorator]

Films *The Duellists* ♦♦♦ (77), Alien ♦♦♦♦ (79), Blade Runner: The Director's Cut ♦♦♦♦ (82), Legend ♦ (85), Someone to Watch Over Me ♦♦♦♦ (87), Black Rain ♦ (89), Thelma & Louise ♦♦♦♦ (91), 1492: Conquest of Paradise ♦ (92)

Steven Seagal [b. 1951]

Films Nico ♦♦ (88), Marked for Death ♦ (90), Hard to Kill ♦ (90), Out for Justice ♦♦ (91), Under Siege ♦♦♦ (92)

Kyra Sedgwick [b. 1965]

Married to Kevin Bacon.

Films Kansas ♦ (88), Born on the Fourth of July ♦♦♦♦ (89), Mr and Mrs Bridge♦♦♦(90) Singles ♦♦♦♦(92), Hearts and Souls (93)

Tom Selleck [b. 194

The Man Who Would Have Been Indy – if he'd been able to get out of his *Magnu*
TV show to be the lead in *Raiders of th*

Lost Ark. In more anonymous days, he appeared a couple of times on US TV's *The Dating Game*: 'I was always Bachelor No. 2 and I was *never* picked.'

Quote 'I'm not Vic Virile.'

Films *Myra Breckinridge* ♦ (b)(70), *Coma* ♦♦♦ (b)(78), High Road to China ♦♦ (83), Lassiter ♦ (84), Runaway ♦♦ (84), Three Men and a Baby ♦♦ (87), An Innocent Man ♦♦ (89), Her Alibi ♦♦ (89), Quigley Down Under ♦♦♦ (90), Three Men and a Little Lady ♦ (90), Christopher Columbus: The Discovery ♦ (92), Folks! ♦ (92)

Ally Sheedy [b. 1962]

Quote 'I go for tough, uncommunicative guys who ride motorcycles.'

Films WarGames ♦♦♦♦ (83), The Bad Boys ♦♦♦ (83), Oxford Blues ♦♦ (84), The Breakfast Club ♦♦ (85), Twice in a Lifetime ♦♦♦ (85), St. Elmo's Fire ♦ (85), Short Circuit ♦♦ (86), Betsy's Wedding ♦ (90), Only the Lonely ♦♦♦ (91), Fear ♦♦ (91), *Man's Best Friend* (93)

Charlie Sheen [b. 1965]

Real name Carlos Irwin Estevez

Son of Martin Sheen and brother of Emilio Estevez.

Films Red Dawn ♦ (84), The Boys Next Door ♦♦ (85), Platoon ♦♦♦ (86), Ferris Bueller's Day Off ♦♦ (c)(86), The Wraith ♦ (86), Wall Street ♦♦♦ (87), No Man's Land ♦♦ (87), Eight Men Out ♦♦ (88), Young Guns ♦♦ (88), Major League ♦♦ (89), Navy SEALS ♦ (90), Men at Work ♦ (90), The Rookie ♦ (90), Stockade ♦♦ (90), Courage Mountain ♦♦ (90), Hot Shots! ♦♦ (91), Catchfire ♦♦♦ (c)(91), National Lampoon's Loaded Weapon 1 ♦♦ (c)(93), Hot Shots! Part Deux ♦♦ (93), *The Three Musketeers* (94), *The Chase* (94)

Martin Short [b. 1950]

Hilarious comic who has been the saving grace of more than one otherwise unremarkable film.

Films ¡Three Amigos! ♦ (86), Innerspace ♦♦ (87), The Big Picture ♦♦♦ (89), Three Fugitives ♦♦ (89), Father of the Bride ♦♦ (91), *Captain Ron* (92), *We're Back* (v)(93), *Clifford* (93)

Elisabeth Shue [b. 1963]

Films The Karate Kid ♦♦♦♦ (84), Link ♦ (86), Adventures in Babysitting ♦♦ (87), Cocktail ♦♦ (88), Back to the Future, Part II ♦♦ (89), Back to the Future, Part III ♦♦♦♦ (90), Soapdish ♦ (91), Too Hot to Handle ♦♦ (91), *Hearts and Souls* (93)

Joel Silver

PRODUCER. Although there are few people in Hollywood who have a good word to say (at least not one that's printable) about Silver as a human being, he's the producer of some of the most successful big-budget action pics of all time. If you like one Joel Silver movie, the chances are that you'll like all of them. Despite being thought of something as a vulgarian, he also appears to have emphasised racially integrated casting in his films, while other more liberal Hollywood types merely pay lip-service to the idea. Feminists are less impressed with him.

Quote 'The only time I use [women], they're either naked or dead.'

Films 48HRS. ♦♦♦ (82), Streets of Fire ♦ (84), Brewster's Millions ♦ (85), Commando ♦♦ (85), Weird Science ♦ (85), Jumpin' Jack Flash ♦♦ (86), Lethal Weapon ♦♦♦ (87), Predator ♦♦ (87), Action Jackson ♦♦ (88), Die Hard ♦♦♦♦ (88), Who Framed Roger Rabbit? ♦♦♦ (88; a only), Lethal Weapon 2 ♦♦♦ (89), Road House ♦♦ (89), The Adventures of Ford Fairlane ♦ (90), Die Hard 2 ♦♦♦ (90), Predator 2 ♦♦ (90), Hudson Hawk ♦ (91), Ricochet ♦♦♦ (91), Last Boy Scout ♦♦♦ (92), Lethal Weapon 3 ♦♦♦♦ (92), Demolition Man (93)

Ron Silver [b. 1946]

Films *Semi-Tough* ♦♦♦ (77), The Entity ♦ (82),

Best Friends ◆◆ (82), Silkwood ◆◆◆ (83),
Lovesick ◆◆ (83), Enemies, A Love Story
◆◆◆ (89), Blue Steel ◆◆ (90), Reversal of
Fortune ◆◆◆◆ (90), Fellow Traveller ◆◆◆
(90), Mr. Saturday Night (92), *Married to
It (93)*

Tom Skerritt [b. 1933]

Films *M*A*S*H* ◆◆◆◆ *(70), Thieves Like Us*
◆◆◆ *(74), The Turning Point* ◆◆ *(77), Alien*
◆◆◆◆ *(79),* The Dead Zone ◆◆◆ (83), Top
Gun ◆◆ (86), Space Camp ◆◆ (86), The
Big Town ◆◆ (87), Poltergeist III ◆ (88),
Steel Magnolias ◆◆ (89), The Rookie ◆
(90), Knight Moves ◆ (92), Singles ◆◆◆◆
(92), A River Runs Through It ◆◆ (92)

Christian Slater [b. 1969]

Real name Christian Hawkins

The actor who is just as famous for his
habit of removing his shirt in every film
as for the roles themselves. Possibly the
only film of his in which his chest remains
unexposed is *Star Trek VI*. For those who
have noticed that his voice, mannerisms
and eyebrows are uncannily like those of
Jack Nicholson, it is interesting that in an
early interview he said: 'Jack Nicholson is
my favourite actor and I'd like to be like
him when I get older'.

Quote 'I do whatever they want [women
who approach him] as long as it's legal. I
sign a piece of paper and shake hands and
say Hello. If they expect something
incredible, I'll do my best.'

Films The Legend of Billie Jean ◆ (85), The
Name of the Rose ◆◆◆◆ (86), Tucker: The
Man and His Dream ◆◆◆ (88), Gleaming
the Cube ◆ (89), Heathers ◆◆ (89), Pump
Up the Volume ◆◆◆ (90), Young Guns II
– Blaze of Glory ◆◆ (90), Robin Hood:
Prince of Thieves ◆◆◆ (91), Tales from the
Darkside: The Movie ◆◆◆ (91), Star Trek
VI: The Undiscovered Country ◆◆◆◆
(c)(91), Kuffs ◆ (92), Mobsters: The Evil
Empire ◆ (92), FernGully...The Last
Rainforest ◆ (v)(92), Untamed Heart ◆◆◆
(93), *True Romance (93)*

Wesley Snipes [b. 1963]

Films Streets of Gold ◆◆ (86), Major
League ◆◆ (89), King of New York ◆◆
(90), Mo' Better Blues ◆◆ (90), Jungle
Fever ◆◆◆ (91), New Jack City ◆◆◆ (91),
White Men Can't Jump ◆◆◆◆ (92), The
Waterdance ◆◆◆◆ (92), Passenger 57 ◆◆
(92), Rising Sun (93), Demolition Man
(93), *Boiling Point (93), Harlem, A Love
Story (93).*

James Spader [b. 1960]

Films *Endless Love ◆ (81),* Tuff Turf ◆ (85),
Pretty in Pink ◆◆ (86), Wall Street ◆◆◆
(87), Baby Boom ◆◆ (87), Mannequin ◆
(87), sex, lies, and videotape ◆◆◆ (89), The
Rachel Papers ◆ (89), Bad Influence ◆◆
(90), White Palace ◆◆◆ (90), Bob Roberts
◆◆◆ (c)(92), Storyville ◆ (92), *Dream
Lover (93), Wolf (94), Stargate (94)*

Vincent Spano [b. 1962]

Films *Over the Edge ◆◆◆ (79),* Baby, It's You
◆◆◆ (83), The Black Stallion Returns ◆◆
(83), Rumble Fish ◆◆◆ (83), Creator ◆◆
(85), Good Morning Babylon ◆◆◆ (87),
And God Created Woman ◆ (88), City of
Hope ◆◆◆ (91), Oscar ◆◆ (91), Alive ◆◆◆
(93), *Tamakawa (93)*

Steven Spielberg [b. 1947]

DIRECTOR. Spielberg, who's made
some of the most phenomenally successful
films ever, appears to be a boy who's
never grown up. A keen film-maker
since childhood, his mother once cooked a
cherries jubilee in a pressure cooker so
that he could film the explosion for a home
horror movie. He wasn't bright enough to
get into film school but regularly bluffed
his way onto the sets of directors like
Hitchcock. After the success of *E.T.*,
Universal built a $3.5m complex for him.
Querying the cost, Spielberg was told that
the revenue from Bolivia alone would
cover it! His divorce from actress Amy
Irving cost a massive $59m and he is now
married to Kate Capshaw, the heroine of
Indiana Jones and the Temple of Doom.

Quote 'I've never been through psycho-analysis. I solve my problems with the pictures I make.'

Quote 'Oh torture. Torture. My pubic hairs went grey.' [On making *E.T.*]

Films *Duel* ◆◆◆◆ (*71*), *The Sugarland Express* ◆◆◆◆ (*74*), *Jaws* ◆◆◆◆ (*75*), *Close Encounters of the Third Kind* ◆◆◆◆ (*77; also s*), *1941* ◆◆ (*79*), *The Blues Brothers* ◆◆◆◆ (*80; a only*), *Raiders of the Lost Ark* ◆◆◆◆ (*81*), *Poltergeist* ◆◆◆◆ (*82; s only*), E.T. *The Extra-Terrestrial* ◆◆◆◆ (*82*), *Twilight Zone – The Movie* ◆◆ (*83*), *Indiana Jones and the Temple of Doom* ◆◆ (*84*), *The Color Purple* ◆◆◆ (*85*), *Empire of the Sun* ◆◆◆ (*87*), *Always* ◆◆ (*89*), *Indiana Jones and the Last Crusade* ◆◆◆◆ (*89*), *Hook* ◆◆◆ (*91*), *Jurassic Park* (*93*), *Schindler's List* (*93*)

Sylvester Stallone [b. 1946]

Real name Michael Sylvester Stallone

Success was a long time coming. A failed trainee beautician, gym instructor at a Swiss girls' finishing school and lion cage cleaner, his early acting career included a nudie revue and the now infamous semi-porn film *The Italian Stallion*. Offered $350,000 for his script of *Rocky* when he was down to his last $100 he refused, insisting that he star. The rest, as they say, is history. He was the first actor to earn $10m for a film and, until Arnie overtook him, held the lead by pulling in over $20m a movie. Divorced noisily and expensively from Brigitte Nielsen, he has a son called Sage Moonblood and apparently believes that he was beheaded in a previous life in 18th-century France. He's a keen collector of art and paints himself. Look out for his brief appearance as an uncredited mugger in Woody Allen's *Bananas*.

Quote 'I tried the kinder, gentler Stallone and it didn't work. Action is where I belong.'

Quote 'You wouldn't believe some of the things they've said about me. Like Rex Reed saying my career is more mysterious than cot death!'

Films *Bananas* ◆◆◆◆ (*b*)(*71*), *The Lords of Flatbush* ◆◆ (*74*), *Farewell, My Lovely* ◆◆◆ (*75*), *Death Race 2000* ◆◆◆ (*75*), *Capone* ◆ (*75*), *The Prisoner of Second Avenue* ◆◆ (*75*), *Cannonball* ◆◆ (*b*)(*76*), *Rocky* ◆◆◆◆ (*76; also s*), *F.I.S.T.* ◆◆◆ (*78; also s*), *Paradise Alley* ◆ (*78; also d&s*), *Rocky II* ◆◆ (*79; also d&s*), *Escape to Victory* ◆ (*81*), *Nighthawks* ◆◆◆ (*81*), *Rocky III* ◆◆◆ (*82; also d&s*), *First Blood* ◆◆ (*82; also s*), *Staying Alive* ◆◆ (*c*)(*83; also d&s*), *Rambo: First Blood Part II* ◆◆ (*85; also s*), *Rocky IV* ◆◆ (*85; also d&s*), *Cobra* ◆ (*86; also s*), *Over the Top* ◆ (*87; also s*), *Rambo III* ◆ (*88; also s*), *Lock Up* ◆ (*89*), *Tango and Cash* ◆◆◆ (*89*), *Rocky V* ◆◆ (*90; also s*), *Oscar* ◆◆ (*91*), *Stop! Or My Mom Will Shoot* ◆ (*92*), *Cliffhanger* (*93*), *Demolition Man* (*93*)

Harry Dean Stanton [b. 1926]

Pre-eminent of those 'I've-seen-his-face-thousands-of-times-before-what-on-earth-is-his-name?' actors. It's almost easier listing the films he's *not* in than the ones he is. These should keep you going for a while.

Films *Cool Hand Luke* ◆◆◆◆ (*67*), *The Godfather, Part II* ◆◆◆◆ (*74*), *Farewell, My Lovely* ◆◆◆ (*75*), *Missouri Breaks* ◆◆ (*76*), *Straight Time* ◆◆◆ (*78*), *Alien* ◆◆◆◆ (*79*), *The Rose* ◆◆ (*79*), *Wise Blood* ◆◆◆ (*79*), *Private Benjamin* ◆◆ (*80*), *Escape from New York* ◆◆◆ (*81*), *One from the Heart* ◆◆ (*82*), *Young Doctors in Love* ◆◆◆ (*82*), *Christine* ◆◆ (*83*), *Paris, Texas* ◆◆ (*84*), *Repo Man* ◆◆ (*84*), *Red Dawn* ◆ (*84*), *Fool for Love* ◆◆ (*85*), *The Care Bears Movie* ◆◆ (*v*)(*85*), *Pretty in Pink* ◆◆ (*86*), *Slamdance* ◆◆ (*87*), *The Last Temptation of Christ* ◆ (*88*), *Mr. North* ◆◆ (*88*), *Stars and Bars* ◆◆ (*88*), *Shadow Makers* ◆◆ (*89*), *Wild at Heart* ◆ (*90*), *The Fourth War* ◆◆ (*90*), *Twin Peaks: Fire Walk With Me* ◆ (*92*), *Man Trouble* ◆ (*92*)

Mary Steenburgen [b. 1953]

Films *Goin' South* ◆◆◆ (*78*), *Time After Time* ◆◆◆◆ (*79*), *Melvin and Howard* ◆◆◆ (*80*), *Ragtime* ◆◆◆ (*81*), *A Midsummer Night's Sex Comedy* ◆◆◆ (*82*), *Cross Creek* ◆◆ (*83*),

Romantic Comedy ◆◆ (83), Dead of Winter ◆◆◆ (87), The Whales of August ◆◆◆ (87), Parenthood ◆◆◆ (89), Miss Firecracker ◆◆◆ (89), Back to the Future, Part III ◆◆◆◆ (90), The Butcher's Wife ◆◆◆ (92), *Philadelphia* (93), *Gilbert Grape* (93), *Clifford* (93)

Daniel Stern [b. 1957]

Films *Breaking Away* ◆◆◆◆ (79), *It's My Turn* ◆◆◆ (80), *Diner* ◆◆◆◆ (82), Blue Thunder ◆◆ (83), Hannah and Her Sisters ◆◆◆◆ (86), D.O.A. (Dead on Arrival) ◆◆ (88), The Milagro Beanfield War ◆◆◆ (88), Leviathan ◆ (89), Home Alone ◆◆ (90), My Blue Heaven ◆◆ (90), City Slickers ◆◆◆◆ (91), Coupe de Ville ◆◆◆◆ (92), Home Alone 2: Lost in New York ◆◆ (92), *Rookie of the Year* (93; also d), City Slickers II (94)

Dean Stockwell [b. 1936]

Despite being in movies (on an off-on basis) since the age of 9, it's only since *Blue Velvet* that Stockwell has been established as one of the most popular character actors in the business.

Films *The Man with the Deadly Lens* ◆◆◆ (82), Dune ◆ (84), Paris, Texas ◆◆ (84), The Legend of Billie Jean ◆ (85), To Live and Die in L.A. ◆◆ (85), Blue Velvet ◆◆ (86), Beverly Hills Cop II ◆ (87), Gardens of Stone ◆◆◆ (87), Married to the Mob ◆◆ (88), Tucker: The Man and His Dream ◆◆◆ (88), Limit Up ◆ (90), Catchfire ◆◆◆ (91), The Player ◆◆◆◆ (92)

Eric Stoltz [b. 1961]

Although he began filming *Back to the Future* as Marty McFly, Stoltz was replaced after five weeks of shooting.

Films *Fast Times at Ridgemont High* ◆◆◆ (b)(82), Highway to Hell ◆◆ (84), Surf II ◆ (84), Mask ◆◆◆ (85), Haunted Summer ◆ (88), Manifesto ◆ (88), The Fly II ◆ (89), Memphis Belle ◆◆ (90), The Waterdance ◆◆◆◆(92), Singles ◆◆◆◆ (c)(92), *Bodies, Rest and Motion* (93), *Naked in New York* (93)

Oliver Stone [b. 1946]

DIRECTOR. Son of a Jewish stockbroker and French Catholic mother, Stone was raised as a Protestant. A drop-out from Yale, he went off to see the world. Returning, he not only volunteeered for the Army but actually asked for combat duty in Vietnam, getting shot in the neck soon afterwards. He served for 15 months, receiving a Bronze Star, but became very bitter about the experience, swinging from the right wing to the left during the shooting of *Salvador*. His screenplay, *Midnight Express*, won him an Oscar but it wasn't until the mid-80s that he made his reputation as a controversial director, bringing his Vietnam experiences into almost every film he makes.

Quote 'The worst nightmare I ever had about Vietnam was that I had to go back. It was a couple of years ago. I woke up in sweat, in total terror.'

Films *Midnight Express* ◆◆◆◆ (78; s only), The Hand ◆ (81; also s), Conan the Barbarian ◆◆ (82; s only), Scarface ◆◆ (83; s only), Year of the Dragon ◆◆◆◆ (85; s only), Platoon ◆◆◆ (86; also a&s), Salvador ◆◆◆◆ (86; also s), Wall Street ◆◆◆ (87; also a&s), Talk Radio ◆◆◆◆ (88; also s), Born on the Fourth of July ◆◆◆◆ (89; also a&s), The Doors ◆◆ (91; also s), JFK ◆◆◆ (91; also s), Dave ◆◆◆ (c) (93), *Heaven and Earth* (93; also s), *Natural Born Killers* (94)

Sharon Stone [b. 1958]

What fun it is looking at the embarrassing early films of future stars. There are so many dogs in Sharon Stone's kennel, you could start an American branch of the Battersea Dogs' Home. It would be nice to say one could see star quality shining through in her performance in *Allan Quatermain and the Lost City of Gold* or *Police Academy 4*. Nice, but totally untrue. However, one below-the-belt shot from a sneaky director in *Basic Instinct* and the world is her's, although a 1990 photo session in Playboy didn't hurt either. She's one of the few beauty contestants to have combined cheesecake posing with a reading of the Gettysburg Address. Now that she's paid $5m a pic, she's only too happy to rubbish actors like Michael Douglas, while Clint Eastwood is apparently no longer a big enough star to appear with her.

Quote 'If you have a vagina *and* an attitude in this town, then that's a lethal combination.'

Films *Stardust Memories* ◆ (b)(80), Irreconcilable Differences ◆ (84), King Solomon's Mines ◆ (85), Allan Quatermain and the Lost City of Gold ◆ (87), Police Academy 4: Citizens on Patrol ◆ (87), Action Jackson ◆◆ (88), Nico ◆◆ (88), Total Recall ◆◆◆ (90), Year of the Gun ◆ (91), Basic Instinct ◆◆ (92), Sliver (93), *Intersection (94), The Flintstones (c)(94), Pin Cushion (94)*

Madeleine Stowe [b. 1958]

Films Stakeout ◆◆◆ (87), Revenge ◆◆ (90), The Two Jakes ◆◆◆◆ (91), Unlawful Entry ◆◆◆ (92), The Last of the Mohicans ◆◆ (92), Blink (93), China Moon (93)

Meryl Streep [b. 1949]

Real name Mary Louise Streep

If producers need a leading actress to play a tortured martyr with an accent, there's only one place they need turn. She's already done Danish ('I haad a faaarm in Aaaafricaaa'), Polish, English, Australian ('A dingow stowl moy boyboi'). Some people love her performances, others find her mannered in the extreme.

Quote 'I could rip Madonna's throat out. I can sing better than she can.'

Quote 'Meryl Streep is an acting machine in the same sense that a shark is a killing machine.' [Cher]

Films Julia ◆◆◆ (77), The Deer Hunter ◆◆◆ (78), Kramer vs. Kramer ◆◆◆ (79), The Seduction of Joe Tynan ◆◆ (79), Manhattan ◆◆◆◆ (79), The French Lieutenant's Woman ◆◆◆ (81), Sophie's Choice ◆◆ (82), Still of the Night ◆◆ (82), Silkwood ◆◆◆ (83), Falling in Love ◆◆ (84), Out of Africa ◆◆◆ (85), Plenty ◆◆ (85), Heartburn ◆ (86), Ironweed ◆◆ (87), A Cry in the Dark ◆◆ (88), She-Devil ◆ (89), Postcards from the Edge ◆◆◆◆ (90), Defending Your Life ◆◆ (91), Death Becomes Her ◆◆◆ (92), The House of the Spirits (93)

Kiefer Sutherland [b. 1966]

Quote 'One thing's for sure. No son of mine will have a name like Kiefer.'

Films The Bay Boy ◆◆ (84), Stand by Me ◆◆ (86), At Close Range ◆◆ (b)(86), The Lost Boys ◆◆ (87), 1969 ◆◆ (88), Young Guns ◆◆ (88), Bright Lights, Big City ◆ (88), Promised Land ◆◆ (88), Renegades ◆◆ (89), Flatliners ◆ (90), Young Guns II – Blaze of Glory ◆◆ (90), Chicago Joe and the Showgirl ◆ (90), Twin Peaks: Fire Walk With Me ◆ (92), A Few Good Men ◆◆◆◆ (92), The Vanishing ◆◆ (93), The Three Musketeers (94)

Patrick Swayze [b. 1954]

Real name Patrick Wayne Swayze

Hard to believe, but Swayze's chosen career was as a ballet dancer. Son of a dancing teacher, he spent time with the Harkness Ballet Company and the Joffrey Ballet, before performing in *Grease* on Broadway. Despite universal female adulation, he's been happily married for almost twenty years. Swayze met his wife Lisa at his mum's dancing school when he was 20 and she 15. He claims to hate his smile, which he thinks lop-sided and has, over the years as a dancer and actor, broken his ribs, his ankle, his foot, all his fingers and, on five occasions, his left knee.

Quote 'I find those [sex] scenes the hardest. I'm always afraid I may get so turned on, I can't stop...It helps somewhat if my wife is on the set – sometimes she has to urge me on from the sidelines, to make me appear more realistic.'

Films The Outsiders ◆◆ (83), Uncommon Valor ◆◆ (83), Red Dawn ◆ (84), Youngblood ◆ (86), Dirty Dancing ◆◆

(87), Tiger Warsaw ✦ (88), Next of Kin ✦✦ (89), Road House ✦✦ (89), Ghost ✦✦✦✦ (90), Point Break ✦✦ (91), City of Joy ✦✦ (92), *Desperado (93)*

D. B. Sweeney [b. 1961]

Real name Daniel Bernard Sweeney

Films No Man's Land ✦✦ (87), Gardens of Stone ✦✦✦ (87), Eight Men Out ✦✦ (88), Memphis Belle ✦✦ (90), The Cutting Edge ✦✦✦ (92), Fire in the Sky ✦✦ (93), *Hear No Evil (93)*

Jessica Tandy [b. 1909]

Although acting most of her long life, London-born Tandy has suddenly become a top star in her 80s, thanks to winning the Oscar for *Driving Miss Daisy*. Her marriage to veteran star Hume Cronyn is one of the longest Hollywood has ever seen, lasting since 1942.

Films Best Friends ✦✦ (82), Still of the Night ✦✦ (82), The World According to Garp ✦✦✦ (82), The Bostonians ✦✦ (84), Cocoon ✦✦ (85), *batteries not included ✦ (87), Cocoon: The Return ✦ (88), The House on Carroll Street ✦✦ (88), Driving Miss Daisy ✦✦✦ (89), Fried Green Tomatoes at the Whistle Stop Cafe ✦✦✦✦ (92), Used People ✦✦ (92)

Emma Thompson [b. 1959]

Married to Kenneth Branagh.

Quote 'Ken and I refer to London as Luvvy Central. We just did Hamlet with Sir John Gielgud and it was so luvvy it wasn't true.'

Films Henry V ✦✦✦✦ (89), The Tall Guy ✦✦ (89), Dead Again ✦✦ (91), Impromptu ✦✦✦ (91), Howard's End ✦✦✦✦ (92), Peter's Friends ✦✦✦ (92), Much Ado About Nothing ✦✦✦ (93), *Remains of the Day (93), The Gerry Conlon Story (93), In the Name of the Father (94)*

Uma Thurman [b. 1970]

Real name Uma Karuna Thurman

Films Dangerous Liaisons ✦✦✦ (88), The Adventures of Baron Munchausen ✦✦✦ (89), Henry and June ✦ (90), Where the Heart Is ✦ (90), Robin Hood ✦✦ (91), Final Analysis ✦✦ (92), Mad Dog and Glory (93), Jennifer 8 ✦✦✦ (92), *Even Cowgirls Get the Blues (93)*

Meg Tilly [b. 1960]

Films The Big Chill ✦✦✦ (83), Psycho II ✦✦ (83), Impulse ✦ (84), Agnes of God ✦✦✦ (85), Masquerade ✦✦ (88), The Two Jakes ✦✦✦✦ (91), Valmont ✦✦✦ (91), *Body Snatchers (93)*

Stephen Tobolowsky [b. 1951]

Another of those excellent supporting actors, he seems to be in every film that Richard Portnow doesn't do.

Films Nobody's Fool ✦✦ (86), True Stories ✦✦ (86; s only), Spaceballs ✦✦ (87), Mississippi Burning ✦✦ (88), Breaking In ✦✦✦✦ (89), Great Balls of Fire ✦✦ (89), In Country ✦✦ (89), Welcome Home, Roxy Carmichael ✦✦✦ (90), Bird on a Wire ✦✦ (90), The Grifters ✦✦✦ (90), Thelma & Louise ✦✦✦✦ (91), Memoirs of an Invisible Man ✦✦ (92), Single White Female ✦✦ (92), Sneakers ✦✦✦ (92), Accidental Hero ✦✦✦✦ (92), Groundhog Day ✦✦✦ (93), *Calendar Girl (93), The Pickle (93)*

Marisa Tomei [b. 1964]

The author's favourite up-and-coming actress. If she's not a star by the end of the 90s, I'll eat my hat.

Films The Flamingo Kid ✦✦✦ (b)(84), Playing for Keeps ✦✦ (86), Oscar ✦✦ (91), Zandalee ✦ (91), My Cousin Vinny ✦✦✦✦ (92), Chaplin ✦✦ (92), Untamed Heart ✦✦✦ (93)

Nancy Travis [b. 1961]

Films Three Men and a Baby ✦✦ (87), Eight Men Out ✦✦ (88), Air America ✦✦ (89), Three Men and a Little Lady ✦ (90), Internal Affairs ✦✦ (90), Chaplin ✦✦ (92), The Vanishing ✦✦ (93), *So I Married an Axe Murderer (93)*

Kathleen Turner [b. 1954]

Starting her dramatic career in the tiniest theatres in New York, she landed a part in long-standing soap *The Doctors*. After failing many film auditions (including one for the sequel to *Love Story*), she burst onto the screen with her sultry debut in *Body Heat*. Here she drove William Hurt and every man in the audience to distraction, including her future husband who made up his mind then to marry her. Despite the success of the film, she was still forced to return to waitressing for a time afterwards! She likes to do her own stunts which, she claims, results in an average of 7 stitches a movie.

Quote 'I know there are nights when I have power, when I could put on something and walk in somewhere, and if there is a man who doesn't look at me, it's because he's gay.'

Quote 'She is her biggest fan. If Kathleen Turner had been a man I would have punched her out long ago.' [Burt Reynolds, co-star of *Switching Channels*]

Films *Body Heat* ✦✦✦✦ *(81)*, The Man With Two Brains ✦✦ (83), Romancing the Stone ✦✦✦ (84), Crimes of Passion ✦ (84), Jewel of the Nile ✦✦ (85), Prizzi's Honour ✦✦ (85), Peggy Sue Got Married ✦✦✦ (86), Who Framed Roger Rabbit? ✦✦✦ (v)(88), The Accidental Tourist ✦✦✦ (88), Switching Channels ✦ (88), The War of the Roses ✦✦(89), V.I. Warshawski ✦✦ (92), *Undercover Blues (93), Naked in New York (93), House of Cards (93), Serial Mom (94)*

John Turturro [b. 1957]

Films Desperately Seeking Susan ✦✦✦ (85), To Live and Die in L.A. ✦✦ (85), The Color of Money ✦✦✦ (86), Gung Ho ✦✦ (86), Hannah and Her Sisters ✦✦✦✦ (86), The Sicilian ✦✦ (87), Five Corners ✦✦ (88), Do the Right Thing ✦✦✦✦ (89), Miller's Crossing ✦✦✦✦ (90), State of Grace ✦✦✦ (90), Mo' Better Blues ✦✦ (90), Jungle Fever ✦✦✦ (91), Catchfire ✦✦✦ (91), Barton Fink ✦ (92), Men of Respect ✦ (92), *Fearless (93), Being Human (93)*

Jean-Claude Van Damme [b. 1961]

Real name Jean–Claude Van Varenberg

Quote 'I've got a talent to act. No matter what any newspaper says about me, I am one of the most sensitive human beings on Earth and I know it.'

Films Black Eagle ✦ (88), Bloodsport ✦✦ (88), Kickboxer ✦✦ (89), A.W.O.L. – Absent Without Leave ✦✦ (90; also s), Death Warrant ✦✦ (90), Universal Soldier ✦✦✦ (92), Double Impact ✦ (92; also s), *Nowhere to Run (93), Hard Target (93)*

Paul Verhoeven [b. 1938]

DIRECTOR. Renowned for stylish movies like *Basic Instinct* with lashings of sex and violence Verhoeven, who grew up during the Nazi occupation of his native Holland, loves courting controversy. After 20 years of making movies in Holland, some with Rutger Hauer, he broke into Hollywood with *Robocop*. He most wants to make the movie, *Christ the Man*. His favourite religious movie is, apparently, *Monty Python's The Life of Brian*.

Quote Fuck Politically Correct. [His response to the protests over *Basic Instinct*]

Films *The Fourth Man* ✦✦✦ *(79)*, Flesh + Blood ✦✦✦ (85; also s), Robocop ✦✦✦ (87), Total Recall ✦✦✦ (90), Basic Instinct ✦✦ (92)

Christopher Walken [b. 1943]

Real name Ronald Walken

One of the most splendidly terrifying actors in the industry, Walken manages to exude menace without actually doing anything.

Films *The Anderson Tapes* ✦✦ *(71)*, Annie Hall ✦✦✦ (77), Roseland ✦✦✦ (77), The Deer Hunter ✦✦✦ (78), Last Embrace ✦✦✦ (79), Heaven's Gate ✦✦✦ (80), Pennies from Heaven ✦✦✦ (81), The Dogs of War ✦✦ (81), Brainstorm ✦✦ (83), The Dead Zone ✦✦✦ (83), A View to a Kill ✦✦ (85), At Close

Range ◆◆ (86), War Zone ◆ (87), Biloxi Blues ◆◆◆ (88), The Milagro Beanfield War ◆◆◆ (88), Homeboy ◆◆ (89), The Comfort of Strangers ◆ (90), King of New York ◆◆ (90), Batman Returns ◆◆◆ (92)

J.T. Walsh

Another of those damn fine supporting actors who can give you sleepless nights if you try to work out where you've seen them before. Now you know.

Films Power ◆◆ (86), Hannah and Her Sisters ◆◆◆◆ (86), Good Morning, Vietnam ◆◆◆ (87), Tin Men ◆◆◆ (87), House of Games ◆◆◆ (87), Tequila Sunrise ◆ (88), Things Change ◆◆◆ (88), The Big Picture ◆◆◆ (89), Dad ◆◆ (89), Wired ◆ (89), Crazy People ◆◆ (90), The Grifters ◆◆◆ (90), Narrow Margin ◆◆ (90), The Russia House ◆◆ (90), Why Me? ◆◆ (90), Misery ◆◆◆◆ (c)(90), True Identity ◆◆ (91), Backdraft ◆◆ (91), Iron Maze ◆ (91), A Few Good Men ◆◆◆◆ (92), Hoffa ◆◆ (92), Sniper ◆◆ (93), Red Rock West ◆◆◆ (93), *Needful Things* (93)

M. Emmet Walsh [b. 1935]

Real name Michael Emmet Walsh

One of the greatest of current Hollywood character actors. You'll know his face, even if you can't put a name to it. No film will be totally duff if M. Emmet Walsh is in it.

Films *Midnight Cowboy* ◆◆◆◆ (69), Serpico ◆◆◆◆ (73), The Prisoner of Second Avenue ◆◆ (75), Straight Time ◆◆◆ (78), Ordinary People (80), Reds ◆◆◆ (81), Blade Runner: The Director's Cut ◆◆◆◆ (82), Silkwood ◆◆◆ (83), Missing in Action ◆ (84), The Pope of Greenwich Village ◆◆ (84), Scandalous ◆ (84), Fletch ◆ (85), Blood Simple ◆◆◆◆ (85), Back to School ◆ (86), Critters ◆ (86), No Man's Land ◆◆ (87), Bigfoot and the Hendersons ◆◆ (87), Raising Arizona ◆◆◆◆ (87), Clean and Sober ◆◆◆ (88), Sunset ◆ (88), War Party ◆◆ (89), The Mighty Quinn ◆◆ (89), Chattahoochee ◆◆ (90), Narrow Margin ◆◆ (90), White Sands ◆◆◆ (92)

Julie Walters [b. 1950]

Quote 'Accents? I can do Irish, Welsh, Manchester, Liverpool, Birmingham, Cockney and New York Jewish lesbian.'

Films Educating Rita ◆◆◆ (83), She'll Be Wearing Pink Pyjamas ◆◆ (85), Car Trouble ◆◆ (86), Personal Services ◆◆ (87), Prick Up Your Ears ◆◆◆ (87), Buster ◆◆ (88), Killing Dad ◆ (89), Stepping Out ◆◆ (91), Just Like a Woman ◆◆ (92)

Rachel Ward [b. 1957]

The niece of the Earl of Dudley. Married to Australian actor Bryan Brown.

Films *The Jerk* ◆◆ (79), Dead Men Don't Wear Plaid ◆◆ (82), Campsite Massacre ◆ (83), Against All Odds ◆◆ (84), The Good Wife ◆◆ (87), How to Get Ahead in Advertising ◆◆ (89), After Dark, My Sweet ◆◆ (90), Christopher Columbus: The Discovery ◆ (92)

Denzel Washington [b. 1954]

Son of a strict minister who wouldn't let his children watch films, Washington's superb acting ability has quickly catapulted him to star status. He and his family now live in the former home of William Holden. As obsessed as Spike Lee with *Malcolm X* (a role he earlier played Off-Broadway), he turned down a co-starring role with Michelle Pfeiffer to do the film.

Films *Carbon Copy* ◆ (81), A Soldier's Story ◆◆◆ (84), Power ◆◆ (86), Cry Freedom ◆◆ (87), Glory ◆◆◆◆ (89), For Queen and Country ◆◆ (89), The Mighty Quinn ◆◆ (89), Heart Condition ◆◆ (90), Mo' Better Blues ◆◆ (90), Ricochet ◆◆◆ (91), Mississippi Masala ◆◆◆ (92), Malcolm X ◆◆◆ (92), Much Ado About Nothing ◆◆◆ (93), *Philadelphia* (93), *The Pelican Brief* (94)

Sigourney Weaver [b. 1949]

Real name Susan Alexandra Weaver

Christened Susan, she named herself Sigourney in her teens after a character in *The Great Gatsby*. The daughter of Pat

Weaver, the man who invented the chat show format, she was a student activist, living for a time in a tree house with a boyfriend while wearing an elf outfit. Her first film role was a blink-and-you-miss-it walk-on appearance at the end of *Annie Hall*. Only with *Alien*, which she did for £30,000, did she become a star. She charges fans for autographs, giving the money to charity.

Quote 'I've always been seen as an ice queen. But I want to strip and be a slut.'

Quote 'I'm an *actor*. An *actress* is someone who wears boa feathers.

Films *Annie Hall* ••• (b)(77), *Alien* •••• (79), *The Janitor* •• (81), *The Year of Living Dangerously* ••• (83), *Ghostbusters* •••• (84), *One Woman or Two* • (85), *Aliens* •••• (86), *Half Moon Street* • (86), *Working Girl* •••• (88), *Gorillas in the Mist* ••• (88), *Ghostbusters II* •• (89), *Alien³* • (92), *1492: Conquest of Paradise* • (92), *Dave* ••• (93)

Joanne Whalley-Kilmer [b. 1964]

Married to Val Kilmer.

Films *The Good Father* ••• (86), *No Surrender* •• (86), *To Kill a Priest* • (88), *Willow* •• (88), *Kill Me Again* ••• (89), *Scandal* •• (89), *The Big Man* •• (90), *Navy SEALS* • (90), *Shattered* •• (91), *Storyville* • (92), *Mother's Boys* (93), *A Good Man in Africa* (93)

Forest Whitaker [b. 1961]

Films *Fast Times at Ridgemont High* ••• (82), *Platoon* ••• (86), *The Color of Money* ••• (86), *Good Morning, Vietnam* ••• (87), *Stakeout* ••• (87), *Bird* ••• (88), *Bloodsport* •• (88), *Johnny Handsome* •• (89), *A Rage in Harlem* ••• (91), *The Crying Game* •• (92), *Consenting Adults* • (92), *Body Snatchers* (93)

Dianne Wiest [b. 1948]

Quote 'All I've won since (getting the Oscar) is three days on *Bright Lights, Big City* – as Michael J. Fox's mother. That's

what an Oscar does for you!'

Films *It's My Turn* ••• (80), *Falling in Love* •• (84), *Footloose* •• (84), *The Purple Rose of Cairo* •• (85), *Hannah and Her Sisters* •••• (86), *September* • (87), *The Lost Boys* •• (87), *Radio Days* ••• (87), *Bright Lights, Big City* • (88), *Parenthood* ••• (89), *Cookie* •• (89), *Edward Scissorhands* ••• (90), *Little Man Tate* ••• (92), *Cops and Robbersons* (93)

JoBeth Williams [b. 1953]

Films *Kramer vs. Kramer* ••• (79), *Stir Crazy* (80), *The Dogs of War* •• (81), *Poltergeist* •••• (82), *The Big Chill* ••• (83), *American Dreamer* • (84), *Teachers* •• (84), *Desert Bloom* ••• (86), *Poltergeist II: The Other Side* • (86), *Welcome Home* • (89), *Switch* •• (91), *Stop! Or My Mom Will Shoot* • (92), *Driving Me Crazy* ••• (92)

Robin Williams [b. 1952]

Unlike so many other comics, Williams had a very comfortable childhood. His father was a senior executive for Ford. He studied drama at the Juilliard School in New York (in the same class as Christopher Reeve) before launching into stand-up. Proud of the fact that he once made $150 a day as a mime on the steps of New York's Metropolitan Museum of Art, it was his manic character in *Mork & Mindy* that first brought him to public attention. The failure of *Popeye* didn't quite kill his film career stone dead and *Good Morning, Vietnam* finally established him as a box-office draw. He left his wife of ten years in 1988, marrying the childrens' nanny shortly afterwards.

Quote 'I was a little fat guy [at school]. And I was picked on. They didn't want so much to beat me up as see me roll. So I got funny.'

Films *Popeye* • (80), *The World According to Garp* ••• (82), *Moscow on the Hudson* ••• (84), *Good Morning, Vietnam* ••• (87), *Dead Poets Society* •••• (89), *The Adventures of Baron Munchausen* •••

(c)(89), Awakenings ••• (90), Cadillac Man •• (90), The Fisher King ••• (91), Hook ••• (91), Dead Again •• (c)(91), FernGully...The Last Rainforest • (v)(92), Aladdin •••• (v)(92), Toys •• (92), *Being Human (93), Mrs. Doubtfire (93), The Mayor of Castro Street (94)*

Bruce Willis [b. 1955]

Real name Walter Bruce Willis

Born in West Germany, Willis was brought up in New York's tough Hell's Kitchen district. Working as a security guard making $4 an hour, he went for acting lessons, landed a part in an off-Broadway play and was on his way. He made his name with TV's *Moonlighting* and almost lost it again with *Hudson Hawk* and *Bonfire of the Vanities*. Married to the ever-popular Demi Moore, the success Willis achieved with *Die Hard* has receded almost as fast as his hairline. As long as they keep making *Die Hard* films, he'll keep getting $6m or $7m a shot.

Quote 'Do people treat me differently now? Well, all my jokes seem to have become a *lot* funnier.'

Films Blind Date • (87), Die Hard •••• (88), Sunset • (88), In Country •• (89), Look Who's Talking ••• (v)(89), The Bonfire of the Vanities • (90), Die Hard 2 ••• (90), Look Who's Talking Too • (v)(90), Mortal Thoughts •• (91), Hudson Hawk • (91), Billy Bathgate •• (92), The Last Boy Scout ••• (92), The Player •••• (c)(92), Death Becomes Her ••• (92), National Lampoon's Loaded Weapon 1 •• (c)(93), *Striking Distance (93), The Color of Night (93), North (94)*

Debra Winger [b. 1955]

Real name Mary Debra Winger

Quote 'I have to spend too much time extricating myself from a reputation I don't particularly want. As to how I got that reputation, all I can say is that a little spunk goes a long way in this business.'

Films *Urban Cowboy* ••• (80), An Officer and a Gentleman •• (82), E.T. The

Extra-Terrestrial •••• (v)(82), Terms of Endearment ••• (83), Legal Eagles ••• (86), Black Widow ••• (87), Made in Heaven •• (c)(87), Betrayed •• (88), Everybody Wins • (90), The Sheltering Sky • (90), Leap of Faith ••• (92), *Wilder Napalm (93), Shadowlands (94)*

Alfre Woodard [b. 1953]

Films *Health* •• (79), Cross Creek •• (83), Extremities •• (86), Scrooged •• (88), Miss Firecracker ••• (89), Grand Canyon •• (91), Rich In Love •• (93), *Passion Fish (92), Bopha (93), Hearts and Souls (93)*

James Woods [b. 1947]

Perhaps the least ingratiating actor in Hollywood, there's probably no back Woods hasn't rubbed up the wrong way. This hostility to his fellow man (and woman, in the case of Sean Young) is what makes him such an electrifying performer on screen. He sued Young for $2m for harrassing him by inundating him with repulsive photographs shortly after they worked together on *The Boost*. Never one to pull his punches, he once referred to the writer of an unflattering piece on him as 'unmitigated puss ripped from the ass of a dead dog'.

Quote 'If I were on a plane and there were an earthquake and all of California fell into the sea and there were no movie actors left, if I landed and called up the studios and said, "Hey, fellas, I'm still here, there's one left", some executive would say, "Well, yeah, but I'm sure there's a football player in Kansas who would be better for the part. Just stay at the airport. We'll get back to you".'

Quote 'Perhaps the most hostile of all American actors.' [Pauline Kael]

Films *The Way We Were* ••• (b)(73), Night Moves ••• (75), The Onion Field ••• (79), The Janitor •• (81), Videodrome ••• (83), Once Upon a Time in America •••• (84), Against All Odds •• (84), Cat's Eye •• (85), Salvador •••• (86), Best Seller ••••

(87), The Boost ✦✦✦ (88), Cop ✦✦✦ (88), The Hard Way ✦✦✦✦ (91), Straight Talk ✦✦✦ (92), Midnight Sting ✦✦✦✦ (92), Chaplin ✦✦ (92), *The Getaway (94)*

Sean Young [b. 1959]

Real name Mary Sean Young

The Woman They Love To Hate. Young's publicity clippings from her films probably take up no more than a filing cabinet, yet the articles about her off-screen behaviour probably occupy the rest of the house. She has a strange knack for being fired from films, she claims because of her refusal to sleep with stars and producers. She was sacked in the midst of filming *Wall Street*, axed from *Dick Tracy* and *Crimes and Misdemeanours*. An unfortunate fall from a horse lost her the female lead in *Batman*, though it's always possible she was pushed. Writer James Dearden has denied that he based the character of Alex in *Fatal Attraction* upon her.

Quote 'The girls [in school] were big and ugly and fat and mean. They used to throw french fries at me.'

Quote 'All right, I'm young, I'm beautiful – but you don't have to hate me.'

Films *Jane Austen in Manhattan* ✦ (80), *Stripes* ✦✦ (81), Young Doctors in Love ✦✦✦ (82), Blade Runner: The Director's Cut ✦✦✦✦ (82), Dune ✦ (84), Baby...Secret of the Lost Legend ✦✦ (85), Wall Street ✦✦✦ (87), No Way Out ✦✦✦ (87), The Boost ✦✦✦ (88), Cousins ✦✦✦ (89), A Kiss Before Dying ✦ (90), Wings of the Apache ✦ (90), Love Crimes ✦ (92), Once upon a Crime ✦ (92), Blue Ice ✦ (92), *Fatal Instinct (93)*

Billy Zane [b. 1967]

Films Back to the Future ✦✦✦✦ (85), Critters ✦ (86), Back to the Future, Part II ✦✦ (89), Dead Calm ✦✦✦✦ (89), Memphis Belle ✦✦ (90), Sniper ✦✦ (93), Orlando ✦✦✦ (93), Dave ✦✦✦ (93)

Robert Zemeckis [b. 1952]

DIRECTOR. Given his break by Steven Spielberg, Zemeckis, who writes his hugely entertaining pictures with friend Bob Gale, is the most financially successful director in the history of the movies, eclipsing the financial record even of his mentor Spielberg. Almost every Zemeckis picture is well worth seeking out for its energy, imagination and humour.

Films *I Wanna Hold Your Hand* ✦✦ *(77; also s), 1941* ✦✦ *(79; s only),* Used Cars ✦✦ *(80; also s),* Romancing the Stone ✦✦✦ (84), Back to the Future ✦✦✦✦ (85; also s), Who Framed Roger Rabbit? ✦✦✦ (88), Back to the Future, Part II ✦✦ (89), Back to the Future, Part III ✦✦✦✦ (90), Death Becomes Her ✦✦✦ (92), Trespass ✦✦✦ (92; s only)

Star Satisfaction Score ...

This is the complete ranking of the average rating of the actors contained
in the rear section of the book. The average is obtained simply by taking
the total rating of every film in the main section of the book an actor has
been in and dividing it by the number of those films.

Actors who have been in fewer than 5 films during the period, where an
average might give a distorted impression, are marked with an asterisk.

SCORE

›3.00: Rosie Perez*; James Woods; Harrison Ford; Joe Pesci.

3.00: Lorraine Bracco; Cher; Billy Crystal; Danny Glover; Woody Harrelson;
Bruno Kirby; Oliver Platt; Laura San Giacomo*; Kyra Sedgwick*; Emma Thompson.

›2.75: Kevin Bacon; Alec Baldwin; Helena Bonham Carter; Matthew Broderick;
Kevin Costner; Ethan Hawke; Dustin Hoffman; Anjelica Huston; Ray Liotta;
Michael Madsen; Mary Stuart Masterson; Mary McDonnell; Frances
McDormand; Bill Murray; Chris O'Donnell*; Sarah Jessica Parker; Bill
Pullman; Aidan Quinn; Mary Steenburgen; Madeleine Stowe; Robin Williams.

›2.50: Bonnie Bedelia; Annette Bening; Tom Berenger; Halle Berry*; Philip
Bosco; Kenneth Branagh; Albert Brooks; Nicolas Cage; Glenn Close; Sean
Connery; John Cusack; Joan Cusack; Geena Davis; Daniel Day-Lewis; Robert
De Niro; Brian Dennehy; Johnny Depp; Danny DeVito; Richard Dreyfuss; Sally
Field; Michael J. Fox; Morgan Freeman; Andy Garcia; Mel Gibson; Gene
Hackman; John Heard; Barbara Hershey; Anthony Hopkins; Samuel L. Jackson;
Julie Kavner; Nicole Kidman; Val Kilmer; Andie MacDowell; Amy Madigan;
John Malkovich; James Marshal*l; Steve Martin; Al Pacino; Dolly Parton; Brad
Pitt*; Robert Redford; Tim Roth; Greta Scacchi; Annabella Sciorra; Ron Silver;
Wesley Snipes; Daniel Stern; Meg Tilly; Stephen Tobolowsky; John Turturro;
Denzel Washington; Forest Whitaker; Billy Zane.

›2.25: Rosanna Arquette; William Baldwin*; Ellen Barkin; Kathy Bates; Lara
Flynn Boyle; Jeff Bridges; Bryan Brown; Tom Cruise; Jamie Lee Curtis; Jeff
Daniels; Judy Davis; Patrick Dempsey; Laura Dern; Mia Farrow; Carrie Fisher;
Jodie Foster; Peter Gallagher; Whoopi Goldberg; Jeff Goldblum; John Goodman;
Richard E. Grant; Melanie Griffith; Julie Hagerty; Daryl Hannah; Rutger Hauer;
Goldie Hawn; Dennis Hopper; William Hurt; Jeremy Irons; Michael Keaton;
Jessica Lange; Juliette Lewis*; Christopher Lloyd; Joe Mantegna; Kelly McGillis;
Elizabeth McGovern; Penelope Ann Miller; Alfred Molina; Demi Moore; Jack
Nicholson; Gary Oldman; Elizabeth Perkins; Michelle Pfeiffer; Lou Diamond
Phillips; River Phoenix; Dennis Quaid; Keanu Reeves; Judge Reinhold; Miranda
Richardson; Alan Rickman; Tim Robbins; Mimi Rogers; Mickey Rourke;
Mercedes Ruehl; Winona Ryder; Susan Sarandon; Ally Sheedy; Elisabeth Shue;
Christian Slater; Vincent Spano; D.B. Sweeney; Uma Thurman; Marisa Tomei;
J.T. Walsh; Sigourney Weaver; Dianne Wiest; Debra Winger.

›2.00: Danny Aiello; Kirstie Alley; Gabrielle Anwar*; Anne Archer; Dan Aykroyd; James Belushi; Patrick Bergin; Gary Busey; Gabriel Byrne; Michael Caine; John Candy; John Cleese; Robbie Coltrane; Macaulay Culkin; Lolita Davidovich; Rebecca De Mornay; Matt Dillon; Amanda Donohoe; Michael Douglas; Charles Durning; Clint Eastwood; Cary Elwes; Richard Gere; Caroline Goodall*; Charles Grodin; Fred Gwynne; Tom Hanks; Bob Hoskins; Tommy Lee Jones; Jeffrey Jones; Raul Julia; Diane Keaton; Moira Kelly*; Kevin Kline; Jennifer Jason Leigh; John Lithgow; Robert Loggia; Jon Lovitz; Dolph Lundgren; Virginia Madsen; Mary Elizabeth Mastrantonio; Michael McKean; Laurie Metcalf; Bette Midler; Helen Mirren; Matthew Modine; Dudley Moore; Rick Moranis; Eddie Murphy; Liam Neeson; Sam Neill; Leslie Nielsen; Nick Nolte; Sean Penn; Richard Portnow; Julia Roberts; Kurt Russell; Meg Ryan; Julian Sands; Arnold Schwarzenegger; Martin Short; Tom Skerritt; James

Busy Bodies Who's the hardest worker?

Using only those films included in the main body of the book, we've ranked the busiest actors included in the back of the book according to the number of their films released in British cinemas from 1983 on*.

22: J.T. Walsh

20: Michael Caine

19: M. Emmet Walsh

18: Robert De Niro, Gene Hackman, Robert Loggia, Liam Neeson; Charlie Sheen, Harry Dean Stanton

17: John Heard, Bob Hoskins

16: Dan Aykroyd, Ellen Barkin, Philip Bosco, Brian Dennehy, Christopher Lloyd, Nick Nolte, Mickey Rourke

15: John Candy, Robbie Coltrane, Kevin Costner, John Goodman, Daryl Hannah, Dennis Hopper, Harvey Keitel, Steve Martin, Michael McKean, Kiefer Sutherland, Stephen Tobolowsky, John Turturro, Bruce Willis

14: Danny Aiello, Nicolas Cage, Willem Dafoe, Danny DeVito, Steve Guttenberg, Tom Hanks, Barbara Hershey, John Malkovich, Susan Sarandon, Christian Slater

13: Kim Basinger, James Belushi, Tom Berenger, Jeff Daniels, Mia Farrow, Bridget Fonda, Mel Gibson, Jeff Goldblum, Raul Julia, John Lithgow, Meryl Streep, Robin Williams, Sean Young

12: Kathy Bates, Jeff Bridges, Gary Busey, Chevy Chase, Glenn Close, Sean Connery, Tom Cruise, Beverly D'Angelo, Michael J. Fox, Morgan Freeman, Richard Gere, Danny Glover, Anthony Hopkins, Anjelica Huston, Kevin Kline, Demi Moore, Rick Moranis, Joe Pesci, Michelle Pfeiffer, Dennis Quaid, Keanu Reeves, Tim Robbins, Julian Sands, Arnold Schwarzenegger, Sylvester Stallone, Dean Stockwell, Dianne Wiest, James Woods.

*Excluded are the 10 1993 Summer blockbusters included in the main book.

Tom & Harry, but where's Dick?

What are the commonest character names in the movies? Here are the most frequent of the 15,500 entries in the database. Poor Dick only gets a look in 14 times.

Jack 126; John 104; Frank 87; Harry 72; David 63; George 62; Michael 59; Tom 59; Mary 54; Paul 53; Charlie 51; Joe 51; Nick 50; Billy 49; Sam 47; Peter 44; Eddie 42; Sarah 41; Larry 40; Bob 37; Sir 37; Ben 36; James 36; Bill 35; Danny 35.

Add in the different variations on the same name, and Jack/John/Johnny and their ilk account for 258, followed by Bill/Billy/William/Willie with 125, Tom/Thomas/Tommy with 105, Ed/Eddie/Ted/Edward with 103 and Charles/Charlie/Chuck with 102. Women's names are far more diverse, with the variations on Elizabeth by far the most common, with 89 appearances in the database.